Are We 'Persons' Y(
Law and Sexuality in Ca1

In 1929, the Privy Council of Canada declared that women were 'persons' under the British North America Act. Seventy years later, a similar move is afoot to establish 'constitutional personhood' for lesbian, gay, bisexual, transsexual, and transgendered people. In *Are We 'Persons' Yet?* Kathleen A. Lahey documents the minimal extent to which human rights laws have improved the legal status of sexual minorities in Canada. She argues that, despite the significant legal progress made with the adoption of the Canadian Charter of Rights and Freedoms, the traditional legal definition of 'persons' continues to limit the legal, social, economic, and political freedom of queer people.

Using an interdisciplinary approach, Lahey presents a historical analysis of litigation relating to sexuality and of the most recent constitutional decisions on sexuality in Canada and the United States. Further discussion concerns immigration law, inheritance law, and same-sex marriage, as well as the widespread exclusion of queers from government census and other statistical surveys.

Are We 'Persons' Yet? provides an excellent model for the analysis of discrimination on the basis of sex, race, sexuality, and marital status and a valuable reference for academics and activists alike.

KATHLEEN A. LAHEY is Professor and Queen's National Scholar, Faculty of Law, and is cross-appointed to the Institute of Women's Studies at Queen's University.

Are We 'Persons' Yet?

Law and Sexuality in Canada

Kathleen A. Lahey

UNIVERSITY OF TORONTO PRESS
Toronto Buffalo London

© University of Toronto Press Incorporated 1999
Toronto Buffalo London
Printed in Canada

Kathleen A. Lahey has asserted the moral right to be identified as the author of this work under the authority of the Copyright Act, RSC 1985, c C-42, s 14.1.

ISBN 0-8020-4205-8 (cloth)
ISBN 0-8020-8062-6 (paper)

∞

Printed on acid-free paper

Canadian Cataloguing in Publication Data

Lahey, Kathleen Ann
　Are we 'persons' yet? : law and sexuality in Canada

　Includes bibliographical references and index.
　ISBN 0-8020-4205-8 (bound)　　ISBN 0-8020-8062-6 (pbk.)

　1. Gays – Legal status, laws, etc. – Canada.　2. Bisexuals – Legal status, laws, etc. – Canada.　3. Transsexuals – Legal status, laws, etc. – Canada.　4. Transvestites – Legal status, laws, etc. – Canada.　5. Canada. Canadian Charter of Rights and Freedoms.　I. Title.

　KE4399.L33 1999　　342.71'087　　C99-930123-3
　KF4483.C576L33 1999

University of Toronto Press acknowledges the financial assistance to its publishing program of the Canada Council for the Arts and the Ontario Arts Council.

This book has been published with the help of a grant from the Humanities and Social Sciences Federation of Canada, using funds provided by the Social Sciences and Humanities Research Council of Canada.

For my wonderful and loving daughters,
Kate Lahey Salter and
Michèle Wadley Lahey

Contents

Preface   xi

Acknowledgments   xxvii

1. **'Full Life,' Human Rights, and Sexuality**   3
   From Criminals to 'Consenting Adults'   6
   Just Ordinary Folks?   8
   Seeking Human Rights for Lesbians and Gays   10
   Protection for 'Sexual Orientation'   13
   Beyond Sexual Orientation Clauses   21
   The Queers Outside the Codes   22
   Conclusions   26

2. **Chart(er)ed Rights**   29
   Drafting the Charter   32
   The 'Moratorium' Years   34
   Implementing 'Equality'   39
   Early Charter Challenges   44
   Conclusions   59

3. **'Demonstrably Justifying' Discrimination**   64
   Egan and Nesbit v *The Queen*   66
   The Other 'Trilogy' Cases   72
   The Impact of *Egan and Nesbit*   77
   The Queers Still Outside the Charter   92
   Conclusions   96

viii   Contents

4. **Human Rights, Charter Rights, and 'Legal Personality'**   100
   Origins of 'Legal Personality'   102
   Deployment of 'Civil Incapacities' in Later Laws   109
   'Personhood' after Edwards   116
   Fundamental Principles Resurfacing   119
   'Core' Rights   125
   Conclusions   126

5. **Are We 'Persons' Yet?**   129
   Participation Rights   132
   Juridical Rights   145
   'Public' Rights   150
   Private Law Rights   156
   Not 'Persons' Yet   171

6. **Counting Queers**   174
   How Many Queer People Are There?   177
   Counting Queer Couples   182
   How Many Children?   187
   Conclusions   190

7. **The High Costs of Being Queer**   192
   Unquantifiable Costs of Discrimination   194
   Employment Discrimination   199
   Discrimination and Income   201
   Net Worth and 'Disposable' Incomes   212
   Conclusions   212

8. **The High Costs of Heterosexuality and the 'Queer Penalty'**   214
   Recognizing Family Sharing   218
   Subsidizing Adult Dependency   224
   The New 'Family Wage' System   231
   The 'Queer Penalty'   235
   Conclusions   237

9. **The 'Benefit' Conundrum and the Politics of Exclusion**   240
   'Benefits' of Being Excluded   243
   Distributional Concerns   249
   Hierarchical Concerns   253
   Deploying Exclusion   261

Rethinking the Benefit Unit   271
Conclusions   279

10. The Costs of 'Incrementalism'   282
Same-Sex Benefits   284
Status of Children   295
Incremental Discrimination   309

11. The Future of Queer Personhood   311
Constitutional Personhood   313
European Models   326
Canadian Models   330
Conclusions   342

Notes   345

Index   457

Preface

What is past is not dead; it is not even past. We cut ourselves off from it; we preferred to be strangers.
Christa Wolf, *A Model Childhood*, trans. Ursula Molinaro and Hedwig Rappolt
(New York: Farrar, Straus and Giroux, 1980), 3

In the cycles of Euro-American history, the legal status of sexual minorities – lesbian, gay, bisexual, transgendered, cross-dressing, and transsexual people – has been a fairly sensitive indicator of the role that the state has played in relation to human rights. From the third millennium B.C.E. until narrowing moral values began to shape Roman state policies in the third century C.E., law codes paid little attention to what would now be called 'same-sex' sexual/emotional/social relations. Although the earliest states were markedly organized on the basis of hierarchies of sexual appropriation, same-sex connections appeared to be generally irrelevant to those policies.[1] Indeed, the research literature suggests that, while same-sex relationships have had widely differing social meanings, they have been tolerated, or even accepted, in many cultures other than Canada and at other times.[2] Even today, marriages between women are openly accepted in some African cultures, and contemporary North American law has finally begun to recognize the importance of Aboriginal traditions that have permitted same-sex unions.[3]

As narrowing morality, and then Christianity, increasingly affected the legal policies of early European states, both reproductivist anti-homosexual policies and anti-Jewish religious policies appear to have been devised to reinforce pre-existing sexual and race/class hierarchies.[4] The first rounds of anti-Semitic, homophobic, and sexist state policies contributed to the construction of legal forms that were given application in later centuries for a wide variety of purposes – the degradation of women's legal status in Norman England, the active state oppression of Jewish persons, the formulation of 'slave codes' in the American states, the control of raced persons when they became socially unpopular, the delimitation of the status of women, and the regulation of sexual minorities at various times.

When the Enlightenment finally resulted in 'liberatory' state policies, many of the links between official state policy and moralist or Christian religious doctrine were broken in Europe. The Napoleonic Code, enacted shortly after the French Revolution, emancipated Jewish persons and decriminalized 'homosexual' existence, resulting in the fuller emergence of queer culture in Europe.[5] Although this new 'liberalism' also spread to England, the United States, and other countries, reactionary trends emerged almost as a symptom of this 'emancipation.'

The newly emancipated were considered to be fascinating, exciting, at the forefront of the 'salon' society because of their differences. But this fascination, itself another manifestation of 'pariah' status, of lack of true acceptance of 'the other,'[6] quickly collapsed in the face of heightening prejudices during the late 1800s as homosexuals, Jewish persons, women, raced persons, and other 'others' were once again subjected to intensifying legal oppression. The recriminalization of 'homosexuality' in Europe culminated in England in 1885, Oscar Wilde was sent to prison in England in 1895, anti-Semitic movements that had emerged in the 1870s led to ghettoization by 1882 in western Europe and state-tolerated pogroms in the early 1900s, and racial lynchings in the United States in the 1880s and 1890s countered movements for Black emancipation. The Enlightenment vision of equality and 'freedom' seemed to incite those motivated by hatred to return to official state violence or state-tolerated violence in order to re-establish old hierarchies.[7]

In a way, the nineteenth and twentieth centuries have seen the working-out, in cycles large and small, of both the premises of the Enlightenment and the fierce reaction they have provoked. Christian religious doctrine has become a prominent conduit for the expression of this reaction. In the hands of nineteenth-century racists in the United States, for example, the emancipation of slaves unleashed passionate appeals to Christian values in an attempt to justify the material reproduction of relations of slavery after 'liberation.'[8] In the hands of the Third Reich, 'god and country' justified the return to violently pro-natalist and heterosexist state policies to reinforce the anti-semitism that formed the central focus of hatred for all things progressive or liberatory.[9] Gay men, cross-dressers, and lesbian women were targeted by the Third Reich because they violated the heterosexist norms on which the new state was posited, while hatred of Jewish persons was often expressed in state propaganda posters by depicting them as child molesters.

In Canada, the legacy of these cycles of 'liberation' and reaction are inscribed in the human rights laws that marked international rejection of state-supported violence of this type. Beginning with the Racial Discrimination Act, 1944, Canadian politicians have repeatedly enacted legislation designed to protect historically disadvantaged groups from future upsurges of hatred.[10] As courts themselves have participated in cycles of tolerance and reaction, these statutes have been read narrowly, read down, or sometimes read not at all because they were not 'entrenched' like the human rights embedded in the U.S. Constitution.[11]

The last half of this century in Canada has seen the growth of human rights legislation at the provincial, federal, and international levels as the unwinding of liberal cycles has generated successively more wide-reaching human rights guarantees. This process culminated, finally, in the 1980s with the adoption of the Canadian Charter of Rights and Freedoms, one of the most complete and progressive constitutional bills of rights anywhere in the world. Yet even this most progressive of all constitutional human rights documents carefully excluded all issues of sexuality from its ambit in deference to the political will of Canadians, continuing the tradition of denying basic legal rights and human rights to sexual minorities despite the by-now centuries-old influence of 'liberal' thought on legal doctrine.

The Plan of This Work

The story I have tried to tell in this book begins with the way in which basic legal rights and human rights were initially denied to sexual minorities in Canada. I have begun here because I have found it very difficult to understand why the twentieth-century human rights movement left sexual minorities out until literally just a few years ago. As I demonstrate in chapter 1, if sexual minorities in Canada still had to rely on human rights codes alone to protect them from the persistent intolerance they have experienced during much of this millennium, they would have no legal protection at all. Before the Charter of Rights came into effect, not one single human rights complaint brought by a lesbian or gay person had ever been resolved in favour of the complainant. Canadian courts found a variety of reasons for ruling against queer complainants, a process that continued even after 'sexual orientation' clauses were added to some human rights codes.

The Charter of Rights has, of course, made all the difference to lesbian women and gay men in Canada. But politicians and courts alike have resisted this effect. As I discuss in chapter 2, all sexual minorities were deliberately excluded from the detailed equality provisions of the Charter during the drafting process. The federal government kept telling lesbian women and gay men that they would be protected by the open-ended language in section 15(1) of the Charter, but when it came time to deliver on that promise, it suddenly evaporated into thin air. It was not until ten years after section 15 of the Charter came into effect that the Supreme Court of Canada ruled that section 15(1) of the Charter does indeed prohibit discrimination on the basis of 'sexual orientation.'[12] Even then, this ruling affected only lesbian women and gay men, not all people characterized by their sexuality.

As I demonstrate in chapter 3, however, the ruling in *Egan and Nesbit* v *The Queen* did establish the bare proposition that sexual minorities had been seeking ever since the Charter was first proposed in the late 1970s: discrimination on the basis of sexuality violates section 15(1) of the Charter. However, *Egan and Nesbit* simultaneously established that state discrimination against lesbians and gays could be 'justified' easily under section 1 of the Charter, at least when the state is defending the restriction of public benefits to 'heterosexuals only.' While growing numbers of cases have come to extend some rights to queers – even relationship-based rights – they are clustered at the 'private' end of the so-called public–private continuum. This has reinscribed the 'keep it private, please' terms on which queer (gay) sex was originally decriminalized in the late 1960s. Even more seriously, the vigour with which the Province of Alberta and the Christian lobby opposed Delwin Vriend's appeal in *Vriend* v *Alberta*[13] has demonstrated that some sexual minorities in Canada can still be deprived of the bare right to work when they are not protected by human rights legislation, and that many registered charitable and religious organizations in Canada are willing to fight for the right to so discriminate.[14] Ironically, the very human rights structures from which the political right attempted to exclude queers have become important ways to funnel conflict over the legal rights of sexual minorities away from the courts and into more 'private' administrative processes as human rights tribunals and labour arbitrators have applied the ruling in

Egan and Nesbit more generously than have many courts. This effect may account for the relatively slow recognition of the rights and duties of sexual minorities under the Charter of Rights itself.

How is it possible, after fifty years of human rights activism in Canada, that queers could have 'equality' without full 'rights' and sometimes 'rights' without 'remedies?'[15] In chapter 4, I argue that, in law-based state/societies, exercise of 'rights' of many kinds is really contingent upon admission to the category of 'legal persons,' and that until courts force the state to recognize the full legal personality of all sexual minorities, queer 'rights' will remain partial, political, and almost purely discretionary. I base this argument on the conclusion that, whenever states have made serious efforts to protect disadvantaged groups from hatred and discrimination, they have begun by safeguarding the fundamental incidents of legal existence –'legal personality.' In documenting this reading of human rights, I trace concepts of legal personality from their crystallization in Roman civil law two millennia ago through their deployment against Jewish persons, queers, women, racialized slaves, and other groups, and then to their emergence in liberatory documents of 'modern' states such as the fourteenth amendment to the U.S. Constitution and the 'Persons' case in Canada in 1929.[16]

The fundamental incidents of legal personality include the right to enter the state, the right to participate in the state, the right to move freely in public, the right to structure a life without violence or appropriation of property, and the right to enter into legally recognized relations sanctioned by property law, contract law, and family law. When those legal capacities are taken away, when groups are not considered to be 'persons' who are the 'end' or subject matter of law, they become unable to access the legal process to secure the rights essential to full functioning as ordinary human beings. They are also unable to effectively access the political process in order to obtain those bare legal rights.

As I have used it, the concept of 'legal personality' is prior to 'equality' claims, and is also prior to 'rights.' It is the grammatical glue that holds statutory and judicial expressions of 'law' together, connecting political and social ideas with living people. The concept of 'legal personality' is both an expression of the minimal content of 'human dignity' and a description of what every human being needs in order to be able to function in state societies and in the world at large.

As I conclude in chapter 5, however, sexual minorities are far from achieving even this bare 'legal personality.' Continued criminalization of sexual expression, denial of physical access to the state on equal terms with non-queers, denial of the right to litigate violations of rights in some circumstances, continued exclusion from basic human institutions like parentage and marriage, workplace discrimination, susceptibility to violence, and denial of basic rights to 'privacy' all add up to incomplete 'personhood' in a country that tells itself that the question of who is a 'person' was resolved in 1929 by the Privy Council.

Queers are, of course, not the only groups in Canada whose legal personality continues to be impaired by state policies. Aboriginal peoples governed by the Indian Act continue to be stripped of almost every incident of legal personality, and Aboriginal women are even more disadvantaged by the combined effects of the Indian Act and their sex. Foreign domestic workers enter Canada on terms not unlike indentured servitude, and have such partial legal personality that they have no legal basis from which to combat their lack of status. Women, visible minorities, immigrants, people disadvantaged by mental or physical limitations, young people, and older people all continue to experience denial of selected incidents of legal personality in contemporary legal policy.

But the story of queer 'non-personhood' has been told not at all, and that is the focus of the remainder of this study. In chapter 6, 'Counting Queers,' I analyse the effects of statistical non-existence on legislative policy. No government in North America has yet made any attempt to tabulate the size of lesbian, gay, bisexual, transgendered, or transsexual populations, and the continued lack of valid data on the demographics of queer communities has made it difficult to engage in informed discussion of the nature of queer existence, whether that discussion is framed by queer communities or by formal levels of government.

The federal government has collected data on queer populations in Canada in its role of official statistician, but instead of making that data available to queer communities, it has kept the information to itself, using it in litigation and in its own internal policy studies to 'prove' that extending social benefits to queers will 'cost' too much.[17] At the same time, the federal government continues to refuse to release its census and survey data on queer existence, and refuses to add questions relating to sexuality to the official census forms so that litigants can meet the federal government on an informed basis in litigation.[18] The result is that the government has monopoly control over the little data that do exist on sexual minorities in Canada, can deploy the information to further its own purposes in litigation, but can continue to deny access to it to the very communities that need it most. Although the federal government has recently agreed to fund a pilot research project into the demographics of selected sectors of queer communities, it is still a long way away from collecting full-sample data on sexual minorities through its official data-collection processes.

In chapters 7, 8, and 9, I report on my detailed examination of the combined effects of the denial of the full incidents of legal personality to sexual minorities and statistical invisibility on queer existence. In chapter 7, I survey what could roughly be referred to as the 'private' effects of discrimination on queers. Although I agree that the 'private' sphere does not really exist in contemporary Canadian society for the simple reason that most 'private' relations are fully regulated by the state, the lack of legal regulation of sexual minorities has, paradoxically, failed to result in enhanced protection of the 'privacy' rights of sexual minorities. Sexuality is expected to remain a 'private' matter from the perspective of most public policy, but queers have few rights to privacy in circumstances in which 'privacy' really matters.

In chapter 7, I look at how the refusal to treat (queer) sexuality as relevant to public policy results in pervasive patterns of discrimination that affect such basic issues as health, security, and relationship functioning. Although the effects of these forms of discrimination cannot easily be quantified, they undeniably affect the well-being of sexual minorities, especially when exacerbated by crisis, age, or death.

Also in chapter 7, I attempt to assess the extent to which employment discrimination affects lesbians and gays. The effects of employment discrimination can be quantified, particularly in terms of incomes. While the lack of reliable data on queer populations is a serious obstacle to such an investigation, existing studies do suggest that employment discrimination reinforces both gender and heterosexual privilege when it comes to incomes: married men have the highest incomes; non-married heterosexual men have the second-highest incomes; gay men have the third-highest incomes; and women's incomes are the lowest, regardless of whether they are lesbian or heterosexual. Because women's earning power is already so impaired by systems of sexual appropriation, lesbian women are less disadvantaged by their sexuality than are gay men. However, the few studies on point do suggest that both women and men pay a high price for being queer.

In chapter 8, 'The High Costs of Heterosexuality and the "Queer Penalty",' I turn the public erasure of sexual minorities around, taking the position that every time the state recognizes heterosexual relations, whether by extending a benefit to heterosexuals or by appearing to place responsibilities on heterosexuals for some policy purpose, it is nonetheless regulating both heterosexual sexuality as well as sexual minorities.

I have developed this analysis of the impact of the public regulation of sexuality in two ways. First, I have calculated 'the costs of heterosexuality' by looking to the measurable state expenditures directed to the subsidy of opposite-sex relationships. In Canada, these expenditures – subsidies for heterosexuals – are the sixty-seventh-largest-government expenditures every year. Second, I have extrapolated from the costs of these heterosexual subsidies a figure I have called 'the queer penalty.' Even though Statistics Canada continues to refuse to measure the size of queer populations, and even though there are no existing valid demographic data on the size of those populations, it is possible, using some indirect data, to make informed guesses as to the minimum and maximum sizes of those populations. Using the costs of the vast 'heterosexual benefit system' as a starting point, it is then possible to project roughly how much being excluded from the public relationship subsidy system costs sexual minorities each year. I refer to this as the 'queer penalty' in order to emphasize the fact that the state plays a critical role in simultaneously encouraging opposite-sex relationships and discouraging same-sex relationships as a matter of public policy.

In chapter 9, 'The "Benefit" Conundrum and the Politics of Exclusion,' I address the other side of the exclusion of sexual minorities from public policy – the fact that some same-sex couples find that it is sometimes to their advantage for the state to refuse to recognize their relationships. For example, same-sex couples who can afford to invest in real estate can actually reap huge income tax advantages from the principal-residence exemption because, unlike opposite-sex couples, they can have two tax-exempt principal residences. For another example, the assumption that 'two can live as cheaply as one' and the use of family-income concepts to set cut-off points for eligibility for social benefits means that two lesbian women living together might sometimes be better off 'uncoupled' than they would be if they could marry or were deemed to be married to their cohabitants.

These types of 'benefits' have attracted considerable attention in the academic and professional literature. Some queer-theorists have pointed out that the exclusion of sexual minorities from public policy can be empowering, because exclusion can create discursive spaces within which identities of resistance can be articulated.[19] Others have argued that queers can 'have it both ways,' reaping the benefits of involuntary singleness under social benefit policies but simultaneously using contracts, wills, trusts, powers of attorney, or rearrangement of property interests to protect their and their partner's interests where they can. Variants of this view have been constructed around the perception that exclusion really means freedom from state regulation of relationships, or that exclusion creates 'choices' not available to others, or that exclusion brings with it the opportunity to construct alternative relationship forms not compatible with hierarchical patristic models. Some commentators have been content with the hypothesis that, on balance, sexual minorities probably receive larger financial benefits from exclusion than they would from inclusion.

Perhaps more than any other strategic issue, the 'benefits of exclusion' have the potential to divide queer communities seriously and to blunt political energies. In the United States, a variant of this issue, known as the 'marriage debate,' has polarized 'pro-marriage' and 'anti-marriage' factions of lesbian, gay, bisexual, and transgendered or transsexual people. As public interest groups in Canada become more representative, the same tensions will undoubtedly arise.

In chapter 9, I trace the dimensions of these divisions and relate them to what is known about class, sexual, race-based, and gender-based hierarchies in queer communities in Canada. What is so particularly difficult about this part of the discourse is that not only have the state and courts made calculated use of the 'benefits of exclusion' in trying to justify continued denial of queer legal personality (as in *Egan and Nesbit*), but some sexual minorities have also tried to deploy these arguments against each other in litigation. When seen from this perspective, the redescription of gaps and omissions in the law as 'opportunities' to fashion creative solutions to problems of legal invisibility can ring somewhat hollow. I question these contentions in light of the practices of those who benefit from them, and test the hypothesis that forced non-existence may not benefit all sexual minorities equally.

I conclude chapter 9 by exploring one of the biggest causes of this apparent double bind: the abandonment of the 'individual' as the unit of social and benefit policy, exacerbated by the use of cost-of-living formulas that presume that economically dependent partners engage in significant levels of non-waged household production. The solution I pose is to move towards the use of the individual as the benefit unit and to rethink low-income cut-offs and cost-of-living formulas in order to take realistic account of how people live.

In chapter 10, 'The Costs of "Incrementalism",' I address another divisive issue that has emerged in contemporary political discourse: the assertion that 'incremental change' will eventually catch up with queer existence, and that this is the best way to pursue change. I examine what I call 'incremental discrimination' from the perspective of two specific areas of ongoing policy concern: the discretion that policies of 'incrementalism' give large administrative agencies like Revenue Canada, and the impact of 'incrementalism' on the status of children who are being raised by same-sex parents. I conclude that, far from being 'neutral' and 'harmless,' policies of 'incrementalism' force queers and their families to live in legal chaos while most governments enjoy the luxury of ignoring the policy and legislative needs of the sexual minorities they are meant to be serving.

In the final chapter, 'The Future of Queer "Personhood",' I return to some of the historical parallels I looked at in chapter 4 in order to comment on the different models of 'liberatory' legislation that queers are being asked to embrace in the political realm. I begin by emphasizing that just because a statute is called a 'civil rights act' or 'human rights code' does not mean that it will be completely salutary. Examples from the post–Civil War anti-slavery legislation and from recent 'human rights' state constitutional amendments of the 1990s in the United States demonstrate just how much damage can be done in the name of civil rights legislation. At the same time, however, European domestic partnership legislation and contemporary legislative models developed in Ontario and British Columbia have done the same sort of thing in more muted form, as new legislative models actually minimize some elements of legal personality at the same time they confirm others. The resulting trend in legislation is towards the creation of second- and third-class status for some sexual minorities in some circumstances, and continuing legal invisibility with all of its attendant problems for others. I conclude that so long as legislatures address queer legal issues only grudgingly, sexual minorities are probably going to fare better, in the longer term, with litigation under the Canadian and Québec charters than with legislation that limits queer legal capacities even as it begins to recognize queer existences.

I conclude chapter 11 by comparing the recent construction of constitutional queer 'personhood' in the United States with the direction that judicial Charter remedies have begun to take in Canada. With the top courts in both countries moving in the direction of declaring classifications based on sexuality to be constitutionally invalid, I posit that it will be the courts that finally reverse the presumption that sexual minorities have no rights or duties unless specifically assigned, and that extend full legal capacity to those who now occupy that jurisprudential space labelled 'sexual orientation.'

'Legal Personality' and Legal Theory

The analysis of law and sexuality that I have carried out here has a history in my own research concerns. On the one hand, I have been interested in tracing the way sex-gender and race-based divisions in law and economics persistently reinforce and reproduce relations of dependency and appropriation despite apparent efforts at 'law reform.' The critical assessment of how hierarchies grounded in race and/or sex-gender are more likely to survive law-reform movements in transformed condition than to be completely eradicated has led me to become deeply suspicious of 'legal' solutions to social, economic, and political problems.

On the other hand, I have known personally and as a researcher that denial of legal rights or legal status can be used very effectively to silence, terrorize, control, or render invisible selected classes of people. The fewer rights groups of people have, the more difficult it becomes for them to find the courage to claim more, or even to claim the benefit of the few that they do have. The rights that lie just out of reach are a good measure of the material locations of specific classes. Compare the situation of a racially 'white' able-bodied male who has been told that he cannot join a women's self-defence class with the situation of a lesbian woman whose lawyer has just advised her that she should defer living openly as a lesbian if she plans to litigate custody of her child. The right that lies just out of reach of the man in this example is qualitatively different from the right that lies just out of reach of this lesbian woman. Add in youth, low income, or racialized identity, and the differences increase dramatically. These differences reflect the very real differences in their hierarchical locations and personal privileges, and these locations and privileges in turn have tremendous impact on what it will cost the lesbian woman in this example to struggle against her condition in comparison with what would be at risk for the male. Focusing on the material implications of legalized discrimination helps explain why, with all its shortcomings and frustrations, law reform continues to be a necessary precondition to 'liberation' for many people, even if it is not, by itself, a complete or even an adequate solution.

This study is in part an effort to work out the contradictions between these two theoretical concerns. A materialist analysis of oppression has enabled me to uncover what appear to me to be the very most fundamental pieces of legal structure that covertly underpin contemporary hierarchies of privilege and power – the elements of civil capacity or 'legal personality.'[20] It is politically so simple to deploy these legal structures, and they are so devastatingly effective once they have been put in place, that it is not at all surprising to find that they have been used widely to promote heterosexual values and to burden non-heterosexual existence. But critical lesbian/queer readings of law-reform measures that are designed to dismantle those structures reveal how resistant they are to genuine change, at least in part because categories of sex-gender, race, and sexuality continue to be treated as 'natural' categories in legal discourse.[21]

Critical lesbian/queer theorists have made particularly important contributions in contesting tendencies towards universalist thought in the liberatory literature of lesbian and gay politics. I have long been a critic of those who would ignore the specificities of lesbian existences in order to reductively include them in references to 'women' or 'feminists,' or in order to downplay the very real differences between lesbian experiences and gay experiences in the interests of promoting coalition politics. I have found that queer impatience with naturalized categories of 'sex'– whether defined medically, biologically, legally, or socially – and 'sexuality' has been particularly helpful in uncovering the arbitrariness of legal categories at the same time that it has further opened up substantive inquiry into the processes of social constructionism that are the 'real' sources of these categories in the first place.[22]

Critical lesbian/queer theorists have shifted legal discourse out of the framework of earlier liberatory studies by acknowledging that law may remain an important system of legitimation at the same time that they reject the necessity of working with pre-existing legal categories, doctrine, or values. The emergence of critical lesbian/queer theory has not completely deprived naturalized categories of their easy lure, however. For example, Nancy Polikoff has suggested that the heavily naturalized language of biological parentage be replaced with concepts of 'functional parenting' within which two lesbian women could be seen as both being legal mothers of their child.[23] Shortly thereafter, however, she was challenged by male queer-theorists who felt that by ignoring potential parental claims by sperm donors, Polikoff's two-parent model too closely 'resemble[s] the law's image of the traditional family.'[24] While the goal of opening family structures up beyond the two-parent model is not particularly problematic, it is somewhat disconcerting to see how Polikoff's critics framed their argument. In arguing in favour of donor visitation, her critics attempted to establish that bare biological connection as a basis for establishing legal parentage was superior to concepts of 'functional parenting,' even though the latter concept was designed to overcome the shortcomings of earlier naturalized biological definitions of 'parent.' Indeed, Polikoff's critics appeared to find critical lesbian attempts to draw the connection between the specificities of lesbian existences and material dispositions of custody/visitation claims to be reactionary and irritating. They went even further, taking the position that lesbian women who might win legal recognition of their parentage by documenting their 'functional parenting' are really being forced to '"lose" the ways in which their lives and relationships differed from those of a traditional heterosexual nuclear family.'[25]

Despite differences among critical lesbian and queer-theorists, however, both perspectives offer strategic insights that can be utilized simultaneously or alone.[26] 'Queer' is a powerful critical term when it is used to open up categories such as 'sex' and 'sexuality' to deconstructive analysis, whether in relation to diverse lesbian sexualities,[27] for example, or in relation to indeterminate identities of those who transgress sex/ual boundaries through cross-dressing, transgenderism, or transsexualism.[28] With its emphasis on articulating the specificities of lesbian existence, critical lesbian theory is a necessary corrective to the universalizing tendencies of sexuality-neutral 'queer' discourse, just as critical race theory is a necessary corrective to race-neutral lesbian, gay, and queer discourses.

'Queer' has other usages as well. It can be used as an inclusive descriptive term that avoids the essentialist connotations of narrower phrases such as 'lesbian and gay' or 'lesbian, gay, and bisexual' (at the moment, I use it to include lesbian, gay, bisexual, cross-dressing, transgender, and transsexual people). There are, of course, many objections to using the term 'queer' in scholarly writing. Many people simply find the word 'queer' to be strongly distasteful, slang, the language of homophobia and hatred. Some feel that it has already lost whatever critical potential it ever had as it has become a shorthand reference for more cumbersome formulations such as 'lesbian and gay.' Others feel that it is politically dangerous to use. At times, it is seriously over-inclusive, as, for example, in discussions of judicial decisions in which the entire record has been constructed around the categories 'lesbian' and 'gay.'[29]

Because 'legal personality' plays such a fundamental role in legal discourse, I have also been able to draw from a wide range of other theoretical traditions. Liberal political theory takes the primacy of 'personhood' as its starting point, with some theorists positing that the basic legal rights associated with personhood should be treated as inviolate.[30] Rights theorists address many of the same doctrinal issues from varying perspectives such as moral philosophy,[31] race theory,[32] and lesbian philosophy,[33] while ethicists begin with the perception that all human beings are 'persons' in deriving justifications for respect of all people that are not grounded in Christian morality.[34] Critical feminists working in the tradition of 'difference' have pinpointed civil capacity as a critical political goal,[35] and semioticians have taken up 'the citizenship question' as a core signifier of social identity, membership, existence, and value, with 'legal persons' being equated with 'citizens' and the banished and exiled treated as having 'zero-value and zero significance.'[36]

All of these discourses have confirmed my own sense that 'legal personality' is a fundamental legal structure, but I have felt that two crucial points have still been missing from these kinds of accounts. First, they fail to consider that the elements of 'legal personality' are really prior to human rights and prior to 'equality' discourse as well. Thus those who lack the full capacities associated with 'legal personality' will not be able to effectively pursue the full range of legal rights needed to function in civil society. Second, they do not grapple with the fact that so long as a state/society denies any incidents of legal personality, the extension of some 'rights' and even the guarantee of technical 'equality' will not solve the problems of social, economic, or political disadvantage either.

Voice and Audience

Although I have written some passages of this work in the first person as an out lesbian feminist, this study is intended not only for lesbian, gay, bisexual, cross-dressing, transgender, and transsexual readers, but for any readers who are concerned with the legal status of sexual minorities in Canada, materialist analysis of oppression, or lesbian/queer turns of critical theory. Having drawn on parallel structures of oppression affecting other 'target' groups in explicating concepts of legal personality, I hope that these parallels might spark further exploration in other contexts.

My decision to write in the first person goes beyond my desire to be unequivocally 'out' in this work. I have occasionally discussed my own perceptions and experiences not only because I think that personal construction of experience is useful data for others, but also because I do think that political positions are affected by personal experience, and I would like readers to know where I am 'coming from' in relation to some of these issues.

Whether this book is ultimately read as a case study in the inequality of lesbians and gays at the end of the second millennium c.e. in Canada, as a critical exegesis of the role that law plays in maintaining heterosexual privilege in relation to all sexual minorities, or as a contribution to 'rights discourse,' my hope is that I have demonstrated that attainment of full 'legal personality' is the first step towards attaining legal equality, and perhaps even social, economic, and political equality, for any group. No more than any other class of people, queers cannot live 'full lives' without the guarantee, as a bare minimum, of basic civil capacities.

Acknowledgments

In preparing this study, I have received tremendous assistance from many people and groups. First and foremost, I have been inspired by my students. They have, year after year, bravely entered the legal profession, knowing what they would be facing. For many years, the only students I met were deeply closeted. Some of them remain in the closet to this day. Some became lawyers but died before being able to come out, or became ill before being able to live the lives they had imagined for themselves. Some are out, are lawyers, and are litigating, writing, organizing, doing everything they can to change the legal status of queers. To all my students, I owe an enormous debt of gratitude for their honesty, courage, and friendship. They have made my work and my professional life 'real' for me, and have given me hope for the future.

I have also been inspired by my friends and colleagues in Canada, the United States, England, and Australia who have, in so many different ways, been able to be queer and be active, as well as by the growing numbers of people who are working to change the social and legal status of sexual minorities and other groups that have been the focus of social prejudice. I owe a particular debt of gratitude to Barry Adam, who was one of the first academics to be 'out' in Canada. He supported me as I came out as a lesbian academic, has had a profound influence on the direction my work has taken over the years, and has offered his colleagues and students an outstanding example of how to combine teaching, scholarship, and activism. I am also deeply grateful to Joe Arvay, who, while we were colleagues at the University of Windsor, took the initiative to confront an administration that looked like it was thinking about what to do with me once news that I was lesbian had spread. I think his confrontation made a difference.

This study owes a great deal to the creative and inventive research assistance I have received from many students at Queen's University. Meredith Cartwright and Ellen Faulkner assisted with the research that enabled me to apply the image 'legal personality' to contemporary law. The research and thinking they did while working with me have enriched my work ever since, and I am deeply grateful to both of them. I have also received inspired research assistance from Nirmala Persaud, Martin Russell, and Joanne Prince, whose creativity has been crucial to the scope of this work, and from Michele Ballagh and Jeff Silver. The Strategic Grants Programme of the Social Sciences and Humanities Research Council of Canada provided funding for this research.

Professionally and personally, I have received wonderful support and inspiration for this work from Terry Hancock, who imagined and organized the first Canadian Bar Association (Ontario) Institute for the Lesbian and Gay Legal Issues Committee around the issues addressed here, and from Patricia LeFebour, whose own work has opened up new critical horizons in queer theory. I have also received valuable feedback from colleagues and friends, including Martha McCarthy, Douglas Elliott, Beverley Baines, Denis Magnusson, Martha Bailey, Meredith Cartwright, and Ellen Faulkner.

My greatest debt of gratitude is to Marguerite Russell, who has helped me shape my thinking on the role of law, human rights, and the Charter generally and in relation to sex/ualities, whose own critical work on the material limitations of human rights remedies, and whose personal support while I was engaged in this study, have been phenomenal, and to my daughters, Kate Lahey Salter and Michèle Wadley Lahey, whose love, creativity, and wonderful approaches to living their own lives have inspired me most of all.

Finally, I would like to thank those who supported the publication of this work: Virgil Duff of the University of Toronto Press, who provided editorial guidance throughout every stage of this project; two anonymous referees, who gave me extremely constructive feedback on the manuscript; Beverley Beetham Endersby, whose copy-editing has enhanced the entire work; Maryellen Symons, a great scholar, lawyer, and friend, whose special genius was critical to the final completion of this project; Denis Marshall, librarian at the Queen's University Faculty of Law Lederman Library; Edna-May McKay, Faculty of Law Staff, who provided printing and formatting assistance; and Vyvien Vella, Faculty of Law Staff and Computer Consultant, who was always there to solve every problem that no one else could handle, and, as ever, put more effort into this project than anyone could imagine. The law described in this book is current to July 1998, but major events such as Supreme Court of Canada decisions have been updated to 1 April 1999.

Kathleen Lahey
Kingston, Ontario

Are We 'Persons' Yet?

Chapter One

'Full Life,' Human Rights, and Sexuality

If a human being wants to become truly herself, if she wants to be a real person, with an individual and indispensable face, then she must not turn away from herself. She has to take her life into her own hands, the same way a sculptor takes material in hand, giving shape to an idea that emerged formlessly from his soul. This requires an incredible amount of courage. It's a path leading through crisis, doubt and uncertainties.

Erzsébet Galgóczi, *Another Love*, trans. Ines Rieder and Felice Newman (Pittsburgh, PA: Cleis, 1991), 89

How did Eva Szalánczky in Galgóczi's book become a 'real person'? Caught in the Hungarian resistance to Soviet occupation in 1959 without the political aptitudes or sexuality necessary for survival, she lived a marginal life of false conformity mingled with ineffective criticism. Alone and too late to plan carefully, she decided that she had to escape from Hungary in order to live the life she needed. In keeping with older traditions of lesbian fiction, death caught her at the border.

Muriel Rukeyser, who also grew up during the middle of the century, used poetry to describe the same choices Galgóczi had explored through her fictional character Eva Szalánczky: 'Wishing to be invisible, you choose / Death of the spirit, stone insanity. / Accepting, take full life.'[1] In this poem, Rukeyser was writing of the choices offered to Jewish persons. She was not able to begin writing of her choices as a lesbian woman until decades after she had written 'Letter to the Front.' Being a Jewish woman during the 1930s and 1940s was the single most defining aspect of her life, but when she did finally grapple in her writing with the sexual dimensions of her identity, her lesbianism, it was muted, cryptic, almost invisible even to lesbian readers, unless they knew what to look for.[2] Describing herself as having been 'split open, unable to speak, in exile from / myself,' she carefully encoded her coming out in these oblique words: 'the fragments join in me with their own music.'[3]

From this tradition of invisibility within the already-invisible, silence among the silenced, obfuscation even by the clearest, how to meet Rukeyser's challenge: 'Accepting, take full life'? How to become a 'real person' who knows what it means to 'take full life'?

Along with growing numbers of sexual minorities around the world, lesbian, bisexual, gay, transgendered, transvestite, and transsexual people in Canada have concluded that they have needed to seek the assistance of the legal system in order to disrupt the vast systems of official homophobia and heterosexual privilege built into the foundations of Canadian culture. One of the most striking things about the use of law – including human rights law – to 'take full life,' however, is that the conception of 'full life' found in legal discourse is radically narrower than Rukeyser's or Galgóczi's, despite the fact that many of the preoccupations of human rights law spring from the same source as these writers' visions: the European genocide of Jewish and other minority persons.[4]

Human rights law is not the only discourse that falls well short of apprehending the essence of what makes people 'human.' The languages of academic 'disciplines'– political science, sociology, jurisprudence, economics – all have scientific-sounding lists of what people need, while the more visionary speak of 'human dignity' in an attempt to convey the deep significance of this project.[5] Thus it is not surprising that when sexual minorities in Canada, heartened by growing social movement and the decriminalization of some aspects of 'homosexual sex,' began to break their silences, to become visible, very little happened, even after the medico-legal phrase 'sexual orientation' was finally formulated to express the essence of queerness and began to become incorporated into human rights codes.

This chapter outlines the first legal strategies employed by sexual minorities to gain recognition of their humanity. Before *Egan and Nesbit* v *The Queen*[6] confirmed that the equality guarantees of the Canadian Charter of Rights and Freedoms do prohibit discrimination on the basis of 'sexual orientation,' and before this Charter of Rights even came into existence, queer communities attempted to rely, first, on ordinary general law; then, on early human rights codes; and, finally, on 'sexual orientation' clauses in human rights codes in order to pursue their civil rights. What the Charter and the *Egan and Nesbit* decision have largely obscured by now is that, on a legal level, none of those sources of law ever really served the interests of queer communities. It was really not until 'sexual orientation' clauses were inserted into some human rights codes that lesbian or gay litigations won any human rights cases at all. And even then, the number of cases decided in favour of lesbian and gay applicants under the rubric of 'sexual orientation' remained shockingly small until the courts began to apply the equality guarantees of the Charter of Rights to those 'sexual orientation' clauses. Despite the growing positive impact of the Supreme Court of Canada decision in *Egan and Nesbit*, success in human rights or Charter litigation is still by no means certain in all contexts.

One of the main reasons that legal doctrine has been able to resist full recognition of the civil and human rights of sexual minorities lies in the social value structure within which law reform has been pursued. The old 'sodomy' provisions that were partially repealed at the end of the 1960s reflected social and moral disapproval of homosexuality, and attempted to use criminal sanctions to discourage its expression. As the use of criminal law to regulate the expression of such personal moral 'choices' came into question, some homosexual offences were decriminalized – but only to the extent that the conduct in question remained 'private.' The implicit 'public–private' dichotomy called up by this new norm immediately began to surface in other areas of legal discourse as civil courts began to struggle with how the legal system ought to deal with the various legal issues that touched on lesbian or gay existence.

One reading of early cases relating to sexuality is that the courts have been consistently reluctant to grant any 'public' status to sexual minorities at all. Whether the context has been general legal doctrine, general provisions of human rights codes, or specific sexual orientation clauses in human rights codes, courts have demonstrated a strong tendency to read all laws as excluding homosexuals. The creation of some non-criminal space within the private sphere seems paradoxically to have helped create the space to which queers have since been confined in civil law as well. Thus the true measure of progress in deploying legal discourse to gain access to 'full life' for sexual minorities lies not in the uses sexual minorities have been able to make of those secret, invisible, and private spaces, but in the extent to which they have been permitted to occupy 'public' space as their 'full selves.'

The legal history sketched in this chapter reveals progress to the extent that almost all human rights codes now expressly prohibit some forms of discrimination on the basis of 'sexual orientation.' But when this history is examined in detail, what also becomes clear is not only that very few sexual-orientation cases have been successful, but that the dividing line between the unsuccessful and the few successful cases appears to track the public–private divide reflected in the first decriminalizing amendments to the Criminal Code. Even more troubling, as the Charter of Rights has come to be applied to issues of sexuality, is the fact that the public–private divide, although transformed and repositioned by Charter discourse, continues to separate successful cases from the unsuccessful.

From Criminals to 'Consenting Adults'

Until the 1960s, sexuality appeared in legal discourse as pathological criminal behaviour. Criminal laws imposed liability for actions described variously as 'lewd and obscene conduct,' 'solicitation,' 'gross indecency,' 'sodomy,' and 'buggery,' while the medico-legal establishment developed theories of 'sexual inversion' and treatment modalities to 'solve' these pathologies.[7] This is not to say that queer people did not also experience employment discrimination; homophobic violence; psychiatrization; exclusion from families, churches, and other social structures; in addition to criminalization, but the visible focus of the legal regulation of sexuality was found in criminal laws.[8]

So deeply entrenched were images of gays, lesbians, bisexuals, and transgendered/sexual people as criminally deviant that when the Allied forces liberated the Nazi concentration camps in 1944, they left some homosexuals who were still alive to serve out their sentences.[9] British and American military jurists had ruled that imprisoned homosexuals were criminals and thus were not to be automatically freed as political prisoners.[10] Even worse, some of those who had served part of prison sentences imposed by the Third Reich courts for homosexuality in camps such as Auschwitz and Dachau were returned to prisons in occupied Germany to re-serve their sentences in prisons, because Allied jurists concluded that their time in the camps should not be counted towards their terms.[11]

It was not until the 1950s that these images began to be challenged. In the late 1940s, Alfred Kinsey and his colleagues reported their finding that nearly half of all men in the United States had had some male–male sexual experience, and that some 10 per cent of all adult males could be classified as 'exclusively homosexual.'[12] Their follow-up study on women resulted in findings on a similar scale.[13] By 1955, the American Law Institute, which drafts highly influential model legislation, had recommended that all consensual relations between adults in 'private' should be excluded from the scope of the criminal law.[14] In 1957, in the United Kingdom, the Wolfenden Report concluded that the criminal-deviance image of gay existence (lesbian existence was scarcely noticed in this report; the sexual deviance of women was called 'prostitution' there) was not as appropriate as the 'modern' images of 'private morality' and 'individual choice.' Locating the condemnation of both homosexuality and prostitution in religious belief, the report concluded that 'it is not ... the function of the law to intervene in the private lives of citizens, or to seek to enforce any particular pattern of behaviour.'[15] This severance of 'private conduct' from religious belief was highly controversial in both countries, and led to the famous 'Hart–Devlin' jurisprudential debate on the relationship between law and morality.[16] These developments did not erase earlier images of 'homosexuals' as deviant.[17] Nonetheless, these developments eventually led, in Canada, to the Trudeau amendments to the Criminal Code in 1969, which decriminalized gay sex to the extent that it was in private, between adults, and consensual.[18]

Shortly after private same-sex sexual relations were decriminalized, gay men began to look to human rights codes for protection from social discrimination. Although one Canada court speculated that decriminalization had led directly to human rights complaints,[19] it is probably more accurate to see both decriminalization and the interest in human rights complaints as reflecting deep changes in social consciousness. The New York Stonewall uprising in 1969 had catapulted queer communities into sight as hundreds of gay organizations, events, and publications were quickly formed in the aftermath.[20] By 1972, the publication of *Lesbian/Woman*[21] formed a focal point for lesbian feminists who had felt isolated from the Stonewall movement, and as the number of organizations and publications grew with each passing year, North American queer communities began to coalesce around concerns over legal discrimination. The movement in Canada first organized formally in late 1969, and grew quickly.[22] As queers affirmed themselves in the face of heterosexist suppression, communities began to explore 'new forms of companionship and kinship' and to challenge 'heterosexist formulas.'[23]

The first human rights complaints in Canada were brought not simply because suppressive criminal laws had suddenly been repealed, but because lesbian and gay people had come to embrace more fully their own humanity. No longer seeing themselves as something less than human, as deserving nothing but the torment, oddity, silence, and invisibility that Radclyffe Hall gave her psychologically correct character

Stephen Gordon in *The Well of Loneliness*,[24] lesbians and gays, along with transgendered and some bisexual persons, began to form community groups, publications, community cultures, and more open relationships in pursuit of the 'full life' that had been denied to them while their very existence had been treated as evidence of criminal conduct. The impassioned cry with which Hall had closed her book in 1928 had finally become a concrete political demand: 'Give us also the right to our existence!'[25]

Just Ordinary Folks?

Being lesbian or gay is a very 'relational' sort of identity. Unlike identification by sex, race, nationality, ability, or age, identification by sexuality presupposes some sort of relational activity, if only on the level of either mere companionship or genital sexual contact. Now it is certainly true that some lesbians and gays have gone their entire lives without forming relationships or having sex with anyone, but my own experience suggests that those individuals are so few that it is generally accurate to say that lesbian or gay identity clearly presupposes – indeed, almost depends upon – some relational element.

I make this point because I think it helps explain why the first attempts by sexual minorities in North America to 'take full life,' to become 'real persons' in legal discourse, were not framed as human rights challenges, but arose out of the simple expectation that they were entitled to be treated like ordinary people in law. This sense that sexual minorities are 'just plain people' is reflected most clearly in the cases involving the status of marriage. Marriage is both a vehicle for assigning rights and responsibilities to couples and a state of considerable anarchy within which two people (or more, where, as in Ontario, polygamy is recognized)[26] can define their relationship across a very wide spectrum of choices, including not even living together.

Thus, in the early 1970s, lesbian and gay couples in both Canada and the United States simply started showing up at local registry offices to obtain marriage licences or to register their marriages. They were usually turned down. I say 'usually' because, as Anthony Sullivan and Richard Adams have related, the County Clerk in Boulder, Colorado, noticed that state law did not say anything about gender, sex, or sexuality in relation to marriage licences. After consulting a county assistant district attorney who gave her a legal opinion to that effect, she then went ahead to issue marriage licences to six same-sex couples – two lesbian couples and four gay couples. As soon as news of those marriages hit the media, the Speaker of the Colorado House of Representatives requested the state attorney general to issue an informal opinion on the point, and the attorney general immediately instructed county clerks to stop issuing such marriage licences on the basis that state law did not recognize same-sex marriages.[27] Although these marriage licences do not appear to have been legally challenged directly by the State of Colorado beyond the issuance of that informal opinion, the federal courts relied on the presumed invalidity of same-sex marriages in later ruling that Adams could not sponsor Sullivan for immigration purposes.[28]

In Canada, much the same expectation led to litigation completely outside the rubric of human rights guarantees. Two gay men in Manitoba, Richard North and Chris Vogel, were united in marriage in a Unitarian Church in 1974. The government refused to accept their certificate of marriage for registration because neither of them was a woman. According to the registrar and provincial lawyers, they simply did not fit the terms of reference. The resulting litigation did not emanate from a human rights complaint, but was merely an appeal from this administrative position.[29] The court upheld the refusal to register their marriage on the basis that no marriage existed to be registered. The court relied on a variety of authorities that all presumed marriage to be limited to heterosexuals, including a case that related not to gay men, but to a transsexual spouse.[30] Interestingly, the last authority relied upon, the *Encyclopaedia Britannica* definition of 'marriage,' was expressed in entirely gender-neutral terms. The court appears to have read sex-specificities into that language on the basis of all the other authorities quoted.

These early legal disputes set in motion two important developments. First, by denying lesbians and gays inclusion in laws that were not necessarily sex- or sexuality-specific, the state/courts made explicit the heterosexual–homosexual dichotomies and hierarchies upon which those laws were implicitly constructed. As these dichotomies began to be articulated by governments and courts, sexual minorities began to assume the position of 'other' in legal discourse. At the same time, they began the deconstructive process of inhabiting and transforming these dichotomies by demanding release from the space assigned to them as 'other' and access to legitimated space. Despite all the legal events that have transpired since then, activists are still engaged in this same transformative process of deconstruction.

Second, quite apart from the reasoning used by the courts in these marriage cases (the courts basically ended up appealing to Christian (or

Judaic) religious doctrine in both cases), references to male partners as being of the 'same sex' helped create a new category of relationships – 'same-sex' relationships – that conflated the realities of queer existences into an abstraction that actually described no one. As transsexual persons have pointed out, the essence of transsexual existence is change of biological sex to fit the person's image of themselves, their 'self-scape.' In contrast, it is attraction to persons of the same legal 'sex' that is thought to define gay and lesbian identity.[31] Thus male-to-female transsexual persons may be transsexual and lesbian, if after sex reassignment they become legally 'female' and relate to women. Or male-to-female transsexual persons may be transsexual and heterosexual, if after reassignment they relate to men.[32] Some people, including myself, often use the general term 'queer' as an inclusive shorthand reference to diverse sexualities/identities that include lesbian, bisexual, gay, intersexed, transgendered, cross-dressing, and transsexual/transsexualing people. But not everyone is queer in the same way. Nor does an analysis that relates to one form of queerness (for example, female bisexuality) necessarily have anything to do with the specificities of either lesbian existence or existence as a female-to-male transgendered person who relates to women.[33]

In comparing the couple in *Corbett* with the couple in *Re North and Matheson*, the court took the first of many steps down the road of legally constructing the abstract category of unrecognized 'same-sex' relationships that were dichotomously distinguished from heterosexual relationships. Once constructed, the opposing categories of 'opposite-sex' and 'same-sex' relationships were used in early human rights complaints to create the unprotected jurisprudential space labelled 'sexual orientation.' By the simple expedient of assigning sexual minorities to this space, their legal claims were presumptively defeated. Subsequent queer embrace of this space and the demand that it be given legal status resulted in judicial construction of further dichotomized and hierarchized pairs – 'status' versus 'conduct,' 'personal rights' versus 'relational' rights, 'private' versus 'public.'

Seeking Human Rights for Lesbians and Gays

Queers in Canada resisted the sex/ual boundaries, the systematic privileging of heterosexuality, and the conflation of transsexual existence with gay existence that become apparent in these early cases. After their attempts to be treated just like everyone else had failed, gay men and lesbian women began to turn to human rights commissions to enforce quite ordinary civil rights. In these early human rights complaints, gays asked to be admitted to existing categories in human rights legislation such as 'sex,' 'marital status,' 'family status,' and, later, 'sexual harassment.'

Like the dichotomy created by courts between heterosexual couples and 'same-sex' couples when gays sought admission to ordinary legal categories, the courts quickly 'otherized' gays who sought human rights protection from discrimination on the basis of 'sex' by creating the category 'sexual orientation.'

This 'otherizing' is clearly visible in the treatment of the first human rights complaint brought by a gay man in Canada – the *Damien* action. John Damien filed a complaint against the Ontario Racing Commission, alleging that he had been dismissed from his position as racetrack groom in 1975 because of 'prejudice against his "sex" and his "sexual preference".' At the same time, he filed an action for wrongful dismissal in provincial court on the basis of 'prejudice and bias against [his] sex.' Neither form of action had gone to trial by the time Damien died in the mid-1980s, but these actions created an opportunity for the legal structure to define issues of sexuality as falling not into the human rights category 'sex,' but into the category 'sexual orientation.'

If Damien had lived to pursue his human rights complaint and his civil action, he may have been able to fight his way into the category 'sex.' At an early stage, it became obvious that he would not be likely to succeed in the human rights process. The Ontario Racing Commission had managed to obtain party standing in the human rights complaint,[34] and, shortly thereafter, the Ontario Human Rights Commission refused to pursue Damien's complaint on the basis that it could not entertain a complaint relating to discrimination on the basis of 'sexual orientation' under the heading 'sex' discrimination.[35] The Ontario Racing Commission then attempted to expunge references to 'sex' from the civil proceeding as well. However, the Divisional Court concluded that the allegation of 'prejudice and bias based on the sex of Damien' should stand, and also rejected the contention that Damien's pleadings should be amended to clarify 'the specific meaning of the word "sex"... used.'[36]

Damien's inability to pursue the civil action closed the door on the opportunity to hear evidence on the relationship between sexuality and sex discrimination. But perhaps the movement to classify sexuality as 'sexual orientation' would have overshadowed the results of the civil action in any event. In 1977, the Ontario Human Rights Commission confirmed that complaints brought by lesbians and gays fell outside its jurisdiction because 'sex' did not cover issues relating to sexuality. The commission did recommend that 'sexual orientation' be added to the legislation,[37] but the overall effect of that recommendation was simply to reinforce the growing perception that prejudice against lesbians and gays had nothing to do with 'sex' discrimination.

The same process was replicated elsewhere in Canada in other human rights complaints, driving the wedge between 'sex' and 'sexual orientation' ever more firmly in place. In *University of Saskatchewan* v *Saskatchewan Human Rights Commission*,[38] the court ruled that the Saskatchewan Human Rights Commission could not accept the complaint filed by Doug Wilson, who had been denied an educational placement because of his sexuality.[39] The court concluded that discrimination on the basis of 'homosexuality' did not constitute discrimination on the basis of 'sex.' As in the *Damien* cases, this result was not inevitable. Just two years later, the Saskatchewan Court of Appeal overruled *University of Saskatchewan* when reviewing the application of 'sex' to pregnancy discrimination in *Re CIP Paper Products Ltd. and Saskatchewan Human Rights Commission*.[40] Concluding that exclusion of pregnancy-related illnesses from coverage under a group insurance policy did not clearly fall outside the meaning of 'sex' discrimination, the court ordered the commission to process the complaint. In reaching this conclusion, the court expressly overruled *University of Saskatchewan*, concluding, as had the Ontario Division Court, that the application of 'sex' to discrimination was a matter to be determined through evidence and fact-finding, and was not governed exclusively by abstract legal doctrine.

The points made in *Damien* and *CIP* did appear to produce some slight change in the legal process. In 1976, the Manitoba Human Rights Commission accepted a complaint filed by Richard North and Chris Vogel, the two men who had been denied a marriage licence in 1974,[41] for denial of same-sex employment benefits. They filed their complaint under the headings 'sex' and 'marital status.' The commission accepted the complaint for processing, and did refer it to a board. However, the board dismissed the complaint on all grounds,[42] relying on a generalized 'heterosexual presumption' to exclude same-sex relationships from the protected category 'marital status.' The board concluded that two men 'may live together but, in my opinion, they do not do so in any legally recognized "marital status".' On the basis that their cohabitation did not have any legal significance, the board then ruled that denial of spousal benefits did not discriminate on the basis of 'sex' either, reasoning that the complainant had been treated just like any other colleague who might have tried to claim benefits for a person whose relationship to him was not legally recognized.

The British Columbia and federal commissions also accepted complaints brought by gay men before sexual orientation was added to their enabling statutes. The B.C. commission accepted a complaint filed by Gay Alliance Toward Equality (GATE) when the *Sun* refused to publish a classified advertisement containing subscription information on the GATE newsletter *Gay Tide*. This complaint was brought under the heading 'denial of any service customarily available to the public without reasonable cause.'[43] Succeeding at the board level, the complaint failed in subsequent appeals. The B.C. Court of Appeal ruled that it was reasonable to deny access to gays; the Supreme Court of Canada concluded that forcing the *Sun* to publish the notice would violate its right to freedom of the press.[44] The federal human rights commission accepted a complaint from Brian Mossop under the head of 'family status' when he was denied bereavement leave by his employer. Although the tribunal found in favour of Mossop, ordering that the collective agreement be read as if it prohibited discrimination on the basis of 'sexual orientation,'[45] the Supreme Court of Canada extended the 'heterosexual presumption' in concluding that this discrimination was not 'really' on the basis of marital status, but was 'really' on the basis of unprotected 'sexual orientation.'[46]

Despite growing criticism of this line of reasoning,[47] *Mossop* confirmed that, in the absence of specific 'sexual orientation' clauses, human rights commissions could not process complaints from lesbian or gay complainants. Although the federal commission had continued to accept complaints during the pendency of *Mossop*, the Federal Court of Appeal ruled that none of those complaints could be processed after the release of *Mossop*, even though, by that time, the Ontario Court of Appeal had actually read 'sexual orientation' into the federal code in *Haig and Birch*.[48]

Protection for 'Sexual Orientation'

Having been named into visibility by a category chiefly characterized by its complete absence of legal rights ('sexual orientation'), it was perhaps inevitable that sexual minorities would embrace that space and attempt to persuade the state to inject into it some of the legal rights they had been denied. Thus the 'sexual orientation' lobby sprang up as soon as the Ontario Human Rights Commission decided that would not accept John Damien's complaint under the heading 'sex.'[49] This movement quickly spread across the country as other complaints failed. Confidence that the inclusion of 'sexual orientation' in human rights legislation would solve lesbian and gay legal problems was bolstered when the Québec Supreme Court ruled in 1979 that a Catholic school had violated the prohibition on discrimination on the basis of 'sexual orientation' in the Québec Charter[50] – the first such clause in the country – when it had refused to rent its premises to a gay group.[51]

To the extent that there was any debate among lobbying groups over the wisdom of demanding that 'sexual orientation' be added to human rights codes, there seemed to be general consensus that it was probably safest to use the same language the courts had employed in describing the space to which they had assigned lesbians, gays, and same-sex couples. At the time, many activists recognized that the term 'sexual orientation' was less explicit or confrontational than the term 'lesbian,' 'gay,' or 'homosexual,' but also realized that it was simply easier for many people to say.[52] In addition, the gender-neutrality of 'sexual orientation' was seen as being consistent with the move away from sex-specific terminology that had been prompted by the women's movement.

Not all lesbians and gays enthusiastically embraced this strategy, of course. Some activists favoured more open-ended formulations such as 'affectional preference,'[53] feeling that it would more obviously apply to relationship-recognition issues like those raised in early human rights decisions. Others felt that focusing on human rights legislation alone was too limited a strategy, because human rights provisions touched so little of 'real life.'[54] Dramatic differences in the specificities of lesbian and gay existences, together with the effects of gender hierarchies and attitudes towards race, class, and ability issues, meant that racially identified lesbians and gays often felt marginalized by activist groups, and that lesbian and gay activists often found it difficult to work together.[55] Many lesbian groups continued to endorse the 'sexual orientation' movement, largely out of a sense of political expedience, but some groups began to resist it in the belief that 'sexual orientation' clauses would privilege gay men at the expense of lesbian women.[56] And the 'sexual orientation' lobby did not attract much support from transgender and transsexual activists, most of whom took the position that they were disadvantaged not by their sexual/affectional preferences or 'orientation,' but by social and legal constructions of 'sex.' Thus, in the end, the 'sexual orientation' lobby was not so much a queer lobby as a gay/lesbian lobby led by gay men.

Although this lobby did eventually achieve a significant degree of success, two factors limited the value of 'sexual orientation' clauses to lesbians and gays until the equality provisions of the Canadian Charter of Rights and Freedoms came to the rescue. The first factor was the rapidly growing movement to inject expressly heterosexual modifiers into statutory definitions of 'spouse' and legally recognized cohabitation. The second was the narrow interpretation initially given to 'sexual orientation' clauses by courts. Both factors sprang from the same source – the continuing governmental search for ways to induce queers to keep their lives as 'private' as possible. If lesbians and gays were to gain some formal civil rights, then at least the 'same-sex'/'opposite-sex' distinction could be used to deny recognition of relationships even while personal rights to employment or housing, for example, began to be recognized.

The 'Opposite-Sex' Movement

At about the same time that the 'sexual orientation' lobby was beginning to organize in the mid-1970s, Parliament began the process of revising the statutory definition of 'spouse' to limit it expressly to heterosexual couples. Whether this process was designed to contain gay demands for relationship recognition or whether it just so happened to coincide with publicity around the Boulder, Colorado, and North–Matheson marriages is not clear, but the timing is suggestive.

During the 'opposite-sex' movement, both sex-specific terms like 'husband' and 'wife' as well as sex/uality-neutral terms like 'common-law spouse' were systematically replaced with the phrase 'persons of the opposite sex.' This simultaneously continued the sex-specific requirement that couples consist of one person from each of the two legally recognized 'sexes' at the same time that it logically required them to be heterosexual in alliance and not 'homo'-sexual.

The 'opposite-sex' movement began in 1974 and 1975 with federal omnibus legislation enacting several recommendations made by the Royal Commission on the Status of Women.[57] Many of the changes were intended to include women on an equal footing in legislation with men, although age distinctions in pension-eligibility formulas, for example, were still drawn. At the same time, all the cohabitation criteria, which had been expressed in terms of sex-specific terms such as 'husband,' 'wife,' 'man,' and 'woman' were replaced with the new 'opposite-sex' formula.[58] The federal government gave two reasons for making this change: the importance of bringing the criteria for identifying conjugal cohabitants who should be deemed to be spouses for purposes of various benefit programs into line with modern social standards,[59] and the need to replace sex-specific language in statutes and regulations with gender-neutral language.

The 'heterosexuals only' dimension of this reform movement was obviously acknowledged in the beginning, although the absence of a queer lobby in Parliament meant that it was not openly debated as such. Most of the controversy focused instead on the effect this formula might have on family stability, the economic security of first wives, and children of first marriages. However, a few comments made along the way of making this latter point clearly assumed widespread distaste for 'a lot of other things' (heavy code for 'same-sex' relationships).[60]

When the 'sexual orientation' movement finally began to make some inroads into legislation, however, the 'heterosexuals only' dimension of the 'opposite sex' definition of 'spouse' was relied upon expressly in the policy process. The Charter compliance process whereby provincial legislation and regulations were brought into line with the equality guarantees of the Charter of Rights in the mid-1980s created an opportunity to take advantage of Charter discourse and the recommendations of the federal parliamentary Committee on Equality to demand inclusion of 'sexual orientation' in the Ontario Human Rights Code.[61] However, the addition of 'sexual orientation' may well have been possible, in the end, only because Bill 7,[62] the Charter compliance statute, was also used to insert the 'opposite-sex' definition of spouse into thirty-three provincial statutes. This feature of Bill 7 was commonly understood as being needed to eliminate sex-specific language that was inconsistent with the new sex-equality guarantees in the Charter. However, it was openly described by the government as ensuring that the new 'sexual orientation' clause in the Human Rights Code would have to be read together with the new 'opposite sex' definitions of 'marital status' and 'spouse' inserted in the Human Rights Code[63] by Bill 7. In the words of the Minister Responsible for the Human Rights Code, the new 'opposite sex' definition of 'marital status' and 'spouse' was one of the main selling features of the proposed 'sexual orientation' clause:

> The third and most commonly repeated argument against this [sexual orientation] amendment has been that it augurs the destruction of the traditional family. There is simply no basis in law or fact for this. The Code is very clear on the meaning of family, marriage and spouse in its definition sections. It leaves no room for doubt. There is no ambiguity in the words used in terms of the opposite sex. The amendment can in no way impair the clarity of these definitions, nor will it.[64]

It was emphasized repeatedly during discussion of the 'sexual orientation' clause that the government was not changing the definition of marriage, and the examples given in debates consistently focused on discrimination in personal rights and not in relation to lesbian or gay couples.[65] Ian Scott, the Attorney General of Ontario, stated in no uncertain terms that the definition of 'spouse' would not include same-sex couples by virtue of this amendment: 'the government has no plans to redefine the family in Ontario legislation to include unmarried couples of the same sex.'[66]

As 'sexual orientation' was later included in other human rights statutes, it often met up with 'opposite sex' definitions of cohabitants and spouses in those statutes or in general laws. This then provided courts and human rights administrators with a powerful justification for applying 'sexual orientation' clauses to discrimination against individual lesbians and gays but not same-sex couples. Although at least one human rights tribunal had already pointed out by 1980 that exclusion of same-sex couples from cohabitation provisions would probably be discriminatory,[67] it took nearly a decade to establish this seemingly obvious point in litigation.[68]

'Sexual Orientation' in the Courts

After Québec and Ontario extended human rights protection to sexual orientation, other jurisdictions slowly followed suit. By the late 1980s, only four jurisdictions prohibited discrimination on the basis of sexual orientation.[69] In 1992, the Ontario Court of Appeal invoked the Charter of Rights equality guarantees to read 'sexual orientation' into the federal human rights code,[70] and, by 1994, four more provinces had added 'sexual orientation' clauses to their statutes.[71] In the wake of the 1995 Supreme Court of Canada decision in *Egan and Nesbit*, a Newfoundland court read sexual orientation into that province's statute,[72] the federal government formally amended its statute in 1996,[73] and, in 1998, the Supreme Court of Canada used the Charter equality guarantees to read 'sexual orientation' into the Alberta statute as Prince Edward Island added 'sexual orientation' to its human rights statute.[74] The Northwest Territories has not yet acted on this issue.

Despite the fact that this movement was to a very great extent pushed along by the equality guarantees of the Charter,[75] courts consistently attempted to give 'sexual orientation' clauses extremely narrow application from the beginning. Charter equality doctrine did eventually widen the scope of 'sexual orientation' clauses as applied in the human rights and labour context, but that process was slow, unfolding in three identifiable phases over a period of nearly ten years.

In the first phase, discussed below, courts kept to the implicitly privatizing notion of 'sexual orientation' clauses as creating merely personal rights. During this phase, they continued to rely on common-law doctrine treating same-sex marriages as nullities in concluding that 'sexual orientation' clauses did not affect the unrecognized nature of same-sex cohabitation. In the second phase, discussed in chapter 2, courts began to give 'sexual orientation' wider meaning, and, in particular, began to treat discrimination against same-sex couples as discrimination on the basis of sexual orientation in some administrative contexts. Early direct Charter challenges to the meaning of terms such as 'family,' 'relative,' and 'spouse,' when used to interpret 'sexual orientation' as it had been read into the federal human rights code by *Haig and Birch*, were critical in initiating this second phase. However, in this second phase, that fact that success could be secured more easily in human rights and labour hearings contributed to the not-so-subtle funnelling of 'sexual orientation' issues into those 'private' dispute-resolution processes and away from direct Charter challenges to the constitutionality of 'public' statutes themselves.

In the third phase, discussed in chapter 3, the impact of *Egan and Nesbit* on the meaning of 'sexual orientation discrimination' further widened the scope given to 'sexual orientation' clauses in human rights codes and collective agreements. While relationship rights that had public or fiscal dimensions were still not always recognized in that context, the success rate in the administrative context remained much higher than in the context of direct Charter challenges. However, in direct challenges as well, it is worth noting that courts were more willing to recognize relational rights under 'private law' than under 'public' benefit systems.

In order to assess the impact of the new 'sexual orientation' clauses on their own, without the benefit of Charter authorities to widen their interpretation, I have identified a group of ten decisions that have addressed 'sexual orientation' issues independently of Charter equality jurisprudence. While these cases do not all pre-date *Haig and Birch*, none of them appears to have been affected by the changes consolidated in that case (although of course it is always possible that the adjudicator was moved by the shift in legal doctrine initiated by *Haig and Birch*).

Only three of these ten cases were successful.[76] The other seven were resolved against the lesbian or gay applicants.[77] All of the successful complaints involved merely 'personal' rights, while five of the seven unsuccessful applications touched on relational issues.[78]

The line of successful 'sexual orientation' cases began with the Québec Supreme Court decision in *L'Association A.D.G.Q.* v *Catholic School Commission of Montreal*. The real issue in this case was whether the Court should recognize some sort of religious exemption; that refusal to rent the premises to the complainant did constitute discrimination on the basis of sexual orientation was not particularly controverted. The Court was not convinced by the school's appeal to religious values, and simply pointed out that the school had not appeared to assess other organizations in light of their activities when renting the space to them.

The fact that three of the ten 'sexual orientation' cases were successful should not be taken as suggesting that lesbian and gay complainants had begun to achieve a steady series of victories. The other two 'personal rights' cases were not decided until nearly fifteen years later, just after the Ontario Court of Appeal read sexual orientation into the federal human rights code on the basis of the Charter in *Haig and Birch*. Although these personal rights cases appear to have been decided independent of *Haig and Birch*, the fact that social attitudes had changed a great deal during that time had to have been a factor in their outcomes. What is striking is that the victories still, despite major changes in social attitudes, related only to personal rights as distinguished from relational rights. In *Waterman v National Life Assurance Co. of Canada*, an Ontario board of inquiry awarded damages to a lesbian women who had been dismissed from her employment because of her sexual orientation.[79] In *Mercedes Homes Inc.* v *Grace*, an Ontario court ruled that landlord's harassment of two gay men on the basis of their sexual orientation violated the Landlord and Tenant Act, and awarded a partial abatement of rent as a remedy.[80]

The seven unsuccessful complaints revealed a continuing preference for narrowing interpretations of 'sexual orientation.' Two complaints failed because they involved harassment on the basis of sexuality, the tribunals ruling that 'sexual harassment' did not include harassment of someone who was lesbian or gay and that discrimination on the basis of 'sexual orientation' did not apply to sexual harassment. Thus the arbitrator in *Re Cami Automotive Inc. and C.A.W., Local 88* dismissed a grievance brought under a collective agreement on the basis that sexual orientation fell outside the ordinary meaning of 'sexual harassment' in the Ontario Human Rights Act, and the complaint in *Roberts* v *Club Exposé* succeeded only because there was a sufficient evidentiary basis upon which to find that the complainant had also been discriminated against on the basis of race. The complainant, an African-Canadian lesbian woman, had lost her job as a stripper because she wished to perform with her lesbian lover. The club owner claimed that she had violated his policy against permitting boyfriends, spouses, and lovers from visiting the club while their partners performed.[81]

The other five complaints, which all involved relationship-recognition issues, were all defeated by the heterosexual presumption. In *Re Carleton University and C.U.P.E., Local 2424*, a grievance arising out of denial of same-sex employment benefits was rejected because other sections of the collective agreement contained the 'opposite-sex' definition of 'spouse.' The arbitrator decided that the opposite-sex definition of spouse should be read as limiting the sexual-orientation clause to personal rights, only, and declined to rule that protection from discrimination on the basis of sexual orientation invalidated the 'opposite-sex' definition of 'spouse.' The Divisional Court upheld this decision on review. Other complaints resulted in similar rulings even in the absence of specifically 'opposite-sex' definitions of 'spouse.' In *Re Treasury Board (Indian and Northern Affairs) and Watson*, the board concluded that the prohibition on discrimination on the basis of sexual orientation did not entitle the grievor to bereavement leave because same-sex partners did not have any entitlement to bereavement leave. In *Re Treasury Board (Public Works) and Hewens*, an arbitrator ruled that the ordinary legal and social meaning of 'marriage' precluded extension of marriage leave to same-sex partners.

This 'heterosexual presumption' was also applied in *Vogel II*, the third legal action brought by Chris Vogel and Richard North.[82] Still struggling for the everyday legal rights of ordinary couples, they waited patiently until the 'sexual orientation' amendment to the Manitoba Human Rights Code[83] had come into effect in 1988. They then filed another complaint with the provincial human rights commission, this time adding 'sexual orientation' to it. Despite the fact that the addition of 'sexual orientation' to the Manitoba code had changed the legal basis for this second complaint, the court ruled that the complaint was an abuse of process because they had unsuccessfully challenged the same issue five years earlier. The court then went on to reject every branch of the complaint, which had been filed under the four headings 'sex,'' family status,' 'marital status,' and 'sexual orientation.' The court ruled that denial of same-sex employment benefits did not constitute discrimination on the basis of 'sex' because 'sex' referred to gender, not to sexual preference; that it was not discrimination on the basis of 'marital status' because that phrase related only to the state of being married or living in a legally recognized common-law heterosexual relationship, which gay men could not do; and that it was not discrimination on the basis of 'family status' because the term 'family' does not refer to a homosexual partnership. (These were the same points that had been made in the 1983 ruling.) The court then went on to rule that the inclusion of 'sexual orientation' in the code did not affect the application of these headings to same-sex couples, because it contained nothing to suggest that the legislature intended to equate homosexual relationships with spousal relationships between man and wife or with heterosexual common-law relationships. Thus the court concluded that denial of same-sex benefits did not constitute discrimination on the basis of sexual orientation either. (The subsequent reversal of this decision in 1995 is discussed in chapter 3.)

An Ontario court reached a similar conclusion in 1994 in *Clinton* v *Ontario Blue Cross* when it ruled that the new 'sexual orientation' clause in the Ontario human rights code did not affect the opposite-sex definition of 'spouse' in the code in the absence of Charter equality arguments. The complainant had not given timely notice of constitutional question, so the case was decided on the basis of the statute alone.[84]

The contrast between the human rights cases decided under 'sexual orientation' clauses alone, without benefit of the Charter, and the post–*Egan and Nesbit* human rights decisions (discussed in chapter 3) is dramatic: once courts and adjudicators began applying *Egan and Nesbit* as the leading authority on the meaning of 'sexual orientation' as used in human rights legislation and collective agreements, only one complaint has failed – even though many of those complaints involved relationship issues. When combined with the much lower rate of success for direct Charter challenges to relational provisions of statutes and regulations, this increased rate of success in the administrative arena has helped funnel sexuality issues into that form of dispute resolution and out of the courts. While these cases do reveal that lesbian women have not necessarily been disadvantaged relative to gay men by 'sexual orientation' clauses, they do demonstrate that it is still fairly easy to define other sexual minorities and other forms of discrimination, such as harassment, as falling outside the scope of 'sexual orientation.'

Beyond Sexual-Orientation Clauses

Courts have absolutely rejected any suggestion that lesbian women or gay men are simply ordinary people who can bring complaints on the basis of 'sex' or 'marital status.' They have also found various ways to narrow the scope of 'sexual orientation,' even in the absence of relationship issues or 'opposite-sex' relationship criteria. However, resistance to recognizing the human rights of sexual minorities does not seem to have extended to include the head of 'disability' in human rights codes. Thus complainants who happen to be gay and who have experienced discrimination on the basis of HIV status or AIDS disability have usually succeeded. Perhaps this is because, as William Flanaghan has suggested, the HIV/AIDS movement has become less identified with gay men in recent years, with the result that homophobic reactions have not gotten in the way of recoveries in these cases.[85]

Thus, in *Fontaine* v *Canadian Pacific Ltd.*,[86] a federal tribunal awarded damages to a Canadian Pacific cook who had been dismissed because of his HIV status.[87] In *A.-G. Canada* v *Thwaites*,[88] the Federal Court upheld a board award of some $150,000 for lost wages and special compensation to an officer who had been discharged from the Armed Forces on the basis of his HIV status.[89] And in *Wood* v *Hinkel*,[90] a board awarded damages to a complainant whose dentist had expressed his dismay that he had learned about his HIV status from the media rather than from him. The board had found that the dentist's reaction amounted to constructive refusal to treat.[91] In none of these cases was there any attempt to characterize the issue as being 'really' about sexuality in order to prevent the complainants from bringing their complaints under the heading 'disability.' What remains to be seen, however, is how the courts will deal with cases involving other dimensions of queer existence, such as discrimination on the basis of sexuality and ability issues in other contexts,[92] or sexuality and Aboriginal culture,[93] sexuality and sexual style,[94] sexuality and race,[95] or sexuality and age.[96] If tribunals and courts would still prefer to avoid talking about sexuality, then they will be likely to avoid dealing with multiple determinants of discrimination and feel more comfortable focusing on less sexual dimensions of complex identities such as Aboriginal origins, race, or age, as the Ontario court did in the *Roberts* case.

The Queers Outside the Codes

Although there is some indication that the Ontario Human Rights Commission and the Canadian Human Rights Commission may be willing, as a matter of policy, to accept complaints brought by transgendered and transsexual persons on the basis of 'sex,' bisexual, intersexed, transvestite, transgendered, and transsexual persons remain very much excluded from sexual-orientation clauses in human rights codes as well as from ordinary legal structures. While the origins and subsequent application of 'sexual orientation' clauses in Canada suggest that it applies only to lesbians and gays, that interpretation is not necessarily inevitable. For example, Minnesota legislation has defined sexual orientation as including 'having or being perceived as having a self-image or identity not traditionally associated with one's biological maleness or femaleness.'[97] Bisexual, transgendered, and transsexual people would appear to be excluded not because Canadian law and culture do not violate their equality rights, but because there appears to be even less sympathy for their status than for that of lesbian women and gay men.

To be fair, bisexual persons have at least been mentioned in passing in a few Charter cases. However, in most cases, the word 'bisexual' seemed to have been used more as a euphemism for 'homosexual,' as a way to avoid saying 'gay,' 'lesbian,' or 'homosexual.'[98] Similarly, bisexuality has been mentioned in some custody cases,[99] but not in the context of human rights claims.

Because transsexual persons are recognized in provincial legislation,[100] the absence of human rights complaints in relation to transgendered and transsexual individuals seems especially likely to be a symptom of disadvantage and lack of access to the legal process. Indeed, many of the fact situations litigated by transgendered and transsexual persons strongly parallel some of the most important human rights and Charter cases that have been brought by lesbians and gays. The fact that transgendered and transsexual persons have not yet been able to bring their cases within the rubric of human rights or Charter rights suggests that they are particularly disadvantaged by the reliance on mutually exclusive concepts of 'sex' and 'sexual orientation.' Instead of being permitted to occupy legal space within either of those two terms or at their convergence, they have been excluded from both.

Just as lesbian and gay couples have been excluded from the categories 'spouse,' 'marriage,' and 'cohabitant' because they have not had one of each of male and female members, so transgendered and transsexual persons who are both legally of the same sex as their partners have been excluded from the definition of 'spouse' when they have not been able to demonstrate that they are of the 'opposite' legal sex. Being more male than female, for example, has not necessarily made the female 'male enough' to meet that requirement. The courts apparently require that in order for transgendered or transsexual persons to receive any of the ordinary legal rights available to ordinary 'men' or 'women,' they must have completely eliminated all physical/hormonal traces of their original sex and taken on all the attributes of their new sex that medical technology can give them. The reported cases illustrate these general principles.

In *B.* v *A.*,[101] B. underwent bilateral mastectomy, pan-hysterectomy, and full hormonal treatment in the early 1970s when she formed a relationship with another woman. This relationship lasted for twenty-one years, during which time B. and A. lived as husband and wife, raised two children together, and become grandparents. When they separated, A. held title to all their accumulated property, and B. accordingly brought an application for support under Part III of the Family Law Act. Even though B. had filed an application under the Vital Statistics Act to change her legal sex to male, and had obtained certificates from two medical practitioners who had certified that the bilateral mastectomy, hysterectomy, and accompanying hormonal treatment of two decades earlier had resulted in 'the anatomical sex structure [having been] changed to a sex other than that which appears on the registration of birth' within the meaning of the Act, the court rejected these certificates – and along with them B.'s application for support – on the basis that the surgery had not gone far enough: 'The genitalia of B., to my understanding, have in no way been touched surgically ... [A] double mastectomy is not within itself an unusual event. [M]any females today undergo a hysterectomy. Indeed, I would anticipate we have many females who have had both surgical treatments, yet who continue completely as female.' The court went on to conclude that social and psychological pressures or desires did not make up for the lack of genital reconfiguration in this case, and ruled that, notwithstanding the medical certificates produced by B., she was not a 'man' within the meaning of the Family Law Act.

Two years later, the court in *L.C.* v *C.C.*[102] relied on *B.* v *A.* to invalidate the marriage between a post-surgical female-to-male transsexual and her wife. After C.C. had begun the transsexual surgical process, he legally changed his name on his driver's licence, and then, on the strength of that driver's licence, was permitted to obtain a marriage licence.[103] It was at this point that C.C. and L.C. married. When C.C. decided against genital surgery, the relationship broke down. L.C. obtained a court declaration that, because C.C. had not undergone that surgery, the marriage had never been consummated and was void *ab initio*.

Although neither B. nor C.C. ever invoked human rights legislation or the Charter, the parallels with the highly successful Charter challenge in *M.* v *H.*[104] are striking. In that case, a lesbian partner won the right to bring an application for support under the Family Law Act despite the fact that it applied only to opposite-sex partners. The courts relied on the non-discrimination provisions of the Charter to delete the opposite-sex qualification from these provisions. *L.C. v C.C.* and *B. v A.* were not Charter challenges, and thus the legal issue in those cases was constructed as genital configuration, not as social gender identification. Thus the outcome in those cases was very different from that in *M. v H*. It will undoubtedly require further Charter litigation to establish that the application of family law depends not on legal (medical) 'sex,' but on the nature of the relationship in question.

The impermeability of the legal boundaries surrounding heterosexuality are also illustrated graphically in *Canada v Owen*.[105] The applicant in this case, Mrs Lillian Owen, had gone through male-to-female sex-reassignment therapy in the early 1950s, began to live as a woman in 1951, and was formally and legally married to Robert Owen in 1955. She was bereaved in 1964, and, when she became sixty years of age in 1989, she applied under the Old Age Security Act for the widowed spouse's allowance. Even though Mrs Owen provided evidence that she had been considered to have been Owen's lawful wife by the Department of Veterans Affairs, which applied the same 'opposite-sex' definition of 'spouse' as set out in the Old Age Security Act, her application for the spouse's allowance was rejected when administrators noticed that her birth certificate identified her as 'male.' She was invited to get her birth certificate amended, but instead she appealed to a review committee. The committee granted her the allowance on the basis that she had lived as a female for nearly four decades, was married, and had remained married until her husband died. Clearly the committee agreed that 'sex' could be constructed through long-standing social identification. The government disagreed, and, on appeal, persuaded the federal court that Lillian Owen was neither a 'married' spouse nor a common-law spouse because she was not of the legal 'sex' opposite to that of her deceased husband.

The court's reasoning centred on the regulation of legal sex categories in the Ontario Vital Statistics Act.[106] Although Lillian Owen had gone through sex-reassignment therapy that was considered to have formed a sufficient basis for her change of name, change of ascribed legal sex in 1951, and formal marriage to a man in 1955, the court found that she had not met the requirements in the act because she had not proven that she had met the test for legal change of sex: 'where the anatomical sex structure ... is changed [through] transsexual surgery.'[107] The court did not inquire into whether, having been bereaved at the age of thirty-five in

1964, what transsexual surgery, if any, would have been available to her; nor did it inquire into what impact her husband's death would have had on her. Even worse, during argument, Lillian Owen had apparently been convinced to concede that she had not had the legal capacity to marry her husband, and that her marriage was legally a nullity.[108] The very process of attempting to secure her ordinary rights through litigation resulted not only in denial of those benefits, but in being stripped even of her long-held sex and sexual identities.[109]

Despite having both the Vital Statistics Act and the legal right to change her legal sex on her side, Lillian Owen ended up being treated exactly like the same-sex gay couple in *Egan and Nesbit* – even though in both sex and sexual identity she was about as different from both of them as she could be.

The Canadian approach to transsexualism and transgender issues may well change as time passes and understanding of the limitations of narrow categories in human rights legislation grows. For example, the European Court of Justice concluded in 1996 that decisions relating to transgender/transsexual discrimination can be challenged as 'sex' discrimination.[110] And, in British Columbia, after going through what the media have described as the 'first same-sex marriage in Canada,' a male-to-female transsexual who now identifies as lesbian has made submissions to the British Columbia Human Rights Commission requesting that 'gender identity' be added to the Human Rights Code.[111]

Conclusions

Since private consensual adult gay sex was decriminalized in 1969, sexual minorities in Canada have no longer had the threat of criminal liability awaiting those who have chosen to be visible. As a result, they have been able to take a look at the rest of life and attempt to claim many of the ordinary rights taken for granted in contemporary Canadian society. Thus the first 'liberation' strategy, from a legal perspective, was simply to demand the same treatment in law that other people received on a routine and unquestioned basis. It appears that this strategy was doomed to failure for the same reason that 'homosexuality' was criminalized and suppressed for so long – social and moral disapproval.

Lesbians and gays then turned to human rights commissions for protection from discrimination. While the first such complaints were brought under the heading 'sex discrimination,' complainants also tried to convince commissions to accept their complaints under relationship headings such as 'marital status' and 'family status.' This second strategy also failed, as courts excluded lesbians and gays from the ambit of those heads of protection and relegated them to the unprotected jurisprudential space labelled 'sexual orientation.' Having been told as part of the criminal-law-reform process that their liberty lay in the 'private' sphere, courts appeared to take that literally, and permitted them no rights under 'public' statutes – not even human rights statutes, which publicly regulate selected 'private' dealings.

Once courts had established that discrimination on the basis of sexuality was properly referred to as discrimination on the basis of sexual orientation, it was more or less inevitable that, as a third strategy, activists would then focus their efforts on lobbying governments to include 'sexual orientation' clauses in human rights codes. As sexuality began to gain a 'public' dimension in human rights legislation, the parallel distinction between status and conduct, or between personal rights and relational rights, brought some of that jurisprudentially unprotected space into the human rights arena as legislatures and courts together agreed that sexual-orientation clauses protected only such personal rights as the right to services, employment, and accommodation, but did not give same-sex relationships any legal status. This limitation on the kind of protection lesbians and gays could expect from sexual-orientation clauses was reinforced by the proliferation of 'opposite-sex' definitions of 'spouse' in statutes, often even in human rights codes themselves.

When the cases involving the application of 'sexual orientation' clauses are examined independent of the effect that Charter equality jurisprudence later had on that term, the record is dire: only three of the ten cases brought strictly as 'sexual orientation' cases ever succeeded, and of the seven that failed, all but two involved relationship issues. The three successful cases involved rental of a church hall in Québec, employment in Ontario, and harassment of gay tenants by a landlord.

Not only did queer communities have to wait until the early 1990s to see two of these three successes, but none of the reported human rights cases has yet touched on issues affecting bisexual, transgendered, or transsexual persons. To date, they have experienced the same jurisprudential 'non-existence' as lesbians and gays, not because of their sexuality, but because of their 'sex' identity. When compared with lesbians and gays, however, transgendered and transsexual persons are even more disadvantaged, for they have not yet gained entry into reported human rights cases. Although the legal category 'sex' is policed at least as heavily as 'sexuality' has been, litigation of these human rights complaints still lies in the future.

Overall, if the legal and social rights of lesbians and gays had ultimately depended solely on human rights codes unaided by Charter equality jurisprudence, I would have to conclude that, despite their 'collective subjectivity' and growing self-affirmation, sexual minorities in Canada would not have been permitted to seek 'full life' or to live as 'real persons.' If it were not for the Charter, human rights codes probably would have given sexual minorities access to but a few isolated and disjointed rights scattered among the thirteen jurisdictions into which Canada is divided. Even if all these limited rights could be rolled up into one jurisdiction, they would still not support the 'full lives' of 'real persons' in the same way that ordinary civil law supports the real and full lives of ordinary people on a day-to-day basis.

Thus it seems fair to say that, absent the Charter, the real effect of human rights litigation relating to sexuality has been to push all queers towards that 'death of the spirit' that Muriel Rukeyser saw as the antithesis of 'full life.'

Chapter Two

Chart(er)ed Rights

chart v.t. to make a map of | | to record on a chart or graph [O.F.].
– *New Webster's Encyclopedic Dictionary* (New York: Lexicon, 1988), 166

CHARTER, n. An instrument emanating from the sovereign power ... to a colony or dependency, and assuring to them certain rights, liberties, or powers. A charter differs from a constitution, in that the former is granted by the sovereign, while the latter is established by the people themselves.
– *Black's Law Dictionary*, Rev. 4th ed. (St Paul, MN: West, 1968), 298

Originally documents with which new sovereigns attempted to reassure their subjects that their rule not only would be no worse than that of their predecessors, but would be better, 'charters' evoke understandably mixed reactions from those who read them as both threat of continued domination and promise of change, perhaps even of liberation.[1]

Such were the mixed feelings with which queer communities greeted the chart(er)ing process in Canada, as disadvantaged groups lined up outside Parliament to lay their cases for recognition/inclusion/liberation in the Charter of Rights and Freedoms that was being drafted not exactly in consultation with the people, but with the appearance of reference to some supposedly representative clusters of organized disadvantaged groups. The process by which women's groups did end up shaping the provisions of section 15 of the Charter had given queer communities ample notice that if they did not make representations on their own behalf, then they ran the risk of being left out of what was beginning to look like a very detailed 'chart' of liberties.

There was never really any question of sitting out the Charter lobbying process. It had already become obvious, even by the late 1970s, that human rights codes alone would not be able to redress the pervasive effects of centuries of homophobia. To be left out of the most important human rights document to be formulated in the entire history of Canada could only entrench legal discrimination on the basis of sexuality more deeply. But it was with considerable trepidation that activists began to work towards the inclusion of 'sexual orientation' in the new Charter. The Charter lobbying process unfolded in several stages, some of which overlapped with lobbying efforts to gain access to human rights legislation that had been inspired by losses in pre-Charter litigation. There was, first, the period during which the provisions of the new Charter were being drafted. Gay input into that process was limited, and lesbian input was almost non-existent. Politicians and lobbyists failed to convince the drafters of section 15 of the Charter to enumerate 'sexual orientation' as one of the heads of protection in that clause, although the drafters did eventually agree to include 'open-ended' language, which it was said would protect sexual minorities.

Widespread unhappiness with the inclusions, exclusions, and effects of the Charter equality guarantees led to a three-year 'moratorium' on the effective date of section 15, during which organizations at all levels looked at the probable impact of these provisions. This was the second stage of lobbying, and it should have led naturally to the enactment of new legislation implementing those recommendations.

This did not happen. After the new Charter was finalized and governments across Canada began to look at amending their own legislation in order to bring it into 'compliance' with its provisions, it became clear that no government in the country was initially willing to recommend such legislation. At the tail end of the three-year 'moratorium' the drafters had imposed on the implementation of section 15, the federal government released a discussion paper and began hearings that inspired another wave of hope that the government could be persuaded to add 'sexual orientation' to section 15 of the Charter, or at least would agree to amend federal human rights legislation to grant lesbians and gays some equal rights.

This hope was also unfounded. When the committee released its report, it appeared to shift most of the responsibility for Charter 'compliance' in relation to sexual minorities back to the human rights structure. All any government appeared to agree on was that section 15 of the Charter, despite its silence on 'sexual orientation,' ought to apply to lesbians and gays.

The only bright spot during this period was the involvement of growing numbers of lesbian and gay activists in the public political process. The Boyer Committee hearings on equality created a forum in which lesbian and gay groups across Canada could bring the full story of lesbian/gay existence into public view. The role that Svend Robinson, then Justice Critic for the opposition, played in these hearings was critical. If it were not for the visibility he gave issues of sexuality in the hearings, it is doubtful whether the other members of the committee would have been as receptive as they were during the weeks and months of submissions on issues relating to sexuality.

Although the testimony in these hearings remains a valuable record of the realities of lesbian and gay existence in Canada during the mid-1980s, little came of this testimony. Nor were transgendered or transsexual persons represented at all in this process, and only one witness was identified as bisexual. In the end, the entire Charter implementation process merely confirmed what many activists had feared all along: Lesbians and gays would have to resort to Charter litigation in order to benefit from section 15, because even the few little changes that the federal government was willing to recommend fell radically short of redressing the effects of long-standing legal discrimination and consequent social/economic discrimination. Thus the process of chart(er)ing the constitutional rights of sexual minorities moved to the courts.

Despite having been assured that the whole purpose behind including 'open-ended' language in section 15 was to ensure that 'the question of whether section 15 has been violated will not turn on questions such as, does "sex" include "sexual orientation",'[2] litigants literally had to start at square one. In Charter challenges, the opponent will almost always be the same governments that had agreed to the non-specific open-ended language in section 15 in the first place, and governments quickly poured massive resources into resisting lesbian and gay claims for inclusion in the Charter.

Instead of proceeding on the basis that section 15 of the Charter of course prohibited discrimination based on sexual orientation, the courts simply recycled the reasoning used in early human rights decisions when queers were forced to frame their complaints on the basis of 'sex,' 'family status,' or 'marital status.' Thus the courts followed a predictable line of reasoning: Discrimination against lesbians and gays did not constitute discrimination on the basis of 'sex' or 'family status' because it was discrimination on the basis of 'sexual orientation,' but discrimination on the basis of 'sexual orientation' was not prohibited by the Charter, and, even if it were, the prohibition did not extend to discrimination based on having a same-sex partner.[3]

In the first ten years of equality litigation under the Charter, lesbians and gays nevertheless did win some half a dozen direct Charter challenges, and a growing number of human rights complaints and labour grievances began to succeed in the first half of the 1990s as well. The pivotal rulings from this period were the British Columbia decision in *Knodel* v *B.C. Medical Services Commission*,[4] in which the court concluded that two gay men could fall into the legal category 'live together as husband and wife,' and the Ontario Court of Appeal decision in *Haig and Birch*,[5] which read 'sexual orientation' into the federal human rights code after the federal government failed to deliver on its own promise to do so as part of the Charter 'compliance' process. *Knodel* treated a same-sex relationship as being equivalent to a spousal relationship, and that new view of same-sex relationships then influenced the interpretation of 'sexual orientation' protection as injected into the federal human rights code and some federal-sector collective agreements by *Haig and Birch*. While these two cases led to a real breakthrough in the numbers of administrative rulings that found in favour of lesbians and gays, they did also have the effect of continuing to funnel lesbian and gay legal claims into dispute-resolution processes largely considered to affect only the 'private' sector.

During the same period of time, a contrary line of authority emanating from the trial court and appellate decisions in *Egan and Nesbit* v *The Queen*[6] threatened even those few gains. Both courts agreed that when Parliament had good reasons for limiting eligibility for publicly funded government benefits to 'opposite-sex' couples, Charter challenges to the definition of 'spouse' were really just attempts to indirectly challenge 'abstract' common-law and statutory definitions of marriage. This reasoning suggested that 'sexual orientation' claims to 'public' benefits might be treated differently than were claims in the human-rights and labour law area to 'private' benefits, at least to the extent that the benefits were premised on relationship status and not on the sexual orientation of a lesbian or gay claiming as a single, unattached person.

Drafting the Charter

The idea of a constitutionally based bill of rights like that in the United States pre-dated the drafting of the Canadian Charter of Rights and Freedoms by several decades. The Canadian Bill of Rights[7] was enacted in 1960 in order to inject the notion of 'equality before the law' into Canadian law. When courts concluded that this bill of rights was merely a statutory instrument that could not constitutionally 'entrench' any human rights, the drafting focus turned to the development of a constitutional bill of rights. The Bill of Rights itself did prohibit discrimination on the basis of 'sex,' but it did not mention sexuality or sexual orientation,[8] and there is no record of any attempts by any sexual minorities to use it to challenge discriminatory legislation.

The current equality guarantees in the Charter of Rights evolved out of more than a dozen drafts proposed by various federal and provincial committees between 1968 and 1981. Not one of these drafts ever contained the words 'sexual orientation' or 'sexuality,' even after it became clear that provincial and federal human rights legislation would not provide any protection to sexual minorities.[9]

The drafting of the current Charter was the direct outcome of Bill C-60,[10] which authorized Parliament to begin the process of amending the Canadian constitution in the late 1970s. Although the Liberal party had adopted a resolution in 1978 to press for equal rights on the basis of sexual orientation, Liberal members of Parliament joined with Conservatives to exclude sexual orientation from the Charter during the drafting process. The committees charged with preparing these drafts were repeatedly requested to include 'sexual orientation' in what became section 15 of the Charter, but this never happened.[11] While the Charter was still in Committee, the vote was 12 to 2 against inclusion. Only the NDP members of the committee supported express inclusion of sexual orientation in the Charter.[12] So hostile were some members of Parliament to the express inclusion of sexual orientation that, when Svend Robinson formally moved the amendment of the Charter to include sexual orientation in 1981, another member scoffed at the amendment, saying that Parliament could not 'include every barnacle and eavestrough in the Constitution of Canada.'[13]

In the end, all that sexual minorities were able to achieve was the assurance that the open-ended language added to section 15(1) of the Charter at the last minute would enable lesbians and gays to invoke the equality guarantees as 'non-enumerated' groups. The final version of section 15(1) guaranteed equality rights 'without discrimination, and in particular, without discrimination based on ...'[14] The drafters of section 15 – including the Honourable Jean Chrétien, then minister of justice – expressly stated that the enumerated grounds were merely exemplary, and it was further pointed out that this open-ended language was necessary to prevent Canada from being in breach of its obligations under international law.[15]

The implications of this open-ended language for lesbians and gays were kept fairly low-profile during the drafting process. Fear was expressed by activists representing other groups that antipathy towards 'homosexuals' could undercut the Charter aspirations of other non-enumerated groups. Some gay activists took the pragmatic view that, if they had to chose between express inclusion in the Charter versus complete exclusion, they were better off with this open-ended language. Remember, by that time only the Québec Charter of Human Rights and Freedoms contained such language,[16] all the cases brought under non-specific human rights provisions had failed, and the second such clause to be enacted was still another six years in the future.[17] In any event, I doubt that any of the proponents of the Charter would have considered for one minute letting controversy over sexuality endanger the chartering process.

Shortly after the Charter finally came into effect in 1982, Hon. Mark MacGuigan, then minister of justice and attorney general of Canada, confirmed that it was understood that section 15 would apply to sexual orientation:

> The list of grounds of discrimination contained in section 15 is not exhaustive. Thus, while it is true that certain grounds of discrimination are expressly prohibited, this enumeration does not detract from the general prohibition found in the section. Therefore, express prohibition of the specific forms of discrimination on the basis of marital status, political affiliation and sexual orientation is not necessary.[18]

This letter had been written in response to concerns that section 15 would not apply to sexual orientation.

If the federal and provincial governments of Canada had adhered to this quiet understanding, fifteen years of expensive and controversial litigation could have been avoided. As history has revealed, however, the government did not exactly keep its promises after the Charter came into effect.

The 'Moratorium' Years

The drafters of the Charter realized that the equality guarantees in section 15 opened up a huge range of issues. At the progressive end of the political spectrum, feminist lobby groups, which were well organized, well funded, and highly visible in comparison with gay and lesbian groups, were poised to press for expansive and substantive interpretation of the new equality guarantees they had already managed to influence during the drafting process.[19] Groups that had not made it into the list of 'enumerated' grounds of discrimination in section 15 – including sexual minorities – were left feeling deeply frustrated and disenfranchised once again, and faced the double challenge of persuading the government to extend equality protections to them and to apply a substantive interpretation to those equality guarantees. At the other end of the political spectrum, institutions such as the Department of National Defence and the Royal Canadian Mounted Police were obviously already planning how to continue justifying the exclusion of women, queers, and other 'equality-seeking' groups from their organizations within the terminology of section 15.

Thus the government decided to defer the effective date of section 15 of the Charter for three additional years – the 'moratorium years'– in order to give all levels of government time to review their policies and legislation, receive submissions from non-governmental groups and members of the public, and begin the legislative 'Charter compliance' process.[20] During that time, groups formed to organize community and professional support, identify their policy positions, draft submissions, and develop structures – journals, litigation groups, educational groups – that could be deployed once section 15 came into effect.

What is very obvious in retrospect is that the same pervasive discrimination that had profoundly suppressed queer existence until the 1970s and that had resulted in the exclusion of sexuality from the enumerated heads of protection in section 15(1) of the Charter had also placed queers at a real disadvantage in the Charter 'compliance' process. But now, added to the effects of centuries of systemic discrimination and homophobia, lesbian and gay groups found themselves competing with other 'equality-seeking' groups for resources, community support, personnel, speech time, and respect in the new fora that were being created as a result of the Charter.

On a broader level, politics of sex, sexuality, feminism, race, and class played a huge role in how the entire 'Charter compliance' process continued to marginalize sexual minorities. But the fragmentation of identities reflected in the language of section 15(1) itself also affected the structure of the equality-seeking process for every group and for every person involved in it. In the end, this fragmentation of identities, interests, and political energies was yet another factor operating to the detriment of queer communities during this part of the chart(er)ing process. Queers were carefully presented as 'lesbian' and 'gay,' and not as 'bisexual,' 'transsexual,' or 'transgendered,' while feminists were carefully imaged as being inclusive in theory but not overtly lesbian in practice.

Lesbians were caught in a very particular bind in the processes that unfolded during the moratorium years. Small local groups of feminist lesbians did form during this period, but for several reasons most lesbian lawyers ended up working with either (non-lesbian) feminist- or gay-dominated groups instead of being able to organize autonomously on the same scale. With several national and provincial organizations already in place, better funding, larger numbers of members, and gay men's seemingly greater ability to be 'out,' most lesbian lawyers seemed to feel that they could not be as effective on their own. Issues of race, class, gender, and sexuality tended to isolate lesbian women who became involved in either feminist or gay(/lesbian) groups, leaving lesbian feminists with the choice of struggling against (non-lesbian) feminist hegemony to gain feminist support for lesbian issues, or struggling for gay support for lesbian issues. Tensions between non-lesbian feminists and some gay groups at the time made those options even more difficult to negotiate.

Like many other feminist lesbians, I ended up spending more time working with (non-lesbian) feminist groups, either as part of the overall group or in smaller lesbian caucuses designed to increase the visibility of lesbian issues. Thus I saw first-hand how the urgency of the political context intersected with group structures to priorize 'getting "equality" right' over 'getting queers into the Charter.'

At the beginning of the moratorium years, I think that I and other lesbian women rather recklessly assumed that, if we joined with (non-lesbian) feminists, we could not only pursue the project of promoting women's equality, but also articulate the needs of lesbian women at the same time. I was certainly naïve in believing that my involvement would be valued not just because of my feminist politics, but because I brought my own experiences of lesbian existence to these projects, and was willing to inject these experiences into work that would, I believed, unfold around all the dimensions of women's existence – sex, gender, marital status, and sexuality, race, ability, age, and class. Speaking for myself only, I perceived the openness of the women's movement to lesbians not as instrumental, using lesbians to image feminism as an inclusive politic, but as simply reflective of the political potential of feminist method.

In retrospect, I think this perception was overly optimistic. When I look at what women's groups accomplished for lesbians during the moratorium years, I mourn for all the silences in myself during those years, even as I worked out lesbian issues in other contexts. While I certainly benefited from participating in the articulation of feminist equality theory at the grass-roots level and in early litigation, from feminist research, and from the networking that went on among (lesbian) feminist lawyers, the aura of disapproval that enveloped the room every time I overtly named my lesbianism or insisted that it be part of every text I touched was difficult to face. At the same time, even though I am sure that most of the people I worked with felt that I already made far too much noise about being a feminist lesbian, I felt that I was being extraordinarily restrained.

I would now describe the way in which lesbian issues kept getting submerged or subordinated to (non-lesbian) feminist issues as a form of appropriation. But it was not a one-sided appropriation: I certainly felt I was making a strategic choice that would generate support by (non-lesbian) feminists for lesbian issues. As time passed and the process became clearer, it was implicitly assumed that lesbian issues were, at best, footnotes to the issues of heterosexual women. While most groups were quite happy to take advantage of the energies and insights of lesbian women (I cannot comment on where gay men were situated in these processes), hierarchies of 'outness' ensured that, from the public perspective, feminist groups were seen as basically heterosexual. Lesbian women who were amenable to closeting their sexuality, or who advocated this stance for various political or theoretical reasons, were more easily tolerated in feminist groups than were those who were 'out.' At the same time, the presence of some 'out' lesbians did help make feminist activities and organizations look perhaps more inclusive and progressive than their agendas actually were. At conferences and strategy meetings, in working sessions and on journal boards, attempts to place lesbianism on the agenda were surrounded with a palpable but inexpressible tension. It was still 'too early' to push the issue of discrimination against lesbians – feminists wanted everyone's energy, lesbian and (non-lesbian) feminist alike, to be devoted to (non-lesbian) feminist issues. Issues of race, ability, age, sexuality, and colour were fairly consistently used not as a basis for substantive exploration, but as a way to answer emerging charges of racism, ableism, classism, or lesbophobia that were beginning to be levelled at the women's movement.

Other lesbian women can tell similar stories, I am sure, which reveal the deep struggle that was going on for 'ownership' and deployment of lesbian energies. Feminist groups obtained some of the most challenging and devoted work from women who were either not yet 'out' or who had made an explicit decision to remain in the closet. Gay groups wanted, needed, lesbian members, but did not always redefine their political agendas quickly enough to attract the same level of commitment from lesbians. In memory, my lobbying experiences with the Coalition for Gay Rights in Ontario (CGRO)are tinged with the sense of being welcome as useful window-dressing, but of being excluded from the 'real' process because of subtle differences between lesbian women who identified as lesbian feminists and those who identified as 'gay' women. (The GCRO became the CLGRO [Coalition for Lesbian and Gay Rights in Ontario] after lesbians complained of exclusion.)

I describe the political tensions I noticed in this detail because I think they help explain why the entire 'Charter industry' that began to develop during the moratorium years seemed to ignore lesbians and gays, sexuality, sexual orientation, and same-sex couples to a great extent.[21] As governments began to bring forward discussion papers and draft 'compliance' legislation, issues of sexuality remained largely invisible. In Ontario, Evelyn Gigantes had to spend a long time convincing the new Liberal government to support Bill 7, but even she was unable to stave off the 'opposite sex' movement within her own caucus that was intended to contain the new 'sexual orientation' clause.[22] Even worse, governments elsewhere began to back off from the position that the open-ended language in section 15 of the Charter would extend the equality guarantees to lesbians and gays.

For example, the Saskatchewan Department of Justice only weakly acknowledged the role of the open-ended language of section 15(1) in its Charter discussion paper: '[Marital status] is not an enumerated ground of discrimination under section 15, but may fall within the scope of that section in any event.'[23] The Ontario government agreed that section 15 was intended to be open-ended, but then quickly pointed out that the judiciary would be the ultimate arbiters: '[T]he real issue seems to be not whether non-enumerated grounds should be given protection, but rather which additional grounds will be judicially recognized.'[24]

Even the federal government appeared to be rethinking its position on the application of section 15 to lesbians and gays. In the federal Charter discussion paper, the attorney general of Canada (by then, Hon. John Crosbie) did maintain that 'the wording of section 15 suggests that ... there could be successful complaints of a denial of equality based on other grounds,'[25] but he went on to minimize and defend discrimination against lesbians and gays in federal legislation: 'Distinctions on the basis of sexual orientation are not made on the face of any federal legislation. However, there are policies excluding homosexuals and lesbians from such bodies as the Canadian Armed Forces.'[26] He then uncritically reiterated the reasons routinely given by the military for excluding gays: fear of offending the laws of other countries to which personnel might be posted; security risks; and the disruption to the institution that would flow from violent attacks on gay personnel that their presence was alleged to invite.[27]

Implementing Equality

Six weeks before section 15 was to come into effect, the government decided to form a parliamentary committee on equality to hold public hearings across the country on issues relating to the Charter. Although the resolution forming the committee instructed it to consider the attorney general's discussion paper, review federal legislation, and ensure that it conformed with 'the letter and spirit of equality and non-discrimination guarantees in the Charter,'[28] this was largely a political move designed to reduce the pressure on the government to take immediate legislative steps to implement equality rights, for the government could then argue that it was actively studying the Charter equality guarantees in consultation with the entire Canadian public.

By 17 April 1985, when the moratorium on section 15 of the Charter ended, not one single government in Canada had enacted any new legislation relating to sexuality. Instead, as the moratorium ended and section 15 first came into effect, the attention of most equality-seeking groups was focused on the hearings being held by the Boyer Committee. The committee, thrown together at the very end of the moratorium period, did not hear from its first non-governmental witnesses until 16 April 1985. A wide cross-section of groups and institutions addressed this committee. Feminists were well represented at all the hearings, and concentrated on urging legislative reforms that would promote the substantive equality of women. The armed forces were there, urging in every way they could the continued exclusion of women, queers, and other groups from the services. Members of the groups that had been enumerated in section 15 of the Charter[29] concentrated in their submissions on identifying the many detailed provisions of federal law that would have to changed in order to remove barriers to equality.

Two things distinguished this process from all the other chart(er)ing processes that had preceded it. First, Svend Robinson, who played an extremely active role in putting the issue of sexual orientation squarely on the agenda of the committee, bravely used his extensive knowledge of discriminatory policies, earlier policy discussions, and the personnel involved to dig out and expose for public view the homophobic attitudes that pervaded federal institutions right from the beginning of the hearings. For example, in one of the earliest sittings, weeks before the committee heard from its first lesbian or gay witnesses, Robinson engaged a representative of the RCMP in a detailed analysis of the RCMP's discriminatory policies by confronting an RCMP witness with the testimony he had given in other hearings on the issue of hiring gays and lesbians: '[T]here are few members of any police organization that are comfortable at this point in our history with people of that persuasion in their midst.'[30] Robinson went on to compare that justification for excluding gays with the reasons given in the past for excluding racial minorities, women, and other groups, and then asked the witness to comment on the impact the Charter might have on those policies. This elicited the statement that 'an organization in order to work has to look a certain way in the public it serves and in itself in order to have a certain view of itself,'[31] and the assertion that if the Charter required the RCMP to change its discretionary policy of exclusion to an exclusionary rule, that it would invoke section 1 of the Charter to justify it.[32]

Throughout the hearings, Robinson got the issue of sexuality onto the pages of Hansard. His questions and comments did not prevent other members of the committee from displaying their homophobia from time to time, but his presence palpably changed the atmosphere in the hearing rooms. He took the trouble to point out to representatives of gay and lesbian groups who were beginning to make potentially damaging personal disclosures that the armed forces had representatives in constant attendance to take notes. He came to the defence of the lesbian witness who had dared to refer to her life-partner as her 'lover' and had been treated to a lecture by Sheila Finestone, who explained at length why she found that term irritating.[33] He followed up points, promoted discussion, and generally supported lesbian and gay witnesses in a way that none of the other members of the committee could or would do. This leadership undoubtedly enhanced the testimony recorded in the pages of Hansard, and made it easier for witnesses to make the points they had come to make.

Second, these hearings were unique because of the sheer numbers of lesbians and gays who came out, made submissions, took the risks of public identification in their communities in order to tell the committee what it was like to live almost completely outside the law. Almost no sittings went by in which at least one or two lesbian or gay groups did not appear, and it was obvious that many more groups had applied to appear or had made written submissions. As a result, the transcripts of the committee hearings contain rich detail on discrimination against lesbians and gays that had never been injected directly into the political process before.

The points made by lesbian and gay witnesses in these hearings are not new or original, but what was new was the fact that they were being made over and over by large numbers of witnesses across the country, all speaking out of their own direct experiences of discrimination. The forms of discrimination identified by the witnesses included: differential ages of consent in the criminal code; exclusion of gays from foreign service postings, the military, the RCMP, and religious ordination; violence against lesbians and gays; lack of support networks for young gays, gays in small towns, and parents who are lesbian or gay; denial of relationship recognition; denial of access to public benefits like the new Spouses Allowance Act;[34] bias against lesbian and gay parents in custody litigation; lack of legal frameworks for resolving disputes on relationship breakdown, including lack of responsibility for child support or division of assets; silence in sex- education programs on the issue of sexuality; entrapment, harassment, interrogation, and expulsion of gays and lesbians in the armed forces; denial of use of public facilities; refusal to extend human rights protections to lesbian and gays; use of Christian religious doctrine to justify employment discrimination in schools; homophobic violence in schools; lack of resources for lesbian and gay youth thrown out of their families of origin; discrimination in legal doctrine relating to wills, insurance, and income taxation; susceptibility to will challenges; lack of affirmation for children with same-sex parents; exclusion from public clubs and restaurants; homophobic values embedded in the general culture; discrimination in employment, housing, and public services; fear of being out in correctional institutions, professions, and the federal civil service; fear of public identification; discrimination in pension plans and adoption policies; denial of marriage rights; lack of rights to consent to medical treatment for a partner or her children; risks of political action to charitable registration status; the impact of all of the above on rates of depression and attempted suicide; discrimination in immigration legislation; lack of access to health care for patients with AIDS; lack of public education on the dangers of homophobia; the extreme costs of litigating human rights cases; homophobic stereotyping and 'joking'; lack of legal prohibitions on hate literature; fear of public identification, to the point of using pseudonyms; lack of sufficient research funding for AIDS; the threat of legal liability for talking to minors about sexual orientation, including in public schools; allegations that gays are more susceptible to 'blackmail'; interference with freedom of expression, assembly, and association, to the point of televising videotapes of gay raids; police harassment of gay publications; the emotional costs of living in the closet; unsubstantiated allegations that all gays are child molesters of some sort; the effects of widespread homophobia on young people coming out; routine 'round-up' operations in parks and other public areas; bath raids and surveillance, entrapment, and perjury in arrests; allegations that gay porn is worse than any other forms of pornography; denial of security clearances on the basis of sexuality; fear of receiving counselling; 'psychiatrization' of sexuality; denial of hospital visiting rights; denial of federal funding for academic research on sexuality and law; exclusion of sexuality from policy agenda; treating sexuality as a 'bona fide occupational impediment'; denial of political asylum on the basis of prosecution of gays and lesbians; denial of immigration rights to those convicted of homosexual offences in other countries; denial of access to public-service broadcasting resources; dismissal of gay teachers on various pretexts; lack of access to classified-advertising sections in newspapers; exclusion of gays from police work out of deference to homophobic public attitudes; breaches of medical confidentiality by homophobic doctors; exclusion from partner benefits related to RRSPs, RPPs, CPP/QPP, health care, and other benefit programs; and denial of same-sex employment benefits.[35]

Some of the witnesses documented the lack of legal remedies for the discrimination they had experienced by pointing to their own unsuccessful court cases.[36] Some of the witnesses had just been expelled from the armed forces or had just lost custody of their children. For some, this was their first appearance in public as lesbian or gay.

The committee's report, published in October 1985,[37] devoted an entire section to 'sexual orientation.' However, the format of the report itself signalled lesbian and gay communities not to expect much from the government from that point onward. The explosion of information the committee had received during the hearings was almost invisible in the pages of the report. The committee recommended only two substantive changes to existing federal legislation and practices: stop denying security clearances on the basis of sexual orientation, and enact uniform ages of consent for private consensual sexual activities.[38] The deep divisions among committee members over sexuality apparently led to a compromise position on how the rest of the issues raised by witnesses should be addressed; the committee merely recommended that 'sexual orientation' be added to the Canadian Human Rights Act, and that, once the Human Rights Act was so amended, the military and the RCMP should bring their employment practices into conformity with it.[39] Remembering that the jurisprudence on 'sexual orientation' was virtually non-existent in 1985, the recommendation that all federal issues touching on sexuality be funnelled into the human rights process was very discouraging, to say the least.

Even more discouraging, the long-standing 'opposite-sex' movement met up with this very limited set of recommendations on 'sexual orientation' right in the pages of this report, building in yet another layer of insulation between discrimination against sexual minorities in relational issues and Charter jurisprudence. Not only did the committee refuse to recommend statutory recognition of same-sex relationships, but it actually recommended, in dealing with what it saw as serious discrimination against non-married cohabitants, that, as the federal government began to enact legislation recognizing non-married cohabitants, the legislation 'require that the parties be of the opposite sex.'[40]

Speaking for the federal government, Hon. John Crosbie, Minister of Justice and Attorney General of Canada, pulled Charter equality discourse even further back towards 'ground zero' when he responded to these recommendations.[41] On the critical point of whether the open-ended language in section 15 would apply to 'sexual orientation,' the response was worrying. When the minister of justice stated that '[t]he Department of Justice is of the view that the courts will find that sexual orientation is encompassed by the guarantees on section 15 of the Charter,'[42] lesbian and gay lawyers realized that the government was probably reluctant to take this step itself, but preferred to shift responsibility for clarifying this point to the courts. This implied that the federal government would probably not be in court by the side of lesbian and gay plaintiffs, but might even be opposing Charter challenges relating to sexual orientation.

The government's other responses were no more encouraging. The government seemed to agree that federal human rights legislation ought to be amended to prohibit discrimination on the basis of sexuality, but also denied that sexuality did actually affect security clearance ('the criteria applied are loyalty to Canada and reliability').[43] Instead of taking the action recommended by the committee on criminal ages of consent, the government merely undertook to study the issue in consultation with the provinces and 'private sector groups.'[44]

The Charter implementation process grew to a close as jurisdiction after jurisdiction enacted Charter 'compliance' legislation that fell short of doing even half of what various committees and policy study groups had recommended. While Ontario, Manitoba, and the Yukon did enact 'sexual orientation' clauses in the late 1980s, no other jurisdiction touched sexuality issues in their Charter 'compliance' legislation. The detailed evidence of massive discrimination against lesbians and gays presented in the federal hearings faded from collective memory as governments acted as if eliminating formal inequalities from statute law was all that was needed to eliminate discrimination.[45]

Queers in Canada thus had to move into their un-chart(er)ed futures with nothing but vague and oblique predictions (no longer promises) that the courts would surely apply section 15 of the Charter to cases of discrimination on the basis of sexual orientation.[46] Driven to the Chart(er) process in the first place by the silences in ordinary legal doctrine and human rights legislation and the overt heterosexual preference in 'opposite sex' definitions of 'spouse,' queers were now being told that their best hope really lay in the silences in the Charter.

Early Charter Challenges

In 1995, the Supreme Court of Canada in *Egan and Nesbit* v *The Queen* did add its authority to the growing body of cases that agreed that section 15(1) of the Charter did prohibit discrimination on the basis of sexual orientation. The Court went even further, concluding that, although exclusion of same-sex couples from the definition of 'spouse' by 'opposite-sex' formulations could be 'demonstrably justified' on policy grounds, it did constitute discrimination on the basis of sexual orientation.

In the ten years it took to achieve that ruling, lesbian, gay, and bisexual people brought growing numbers of Charter challenges to both federal and provincial legislation in the search for a way to bridge the gap between their almost 'right-less' existence and the 'full lives' many were attempting to live. (As is true of earlier human rights cases, no Charter challenges were brought by transgender, transsexual, intersexed, or cross-dressing persons.)

Despite the energy that went into these early Charter challenges, however, the litigation record before the Supreme Court of Canada ruled on

Egan and Nesbit was not very reassuring. Out of some nineteen direct Charter challenges to federal and provincial legislation brought during this period, plaintiffs won clear Charter victories in only six of these cases, and one of those victories – the trial court ruling in *Vriend* v *Alberta* – remained in abeyance during appeals that were not resolved until 1998.[47] Paradoxically, the Charter had much more impact on the application of 'sexual orientation' clauses in human rights codes and collective agreements. During the same period of time, a dozen such cases were heard, and all but four of them were successful.

Although most Charter challenges during this period were unsuccessful, several important developments took place between 1985 and 1995. First, all levels of government attempted to combat the contention that the open-ended language in section 15(1) of the Charter could be read as including 'sexual orientation' as an analogous ground. Lesbian and gay litigants had to establish this point the hard way. Second, even though the language of section 15(1) focuses not on common-law doctrine, but on establishing that 'discrimination' occurred, governments attempted to read the prohibition on discrimination on the basis of 'sexual orientation' narrowly, especially when the rights in question were not merely personal or 'status' rights but touched on relationship issues in some way. Thus it was necessary for lesbians and gays to find a way to characterize discrimination on the basis of relationship as discrimination on the grounds of 'sexual orientation.' It took quite a long time to achieve rulings that rejected both of these narrowing points. Once the decision in *Haig and Birch* v *Canada* consolidated the favourable authorities that had begun to emerge on both points, most of the successful Charter challenges before 1995 were heavily influenced by this decision. The main exceptions to this were the lower-court decisions in *Egan and Nesbit*.

The same sequence of events is reflected in administrative rulings of this era. Beginning with narrow doctrinal stances in relation to same-sex couples, benefit rights, and harassment issues, arbitrators and boards finally began to rule in favour of lesbians and gays when the impact of *Haig and Birch* became clear. In general, this shift was due to the new framework of analysis applied in *Andrews* v *Law Society of British Columbia*, which shifted the emphasis away from non-recognition of same-sex relationships in law and placed it on whether 'discrimination' had taken place. The authority of *Haig and Birch* enhanced the authority of lower-court rulings that had applied section 15(1) of the Charter to relationship issues, and thus the outcomes in these cases changed dramatically.

46 Are We 'Persons' Yet?

Challenges to Federal Legislation

Ten Charter challenges to federal legislation were brought by lesbians and gays in the period leading up to the Supreme Court of Canada decision in *Egan and Nesbit*, and one case raised issues relating to bisexual persons.[48] Two of the eleven cases were merely procedural rulings,[49] one case was dismissed on the basis that it arose before the Charter came into effect,[50] and one case was settled out of court.[51] The procedural rulings and the settlement were all military/RCMP cases that did manage to establish the bare proposition that these institutions were answerable under section 15(1) of the Charter. However, because these cases were all settled out of court, the courts were denied the opportunity to discuss discrimination in these organizations in any detail.

Of the seven Charter challenges resolved on the merits, four were section 15 equality cases, and three were brought under section 7 or 12 of the Charter. The latter three all failed,[52] one of the equality challenges was ultimately decided on other grounds on appeal,[53] and two of the three section 15 cases were successful.[54] In terms of substance, two of the section 15 cases touched on relationship issues (*Veysey* and *Egan and Nesbit*). The others involved denial of personal rights or discrimination on the basis of status as 'homosexual.'

The three section 7 or 12 cases exhibit the same narrowness of reasoning that first appeared in rulings under general human provisions. In *Sylvestre* v *Canada*, the Federal Court of Appeal concluded that the government had not violated a lesbian woman's right to security of the person under section 7 of the Charter when it dismissed her from the Canadian Armed Forces for lesbianism. The court reasoned that her discharge from the service did not deprive her of 'liberty to be a homosexual' – it merely deprived her of her right to be in the Armed Forces. In *Piche* v *Canada (Sol. Gen.)*, the court ruled that double-bunking federal inmates did not violate section 7 or 12 of the Charter, even though there was evidence that prison officials had apparently secured initial inmate consent to double-bunking by offering bisexual inmates the opportunity to share cells with their partners. Once these arrangements proved to be problematic, those inmates sought to revoke their consent, hence the Charter challenge. And in *Glad Day Bookshop Inc.* v *M.N.R.*, the court ruled that the seizure of gay material did not unreasonably violate freedom of expression even though some of it merely depicted anal intercourse. The court concluded that the material was 'degrading' and therefore posed a risk of harm to the community. Once again, gay freedom of expression was given very limited meaning.

The four equality cases that were decided on the merits were all brought by gay men. Because *Veysey* v *Canada (Correctional Services)*[55] raised relational issues, it played an important role in the early development of equality doctrine relating to same-sex relationships. The case also confirmed that section 15 of the Charter did apply to 'sexual orientation.' *Veysey* arose out of exclusion of a gay inmate from a 'family visiting program.' Although the description of the program did not clearly specify whether the 'relatives' or 'connections' who were permitted to visit under this program excluded same-sex partners, the prison refused to admit Veysey's partner to the program. Thus he invoked section 15(1) of the Charter in asking the court to order Corrections Canada to administer the program in a way that did not discriminate against him on the basis of his sexual orientation.

At the time of the trial court ruling in *Veysey* – 1989 – no court in Canada had ever extended 'sexual orientation' protection to same-sex relationships on any basis. Thus the full weight of prior authorities ran completely against Veysey. But by the time the trial court in *Veysey* went to draft its opinion, the Supreme Court of Canada had released its decision in *Andrews* v *Law Society of British Columbia*, in which it set out the general framework of analysis to be used in applying section 15 of the Charter. Although the court in *Veysey* could find no existing authority upon which to base a favourable ruling, when it went to work through the elements of the new *Andrews* test, it concluded that 'sexual orientation' was analogous to the grounds enumerated in section 15 and that exclusion of gay partners from the program constituted discrimination within the meaning of section 15 of the Charter.

While the court's application of the *Andrews* test was not particularly innovative, it had taken a completely fresh approach to an issue that had already been heavily litigated in general law and in human rights law to produce a long line of authorities that all supported the government's position. The court concluded, however, that the earlier line of 'relationship' authorities simply had no application to the facts of *Veysey* once the Supreme Court had set out the procedure for evaluating equality claims under section 15(1) of the Charter. Of course, later cases demonstrated that there was still a great deal of room within the elements of the sections 15 and 1 tests to interpret them narrowly against lesbians and gays, but what was critical about the trial court decision in *Veysey* was that it chart(er)ed a new path through old issues that had inevitably been resolved by recourse to the 'heterosexual presumption' or the proliferating 'opposite sex' definitions of 'spouse.' Especially since provincial Charter challenges had not been able to displace the older view of same-sex relationship issues, the trial court ruling in *Veysey* was all the more critical.

The breakthrough in *Veysey* was, however, short-lived. When the government appealed this decision, the Federal Court of Appeal affirmed the trial court as to result, but instead of basing its decision on the Charter, it based its decision on the narrower and non-constitutional grounds of canons of statutory construction. Looking directly at the language describing the visiting program, the court concluded that the general wording used in the policy, especially when read in light of the reintegrative purpose of the program, 'opens the door to applications by common law partners of the same sex.' The court was perfectly aware that it had diverged from the established weight of pre-Charter authority denying that same-sex relationships could ever have any legal significance, but it distinguished the facts before it from that line of authority on the basis of the uniqueness of the context: 'We are here dealing with very special and unusual expressions found in a unique document obviously not drafted by legal experts and directed at a specific program of integration of inmates in society.'[56]

Even as narrowed by the appellate court and limited by its unique context, the trial court's application of the *Andrews* test to a case involving 'sexual orientation' plus the Federal Court of Appeal's slight movement away from the weight of the older cases that refused to recognize same-sex relationships laid the basis for further movement in that direction in later cases. When a British Columbia court again applied *Andrews* to a relationship issue raised by provincial legislation in *Knodel* v *B.C. Medical Services Commission* (discussed under 'Challenges to Provincial Legislation,' below), this trend was strengthened further.

That line of cases was, however, threatened by the federal court rulings in *Egan and Nesbit*. James Egan and John Nesbit had sought to be treated as spouses for purposes of qualifying for the spousal allowance under the Old Age Security Act. Turned away because the definition of 'spouse' in that act had been amended in 1975 to include cohabitants only if they were of the 'opposite sex,' they brought a Charter challenge to that definition, contending that it discriminated against them on the basis of 'sex' and 'sexual orientation.' Martin J. of the Federal Court Trial Division concluded that this definition of 'spouse' did not violate section 15 of the Charter because it had really only been intended to form a basis for differentiating spousal relationships, which were traditionally between a man and a woman, from non-spousal relationships that had no legal significance.[57] Upholding this reasoning on appeal, the Federal Court of Appeal added a second reason for dismissing the challenge: the plaintiffs were really just attempting to challenge the common-law and statutory definitions of 'marriage' indirectly, which the court could not address, even through the mechanism of the Charter. When examining prior authorities, the appellate court also began to describe the issue in some of the cases as involving government benefits, although it did not base its decision on that point.[58]

The other two federal Charter challenges involved personal or status issues, not relational issues. The Charter challenge in *Haig and Birch* v *Canada* arose out of the military's policies of harassment and exclusion of 'homosexuals.' Joshua Birch, a member of the Canadian Armed Forces, had been told, like Michelle Douglas, that his sexual orientation disqualified him for promotions, postings, or further military career training. He was then released from the service on medical grounds. Phil MacAdam, the Ottawa lawyer who was advising Birch, recommended that he file a complaint with the Human Rights Commission of Canada instead of trying to challenge the forces' policies directly in federal court under the Charter. The federal commission turned Birch away on the familiar basis that it was not directly empowered by the Canadian Human Rights Act to process complaints relating to 'sexual orientation.' At this point, however, MacAdam launched a section 15 challenge to the exclusion of 'sexual orientation' from the federal human rights code. The Ontario Court General Division issued a declaration that the omission of 'sexual orientation' from the Canadian Human Rights Act violated Birch's equality rights, declared the grounds provisions of the act to be inoperative,[59] and temporarily suspended the declaration of invalidity during the resulting appeals.

The Court of Appeal heard the government's appeal and Birch's cross-appeal, but replaced the remedy ordered by the trial court with the remedy of 'reading in.' In the course of this ruling, the Court of Appeal confirmed that 'sexual orientation' is an 'analogous' ground of discrimination in section 15(1) of the Charter of Rights. The government did not attempt to invoke section 1 of the Charter to justify the omission of sexual orientation from the act. Nor did the government appeal this decision.

In retrospect, *Haig and Birch* appears to have formed the real turning point in the jurisprudence on 'sexual orientation.' Not only did it place the imprimatur of the prestigious Ontario Court of Appeal on the inclusion of 'sexual orientation' as an analogous ground under section 15(1) of the Charter, but it also employed the innovative 'reading in' remedy in relation to 'sexual orientation.' Because discrimination on the basis of sexuality has so often resulted in legislative 'silence' rather than in facially discriminatory provisions, use of the 'reading in' remedy gave courts a concrete way to eliminate discrimination. Despite the fact that *Haig and Birch* involved personal or 'status' rights and not relational rights, it consolidated at the appellate level the reasoning in *Veysey* and *Knodel*, both of which did involve relational issues. In purely chronological terms, only one more pre–*Egan and Nesbit* direct Charter challenge failed after *Haig and Birch* was decided, and only one out of more than a dozen administrative cases decided after *Haig and Birch* went against the complainant.

Viewing *Haig and Birch* in the context of the time at which Krever J. formulated the Ontario Court of Appeal decision, several factors appear to have intersected to produce this result. First, the trial court decision in *Veysey* had outlined quite persuasively how the *Andrews* framework could be applied to an issue involving those who have 'deviated from accepted sexual norms.' Second, the substantive test in *Andrews* was designed to identify legislative distinctions that selectively burdened historically disadvantaged groups, and the factual record relating to sexuality made it possible to make a very satisfying case on the conceptual level. Third, the abstract elements of the *Andrews* framework took the emphasis away from older common-law authorities and away from questions of 'natural,' 'biological,' or acceptable beliefs, placing it instead on the claimant's experiences of discrimination. When combined with the fact that several other decisions had at least confirmed that 'sexual orientation' was an analogous ground under section 15 of the Charter, the court was able to craft a decision that advanced all of these elements in the direction of affirming the fundamental human rights of lesbians and gays. And although *Haig and Birch* involved personal or 'status' types of rights, it was conceptually not illogical for the court to draw on cases involving relational types of interests, because the *Andrews* framework had helped minimize the differences in the way the two types of cases were processed in Charter equality discourse.

The Ontario Court of Appeal decision in *Haig and Birch* does not explain all the subsequent Charter victories leading up to *Egan and Nesbit*. But it did appear to help create a greater willingness on the part of courts to consider how other forms of discrimination on the basis of sexual orientation might be affected by section 15 of the Charter. For example, in the other successful federal Charter challenge in the period leading up to the decision in *Egan and Nesbit*, *Halm* v *Minister of Employment and Immigration*, the federal court found that section 159 of the Canadian Criminal Code violated section 15 of the Charter on the grounds of both age and sexual orientation. This Charter challenge arose out of an appeal from a conditional deportation order that was made when Immigration Canada discovered that the appellant had failed to disclose a prior conviction for sodomy involving fifteen- and sixteen-year-old boys to immigration officials when he came into Canada. The court vacated the deportation order after concluding that section 159 of the Criminal Code, which prohibited anal intercourse with persons under the age of eighteen, unjustifiably violated sections 7 and 15 of the Charter. Once the court had found that this provision was constitutionally invalid, the offence of which Halm had been convicted in the United States had no equivalent in Canada, and he was therefore no longer subject to deportation. Unfortunately, Halm had sought sanctuary in Canada on the day he was to have been sentenced in the United States, and Immigration Canada promptly issued a new deportation order on the basis that he had technically 'jumped bail' in the United States – an offence for which there was an equivalent in Canada.[60]

Challenges to Provincial Legislation

Initially, courts appeared to be somewhat more reluctant to disturb the established case law relating to 'sexual orientation' in Charter challenges to provincial legislation. Of the eight challenges to provincial legislation under various provisions of the Charter of Rights during the first ten years of Charter litigation,[61] four were successful,[62] but the first favourable ruling was not issued until 1991. Some of the earlier losses can be explained in terms of procedural rulings or problems of timing. Overall, the chronology of the cases reveals that *Haig and Birch* had a great deal of influence in these cases.

The real problem in the earlier challenges to provincial legislation appeared to be that they immediately focused not on personal or status-type issues, but on relational issues. Both *Anderson* v *Luoma* and *Andrews* v *Minister of Health* involved lesbian women who had formed families and were raising children. At the heart of the reasoning in both cases lay the perception that relationships between lesbian women, even when they had children, had no legal significance, and that the relationship between non-biological parents and their children was legally a nullity.

On an ontological level, this is yet another extension of the common-law view that same-sex couples do not have the 'capacity' to marry. Because the courts in these cases were not able to see lesbian couples as 'real' couples, neither court found any violations of section 15(1).

In *Anderson v Luoma*, the plaintiff and defendant had had two children through artificial insemination during their relationship. When Arlene Luoma became involved with another woman, she demanded that Penny Anderson and their two children move out of the house. Anderson, who had become economically dependent on Luoma as she withdrew from waged work to have their children and care for the family, relied on the Charter to back up her application for maintenance and child support under provincial family law.[63] Luoma took the position that her former partner was just a friend, not a former partner entitled to support, and that she was not liable for child support because the children were not biologically connected to her. The court summarily rejected the Charter part of the application, merely stating that it did not apply, and that, if it did, exclusion of same-sex couples from the support provisions was justifiable under section 1 of the Charter. The court then went on to conclude that Anderson was not entitled to the benefit of family-law support provisions because the court did not believe that those provisions had been enacted for the purpose of providing support for children born to another woman through artificial insemination.[64] The court did invoke the equitable remedy of constructive trust to award a share of the couple's real estate to Anderson; the application of equitable doctrine did not depend on establishing the existence of opposite-sex conjugal relationships of the sort contemplated by the support legislation.[65]

In *Andrews v Minister of Health*, Karen Andrews had sought to have her partner treated as her 'spouse' for purposes of the Ontario health insurance plan. She and her partner were raising two children together, and thought of themselves as a family unit. Although neither the Health Insurance Act[66] nor the regulations[67] contained any definition of 'spouse,' the government took the position that two persons of the same sex could not be spouses, even if they cohabited together. Andrews brought a Charter challenge under section 15(1) to that administrative position, arguing that this constituted discrimination on the basis of sexual orientation. As in *Re North and Matheson*[68] and the earliest human rights cases, the court applied the 'heterosexual presumption' to fill in the missing definition of 'spouse.' MacRae J. looked to the seventy-nine 'opposite-sex' definitions of 'spouse' in Ontario legislation and concluded that 'spouse' 'always refers to a person of the opposite sex.'[69] Thus even when not so defined in positive law, the court concluded that it must be read as if it were.

Although the courts in the other two unsuccessful challenges to provincial legislation also employed very narrow reasoning, they were somewhat more favourable to the gay plaintiffs in that both courts did acknowledge that section 15(1) of the Charter prohibited discrimination on the basis of 'sexual orientation.' However, both courts went on to conclude, as in *Anderson* and *Andrews*, that the actions in issue did not constitute 'discrimination' within the meaning of section 15(1). In *Brown v Minister of Health*, the court ruled that the provincial government's refusal to cover the entire costs of AZT for AIDS patients did not violate section 15 of the Charter because it was not 'direct discrimination' against gay men. The court refused to treat evidence that this funding decision fell most heavily on gay men, who accounted for some 90 per cent of all AIDS patients at the time the case was heard, as establishing 'direct' impact on gay men on the basis of their sexuality. And in *Layland and Beaulne v Ontario (Minister of Consumer & Commercial Relations)*, an Ontario court ruled that the refusal to grant a marriage licence to two men did not constitute 'discrimination' because they could still marry persons of the opposite sex. Undeterred by the *Andrews* framework of analysis, the court relied on the line of relationship cases that began with the transsexual case of *Corbett* v *Corbett* to conclude that persons of the same sex do not have the capacity to marry each other under the common law of Canada.[70]

Three of the four successful provincial Charter challenges, however, did involve various relational issues. The influence of *Veysey* and *Haig and Birch* is evident in all these cases. In *Knodel* v *B.C. Medical Services Commission*, the British Columbia Supreme Court ruled that the government had discriminated against Knodel on the basis of his sexual orientation when it had denied coverage to his partner under the provincial medical services program.[71] His partner, who had AIDS, had lost his own insurance coverage when he became unemployed. The court ordered the government to interpret the definition of 'spouse' to include the applicant and his partner.[72] In this decision, the court more or less ignored the older cases on relationship status, and placed its focus on helpful passages in *Veysey* and the *Andrews* framework.

Just a few weeks after the Ontario Court of Appeal decision in *Haig and Birch* was published, the Board of Inquiry in *Leshner* v *The Queen* was influenced by the earlier decisions in *Veysey*, *Knodel*, and *Haig and Birch* to conclude that the denial of same-sex survivor rights under employee pension plans also violated the Charter. Whereas the government in *Haig and Birch* did not seek to assert section 1 of the Charter, the government in *Leshner* did not contest the section 15 part of the case, but rested its case on section 1, arguing that the 'opposite-sex' definition of spouse in federal income tax legislation[73] formed the real basis for the discrimination. In the course of setting out its reasons, the majority of the board concluded that the 'opposite-sex' definition of spouse in the Ontario Human Rights Code that exempted such pension plan provisions from the Code unjustifiably violated section 15 of the Charter.[74] Constitutionally correcting the act and other provincial statutes to conform with the Charter,[75] the board then ordered the employer, which was the provincial government, to provide equivalent survivor benefits in an 'off-side' plan to fully fund that plan if the Income Tax Act were not amended within three years to bring such benefits within the terms of the federal legislation.[76]

Not surprisingly, *Haig and Birch* played a significant role in persuading the Alberta Queen's Bench to read 'sexual orientation' into the Individual's Rights Protection Act in the 1994 decision in *Vriend* v *Alberta*. With facts similar to those in *Haig and Birch* – Delwin Vriend had been fired from teaching because of his sexuality, but the Alberta commission refused to let him file a human rights complaint because the legislation did not mention 'sexual orientation' – Russell J. took judicial notice that lesbian women and gay men suffer from discrimination, even though there had been no evidence led on that issue during the trial, and ordered the statutory provisions in question to 'be interpreted, applied and administered as though they contained the words "sexual orientation".' This decision would then have given the commission jurisdiction to process the complaint filed by Delwin Vriend, who was dismissed by King's College for being gay. However, in a surprisingly vitriolic decision, the Alberta Court of Appeal reversed the trial court shortly after *Egan and Nesbit* was published,[77] contending that the Charter could not be read as forcing provinces to extend human rights protections to any particular group when the only 'action' the legislature had taken was to remain 'silent' on the issue. It was not until 1998 that the Supreme Court of Canada finally reinstated the trial court decision,[78] during which period the commission was not able to accept any complaints on the basis of sexuality.

In *Re K.*, four non-biological lesbian mothers who had co-parented their children since birth were given permission to adopt under them under the 'step-parent' provisions of the Child and Family Services

Act.[79] This application was necessary because the act incorporated by reference the human rights definition of 'spouse' for purposes of regulating access to step-parent adoption,[80] and if the non-biological co-mothers could not adopt as step-parents, any adoption order in their favour would have had the effect of terminating the birth mothers' parental status. Nevins J. applied section 15(1) of the Charter to invalidate the opposite-sex definition of 'spouse' in the act, and read a same-sex definition of conjugal relationships into the provisions.[81]

'Sexual Orientation' Outside the Charter

As Charter authorities like *Haig and Birch* and *Leshner* came to the attention of arbitrators and human rights boards of inquiry, the narrower interpretations given to sexual orientation in the human rights tradition began to give way to the discrimination-based reasoning invoked by the Charter, even though these administrative rulings were not themselves Charter challenges. These Charter rulings were used as authorities in human rights hearings and arbitrations simply because they had became the leading precedents on the meaning of sexual orientation. When faced with the choice of following older board rulings or arbitration awards, on the one hand, and carefully reasoned Charter rulings, on the other hand, administrative-hearing officers began, after some prompting, to adopt the reasoning in the new Charter case law.

Although I have located the point of this transition roughly in 1993, there is in fact no moment at which the focus shifted from older non-Charter cases to the Charter analysis of 'sexual orientation' discrimination. As late as 1994, some arbitrators still found nothing of assistance in the Charter cases on sexual orientation,[82] and, in 1996, a federal human rights tribunal still permitted an employer to exclude same-sex employees from some pension benefit features.[83] Although arbitrators continued to refer to the narrower understanding of sexual orientation, sometimes even making reference to the pre–sexual orientation *Mossop*[84] case, this did not happen much beyond 1993. The focus then shifted to defining both discrimination and sexual orientation as it was understood in Charter jurisprudence.

Eleven administrative cases involving sexual orientation were decided between 1992 and 1995.[85] Lesbian and gay applicants won all but four of these cases.[86] Of the eight successful decisions, seven raised relational issues. By the end of this series of decisions, it was well established in the administrative jurisprudence that denial of either personal or relational rights in human rights codes or employment arrangements violated statutory and contractual sexual-orientation clauses.

When these administrative rulings are examined in chronological order, it is possible to see how the new Charter jurisprudence on the meaning of 'discrimination on the basis of sexual orientation' was resisted initially. In *Parkwood Hospital*, an employee sought same-sex 'family' benefits for his partner under a collective agreement that did not contain a 'sexual orientation' clause or a definition of 'spouse.' The union argued that the prohibition on sexual-orientation discrimination in the Ontario Human Rights Code should be applied to the collective agreement, and that the Charter cases *Knodel* and *Veysey* were the leading authorities on the application of 'sexual orientation' protections to relational issues. The arbitrator refused to go down this path, and concluded instead that the dependency requirement in the collective agreement should govern the outcome. Thus the grievance was dismissed on the basis that there was no factual evidence that the employee's partner was actually economically dependent on him. A similar fact-based approach was taken in the *Smith* arbitration, in which an employee had been dismissed for allegedly sexually harassing two women she supervised. The arbitrator inferentially minimized the protection given those two workers, relying on the grievor's contention that she was heterosexual and that, while she admitted that the incidents took place, she was not sexually interested in them, in concluding that, factually, sexual harassment had not occurred. The grievor was reinstated despite 'ill advised' and 'rude' behaviour.

During a series of grievances brought by the Public Service Alliance of Canada (PSAC) against Canada Post, the shift away from the narrow human rights jurisprudence on the scope of 'sexual orientation' discrimination to the new Charter-based jurisprudence took place. In *Canada Post I*, the arbitrator ruled that the collective agreement did not prohibit Canada Post from excluding a gay cohabitant from the opposite-sex definition of 'common-law spouse' for purposes of medical benefits. The collective agreement did not contain an express 'sexual orientation' clause, but stated that the employer would adhere to the federal human rights statute. The arbitrator relied on the Supreme Court decision in *Mossop* in concluding that 'sexual orientation' was not included in any of the heads of coverage enumerated in the non-discrimination clause, and that the employee's partner therefore could not be considered to be his 'common-law spouse' for purposes of the agreement.

Later that same year, the arbitrator in *Lorenzen*, which also raised benefit issues that touched on relationship recognition, relied on the very different approach found in *Haig and Birch* in granting that grievance. That collective agreement did contain a 'sexual orientation' clause, but the employer argued that the scope of that clause had to be limited where family-type benefits were involved, because the agreement also contained an 'opposite-sex' definition of 'spouse.' Relying on *Haig and Birch*, the arbitrator concluded that, since 'sexual orientation' had been read into the federal human rights code, the denial of leave was contrary to the code and to the collective agreement. The arbitrator flatly concluded that having a 'spouse a person of the same sex cannot be separated from his sexual orientation' and thus granted this grievance.

Lorenzen was published roughly two weeks before *Canada Post II* was decided. *Canada Post II* arose out of denial of vision care benefits to a same-sex spouse. This arbitrator relied not on *Lorenzen*, but on *Canada Post I*, and dismissed the grievance on the basis that the prior award in *Canada Post I* had to be followed unless it had been 'clearly wrong.' A few months after that, however, in *Canada Post III*, which arose out of denial of insured benefits to a same-sex partner, the arbitrator ruled that *Canada Post I* had been 'clearly wrong' and followed *Lorenzen* instead. The arbitrator concluded that *Mossop* was not inconsistent with *Haig and Birch*, and that the 'opposite-sex' definition of 'spouse' in the collective agreement could no longer exclude same-sex partners now that *Haig and Birch* had read 'sexual orientation' into the federal human rights code. Reading 'sexual orientation' into the federal code effectively read it into the collective agreement as well, because the agreement incorporated the code by reference.

What is notable about *Canada Post III* and *Lorenzen* is that, while applying *Haig and Birch* for the proposition that 'sexual orientation' had become protected by the federal code, these awards looked beyond the facts of *Haig and Birch* to apply the prohibition on sexual-orientation discrimination to both relational issues as well as personal or status issues. The Charter rulings in *Knodel* and *Veysey* had brought new substantive scope to sexual orientation, and by reading 'sexual orientation' into the federal code, and thus into collective agreements that were governed by it, *Haig and Birch* had opened the door to using those precedents in applying 'sexual orientation' both within the context of the code and as incorporated by reference into private agreements.

The *Lorenzen–Canada Post* series formed the turning point in the administrative rulings. After *Canada Post III* was decided, all of the other grievances leading up to *Egan and Nesbit* followed that same general line of analysis. In *University of Lethbridge*, in which the collective agreement prohibited sexual-orientation discrimination and did not limit the definition of 'family' to opposite-sex couples, the arbitrator actually treated the *Andrews* framework as having set out a new common-law definition of 'discrimination' that was to be applied in interpreting the collective agreement. Between adopting the substantive *Andrews* approach to defining discrimination and Charter-based definitions of 'sexual orientation,' the arbitrator had no difficulty in reaching the conclusion that the collective agreement required the employer to extend the same family benefits to employees with same-sex partners as to those with opposite-sex partners. That the arbitrator would take this line is even more impressive when it is remembered that, by this time, the federal courts had begun the process of limiting the scope of 'sexual orientation' in section 15 of the Charter itself in *Egan and Nesbit* to exclude same-sex benefits deriving from government expenditure programs.[87]

In *Bell Canada*, another arbitrator cited *Haig and Birch* for the proposition that the refusal to extend spousal benefits to same-sex partners violated prohibitions in both a collective agreement and the Canadian Human Rights Act on discrimination on basis of sexual orientation. And in *Canadian Broadcasting Corp.*, the arbitrator followed the *Bell Canada* award in ruling that the combined effect of the Canadian Human Rights Act, as extended by *Haig and Birch*, and the sexual-orientation clause in the collective agreement made it necessary for the CBC to extend medical and dental benefits to same-sex couples. The arbitrator directed the employer 'to rid the disputed benefit plans of all discrimination based on sexual orientation,' even though the employer by this time could argue that the Supreme Court of Canada decision in *Egan and Nesbit* had overtaken the award at least in relation to the pension issues.

During the same period of time, human rights tribunals charged with applying sexual-orientation clauses were also looking to Charter jurisprudence for authoritative interpretations of 'discrimination' and 'sexual orientation.' For once sexual orientation had been read into the federal human rights codes, complaints could be brought under it in the same way as if it had been legislatively inserted. Thus in *McAleer v Canada (H.R.C.)*,[88] the Supreme Court of Canada upheld a tribunal finding that recorded telephone messages were designed to incite hatred on the basis of sexual orientation. The meaning of 'sexual orientation' continued to expand in provincial human rights law as well. In *O'Neill and Coles v The Queen*,[89] an Ontario board of inquiry ruled that same-sex partners were entitled to transfer ownership of vehicles between themselves without obtaining safety certification, just like opposite-sex cohabitants and married couples. Although the order was limited to the complainants personally and did not include any declaration as to the validity of the legislation or regulations that were challenged in this case, it gave further substance to the recognition of same-sex relationship rights in provincial human rights law.

Although *Egan and Nesbit* did quickly overtake and limit the lines of cases discussed in this chapter, judicial confirmation that 'sexual orientation' was a non-enumerated head of protection in section 15(1) of the Charter displaced a truly bleak litigation record under human rights codes with a body of jurisprudence that slowly began to overcome decades of narrow interpretations. The effects of the early Charter relational cases – *Veysey* and *Knodel*, as reinforced by *Leshner* and *Re K.* – have been noticeable, all the more so because *Haig and Birch* then read 'sexual orientation' into the federal human rights code.

The trickle of complaints that *Haig and Birch* empowered the federal commission to accept will undoubtedly grow quite rapidly. In *Nielsen v Canada (Employment and Immigration Commission)*,[90] the Federal Court of Appeal ruled that *Haig and Birch* added 'sexual orientation' to the federal human rights code retroactively, and that the commission, as a party to *Haig and Birch*, was bound by it before the legislation was actually amended later on. This ruling enabled the commission to process Nielsen's complaint, which had been placed in abeyance during the pendency of *Mossop*.[91] Since at least another fifty-one complaints had also been placed on hold during that period of time, many of those are now also moving through the commission process. The *Nielsen* complaint arose out of denial of same-sex employment benefits, and will certainly not be alone in testing the limits of the new 'sexual orientation' clause in the federal human rights statute.

Conclusions

When courts refused to apply either ordinary legal doctrine or existing human rights provisions to lesbians and gays, they turned their efforts to two basic strategies for legal reform: they lobbied for the addition of 'sexual orientation' clauses to human rights codes, and they attempted to secure the inclusion of 'sexual orientation' in the new Charter of Rights equality guarantees. The first strategy was designed to overcome the virtually total exclusion of lesbians and gays from 'private' legal doctrine and from 'public' regulation of some forms of 'private' and state discrimination. The second strategy was designed to ensure that the Charter, which was designed to reach discriminatory actions of governments themselves, would give lesbians and gays equal rights in the entire 'public' sphere.

Although the lobby for human rights protection pre-dated the drafting of the Charter of Rights and Freedoms, the inclusion of 'sexual orientation' in human rights codes occurred so slowly that it was not until the Charter equality guarantees came into effect in 1985 that Charter discourse helped spur the reform of the codes. At the same time, the federal government consistently refused to include 'sexual orientation' in section 15 of the Charter itself. The most that could be achieved was the addition of open-ended language to section 15 that would enable courts to apply it to discrimination on the basis of 'sexual orientation.' Government assurances that it considered that open-ended language to apply to lesbians and gays were muted and delivered in carefully guarded language to select audiences.

Lesbians and gays remained very much on the 'outside' during the entire Charter drafting process. If it had not been for the astute work that Svend Robinson did as a member of the Parliamentary Committee on Equality in 1985, the voices of lesbians and gays would have remained much more silent during the entire chart(er)ing process. Robinson brought his own experience of government discrimination into the hearings and interacted with committee members and witnesses – many of whom took huge personal risks to testify in such an open forum – to create a stunning record of pervasive discrimination on the basis of sexuality in Canada.

The promise of those hearings was quickly shattered, however, when the committee made only limited policy recommendations in its final report. Instead of finding that the government should take immediate steps to include sexual orientation in section 15 of the Charter, the committee made only three substantive recommendations: stop using 'homosexuality' as a basis for withdrawing security clearances; eliminate disparities in criminal age-of- consent provisions; and amend the federal human rights code to prohibit discrimination on the basis of 'sexual orientation.' These recommendations reinforced the perception that most forms of discrimination on the basis of sexuality should be funnelled into the human rights process and that state discrimination was not serious enough to merit direct attention in more than the two areas of the military and the criminal age of consent.

Given that one of the strongest justifications for entrenching human rights in a constitutional charter was that courts had concluded that human rights codes could not be used to invalidate other legislation, the recommendation that the huge range of issues affecting sexual minorities could be addressed through the mechanism of human rights codes signalled lack of serious government commitment to change in this area. Even more concerning, the committee recommended that the 'opposite-sex' definition of 'spouse' be inserted in all federal legislation in order to continue promoting the equality of non-married heterosexual partners.

In a very real sense, the committee recommendations threatened to collapse the two solutions sought by queers – getting 'sexual orientation' into human rights codes and into the Charter – into a single solution – get 'sexual orientation' into human rights codes. Thus lesbians and gays decided to turn to the courts in the hope of receiving some support under the Charter. At that point, litigants began to discover that many of the same governments that had been promising them human rights, some protection under the Charter, or some statutory recognition were now their very powerful opponents in Charter litigation.

The Charter challenges that led up to the Supreme Court decision in *Egan and Nesbit* produced but a handful of favourable rulings, and several of those rulings were either vacated by appellate courts or suspended for so long during the appellate process that they had little immediate impact. A smattering of cases began to acknowledge that 'sexual orientation' was analogous to the heads of protection enumerated in section 15 of the Charter. Thus the first criminal age-of-consent provision was successfully challenged in *Halm*, a provincial employee obtained same-sex survivor benefits for his partner in *Leshner*, lesbian and gay co-parents became able to co-adopt their children in *Re K.*, and *Knodel* extended 'family coverage' for purposes of medical services to same-sex couples in British Columbia. The non-recognition of same-sex relationships that so characterized the jurisprudence under general law and human rights codes began to fade away as the substantive analysis of equality exemplified in *Andrews* v *Law Society of British Columbia* became the leading authority on the meaning of 'discrimination.' Some courts that applied this framework of analysis were able to circumvent the older case law on same-sex relationships, and to approach discrimination in relational issues in terms that avoided falling back into those lines of authority.

In human rights cases and labour arbitrations, the older jurisprudence retained its vitality until the Ontario Court of Appeal decision in *Haig and Birch* consolidated the authority of trial court decisions like *Veysey* and *Knodel* in a powerful section 15 analysis of discrimination in the structure of the federal human rights code itself. *Haig and Birch* generated a number of critical changes in Charter discourse relating to sexuality. Doctrinally, it became the leading authority on how the *Andrews* framework was to be applied to issues of sexuality. Although the facts of *Haig and Birch* related only to 'personal' employment issues and not to relational or conduct issues, the analysis was set out in terms that provided no basis for making that distinction. Structurally, by reading 'sexual orientation' into the federal human rights code, it literally opened the doors of that commission to sexual minorities. It also opened collective agreements across the country up to grievances on the basis of 'sexual orientation' as unions realized that the language of the federal code was in some cases incorporated by reference into some collective agreements.

As the result of these changes, the conflict between the older 'heterosexual presumption' that sexual-orientation clauses protected only personal rights and not relational or conduct rights, on the one hand, and emerging Charter equality discourse on sexual orientation discrimination, on the other hand, was quietly played out in low-profile grievance and human rights hearings within federal jurisdiction. The turning point in the jurisprudence can be found in a series of grievances against Canada Post as the impacts of *Haig and Birch*, *Knodel*, *Veysey*, and then *Leshner* worked their way into the interpretation of sexual-orientation clauses in that collective agreement.

Jurisprudentially, the effect of this line of cases spiralled out into more board and arbitration rulings in the mid-1990s, until there were some seven decisions that applied sexual-orientation clauses to relational issues. The sequencing of these rulings suggested that this spiral would continue to expand. In total numbers, the overall litigation record was still daunting. The number of successful Charter challenges was still small. But the opening created by *Haig and Birch* led to the hope that genuine change could take place.

Critics were still cautious, of course. The effect of the Charter in the area of human rights did have exactly the effect the federal Committee on Equality had recommended: that most issues of discrimination on the basis of sexuality be funnelled into the human rights mechanism. Critics had many concerns: that human rights commissions could deal only with some 'private' rights and government action that could be classified as 'services,' 'employment,' 'contracts,' or 'housing'; that human rights codes could not be used to invalidate concurrent legislation; that human rights codes themselves discriminated on the basis of sexuality when they defined words like 'spouse' in terms of 'opposite-sex' partners; and that boards could order only limited remedies.

But of perhaps greatest concern was the effect of the appeal in *Egan and Nesbit* to the Supreme Court of Canada. If that appeal were successful, it could bring the 'opposite-sex' movement to an end, ensure that section 15 of the Charter could be used to challenge the full 'public' functions of governments, invalidate or amend legislation when necessary to eliminate discrimination, and form a jurisprudential basis for achieving genuine structural change. Or, if it failed, it could wipe out even the limited litigation gains that had been achieved by 1995.

Chapter Three

'Demonstrably Justifying' Discrimination

The Canadian Charter of Rights and Freedoms guarantees the rights and freedoms set out in it subject only to such reasonable limits prescribed by law as can be demonstrably justified in a free and democratic society.
> Canadian Charter of Rights and Freedoms, section 1

By the time *Egan and Nesbit* v *The Queen*[1] came before the Supreme Court of Canada, many courts had agreed that 'sexual orientation' was included in the open-ended language in section 15(1) of the Charter. However, most direct Charter challenges had failed anyway, and it was by no means clear just how far the presumed prohibition on discrimination on the basis of sexuality would extend once the Supreme Court of Canada had a chance to rule on the issues.

On the doctrinal level, the successful Charter challenges were not very reassuring. Only a few cases involving 'personal rights' had been filed, and the ones that had the most potential to establish Charter doctrine on basic personal rights such as the right to employment had been persistently settled by the federal government.[2] The clearest victories in this area were the Charter challenges to the omission of 'sexual orientation' from existing human rights codes, which could be considered to violate the personal right to access dispute-resolution services. The case law in this area was fragile, with *Vriend* v *Alberta*[3] under appeal and *Haig and Birch*[4] remaining a provincial authority. In any event, with the strongest successes in the area of access to the human rights process, there was the concern that funnelling issues of 'sexual orientation' into the human rights process, which has traditionally been considered to be concerned only with discrimination in 'private' dealings and government services,

'Demonstrably Justifying' Discrimination   65

could inhibit the long-term goal of achieving full legal recognition for sexual minorities.[5]

Even more fragile were the gains in the group of cases that touched on 'conduct, 'relational,' or 'public' rights. The success in *Knodel*[6] in achieving same-sex coverage under provincial health care plans was overbalanced by the losses in *Andrews* v *Minister of Health*[7] and *Brown* v *Minister of Health*,[8] both cases directly on point. The initial success in *Veysey* v *Correctional Service of Canada*[9] had been wiped out in the appeal in that case, and by the later decisions of the federal court in *Egan and Nesbit*. *Leshner*[10] had established a limited right to same-sex survivor rights under employment pensions, *Re K.*[11] did stand unchallenged in establishing the right to memorialize parental status in lesbian and gay families, and *Halm* v *Minister of Employment and Immigration*[12] did invalidate the age-of-consent rules in criminal law that stood in the way of relationships involving younger queers. However, nowhere was there any clear authority establishing that the Charter of Rights guaranteed sexual minorities equal protection of the law when they acted on their sexuality, sought rights created by the 'public' sphere, or sought recognition of 'same-sex' relationships. Indeed, the early decision in *Anderson* v *Luoma*[13] suggested that even 'private' types of rights regulated by 'public' legislation (such as in family law) might not be protected by the Charter.

Given the splits and reluctances exhibited in the existing case law, *Egan and Nesbit* was a high-risk Charter challenge to bring before the Supreme Court of Canada. Arising out of the 'opposite-sex' definition of 'spouse' in the Old Age Security Act – one of the very first 'opposite-sex' provisions to be enacted in Canada – *Egan and Nesbit* not only involved 'conduct' instead of 'status' and 'relational' rights instead of 'personal' rights, but also pitted the statutory 'opposite-sex' definition of 'spouse' against the untried 'sexual orientation' protection in section 15 of the Charter, and in the context of the demand that government-funded direct spousal benefits be extended to same-sex couples.

Not surprisingly, both the government and lesbians and gays were able to point to some victories in the way the appeal was resolved by the Court. Lesbians and gays were reassured that a majority of the Court had confirmed that 'sexual orientation' was indeed protected by the open-ended language in section 15(1) of the Charter,[14] and that 'opposite-sex' definitions of 'spouse' in direct benefit programs did violate section 15(1) of the Charter. But that reassurance turned out to be more theoretical and abstract than real, because another majority of the Court then went on to conclude that even if such legislation did violate section 15(1) of the

Charter, it was 'a reasonable limit' under section 1 of the Charter that could be 'demonstrably justified in a free and democratic society.' Thus Egan and Nesbit lost their application for the Old Age Security Act spousal allowance.

The results in this appeal were particularly disappointing to lesbians and gays because it was released together with *Miron* v *Trudel*,[15] in which non-married opposite-sex cohabitants who were also excluded from a statutory definition of 'spouse' were entirely successful. At the same time, the Court narrowed its definition of 'discrimination' in the third case in this 'equality trilogy,' *Thibaudeau* v *The Queen*,[16] concluding that the differential impact of the income tax treatment of taxable child support payments on women did not constitute discrimination when it could be shown that such provisions conferred an overall tax benefit on a large percentage of divorced or separated couples with children.

Predictably, the ambivalence and genuine limitations reflected in *Egan and Nesbit* have had significant impact on further attempts to challenge discriminatory legislation and government policies. While the 1998 Supreme Court decision in *Vriend* has now confirmed that continued exclusion of 'sexual orientation' from human rights codes does unjustifiably violate section 15 of the Charter, and while nearly every administrative decision released since *Egan and Nesbit* has been successful, governments are still strongly contesting the extension of simple 'private' rights under provincial family law[17] or of publicly regulated 'private' compensation benefits to lesbians and gays,[18] and other sexual minorities such as bisexual or transsexual persons have yet to bring their first Charter challenge.

In this chapter, I discuss the way the Court decided *Egan and Nesbit* and the other two 'trilogy' cases, and then look at the impact of these decisions on subsequent Charter challenges and administrative decisions. The conclusion I reach is that, instead of clarifying the constitutional status of sexual minorities, the decision in *Egan and Nesbit* has ensured that, until legislatures take responsibility for changing the legal status of sexual minorities, queers will have to continue to turn to the courts in selective, expensive, and high-risk litigation in order to secure fundamental civil rights and human rights.

Egan and Nesbit v The Queen

Egan and Nesbit v *The Queen* was a direct Charter challenge to the opposite-sex definition of 'spouse' in the federal Old Age Security Act spousal allowance rules (SPA). In this case, two gay partners had sought the spousal allowance for the younger of them, John Nesbit, on the same basis that a married or cohabiting heterosexual spouse would have received it.[19] This case, along with the others that form the 'equality trilogy,'[20] not only tested the availability of Charter remedies to non-enumerated groups, but also tested in terms of subject matter the types of Charter challenges that could be expected to succeed in the future.

The Court could not have divided more deeply over the issues in *Egan and Nesbit* if it had tried. The first issue in the case was whether denying the SPA violated section 15(1). A bare majority of the Court – five out of nine justices – agreed that it did. The second issue was whether this discrimination could be 'demonstrably justified' under section 1 of the Charter. A different bare majority of five justices agreed that it was justifiable discrimination. Nor could the Court have created more confusion over just what the reasons for each of these two rulings were. The five justices who agreed that the discrimination was justifiable under section 1 did not agree among themselves on the precise legal reasons for that result. Justices La Forest, Gonthier, Major, and Lamer concluded that denying the spousal allowance to gay partners did not even violate section 15(1) of the Charter, so they did not actually write opinions on how section 1 led to the conclusion that this discrimination was justified. The only section 1 opinion in this case was written by Justice Sopinka, and his opinion departed so markedly from earlier section 1 jurisprudence that it was not clear how much weight should be given to it, especially in light of the lack of comment by the other majority justices on his reasoning. At the same time, the fact that Justice Sopinka had joined Cory, Iacobucci, McLachlin, and L'Heureux-Dubé to agree that denial of the SPA did violate section 15(1) meant that it was not clear whether the section 15(1) analysis authored by the justices who defeated the challenge on the basis of section 1 should be treated as the authoritative section 15(1) analysis arising from this case, or whether Justice Cory's opinion was the authoritative one.

The Section 15(1) Opinions

Because of these splits in the Court, there has been considerable confusion over how section 15(1) of the Charter should be read and applied. Three competing views could be taken.

One view was expressed in the editorial head note to *Egan and Nesbit* in the *Supreme Court Reports*, which treated La Forest J.'s section 15(1) opinion as the majority section 15(1) opinion even though only three other justices concurred with his analysis. Justice La Forest had concluded that denial of the SPA did not violate section 15(1) because the 'functional value' of the spousal allowance was to extend some retirement funding to women who had worked in the home and who continued to be dependent on their husbands for money. Attempting to 'contextualize' the section 15(1) issue by considering the legislative objectives of the spousal allowance, social values, and related legislation, La Forest J. concluded that the 'functional value' served by the spousal allowance really had nothing to do with sexuality. La Forest J. was of the opinion that denial of the allowance did not burden gay partners any more than it burdened roommates or siblings who lived together, because the opposite-sex definition of spouse was consistent with the 'functional values' connected with heterosexual reproduction.

A second view that can be taken of the section 15(1) issue in *Egan and Nesbit* is that the splits in the Court and the failure of the differing factions to join in a common substantive analysis have deprived *Egan and Nesbit* of much authority beyond its particular facts, leaving the section 15(1) analysis authored by Justice McLachlin in *Miron v Trudel* as the authoritative section 15 analysis to emerge from the 'trilogy' cases.

The third view is that Justice Cory's section 15(1) opinion in fact contains the *ratio decidendi* in this case because it is the opinion with which four other justices did in fact agree. Justice Sopinka – the fifth justice needed to make up a numerical majority – actually disagreed with La Forest J.'s 'functional values' analysis and agreed with Justice Cory's section 15(1) opinion. Justice Iacobucci completely agreed with Justice Cory's section 15(1) opinion, Justice McLachlin declared that she was 'in substantial agreement' with his section 15(1) analysis, and, although Justice L'Heureux-Dubé went considerably further than Cory J. had in her own concurring opinion, she certainly agreed with him on all the points essential to his ruling. Thus on a strict reading of the rules of precedent in split decisions, La Forest J.'s section 15 opinion is merely a dissenting opinion.[21]

In his section 15 opinion, Justice Cory followed the path that had been clearly marked out in *Andrews*,[22] *Turpin*,[23] *Symes*,[24] and *Miron*. He concluded that the 'opposite-sex' definition of 'spouse' in section 2 of the Old Age Security Act violated section 15(1) because it created a distinction that denied the equal benefit of the law and that burdened people characterized by their sexual orientation. He reasoned that, despite its historical origins, the spousal allowance in its current form was no longer specifically aimed at economically dependent women, but was now more generally designed to alleviate the poverty of both women and men who were dependent on their retiring partners. When considered from this perspective, he concluded, denying the spousal allowance to 'homosexual common-law couples' under circumstances in which it would be available to heterosexual common-law couples was clearly a denial of the equal benefit and protection of the law. He gave the concept of 'equal benefit' expansive meaning, reading it as including both economic benefits and the social and psychic benefits that flow from state recognition of the legitimacy of the status of particular relationships. He confirmed that the relational nature of the claim was no obstacle to the application of section 15, pointing out that 'choice of a spouse is a matter of great importance to the individuals involved' that touches the 'inherent dignity' of human beings (at 595).

The government had argued that the applicants were not disadvantaged by being treated as individuals because they were receiving adequate social assistance benefits from the province as individuals. Justice Cory rejected that contention, saying that it actually invited lesbians and gays to hide the nature of their relationships, 'imprisoning them in their privileges' (at 593–4). He went on to conclude that there was ample evidence that lesbians and gays were members of a disadvantaged group, and that denial of the spousal allowance thus violated section of the Charter.

Justice L'Heureux-Dubé agreed with much of Justice Cory's opinion, but she wrote a separate opinion in which she warned that the Court had begun to drift away from giving effect to the anti-discrimination purposes of section 15(1) by placing too much emphasis on 'grounds.' She urged the Court to 'put discrimination first' in order to give 'discrimination' greater independent content. She was of the view that legislative distinctions that treat some people as 'second-class citizens' are discriminatory, and elaborated an 'effects-sensitive matrix' which she proposed be used in analysing these types of issues.

The Section 1 Opinion

By adopting Justice Cory's section 15(1) analysis, Justice Sopinka ensured that Justice La Forest's 'contextual,' 'comparative,' or 'functional' approach to section 15(1) did not gain the support of a majority of the Court in *Egan and Nesbit*. Thus he preserved the methodological separation between section 15(1) and section 1 of the Charter. However, he went on to conclude that this violation of section 15(1) was 'justifiable' under section 1 of the Charter, and it was because of his section 1 opinion that Egan and Nesbit's challenge failed.

Justice Sopinka's section 1 opinion is unique in the sense that he gave the authoritative *'Oakes* test' developed by Chief Justice Dickson for the application of section 1 an unusual application.[25] The *Oakes* test consists of two basic steps: identifying the legislative objectives of the measures in question to see if they are 'pressing and substantial,' and then assessing whether that legislative objective is proportionate to its discriminatory effect in order to decide whether that effect can be considered to be 'rationally connected' to the objective. On a formal level, Justice Sopinka did not apply these elements of the *Oakes* test so directly to the facts in *Egan and Nesbit*. Instead, he reframed the *Oakes* test by incorporating an element of 'judicial deference' to legislative change that takes place incrementally and by 'balancing' the interests of competing factions in society. He found authority for this application of section 1 in *McKinney* v *University of Guelph*,[26] which had spoken of giving legislatures 'reasonable leeway' in making 'choices between disadvantaged groups' and the authorities relied upon in that decision, *R.* v *Edwards Books and Art Ltd.*[27] and *Williamson* v *Lee Optical of Oklahoma*[28] in the United States. Relying on the language in those cases, he concluded that the Charter should not be used to 'second-guess legislative judgment' as 'the recognition of human rights emerges slowly out of the human condition' with 'short or incremental steps ... a harbinger of a developing right, a further step in the long journey towards full and ungrudging recognition of the dignity of the human person' (at 574).

Despite the fact that all these decisions are quite distinguishable from *Egan and Nesbit* in terms of both their facts and the legal issues they raised,[29] Justice Sopinka used this line of authority to establish that the legislative objective of statutes involving 'opposite-sex' definitions of 'spouse' is the pursuit of 'incremental change' in the recognition of human rights. He then used the formal elements of the *Oakes* test to demonstrate how the history of the opposite-sex definition of spouse actually met that legislative objective – the objective of 'incremental change' (at 574–6). He agreed with the government that the opposite-sex definition of 'spouse' in the SPA was intended to alleviate the poverty of elderly spouses in an 'incremental' fashion by focusing on those in greatest need, beginning first with extension of the benefit to economically dependent cohabitants in 1975, followed by certain widowed spouses in 1979, and then to all unmarried widows and widowers in 1985. He seemed to assume that this objective was 'pressing or substantial,' and then read an 'incremental' element into the rest of the elements of the *Oakes* test as well. Thus he concluded that the opposite-sex definition of spouse met the 'proportionality' branch of the test because it could be 'regarded as a substantial step in an incremental approach to include all those who are shown to be in serious need of financial assistance due to the retirement or death of a supporting spouse,' 'minimally impaired' the Charter rights of same-sex couples because the government had to 'mediate between competing groups' in allocating these benefits, with the result that the legislation 'reasonably balances competing social demands which our society must address,' and was 'proportionate' because 'The proper balance was struck by Parliament in providing financial assistance to those who were shown to be in the greatest need of financial assistance' (at 575-6).

Justice Sopinka himself considered that his biggest contribution in *Egan and Nesbit* was the elaboration of what he called his theory of judicial deference or 'incremental' change.[30] It is not entirely clear whether he was motivated to take this direction out of genuine concern for government flexibility and finances, or whether it reflected his own reluctance to grant substantive equality to controversial minority groups such as Aboriginal women[31] and queers ('a novel concept'). Whatever his motivations, the biggest problem with his reading of section 1 is that it substantively reduces the rich and detailed elements of the *Oakes* test to the repetitive mantra of gradualism: 'the goal is gradual achievement of the objective,' 'gradual change is rational,' 'gradual change minimally impairs rights because it balances competing groups,' 'gradual change is "proportionate" because it balances gradual change against gradual achievement of the objective.' Tautological where the *Oakes* test is substantive, abstract where *Oakes* appeals to actual impact on real people, this theory of 'incremental change' lacks substantive content beyond the notion of deference to the legislature.

While Justice Sopinka's opinion can be read as setting up a 'sunset clause' giving the federal government some additional but limited time to address issues of sexuality,[32] he was criticized quite harshly by other justices in their dissenting opinions. Justices Iacobucci and Sopinka both agreed that the goal of the spousal allowance was to alleviate the poverty of elderly couples, but Justice Iacobucci concluded that the real legislative objective of the 'opposite-sex' definition of 'spouse' was the exclusion of same-sex couples from the SPA on the basis of their sexuality. He pointed out that excluding same-sex common-law couples from the program could not be considered to be proportionate to the goals of the program unless the real motivation behind the exclusion was 'fostering the existence of elderly heterosexual couples only'– an objective which he considered to be constitutionally impermissible (at 616). He also felt that the government policy really reflected fear of homosexuals, rejected the 'family values' argument against including same-sex couples, and systematically criticized all the other elements of Justice Sopinka's opinion.

Justice L'Heureux-Dubé made many of the same points, and particularly rejected the biologist nature of the government's justifications as smacking of the reductionist analysis in the now-discredited decision in *Bliss*.[33] Academic comments were similarly critical of Justice Sopinka's section 1 analysis,[34] and the Court itself has surpassed this decision. Building on Charron J.'s section 1 analysis in *M. v H.* in its 1998 decision in *Vriend* v *Alberta*, the Supreme Court of Canada has now emphasized that it is the legislative objective of discriminatory provisions themselves that must pass scrutiny under the *Oakes* test. It is unlikely that conscientious application of this new standard will leave much room for theories of 'incremental change' or 'gradualism.'

The Other 'Trilogy' Cases

Egan and Nesbit was released together with two other equality cases. In *Miron* v *Trudel*, the Court ruled that the exclusion of opposite-sex cohabitants from the definition of 'spouse' in the 1980 Insurance Act standard auto policy unjustifiably violated section 15(1). The Court read cohabiting partners into the definition of 'spouse.' In *The Queen* v *Thibaudeau*,[35] the Court concluded that section 56 of the Income Tax Act did not discriminate against women who received child support payments when it included them in their taxable income.

Miron v *Trudel*

Miron v *Trudel* is of particular interest because it closely paralleled *Egan and Nesbit*, yet led to a dramatically different result. Although another split decision, the Court in *Miron* rejected the government's section 1 justifications for excluding opposite-sex common-law partners from the definition of spouse. The majority justices concluded that the legislative objective of the standard-form definition of 'spouse' was to sustain families when one of them was injured in an automobile accident and to reduce the economic dislocation resulting from such injuries. In light of those objectives, which they considered to be 'pressing and substantial,' they concluded that limiting the definition of 'spouse' to married couples did not meet the 'rational connection' or 'minimal impairment' tests, because it was not the best 'group marker' that could be used to promote such an objective. Because the legislation failed the 'rational connection' step of the *Oakes* test, the Court did not even go on to consider whether the impairment was proportionate to the legislative goal. All the majority justices agreed that common-law spouses should be read into the definition of 'spouse' in the policy, reasoning that the legislature would have done exactly this if they had an opportunity to address the issue.[36]

In this ground-breaking decision, Justice McLachlin demonstrated that the human rights movement remains the philosophical fountainhead of the Charter equality guarantees by relating each element in the Charter analysis to the protection of 'essential human dignity' (at 590–1). She unequivocally declared that distinctions based on relationships violated these fundamental human rights, describing 'the individual's freedom to live life with the mate of one's choice in the fashion of one's choice' as a 'matter of defining importance to individuals' (at 591). Justice L'Heureux-Dubé warned that leaving the decision to formally marry to individual 'choice' or 'autonomy' could actually create opportunities for dominant partners to exploit or unjustly enrich themselves at the expense of the partner with less power (at 569–72).

Because Justice McLachlin had said, in her brief concurring opinion in *Egan and Nesbit*, that she would have applied the principles she had set out in *Miron* v *Trudel* to *Egan and Nesbit* to reach the same result, it is useful to consider how those two majority opinions fit together. Because the majority opinions in *Miron* are written in sexuality-neutral language, the principles in *Miron* clearly apply just as fully to same-sex common-law couples as they do to opposite-sex common-law couples. Indeed, the same arguments could be made even more forcefully in relation to same-sex common-law couples. Thus in any case in which the legislative facts are not precisely identical to those in *Egan and Nesbit*, it is certainly open to litigants to base their arguments on the authority of *Miron* rather than in *Egan and Nesbit*, and to distinguish *Egan and Nesbit* on as many points as possible. For example, the legislation in *Miron* involved private rights under privately owned insurance policies, the public interest being limited to regulating this area of private contract, whereas the legislation in *Egan and Nesbit* involved public social assistance payments funded out of government budgetary revenues. Since the discussion of stereotyped relationships and the effects of prejudice in *Miron* would obviously apply to any lesbian or gay relationship, it would be completely reasonable to base Charter challenges to legislation which merely regulates other types of 'private' relations on the majority judgments in *Miron* as being more closely analogous than *Egan and Nesbit*.

It is certainly true that by issuing *Egan and Nesbit* together with *Miron*, the Court made it impossible for future litigants to treat *Miron* as having implicitly narrowed or reversed *Egan and Nesbit*. However, by issuing the two decisions together, the Court also made it impossible for future litigants to treat *Egan and Nesbit* as completely ousting *Miron* as authority in relation to 'common-law couples,' which is what lesbian and gay couples are so long as their relationships have no legal status. The list of factual considerations that moved Justice McLachlin and the other members of the *Miron* majority form a useful template for the types of evidence that could well be considered to be persuasive in future challenges. Her 'grounds' analysis provides an excellent outline within which to particularize how the invisibility, exclusion, and stigmatization of lesbian women and gay men as sexual minorities have affected lesbian and gay relationships and lesbian/gay couples.[37]

The Queen v *Thibaudeau*

Of the trilogy cases, the Charter challenge in *The Queen* v *Thibaudeau* was the least successful. The majority of the Court concluded that the income tax provision in question did not even violate section 15 of the Charter. Although the case was brought by Suzanne Thibaudeau on her own, and not by the Thibaudeau family as a unit, the Court refused to evaluate the impact of section 56 of the Income Tax Act on her as an individual, and instead looked at how both sections 56 and 60, which gave her former husband tax deductions for his support payments, affected the 'post-divorce "family unit"' (at 702).

Because the majority justices treated the taxpayer and her former husband as a unit, none of them analysed the impact of the child-support tax rules on custodial mothers as individuals with autonomous financial responsibilities. Being unable to envision divorced women as being functionally separate from the 'post-divorce "family unit",' they could not see how these provisions burdened or discriminated against divorced women as 'individuals' within the meaning of the opening words of section 15(1) of the Charter. This decision offers little in the way of direct assistance to lesbian and gay litigants, but it does ironically emphasize, when read with *Egan and Nesbit*, that the Supreme Court of Canada could see the 'coupled-ness' of divorced women more clearly than they could see an intact gay couple as forming any recognizable relationship.[38]

In the end, the real significance of *Miron, Thibaudeau,* and *Egan and Nesbit* lies in the extent to which courts will extend Charter protections to 'non-traditional' relationships. The litigants in these cases all violated that norm in one way or another: Suzanne Thibaudeau was a divorced single mother; John Miron was not married to the woman he lived with; James Egan and John Nesbit were neither married nor heterosexual.[39] In a very concrete way, these three cases redescribe and reinforce the powerful boundaries that the state has constructed around heterosexual privilege. Even though Suzanne Thibaudeau had become economically, legally, and socially self-dependent, she was not permitted, in a very material way, to leave the heterosexual unit she had formed with her former husband. And despite their long-term and deeply committed relationship – a relationship of much longer duration than the average heterosexual relationship in Canada today – James Egan and John Nesbit were not permitted to breach that boundary from the other direction, to gain admittance to the state of marriage even by way of common-law cohabitation. In contrast to the inescapability of marriage for Suzanne Thibaudeau and the unattainability of even common-law cohabitation for James Egan and John Nesbit, however, John Miron found the state eager to admit him to the condition of deemed marriage by virtue of common-law cohabitation after a mere four years.

The impermeability of these boundaries is even more graphically emphasized when the 'trilogy' cases are compared with *Canada* v *Owen*.[40] In that case, Mrs Lillian Owen, after going through sex-reassignment therapy, began to live as a woman in 1951, was formally and legally married to Robert Owen in 1955, was bereaved in 1964, and, upon becoming sixty years of age in 1989, applied under the Old Age Security Act for the widowed spouse's allowance. Even though she had provided evidence that she had been considered to have been Owen's lawful wife by the Department of Veterans Affairs, her application for the spouse's allowance was rejected on the basis that her birth certificate stated that she was male. She also eventually lost her appeal on the basis that she had not had sufficient surgery to complete her sex reassignment. The Court refused to consider the long period of time she had lived as a woman as having anything to do with her legal sex, and ruled that she was neither a 'married' spouse nor a common-law spouse because she was not of the sex opposite to that of her husband.[41]

When the trilogy cases and the *Owen* case are read together, they demonstrate that heterosexual hierarchies of privilege have not yet been significantly disrupted despite the fact that the Euro-Canadian nuclear model of the 'couple' is becoming de-centred in Canadian society. Of the 'irregular' family structures considered in these cases, the only one that received judicial recognition was the biologically heterosexual cohabiting couple. Same-sex couples, divorced mothers, and transsexual spouses did not.

Reading these four decisions together makes it possible to see how the simultaneous appropriation of women's procreative and productive labours and the exclusion of same-sex couples (whether of the same sex or the opposite social sex) from the network of social benefits surrounding heterosexual couples perpetuates the heterosexual male privilege that lies at the heart of structures of power in Canada today. By continuing to support the constitutionality of social benefit provisions that set women up for appropriative transactions, and by insisting at the same time that lesbian or gay partners do not fit the traditional model of the 'family' or 'couple,' or should not fit it, liberal legal reasoning has been deployed to shore up hierarchies of relationships, in which single-earner male-headed heterosexual married couples stand at the apex of these hierarchies – all without even having to admit that these hierarchies discriminate against women or sexual minorities.

With divorced women being treated as if they were still 'locked in' to the married couple even after divorce, and with same-sex couples continuing to be 'locked out' of it unless one of them has gone through complete surgical change, the complex system of rewards, incentives, and benefits for married couples continues to promote heterosexual relations at the same time that it continues to set women up for exploitation within those heterosexual relations. Rewarding even non-reproducing heterosexuals for being heterosexual obviously reinforces the institutions of marriage and deemed marriage, and it simultaneously provides disincentives both to women who might prefer to raise children as single mothers and to lesbian women, gay men, and transsexual or transgendered persons.

The benefits of participating in recognized relationships are vast and valuable. More than 360 provisions of federal law contain special rules relating to 'spouses,' the vast majority of which confer benefits, not liabilities, on such persons.[42] Provincial laws also contain extensive special provisions relating to 'spouses.' Despite the fact that Ontario legislation has begun to include same-sex couples in some statutory schemes, hundreds of statutory provisions continue to refer only to heterosexual couples, and, on the whole, provide special treatment in the form of benefits and responsibilities that are intended to recognize and nurture these types of relationships. And the disadvantaged status of single parents – even when receiving some child support payments – is well documented.[43]

The members of the Supreme Court were well aware of the deep contradictions in the trilogy cases. In *Egan and Nesbit*, Justice Sopinka initially relied on concerns about 'cost,' but he quickly moved on to base his opinion on his theory of 'incremental change.' Justice La Forest had agreed with the other male justices in *Thibaudeau* that the impact of section 56(1)(b) of the Income Tax Act on women as individuals was not constitutionally relevant, but in *Egan and Nesbit* he suddenly waxed eloquent about the poverty of single mothers in an attempt to explain why same-sex couples should not receive the spousal allowance: 'children brought up by single parents more often end up in poverty and impose greater burdens on society' (at 537). In *Miron*, the fact that some heterosexual cohabitants did not physically reproduce with each other was considered to be irrelevant, because the Court observed that 'many' such couples either did or could physically reproduce with each other – yet in *Egan and Nesbit* the fact that many same-sex couples do raise children together was seen as irrelevant, while in *Thibaudeau* the fact that the taxpayer mother had physically reproduced and was paying a high financial cost for having done so was also seen as irrelevant. And in *Owen*, Justice Rouleau accepted the fact that Lillian Owen has lived for over forty years as a woman, yet went on to conclude that 'Parliament has seen fit to make the sex of an individual ... an essential element of the common law relationship' despite the complete absence of any discussion in federal law of what constitutes being a 'woman' or how 'sex' is defined legally.

The Impact of *Egan and Nesbit*

Ironically, lesbian women and gay men might have been better off if *Egan and Nesbit* had not been pursued, because Justice McLachlin's majority opinion in *Miron* v *Trudel* would then have formed the main authority on the constitutional status of 'non-traditional' relationships. However, it does appear that the Court went to some effort to issue those two decisions together, so if *Egan and Nesbit* could not have been used to narrow the ambit of *Miron*, the Court probably might well have found some other way to achieve the same result.

This admittedly wishful thinking aside, the impact of *Egan and Nesbit* has been complex. On the positive side, the Court did confirm that 'sexual orientation' is included in the open-ended language in section 15(1) of the Charter, and that 'opposite-sex' definitions of 'spouse' do violate section 15(1). This aspect of the ruling has had far-reaching influence as time has passed. On the negative side, the conclusion that denial of public benefits to same-sex partners is demonstrably justified under the Charter has made the pursuit of other legal benefits more difficult. Certainly the litigation climate has improved since *Egan and Nesbit* was released in 1995; of the thirteen direct Charter challenges decided since then, only four have been complete failures.

Challenges to Federal Legislation

Since *Egan and Nesbit* was decided, courts and tribunals have dealt with six direct Charter challenges to federal legislation.[44] The first decision to be released was the trial court decision in *Rosenberg* v *A.-G. Canada*,[45] in which an employer had contested the opposite-sex definition of 'spouse' in the Income Tax Act registered pension-plan survivor provisions. The *Rosenberg* challenge was the logical follow-up to the 1992 *Leshner* ruling on registered pension plan (RPP) survivor benefits,[46] in which a board of inquiry had ordered the Province of Ontario to fund a segregated 'offside' pension plan out of current provincial budgetary revenues. The board in *Leshner* had refrained from making any determination in relation to the income tax legislation that had caused the problem in the first place, but seemed to assume that the definition of 'spouse' in the registered pension plan rules would be amended to include same-sex couples in due course.[47] The government did then amend the definition of 'spouse,' but instead of dropping the 'opposite-sex' requirement, it extended it to all heterosexual cohabitants, married as well as non-married, with the result that in 1993, opposite-sex cohabitants became deemed to be spouses for purposes of the entire Income Tax Act.[48]

The Charter challenge in *Rosenberg* arose when the Canadian Union of Public Employees (CUPE), acting as an employer, attempted to secure Revenue Canada approval for an amendment to the trust agreement comprising its RPP that would have given employees with same-sex partners the same survivor options given to employees with opposite-sex partners. Revenue Canada refused to approve the amendment on the basis that it could not approve plan terms that were not consistent with the relevant provisions of income tax legislation, and threatened to 'deregister' the plan if CUPE went ahead and made the change without approval. CUPE appealed that administrative position to the Federal Court of Appeal,[49] which upheld Revenue Canada's position.

As soon as the Federal Court ruled in favour of the Minister of National Revenue, the government literally had CUPE over a barrel: if CUPE went ahead with its obligations under the collective agreement, the government claimed that it could 'deregister' the entire pension plan.[50] Even if this claim were not well founded in law, this was a risk that CUPE did not want to take. Thus CUPE filed a challenge under section 15(1) of the Charter in provincial court, taking the position that the 'opposite-sex' definition of 'spouse' in the Income Tax Act violated the prohibition on discrimination on the basis of sexual orientation.

Charron J. delayed releasing her opinion until the Supreme Court of Canada had decided *Egan and Nesbit*, and the hope was that she would take the opportunity to distinguish *Egan and Nesbit*. This did not happen. After reading *Egan and Nesbit*, she applied Justice Sopinka's section 1 analysis in *Egan and Nesbit* to the definition of 'spouse' in the Income Tax Act to conclude that the RPP survivor rules could not be distinguished from the Old Age Security Act spousal allowance. Rejecting the plaintiff's contention that privately funded employer pensions were appreciably different from publicly funded spousal benefits, she accepted the government's submission that the RPP scheme was merely one part of a three-part public retirement scheme consisting of: (1) the non-contributory public pensions under the Old Age Security Act litigated in *Egan and Nesbit*; (2) compulsory government-run contributory plans (CPP and QPP); and (3) private plans, including 'employer-sponsored pension plans' such as the CUPE plan and individual savings. Thus Charron J. found that the 'overall' objective of this 'overall legislative scheme' was 'to alleviate poverty in the elderly' and treated the direct cash expenditures from government budgetary revenues in *Egan and Nesbit* as the functional equivalent of the costs of tax deferral associated with registered pension plans.[51]

It took until 1998 to gain reversal of this decision by the Ontario Court of Appeal.[52] By this time, Abella J., who wrote the majority decision, was able to point to a growing body of section 1 decisions that focused the analysis not on the legislative objectives of the overall statute within which offending language might be located, but on the offending language itself. Thus she was able to conclude that the exclusion of same-sex couples from the RPP portion of the government's 'three-tier' retirement security program was neither a 'reasonable limit' on equality rights nor 'demonstrably justified.' She concluded that it could not be 'a pressing and substantial objective to single out for exclusive recognition, the income protection of those older Canadians whose sexual preferences are heterosexual' (para. 28), that exclusion of lesbians or gays was not a reasonable means of achieving the overall objective of the 'three-tier' system (paras. 34–42), and that the effect of exclusion on lesbians and gays was in no way proportional to the beneficial effects of the scheme on other beneficiaries (paras. 46 and 47). Thus she ordered that the 'opposite-sex' definition of 'spouse' in the legislation be read to apply to those of 'the same sex.' Although the government has decided not to appeal this decision further, no doubt trying to avoid giving it more authority than it has now, other cases on the same point are either under appeal or have been decided negatively, and so the issue remains unsettled at least in those cases in which the employer does not voluntarily extend survivor benefits to same-sex couples.[53]

Because the trial court decision in *Rosenberg* was released so soon after *Egan and Nesbit* was published, that application of *Egan and Nesbit* has played a significant role in other Charter challenges to pension-related provisions. Thus in the *Hodder* and *Fisk* decisions, administrative tribunals hearing Charter challenges to the 'opposite-sex' definition of 'spouse' in the Canadian Pension Plan provisions have applied Justice Sopinka's section 1 analysis in *Egan and Nesbit* in ruling that the denial of survivor pensions to same-sex partners justifiably violated the equality rights of gay men. Fortunately, this position has not been accepted without question; in *Boulais*, another review tribunal (chaired by the same person who chaired the challenge in *Hodder*) distinguished Justice Sopinka's analysis in *Egan and Nesbit* and followed more recent decisions in Ontario litigation. Further Charter challenges are being prepared in this area, and it will undoubtedly take quite some time and expense to clarify the implications of *Egan and Nesbit* for contributory public pension schemes like Canada/Québec Pension Plan (C/QPP), as well as for the various pension plans administered by the federal government, many of which involve varying degrees of contribution.

The court in *Silva* was not particularly affected by *Egan and Nesbit*. In that case, a gay man who had been charged with public indecency challenged the use of videotapes obtained in non-consensual police surveillance of public washrooms as evidence in his trial under sections 7 and 8 of the Charter. The court allowed the appeal, concluding that he had had a 'reasonable expectation of privacy' in the public washroom, and that even intermittent videotape surveillance directed only at gay men suspected of using the cubicles for sexual purposes brought the administration of justice into disrepute and thus constituted an unreasonable search and seizure. No equality issues were raised in this case.

In *Little Sisters*, the Supreme Court of Canada decision in *Egan and Nesbit* played a critical role. The plaintiff had challenged the criminal obscenity provisions administered by Canada Customs on the basis that they violated section 15(1) of the Charter. Relying on Justice La Forest's section 15(1) analysis in *Egan and Nesbit* and on Justice Gonthier's parallel analysis in *Miron v Trudel*, including the new 'functional values of the legislation' element both of them believed to be part of the analysis,[54] the British Columbia court concluded that the legislation did not violate section 15(1), reasoning that 'homosexual obscenity is proscribed because it is obscene, not because it is homosexual.'[55] The court did go on to conclude that the way in which Canada Customs administered the criteria in the code unjustifiably violated section 15(1) because it treated depictions of anal sex as being in themselves 'obscene,' and later granted an injunction on this exercise of administrative discretion.[56] The government has appealed this ruling, and the accused has cross-appealed on the issue of the validity of the underlying law itself. At the very least, the court's reliance on the non-majority analysis of section 15(1) ought to be seen as incorrect.

Challenges to Provincial Legislation

Overall, most of the eight post–*Egan and Nesbit* Charter challenges to provincial legislation have been successful.[57] The only failures have been in the *Canadian AIDS Society* and *Obringer* cases. However, it is worth noting that so influential was the trial court decision in *Rosenberg* that, in formulating the Charter challenge in *Dwyer*, the federal RPP rules were deliberately omitted. The same pattern of deference to *Egan and Nesbit* by way of Charron J.'s analysis of the RPP rules in *Rosenberg* appears in the administrative rulings discussed under 'Impact on Administrative Decisions,' below. The successful challenges should be treated with some caution, because at least two of them are still under appeal (*M. v H.* was argued before the Supreme Court of Canada on 18 March 1998, and *Dwyer* is under appeal to the Ontario Court of Appeal).

Three of these challenges to provincial legislation can be considered to have involved the denial of 'personal' rights. In *Nolan and Barry* and *Vriend*, the courts concluded that denial of access to the human rights process on the basis of 'sexual orientation' unjustifiably violated section

15(1) of the Charter. While the two cases took entirely different routes to the same conclusion, neither of them can be considered to have established global rights under 'sexual orientation,' but only the more limited personal rights addressed in human rights legislation.

The Charter challenge in *Nolan and Barry* arose when Brian Nolan was not permitted to file a complaint with the Newfoundland and Labrador Human Rights Commission relating to police conduct. When Nolan had been arrested by the Royal Newfoundland Constabulary for no valid reason, they referred to him as 'queer' and 'faggot' during the arrest, and left him at the mercy of a warder, who assaulted him and called him 'faggot' and 'queer.' The commission and Nolan joined together in an application to the court for a ruling that the omission of sexual orientation from the Code violated section 15(1) of the Charter of Rights. The court had no difficulty granting the application, relying on *Egan and Nesbit* and *Miron* to support its conclusion that the exclusion from the Human Rights Act prejudicially affected homosexuals by withholding from them 'the opportunities, benefits and advantages granted to others by protection from discrimination,'[58] and buttressing its analysis with references to *Haig and Birch* and the trial court decision in *Vriend v Alberta*.

One of the most interesting aspects of the decision in *Nolan and Barry* is the extent to which the court felt comfortable distancing itself from Justice Sopinka's section 1 analysis in *Egan and Nesbit*. The court flatly rejected the suggestion that the legislature should be permitted to take 'incremental' measures, and rejected the contention that legislatures should be guided by social disapproval of homosexuality. The Charter challenge in *Vriend*, which involved similar facts, led to the opposite result. Early in 1996, the Alberta Court of Appeal reversed the trial court on even narrower grounds than those the Supreme Court had relied upon in *Egan and Nesbit*. The court concluded that, because the Alberta human rights code was completely silent as to sexuality, it drew no distinctions between individuals on the basis of their sexual orientation, and thus did not discriminate on the basis of sexuality. Instead of applying the analysis of discrimination developed in Charter jurisprudence, the court appealed to the already-discredited reasoning used in the *Bliss* decision under the Canadian Bill of Rights to conclude that '[a]ny distinction between the way that homosexuals and heterosexuals are treated is not due to the IRPA [Individual's Rights Protection Act], but rather exists independently of the legislation. [T]he IRPA provides protection ... [but is not] responsible for some individuals being "worse off" than others, not even by adverse effect of the legislation.'[59]

This decision was finally reversed by the Supreme Court of Canada, which reinstated the order of the trial court. Thus the government of Alberta was ordered to administer its human rights legislation on the basis that 'sexual orientation' be read into all the protective provisions of the statute, not just the provisions relating to employment. In drafting that opinion, Lamer C.J. confirmed that Corey J.'s opinion in *Egan and Nesbit* contained the proper test of section 15(1), not the 'functional values' test applied by La Forest J. Lamer C.J. also took the opportunity to clarify the Court's approach to section 1, and firmly rejected Sopinka J.'s 'incremental' section 1 analysis. With a majority of the Court clearly behind him, he ruled that the omission of sexual orientation from human rights legislation could scarcely be considered to be rationally connected to the objective of the statute, but was 'antithetical to that goal.'[60] While speculation as to a governmental override under section 33 of the Charter has boiled up since this decision was released, the government of Alberta has not yet taken any steps in that direction.[61]

Although the Court read sexual orientation into all heads of protection in the Alberta statute, the *Vriend* case did, nonetheless, involve only 'personal' rights. The only other provincial Charter challenge involving 'personal' rights was *Canadian AIDS Society* v *Ontario*, in which the Ontario courts have ruled that, although section 7 of the Canadian Charter did protect HIV-positive donors from disclosure of test results by the Red Cross, this disclosure – despite the harm to those who tested positive – was a justifiable invasion of the donors' privacy rights because it was in accordance with principles of fundamental justice. The court further ruled that reporting the donors' HIV-positive status did not infringe the prohibition on unreasonable seizures in section 8 of the Charter. This ruling clearly gives the privacy interests of HIV-positive persons lower priority than other social interests, and gratuitously so, because the testing was done years after the initial donations and the donors could not have been considered to have consented to either testing or disclosure.

The remaining Charter challenges all touched on relational issues of various kinds, and could be considered to challenge the exclusion of same-sex couples from 'public' legislation governing ordinary family-law issues. *Re C.E.G. [(No. 1]* was a non-controversial application of the earlier ruling in *Re K.*, which permitted non-biological lesbian co-mothers to use the 'step-parent' adoption provision to memorialize the parent–child relationship, to the same situation in another court district. The other three decisions, all much more controversial, challenged the exclusion of same-sex couples from 'opposite-sex' definitions of 'spouse' in support law, dependent relief and inheritance law, and provincial provisions governing pensions for public-sector employees.

Of these three decisions, the rulings in *M. v H.* have been the most significant. Coming as it did shortly after *Egan and Nesbit* was decided by the Supreme Court of Canada, Epstein J.'s decision in *M. v H.*[62] offered an important reading of *Egan and Nesbit*. Epstein J. ruled that the 'man or woman' definition of cohabitants who can claim support under Part III of the Family Law Act[63] includes same-sex couples for purposes of support obligations. In a decision that focused on section 1 justifications, Epstein J. defined the legislative objective of these support provisions as being to 'protect those who have become economically dependent upon a relationship marked by marriage or intimate cohabitation, and who require assistance in becoming self-sufficient upon the breakdown of that relationship' (at 610). Epstein J. concluded that excluding economically dependent lesbian partners was not rationally connected to that objective, was not offset by the opportunity to bring an application in relation to capital property, and was disproportionate to the objective of providing support for dependent heterosexual cohabitants because 'it eludes me how giving same-sex partners access ... affects the formation of heterosexual unions' (at 614). Epstein J. did not entirely reject Justice Sopinka's section 1 analysis in *Egan and Nesbit*. She treated it as having added an element of 'judicial deference' to the *Oakes* test, thus permitting her to consider whether legislation could be regarded as a 'substantial step in an incremental approach' to the achievement of the relevant legislative objective (at 615). However, she distinguished his version of 'judicial deference' in three ways: (1) His deference analysis was 'specific to that case and particularly to the nature of the impugned legislation'; (2) cost considerations were not relevant to the application of Charter rights; and (3) the application in question had the potential to reduce government expenditures rather than increase them because 'fewer people would have to look to social assistance upon the breakdown of their relationship' (at 615–16). Epstein J. then amended the heterosexual limitation in section 29 of the Family Law Act, ordered the defendant to submit a financial statement within thirty days, and set the matter down for hearing on interim support.

The impact of the trial decision in *M. v H.* in overcoming the problems with Justice Sopinka's section 1 analysis was further strengthened by the Ontario Court of Appeal. Writing for the court, Charron J., who had written the trial court decision in the *Rosenberg* case, authored this decision.[64] In a breakthrough section 1 analysis, Charron J. set out an approach to section 1 that was shortly thereafter applied by that court in the *Rosenberg* appeal and then approved by the Supreme Court of Canada in *Vriend*. Charron J. applied section 1 by looking to 'legislative purpose' in light of the overall purpose of the legislation as a whole, the function of the provision in question, and the purpose of the specific discriminatory language. Applying that approach to the support obligations under provincial family law, she concluded that the denial of support rights to same-sex partners was completely antithetical to the purposes of the support provisions generally, as well as to the purpose of extending those provisions to non-married heterosexual cohabitants.

Despite the powerful rulings in *M. v H.*, however, the court in *Obringer v Kennedy Estate* refused to extend other statutory definitions of 'spouse' to give a gay man a share in his intestate partner's estate. When his partner left an estate valued at nearly $.5 million upon his death, all of which was claimed by a distant relative, Obringer challenged four provisions of family property law that would have given him some share of the estate if he had been a surviving heterosexual partner. These were the heterosexual definitions of 'spouse' under section 44 of the Succession Law Reform Act,[65] under which he claimed the whole of the estate as a surviving spouse; the definition of 'dependent spouse' under Part V of that act, which would have given him the right to claim support from the estate; the definition of 'spouse' under section 5 of the Family Law Act,[66] which would have entitled to him to equalization benefits; and the definitions of cohabitants or 'spouse' under Part III of that act, which would have given him a claim to support from the estate.[67] This last point challenged the same statutory definition that had been litigated in *M. v H.*, although it was obviously a different context. The court rejected Obringer's claims to be treated as a formally married spouse on the basis of *Layland and Beaulne*,[68] in which an Ontario court had ruled that the prohibition on same-sex marriages did not violate section 15(1) of the Charter. The claims to be given the rights of non-married cohabitant also failed, not on the basis of the Charter, but because the court found that Obringer had not established that he was, in fact, 'cohabiting' with Kennedy at the time of his death. Thus the court concluded that he did not have standing to challenge the definitions of dependent cohabitant or 'man or woman' cohabitant that barred him from a share in the estate. Pointing to the fact that Obringer continued to work for the New York Thruway Authority despite his twenty-year relationship with Kennedy, the court found that he did not live with Kennedy continuously enough to be considered to be a cohabitant.

While the court in *Obringer* did seem to suggest that the ruling in *M. v H.* could be applied when same-sex partners do meet the factual definition of 'cohabitant,' the court's factual analysis of the realities of maintaining a transborder commuting relationship appeared to underrate the severity of the constraints this couple faced. For example, it would not have been until shortly before Kennedy died that he could have sponsored Obringer for immigration into Canada under new same-sex sponsorship policies. Before that, it is not clear that someone who was essentially a civil servant would have been able to meet the criteria applied by Immigration Canada for independent immigration.[69]

The cumulative effect of the rulings in *M. v H.* and *Rosenberg* appear to have once again improved the litigation climate surrounding lesbian and gay issues. The two most recent Charter challenges to provincial legislation, both resolved in favour of lesbian or gay plaintiffs, took pains to distinguish *Egan and Nesbit*. In *Dwyer* v *Toronto (Metropolitan)*, an Ontario board of inquiry ruled that if and when the Income Tax Act were ever amended (legislatively or judicially) to permit extension of survivor benefits to same-sex partners, then municipal employers would be required to provide such benefits. The board also extended all the provincial statutes that limited such benefits to opposite-sex spouses to include same-sex partners. The tribunal ordered the municipal employer to extend other employment benefits to same-sex couples, although Revenue Canada had by that time changed its position with respect to the tax treatment of such benefits, which was the main reason given by the employer for denial of same-sex benefits. In dealing with the respondent's contention that, on the section 1 analysis in *Egan and Nesbit*, the exclusion of same-sex partners was justifiable, the board distinguished the two situations on the basis that the benefits sought in *Egan and Nesbit* were 'social benefits,' whereas the benefits sought in *Dwyer* were 'employment benefits' of the sort directly referenced by way of comparison by Justice Sopinka himself in *Egan and Nesbit*. Sopinka J. had stated that human rights legislation, which 'operates in the field of employment, housing, use of public facilities and the like ... can hardly be equated with the problems faced by the federal government' in extending some fifty 'opposite-sex' definitions of 'spouse' to same-sex couples as had been demanded in *Egan and Nesbit*.

The *Dwyer* decision reveals the extent to which the authority of *Egan and Nesbit* had already been eroded by Charron J.'s application of section 1 in *M. v H.* The board had no hesitation in distinguishing the tax deferral associated with the RPP system from the direct expenditures authorized by the Old Age Security Act. Pointing out that private pension plans are funded by contributions from the employee and the employer commonly considered to represent deferred wages earned by the employee, the board distinguished both *Egan and Nesbit* and the trial court decision in *Rosenberg*, which was the most recent ruling on point at that time.

The influence of the decisions in *M. v H.* was also apparent in the decision in *Kane v Ontario (A.-G.)*, in which an Ontario court concluded that the omission of lesbian partners from the definition of 'spouse' in insurance legislation as being limited to 'a man and a women' who have married or cohabited violated section 15(1) of the Charter. Coo J. flatly rejected the asserted authority of *Egan and Nesbit*: 'I do not accept that *Egan* governs the circumstances with which I am faced.' The court concluded that it was bound by *M. v H.* because the facts of *Egan and Nesbit* were distinguished from commercial insurance policies, and on the basis that the cost issues actually ran 'in the opposite direction' because of the essentially private nature of the contract.

Impact on Administrative Decisions

While it took courts several years to distance themselves enough from the reasoning in the Supreme Court of Canada decision in *Egan and Nesbit* to begin distinguishing cases and relying on the more sophisticated section 1 analysis developed by Charron J. in *M. v H.*, decision makers sitting on human rights boards, arbitrations, review tribunals, and courts reviewing such decisions were able to move more quickly to apply the new and authoritative definitions of 'discrimination' and 'sexual orientation' set out in *Egan and Nesbit*. During the same period of time in which litigants in direct Charter challenges had to undergo lengthy and expensive appeals, and still ended up losing at least four critical Charter challenges, all but one of the sixteen administrative cases decided during that time were resolved in favour of lesbian and gay applicants.[70]

None of these decisions were themselves Charter challenges. But *Egan and Nesbit* became an important precedent in administrative hearings because it provided, at the highest level of judicial authority, a detailed definition of what constitutes 'discrimination,' as well as an authoritative precedent on how 'sexual orientation' applies to relational rights, personal rights, harassment, and the basic categories of human rights protection. Thus *Egan and Nesbit* emerged in this area of litigation not as the leading Charter authority, but as the leading judicial authority on the interpretation of 'sexual orientation.'

Because *Egan and Nesbit* was used as an interpretive authority only, Justice Sopinka's section 1 opinion in *Egan and Nesbit* did not cause any problems in these cases. While violations of Charter rights can always be justified under section 1 of the Charter in Charter challenges, boards and arbitrators consistently confirmed that section 1 of the Charter does not apply to human rights codes, collective agreements, or other employment standards when Charter rights have not actually been invoked. This explains why so many favourable decisions could have been based on an authority that was, in the context of subsequent Charter challenges, not a particularly strong precedent upon which to base equality claims. But in the context of administrative proceedings, *Egan and Nesbit* has continued to be treated as the leading authority, and Sopinka J.'s theory of 'incremental change' has had no impact in these cases. Because the Supreme Court of Canada decision in *Egan and Nesbit* established that excluding same-sex couples from the 'opposite-sex' definition of 'spouse' or 'cohabitant' constitutes 'discrimination on the basis of sexual orientation,' *Egan and Nesbit* has been squarely on point with a large number of administrative cases.

Most of these administrative cases have revolved around relationship issues. The leading case in this group of decisions is *Vogel v Manitoba [Vogel II]*, which was decided by the Manitoba Court of Appeal just a few weeks after the Supreme Court of Canada decided *Egan and Nesbit*. This was a further appeal from Chris Vogel and Richard North's attempt, after the Manitoba Human Rights Code had been amended in the late 1980s to include 'sexual orientation,' to obtain same-sex employment benefits. (The trial court ruling is discussed in chapter 2.) Even after 'sexual orientation' had been added to the Manitoba code, an adjudicator and a court had ruled that the denial of same-sex benefits to the couple did not discriminate on the basis of either sexual orientation or other grounds such as family status because the partners were of the same sex, and the benefit plans to which they sought access contained an 'opposite-sex' definition of 'spouse.' Shortly after the Supreme Court of Canada decision in *Egan and Nesbit* was released, however, the Manitoba Court of Appeal directed the adjudicator to reopen the hearing and to treat the complaint as one relating to 'sexual orientation.' This direction does not determine how the adjudicator will deal with the substance of the complaint itself, but the court did rely on *Egan and Nesbit* to conclude that exclusion of same-sex partners from an 'opposite-sex' definition of 'spouse' could constitute discrimination on the basis of sexual orientation, and that the new code provision did not extend merely to personal rights. The court dealt with the section 1 aspect of the *Egan and Nesbit* decision very simply, reasoning that the Manitoba code 'does not have a general qualifying provision similar to section 1.' Thus the adjudicator was ordered to continue the adjudication in accordance with the court's decision.

The federal tribunal in *Moore and Akerstrom* reached a similar conclusion. This case arose from a complaint filed with the federal human rights commission after the Ontario Court of Appeal had read sexual orientation into the Canadian human rights code in *Haig and Birch*. Emphasizing that this was a complaint originating with the Canadian human rights commission and not a Charter case, the tribunal applied *Egan and Nesbit* to conclude that denying federal employees the full range of spousal benefits when their partners were of the same sex violated the sexual-orientation clause of the act. When the government argued that the tribunal should apply the section 1 portion of *Egan and Nesbit* as well, the tribunal distinguished this proceeding from a Charter challenge: 'Here, we are dealing with an employer who happens to be the government. The government as employer can no more rely upon s. 1 of the Charter to justify discrimination on a ground prohibited under this Act than can a private employer who is federally regulated' (para. 79), and '[t]his case is not a Charter case. The defences available to the Respondent are the defences provided in the Act. S. 1 of the Charter is not one of those defences' (para. 82). More recently, this application of *Egan and Nesbit* has been confirmed in the context of *McCallum* v *Toronto Transit Commission*, in which the parties settled a complaint arising out of the denial of spousal benefits to same-sex partners of employees on the same terms as *Dwyer* by agreement of the parties. Although *McCallum* did not directly rely upon *Egan and Nesbit*, *Dwyer* had.

It has been interesting to see that, as human rights commissions have accepted complaints in relation to sexual orientation, concern over the common-law status of same-sex relationships has receded into the background, and commissions have generally been able to process complaints such as the one in *McCallum* under the heading 'discrimination in employment.' In other complaints where discrimination has taken the form of refusal to recognize same-sex relationships for various legal purposes, complaints have been classified as arising under 'services' provisions of human rights codes. For example, in *Bewley* v *Ontario*, the complaint arose out of the refusal to permit a lesbian couple to register new hyphenated last names after going through a commitment ceremony. The commission and board treated the complaint as arising out of the 'denial of the right to equal treatment with respect to services because of sexual orientation,' and the board ruled in favour of the complainant.

The elasticity of the categories 'services' and 'employment' are sweeping up more and more forms of discrimination. This in turn is blurring the distinction between 'public' benefits as litigated in *Egan and Nesbit* versus 'private' rights at the same time that it is funnelling growing numbers of discrimination cases involving lesbians and gays into the human rights process. Two surviving gay partners who had brought Charter challenges to the denial of survivor benefits under the Canada Pension Plan – allegedly 'public' benefits in *Boulais* and *Hodder* – have also been permitted to file human rights complaints for denial of services against employer-administered pension plans. In *Nova Scotia (Minister of Finance) v Hodder*, the Nova Scotia commission referred a complaint that the Nova Scotia Department of Finance and the Nova Scotia Teachers' Union had discriminated against the complainant in the provision of services by excluding same-sex partners from the term 'spouse' as used in the Public Service Superannuation Act[71] to a board. The respondents challenged the board's jurisdiction to hear such a complaint, but the Nova Scotia Court of Appeal ordered the inquiry to proceed. A similar jurisdictional challenge was considered in *Nova Scotia (Minister of Finance) v MacNeil Estate*, which involved the complaint brought by MacNeil's surviving partner, the plaintiff in the Charter challenge to the CPP survivor rules in *Boulais*.

With human rights commissions and boards treating denial of same-sex benefits of various kinds as discrimination in relation to 'employment' or 'services,' it is not surprising to see that the category of 'services' has come to be applied expansively. Thus in *Korn v Potter and Benson*, the British Columbia Supreme Court upheld a board ruling that denying lesbian women access to alternative insemination services constituted discrimination on the basis of sexual orientation.[72] And in *Hudler v London (City)*, a board concluded that refusal to proclaim Pride Day in London, Ontario, constituted discrimination in the provision of services.

Not all of these kinds of complaints have been completely successful. The early trial court decision in *Rosenberg* has cast a long shadow, dissuading the complainant in *Dwyer* from directly challenging the validity of the RPP rules in the federal Income Tax Act, and convincing the federal tribunal in *Moore and Akerstrom* that it should not deal with the RPP issue in its comprehensive order. One of the consequences of the uncertainty surrounding this particular form of discrimination has been the decision in *Laessoe* v *Air Canada*, in which the tribunal concluded that a 'private sector' employer did not violate the federal human rights statute when it denied same-sex survivor benefits to a gay employee. The members of the tribunal reasoned that extension of survivor options to same-sex employees would impose too heavy a burden on private employers, especially when the federal government itself, when acting as an employer, was still not under any duty to offer such benefits. In justifying this conclusion, the tribunal pointed to the indeterminate costs of extending survivor benefits to same-sex partners of employees, the obvious administrative burden associated with such a program, and the fact that no 'off side' arrangement could ever fully equalize the benefits without imposing excessive costs on the employer.

Egan and Nesbit has had similar influence in the interpretation of 'sexual orientation' clauses in collective agreements. While the precise focus of the grievance in *Re Metro Toronto Reference Library* was a little murky, the arbitrators did decide, in the end, that denial of bereavement leave to a same-sex partner on the basis of the 'man and woman' definition of spouse that had been incorporated into the collective agreement violated both the prohibition on discrimination on the basis of sexual orientation in the agreement and the federal human rights code as corrected by *Haig and Birch*. The panel appeared to have cast the main issue in this grievance as whether the denial of leave violated section 15(1) of the Charter as applied in *Egan and Nesbit*, but that part of the decision was not necessary to the overall result. The board did not deal with section 1 of the Charter in that context because it had not been argued by the employer.

The adjudicator in *Re Treasury Board (Agriculture and Agri-Food Canada) and Yarrow* (bereavement leave) and *Re Treasury Board (Canadian Grain Commission) and Sarson* (unpaid leave during spousal relocation) was much more precise in formulating the issues. While the grievance had contained a Charter challenge in the beginning, that was dropped, and the grievance, arising again out of the denial of bereavement leave to a gay employee, was dealt with on the basis of the interpretation of the 'opposite-sex' definition of spouse in the collective agreement, arbitral decisions, the provisions of the federal human rights code as corrected by *Haig and Birch*, and the decisions thereunder. The adjudicator was guarded in applying the law, and did not mention *Egan and Nesbit* as the specific authority for her decision, but instead made more general references to 'the law of the land' as embodied in the federal code and previous arbitral and human rights decisions on the scope of 'sexual orientation' in collective agreements. No section 1 justification was entertained because there was no Charter challenge in either of these grievances.

Most recently, the Canada Public Service Staff Relations Board extended this line of reasoning to include marriage leave in *Re Boutilier and Treasury Board (Natural Resources)*. Applying a collective agreement that did not make express reference to 'sexual orientation' in its non-discrimination clause, this decision reveals how the breakthrough decision in *Haig and Birch* can intersect with the Supreme Court of Canada's understanding of discrimination on the basis of sexual orientation in order to extend spousal rights under collective agreements to lesbian and gay employees. The board concluded that because the agreement did stipulate that it could not be applied in a manner that abridged the constitutional or statutory rights of employees, the 'sexual orientation' clause read into the Canadian human rights code by *Haig and Birch* inserted that head of protection into the agreement. The board then applied the jurisprudence on sexual-orientation discrimination to the interpretation of that clause, and concluded that denial of marriage leave violated the agreement. The grievor's representative had wanted the board to find that 'marriage' in the agreement should be interpreted as applying to the 'only marriage possible between the Grievor and his partner,' but the board made the more cautious finding that denial of this grievance would 'amount to denying to Mr. Boutilier the equal benefit of the collective agreement as required by the Canadian Human Rights Act.'[73]

The Queers Still Outside the Charter

In contrast to the burgeoning numbers of cases and administrative rulings relating to lesbians and gays, the continued invisibility of other sexual minorities in Charter and human rights discourse is cause for concern. With the exception of *Piche*, which involved federal inmates who were described as 'bisexual,' only one case, *Sheridan*, involving the application of human rights or Charter rights to sexuality has been brought by transgendered, bisexual, or transsexual persons, and only one human rights complaint, *Roberts*, has focused on the dimension of racial identity in relation to sexuality.

The explanation for this invisibility and silence is, in my opinion, the hierarchical construction of categories in legal discourse, especially of human rights and constitutional rights discourse. The very forces that have necessitated the creation of special legal mechanisms to protect minimal rights – racism, sexism, heterosexism, and other forms of prejudice – have also exerted pressure on governments, administrators, and courts to construe and apply those rights as narrowly as possible. Thus provisions initially intended to redress discrimination on the basis of 'sex' were read down to exclude any other group, such as lesbians or gays, and I have no doubt that when other sexual minorities begin to seek recognition of their civil, human, or constitutional rights, their political opponents will also seek to read terms like 'sexual orientation' as narrowly as possible in order to eliminate grounds of protection.

This is a political or critical reading of how 'rights' discourse unfolds and is constrained, and I think it is a realistic assessment of how liberal claims are disrupted, diverted, and undermined. The blame is not on the groups that have failed to achieve legal recognition or protection. Nor does the solution lie in 'getting it right.' I make this point because there are critics who do seem to feel that if only 'categorical thinking' could be surpassed, or if only 'intersectional grounds' could be recognized by courts, the problems of those still outside rights discourse would be solved.

Nitya Iyer has written a fine critique of how equality rights have been constructed to force claimants to fit themselves into categories that are defined so narrowly that they leave out a great deal of their real selves and experiences. While this analysis effectively speaks to the continued use of categorical thinking by decision makers, the critique is quite decontextualized in the sense that the sources of legal categories are not explored, the politics of law are ignored, and existing legal categories are treated almost as if they had *a priori* existence. By failing to consider the hierarchical sources of existing categories, the solutions suggested – 'open up the pockets and permit them to intersect' by looking to all characteristics of all parties[74] – have abstract appeal, but little pragmatic potential. The real problem is power, not terminology. The real solution is changing hierarchies of privilege, for without changing the allocation of political power, changes in the definitions of categories will not, by themselves, change the method of the law in this regard.

While the 'blame' for the emphasis on 'sexual orientation' as the vehicle for redressing the social and legal discrimination against lesbians and gays certainly belongs primarily to policy makers and courts, lesbian and gay activists do of course bear some responsibility for deciding to work within that framework instead of creating other strategies. But their responsibility is more that of making the best of a bad set of choices, and not responsibility for having constructed the choices in the first place.

The further people move from the paradigm of racially 'white' dualistic categories of 'lesbian' and 'gay,' the less relevant the pigeon-holes called 'grounds' in human rights codes and section 15(1) of the Charter will be to lived experiences, especially when 'sexuality' is not conceived merely as monogamous same-sex sexuality, and 'identity' comes to be understood as being constructed simultaneously along dimensions such as race, legal sex, perceived biological sex, assigned sex of partner, sexual enjoyment and sexual preferences, class, economic location, ability, or sex as gender. In 'real life,' as Audre Lorde has expressed so poignantly, identity is fluid, contextual, in constant discourse with others as well as with 'self':

[W]hen the sisters think you're crazy and embarrassing; and the brothers want to break you open to see what makes you work inside; and the white girls look at you like some exotic morsel that has just crawled out of the walls onto their plate (but don't they love to rub their straight skirts up against the edge of your desk in the college literary magazine office after class); and the white boys all talk either money or revolution but can never quite get it up – then it doesn't really matter too much if you have an Afro long before the word even existed.[75]

Heterosexual and lesbian women of colour; lesbian and heterosexual men of colour; lesbians who are 'white' and lesbians who are women of colour; lesbian women of colour and heterosexual 'white' men – the polarities and permutations go on and on, but the hierarchies of race, sex, and sexuality fold and unfold, continuously reproducing sometimes smaller and sometimes larger pyramids of privilege and burden. Until Charter law can trace discrimination through these unfoldings of social reality, it can never begin to apprehend 'full life.' But the solution is not to castigate existing categories for their narrowness and artificiality; certainly it lies more in the direction of insisting that rule makers and courts listen to the complex realities of the people who bring their lives before them.

The open-ended language in section 15(1) of the Charter may present a basis from which to address this fundamental problem. The progressive spin on this open-ended language is that it was included not only to ensure that groups like lesbians and gays would be able to gain access to the Charter without drawing too much political attention to that possibility, but also to ensure that, as other dimensions of discrimination could be expressed, there would be room in the Charter to address them. Just as discrimination claims relating to 'sexual orientation' have not been litigated within the rubric of 'sex,' 'lesbian' does not have to be litigated within the category 'sexual orientation,' 'transgender' or 'transsexual' does not have to be litigated as discrimination on the basis of either 'sexual orientation' or 'sex,' and 'bisexual' can be treated as the differentiated identity that it is.[76]

The open-ended language in section 15 may also make it feasible to frame issues of discrimination on the basis of specific aspects of queer existence. Non-monogamous, non-cohabiting, non-sexual, or only-sexual relationships can be named as the specificities of queer existences that they are, and litigants can demand recognition of those specificities for what they are, as unique to the often uniquely disadvantaged status of those ways of relating. The litigation framework has already been constructed within which such challenges could be developed in *Miron v Trudel*.

This suggestion runs deeply counter to most accepted approaches to the litigation of entrenched rights. In Europe, the tendency has been to litigate transsexual issues within the rubric of 'sex discrimination.'[77] Building on early successes with that approach, this is now perceived to be such a strong trend that there has been recent serious suggestion that the new charter promised by the Labour government in the United Kingdom might well do better to omit 'sexual orientation' so that all sexual minorities could bring their claims under the heading of 'sex.'[78] Lesbian women in Canada continue to debate whether to bring Charter challenges relating to lesbians under the headings 'sexual orientation' or 'sex,' but there has been no suggestion to date that they should be brought under the heading 'discrimination based on lesbianism.'[79] Some transgendered and transsexual activists in Canada have decided to seek inclusion in the category 'sex' rather than struggle for recognition of other new categories.[80] Limited in most states to equal-rights amendments that expressly extend to 'sex' discrimination, lesbian and gay litigants in the Hawaii 'marriage case' have managed to win a constitutional challenge to exclusion of same-sex couples from the institution of marriage by framing their case under the heading 'sex.'[81]

Whichever strategy is selected, however, the invisibility of bisexual, transgendered, racially identified queer, and transsexual persons in the chart(er)ing process is largely a reflection of existing hierarchies of privilege, and not just a function of uninspired legal imagination or the impossibility of fully expressing the realities of human existence in the legal process. The historical record certainly demonstrates that legal discourse is uniquely impervious to the difficulties of expressing all the dimensions of human identity and experience through the fragmented and fragmenting vocabularies of rights discourse, but the problem most certainly is, for the queers who remain outside the Charter, hierarchized access to legal services and judicial sympathy.[82] As contemporary critical pragmatists have pointed out, both rights discourse and hierarchies of privilege are here to stay, and more fundamental change may well have to be pursued not only in the courts, or even in the legislatures, but in the streets.[83]

Conclusions

Lesbian, gay, bisexual, transgendered, and transsexual persons have been actively seeking simple legal equality in Canada for nearly half a century. This struggle began with the belief that, despite differences from the 'heterosexual' majority, they were still just 'ordinary people' with 'ordinary' legal rights. Early litigation quickly established that they were not, and that discrimination against queers had become successfully embedded in every form of legal structure in Canada, including common-law doctrine, vast numbers of statutes, and even the very human rights statutes that had been developed to protect fundamental human integrity.

This exclusion from 'ordinary' legal structures relating to 'ordinary' life left sexual minorities with little choice but to seek some recognition under human rights statutes. Before 'sexual orientation' clauses began to be included in human rights codes, however, courts repeatedly ruled that human rights legislation did not impliedly prohibit discrimination on the basis of sexuality, and that other heads of protection, such as 'sex' or 'marital status,' did not apply to lesbian women and gay men because discrimination against them was based on their 'sexual orientation.' When 'sexual orientation' clauses were finally added to some human rights statutes, lesbian women and gay men continued to be denied legal protection for a variety of reasons, including the proposition that the prohibition on discrimination on the basis of sexual orientation did not affect the legal recognition of lesbian or gay relationships, but merely protected 'personal' or 'status' rights such as the right to employment.

As sexual minorities became imprisoned within the category labelled 'sexual orientation,' hopes for 'ordinary rights' became pinned on the drafting, application, and interpretation of the Charter of Rights and Freedoms. But the pattern of exclusion seen in ordinary legal doctrine and human rights law was replicated once again during the chart(er)ing process. The drafters of the Charter refused to include references to 'sexual orientation' in the Charter. Early Charter decisions established that discrimination against lesbian women and gay men was not prohibited because, as discrimination on the basis of sexual orientation, it did not constitute discrimination on the basis of 'sex' or 'family status,' and that the Charter did not prohibit discrimination on the basis of sexual orientation. Thus assigned to the jurisprudential space labelled 'sexual orientation' by these early Charter decisions, the law did not appear to support queer existences beyond the confines of 'the lesbian/gay realm of existence' in which positive rights existed only to the extent expressly conferred by judicial or legislative action.

The chart(er)ing process did generate two key changes that have finally interacted to produce some significant changes in the legal status of lesbians and gays. The inclusion of open-ended language in section 15 of the Charter made it possible for courts to extend equality guarantees to queers. And the articulation of a substantive concept of 'discrimination' in the section 15 jurisprudence resulted in a line of cases that slowly built upon each other to result, first, in the breakthrough ruling in *Haig and Birch*, reading 'sexual orientation' into the federal human rights code and from there into collective agreements, and, second, in the substantive understanding of discrimination on the basis of sexual orientation set out in *Egan and Nesbit*.

However, even as the emphasis on older concepts of protected 'personal' rights versus unprotected 'relational' rights has began to fade away in the face of the 'burden' approach to 'discrimination' developed in Charter equality jurisprudence, courts have began to rely on section 1 of the Charter to find that the continued denial of some relational rights can be 'demonstrably justified' even under the Charter. This effect has been most noticeable where 'opposite-sex' definitions of 'spouse' have been read as narrowing the scope of sexual orientation clauses in human rights codes or the Charter itself. At the same time, the differences in outcome in *Egan and Nesbit*, which involved the rights of same-sex partners to public income support, and *M. v H.* or *Rosenberg*, which involved the rights of same-sex partners to a share in 'private' incomes or savings of their partner, has begun to construct within Charter equality discourse a 'public'/'private' divide between rights in 'public' legislation that can still be denied despite the Charter and rights in 'public' legislation that cannot be so denied.

Despite all these problems in the jurisprudence, the sheer numbers of

98   Are We 'Persons' Yet?

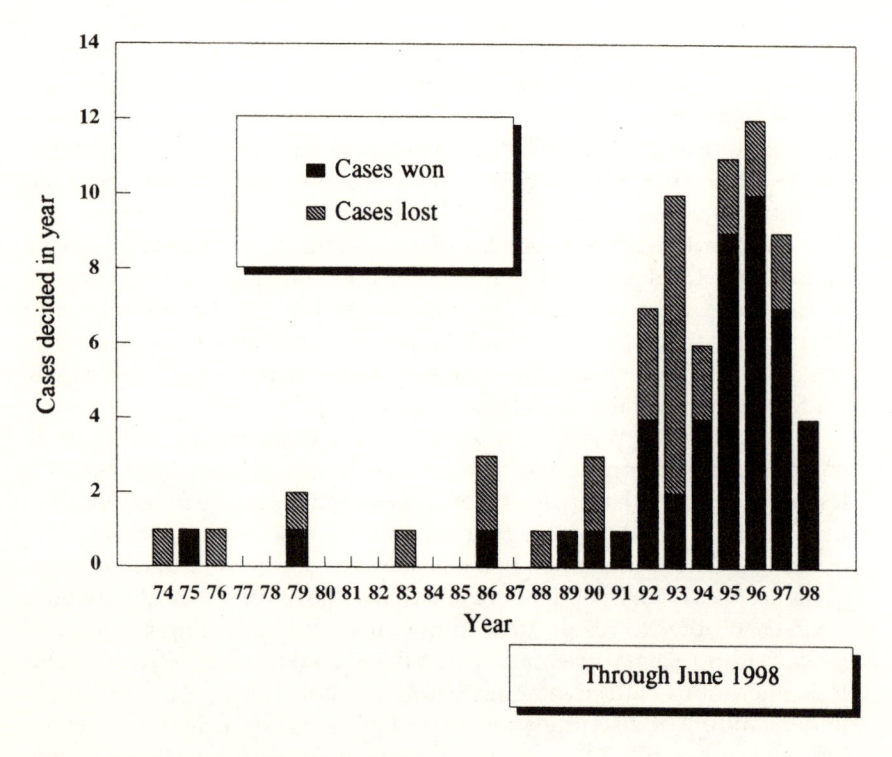

Figure 3.1. Litigation Record, 1974–98

cases touching on queer existence have grown dramatically over the last twenty-five years. And, as the result of the chart(er)ing process, the proportion of cases being decided in favour of lesbian and gay litigants, as shown in figure 3.1, has begun to increase radically as well.

As reassuring as the results reflected in figure 3.1 are, however, they do not reveal two troubling trends. First, the unsuccessful cases still fall within what could be described as the 'public' end of the spectrum of rights created by 'public' legislation when those rights are arrayed along a 'public'–'private' continuum. Second, the single biggest gains in numbers of cases brought and in numbers of cases decided in favour of lesbian or gay litigants are attributable to the relatively greater success of cases decided administratively rather than judicially.

These two trends are mutually reinforcing. Charter challenges to same-sex survivor rights under 'public' pension plans, one of the types of 'public' benefits most completely denied to same-sex couples as the result of the Supreme Court of Canada decision in *Egan and Nesbit*, are still not consistently successful, whereas similar challenges framed as complaints in human rights legislation or grievances under collective agreements have a better rate of success. This is symptomatic of the larger structural transformation that is going on in the face of increasing legal recognition of the rights of lesbians and gays: As the scope of 'sexual orientation' clauses in human rights codes and collective agreements continues to expand, claims that could have been framed as Charter challenges to general or ordinary legal structures may be increasingly funnelled into administrative channels, which tend to grant more individualized and limited remedies than do courts dealing with direct Charter challenges.[84] When viewed from that perspective, it could be said that increasing success in litigation is having less impact on general or ordinary legal structures as lesbian and gay rights are becoming increasingly dependent upon specialized administrative structures. In this sense, sexual minorities are not gaining genuine equality in ordinary legal doctrine. Instead, lesbians and gays – along with other marginalized groups – are merely gaining limited special rights located in human rights codes and private agreements, the 'lesbian coffee houses' of law, carefully segregated from ordinary legal structures.[85]

Chapter Four

Human Rights, Charter Rights, and 'Legal Personality'

However generously interpreted, section 15 represents only the legal minimum that must be respected by governments. Its scope will not evolve as it should if governments and people base their actions and policies only on that minimum ... A look into the past is suggestive ... It was only in 1927 that the term 'person'... was ruled to include women ...

Hon. John Crosbie, *Toward Equality* (Ottawa: MSSC, 1986), 3

The human rights movement has existed in North America for at least two centuries, yet lesbian, gay, bisexual, transsexual, and transgendered people have begun to obtain recognition for their human rights only in the last few decades. Nor are the gains that have been made to date particularly secure. Despite the fact that increasing numbers of cases have been filed and won in recent years, cases such as *Vriend* v *Alberta*[1] demonstrate that access to statutory and constitutional protections as well as to the full range of 'ordinary' legal rights that surround and support 'full life' are almost completely contingent on judicial opinion.

The road to recognizing and protecting human rights has, of course, never been smoothly or quickly traversed. It is no secret that the mere enactment of statutory or constitutional human rights guarantees does not necessarily eradicate discrimination. Richard Bardolph's detailed legal history of the statutes, cases, and constitutional provisions relating to racial discrimination in the United States demonstrates more graphically than any theoretical analysis could ever do how long it takes to reshape legal structures, how progressive reforms can be transformed into new structures of oppression or exclusion, and how little impact law reform alone has on social and economic practices.[2] More recently, critical scholars across the disciplines have recognized how deeply contradictory, frustrating, and useless 'rights discourse' can be.[3] My favourite image of these contradictions is the one created by Pat Williams: 'At the bottom of the Deep Blue Sea, drowning mortals reached silently and desperately for drifting anchors dangling from short chains far, far overhead, which they thought were lifelines meant for them.'[4]

The experiences of lesbian, gay, bisexual, transsexual, and transgendered people with 'ordinary' legal doctrine, human rights guarantees, and constitutional 'equality' guarantees starkly illustrate the difficulties of achieving genuine change in legal norms. The recognition of queer rights in both human rights and constitutional discourse appears to be running into almost the very same barriers that other disadvantaged groups have encountered in their struggles, with conservatives claiming that any recognition of such rights constitutes 'special treatment,' and courts finding endless ways to read protective legislation as excluding sexual minorities.[5]

In this chapter, I argue that human rights codes, and even constitutional guarantees of 'rights' or 'equality,' will remain but 'drifting anchors' unless their historical disconnection from the 'ground' of 'legal personality' can be repaired. Although it may well be that the very structures of law themselves will always ensure that legal capacity will serve as anchors only for the privileges of dominant groups in state/society, I would like to test that critical hypothesis one last time before giving up. Indeed, what is the alternative?

Thus I locate the struggle over the rights of disadvantaged groups generally, and more particularly the rights of sexual minorities, in the larger struggle that has unfolded in state societies over the civil capacities of 'persons.' I have chosen to evaluate the status of lesbian, transgender/sexual, bisexual, and gay people in this fashion because I have concluded that the contemporary human rights movement became possible only when state societies began to reach consensus that older notions of 'civil incapacities'[6] – such as the lack of legal capacity assigned to women by virtue of marriage – should no longer be used to delimit different classes of adults.

Reading human rights law in this historical context has led me to conclude that the 'human rights' movement has had a dual function; it has served to bring to an end the political practice of using 'legal incapacities' to strip some human beings of their social and economic power, and it has protected members of groups that have historically been denied full legal personhood from wide-ranging forms of injury to their 'human dignity.' Although most commentators have used the notions of personhood and human dignity almost interchangeably,[7] I differentiate those concepts here. Even though human rights guarantees were originally designed to secure the basic incidents of full legal personality to disadvantaged groups, merely securing the 'human dignity' of people who remain 'civilly incapacitated' in any way will not have much effect on deep-seated hierarchies of privilege.

Thus I argue that, until lesbians, transgendered, transsexual persons, gays, and bisexuals are accorded the full legal capacities of 'persons' in Canadian law, it will be difficult for courts to see beyond the social practices and beliefs that normalize the denial of equal rights to queers. So long as the older discourse around 'legal personhood' is still the unarticulated text in rights cases involving sexual minorities, the values that supposedly drive human rights discourse –'human dignity,' 'integrity,' 'equal respect'– cannot form an adequate ground upon which to base equality claims of lesbians, gays, bisexual, transsexual, and transgendered people.[8]

In this chapter, I trace the origins of 'legal personhood' from the emergence of legal categories of people in the earliest surviving law codes to the subsequent crystallization of the law of 'persons' in Roman civil law. I then document how the Roman model of regulating juridical rights through the imposition of 'legal incapacities' was deployed in later cultures to maintain domination over selected groups, including women of the ruling classes. The purpose of this section is to demonstrate that concepts of 'personhood' and 'legal capacity' are integral to the delineation of the legal status of disadvantaged groups. I then review recent court decisions that reveal how the older debate around 'legal personhood,' while submerged in Canada since 1930, has lurked just below the surface in human rights and constitutional jurisprudence since then.[9] In chapter 5, I apply this analytic framework to the particular situation of sexual minorities in order to assess whether any sexual minorities can be considered to be 'persons' yet, even within the narrow and classical meaning of the term.

Origins of 'Legal Personality'

My interest in exploring the extent to which members of disadvantaged groups have become 'persons' was initially sparked by the legal history of racial oppression in North America and by texts of the early women's movement, both of which documented the crucial role that 'civil incapacities' based on race, involuntary servitude, or marriage have played in maintaining historical patterns of oppression and exploitation. Civil disabilities produced entire classes of people whose acts had no legal significance, but were, at best, considered to be the acts of an owner, parent, husband, or guardian. It was commonplace to refer to people so incapacitated as being civilly or juridically 'dead.'[10]

Until the 'trilogy' cases[11] began to work their way up to the Supreme Court of Canada, I had considered 'personhood' or 'civil capacity' to be instructive artifacts of legal history that had only technical relevance in contemporary law.[12] After all, the Privy Council had ruled in 1929 that married women were 'persons' for purposes of interpreting legislative formulations that prior common-law doctrine had treated as excluding married women,[13] and one of the last major U.S. constitutional cases involving the 'personhood' of African Americans declared it constitutionally impermissible for states to impose civil incapacities on people by race over three decades ago.[14] However, as conflict over just how far courts should go in shaping the legal status of queers has intensified, I felt drawn to trace concepts of 'legal personality' and legal discrimination against sexual minorities back to their origins to clarify the relationships among 'legal capacity,' 'discrimination,' and sexuality in an assessment of how the full humanity of queers could be discussed in the admittedly dehumanizing language of law.

Early Law Codes

What I discovered is that the contemporary human rights movement has its origins in the categorical way in which status was initially delimited in the earliest law codes.[15] What is striking about these codes is how 'modern' they seem in some regards. Like contemporary legislation, these codes do not set out the capacities and rights of privileged members of the state so much as they set out the incapacities, liabilities, and constraints of those lower in various social hierarchies. Categorization and delimitation of status was not used to spell out the prerogatives of members of ruling classes, but was used to define and control certain classes of people, animals, and things. The result was that the lives of those who fell into status categories are clearly depicted in many of these old codes, while we are left to guess at the rights and responsibilities of privileged people.

All these early civil states were patristic in structure, because all indications point to the more or less coterminous emergence of patrifocal social structures, 'state' political structures, and 'law.'[16] Early states used legal categories to control reproduction, family formation, property ownership, inheritance, and productive labour. In law, marriage gave husbands nearly absolute control over their wives, and heterosexual marriage was constructed as a 'status' similar to that of 'slavery,' which also featured prominently in all these codes. For example, the Hammurabi Code penalized by death the theft of religious items, freeing or harbouring a slave, adultery by married women, or poor housekeeping.[17] In contrast, a man who had abandoned his home and family might, at worst, have to make some payment to his wife.[18] There is nothing in the code to suggest that either male adultery or poor husbandry had any legal significance at all.

Although the Laws of Eshnunna and the Laws of Hammurabi appear, from our vantage point, to be harsh, violent, and cruel in many regards (and in that regard, not 'modern'), they nonetheless have played a tremendously important role in the construction of our own legal culture. Mediated by Roman law, by the various laws that replaced Roman law during the Middle Ages, and then by the legal regimes that emerged in this millennium C.E. in England, Europe, and North America, positive law has for more than 4,000 years now exercised strict control over 'legal capacity' and the legal status of 'persons.'

'Legal capacity' came to describe what, in law, a human being could do within the framework of the legal process. 'Legal capacity' included political and social rights as well as legal rights, while the category 'person' came to be a short-hand expression for a human being who had the full capacities that law could confer. Sex, marital status, race, class, and age continued to animate these categories during the entire 4,000-year period discussed here, and nearly 2,000 years ago, sexuality came to be a category of classification as well.

Roman Civil Law

Under Roman civil law, the concept of 'personhood' crystallized around the various elements of legal capacity in order to give legal expression to the social hierarchies that were fundamental to the Roman state. This was achieved with the legal fiction of the *unitas personae* (one person, unitary person) that was used to shift the legal existence of children, women, slaves, and so on, into the hands of the father/husband/owner. This legal fiction then justified the denial of all legal capacity to children and others – even past the age of majority, until the death of the father or the marriage *cum manu* of daughters – on the basis that the father into whose legal existence their legal personality was incorporated held all those capacities.[19] As Roman law evolved, a complex set of categories was developed to articulate the implications of the basic principle of the *unitas personae* for different classes of people.

Children: Under Roman civil law, the power of fathers (*patriapotestas*) was unlimited: a father literally held power of life or death over his children, and could kill or sell a son into slavery even if he held high public office. Children's lack of legal personality translated into a series of legal incapacities: they could not own property, enter into contracts, marry, divorce, make custodial decisions in relation to their own children, make testamentary dispositions, or make any other legally significant decisions without the consent of the father.[20] In contrast to daughters, sons did have some juridical existence in relation to the 'public' sphere in that sons could hold public office. However, in relation to the legal process, the doctrine of *unitas personae* precluded them from acting as anything but agent for their fathers, and then only upon consent.

Slaves: The same types of rules were adapted to define the legal incapacities of women and slaves. Although slaves were technically *personae* simply because they were human beings, their legal personality was fully incorporated into the legal personality of their masters.[21] Thus slaves did not have the legal capacity to own property; enter into contracts; marry; have custody of their children; inherit; participate in the legal process as witness, party, or juror; or hold public office. Any family relations slaves might enter into were purely *de facto*, had no legal effect or status, and could be terminated immediately by their owners. Any property in their *de facto* possession was in law considered to be the property of the master. Any damage done by slaves became the delicts of the master, who thereby became liable on them. In the later Roman Empire, some of these attributes were vitiated by statute, but this in no way displaced the underlying legal doctrine of *unitas personae*.[22]

Women: Women's legal incapacities were virtually identical to those of children and slaves, with three exceptions: unlike adult sons, daughters could never hold public office; unlike slaves, women could legally marry with their father's consent; unlike either sons or male slaves, women could never become emancipated, but remained always under the power of a male relative or a guardian. Marriage *cum manu* would transfer the power of the father over a daughter to her husband (or to the husband's *paterfamilias*, if he was still alive),[23] but marriage *sine manu* had no such effect, leaving a daughter under the *patriapotestas* of her father even after she began cohabiting with her husband. Thus, under Roman law, women could not own property; enter into contracts; engage in the legal process as litigant, witness, or juror; hold public office; marry; or hold custody of their children.[24]

Some of these features underwent transformation in the later empire as some women managed to free themselves from the powers of their male relatives and pass into the power of guardians who acted legally for them. In practice, sympathetic guardians might take considerable direction from women in relation to property or contractual transactions, for example, and in some instances women were permitted to participate more or less directly in legal proceedings, under the (reversed) legal fiction that they were really still acting only with the permission of their guardians.[25] Thus there has been some ambiguity surrounding the legal capacities of women in the later empire, and it is certainly true that, as the centuries passed, women became functionally freed from the more extreme applications of the doctrines of *patriapotestas* and *unitas personae* even though those doctrines continued to apply to them on a technical legal level.

Roman civil law was not static, but exhibited the same tendency to change that is evident in Canadian law. Before the Roman state incorporated Christian religious doctrine into legal doctrine, marriage laws changed dramatically to include mere cohabitation and unions between men, both of which were widely recognized and came to have the same legal effect as opposite-sex marriages. In the later empire, moralist attitudes held by some rulers apparently inspired the deployment of property and taxation laws to create incentives to reproduce within the structure of heterosexual marriage. These laws at least implicitly formed incentives to functional bisexually.

Marriage in Roman civil law took two forms, the defining feature of which was whether the *patriapotestas* of the father was transferred to the husband or remained with the father. Marriage *cum manu* placed the husband very much in the same position the father had held in relation to the wife. Marriage *cum manu* could be achieved in one of three ways: religious ceremony requiring the presence of a leading priest; *mancipatio*, based in legal form on adoption; or through cohabitation. Marriage *sine manu* left the woman under the power of her father or guardian. *Mancipatio* was a generalized legal form through which formal legal powers could be transferred in a wide range of circumstances such as marriage, making wills, adopting children, freeing children from paternal power, and transferring women to the power of a guardian. The use of *mancipatio* to create marriage *cum manu* was essentially an adoption, down to the legal fiction that the woman was adopted into the husband's family, became his sister, and passed into the power of the husband's father. In this form of marriage, the wife did not pass into the power of the husband until after the father-in-law died.[26] Marriage *cum manu* was established through cohabitation if a woman who lived with a man did not absent herself from him for at least three successive nights within each year. Marriage *sine manu*, which did not transfer power over a woman to her husband but left it with her father or guardians, also arose through cohabitation. There were no time limits associated with marriage *sine manu*; it required only the intention to marry and provision of a dowry.[27] Bare cohabitation thus could give rise to one of three possible relationships: mere concubinage, if there was no intention to marry or no dowry; marriage *sine manu*, if the wife did absent herself from her husband's home at least three successive nights each year but the elements of intention and dowry were satisfied; or marriage *cum manu*, if cohabitation was continuous and the elements of intention and dowry were satisfied. These differing routes to relationship recognition were of course available only to the 'free' classes. Even when persons of slave classes cohabited continuously, their relationships did not have any legal status.[28]

Controversial research has suggested that *mancipatio* was also used to set up legal relations between men (or sometimes between women) through adoption that had the same functional effect as formal marriages.[29] Unlike paternal adoption by the father of another son, under which the new son would pass into the power of the father, adoption as brothers would constitute the adopted brother as heir of the adopting brother, but the adopted brother was not thought to come under the power of the adopting brother, nor change his name.[30] Like later forms of marriage, it could be accomplished merely by making declarations in front of witnesses.[31] The fact of such legal unions between men is not controversial; it is the conclusion that they sometimes were used to establish a marriage-like relationship between two men, or that such a marriage-like relationship involved sexual, social, or emotional dimensions associated with contemporary marriage that is so controversial.

What is clear from the historical record, however, is that, during the later empire, legal policy was deployed to reinforce hierarchical reproductivist heterosexual relationships. It is difficult to assess whether these laws were primarily designed to counter the increasing freedom of women[32] or to make it less attractive for men who controlled family property to leave it to someone other than their wives and children, but there is some basis for concluding that same-sex 'marriages' did come to be perceived as a problem. In 18 B.C.E., Augustus enacted the restrictive Julian laws, which imposed severe penalties for adultery, limitations on inheritance by women, and special awards for women who had three or more children. These laws were designed to promote heterosexual marriage, monogamy within marriage, and biological reproduction of the ruling classes; they were also designed to induce women to adhere to Augustus's personal image of how women should act socially and sexually.[33] Estate taxation was used to penalize bequests that were made to those outside the nuclear heterosexual family. Testators could avoid these new estate taxes only by leaving everything to their children, and not even wives could inherit under these new laws unless they had borne three or more children. In the late empire, new policies were enacted to place express limitations on same-sex unions, beginning with the Theodosian prohibition on same-sex marriages.[34] While these policies pre-dated the rise of Christianity in Rome, Christianity became a conduit through which the 'narrower morality' of the later Roman Empire was deployed, and this morality contained elements of disapproval for 'homosexual' connections.[35]

The Elements of 'Civil Capacity'

By the end of the Roman Empire, Roman civil law had generated quite detailed rules relating to civil capacities of every social class. Each status was defined by withholding or extending 'civil capacities.' Juridical 'persons,' then, were human beings who could engage fully in the state, the 'public' sphere, and the legal process, with the consequence that their acts, both public and private, were legally recognized. These incidents of legal capacity fall under four general headings:

1 Juridical rights: the capacity to sue or be sued, act as a witness in legal proceedings, sit as a juror;
2 Participation rights: membership in the state as 'citizen'; capacity to vote, hold public office;
3 Public rights: state protection from violence; right to meet in public, speak, attend entertainment, or perform;

4 Private-law rights: the capacity to own property, own the produce of one's own labour, enter into contracts, marry, adopt, have custody of children.[36]

Roman social and legal policy exhibited considerable fluidity as political and economic conditions changed. However, all those changes took place within this framework. Legally incapacitated groups measured their progress, relative to adult male citizens, by the extent to which they acquired each of these incidents of 'legal personality.'

So resilient has this framework been that it has formed the mechanism by which diverse governments in Europe and in North America defined the civil status of subordinate groups wherever and whenever they wished to establish or vary social and economic hierarchies. While the evidence concerning the impact of growing intolerance of same-sex relationships on the laws of civil status in Roman law remains sketchy and speculative,[37] the civil status of 'homosexuals' has certainly been controlled through the use of this mechanism in later laws.

Deployment of 'Civil Incapacities' in Later Laws

The Roman Empire came to an end when the Visigoths, who had been invited into some of the northern reaches of the empire to help Rome defend itself against other encroachers, took over. These Germanic peoples brought their own customary laws with them, but over the centuries of Visigoth rule successive codifications of Visigoth law vacillated between these Germanic customary laws and Roman civil law.[38] The deployment of 'civil incapacities' in later law began as the Visigoths drew upon the Roman civil law of persons. It would be nice to say that these models no longer animate contemporary law, but examples as immediate as the present-day Indian Act demonstrate that this misperceives contemporary law.

Visigoth Law

Visigoth culture was heavily stratified, with distinct classes ranging from slaves, indentured bondsmen, and serfs at the bottom, to nobles and kings at the top.[39] The Roman civil law of persons offered a ready framework within which this class structure could be codified. The militant conversion of some Visigoth rulers to Christianity resulted in the radical incorporation of Christian doctrine into civil law. The combined effect of Christian religious doctrine, the power of the state, and the use of civil law to categorize people and impose civil disabilities on them by categories resulted in the deployment of law to enforce the Roman Christian ideal of purely procreative heterosexual marriage, suppress male homosexual existence,[40] and place tremendous pressure on Jewish persons to embrace Christianity.

The connection between militant Christian intolerance and the deployment of the Roman model of legal incapacities in Visigoth law to force adherence to Christian values on every level – religious/cultural practice, heterosexual sexuality even within marriage, and same-sex culture – is tremendously important in understanding the history of the human rights movement. Prejudice towards lesbian women/gay men and that towards Jewish persons spring from the same source. Beginning with Visigoth laws relating to Jewish persons, this prejudice took the form that would later, in the 1200s in Europe, be applied just as systematically to queers.

Jewish persons were completely excluded from participation in the dominant culture by denying them all civil and religious rights, purportedly to give them every incentive to convert to Christianity. Under the Visigothic Code, Jewish persons had no juridical rights; they were not allowed to sue, testify in court, or defend a legal action except in relation to other Jewish persons. They had no participation rights; they could not hold public office, nor were they permitted to emigrate or immigrate freely. 'Public rights' such as protection from violence were turned upside down because the state did not protect Jewish persons from violence, but instead imposed penalties on anyone who attempted to protect Jewish persons from state or individual violence or who harboured fugitives, and on judges and priests who did not enforce all the laws relating to Jewish persons. Private-law rights relating to property, contracts, and so on did not apply to Jewish persons; in their stead, numerous provisions prohibited Jewish persons from marrying according to their own laws, marrying non-Jews, hiring or working for non-Jews, owning Christian slaves, observing their own religion, or participating in their own cultural practices. Other 'public' laws placed tremendous pressure on Jewish persons to convert to Christianity.[41] As Scott relates, the 'cruel and unrelenting pursuit of the Jews, commanded by the Visigothic Code, was the foundation of the Spanish Inquisition and its diabolical procedure.'[42]

Anglo-Norman Law

After the Arabs drove the Visigoths from most of their territory, and after the Arabs themselves slowly withdrew from Europe towards the end of the first millennium C.E., Roman civil law remained in abeyance for several centuries as localized feudal structures took over law-making functions previously performed by empires. The disintegration of state structures into localized feudal structures opened the door for the re-emergence of customary laws. Thus Roman civil law did not again play a dominant role in legal culture until selected elements of it were incorporated into the 'common law' of England after the Norman Conquest in 1066.

Unlike the rest of Europe, which gradually developed civil laws based on either remnants of the Visigothic Code or customary laws (thus picking up elements of Roman law through that route), Norman England quickly organized a national legal system that extended feudal hierarchies to new lengths and within which was embedded a deeply patriarchal system of legal rights and property ownership. In the course of elaborating legal rules designed to bond soldier to lord, and baron to king, in a series of exchanges of oaths and grants of property, the emerging common law dipped into Roman civil law to define the status of women in terms that would not get in the way of this male-to-male system of military power and ownership. Thus the common law of England arguably went even further than Roman civil law had gone in turning married women into 'legal minors,' in the sense that, during coverture, they 'became one' with their husbands when husbands absorbed all their wives' legal capacities through marriage.

Thus Norman-Anglo common law revitalized Roman civil disabilities in constructing, for the purposes of a military colonial regime, 'civil death' for women who married. Under Blackstone's codification of the common law relating to women, as it emerged during the 1100s and 1200s, married women in England had no juridical rights, participation rights, or private-law rights.[43] Any legal rights married women might have had if they had been unmarried passed to their husbands upon marriage. Even if wives survived their husbands, these rights were given back to them in severely attenuated form, if at all.[44] Although private settlements, equitable doctrine, and various statutes were enacted from time to time to ameliorate these legal incapacities in England, they were not systemically displaced until 1935, when married women were given most of the same private-law rights of the *feme sole*.[45] By the time the private-law incapacities of married women came under political attack by the emerging women's movement, women's generalized lack of capacity had become so entrenched that it was widely believed by jurists that women could not participate in public life in any way. Thus public rights such as voting rights and the right to hold public office, even if clearly enjoyed by women under customary feudal laws before the Norman Conquest, could not be exercised until clarifying legislation was passed.

North American Law

The legal disabilities associated with women in North America are clearly a product of European colonialism.[46] They also served as a template for the drafting of other laws that imposed civil disabilities on other groups. African slaves were governed by 'slave codes' and 'black codes' of the U.S. South that were constructed around the wholesale and detailed withdrawal of civil capacities.[47] Even without slave codes of the scale and detail found in U.S. legal history, slaves in Canada were presumed to lack civil capacities not expressly extended to them by legislation.[48] Aboriginal persons were governed by legislation that quickly came to suspend all of the classical elements of 'legal personality' for 'status' Indians.[49] This model then inspired extensive legislative erasure of Chinese civil capacities in British Columbia[50] and later provisions relating to Japanese persons during the 1940s internments of the Second World War.[51] During the colonial period, this model formed the template for similar types of laws around the globe.[52]

The North American legal context also gave rise to the human rights movement, in that it was in North America that legal strategists first hit upon the notion of enacting laws of general reference and wide application to invalidate the layers of civil incapacities that had built up over the centuries.

The Seneca Falls Declaration of Sentiments, adopted by an early feminist convention in Seneca Falls, New York, in the mid-1800s, after enumerating the ways in which legal disabilities and social prejudice ran together to construct the disadvantaged status of women,[53] passed a resolution proposing the use of law to eradicate those incapacities: 'Be it resolved ... [t]hat such laws as conflict, in any way, with the true and substantial happiness of woman, are contrary to the great precept of nature and of no validity...and therefor of no force or authority.'[54] The

Thirteenth Amendment to the U.S. Constitution attempted to undo the enslavement of African Americans by declaring the status of 'involuntary servitude' to be abolished. When formalistic legal reasoning was used to uphold the spirit of slavery under other names, the Fourteenth Amendment was then adopted to invalidate the whole range of legal provisions that buttressed *de facto* slavery: 'No State shall make or enforce any law which shall abridge the privileges or immunities of citizens of the United States; nor shall any state ... deny to any person within its jurisdiction the equal protection of the laws.'[55]

As activists began to realize how far courts were willing to go in order to uphold the denial of women's 'legal personality,' they turned their energies towards trying to obtain the enactment of blanket protections like those of the Fourteenth Amendment. The first such effort, known as the Women's Bill of Rights (Wisconsin), contained both a detailed list of specific 'capacities' that were to be considered to be inviolate and a blanket extension of civil capacity to women. (The blanket clause evolved through successive drafts to become the Equal Rights Amendment [ERA] that U.S. feminists lobbied for until it was decisively defeated in 1979.) Thus the draft stipulated that women would have the same 'rights and privileges under the law as men in the exercise of suffrage, freedom of contract, choice of residence for voting purposes, jury service, holding office, holding and conveying property, care and custody of children and in all other respects,' and that courts would read references to the masculine gender to include the feminine gender 'unless such construction will deny to females the special protection and privileges which they now enjoy for the general welfare.'[56] This model eventually gained influence in Canada as well as in the United States, as human rights legislation began to crystallize around the protection of core incidents of legal capacity from public or private infringement.

However, as the human rights movement gained momentum, and fuelled by outrage at the German manipulation of law to support genocidal policies in the 1930s and 1940s, the language of 'legal capacity' did not seem to adequately communicate the essence of human existence that modern liberals believed the state/society should protect.[57] It was at that point that drafters of human rights legislation began to include references to 'human dignity' and 'human integrity' in order to prevent conservative courts from following older patterns of legal reasoning to gut 'civil capacities' of their legal effect. Long experience had demonstrated time and time again that regardless of the drafting strategy used to remove 'civil incapacities,' however expressed in law, provisions designed to nullify civil incapacities all contained one weakness: Although such provisions appeared to apply universally to all human beings, conservative courts could simply circumvent them by reaching back into legal doctrine surrounding the understanding of the meaning of 'person,' 'citizen,' 'people,' or 'individual' to rule that they did not apply to classes of human beings who were not 'persons.'[58] This interpretive strategy simultaneously entrenched the elements of non-personhood in general law and narrowed human rights provisions.

Thus, for example, the Alberta Individual's Rights Protection Act (IRPA),[59] which is quite similar to all the other human rights statutes in Canada,[60] now combines both a declaration of the primacy of human 'dignity' and specific protections for fundamental legal capacities. The preamble to the Individual's Rights Protection Act contains the following declaration:

> Recognition of the inherent dignity and the equal and inalienable rights of all persons is the foundation of freedom, justice and peace in the world.
>
> [It is] a fundamental principle and ... a matter of public policy that all persons are equal in dignity and rights without regard to race, religious beliefs, colour, gender, physical disability, mental disability, age, ancestry or place of origin.[61]

At the same time, the working provisions of the statute grant quite specific remedies for the infringement of basic legal capacities: Section 2 prohibits public announcements of intention to exclude classes of people; section 3 secures the right to equal access to public accommodation, services, and facilities; section 4 prohibits discrimination in obtaining rental accommodation; section 6 relates to wage equality; sections 7 and 8 protect the right to work; and section 10 prohibits discrimination in memberships of trade unions or worker organizations. The actual terms of the IRPA thus reveal that, despite the sweeping general statement of purpose in the preamble, the statute is really cast as a 'persons' statute. That is, it has really been designed to secure the incidents of legal capacity to those groups it is intended to protect.

Going back to the elements of legal capacity that crystallized in Roman civil law, the IRPA thus can be seen as completing the reconstruction of civil capacities that had been denied historically to disadvantaged groups. Married women's property legislation, voting laws, family law, the 'Persons' Case in Canada, and interpretation statutes have come to secure many of the juridical and participation rights previously denied to women, racialized persons, members of religious groups, and married women. Human rights codes – and the Charter of Rights which grew out of them – were intended to complete the restoration of full civil status to members of these groups by securing the remaining public rights (such as the right to meet in public, speak, attend entertainment, share in public resources) and private-law rights (such as the capacity to rent property and enter into contracts) associated with full legal personhood.

The shift of emphasis from narrow concepts of 'legal capacity' to the seemingly wider concern with human dignity and equality in human rights law has of course been a tremendously crucial development. However, this shift has obscured the fact that 'equality' guarantees originally meant, and still mean, that it is illegal to use civil disabilities to deprive some groups of people of access to the legal process. A private employer's refusal to hire a person because of gender, for example, has the same effect as judicial doctrine that says that women do not have the legal capacity to enter into contracts, including employment contracts. A movie theatre's refusal to let a racialized person enter the premises has the same effect as statutes that deprive persons of colour from freedom of movement, or that restrict them to segregated facilities.

To get more directly to the point I am trying to make, I think it is still important to talk about legal personhood or civil capacity, because if courts lose the ability to see how tolerating differential legal treatment actually impairs legal personality, then human rights laws – including the Charter of Rights – can become just another legal tool that gives civil incapacities legal effect. I am not attacking the value of declarations of commitment to deep social values. But appeals to 'human dignity' or 'human integrity' have often failed to move conservative courts, perhaps because they are quite abstract, so fundamentally not 'legal' in connotation. Thus the gap between concepts of 'human dignity' found in human rights legislation and the actual legal rights and social status of disadvantaged groups remains difficult to bridge. For this reason, I have concluded that, until the connection between historic denial of 'legal personality' as classically conceived and the purposes of human rights or constitutional provisions is articulated in legal doctrine, it may be useful to identify the extent to which contemporary laws continue to deny the full legal personhood of some human beings. Until a human being can exercise all of the incidents of legal personality, neither general human rights guarantees nor constitutional guarantees have much genuine impact on 'ordinary life.'

'Personhood' after *Edwards*

With the emergence of the human rights movement in the first half of this century, legislative and judicial thinking shifted from global declarations of 'equality' to formulating effective prohibitions on 'discrimination.' Although the Bill of Rights in the United States kept 'personhood' at the forefront of U.S. constitutional discourse, in Canada, the lack of constitutional-level rights provisions meant that there was little legal basis for framing issues in terms of 'personhood.' Indeed, the 'Persons' Case[62] itself has never been cited for the substantive proposition that it addressed, but instead has operated merely at the symbolic and interpretive level as the source of Lord Sankey's often-quoted description of the Constitution of Canada as a 'living tree capable of growth and expansion within its natural limits.'[63]

The image of the 'living tree' has of course been an important dimension of Canadian constitutional theory, and it has particularly vitalized Charter jurisprudence.[64] In *Southam Inc. v The Queen*,[65] one of the first the judicial rulings on a Charter challenge, MacKinnon A.C.J.O. relied eloquently on the image of the 'living tree' as a principle of constitutional interpretation in a passage that has been quoted almost automatically in subsequent Charter cases. Concluding that the Charter should receive 'large and liberal construction,' MacKinnon A.C.J.O. stated that '[t]he spirit of this new "living tree" planted in friendly Canadian soil should not be stultified by narrow, technical, literal interpretations.'[66] As this passage in turn came to be cited as the source of the 'living tree' image in Charter jurisprudence, however, it was quickly cut from its own roots in the 'Persons' Case as courts have either forgotten or ignored its origins.[67] Thus the case that most profoundly set human rights in Canada on a new basis by including women in the legal category of 'qualified person' was pushed into the shadows of canons of constitutional construction, while the new generation of constitutional human rights guarantees largely ignore the fact that the fundamental human right litigated in that case was the right to be considered to be an ordinary human being – a 'person' – in law.

I am not suggesting that constitutional human rights guarantees do not relate to the legal concept of 'civil capacities' or legal personality. Many of them do. For example, in *Reference re Provincial Electoral Boundaries (Sask.)*,[68] a direct connection was drawn between voting rights – one of the classical elements of legal personality – with 'the inherent dignity of the human person, commitment to social justice and equality, respect for cultural and group identity, and faith in social and political institutions which enhance the participation of individuals in society.' But Charter discourse had by this time also become completely dissociated from the earlier concern with the incidents of legal personality, and had shifted analytic focus to more open-ended concepts like 'inherent dignity.'

Human rights legislation and the Charter of Rights have not rendered concepts of 'personhood' completely irrelevant. Since 1930, however, Canadian courts have tended to give 'personhood' cryptic and shifting connotations. In addition to using 'personhood' to denote the bundle of civil capacities that construct 'legal personality,' courts have begun to use 'personhood' as a synonym for 'human personality' or 'sense of self' in the social sense, and have also used it to test the existential boundaries surrounding 'personhood' in relation to birth and death.

Synonym for 'Sense of Self'

The use of 'personhood' as being interchangeable with 'human personality' or 'sense of self' in a social context appears to have emerged in *Moge v Moge*,[69] in which the Supreme Court of Canada, in ruling that a wife was entitled to long-term support after divorce, stated that marriage and the family 'serves vital personal interests, and may be linked to building a "comprehensive sense of personhood". Marriage and the family are a superb environment for raising and nurturing the young of our society by providing the initial environment for the development of social skills.'

In the later decision in *A.-G. Canada v Mossop*,[70] the Supreme Court of Canada had an opportunity to extend this understanding of 'personhood' to lesbians and gays. The federal human rights tribunal that heard this complaint had concluded that excluding a gay partner from the opposite-sex definition of 'immediate family' in a collective agreement violated federal human rights legislation, and relied directly on this passage in *Moge* to conclude that denial of family benefits denied Mossop's essential 'personhood.' When the government appealed this ruling to the Supreme Court of Canada, that Court reversed the tribunal's decision, concluding that denial of bereavement leave did not relate to the appellant's 'family status,' but was really based on his statutorily unprotected 'sexual orientation.' Although the Court quoted the entire passage from *Moge v Moge* in explaining how the tribunal had reached its decision, the Court rejected this link between definitions of 'family' and the wide social understanding of 'personhood.'

Existential Boundary Marker

Cases that have tested the existential boundaries of 'personhood' in relation to unborn foetuses and deceased people have invoked the older understanding that classification as a 'person' is a precondition to the recognition of legal capacities. In a variety of contexts, the courts have consistently ruled that, before birth and after death, there is no 'personhood' in the legal sense. Thus in tort law and pre-Charter abortion law, the courts ruled that unborn foetuses were not 'persons,'[71] and this position has been maintained in Charter decisions.[72] Nor is a deceased human being a 'person' in law, whether for purposes of charging vandals for 'offering indignities to human remains' or for purposes of balancing publication interests with privacy interests.[73]

Bundle of Legal Capacities

Despite varying connotations of 'personhood' in Canadian jurisprudence, the term has been used to denote full legal capacity or legal personality in three Supreme Court of Canada Charter decisions. In *Andrews* v *Law Society of British Columbia*,[74] the first section 15(1) case to be heard by the Court, Justice McIntyre, dissenting from the decision to permit landed immigrants who were not yet citizens of Canada to practise law, made reference to 'personhood' in the classical sense of a legal category to which juridical or civil capacities are attached. Stating that 'the characteristic of citizenship is one typically not within the control of the individual,'[75] Justice McIntyre referred to the long-standing tendency to limit rights such as the right to work for wages, own property, or vote to those who are citizens. Although he framed his analysis of these civil disabilities in terms of 'discrimination' within the meaning of section 15(1) of the Charter, he certainly appeared to be aware that 'discrimination' had simply become a new way to talk about the validity of legislation that used legal categories to confer and deny legal incidents of juridical personhood.

This discussion of 'personhood' has had an important impact on Charter equality jurisprudence. Justice McIntyre's reference to the individual's 'control' over 'characteristics' such as citizenship has led to the development of the 'immutable characteristic' branch of analysis in Charter equality jurisprudence. Since section 15(1) of the Charter prohibits discrimination against listed groups, and since 'discrimination' is the contemporary method of describing actions or laws which regulate civil capacities by creating classes of people, the courts have tended to look for ways to measure 'immutability' of characteristics according to which people are placed into such classes. Thus in *A.-G. Canada* v *Ward*,[76] the Court, in dealing with a Charter challenge to persecution provisions of immigration law, quoted McIntyre J.'s statement that citizenship is a characteristic of personhood. More recently, Justices Cory and Iacobucci drew deeply on the connection between racist speech, the responsibilities of the state, and juridical rights of personhood in dissenting from the vacation of Ernst Zundel's conviction for publishing holocaust denial material in *R.* v *Zundel*.[77] Accusing the government of having denied the 'personhood' of Jewish persons by denying legal recourse for hate propaganda,[78] this part of their opinion clearly links back into U.S. constitutional jurisprudence, which treats 'personhood' as consisting of, at a minimum, the bare juridical right of admission to the state and the right to be protected from violence within or at the hands of the state. The same link has been considered in two other Charter cases. In *R.* v *LeBeau*,[79] two gay men had been convicted of gross indecency on the basis of evidence collected through monitored videotape surveillance of a public washroom. They brought a Charter challenge on the basis that their rights of speech, expression, privacy, and personhood under section 2(b) of the Charter had been infringed. And in *Rodriguez* v *A.-G. B.C.*,[80] a terminally ill woman challenged the prohibition on assisting suicide on the basis that it infringed her Charter rights, including her rights of 'privacy and personhood' under section 7 of the Charter. While neither of these submissions relating to personhood was accepted by the Supreme Court of Canada, they demonstrate that the relationship between 'personhood,' civil capacities, and human rights has never disappeared entirely from view in Canadian law.

Fundamental Principles Resurfacing

As legal discrimination continues to be an ineradicable feature of contemporary life, concepts of 'personhood' have begun to resurface in key constitutional cases. Dissenting justices in both *Egan and Nesbit* and *Thibaudeau* have directly invoked the 'Persons' Case in an effort to jolt the majority of the courts into an awareness of the impact those decisions have had on fundamental civil rights. And the connections among human rights, constitutional rights, and fundamental civil capacities was discussed directly and at some length in the recent United States Supreme Court decision in *Romer* v *Evans*,[81] which involved state denial of the human rights of lesbian, gay, and bisexual people.

The Equality Trilogy

In his dissenting opinion in *Egan and Nesbit* v *The Queen*,[82] Justice Linden emphasized the connection between the historic denial of women's 'personhood' in Euro–North American legal theory and the equally long tradition of imposing categorical disabilities on members of all oppressed groups by excluding them from the categories such as 'persons,' 'people,' and 'citizens.' He reminded the other members of the Court of the 1856 United States Supreme Court ruling in *Dred Scott* v *Sandford*,[83] which established that individuals whose ancestors had been brought to the United States from Africa and sold as slaves were not citizens under the Constitution, and he quoted directly from Chief Justice Tanney's opinion, in which he had stated that the words 'people of the United States' and 'citizens' did not include African Americans. Linden J. then compared this decision with the 1928 the Supreme Court of Canada ruling in the 'Persons' Case, in which the Court compared women to 'criminals and lunatics and minors' when it ruled that they were not 'qualified persons' within the meaning of section 24 of the Constitution Act, 1867, and therefore could not be appointed to the Senate.[84]

The key point made by Justice Linden was that various forms of discrimination were justified by courts not by relying directly on widespread acceptance of social prejudice against members of the groups in question, but by imposing strikingly similar 'civil incapacities' on any group that did not enjoy the same social status as adult 'Caucasian' males. These 'civil incapacities' attached not only to former slaves in the United States, but to other categories of humans as well, including convicted criminals, 'lunatics,' children, married women, immigrants, persons who did not own real property, members of various religious groups, and so on. The result of these categorical denials of status resulted in the creation of huge functional distinctions between 'persons' and 'non-persons'– those whose existence, in Kantian terms, was not the 'end' of the state, but who could be treated as 'means.'

By linking the (non-)recognition of women's 'personhood' with categorical exclusion of other types of people, Justice Linden has clarified the relationship between the older legal fiction of denying that some people are 'persons' and the goals of the human rights movement, of which the Charter of Rights, like the U.S. Bill of Rights before it, is part: Both statutory and constitutional human rights guarantees are intended, as a minimum, to eradicate traditional civil disabilities, undo the exclusion that they categorically produced, and redress the social inequalities that have in turn inspired such exclusion and are the continuing result of historical exclusion and disadvantage. As Justice Linden warned, failure to admit 'new grounds of discrimination' such as sexual orientation to the Charter would 'perpetuate that discrimination' instead of nurturing the 'living tree' that the Privy Council had found had been planted in Canadian jurisprudence by the British North America Act (at 428–9). Emphasizing that the Supreme Court of Canada had already ruled that the 'living tree' doctrine applies to the Charter of Rights,[85] he concluded that, like 'sex' and 'marital status' before it, sexual orientation has also been 'a basis for discrimination and persecution throughout history' that deserved protection in the Charter of Rights (at 429–30).

Civil capacities were also very obviously in contention in the *Thibaudeau* case at the Supreme Court of Canada. Suzanne Thibaudeau, a divorced custodial mother who received child support, took the position that requiring her to treat those payments as her own taxable income violated her Charter equality rights. The majority of the Court rejected this challenge, not on the basis that it was justifiable discrimination, but on the basis that there was no discrimination in the first place because the tax provisions affected Thibaudeau not as an 'individual,' but as a member of a former married couple. The majority of the Court reasoned that, since the tax provisions in question were but one part of a larger statutory mechanism that was designed to shift income out of the husband's tax base and into the wife's tax base, the entire mechanism should be evaluated in terms of how it affected the group consisting of 'separated or divorced couples' or the 'post-divorce 'family unit.'

Justices McLachlin and L'Heureux-Dubé strenuously objected to this line of analysis, and pointed out how this position literally resurrected the age-old civil incapacities of women and the exclusion of women from the status of 'persons' in Canadian law. Justice McLachlin linked the issue directly to the language of section 15, contending that it was women as 'individuals' and not 'the fractured family' who were protected by the equality provisions of the Charter. She emphasized that section 15(1) of the Charter was designed to protect individuals from unequal treatment, and that where unequal treatment of one individual, as compared with another, is established, 'it is no answer to the inequality to say that a social unit of which the individual is a member has, viewed globally, been fairly treated.' Beginning from the premise that '[i]nequality is inequality and discrimination is discrimination, whatever the legislative source,' Justice L'Heureux-Dubé made the same point. She rejected the government's contention that 'the appropriate unit of analysis is the couple,' and concluded that the use of the couple to evaluate the constitutionality of a provision that burdened one member of the couple for the benefit of the other was not acceptable. She made the quite obvious point that, if the couple were the only unit of constitutional analysis, even the old Marital Property Acts of the nineteenth century, which unequally burden women because they automatically gave a husband powers over his wife's assets, would not be considered to violate section 15 of the Charter. Both Justices L'Heureux-Dubé and McLachlin then went on to analyse the impact of section 56(1)(b) by itself on the taxpayer as an individual, concluding that it violated her equality rights.

Thinking again about how equality discourse tends to reflect and reinforce existing hierarchies of privilege, it is easy enough to see how the refusal by the majority of the courts to assess these cases in terms of the 'legal personality' of the claimants made it possible for the court to avoid dismantling those hierarchies. Jean Miron wanted access to the legal benefits of being considered to be married, even though he had apparently never actually exercised his right to become married. As a heterosexual male, he was accorded this benefit when he asked for it. Suzanne Thibaudeau wanted out of the paradigm of marriage when she became divorced because it indirectly deprived her of economic power by imposing additional tax liability on her in order to finance tax benefits given to her former husband even after their marriage ended. Suzanne Thibaudeau merely wanted to be treated fiscally like the person she had become: a non-married woman. But she was not permitted exit from deemed marriage, even after divorce. James Egan and John Nesbit wanted access to the legal benefits of being considered to be legally recognized cohabitants, but, because they were both of the same legal 'sex,' they were denied access to even the lesser status of cohabitation. And referring again to the non-Charter case of *Owen* v *Canada*,[86] Lillian Owen, a male-to-female transsexual who had been denied the spousal allowance under the same legislation challenged by *Egan and Nesbit*, wanted access to the legal benefits of being considered to be formally married – which she had been in 1951 – but because her physical 'sex' had not changed enough to command a change in her 'legal' sex, she was denied the benefits of the legal status she had had for most of her adult life. Thus contemporary equality jurisprudence actually operates to reserve the social, economic, and legal benefits of marriage to men who are married, who used to be married, or who live as if they were married even though they are not, while it denies women exit from the marital unit even after divorce and denies same-sex couples and transsexuals access to this privileged status.

So long as these hierarchies remain beyond challenge in Charter jurisprudence, the benefits of marriage to men remain larger and more valuable than if women were permitted exit or if the benefits of marriage had to be shared with a larger group of people. Indeed, the continued existence of this hierarchy also makes it unlikely that the remaining vestiges of married women's civil incapacities can be challenged effectively under the Charter.[87]

Romer v *Evans; Vriend* v *Alberta*

The recent decision of the U.S. Supreme Court in *Romer* v *Evans*[88] demonstrates that Justice Linden in *Egan and Nesbit* and Justices L'Heureux-Dubé and McLachlin in *Thibaudeau* are in close touch with the wellspring of human rights in North America. In yet another application of the long line of U.S. Supreme Court constitutional decisions that have invalidated legislative attempts to curtail the legal personality of one class of people or another since the late 1800s, the U.S. Supreme Court unequivocally ruled that state constitutional provisions intended to invalidate state or municipal 'sexual orientation' human rights provisions violate the equal protection clause of the Fourteenth Amendment. Justice Kennedy concluded that this constitutional provision (known as Amendment 2) deprived one class of persons of ordinary legal protections that most people have come to take for granted:

> [W]e cannot accept the view that Amendment 2's prohibition on specific legal protections does no more than deprive homosexuals of special rights. To the contrary, the amendment imposes a special disability upon those persons alone. Homosexuals are forbidden the safeguards that others enjoy or may seek without constraint ... These are protections taken for granted by most people either because they already have them or do not need them; these are protections against exclusion from an almost limitless number of transactions and endeavors that constitute ordinary civic life in a free society. (1626–7)

Justice Kennedy went on to state that '[e]qual protection of the laws is not achieved through indiscriminate imposition of inequalities,' that 'laws singling out a certain class of citizens for disfavoured legal status or general hardships are ... a denial of equal protection of the laws in the most literal sense,' that the amendment 'classifies homosexuals not to further a proper legislative end but to make them unequal to everyone else,' and that 'a State cannot so deem a class of persons a stranger to its laws' (1628–9).

The majority opinion in *Romer* v *Evans* is unquestionably grounded in the long line of constitutional decisions that began the slow process of abolishing civil incapacities on this continent. Justice Kennedy opened the majority opinion with the reminder that laws that create racial classifications of citizens had been upheld in *Plessy* v *Ferguson*,[89] but that the equal protection clause of the Fourteenth Amendment has come to be understood to reflect a commitment to the neutrality of law 'where the rights of persons are at stake' (1623). In *Plessy* v *Ferguson*, an African-American man had been arrested when he refused to leave the 'white' compartment in a segregated railway train. The majority of the Court, in which Justice Harlan was the lone dissenter, had ruled that the segregated facilities did not violate the equal-protection clause of the Fourteenth Amendment if they were 'substantially equal.' This principle of constitutional law remained unchanged until 1954.[90]

Justice Kennedy's decision to frame his opinion in *Romer* v *Evans* around the changes in the legal status of African Americans over this last century clearly locates the issues relating to the human rights of sexual minorities in the larger debate over full legal personhood.[91] This connection was not lost on the Supreme Court of Canada when it came to rule on the similar exclusion of lesbians and gays from the Alberta human rights statute in *Vriend* v *Alberta*. The Court quoted some of the key passages in *Romer* v *Evans* in reaching the conclusion that the refusal to include 'sexual orientation' in provincial human rights legislation unjustifiably violated section 15(1) of the Charter. Explaining why the denial of access to the human rights process on the basis of sexuality has 'dire and demeaning consequences,' Lamer C.J. quoted from *Romer* v *Evans*:

> [T]he [exclusion] imposes a special disability upon those persons alone. Homosexuals are forbidden the safeguards that others enjoy or may seek without constraint ... These are protections taken for granted by most people either because they already have them or do not need them; these are protections against exclusion from an almost limitless number of transactions and endeavors that constitute ordinary civic life in a free society. (para. 98)

The Chief Justice then went on to conclude that, although the ways the exclusions in the two cases had come into existence were different, the effect of the Alberta exclusion was similar.

'Core' Rights

In Canada, gay and lesbian people stand on the brink of full personhood, and fuller recognition of the legal capacities of bisexual, transgendered, and transsexual people may follow. If the impending appeals in *Dwyer* v *Toronto (Metropolitan)*[92] and *M.* v *H.*[93] are resolved in favour of the lesbian and gay parties, some sexual minorities will have obtained full inclusion in human rights codes, full recognition of same-sex cohabitants in the federal employment sector, and the beginnings of relationship recognition in provincial family law. If these appeals are lost, however, it will be impossible to achieve full personhood in this millennium, because legislatures will have discovered that, even when they cannot exclude sexual minorities from human rights codes, they can still 'justify' denying same-sex couples 'private' as well as 'public' benefits, leaving same-sex couples in the outlaw position accorded all *de facto* relationships. If the Charter protection extended to people characterized by their 'sexual orientation' affects only 'personal' rights and only 'private' variants of 'relationship' rights, then the recognition of the 'personhood' of sexual minorities will also remain partial and politically contingent.

As these and other issues work their way through the legal and political processes, I suggest that keeping an eye on the core incidents of legal personality will clarify the long-term implications of seemingly disparate and isolated issues. The idea that some rights may be more critical than others is nothing new. Every 'rights' decision implicitly ranks rights. Courts have often described rights that they have gone on to protect as 'fundamental' or 'essential,'[94] and legal scholars have tried to identify 'core' or 'penumbral' rights.[95] Although the Alberta Court of Appeal disapproved of this approach to rights analysis in *Black* v *Law Society of Alberta*,[96] the court did nonetheless agree that it was always important 'to evaluate the importance of the right in question' and 'the nature of the violation.' In addition, the court agreed that there was room in Canadian constitutional jurisprudence for the principle of *de minimis non curat cartula*.

The most sophisticated approach to weighing the relative importance of rights in Charter jurisprudence is Justice L'Heureux-Dubé's analysis in *Egan and Nesbit*. Building on Justice McIntyre's conclusion in *Big M Drug Mart Ltd.* v *R.*[97] that 'inherent human dignity is at the heart of individual rights,' Justice L'Heureux-Dubé posited that the criticalness of rights depended upon two factors: the nature of the group adversely affected by a distinction, and the nature of the interest adversely affected. She examined how these two factors operate by developing this analogy: 'If a projectile were thrown against a soft surface, then it would leave a larger scar than if it were thrown against a resilient surface. In fact, the depth of the scar inflicted will generally be a function of both the nature of the affected surface and the nature of the projectile used' (553). Justice L'Heureux-Dubé posited that some 'scars' might be 'trivial,' whereas some might be more serious. She concluded that, 'if the projectile is dense enough and thrown hard enough, then it will leave a mark on even the most resilient of surfaces.' Moving from analogy to constitutional language, she stated that 'the more fundamental the interest affected or the more serious the consequences of the distinction, the more likely that the impugned distinction will have a discriminatory impact even with respect to groups that occupy a position of advantage in society' (556). Although Justice L'Heureux-Dubé did refer in passing to how excluding the appellants from the category of 'spouse' on the basis of their sexuality affected their 'personhood,' she used these two factors (nature of group, nature of interest affected) to assess how this exclusion affected the appellants in terms of the 'concern, respect, and consideration' accorded them (566).

While these elements undeniably lie at the heart of 'human dignity,' taking the notion of 'personhood' back to its original elements may perhaps help clarify the significance of relationships to sexual minorities even more than do notions of 'dignity,' 'respect,' or 'concern.' Many people who continue to be affected by social prejudice against lesbians and gays (let alone against bisexual, transgendered, transsexual, or bi/transgendered persons) cannot 'see' their own lack of respect or concern because they are caught up in their own internal reactions or value structures. It may be easier to cast the issues in terms of legal capacity to function, and relate those issues to the class structures that legal incapacities support, than it is to convince people to 'care.'

Conclusions

In this chapter, I have argued that concepts of 'legal personality,' 'civil capacity,' and 'personhood' are the fundamental building blocks of much Euro-Canadian law. Emerging from ancient legal texts that legislated almost completely by categories and status, Roman civil law crystallized 'legal personality' around the classical elements I have described as juridical rights, participation rights, private-law rights, and public rights. These classical elements of legal personality have been used for nearly two millennia to strip selected classes of human beings of their capacity to act in civil society. The purpose of the resulting 'legal incapacities'– denial of the elements of personality, or transfer of those capacities to an owner, husband, parent, or master – was to solidify social and economic hierarchies and to maintain privilege. So efficient are 'legal incapacities' in achieving this legislative objective that they have been deployed repeatedly over the last two millennia to control Jewish persons in numerous different countries and at different times, as well as women, slaves, Aboriginal persons, victims of colonization, enemies, non-citizens, and sexual minorities.

The emergence of liberal legalism has only slowly moved to eradicate these 'incapacities.' Married women's property legislation, the 1862 Emancipation Proclamation in the United States after the civil war, the 'Persons' Case in the Privy Council, international declarations of human rights, the only partly successful United States Equal Rights Amendment (ERA), provincial human rights codes, and, most recently, the Canadian Charter of Rights and Freedoms have all been devised to restore at least some of the vast array of ordinary legal rights that have been expunged by 'legal incapacities.' The fact that none of these legal mechanisms has generated adequate results demonstrates that until fundamental legal capacities are secured to all adults, 'equality' guarantees will not be enough.

Important litigation involving lesbians, gays, and bisexuals in both Canada and the United States has already considered whether provisions that discriminate on the basis of sexuality impose 'civil incapacities' on them. This analysis is still submerged in the larger legal discourse surrounding 'discrimination' and the 'justification' of discrimination. Although the analytic connections between constitutional 'personhood' and discrimination on the basis of sexuality have recently been considered explicitly by Justice Kennedy in *Romer* v *Evans* and have now formed part of the reasons for decision in the Supreme Court of Canada decision in *Vriend* v *Alberta*, long-standing discrimination on the basis of sexuality has had a pervasive impact on the many legal capacities that shape civil existence.

As I have framed the argument, the legal incidents of personhood should be treated as 'core' values that must be protected at all costs. My reason for this is fairly simple: Without these rights, individuals do not have the civil capacity to function in the modern state. Without the civil capacities that are constitutive of the 'individual' who can act in law, antidiscrimination laws, Charter guarantees, and other human rights protections can do very little to alter patterns of bias and exclusion. Empowering everyone to act in law frees individuals to care for themselves instead of relying on the state or other structures, and it makes everyone's energies more fully available to themselves and to the society in which they live.

In chapter 5, I explore the extent to which queers in Canada can be considered to have become 'persons' in this sense yet.

Chapter Five

Are We 'Persons' Yet?

I would like for my grandchildren ... and the grandchildren of all of us, to know that they are persons under the law. I am a person because I am a woman under the laws of Canada, but as a gay woman I am not a person with any right to exist under the law. If our future generations would not have to go through the pain, the hiding, the insidious violence that all of us here have been through, that would make my golden age ever so much more happy. Thank you very much.
– Susan Rieke, Gay Alliance Towards Equality, testifying before Parliamentary Committee on Equality (29 May 1985, at 10:17)

By 1985, even after the Charter equality guarantees came into effect, lesbian, gay, bisexual, transgendered, and transsexual people were acutely aware that they were still not really full 'persons' in law. The question I pose in this chapter is whether, now that we have seen well over twenty years of human rights activism and more than fifteen years of Charter discourse, we can now say that people who are characterized by their sexuality have become full 'persons' in law yet.

In my opinion, the answer is 'Not yet.' Some important changes in some areas of legal doctrine have given some sexual minorities increasing rights and responsibilities. Growing recognition of the human rights and Charter rights of lesbians and gays has accelerated that process. But laws that still distinguish on the basis of sexuality are presumed to be legitimate until challenged. And when they are challenged, they may still be 'justified,' even under the Charter of Rights.

In this chapter, I review the legal status of sexual minorities in relation to the classical elements of 'legal personality.' I weigh the legal rights of sexual minorities against the rights historically associated with full 'legal capacity' – participation rights to enter into the state, juridical rights to engage the legal process, 'public' rights, and private-law rights. In this review, I look at the human rights and Charter cases discussed in earlier chapters as well as to the large numbers of cases that have litigated 'ordinary' legal rights. I comment on where the incidents of 'legal personality' appear to be most secure, where they are most vulnerable, and where they appear to remain unavailable.

Applying the paradigm of 'legal personality' to any group involves not only familiarity with 'law,' but also an understanding of the realities of day-to-day existence for members of that group. While I have been able to draw extensively on my own life as a lesbian woman, my sex, sexuality, race, class, and abilities have shaped my experiences at the same time they have limited them. It is my hope that others will fill in the gaps beyond my own experiences.

However, I have been able to see enough of the picture I am concerned with here to have realized that, paradoxically, the defining characteristics of 'personhood' are most visible in their absence from actual legal texts. Until they are actually challenged, legal concepts like 'person,' 'individual,' or 'citizen' just seem to provide the non-remarkable nouns that glue more active grammatical elements together. Human rights legislation and international documents have certainly tried to move the discussion beyond the limiting issue of whether a claimant is a 'person' covered by some legal provision or other, and instead have placed the emphasis on formulating global guarantees of social, economic, political, and legal equality. But, as *Egan and Nesbit* v *Canada*[1] and *The Queen* v *Thibaudeau*[2] have demonstrated, these global guarantees can be circumvented easily by going back to the prior question of whether a claimant is indeed a 'person' who can invoke them at all. 'Personhood' can come fully into view only when it is sought by those to whom it is denied.

There has been a further, particular difficulty in uncovering the extent to which sexual minorities are not considered to have the full capacities of 'persons' in contemporary law. This difficulty arises out of the way in which 'personhood' has functioned in the dominant legal culture. The personhood or legal capacities of disadvantaged groups such as women, children, slaves, and Aboriginal peoples have been considered to have been somehow suspended or incorporated into the legal capacities of husbands, fathers, masters, or governments in the formation of various kinds of relationships. Submerged in 'the household,' 'the family,' 'the master,' or 'the state,' the legal capacities of children, wives, servants, or Aboriginal peoples have not been completely extinguished, but have been shifted over to and located in another physical person or legal entity.

In contrast, the legal capacities of groups that are the targets of genocidal hatred have not been merely suspended, absorbed by others, or even carved up among other people, but literally have been extinguished. This has been the experience of lesbian, bisexual, transgender, transsexual, and gay people during times of oppressive hatred. Key legal capacities have simply been erased, negatived, nullified. No one else has held those capacities for civilly 'dead' queers.

Sexual minorities have often attempted to counter this process of erasure, negation, nullification by erasing, negating, nullifying their queerness – sometimes referred to as 'staying in the closet.' Criminal law and all the other legal/political/social/economic suppressions of queerness have literally driven queerness into hiding in the psyches of those who attempted to retain some ordinary legal capacities by keeping 'in the closet' the parts of their identities that would attract civil death. I am not suggesting that sexual minorities are the only people who have been forced to hide or 'pass' as someone else. It is notorious that biracial people or people characterized by their religion, culture, or class have all too often been given the choice between 'passing' as non-Jewish, non-Muslim, or non-working class, to give just a few examples, versus bearing the consequences of being known as their 'real' selves.

The specificities of sexuality shape the way this 'passing' or closetry is worked out in queer lives. Thus, to the extent that lesbian, gay, bisexual, transgendered, or transsexual people look like heterosexuals (by marrying or by having children heterosexually) or look like single persons (by hiding their partners, or by not getting involved with anyone), they can appear to have full legal capacity. Often, it is only when sexual minorities try to claim their identities and seek open acceptance of their life choices that they begin to run into the 'for heterosexuals only' rules that underpin Canadian culture.[3]

Individual queers may be presumptively considered to be 'persons' for purposes of voting rights and so on, but the more closely an incident of legal personality touches on identity and relationship issues, the more profoundly sexual minorities continue to be denied many of the elements of full legal personality. With the proliferation of 'opposite-sex' definitions of 'spouse' in the last twenty-five years, many of these presumptions have been made more visible, which may mean that the presumed legitimacy of this system is becoming more difficult to sustain.

The discussion in this chapter centres on the layers of functioning that are regulated in law by the concept of 'legal personality.' Participation rights are discussed first, because it is the right to enter the state, the right to be oneself in the state, the political rights to hold public office and vote, which form the threshold that sexual minorities must cross over before any other functioning can become an issue. To the extent that queers are either prohibited from existing in Canada or are exiled from Canada, they do not have participation rights. I then discuss juridical rights, or rights to participate in the legal process, because, once physically present in 'the state,' queers will remain permanently disadvantaged unless they can fully and freely function in law as parties to litigation, as witnesses, and as members of juries. Because 'law' is the discourse through which the other elements of legal personality are constructed – defining rules of entry and existence, participation and benefit, 'public' ordering and 'private' ordering – juridical rights are of pervasive importance to those who seek to become full 'persons.'

I then discuss the extent to which sexual minorities can be considered to have 'public' and 'private law' rights. The 'public/private distinction' is largely illusory, and no two commentators agree on just where the line between these two spheres is to be drawn.[4] But for purposes of this discussion, I have defined 'public' rights as relating to state ordering of civil society through law. 'Private law' rights have also become increasingly subject to state ordering, so I am largely concerned to look at how the personal choices sexual minorities have in fact made for their lives have been affected or altered by that public law state ordering. To the extent that many sexual minorities are deprived by public laws of the power to privately order their lives, they cannot be considered to have the 'private law' rights of ordinary persons either.

Participation Rights

Participation rights enable people to enter, exist in, and act in 'the state.' In some ways, participation rights are the most basic elements of legal personality, even more basic than 'civil rights.' Participation rights are an absolute precondition to 'civil life,' to entry into society, to the interaction of one human being with another that is the beginning of 'human community.' The history of the emergence of the 'state' is the history of the articulation of the elemental status 'citizen.'[5] Citizens not only had the right of free passage into and out of the state, but had all the prerogatives in politics, law, and civil existence that the state could extend. The denial of citizenship was initially used as a rough tool to withhold other civil rights, ranging from the right to be physically present in the state, the right to act as oneself, and the right to act in law, politics, public life, and private activities. Those who transgressed the dominant social order were subjected to varying degrees of 'civil death.' Over the last two millennia, 'civil death' has been expressed in many different ways – physical execution; expulsion from the state; incarceration, with or without the loss of other elements of legal personality; denial of refuge; and the imposition of some or all 'legal incapacities.'

In most state societies today, citizenship and criminal conviction regulate participation in the state. Citizenship regulates both the right of physical entry into the state and rights to participate in the political functioning of the state through voting and holding public office. The older pattern has been to limit all other civil capacities to citizens. Now some of the capacities of 'citizens' have been extended to landed immigrants in Canada, or to resident aliens in the United States; the right to practise law is a good example of this trend.[6] However, other fundamental legal capacities such as voting rights are still limited to citizens in some jurisdictions.[7] Criminal liability is used to regulate those who are already citizens in much the same way. By withdrawing convicted criminals from civil society, from day-to-day contact with other people, that class of people loses the right of physical movement in the state, the right of easy communication and action in social processes, and, depending on the crime and other state laws, at least some of the elements of legal personality such as the right to hold public office.[8]

Historically, basic participation rights have been among the first types of rights to be denied during periods of oppression. Sometimes this has been accomplished by withdrawing the status 'citizen' from the target group. Sometimes it has been accomplished by criminalizing disfavoured groups, or by combining criminalization with the denial of citizenship. The way this is done in modern constitutional states is highlighted by the legal provisions enacted by the Third Reich in Germany to control both Jewish and queer populations in the 1930s. One of the first steps taken by the Third Reich in laying the legal foundation for the genocide of Jewish persons was to extinguish the right of citizenship of Jewish persons.[9] The right to vote and the right to hold public office – which could be exercised only by citizens – were then withdrawn from Jewish persons.[10] The ideological justification for the denial of basic participation rights was the claim that 'purity of German blood [was] essential to the further existence of the German people.'[11] As time passed and the Third Reich withdrew more and more elements of legal personality from Jewish persons, criminalized more and more features of Jewish existence, the legal machinery for incarcerating and executing massive numbers of Jewish persons was set in motion. At the same time, the Third Reich invoked an ideology of 'purity of sexuality' to declare sexual minorities to be 'criminals': 'simple contemplation of desired object (abstract coitus)' was made a criminal offence.[12] Criminalization of queer sexual desire established the legal basis for then incarcerating and killing many sexual minorities during the 1930s and 1940s, including gay men, lesbian women, and cross-dressing people. Through criminalization, and then incarceration, these queers also lost many basic political and legal rights.

The Nazi 'criminal contemplation' laws and 'purity of blood' laws went far beyond earlier forms of civil death used by European states. The Visigoth laws relating to Jewish persons were designed to place inexorable pressure on Jewish persons to embrace Christianity. Full civil capacity was then restored to those Jewish persons who did successfully convince the authorities that they had become Christian.[13] Not so the laws of the Third Reich; the simple fact of having 'ancestral blood' stripped Jewish persons of their juridical and political rights, and no degree of 'passing' could change that once the Law for the Protection of German Blood had come into effect.[14] Similarly, laws relating to sexuality dating back at least to the Visigoth period in Europe were concerned with behaviour, not with 'purity of desire.' But no degree of heterosexual conduct could insulate queers from scrutiny under the criminal contemplation laws of the Third Reich. Women and men alike were subjected to intense scrutiny by hostile inquisitors for any hint that they harboured homosexual desire.[15]

The international human rights movement continues to struggle to eradicate racial, religious, and cultural grounds for denial of juridical and participation rights. But while the international human rights movement grew rapidly after the end of the Second World War, the ideology of 'criminalized desire' was quietly incorporated into the medico-legal regulation of sexuality in English law in the 1950s. Subsequent 'reforms' of those laws – and of Canadian laws patterned on English criminal sexuality law – have concentrated not on decriminalizing desire, but on trying to make homosexual acts disappear into a space beyond the law – into the so-called private sphere. Although criminal liability by itself does not strip people of all political rights, the fact that many sexual minorities were until the very recent past considered to be criminals in Canada has powerfully affected attitudes in law and in politics. Some forms of queer sexual expression continue to be criminalized. Immigration law, which started from the position that 'practising homosexuals' were 'undesirable aliens,' still constrains queer immigration to Canada in ways that do not affect non-queer immigration. In addition, social attitudes towards queers are powerful deterrents to 'coming out,' to running for public office as an open queer, and thus to the exercise of voting rights.

Criminalization of Sexual Expression

Pierre Trudeau made legal history when, under his leadership, the government decriminalized 'private' consensual sex between adults in the late 1960s.[16] This made it possible for gay men (and inferentially, for lesbian women) to acknowledge their sexuality without fear that such acknowledgement would constitute an admission of criminal activity. This was an important step, because admission of criminal activity could disqualify a person from being admitted to various professions, from holding public office, and from holding positions of trust.[17]

Read in historical context, however, the Trudeau amendments and the law-reform studies that inspired them[18] really helped obscure the importation into English and Canadian criminal law of the deep anti-queer biases that had been so blatantly manipulated in Third Reich law. The Wolfenden Report recommended the decriminalization of 'private' sexual activities between 'consenting adults.' However, this one liberalizing recommendation was embedded in a report that gave new and seemingly liberal voice to deep biases against queers. The report differentiated homosexual sexual identity from sexual behaviour, and accepted the suggestion that 'homosexual identity' could be validly inferred from a person's outlook, judgment, occupation, or even his or her interest in youth movements.[19] While the report did recommend that private consensual adult sex be decriminalized, it also recommended heavier penalties for underage sex, higher ages of consent for same-sex sex, criminalization of homosexuality in the military, and prohibitions on marriage.[20]

Thus it would be more accurate to describe the Wolfenden Report as having inspired not the decriminalization of queer existence, but the rearrangement of existing criminal sexual offences around the concept of 'homosexual offences.' These 'homosexual offences' were considered to include buggery, attempted buggery, assault with intent to commit buggery, indecent assault on male by male or female by female, acts of gross indecency between men, procuring and attempts to procure acts of gross indecency between males, persistent soliciting, importuning of males by males for immoral purposes, and violations of indecency by-laws.[21]

Despite the Trudeau amendments decriminalizing 'private' 'adult' 'consensual' acts of 'gross indecency,' the age of consent in that original amendment was twenty-one years of age. In 1987, that age of consent was lowered to eighteen years of age, but, at the same time, the gross- indecency provision was replaced with a prohibition on 'anal intercourse' that carried a penalty of ten years in prison.[22] Not only was this age of consent higher than for heterosexuals, but the Criminal Code continued to contain numerous other charges that were easily applied to gay men and sometimes to lesbian women: bestiality,[23] sexual assault,[24] the bawdy-house crimes,[25] and the sentencing rules for dangerous offenders.[26] The continued use of higher ages of consent for same-sex sex than for opposite-sex sex criminalizes queer youth in circumstances that do not apply to non-queer youth.[27]

Even though the Parliamentary Committee on Equality Rights received repeated submissions protesting the discriminatory effects of these criminal provisions, the committee recommendations touched only on the age-of- consent rules in the Criminal Code.[28] To the disappointment of queer communities, the committee did not recommend the repeal or amendment of the substantive 'homosexual offences' themselves. And even though the government promised, when reviewing that report, that it would 'give careful consideration to the possibility of amending' the age-of-consent rules,[29] the most important changes in this area of law have resulted from Charter litigation and feminist critiques of the way various sexual offences affected women.[30]

To date, the only age-of-consent provision that has been invalidated as the result of Charter litigation has been the prohibition on anal intercourse. Because the provinces enforce the federal criminal code, it is not clear just how far current rulings extend. In *R. v Carmen M.*,[31] the Ontario Court of Appeal ruled that the age-of-consent rules relating to anal intercourse violate the prohibition on discrimination based on age in section 15(1) of the Charter. The defendant in that case was actually heterosexual, but the court ruled that section 159 violated the Charter equality guarantees because of the differential ages of consent for gays and heterosexuals (majority), and because of the impact of section 159 on gay men (minority). The Crown had argued that the higher age of consent in section 159 was intended to protect young persons from the various risks of anal intercourse, including the transmission of HIV; the court rejected this justification for want of rational connection. *R. v Carmen M.* has been followed in several other cases that have involved gay men, suggesting that the issue has been settled in Ontario.[32] A federal court also reached the same conclusion in *Halm* v *Canada*,[33] which related to the administration of federal immigration legislation. Whether a ruling by a federal court will be considered to be binding on other provinces administering the criminal code in other contexts is unclear, although the weight of *Carmen M.* will be influential, as demonstrated the Québec Court of Appeal decision in *R.* v *Roy*.[34] Charter challenges to other 'homosexual offences' have been less successful,[35] and policing of so-called homosexual offences continues to be intense. But where earlier courts tended to be critical of police readings of gay existence,[36] cases like *R.* v *LeBeau*; *R.* v *Lofthouse*[37] suggest that, when applying the Charter, some courts continue to see gay sex as inherently violative of public order. In *LeBeau* and *Lofthouse*, police had used secret video-surveillance cameras in park washrooms in developing charges for gross indecency. The Ontario Court of Appeal ruled that section 157 of the Criminal Code[38] was not unconstitutionally vague, and that video surveillance did not violate the Charter. Although *R.* v *Silva*[39] came to the opposite conclusion, that decision, which turned on the admissibility of videotape evidence, did not challenge the prohibition on public indecency in section 173 of the Criminal Code, has not been appealed, and is of uncertain impact in light of subsequent amendments to the provisions relating to videotape surveillance in 'private' circumstances.[40]

When cases like *LeBeau* and *Lofthouse* are read together with older decisions like *Klippert* v *The Queen*,[41] in which the Supreme Court of Canada upheld sentencing under the dangerous-sexual-offender provisions for unspecified acts of gross indecency with consenting male partners, it is clear that gay sex continues to be criminalized in circumstances unique to gay existence. This in turn means that sexual minorities continue to be at greater risk of losing other civil rights that depend upon not having a criminal record, including the right of entry into Canada.[42]

The continued criminalization of queer sexual expression fundamentally impairs the legal personality of sexual minorities in several ways. First, it continues to create opportunities to focus criminal enforcement activities on an already-hated sector of Canadian society, turning queer sex into a way to differentially arrest, try, and incarcerate sexual minorities.[43] Second, it helps feed the image of queers as not only hateful, but dangerous, deviant, 'undesirable,' which in turn supports policies of exclusion in a wide array of other political and legal contexts. And, third, it creates a continuing basis to deny queers who have engaged in similar activities in other countries the right to visit or emigrate to Canada, whether as independent applicants, sponsored immigrants, or refugees.

Even in cases of extreme political persecution of queers, it is difficult to be seen as a political victim when the allegedly criminal activities that are the basis for persecution are also liable to attract criminal charges in Canada.

Entry into the State

Entry into the country is one of the most basic rights of 'citizens.' But for queers who are not citizens of Canada, gaining the right of physical entry into the country is often more difficult than for non-queers. The older view that homosexuals are undesirable aliens has not yet been completely displaced, the application of refugee rules to sexual minorities remains uneven and uncertain, and queer citizens do not have the same legal rights as other Canadian citizens in terms of their rights to sponsor their partners' immigration.

'Undesirable Aliens': Because immigration law regulates physical entry into the state, it has frequently been used to filter out classes of people thought to be destructive of the fabric of society – 'undesirable aliens.' Two such classes of 'undesirable aliens' have been those with criminal records, and, earlier in the history of immigration law, 'homosexuals' and those who practised 'homosexualism.'[44]

Immigration Canada has always taken a very wide view of the meaning of 'homosexuality.' For example, in *Sherwood Atkinson (Sheri de Cartier)*,[45] the applicant was a post-operative male-to-female transsexual person who, after completing the sex-reassignment process, was charged with pursuing sexual activities with a male. Despite her sex reassignment, the applicant was considered to have practised 'homosexualism.' She was thus denied entry into Canada on the basis of sexuality because the pre-1978 Immigration Act prohibited entry by those who had engaged in homosexual conduct.

Although that clause of the Immigration Act has now been repealed, the continued criminalization of 'homosexuality' in many countries around the globe[46] has meant that queer immigrants still lack the legal capacity to enter Canada in two sets of circumstances that arise directly out of this criminalization. First, when queer immigrants have been criminally charged or convicted under 'homosexual offences' in other countries, they continue to be denied entry into Canada on the basis of having a criminal record. Second, even when a lesbian or gay refugee has been able to demonstrate that criminal liability has been used to suppress

Are We 'Persons' Yet?   139

sexual minorities in their country of origin, immigration officials have tended to see 'homosexual offences' more as ordinary criminal activity than as political misuse of criminal powers to violate human rights. Surprisingly, this has been true even when the Third Reich concept of 'homosexual offences' has been directly implicated in the exclusion of 'criminal' queer immigrants. Thus, in 1992, Immigration Canada denied a Dutch gay man's application for landed-immigrant status on the basis of a criminal record that had arisen out of charges laid against him for 'homosexual offences' by Nazi occupiers of Holland during the Second World War.[47] Immigration Canada was not willing to look behind the fact of this 'record' to the nature of the charges themselves in considering his application.

The recent decision in *Halm* v *The Queen*[48] suggests that courts (if not immigration officials) have become willing to look behind the mere fact that a gay applicant has a criminal record. Halm, a gay man, had been held in a Toronto detention centre pending a Charter challenge to a deportation order that had been issued on the basis of his criminal record. This record consisted of convictions for engaging in sodomy with fifteen- and sixteen-year-old boys. The court invalidated the deportation order on the basis that the equivalent offence for such conduct in Canada, section 159 of the Criminal Code, violated the Charter. Unfortunately, the fact that Halm had 'jumped bail' in the United States to come to Canada before he was tried was used as the basis for a second deportation order that was upheld by the courts. Thus he was ultimately removed from Canada in any event.[49]

The possibility that the Charter may invalidate other 'homosexual offences' in Canada does not solve the problem faced by queer immigrants whose sexuality has been criminalized elsewhere. It merely creates a three-way bind that still effectively denies queers the right of entry into Canada on the basis of their sexuality: If they disclose prior criminalization before entry, even if those laws are unconstitutional in Canada, they can be denied entry as 'undesirable aliens' without right of appeal. If they do not disclose prior criminalization, they can be deported for non-disclosure of that prior record even if the underlying charges would be invalid here. And if they disclose prior criminalization but ask for refugee status, it is unlikely that mere threat of criminal liability for queer sexuality in their country of origin would result in receiving refugee status.

Queer Refugees: Along with other people who seek refuge in Canada 'by reason of a well-founded fear of persecution for reasons of race, religion, nationality, membership in a particular group or political opinion,'[50] sexual minorities can seek entry into Canada as 'Convention refugees.' In 1993, the Supreme Court of Canada declared that membership in a 'particular social group' for purposes of Convention-refugee claims included 'innate, unchangeable' characteristics like sexual orientation,[51] and, by early 1995, officials at the Immigration and Refugee Board reported that nearly two-thirds of the 'significant number' of refugee claims made on the basis of sexual orientation have been successful.[52] However, most claims based on sexual orientation appeared to originate almost exclusively in Central and South America, Eastern Europe, and India. Examination of the reported cases also reveals that no successful refugee or compassionate/humanitarian application appears to have been granted on the basis of U.S. or Western European laws. This is undoubtedly because the test of refugee status is the likelihood of 'persecution' on the basis of homosexuality. Mere variations in the legal status of same-sex sexual activities does not, by itself, appear to constitute 'persecution.'[53] In addition, the reported cases demonstrate that the concept of 'persecution' is applied narrowly. For example, in *Tchernilevski v M.C.I.*,[54] the court denied an appeal brought against the board by a gay man who sought refugee status on the basis that, if he were forced to return to Moldova, he would be tried under Article 106 of the Moldovian penal code, which outlawed homosexuality. The board had found, on the basis of a report by Amnesty International, that this fear was not 'objective' because that code section was no longer being enforced and was slated for repeal.[55] In other cases, such claims have been denied because the claimant lacked 'credibility.'[56]

Even though Canada has been expanding the criteria it applies to refugees from other countries, lesbians and gays who have sought asylum on the basis that they would be subject to anything from the death penalty to torture, other serious risks to their safety, or denied AIDS treatment if they were forced to return to their country of origin have only recently been successful in seeking refugee status.[57]

The fact that many such applications are now successful does not diminish the seriousness of denial of refugee status in unsuccessful claims. Consider for example *L.J. v M.C.I.*,[58] in which a lesbian woman from Trinidad was denied refugee status because, 'objectively,' she was found not to have a 'well-founded fear of persecution' for lesbianism, and because her claim lacked 'credibility.' At her board hearing, L.J. had testified that she had always tried to keep her sexuality secret in Trinidad because of the very strong 'taboo' surrounding homosexuality there, and had, after coming to North America, tried to use religion to keep her preferences at bay. Partly because of her appearance ('butchie femme'), she was harassed during her school days, banned from her father's home, gang-raped by five men in Guayaguayare who accused her of being a lesbian, turned away by the police when they learned that she was 'a queer,' followed when she moved to another town by one of the rapists, raped by an employer who had learned she was lesbian, and deprived of family support on all fronts. She then stowed away on a boat to illegally emigrate to Grenada, and finally got help in travelling to Canada in 1988. L.J.'s experiences in Canada were a muted replay of the dynamics she had faced in Trinidad. Her Canadian cousins were strongly religious, and she herself adopted their views of homosexuality. When she finally come out at the age of twenty-six, her claim for Convention- refugee status was denied on the basis that she was not 'objectively' in danger of being criminally charged for lesbianism in Trinidad, her fears of being charged were 'mere speculation,' and the evidence of harassment and violence was of 'questionable reliability and uncorroborated.'

It is this kind of thinking that intensifies the legal incapacities imposed by Canadian law on lesbian women from other countries. Lesbian women like L.J. cannot seek sponsorship from a husband, because they are queer. Family sponsorship is conditional on embracing heterosexual norms. The forms that persecution against lesbians takes in other countries are not as well-known or documented as persecution of gays. As a sex class, women have fewer economic resources, lower earnings, and much less chance of obtaining employer sponsorship. Thus they are set up by global patterns of sex discrimination and lesbian oppression for entry into Canada through the 'foreign domestic worker' program, which itself systematically strips women workers of legal capacities: applicants who do have children usually have to deny their existence in order to gain entry through this program; they are expected to send a large portion of their wages to their families abroad to held support them; they cannot receive social assistance if they are fired or leave their job; their bare presence in Canada is completely conditional on remaining employed by their domestic sponsor, which obviously forecloses living openly as lesbian in most cases. Thus the way the refugee standards are applied to lesbian women intersects with the foreign-domestic-worker immigration rules to place extreme constraints on their legal capacities when they turn to Canada to avoid persecution as lesbian in their countries of origin. The civil capacities of lesbian women refugees are even more constrained when they seek immigration status through the legally constructed closet of the foreign-domestic-worker program.[59]

Family-Sponsored Immigration: Criminalization of sexuality and tough refugee standards are the first two dimensions of the 'triple bind' faced by sexual minorities who seek entry into Canada. The third dimension of this bind is the fact that same-sex partners are not officially permitted by immigration law to sponsor their partners. These three dimensions often play against one another to exclude queers, no matter how the application has been framed. Thus, in *Sherwood Atkinson (Sheri de Cartier)*, being a post-operative female did not take Cartier out of the category 'male,' which meant that her relationship with a man, which was criminalized at that time, made her an 'undesirable alien.' After being homosexual was no longer a bar to immigration, however, even a transsexual wife was not treated as a 'spouse' for purposes of the immigration regulations, and could not be sponsored by her husband.[60] Even after the equality guarantees of the Charter of Rights came into effect and had been applied to some cases involving relational rights, it was automatically assumed that same-sex partners could not be sponsored, and queers were routinely advised that their partners should make independent applications or applications under other categories.[61] When Charter challenges were initiated against Immigration Canada in 1992, the government continued to take the position that only opposite-sex couples by birth qualified under the 'family class' sponsorship provisions.[62] Obviously worried that court rulings could rewrite this area of immigration law, the government settled these applications by granting permanent-resident status to the applicants on an individual basis rather than on the basis of family sponsorship.

Because these applications were settled in this way, the actual law governing family sponsorship and the definition of 'spouse' for sponsorship purposes have not changed at all. This has left the government with considerable power to continue administering the law on the basis that only opposite-sex couples – married or cohabiting – can qualify. Internal policies have been changed as the result of a confidential memorandum setting out how same-sex partners can be granted landed-immigrant status on 'humanitarian and compassionate grounds,'[63] but only those applicants who know about these two settlement cases and this internal policy can obtain family sponsorship. Immigration Canada, of course, does not want litigation in this area, so the internal procedures do work for those applicants who know how to frame their applications to meet these invisible criteria.

These covert changes in official policy have relieved the triple bind facing queer immigrants somewhat. Reports of community groups providing support for these types of applications indicate that as many as two hundred sponsored applications have been processed successfully since then.[64] But not all recent applications are successful. For example, Todd Layland and Pierre Beaulne originally attempted to obtain a marriage licence to solve their immigration problem. When litigation surrounding that application was unsuccessful, they then applied for a special immigration permit, which was denied.[65] More recently, community members have reported that some Immigration Canada offices appear to have been interpreting the June 1994 policy restrictively in some types of cases. The invisibility and inaccessibility of queer-sponsorship procedures, together with geographic and temporal variations in the way they are administered, however, means that queer couples have to take care to obtain up-to-date information on how and where best to apply. 'Official' information that is now available on this process still has to be approached carefully, even though the government released a review of immigration legislation in 1997 that recommended extending deemed spouse status to same-sex partners.[66]

Holding Public Office

Narrowly defined, 'public office' refers to elective or appointive positions such as member of Parliament or judge. There has never been any litigation over denial of the right to hold elective public office in Canada on the basis of sexuality. This does not mean that sexual minorities have full legal capacity to hold public office. The virtual absence of queers from Parliament until Svend Robinson 'came out,' and the invisibility of lesbians or gays in top civil service positions, on the bench, and in other elective or appointive offices, demonstrate that parties and governments deny this civil capacity not through written laws like the ones that were thought to keep women out of the Senate until 1929,[67] but through political practice.

Svend Robinson, long-time Justice Critic and NDP member of Parliament, was a strong contender for the NDP leadership position in 1997, but stepped back for Alexa McDonough. Informed observers concluded that he (or members of the party?) felt that his open gay identity was still too much of a problem for a party that was fighting for a larger share of the votes. Until prejudice against queers eases off, Robinson's role in the party is unlikely to change. This form of political discipline is pervasive.

Citing the assassination of San Francisco mayor George Moscone for sympathizing with the homosexual community and Toronto mayor John Sewell's defeat because he supported his gay constituents, the *Alberta Report* described in detail how homophobic fury over Calgary mayor Ralph Klein's appearance at a non-partisan gay function had convinced him to keep his distance from the lesbian and gay community.[68] That was in 1981. As recently as June 1997, Klein, by then the premier of Alberta, refused to endorse Calgary's bid to host the sixth annual Gala Choruses Festival in 2000 for fear of the political repercussions of supporting homosexuals.[69] In the face of this history, the election of Glen Murray, an openly gay man, as mayor of Winnipeg in October 1998 is all the more heartening.

Because of the realities of the political process, even queer candidates who are comfortable with being 'out' face unique strategic issues. Jamie Lee Hamilton, a candidate for Vancouver city council, received more attention in the media because she was transsexual than she did on the merits of her campaign. She then had to balance her prior decision to downplay her personal history with the political benefits of that type of attention. Other transsexual candidates in municipal politics appear to have realized, after the fact, that it may be better to play up such information precisely because of the attention it attracts. It is obviously a balancing act, no matter where the balance is struck,[70] and the smaller the municipality, the less visible any queers tend to be.

Do sexual minorities have clear-cut rights to hold lesser public offices – rights to serve as police or military officers, teachers, lawyers, or in other civil appointments? Certainly queers in Canada have been excluded from every conceivable type of public position, from racing steward[71] to Santa Claus,[72] on the basis of their sexuality. The armed forces, intelligence service, and the RCMP have continued to attempt to justify the exclusion of queers from those types of public offices,[73] but, as with the immigration cases, the federal government has pursued a policy of either aggressively defending such actions or settling them in order to avoid the creation of binding legal precedents.[74] The recent addition of 'sexual orientation' to the federal human rights code[75] may be enough to secure the right to hold these forms of public office, because human rights complaints are not vulnerable to 'demonstrable justification' under section 1 of the Charter. However, from the perspective of measuring the extent to which sexual minorities in Canada now have received concrete assurances of full legal capacity, the partial and uncertain nature of these legal developments can scarcely be read as absolutely assuring sexual minorities full rights to hold all types of public offices. Too little has been gained in that regard to support such a strong statement. And while lesbians and gays have been struggling to gain admittance through the front door of the services and police, the services and police have been quietly finding new grounds for removing them through the side and back doors. Thus in *Nuosci* v *Canada (H.R.C.)*,[76] the Federal Court of Appeal upheld the dismissal of a gay man from the RCMP on basis of HIV-positive status. The Armed Forces also discharged an officer on the basis of his HIV status, but, in that case, *A.-G. Canada* v *Thwaites*,[77] the federal court upheld the board's award, which included both lost wages and special compensations.[78] Delwin Vriend has now won the right to bring complaints arising out of denial of a teaching position before the Alberta Human Rights Commission, but he has decided not to pursue that right, and the government of Alberta is now looking at how being not gay can be used as a *bona fide* occupational qualification.[79]

Voting Rights

Voting rights have never been denied on the basis of sexuality in Canada. But it is worth noting that the same forces that tend to exclude openly queer candidates from running from public office, that tend to keep queer politicians in the closet, that discipline openly queer politicians in the positions they are rewarded for taking, and that tend to frighten sympathetic politicians away from their queer constituents and queer issues also operate indirectly to diminish the voting rights of sexual minorities. Already minorities, there is little incentive to get involved in political campaigns or to vote when the entire political process excludes queer issues. So long as homophobia in the political process deprives sexual minorities of the opportunity to vote for politicians who might be willing to treat them like other constituents, the right to vote continues to mean less for sexual minorities than it does for other groups in Canada.

Juridical Rights

Juridical rights enable human beings to act in 'law.' Juridical rights include the legal capacity to sue or to be sued, to testify in legal proceedings, or to sit on a jury. These are some of the most basic legal rights that exist in liberal legal culture. Without 'persons' who can access the legal process, initiate legal proceedings, and play the various roles upon which the process depends, the legal process could not function. When some classes of people can use the legal process to enforce their rights and others cannot, those who cannot are 'outlaws' in the truest sense of the word, being both without laws and without recourse against those who can use law. During liberatory periods, juridical rights are among the first types of rights to be extended to disenfranchised groups. For example, when the U.S. southern states attempted to reproduce the legal and social status of 'involuntary servitude' in defiance of the Emancipation Proclamation after the conclusion of the Civil War, they nonetheless had to concede that former slaves had the rights to 'sue and be sued ... in all the courts of law and equity' and to testify in all civil and criminal proceedings.[80]

At first glance, it may be difficult to imagine how any of these basic juridical rights could still be denied to any group in Canada today, let alone to sexual minorities. After all, there is nothing obviously 'sexual' about having the ability to sue, to give evidence in court, or to exercise jury rights. However, closer examination reveals that even these basic legal rights are still denied to some queers in Canada. Sexual minorities are still barred in a few jurisdictions in Canada from using the legal process to address discrimination in housing, employment, services, or contracts. Even where queers can look to the legal process for remedies, they may still be prevented from exercising their basic juridical rights because they may have to 'come out' in order to gain legal protection. They are vulnerable to being discredited as witnesses on the basis of their sexuality, to being exposed as queer as witnesses in the legal process, and to being judged by juries that may contain biased members. Thus some of these basic legal rights – the right to sue or be sued, the right to give evidence in legal proceedings, and jury rights – are either denied to some sexual minorities in Canada, or can, at best, be exercised only at considerable risk.

Capacity to Sue and Be Sued

On the surface, sexual minorities appear to have unquestioned rights to use the legal process – to sue and be sued. If a gay man entered into a contract to sell his house to a purchaser who then breaches that contract, nothing about his sexuality would prevent him from suing the purchaser for breach of contract. But the more closely legal issues touch upon sexuality, the more likely sexual minorities are to lack full legal capacity to prosecute or defend an action. The best example of how this lack of legal capacity to sue can still be constructed in contemporary law is found in *Vriend v Alberta*. In that case, Delwin Vriend had lost his job as a laboratory instructor at King's College in Edmonton, Alberta, because he was gay. When he took his complaint of employment discrimination to the Alberta Human Rights Commission, it attempted to refer the complaint to a tribunal constituted under the Individual's Rights Protection Act, but when challenged on lack of jurisdiction to hear complaints relating to 'sexual orientation,' the matter ended up in front of the Queen's Bench. The court ruled that the provincial human rights code should be read as if it prohibited discrimination on the basis of 'sexual orientation,' but the Alberta Court of Appeal reversed the lower court in extremely strong terms. Thus an appeal to the Supreme Court of Canada was necessary, and it was not until 1998 that the lower-court ruling was reinstated, permitting such complaints to go forward. Of course the *Vriend* decision most likely applies to the few remaining human rights codes that do not extend protection expressly to sexual minorities, but the point here is that access to the legal process in areas that are of critical importance to human functioning is still entirely contingent upon court rulings like this, and can still be cut off by any jurisdiction that decides to insert *bona fide* occupational qualifications into human rights or employment statutes, or that would even go so far as to invoke section 33 of the Charter to override such a judicial ruling.

This vulnerability is intensified by the fact that, without legal recourse to human rights commissions, people in Delwin Vriend's position would have to enter even murkier areas of the law in search of a common-law tort of discrimination, the development of which has been severely curtailed by human rights legislation.[81]

Sexual minorities also have to deal with the fact that being identified in the legal process by sexuality can force someone who is 'in the closet' to come 'out' in order to gain his or her full legal rights. The 'outing' dimension of capacity to sue or be sued depends entirely on the circumstances of each situation. When the subject matter of the litigation itself, or of related matters, is of tremendous importance to someone who is 'in the closet,' the risk of being 'outed' can induce the person to forgo all their legal rights entirely. Women involved in custody, access, or other family litigation are often labelled 'lesbian' in order to induce them to drop the contest completely. Parents who fear that they will lose custody of their children because of their sexuality and that they will then lose their job when 'outed' by litigation can sometimes be persuaded to surrender custody without a fight. Allegations relating to sexuality are privileged when made during litigation, and unless courts are willing to seal files and impose publication bans out of concern for children, there is nothing litigants can do to protect themselves against such tactics. Many people chose to put up with unreasonable and even damaging settlements or infringements of their rights rather than put themselves, their children, or other members of their families through such searing processes. Although courts are willing to prohibit publication of names, at the community level, this does not always solve the problem.

Community pressures add to this double bind. Lesbian women who are assaulted by other lesbians are often told that 'outing' their assailant would do her far more harm than the initial battery did to the victim. Thus many victims of lesbian violence avoid laying charges out of a sense of responsibility for the assailant, as well as for fear of being identified as lesbian themselves.[82] Even routine litigation arising out of accidents can 'out' people when sexuality has nothing to do with the cause of the accident.[83]

Queer Witnesses

If sexual minorities had full legal capacity to testify in legal proceedings as witnesses, they would not only have the bare legal right to testify, but would not face any social or legal risks as the result of being identified as lesbian, gay, transsexual, transgendered, or bisexual in legal proceedings.

This is, of course, not the case, as demonstrated by several rulings which have treated revelation of a witnesses' sexuality as inappropriate and even as reversible error, depending on the circumstances. Thus in *R. v Wilson*,[84] a man who had been accused of touching a male child for sexual purposes was given a new trial because the Crown had given the impression in its questions that the accused was gay.[85] In *R. v Paterson*,[86] the court ordered a ban on publication of the identity of three gay witnesses out of concern for the consequences to them outside the courtroom of being known as gay. And in at least one case, courts have refused to let counsel cross-examine on sexuality out of concern for prejudice.[87]

Jury Rights

Basic jury rights include the right to sit on a jury, the right to be judged by a 'jury of peers,' and the right to exclude people from juries when they appear to have prejudged the case on the basis of personal bias such as racism. The Criminal Code guarantees the right to sit on a jury to women, reversing the common-law denial of that capacity.[88] *R. v Parks*[89] has established that Black accuseds have the right to question potential jurors for racial bias when there is a 'realistic possibility' that one or more jurors drawn from that community would discriminate against Black accuseds.[90]

However, neither the courts nor Parliament have done anything to counter bias against sexual minorities in the selection and composition of juries. Indeed, when Muzum Alli attempted to extend the *Parks* ruling to gays and other visible minorities, the Ontario Court of Appeal refused, ruling that denying the right to question potential jurors on anti-gay bias was not reversible error.[91] Alli, who was Guyanese, had been charged with sexually assaulting another male prisoner while they were both confined to the 'drunk tank' in the local lock-up. Perhaps even more startling is the fact that the court in *R. v Paterson*, which had banned publication of the identity of three gay witnesses, refused to permit the defendant to question potential jurors in relation to homophobia – despite the fact that it had found as a matter of fact 'that there is a high degree of homophobia in our society.' It does not make much sense that homophobia might affect gay witnesses while it does not affect accuseds.

When taken together, the three rulings in *Parks*, *Alli*, and *Paterson* are not consistent. The court in *Parks* had taken the initiative of seeking out socio-legal information on the existence of anti-Black bias in Canadian society. The court in *Alli* apparently thought it had done the same thing when it asked a staff lawyer at the Correctional Law Project at Queen's Faculty of Law to prepare written submissions on behalf of Alli, who represented himself, on potential prejudice on the basis of race and homosexuality. The court in *Paterson* had actually made findings of fact as to homophobic bias in Canadian society in support of its ban on publication of any information tending to identify three gay witnesses. Yet the court in *Alli* gave the impression that the fault in that case lay with the accused: 'Where, as in this case, there was no evidence offered at trial to support the proposed extension, the court should decline to interfere with the trial judge's exercise of his or her discretion' and concluded that any extension of *Parks* to questions about anti-gay prejudice would depend on the production of socio-legal evidence that homophobia is as widespread as prejudice against Blacks in Canada. The court in *Paterson* had such evidence before it in the form of expert testimony led by the Crown in support of application for a publication ban, yet that still did not satisfy the burden borne by the defence in its request for the right to question potential jurors.[92]

Sexual minorities do have the bare juridical right to sit on a jury, but they do not have the right to question potential jurors on their biases against sexual minorities. The related question – whether sexual minorities have a right to be judged by juries that include representative numbers of queers – has not yet been addressed.

'Public' Rights

So-called public rights relate to life outside the 'household.' In the classic liberal sense, the 'public' sphere is thought to correspond with markets and institutions funded through government expenditures, yet even in that sense it is larger than any of these, including everything from group meetings outside the home and forms of entertainment to various types of media and walking around outside.[93] The so-called public sphere need not necessarily exist; in some cultures, human activities can be so fully integrated into each other on every dimension that nothing occurs outside dwelling houses that does not also occur within, and group activities move without boundaries from dwellings to the out-of-doors, to other locations, to other dwellings. But Canadian culture does of course differentiate between various types of common spaces and activities versus 'households.' Thus it becomes useful to ask whether sexual minorities are under any particular constraints in relation to the 'public' dimension of existence, in terms of freedom to meet 'in public,' speak together in groups, move about, or attend events and locations generally considered to be open to 'the public.' Fundamental to these 'public' capacities is the assurance that the state will protect sexual minorities from violence expressive of prejudice.

State Protection from Violence

Like criminalization of sexual expression, the freedom to walk down the street or to move without fear in other 'public' spaces is fundamental to the functioning of a state that considers itself to be 'democratic.' Violence in public or in private spaces has long been closely identified with maintaining the non-personhood of some classes of people, ranging from the right of Roman males to kill their own children at will to compulsory service in 'slave patrols' in the southern United States during the slave-owning era to prevent slaves from moving off the plantation without written permission,[94] or the refusal in the Third Reich to treat violence against Jewish persons as culpable conduct of any kind. Like criminalization of sexual expression, the reluctance of the state to protect lesbian women and gay men who enter public spaces as their true selves is a strong reminder that not all persons do receive 'equal protection of the law' in even this bare physical sense. Study after study has disclosed the disproportionate amount of violence that lesbian women and gay men experience when they do not carefully avoid giving even a suggestion that they might be lesbian or gay.[95] The federal government has enacted special sentencing provisions relating to hate crimes motivated by hatred of sexual orientation,[96] yet the violence goes on.[97]

The right to live free of violence has never been treated as an element of legal personhood, but bare physical survival is a precondition to the exercise of whatever civil capacities a person might in fact have. Freedom from violence and from the public expression of hatred is also supposedly one of the justifications for the existence of the state in the first place: to provide mutual protection for everyone.[98] 'Private' violence is also a 'public' issue as well, and there are concerns here as well. Gay men are no safer with partners, former partners, friends, neighbours, or new acquaintances in their own homes, so deeply does hatred of gays run. The documentation of violence between lesbian women is increasing as well. Although lesbian women and gay men are willing to speak out around issues of 'public' violence, violence in lesbian and gay relationships is more difficult to address. Some members of queer communities feel that the accused is at greater risk in the criminal justice system than victims can ever be in queer communities. The result is a great deal of invisible 'private' violence within queer relationships that undercuts what little freedoms sexual minorities might feel in their own 'private' spheres.[99]

Right to Identity

Both sexual identity and sex identity are carefully policed in Canadian culture. Along with the strong preference for opposite-sex sexual orientation embedded in Canadian legal policy is the belief that all people fall into one of two clearly identified sexes – 'male' and 'female.' This binary image of biological sex is buttressed with rules that regulate entry into and exit from these two 'sexes.' The psycho-medicalization of transsexualism (and, in different ways, of transgender existence) has resulted in legal rules that do permit some people to traverse the supposed biological/legal sex line: When the clarification or alteration of a person's biological sex is medically inconsistent with the legal sex registered at his or her birth, then that person can apply to court for a legal change of sex in some jurisdictions.[100] The standard of proof is that 'the anatomical sex structure [must have been] changed to a sex other than that which appears on the registration of birth.'[101] Two medical certificates must be filed to meet that standard. People who are in the process of changing their birth sex are permitted to legally change their names in preparation for completion of the process.[102] This legislation does not stipulate what medical/surgical steps must be taken in order to qualify an applicant for legal sex reassignment. Nonetheless, the courts have applied such provisions very narrowly, essentially requiring that the procedures take the applicant beyond the realm of reversibility in order to qualify.[103]

Especially when these rulings are completely at odds with the way transgendered or transsexual people have actually lived their lives, they fundamentally violate 'public' rights to present oneself openly in the public sphere without fear of injury or violation. 'Common-law spouses' have long been recognized in Canadian law, yet 'common-law women' and 'common-law men' run the risk of losing everything, from marriage and property rights to public benefits, if they do not adhere to the medical definition of sex 'change.' Thus the transgender and transsexual rules form another type of closet that prevents people from moving freely between the two polar sex identities recognized in law. And to the extent that people who have not met the legal standards of sex change are in relationships with partners who are of the same legal sex, transgendered and transsexual people are forced to assume the sexual identify of 'homosexual' even when that is not how they think of themselves at all.[104]

The denial of the right to identity triggers the denial of other public rights. Transgendered and transsexual persons report that they are disproportionately targeted in police raids of clubs, bath houses, and parks. If incarcerated for any reason, transgendered and transsexual persons may well be assigned to prison on the basis of their legal sex of origin, stripped of the support they have built up, and abruptly denied supporting drug therapy. Although the use of the legal system to deny the full incidents of legal personality to lesbians, gays, and bisexuals obviously denies them the right to identity, the extraordinary measures taken in Canadian law to police the biological/legal gender line denies the rights of transgendered and transsexual persons to their sex and sexual identities in specific and unique ways.

Speech Rights

The liberal-democratic state prides itself on the extent to which members of the state enjoy not only freedom from violence, but freedom of expression as well. For sexual minorities, however, 'free speech' is a legal fiction that can actually suppress queer existence, for sexual minorities have freedom of speech and personal expression largely to the extent that they are willing to leave their true selves at home, carefully hidden from public view. Thus when the *Vancouver Sun* refused to accept a small

Are We 'Persons' Yet? 153

advertisement from a gay organization, Gay Alliance Toward Equality (GATE), the Supreme Court of Canada ruled that the newspaper had refused to publish the advertisement for reasonable cause because it felt that the content of the advertisement would offend public decency.[105] Changes in human rights laws and the jurisprudence relating to sexuality might well produce a different outcome in these types of cases in the future, but the *GATE* case remains highly visible.[106]

Sexual minorities also face greater obstacles to the exercise of the quite ordinary right to appear in public, meet in public, and celebrate their identities in public. Case reports suggest that queers cannot always even count on being served in public facilities[107] or being permitted to dance together.[108] Nor do sexual minorities appear to have the right to cultural expression in public spaces on a footing of complete equality with heterosexual groups.[109] Hostility by municipal governments to annual Pride Day affirmations, celebrating the 1969 Stonewall uprisings, illustrate how narrow queer 'public' space is in practice. Municipalities have refused to issue parade permits, have revoked Pride Day proclamations, or refused to proclaim Pride Day. Legal action to secure permits or proclamations have been subject to applications for stays, transfers to other courts, and so on, before orders could be obtained under human rights legislation.[110] In Saskatchewan, complainants who had been refused parade permits had to take an order of prohibition to the Court of Appeal in order to clear the way for a human rights inquiry that would establish the right to public expression.[111] In London, Ontario, the mayor refused to proclaim Pride Day because she insisted that doing so would violate her strongly held personal religious convictions, and it took the order by a board of inquiry to obtain the proclamation.[112] Other communities have had to consider human rights complaints before municipalities have finally issued proclamations.[113]

Sexually explicit lesbian and gay print/film/videotape material raises particularly controversial questions of public expression. All 'freedoms' are bounded; very few people, I suspect, would seriously argue that 'sexual freedom' would permit the public enactment of paedophilia, rape, or fatal violence, yet heterosexual erotica and pornography that draws upon that iconography is generally accepted in contemporary Canadian society. But as soon as sexually explicit material takes on lesbian, gay, transgendered, or transsexual character – whether it is 'really' lesbian or gay material or is material manufactured for heterosexual audiences who like lesbian or gay images – it somehow becomes worse, more culpable, more likely to be censored. Thus, an appeal from a decision by Customs Canada to deny importation to a range of magazines directed at gay men failed not because the types of activities were somehow more offensive than those permitted to be imported for heterosexual audiences, but because 'the community standard of contemporary Canada remained less tolerant with regard to overt homosexual acts than with regard to similar acts committed between persons of opposite sexes.'[114] Certainly if the mere depiction of heterosexual sadomasochism, cruelty and bondage, group activities, advertising prostitutes, couplings, and masturbation were sufficient to offend the customs tariffs, the *Butler* appeal[115] would never have been necessary, and there would be a lot less explicit pornography on the shelves of the drug stores, convenience stores, and run-of-the-mill bookstores. The suspicion that Customs Canada continues to overregulate sexually explicit lesbian and gay material is borne out by the fact that some of the material apprehended by Customs in the *Little Sisters* and *Glad Day* cases had ended up on the shelves of other stores without any question.[116]

The most successful Charter challenge to this censorship has been *Little Sisters Book and Art Emporium* v *The Queen*,[117] However, even in that case, the court refused to find that the provisions of the Customs Act under which Canada Customs seized the material in question violated the plaintiff's Charter rights, and instead merely ruled that it was Customs Canada's application of the act that violated the Charter. The court did not actually order any remedy in the main case. The bookstore had to bring a subsequent application for an injunction in order to obtain any relief.[118]

It is probably accurate to say that, even though sexual minorities are slowly gaining equal rights of expression and speech, it appears to be true only for those queers who are willing and able to litigate as far as necessary to secure those rights. They are not yet freely recognized.

Other 'Public' Rights

As the state increasingly diverts economic power to public benefit systems like the health care system, social assistance, and retirement funding, 'public' rights have come to encompass issues like equality of claims for health care and rights to equal treatment, notwithstanding HIV status or AIDS disability. Although these issues certainly overlap to some extent with participation rights such as the right to hold public office, HIV/AIDS and other health care issues raise fundamental safety issues as well.

Cases like *Brown v B.C. Minister of Health*[119] demonstrate that public health officials cannot be trusted to provide the full range of health care for people with AIDS, despite the fact that provincial health care systems are meant to be universal,[120] while *Canadian AIDS Society v Ontario*[121] demonstrates that HIV-positive people have fewer privacy rights and rights to consent to treatment than do other members of the population.[122] *Korn v Potter and Benson*[123] has confirmed that lesbian couples may receive artificial-insemination services in British Columbia, but that application was also fought bitterly by the medical practitioner who denied them services in the first place. Denial of the spousal allowance under the Old Age Security Act funded out of general tax revenues (*Egan and Nesbit*) and continuing contestation of survivor options under private employment pensions (despite the successful Charter challenge in *Rosenberg v Canada*[124]) as well as under the federally managed pension plan (*Hodder and Fisk*) make it all too clear that sexual minorities are not expected to benefit equally from the wide array of public programs.

Beyond publicly funded resources like health care, the state now regulates access to privately owned business and spaces that are considered to be open to 'the public.' The large amount of litigation in this area suggests that people across Canada still feel that they can enforce 'no queers allowed' policies in such contexts.[125] Historically, discrimination in the provision of such goods and services has been the focus of human rights legislation from the very beginning in Canada. However, to the extent that sexual minorities are still denied access to the human rights process in some parts of Canada, they are also denied access to those 'public' spaces and activities.

The range of 'public' rights that attach to those people who are considered to be full and equal members of the state is of course unlimited. What is disturbing about this selection of cases is the 'tilt' in all the contexts described in these cases: sexual minorities still experience a disproportionately intense level of violence directed at them by virtue of their sexual orientation, yet they also have a disproportionately small claim on 'public' rights, ranging from advertising and entertainment rights to rights to participate in cultural events as themselves or to receive the health care or other government benefits they need. Although a gratifying number of complainants won the cases discussed in this section, it should not be forgotten that simply having to bear the burden of taking legal proceedings to secure basic rights is itself a reflection of the presumed absence of those rights.

Private-Law Rights

'Private law' rights, which enable ordinary people to structure their own relationships, encompass much of the 'everyday-ness' of life – work relations, economic transactions, domestic relations, reproduction issues, and the range of activities that construct the 'private' sphere or 'privacy.' Going back to the elements of legal personhood in Roman civil law, 'private law' has long been thought to govern property ownership and other property transactions; the right to work for wages or otherwise own the fruits of one's own labour; recognition of inheritance rights and testamentary dispositions; the right to demand that the state enforce contracts; the right to legal recognition of families, including the right to form legally recognized marriages, adopt, and have custody of children.

That is the legal theory of private-law rights. In practice, however, the private-law rights of sexual minorities have been honoured as much in the breach as in the enforcement, because relational issues play a prominent role in the 'private' sphere at the same time that 'private' persons, shielded somewhat from the kinds of scrutiny focused on governmental actors, give expression to personal prejudice. Thus lesbian women and gay men have been deprived of important dimensions of legal capacity that have been accorded more or less automatically to other members of the Canadian state.[126]

Property

Cases involving ownership or use of property tend to fall into two distinct categories: the use of business premises, and property claims between lesbian or gay partners who have been disadvantaged by their partner's property dealings. The courts have tended to take the property rights of business entrepreneurs seriously. For example, an Alberta court granted an injunction to a business tenant which had been locked out of premises by the landlord when the tenant tried to turn the lounge section of the rental premises into a private gay nightclub. The injunction was granted pending trial of the main action.[127] There is some suggestion that HIV status or AIDS can give rise to bias in this type of litigation, at least when there is some basis for the court to question whether the complainant has been behaving 'reasonably.' For example, in *Mercedes Homes Inc.* v *Grace*,[128] a case which arose when two gay men filed a human rights complaint arising out of harassment by their landlord, the court seemed to be preoccupied with their health. The court made repeated references to the fact that their health condition had to be a major source of anxiety, a big factor in their reaction to the landlord's harassment, and a reason for them to pursue not only a human rights complaint but also publicity in the gay community. The court speculated that the litigation gave them a sense of 'the meaning of their lives' as they faced deteriorating health.[129]

Domestic relations, of course, raise numerous property issues. In the eyes of courts, most same-sex relationships are merely *de facto* relationships, not *de jure*. This lack of legal status in turn has profound impact on the kinds of property claims that can be made between lesbian and gay partners. When litigation arises between formerly heterosexually married lesbians or gays and their former partners, lesbians and gays may experience this invisibility as an advantage: Unlike in custody litigation, courts tend to ignore subsequent same-sex relationships when calculating support or property awards. Thus when the former husband of a lesbian woman sought reduction of his alimony and child support payments on the basis that his former wife was living in a relationship with another woman who contributed to domestic expenses, the court ruled that the unenforceable nature of the 'companion's' contributions made them irrelevant to the calculation of support.[130]

Contests over support or family assets become more difficult as soon as both of the separating partners are lesbian women or gay men, for the courts have held that this fact takes the dispute entirely outside the boundaries of family support or property law, leaving the injured partner with no remedy but those available under equitable doctrine. In *Anderson v Luoma*,[131] the court refused to award any child support to the biological mother of the couple's two children.[132] The court concluded that, even though the applicant had quit her paid employment to work full-time in the home, the defendant could not be charged with support because she was not a 'father' within the meaning of the common law, not a 'parent' or 'spouse' under matrimonial law, and not under any express or implied contractual obligation to pay support.[133] However, the court did award the applicant an equal share in the residence and a 20 per cent interest in a vacation property, both of which had been in the defendant's name alone, on the basis of the doctrine of constructive trust. The applicant had assumed household duties, worked in the defendant's office, thereby giving the defendant *gratis* the benefits of her work and depriving the applicant of the ability to hold property of her own. The court noted that it was 'reasonable' for the applicant to expect to share the defendant's assets because of the nature of their relationship.[134]

Epstein J.'s decisions in *M. v H.*[135] represent major departures from this limited approach. In a Charter challenge, the applicant in *M.* v *H.* was awarded interim support through an oppression remedy in corporate law, interim use of jointly owned property from which she has been excluded,[136] and the right to a hearing on support payments under Part III of the Family Law Act[137] as well.

The right to apply for support as a 'cohabitant' under Part III of the Family Law Act secures an important element of legal personality, because the inability to share in the assets or income of a former partner is just one aspect of the deeply appropriative nature of the common-law incapacities arising from fictions of conjugal unity. Married women have managed to remove themselves from this appropriative legal fiction,[138] as have opposite-sex cohabitants who are excluded from the asset-sharing provisions of reformed family property law.[139] The rulings in *M.* v *H.* enable lesbian cohabitants to remove themselves from appropriative relations as well, and also offer a solution to the problems revealed by *B. v. A.*,[140] the case in which a woman who had undergone extensive surgery and subsequent hormonal treatment for twenty-one years, raised two children, and become a grandparent with her female partner, was denied the right to apply for support under Part III of the Family Law Act because the surgical changes were not extensive enough to make her a 'man.' This ruling left B. with no property (her former partner held title to all their property) and no income. *M.* v *H.* removes the sex qualifications in Part III as well as the sexuality qualifications, which means that this ruling will benefit bisexual, transgendered, and transsexual people as well as lesbians and gays.

Until the Supreme Court of Canada rules on the government's appeal in *M.* v *H.*, of course, property relations between same-sex partners still remain largely in the shadows of the law. Although former partners can voluntarily agree to negotiate with each other, sign settlement agreements, and probably also sign binding cohabitation agreements, these arrangements are governed not by domestic property law, as they would be for opposite-sex couples, but by the general laws of property and contract.[141]

Wills, Trusts, and Estates

An Ontario court has recently confirmed that surviving lesbian and gay partners cannot receive the benefit of intestacy legislation when their partners die without leaving a will, insurance, or a trust. *Obringer* v *Kennedy Estate*[142] arose because David Kennedy, a university professor, had died intestate, leaving an estate valued at just under $500,000. Because Kennedy appeared to be a single man with no family when he died, the Public Trustee initially received letters of administration which were vacated when a distant relative was finally located (the daughter of a first cousin). Kennedy's surviving partner, John Obringer, then filed an application for letters of administration, appointment as trustee of the estate,[143] and a declaration of his interest in the estate.

In his application, Obringer argued that he was either Kennedy's surviving spouse, or that he was a surviving cohabitant. As surviving spouse, he could have received either the entire estate[144] or half of it as an 'equalization payment.'[145] As a surviving cohabitant, he could have received support payments or a smaller share only if he had been able to show that he was 'dependent.'[146] The court rejected Obringer's application completely. The court reasoned that Obringer could not be treated as being a formally married spouse for the reasons given in *Layland and Beaulne*,[147] because, even under the Charter, Ontario law does not permit persons of the same sex to legally marry. And the court refused to let Obringer raise section 15 of the Charter to show that he should be given the more limited benefits ordinarily accorded to surviving cohabitants because Obringer had not established that factually he was either a cohabitant or a dependant.

This case is somewhat encouraging in the sense that it may well be, in a future case, that a court would accept another partner as a factual 'cohabitant' and thus would apply the analysis developed in *M. v H.* Certainly there is no reason to treat same-sex cohabitants as cohabitants for purposes of support under family law legislation and to deny them that status under identical support provisions in succession law. But that issue was avoided in *Obringer* because the court refused to find that spending every weekend together, taking vacations together, and planning for retirement together constituted cohabitation. The court relied on the elaborate formulas in *Molodowich v Penttinen*[148] to conclude that Obringer and Kennedy did not cohabit to the extent required under succession law.

For estate-planning purposes, the *Obringer* case suggests that, at best, lesbian and gay partners may attempt to establish that they are entitled to the limited benefits for cohabitants under intestacy law, but it is not clear just what it would take to establish factual cohabitation. Certainly it would be important for the parties to live together and to not maintain separate residences.[149] But factual cohabitants would still be entitled only to 'support,' and support, whether as a surviving cohabitant or as a 'dependent,' can be demonstrated legally only by showing factual economic dependency. Where the partners are both employed, absent other compelling factors, it might still be difficult to meet that test as well.

The lesson in *Obringer* is that same-sex couples must carefully document their testamentary intentions; they cannot rely upon general law to protect their partners. However, even the most careful estate plan is vulnerable to attack, and thus to expensive litigation, because of longstanding bias against queers reflected in notions like 'undue influence' and 'lack of testamentary capacity.' Particularly when the deceased had AIDS, the fears left in the wake of *In re Kaufman's Will*[150] continue to be realistic, and appropriate steps must be taken to safeguard the testamentary arrangements from such attacks.[151]

For example, in *Oates* v *Baker Estate*,[152] two brothers challenged the will of a gay man with AIDS on the basis of both testamentary capacity and undue influence in an effort to invalidate the testator's bequest of shares to a third brother. The brothers argued that the bequest was the result of 'AIDS dementia' and attempted to prove that the testator's lawyer, who also received a small bequest, had acted inappropriately. Fortunately, the court was able to see through these homophobic assertions, and found that testamentary capacity had been clearly established and documented, there was no evidence of undue influence, and the lawyer, who had arranged for medical examination, medical witnesses, and clear instructions from his client, had acted in an 'exemplary' manner.

Oates v *Baker Estate* has not, however, solved all the problems surrounding estate planning for same-sex partners – especially if the testator had AIDS. Anecdotal accounts demonstrate how useless wills can be in ordinary situations, where the estate is small or the surviving partner does not have the resources to defend his or her interests. In one situation, the family of a gay man who had had AIDS came to the apartment he shared with his partner shortly after he died, packed up all his belongings without any notice to the partner, and disposed of them, leaving the partner with full responsibility for the rent on the lease until it expired. The value of the net estate was slight, consisting largely of personal possessions they had accumulated together, many of which were owned either by both of them together or by the surviving partner. By the time the surviving partner realized that he might have had legal remedies, at least with regard to retrieving his own possessions, virtually nothing was left. In another situation, the testator had died of AIDS. Before he died, his family and his partner had all gathered together to help him write a holographic will, in which he gave special possessions and original works of art to carefully selected friends. But as soon as he died, his parents ripped up the will and hauled all the artwork they did not like and other possessions to a landfill site.

Other reports suggest that when the estate has not only sentimental value, but significant net financial value, allegations of 'AIDS dementia' are being used to discourage litigation. The beneficiary in *Baker Estate* was a brother, and the people trying to attack the will were the decedent's other two brothers. It may well be that when the beneficiary is a surviving lesbian or gay partner, and the will contest is launched by a family of origin, that 'testamentary capacity,' 'undue influence,' or even 'AIDS dementia' will become persuasive. Continuing uncertainty as to constitutional rights and the application of intestacy legislation, combined with cases like *Baker Estate* and the behaviour of families, means that queers do not have full testamentary rights in Canadian law.[153]

Enforcement of Contracts

Lesbian women and gay men appear to have full capacity to contract in Canadian law. This is not surprising, since contractual capacity does not have any relational qualities unique to sexuality. However, the right to work for wages, which is an aspect of contractual rights, is still only partial. Although the Supreme Court of Canada has now ruled in *Vriend*[154] that complaints of employment discrimination on the basis of sexual orientation can be brought under the Individual's Rights Protection Act,[155] continuing pressure from employees for *bona fide* occupational qualifications relating to sexuality, the inability of human rights commissions to restore employment contracts or affect workplace attitudes, and the limited remedies available to complainants all pose significant barriers to equality in the workplace.

In jurisdictions that do prohibit employment discrimination on the basis of sexual orientation, there are still uncertainties as to how far they extend. In *Waterman v National Life Assurance Co. of Canada (No. 2)*,[156] a board of inquiry did find that refusal to offer a permanent position to a lesbian woman violated the Human Rights Act on the ground of sexual orientation. However, detailed considerations relating to the lesbian's attitude and dress seemed to occupy the board overly much. In *Chaychuk v Best CTV*,[157] the court dismissed an action for sexual harassment, sexual discrimination, and wrongful dismissal brought by a lesbian woman who claimed to have been harassed by her female supervisor, because the court found that the dismissal of the lesbian was justified by her disobedience. In *Re Cami Automotive Inc. and C.A.W., Local 88*,[158] an arbitrator ruled that nothing in the collective agreement or Human Rights Code of Ontario provided relief for harassment on basis of sexual orientation. However, in another recent decision, *Crozier* v *Asselstine*,[159] the board concluded that employee harassment on the basis of sexual orientation did constitute discrimination on the ground of sexual orientation, thus extending discrimination in employment somewhat further in Ontario.[160]

That courts in Canada will protect transgendered or transsexual persons from discriminatory breach of employment contracts is also uncertain. Some transsexual persons in Canada have expressed the view that such discrimination should be processed under the heading 'sex discrimination' instead of as discrimination on the basis of sexual orientation. This would be consistent with emerging trends in Europe. For example, in *P.* v *S.*,[161] the Court of Justice concluded that dismissal of a transsexual man who was going through sex reassignment was precluded by the Community directive on equal treatment in employment. No similar cases have been published in Canada.

Custody and Parentage

Many lesbian, gay, bisexual, transgendered, and transsexual people have children at some point in their lives, either before they come out or adopt an openly queer lifestyle, after they come out as single parents, or with partners by way of adoption, step-parenting, or alternative insemination leading to the birth of their child. Although the legal rights to custody, access, or even recognition of the parent–child relationship are fundamental elements of legal personality, they have all too often been denied to queer parents in Canada. However, this disadvantage is not described in the cases as flowing from 'legal incapacity,' but is usually framed in terms of the 'best interests of the child.'

Custody and Access Issues: It is trite law that 'homosexuality' is not a bar to custody.[162] Thus simple allegations that a parent is lesbian, gay, bisexual, transgendered, or transsexual will not, by itself, ensure that the other parent will receive custody. But more than in many other forms of litigation, the simple threat of 'outing' the other parent – even if that parent is completely heterosexual – is often used as a way to create an advantage in custody litigation, and there are many queer parents in Canada who have immediately backed off any custody or access litigation rather than be identified publicly as queer. Some cases where these kinds of ungrounded allegations have been made have gone to trial, and account for the fact that, even today, the occasional allegation of lesbianism, for example, will float through a custody decision with little appearance of reality.

But this 'trite law' gives an appearance of judicial neutrality that is not borne out by the cases on custody and access. Sometimes courts have actually gone so far as to say that, while homosexuality is not a bar to custody, it is nonetheless a negative element.[163] Sometimes courts impose conditions on lesbians receiving custody, the most usual condition being that they not live with a lover or engage in openly lesbian activities.[164] Frequently courts make references to the fact that the queer parent receiving custody is 'discreet' in his or her sexuality, the underlying warning being that ceasing to be 'discreet' might result in the loss of custody.[165] But sometimes even being 'discreet' is not enough.[166] And in some cases, loss of custody appears to be linked to fears or prejudices associated with the parent's sexuality, as in the belief that a lesbian mother's life or relationships might not be as 'stable' as those of the other parent.[167] When judicial beliefs of these types come into play, the desires of the children appear to be irrelevant.[168]

Not all courts fall into these lines of thinking. In many decisions, lesbian mothers have ended up with non-conditional custody of their children, and the courts do not appear to have been concerned about their lesbianism to any great extent.[169] However, gay fathers do not appear to have ever received custody in contested applications,[170] and, given a choice between a gay father and a lesbian mother, in the one case on point, the court not surprisingly awarded custody to the lesbian mother.[171] Whether it is the long-standing belief that children should be raised by their mothers, or covert fear that gay men are somehow naturally child molesters, the big legal issues for gay fathers have centred not around child custody, but around simple access and overnight access. Thus courts tend to either deny overnight access to gay fathers who live with their partners,[172] or order the father to sleep separately when the children are with them.[173] In only one case has a father tried to so limit a lesbian mother's overnight access; the court struck this clause from the separation agreement on the basis that it violated the Québec Charter of Rights.[174]

Bisexual parents do not seem to face the same obstacles in custody and access litigation. In *Guppy* v *Guppy*,[175] a mother who was alleged to be bisexual received custody without any hesitation on the part of the court. Twenty years ago, an Ontario court awarded custody to a bisexual father,[176] and in *Ouellet* v *Ouellet*,[177] an Ontario court found that a bisexual mother's sexuality was not relevant except to the extent that it affected the children's well-being, and awarded custody to her. Especially in relation to the bisexual father, it may be that bisexuality is less threatening to courts than lesbian or gay identity.

Transsexual and cross-dressing parents have endured detailed scrutiny of their sexuality, sexual practices, and parenting, but, in two of the three reported cases, they have actually been allowed to retain child custody. In *Ghidoni* v *Ghidoni*,[178] the father had begun consultations leading to sex reassignment, and often cross-dressed. Based on the merits of his parenting and the older daughter's preferences, the court ordered joint custody with primary residence of the two children (the other was a school-age boy) with him. In *Chernoff* v *Pyne*,[179] the fact that the father engaged in 'erotic cross-dressing' as 'foreplay' to heterosexual sex was not considered to be a bar to his continued custody of his young daughter. However, this decision appeared to be heavily influenced by the fact that the mother had originally transferred custody to the father voluntarily, and had serious emotional problems that interfered with her parenting. In *H.I.M.* v *W.A.M.*,[180] the court ordered supervised access for a father it described as 'transvestite,' and ordered the father during access to not dress 'in feminine attire,' 'expose them to pornography or indecent behaviour' nor 'use foul language or assault them.'

Parental Status: Over the last twenty years, increasing numbers of lesbian women, both single and in couples, have been becoming parents through adoption and artificial insemination. Although many gay men have also become parents through artificial insemination, gay men have not as often maintained relationships with children so conceived, either because they have donated sperm by way of a sperm bank or because they have agreed with the recipients of their donations that they would not play any social role in the child's life. Whenever a lesbian woman or gay man who is the birth or adoptive parent of a child lives in a conjugal relationship, and whenever a lesbian woman or gay man becomes involved in a conjugal relationship with an adoptive or birth parent, however, issues of parental status arise. Relative to lesbian women, gay men are at a disadvantage in this area of domestic law.

Ontario is on the forefront of jurisdictions that accord lesbian women the legal capacity to form family relationships with children they have not adopted or birthed. In *Re L. and S.*,[181] a family court granted interim sole custody of two children, one adopted legally by the applicant and the other conceived by artificial insemination by her partner during their relationship, to the applicant on the basis of the definition of 'parent' and 'child' in the Children's Law Reform Act, which defines 'parent' as any person who has acted consistent with a settled intention to serve as a parent. On consent, the court ordered that the applicant retain sole custody of the adopted child, joint legal custody of the other child, and that the children continue to be primarily resident with the applicant.[182] In *Buist* v *Greaves*,[183] another family court recognized the parental status of a non-biological lesbian mother, denying her application for sole custody in favour of the birth mother so she could move to Vancouver, but ordering her to pay monthly child support of $450. Buist received liberal access and was permitted to continue playing an important role in her son's life. In *Re K.*,[184] a provincial court applied section 15(1) of the Charter to read same-sex couples into the definition of 'spouse' in the step-parent provisions of provincial adoption law, with the result that the co-mothers of children conceived by artificial insemination were permitted to memorialize their parent–child relationship without terminating the parental status of the birth mothers.[185]

The orders in *Re L. and S.*, *Buist* v *Greaves*, and *Re K.* establish two important methods by which the parental status of both adults in lesbian relationships can obtain legal recognition – through the provisions of the Children's Law Reform Act, and through formal legal adoption. This has important consequences for the parent–child relationship on virtually every level, ranging from the simple ability to meet with schoolteachers and give consent for school trips to being able to maintain parent–child relationships should the adult relationships break down. They also form the basis for future applications for child support in situations of relationship breakdown.[186]

Compared with lesbian women, gay men have fewer ways to exercise their potential capacity to form families outside heterosexual marriage or deemed marriage. For example, in *Re Fink*,[187] a gay man had entered into an agreement with a woman who had conceived through artificial insemination with his sperm; the agreement provided that the father would take full custody of the child immediately after it was delivered by Caesarean section. The application was denied because the court apparently was convinced that the agreement was motivated by fear that the child would be apprehended by Social Services at birth, because the birth mother had pleaded guilty to manslaughter in relation to the death of an older child, and refused to 'lend itself to such an evasion of the child's normal safeguards.' Factually, this case is very unclear, and should not foreclose gay men's legal capacity to form parental relationships through adoption, artificial insemination, or co-parenting.[188]

No Canadian cases have considered the legal status of transsexual parents. However, in *X, Y, and Z v UK*,[189] the European Commission on Human Rights issued an opinion that a female-to-male transsexual was the father of a child born to his partner as the result of artificial insemination. The commission based this opinion on three factors: Article 8 of the Convention for the Protection of Human Rights and Fundamental Freedoms, which guaranteed the right to family life; donor legislation, which deemed a man who consented to his partner's insemination to be the father; and the *de facto* father–child relationship that had existed since birth.[190]

Recognition of Relationships

At the present time in Canada, relationships are recognized in law either as formal marriage religiously or civilly conducted and registered with the state, or as cohabitation with conjugal intent or effect. To this day, the courts have refused to recognize marriages between same-sex partners, even when one of the partners has been living as a person of the other sex for decades. Actual formal marriages involving a transsexual partner have been invalidated when medical/surgical sex reassignment has not resulted in formal legal change of sex. The courts are slowly expanding the definition of 'cohabitants' to include same-sex partners in some circumstances. As that list of circumstances has slowly grown, queer relationships have begun to move out of their previous 'outlaw' status and into the realm of legal regulation. However, relationship recognition remains one of the most contested elements of full legal capacity for lesbians and gays.

Same-Sex Marriage: Every attempt by lesbian or gay couples to formally and legally marry in Canada as same-sex couples has failed. According to all the precedents on point, two persons of the same sex cannot receive a marriage licence, because they are considered to lack the legal capacity to enter into marriage with each other. In each case, this lack of legal capacity has been founded on Christian religious doctrine, which allegedly requires sexual expression to be limited to procreation within formal marriage.[191] So rigorously is this 'no queers allowed' boundary maintained that, despite the proliferation of favourable same-sex employment benefit cases (discussed below), at least one administrative board has ruled that denial of marriage leave to a queer employee was found to not violate the collective agreement because same-sex partners could not 'marry.'[192]

Transsexual Marriage: Transsexual persons have had much more success crossing that boundary. The reason for this is not difficult to find: transsexual persons who seek to marry a person of the sex opposite to their own 'new' sex usually consider themselves to be more 'heterosexual' than 'homosexual.' The more completely a transsexual person has come to appear to be of the biological sex 'opposite' to that of his or her partner, the more likely that person is to be able to obtain a marriage licence and legally register the marriage. Thus several transsexual women and men who have been in the process of medical/surgical sex reassignment have legally changed their names and formally married.[193]

Now, of course, the origin of the legal proposition that same-sex couples do not have the legal capacity to marry because they do not have the biological capacity to procreate together lies in cases testing the validity of marriages involving transsexuals.[194] But the enactment of the Vital Statistics Act sex-reassignment rules, together with the language in some of the subsequent cases on marriage validity, suggests that if a transsexual person legally changes his or her sex, that person could validly marry a person of the sex opposite to his or her new sex. For example, in *Canada v Owen*,[195] the court looked to the Vital Statistics Act for information on what would be required to determine that a person had legally changed his or her sex. Although that case certainly did not result in a ruling that Lillian Owen had become a woman as the result of her surgery and treatment in the 1950s, it suggests that when a person has legally changed his or her sex, formal marriage occurring after that change would be legally recognized. The obstacle in Owen's case, according to the court, was that the surgery had never been completed, and the court was unwilling to find that Owen had become a 'common-law' female by marrying and living as female for most of her adult life.

When transsexual persons have not met the courts' requirements for establishing a new legal sex, however, they have no more marriage rights than do same-sex couples.[196] The further question of whether transsexual persons in such circumstances could claim the rights of same-sex cohabitants has not yet been raised in litigation.

Same-Sex Cohabitants: From a strictly legal perspective, it is completely unclear whether, at the end of the day, lesbians, gays, or bisexuals will be considered to have the legal capacity to form legally recognized same-sex relationships.[197] The reason for this lack of clarity is the particular way in which the Supreme Court of Canada dealt with the appeal in *Egan and Nesbit*. Although the section 1 analysis in *Vriend v Alberta* is much more satisfying than Justice Sopinka's section 1 opinion, that case merely involved personal juridical rights, and it is not yet certain how that section 1 analysis will affect the application of *Egan and Nesbit*.

Read narrowly, *Egan and Nesbit* established that same-sex couples cannot claim the same legal rights as opposite-sex cohabitants. Certainly that was the result of their application for the spousal allowance under the Old Age Security Act.[198] A more generous reading of *Egan and Nesbit* is that it was merely concerned with same-sex access to publicly funded spousal benefits like the spousal allowance, and that it leaves the door open to recognizing same-sex couples for purposes of other types of statutes. Justice Sopinka appeared to contemplate in his section 1 analysis a 'sunset' by which governments would have to extend the definition of 'cohabitant' to include same-sex couples, and the section 1 analysis in *Vriend* would appear to be much more favourable to recognition of same-sex marriages.

In any event, nearly two-thirds of all the court, administrative, and arbitration rulings on the legal status of same-sex couples have extended, in one context or another, some legal recognition to same-sex relationships. As the numbers of these rulings continue to grow, same-sex couples will undoubtedly obtain the status of 'cohabitant.' However, it is worth noting that increasing numbers of these favourable rulings are being issued by human rights tribunals, which means that relationship recognition may be easier to achieve in that forum than in courts applying section 15(1) of the Charter.

Before reviewing the circumstances in which same-sex couples will be recognized, however, it is worth noting that even opposite-sex cohabiting relationships are still not recognized to the same extent as formal marriage. Although *Miron v Trudel*[199] established that, at least for purposes of interpreting insurance policies, opposite-sex cohabitants should be equated with married spouses, the extent to which that ruling will expand the meaning of 'spouse' in other contexts is unclear. Thus, for example, the Ontario Family Law Act continues to exclude opposite-sex cohabitants from Part II, which creates presumptive 50-50 interests between married spouses. So when looking at the cases relating to same-sex couples, there are two layers of uncertainty in this area of law: it is not clear how far cases equating same-sex couples with opposite-sex cohabitants will extend, and it is not clear how far *Miron* extends in equating opposite-sex couples with married couples. In the not-too-distant future, courts may link the two lines of authority to give all three types of couples the same legal status. Or they might use *Egan and Nesbit* to limit the legal status of same-sex couples.

After *Egan and Nesbit*, the most authoritative decision relating to the capacity of lesbians and gays to form legally recognized relationships is the Ontario Court of Appeal decision in *M. v H*. In this decision, the court distinguished *Egan and Nesbit* in concluding that same-sex partners had a legal obligation to provide support for each other upon relationship breakdown. However, this decision should not be taken as completely final, because the Ontario government has appealed it to the Supreme Court of Canada. In the meantime, however, the federal government has abandoned its appeal against the Ontario Court of Appeal decision in *Rosenberg*, in which the court permitted employers to extend registered pension plan survivor options to lesbian and gay employees.

The *M. v H.* appeal is critical. If the Supreme Court ends up equating private obligations like the obligation of support after relationship breakdown with public spousal benefits, then the legal recognition of same-sex partners can be obtained only under special legislation such as human rights legislation or via special contracts such as collective agreements. However, if the Court rejects the government's appeal, it will extend this element of legal capacity at least to other 'private' types of legal obligations, even if the Court is not willing to reverse the position it took in *Egan and Nesbit*.

Aside from *M. v H.* and *Rosenberg*, two other appellate court decisions have recognized same-sex relationships – *Vogel v Manitoba*[200] and *Knodel v British Columbia (Medical Services Commission)*.[201] Neither has the same precedential value as *M. v H.* or *Rosenberg*. In *Knodel*, the B.C. Supreme Court extended spousal-type benefits to a gay cohabitant for purposes of provincial medical benefits coverage. In *Vogel II*, the Court ruled that denial of same-sex employment benefits can violate 'sexual orientation' clauses in human rights legislation, which also circumvents the section 1 issue addressed in *M. v H.* and *Rosenberg*.[202]

Thus *M. v H.* and *Rosenberg* continue to stand as the leading appellate authorities squarely dealing with the legal recognition of same-sex relationships. These two decisions are backed up by growing numbers of trial court decisions, a growing bevy of human rights tribunal decisions, administrative rulings, and arbitral decisions, but the application of human rights provisions is not subject to section 1 of the Charter, grievances are not subject to section 1 of the Charter, and many of the other administrative decisions were based on the particular provisions of unique agreements and policies. Given the age of the unfavourable authorities, the fact that relatively few recent labour arbitrations have gone the other way, and the Supreme Court's adoption of the Ontario Court of Appeal's section 1 analysis in *Rosenberg* in its own ruling in *Vriend*, it seems inconceivable that the Supreme Court of Canada would reverse the Ontario Court of Appeal in *M. v H.* However, until further decisions consistently supersede the more negative possible applications of *Egan and Nesbit*, legal recognition of same-sex relationships remains on shaky jurisprudential ground. As yet, such recognition as does exist is restricted to but a few relatively 'private' contexts in general law, is dependent upon the terms of special legislation like human rights codes or special contracts like collective agreements, or must be obtained by way of formal legislation, as found in British Columbia, and, on a much narrower scale, in Ontario.[203]

Sexual minorities are still a long way away from having the same three choices that are open to opposite-sex couples: formal marriage, legally recognized cohabitation, or *de facto* relating without full-time cohabitation.[204] In a sense, queers are simply asking that the state at least grant legal recognition to queer customary relational practices in the same way that it has recognized the customary practices of opposite-sex couples. Two millennia ago, Roman civil law clearly reflected the fact that, in non-Christian cultures, the legal relation of 'marriage' is founded not in religious ceremony, but in the practice of cohabiting with intent to marry. Before Christian beliefs became fully incorporated into Canadian matrimonial law, nineteenth-century courts recognized the validity of customary forms of marriage: Canadian courts in the 1800s recognized marriage *à la façon du pays* ('according to the fashion of the country') between Aboriginal women and European Canadians, at least until Christian doctrine became considered to be an element of Canadian matrimonial law.[205] And throughout history and around the globe, same-sex marriages have been recognized in the customary laws of many cultures, including not only in some aspects of Roman civil law, but also by cultures as diverse as the Zuni of North America;[206] the Azande people of Sudan;[207] the Ibo and Nuer of Nigeria, Dahomey, and South Africa;[208] the Hawai'i;[209] among many others.[210] It is notable that these accounts either pre-dated the Christianization of indigenous peoples or related to cultures that have managed to survive Christian influences in some degree.

Not 'Persons' Yet

Denial of legal personality by the state is always instrumental. The 'civil death' imposed on Jewish persons under the Visigothic Code of the first millennium C.E. was designed to place as much legal, social, economic, and physical pressure as possible on Jewish persons to induce them to genuinely convert to Christianity. The specific form of civil death that was developed by the Third Reich was instead designed to erase Jewish existence from Europe completely, and to appropriate any property or other things of value owned by Jewish persons for the enrichment of the Reich. The civil death imposed on African Americans under conditions of legal slavery was designed to appropriate the labour and reproductive power of this class of people while stripping them of all other aspects of existence.

The particular form of civil death that is still imposed on people characterized by their sexuality or sex identity ('queers') is designed to eradicate queer existence not by eradicating queers, but by placing as much legal, social, economic, and physical pressure as possible on sexual minorities to induce them to embrace non-queer existence. Thus the more completely queers wish to be their actual selves in all aspects of life, the more completely their legal personality is constrained and impaired.

At the heart of queer-shaped 'civil death' is the long-standing criminalization of many forms of queer sexual expression. The disproportionate criminalization of sexual expression has meant that in relation to the first cluster of civil capacities – participation rights – sexual minorities who have criminal records arising out of sexual expression will be denied entry to Canada both as individual applicants and as sponsored applicants. It also means that, although lesbians and gays can now seek Convention-refugee status, evidence of 'persecution' on the basis of sexuality cannot rest on the fact of charges or convictions arising out of activities that are still prohibited in Canadian law. And the right to sponsor same-sex partners is still extended through governmental discretion; despite Charter litigation, this right has still not been enshrined in positive law. Denial of entry into Canada is intensified when other dimensions of queer existence such as gender, race, ability, and economic class come into play as well.

Sexual minorities also still face barriers in gaining access to public office. Social prejudice against sexual minorities has kept the numbers of open lesbians and gays in politics very low, has dissuaded politicians from pursuing issues of sexuality in politics, and has continued to support discriminatory employment policies in public institutions ranging from the military and police to schools and public agencies. As with same-sex sponsored-immigration policies, new policies of non-discrimination in the military and police, for example, continue to be expressed in court settlements and internal policy memoranda, not in the form of legal provisions. Thus the legal basis for claiming these elements of legal personality continues to be found in ephemeral and discretionary administrative policies.

The second cluster of civil capacities that are fundamental to legal existence – juridical rights, or rights to engage the legal process – are also denied in several critical regards. Only very recently have lesbians and gays gained the right to sue for discrimination in employment, accommodation, services, or police protection. In litigation, they are still vulnerable to bias on the part of jurors, courts, and lawyers. Attempts to obtain the right to question potential jurors for homophobic bias have failed, and the best the courts can do to protect lesbian or gay witnesses, accuseds, and other parties is to keep their sexuality from the jury, prohibit publication of their identities, or limit cross-examination on their sexuality. These are merely ameliorative steps that do not address the underlying prejudice that makes these measures necessary in the first place, and they are rarely taken, in any event.

Sexual minorities continue to be denied a wide array of 'public' rights, beginning with not only the right to protection from violence, but the right to protection from police violence. The right to identity is completely denied to all but fully post-operative transsexual people; speech rights are, at best, secured by orders at the administrative level or only upon litigation; and, as is explored in greater detail in chapters 7 and 8, almost no publicly funded benefits are available to lesbians and gays on the basis of their relationships.

Even in 'private' law, which was originally thought to be the one area of life into which law and legal policy could not intrude, sexual minorities are denied the right to privately order their lives in the ways they wish. Statutory regimes that order property rights between conjugal partners exclude same-sex partners, which leaves some partners vulnerable in situations of power imbalance or oppression, and places a heavy duty on all same-sex couples to set up their own contractual arrangements, or content themselves with general equitable doctrine. Landlords continue to discriminate on the basis of sexuality; families of origin and courts continue to ignore same-sex partners in looking at testamentary dispositions; and queers of all kinds face very serious impediments to obtaining custody of their children, access, or overnight access because courts still give free rein to fears about children. Although private ordering via collective agreements has made some inroads into the denial of same-sex employment benefits, as has special legislation via human rights codes, only two appellate decisions in Canada have actually extended legal recognition to same-sex partners in full-scale Charter reviews – *M.* v *H.* and *Rosenberg* – and the partnership rights pursued in both cases were 'private' rights merely regulated by 'public' legislation.

A full-scale comparison between the continuing civil incapacities imposed on sexual minorities and other groups in Canada is beyond the scope of this work. I would predict that such a comparison would reveal that, along with Aboriginal persons, foreign domestic workers, and raced persons, sexual minorities continue to face some of the most formal constraints of legal personality inscribed in contemporary law. But what is unique to the way legal personality is abridged in relation to sexual minorities is that the more obviously a right or status touches on the sexual or relational aspects of queer existence, or contains elements that could be seen as 'public' benefits, the more completely that right or status continues to be denied on the basis of sexuality.

This is not just an abstract or theoretical jurisprudential conclusion. Because the elements of legal personality form the concrete legal capacity to act in law, and thus in the state, in public, and in the 'private' sphere as constituted by legal doctrine, denial of any element of civil capacity radiates out through the thousands of provisions of contemporary law and, through them, touches countless moments of 'real' life to continually reinforce and actualize these incapacities.

In order to demonstrate how pervasively the denial of full legal personality still affects sexual minorities in Canada, I address, in the next five chapters, some of the specific implications of even partial 'civil death' based on sexuality today. I attempt at as many points as possible to link this constrained status with the real lives of sexual minorities in order to form a solid basis from which to look at how these remnants of civil incapacity should best be eradicated.

Chapter Six

Counting Queers

Legal concepts such as 'discrimination,' 'equality,' 'rights,' or even 'legal personality' ultimately have no real meaning. What most genuinely matters to most people is the emotional, spiritual, and material quality of life: well-being. Despite the proliferation of liberatory scholarship in the last few decades, there are no accepted measures of 'well-being.' Indeed, so long as income disparities remain pronounced, 'well-being' will mean very different things to people with different income levels. Other differences also affect what counts as 'well-being.'[1] In order to concretize the effects of denial of legal personality on the basis of sexuality, I have selected five aspects of discrimination that can be isolated and analysed either qualitatively or quantitatively: The failure to collect demographic data on sexual minorities for use in the policy-formation process; the pervasive effects of exclusion from legal norms on so-called private arrangements; the systematic exclusion of same-sex couples from the 'heterosexual benefit system'; living with 'incremental discrimination' in the wake of the Supreme Court of Canada decision in *Egan and Nesbit*;[2] and the impact of various models of 'civil rights' legislation that have been developed to restore some incidents of legal personality to some sexual minorities.

In this chapter, I focus on demographic data. I have chosen that as a starting point for the simple reason that the continuing refusal of governments such as the federal government in Canada to enumerate queer populations says very clearly that 'queers do not count.' I know that I am going somewhat against the political mainstream in queer communities by saying that numbers do matter, if only symbolically. Several scholars have taken the position that it is numbers that do not count, that what really matters is qualitative experiences of discrimination on the basis of sexuality.³ While I agree with the substance of this position, I do not agree that numbers do not matter. I think this view ignores the realities of numbers and political power, for several reasons.

First, one has only to look to the conduct of Canadian governments around the 'numbers' issue to understand that demographic data are critical to contemporary social-policy processes. Despite the fact that the numbers of sexual minorities in Canada are probably roughly the same as the numbers of racial minorities in Canada, the complete lack of valid data on numbers makes it impossible for queer litigants or policy critics to talk convincingly about the financial implications of legal policy. And the federal government's continuing refusal to collect such data through its census power appears to be unshakeable. Although Census Canada did permit queers to record same-sex relationships in the 1991 census, it apparently took a policy decision to 'destroy' the demographic information attached to those respondents, and still refuses to release the aggregate numbers of couples who so identified themselves.⁴ When lesbian and gay activists contacted Census Canada about how to record themselves and their relationships in the 1996 survey, Census Canada actually gave groups detailed information on how best to report same-sex relationships, but subsequently decided that it would not release these data because they are not statistically valid.⁵

In the meantime, major policy studies continue to proceed on the assumption that the only people who are relevant to policy analysis are heterosexual. For example, Maureen Baker recently published a comprehensive cross-cultural study on contemporary family policies that made extensive use of demographic and fiscal data.⁶ In order for the study to have any validity, she really had no choice but to adopt official government concepts of the heterosexual 'census family' (married couples and lone parents plus non-married children) and the heterosexual 'economic family' (two or more people living together and related by blood, adoption, or marriage), for her study. She was forced to leave same-sex couples out of this wide-ranging and detailed study, even though she recognized that same-sex couples are becoming just one of many diverse family forms in contemporary Canada.⁷

Second, in the absence of valid data, homophobic politicians and courts find it relatively easy to assert or assume low numbers, which can be used to argue that legislative reforms or administrative measures that recognize sexual minorities are just 'special interest' policies, or that there are too few sexual minorities to matter,⁸ or that the percentage of the gay population affected by HIV/AIDS, for example, is quite high. Without valid data on incomes and assets, it is also much easier to get away with claims like 'all gays are rich'[9] or that 'all,'[10] or at least 'most' children, are born into heterosexual families.[11]

Third, queer activists need reliable data on all of these issues and more in order to engage in informed analysis and debate at the community level, in order to formulate priorities for lobbying purposes, and in order to present credible expert evidence in litigation. Cases like *Baehr* v *Miike*[12] have been won by lawyers who have understood how to work effectively with valid social science research data. Yet in Canada, most of the data that are available are of the 'projection' or 'guesstimate' nature, developed by using rough summaries of research in other countries to make even rougher calculations based on the size of the overall Canadian population, for example.

Fourth, the fact that the federal government holds a monopoly on the collection of census data and other large surveys, yet refuses to release this data for open analysis and debate, enables it to quietly use that monopoly power to develop convincing-looking and detailed data for use against queer litigants in Charter cases. Lawyers in *Egan and Nesbit* did manage to convince the Supreme Court that these data were so speculative as to be completely unreliable, but the government continues to develop even more complex 'data' as it continues to resist the extension of ordinary legal rights to queers. Not all lawyers appear to be comfortable enough with data to build a record that reveals how useless they really are, and as soon as these figures become judicial findings of fact, they take on a life of their own in subsequent litigation.[13]

This is not to say that there are absolutely no data available anywhere on the demographics of the queer population. There are quite a lot. But with the exception of a small set of census data relating to same-sex couples in the United States and data collected in the 1996 Australian census, none of the data have been derived through large-scale governmental demographic studies, and researchers have used a wide array of methodologies to produce what look, at first glance, like conflicting findings.

What I have done in this chapter is to discuss the leading sources of data in the United States and Canada in order to illustrate the research issues that bear on answering three basic questions: How many lesbians and gays are there, as a percentage of the adult population? (The research data have almost completely ignored bisexual, transgendered, and transsexual people to date.) How many same-sex couples are there? And how many children are living in queer families? Although it is not possible to answer these questions with any precision at this time, it is possible to identify the shortcomings of existing studies and to get a sense of the probable range of valid data.

How Many Queers Are There?

Research Findings

The controversial research done in the middle of the century by Alfred Kinsey and his associates[14] appears to have led to the contemporary perception that 10 per cent of the entire population is lesbian or gay. In fact, the specific finding was that 10 per cent of the male population was 'exclusively homosexual.'[15] However, the findings and the methodologies in these studies are much more complex than that.

Kinsey and his colleagues found a quite high level of homosexual experience in the U.S. population. They also found that they got widely divergent responses to their questions depending on how they defined sexuality and how they framed their questions. Specifically, Kinsey and his colleagues found that if they asked their subjects whether they had ever had either any sexual contact with other men or experienced homosexual desire or attraction, even in fantasy, 50 per cent answered in the affirmative.[16] When the questions focused on actual physical sexual contact to the point of orgasm, the response rate dropped to 37 per cent. The response rate dropped further – to 25 per cent – when subjects were asked if they had had 'distinct and continued homosexual experience' during at least part of their lives.[17] Kinsey found that 10 per cent of the men in the study were 'more or less exclusively homosexual' during part of their lives, but that only 4 per cent were 'exclusively homosexual throughout their lives.'[18] On the basis of this range of findings, Kinsey and his colleagues concluded that 13 per cent of U.S. males could be classified as 'homosexual.'[19] In later work, they concluded that women reported roughly a half to a third the levels of homosexual activity of men, putting the equivalent figure for women at 7 per cent.[20]

The 10 per cent figure that is popularly used is probably either a mistaken attribution of the results relating to men to women, or is a rough average of the 13 per cent figure for men and the 7 per cent figure for women. But no matter how that 10 per cent is derived, it seriously overshadows the overall conclusions based on subjects' reports of their most recent sexual activities. Depending on race, age, education categories, between 10 and 49 per cent of male respondents who were never married reported that during the most recent time period, they had had homosexual relations to orgasm. The equivalent figures for women were 2 to 11 per cent.[21]

The Kinsey studies continue to remain unique. Kinsey and his colleagues interviewed more than 20,000 subjects. Their samples were not representative, and it appears that they made an effort to make sure that they included people with a variety of same-sex sexual experiences. The interview technique was designed to put subjects at ease, with the interviewers inviting openness by making it clear to subjects who disclosed same-sex fantasies or contact that they would not be criticized in any way, and the interviewers were taught how to ask questions and relate in a manner calculated to elicit information not easily shared.[22]

The findings reported in more recent studies of sexual minorities have been quite diverse. In 1972, Gebhard found that studies had come up with figures ranging from 2 per cent to 5 per cent of 'exclusive homosexuals.'[23] In 1985, the author of a textbook on psychiatry reported that studies had established that 4 to 6 per cent of the population was exclusively homosexual.[24] The General Social Survey of National Opinion Research Center at the University of Chicago in 1989 found that 4.8 per cent of the general population was lesbian, gay, or bisexual,[25] while a cross-cultural study of men in France, the United Kingdom, and the United States found levels of 11.6 per cent, 7.8 per cent, and 11.6 per cent, respectively, in 1990.[26] More recent studies have widened the range of figures, with a low of 1 per cent and a high of 20 per cent. At the low end, researchers at the Battelle Human Affairs Research Center concluded in 1993 that gays make up only 1.5 per cent of the population[27] and a University of Chicago study published in 1994 found that only 2.8 per cent of men identified as gay.[28] In 1996, the National Gay and Lesbian Task Force in Washington, DC, which sponsored a study directed by John D'Emilio, concluded that at least 3.2 per cent of U.S. voters are gay.[29] At the other extreme, a 1994 study concluded that some 20 per cent of the U.S. population experiences 'homosexual attraction'.[30]

Three basic factors account for the disparities in these figures: the definition of 'homosexual,' 'lesbian,' or 'gay' used in the study; the actual methodology employed in the study; and what has been called the 'spiral of silence' or the effect of fear of disclosure. At the methodological level, the Kinsey research suggests that the subjects' comfort level, the perceived degree of risk or confidentiality, the representativeness of the sample, the way the researchers or the subjects define sexuality, the time frame to which the questions relate, the age of the respondents, and the personal ethics of the researchers will all affect the research findings.

At one extreme, some researchers appear to be primarily motivated by political objectives. For example, low estimates of the size of the homosexual population can be used to inflate figures on the incidence of HIV infection among gay men. When the number of gay men who are HIV-positive is divided by a small number of gay men in the total population, the infection rate will appear to be higher than when it is divided by a larger number.[31]

For purposes of legal policy, probably the most important of the factors that affect findings is the definition of sexuality used in the study. As the Kinsey studies made very clear, 'sexuality' is a complex set of phenomena, experienced not only physically and socially, but also emotionally and psychically. Persons who are asked 'Are you gay?' or 'Are you lesbian?' might not necessarily feel comfortable saying 'Yes' even if they have had same-sex sexual contact or are in a continuing same-sex relationship.

Following Kinsey, Laumann et al. have isolated what they consider to be the three most important components of sexuality – desire, behaviour, and identity.[32] They found that the response rates of both men and women to each of these elements of sexuality varied quite markedly. Fifty-nine per cent of the women and 44 per cent of the men reported desire, but did not report either same-sex behaviour or any form of homosexual, 'gay,' or 'lesbian' identity. Only 15 per cent of the women and 24 per cent of the men reported 'lesbian' or 'gay' identity and same-sex sexual behaviour, while only 2.8 per cent of the men and 1.4 per cent of the women disclosed 'identity.'[33] Overall, they found that 9 per cent of the men and a little over 4 per cent of the women had engaged in some same-sex sexual activity.[34] When they measured the 'identity' dimension of sexuality instead of sexual behaviour, however, they came out with much lower figures.

Other factors such as time frame, age, and fear of disclosure have also been shown to affect response rates. When Sell et al. asked subjects about their sexual behaviour since the age of fifteen, 11.6 per cent, 7.8 per cent, and 11.6 per cent of the respondents in France, the United Kingdom, and the United States disclosed same-sex sexual behaviour. When the time frame was restricted to the immediate past five years, the affirmative responses fell to 10.8 per cent, 4.7 per cent, and 6.3 per cent, respectively.[35]

Kenneth Sherrill has studied the impact of age and fear of disclosure on response rates, and has concluded that social and legal pressures tend to induce sexual minorities to make themselves invisible in all but the safest contexts.[36] As he pointed out, Kinsey and his colleagues had created a very supportive context by making statements like 'we would not be surprised if he had had such experience' because '[w]e always assume that everyone has engaged in every type of activity.'[37] He concluded that the more open and public the interview methodology, the less likely people would be to disclose sexualities that diverge from the favoured norm. Sherrill illustrated this effect by comparing the methodologies used in two recent studies. In the Yankelovich survey, subjects were given a card with codes on it, and the surveyors did not know what the codes stood for. In the University of Chicago study, researchers asked respondents directly who they had had sexual relations with in the past year, and how often. The response rates in the Yankelovich survey were higher, which Sherrill attributed to the degree of disclosure, in the absence of reassuring statements like those made by Kinsey and colleagues, required by each methodology. Calling this fear factor the 'spiral of silence,'[38] Sherrill contrasted the Kinsey data with the results of a 1990 voter exit poll.[39] He concluded that as many as 90 per cent of sexual minorities are unwilling to reveal their sexuality even in completely anonymous ballots.[40]

The 'spiral of silence' appears to be linked with age. Sherrill found that 48 per cent of voters who identified as lesbian or gay in the exit poll were age thirty to forty-four, while only 20 per cent were age forty-five to fifty-nine.[41] Not only do lesbians and gays seem to have begun to come out at younger ages, probably because of increasing levels of social acceptance and legal protection, but lesbians and gays over the age of forty-five are perhaps more likely to hold cultural memories of how official lists and records of the lesbian and gay populations have been used in living memory by police to control queer communities. Indeed, many queers in that age group may well have begun their political lives campaigning for demands that included destruction of police lists of local queers that had been developed during the McCarthy era.[42]

Canadian Projections

Although there have been some Canadian studies of partnered gay men, none of the large-scale demographic studies routinely carried out in Canada has ever attempted to measure the size of the queer population. This includes the Canada Census and the Survey of Consumer Finances, neither of which give respondents an opportunity to identify by sexuality or by same-sex relationship. Nor have funded academic researchers ever attempted to carry out such a study. Canadian policy makers and researchers have dismissed this gap in the literature with a rather cavalier attitude. For example, in the Ontario Law Reform Commission's 1993 report on the wisdom of recognizing same-sex couples in family law, the commission dismissed the question of how many lesbian or gay people might be affected by such legislation with the cursory comment that '[s]tudies report numbers that vary from four percent to seventeen percent.'[43] The only reference given for this statement was the essays collected in Gonsiorek and Weinrich's 1991 book,[44] all of which were based on older U.S. research data.[45] The commission did not subject the various research references in this book to any kind of analysis. Nor did it discuss the fact that the wide range of results discussed in Gonsiorek and Weinrich employed quite divergent research methodologies, making generalized conclusions about the findings invalid. Experts testifying in litigation over sexuality discrimination have also had to rely on U.S. data, sometimes merely referencing the global figure of 10 per cent associated with Kinsey and colleagues,[46] and sometimes being examined on the basis of newspaper accounts of quite different types of research studies.[47]

This means that Canadian researchers who have wanted to do any data-based work on policy issues affecting sexual minorities have had to rely not on Canadian data, but on projections derived from another country. And, lack of critical analysis of the methodologies used to generate U.S. data has meant that the connection between methodology and data has been lost to the policy-formation process. For example, when considering the need for hate-crimes provisions, it makes sense to take into account how many people in Canada might be considered to be 'queer' in the widest possible terms, because hate crimes are often motivated by perceptions that a person has a hated characteristic. But when looking at the fiscal implications of same-sex benefits, for example, it might make more sense to work not with the data collected by Kinsey and colleagues, but with, perhaps, those gathered by Laumann and colleagues on self-identifying persons, which are roughly 7 per cent for men and 4.4 per cent for women. This suggestion is based on the (untested) assumption that those sexual minorities who are unwilling to self-identify for purposes of an anonymous survey are also less likely to self-identify in order to claim same-sex benefits.[48]

At this time, there appears to be little hope that Canadian national surveys or the Canadian census will be used to obtain information on sexuality in the near future. Although there have been ongoing discussions about collecting data on same-sex couples, the separate issue of trying to collect individual data on sexuality or sex identity has not even been considered seriously. Thus Canadian policy analysts have to content themselves with the very roughest of projections. For purposes of this study, this is the approach I have adopted. In order to get some sense of revenue implications and government costs of some government policies, I have used projections based on the Laumann and colleagues self-identification study. Applying those results to the Canadian population, I have speculated that at least some 769,378 men in Canada have had sexual contact with other men, but do not necessarily identify as 'gay' or 'homosexual,' and that some 503,369 women have had sexual contact with other women, but do not necessarily think of themselves as 'lesbian,' 'gay,' or 'homosexual.'[49] This would translate into 5.7 per cent of the adult population as a whole. Since there were as many as 650,000 people at the Toronto Gay Pride celebrations in 1996,[50] this figure is more than likely on the low side. How differing research methodologies would affect any of these projections remains an open question at this time.

Counting Queer Couples

The intact opposite-sex couple has had a strong hold on the Canadian political imagination for much of this century. In the 1920s, parliamentarians routinely invoked the image of the 'couple' to justify a range of social-policy measures that were obviously, and sometimes even expressly, designed to promote the heterosexuality of men, the economic dependency of women, and the sense of obligation to reproduce within such relationships. The 'family values' lobby has continued with the politics of the family, attempting to persuade courts across the United States and Canada that the opposite-sex couple ought to be the only unit of social policy. Despite the difficulties of measuring the queer population as a whole, measuring the number of same-sex couples is somewhat more advanced. That is because there is considerable research on the growing diversity in family forms, and some U.S. and Australian census surveys have even begun to identify some same-sex couples on a national basis.

U.S. and Australian Data

Figures on the numbers of same-sex couples remain highly speculative. Kathy Roberson has estimated that some 38 per cent of the 8.4 million adults currently living in some sort of non-married domestic partnership in the United States are living in same-sex couples. Based on this estimate, there are 1.6 million same-sex couples in the United States, or an average of 32,000 same-sex couples per state.[51] Using U.S. census data on self-identified same-sex couples, Klawitter and Flatt have placed that figure at 136,000 couples for the entire country, or an average of 2,720 per state.[52] Badgett and Goldfoot have estimated that there are perhaps 10,000 two-earner same-sex couples in California, a state with a large population overall, and large lesbian and gay populations as well.[53] The 1996 Australian census, which has included tabulations of self-identifying same-sex couples, reported 10,217 same-sex couples for the entire country.[54]

It is not clear how many of these couples are lesbian versus gay. Despite studies that have suggested that there are perhaps twice as many gay men as there are lesbian women, Klawitter and Flatt found roughly equal numbers of lesbian and gay couples.[55] They concluded, on the basis of a study of the coupling behaviour of lesbian women and gay men,[56] that this was consistent with findings that lesbian women form committed relationships more quickly than do gay men. Thus they predict that a larger percentage of the lesbian population will be coupled at any one time.[57] Of the 10,217 same-sex couples tabulated in the 1996 Australian census data, 42 per cent were female and 58 per cent were male.[58]

Canadian Data

There have been no systematic studies of same-sex couples in Canada. A 1993 study by Ted Myers found that 36 per cent of the gay men surveyed described themselves as being in an intimate relationship, and half of them described their relationships as monogamous.[59] A 1995 study by Stephen Samis found that 45.7 per cent of 420 lesbians and gays in the Vancouver area were in relationships, and 63.5 per cent of those respondents were cohabiting.[60] The 1997 Coalition for Lesbian and Gay Rights in Ontario (CLGRO) survey found that in a sample of 1,233, containing slightly more men than women (54 per cent versus 45 per cent), 75 per cent of the women were in same-sex relationships, compared with only 58 per cent of the men.[61]

While studies like these can be used to project the rates of coupling in the lesbian and gay population, they cannot be used to calculate the total number of same-sex couples in Canada, because they are geographically limited and urban-based, and can, at best, be used only to make a projection on a projection. That is, if there were 10,991,110 men over the age of eighteen in Canada in 1995, and if 7 per cent of men over the age of eighteen are gay (769,378), then 36 per cent (276,976) were coupled in that year, and 18 per cent (197,840) were monogamously coupled. And if there were a total of 22,431,315 women and men over the age of eighteen in Canada in 1995, and if 10 per cent of them were lesbian or gay (2,243,131), then 45.7 per cent (1,026,024) were in a relationship that year, 63.5 per cent of whom were living together (651,525).[62]

The numbers of lesbian and gay cohabitants are unlikely to be this high. However, the lack of precision in Census Canada questions means that general census data can shed very little light on the issue. For example, the 1991 census found that there were only 391,010 two-person 'non-family' households, and a total of only 485,980 non-family households of two or more persons.[63] These 'non-family' households included students, friends living together, group homes, boarding houses, and other non-related groups, as well as same-sex couples who could not identify themselves as 'spouses' or 'cohabitants' on the census form. Without disaggregating data on these non-related groups of respondents, it is difficult to identify those who might be same-sex couples.

Although researchers, governments, and public-interest groups have legitimate interests in being able to obtain accurate data on same-sex couples, Statistics Canada has thus far refused to collect such data, and apparently for purely political reasons. In the consultation document distributed as part of the process of planning for the 1996 census, Statistics Canada spoke of this issue not in terms of the need for information about same-sex couples, but as the 'demand to legitimize the status of same-sex unions by including them as a response option.' The consultation guide then went on to discuss 'public resistance to identifying same-sex unions on the census' and resistance by gay/lesbian couples who see such an option as 'potentially threatening.'[64] Reporting later on feedback received on this issue in the consultation process, Statistics Canada concluded that it would be too 'controversial' to collect such data 'even though there might be a strong, legitimate reason' to do so. This agency then went on to speculate that, if people 'boycotted the census as the result of negative feeling, it would jeopardize overall census results,' and argued that terminology general enough to avoid such controversy might well be incomprehensible or unacceptable. These last two factors, it was contended, would then call the accuracy of the data into question.[65]

The real reason for leaving sexuality out of the 1996 census, however, appeared to be the federal government's vigorously defended legal position – that same-sex couples have no legal status, and that governments can justifiably leave same-sex couples out of benefit programs: 'The census must reflect the legal definitions of marriage, separation, divorce, and common-law union as they exist now. Despite recent Supreme Court decisions relative to the Canadian Human Rights Act, legal marriage is not permitted between persons of the same sex.'[66]

In the end, the 1996 census did not list same-sex couples as a response option on the form. Statistics Canada did give detailed directions on how same-sex partners could self-identify,[67] and had previously said that they intended to count the numbers of same-sex couples reported this way and to run cross-tabs with other data 'if the quality assessment of this type of data meet our quality and accuracy standards.'[68] On the strength of these statements, several groups made concerted efforts to get this information out to queer communities. However, Statistics Canada has now taken the position that it will not release this information, nor will it be possible to find it in the Statistics Canada's Public Use Microdata Files.[69]

Prospects do not appear to be any better for the 2001 census. Although Statistics Canada conceded in 1997 that '[t]he issue of the extension of legislated rights and benefits to same-sex couples is being debated and addressed in both the political and public arenas,' and once again asked for comments on whether and how this information should be collected or published,[70] the most that the federal government appears to be willing to do in this area is to fund a national survey of lesbians, gays, and bisexuals. Not to be confused with a census or Statistics Canada survey, this survey will be limited to self-identifying queer respondents and will be neither comprehensive nor multivariate in structure.[71] While it will be useful to obtain further information on selected queer populations, this survey will be much larger than other surveys undertaken to date, but it will not be appreciably different from other non-representative surveys like that recently carried out by CLGRO.[72] Thus the burden of obtaining realistic data on the size of queer populations remains entirely on queer activists. Until such data do become available, it will remain completely impossible to break the 485,980 'non-family' households down into queer and non-queer households or to develop detailed demographic data on members of such households.

The government, of course, is not hampered by this lack of data. Empowered by law to collect census data[73] and to run other surveys like the Survey of Consumer Finances, required by law to keep these data completely confidential unless they do meet Statistics Canada's 'quality and accuracy standards,'[74] and financing the collection of these data out of tax revenues, the federal government thus has access to the best data available in Canada on same-sex couples – and has no qualms about using it to its own advantage in Charter litigation.

Thus in preparing its defence in *Rosenberg* v *The Queen*, the Department of Justice was able to use government resources to develop a detailed statistical model of same-sex couples in Canada for the year 1994. The data out of which this model was constructed were based on the Statistics Canada 1990 Survey of Consumer Finances, adjusted to 1994. All two-adult households containing unrelated adults of the same sex in the sample of 39,000 households were identified, excluding full-time students. The resulting percentage was then used as a basis for projecting the number of same-sex households in Canada. The department concluded that there were approximately 134,700 same-sex couples in Canada in 1994, or about 1.6 per cent of all households with more than one person. This data was used to model detailed characteristics of these purported same-sex households, the purpose being to calculate the tax costs and tax benefits of being recognized as couples under the Income Tax Act. The income tax projections produced with this model were then presented to the trial court that heard *Rosenberg* v *The Queen* by Albert Wakkary, a Tax Policy Officer in the Department of Finance.[75] The point of his testimony – which was not cross-examined in any detail or supported by delivery of a copy of the statistical database or model – was to demonstrate that lesbians and gays had more to lose than to gain by winning the Charter challenge in *Rosenberg*.

Because the federal government holds a monopoly over the collection, analysis, and publication of the very data upon which it has now come to rely in litigation, it has become even more urgent to gain access to both the 1991 and 1996 census data on same-sex households, whether those figures are part of the 'approved' data or not. The government's continued control over this whole area of knowledge has placed queer communities at a severe disadvantage through its abuse of this monopoly. Even if this 1996 census data does become available, however, it will not give an accurate picture of the number of same-sex couples in Canada for several reasons. First, only people who were 'in the know' or who were willing to put some thought into how to report their relationships will have filled the form out in the manner specified. Second, the 'spiral of silence' effect will doubtless have kept many couples from making any disclosure of their relationship or sexuality at all on this official survey form.[76] And even if Census Canada were to include questions on sexuality in the 2001 census, the 'spiral of silence' and the census methodology will probably result in significant underreporting of sexuality or of relationship status to an unmeasured extent.

How Many Children?

Given the barriers to accurate measurement of the queer population as a whole in either the United States or Canada, and the fact that there is little but speculative guesses at the numbers of same-sex couples, it is even more difficult to estimate the number of children with same-sex parents. Counting children is even more complicated because of the many ways children come to have same-sex parents. Children can be born to parents who were married at the time of conception or birth, but who separated or divorced later. Children can be adopted by an individual or by a same-sex couple, before or after he or she forms a relationship. Children can be born to an individual or to a couple as the result of alternative insemination, and even children born by an individual can end up being raised in a two-parent household. And children can become 'foster children,' 'stepchildren,' or 'adopted' children in relation to second, third, or fourth parents. Children with same-sex parents cannot simply be identified by finding their first parents or their custodial parents, and I am not even sure that there is any one adjective or phrase that would be widely understood as referring to all children with same-sex parents. Nonetheless, these complexities have not prevented researchers from making some estimates as to the number of children with same-sex parents or who are living in same-sex households.

U.S. and Australian Estimates

Despite these methodological problems, U.S. researchers have made some estimates of the numbers of children with lesbian or gay parents, or who live with same-sex parents. Drawing a number of these studies together, Patricia J. Falk[77] has found that the estimates range from 3 to 5 million children living with lesbian mothers,[78] and from 6 to 14 million living with gay parents.[79] Barret and Robinson found studies that indicated that over 1 million gay fathers live in the whole of North America,[80] a figure that reflects the fact that as many as 20 per cent of all gay men and 35 per cent of lesbian women were previously married.[81] Even if children born to or adopted by same-sex parents are left completely out of the calculation, approximately half of previously married lesbians and gays are parents.[82]

The Blumstein and Schwartz study, *American Couples*, has produced some information on the number of children with same-sex parents. Thirteen per cent of the individuals in this study were lesbian, and the authors found that 14 per cent of these women had children from a past or current relationship. Eight per cent of them had as many as three children living at home more than six months per year. (They did not ask gay men about their children).[83] On the basis of the Blumstein and Schwartz data, it could be projected that 14 per cent of all lesbian women will each have 1.79 children from a past or current relationship, and that 8 per cent of all lesbian women will each live with 1.38 children.[84] These figures are consistent with the data on children with same-sex parents in the 1996 Australian census data, which reveal that almost 8 percent of the total same-sex couple population had dependants, 86 per cent of whom were female couples and 14 per cent of whom were male couples. Overall, 16 per cent of all the female couples had children living with them as dependants, compared with just under 2 per cent of the male couples.[85]

Canadian Projections

There are two sources of information on the numbers of children with same-sex parents in Canada: some small local surveys of lesbian and gay communities, and the data in the Department of Justice litigation database on same-sex couples. Alan Cornwall, one of my students at the University of Windsor, carried out a small survey of lesbians and gays in Windsor and Detroit in 1986. He found that 19 per cent of the lesbian women in his sample lived alone, another 19 per cent lived as single parents with their children, and 62 per cent were cohabiting with their partner. Of the partnered lesbian mothers, 40 per cent (or 25 per cent of the entire sample) were raising their children with their partner. He did not report on the total number of children, but it is useful to know that 25 per cent of the lesbian women in the sample were raising children together. He found that none of the gay men in the sample had custody of their children, but that 14 per cent were providing support for their children.[86]

Later localized surveys report similar figures. In his survey of 420 lesbians and gays in the Vancouver area, Stephen Samis found that 17.2 per cent of lesbians had children, and 12.3 per cent had custody of those children. Eleven per cent of the gay men in the sample had

Table 6.1. Same-Sex Couples with and without Children, by Household Income, 1994

Total house-hold income	With children	Without children
Under $10,000	–	1,100
$10,000–$20,000	–	5,200
$20,000–$30,000	300	13,000
$30,000–$40,000	900	15,900
$40,000–$50,000	1,100	18,100
$50,000–$750,000	2,200	42,000
Over $75,000	300	34,600
Total households	4,800	129,900
Average household income	$54,950	$60,880
Percentage of all couples	3.6	96.4

SOURCE: Derived from Affidavit of Albert Wakkary, filed in *Rosenberg* v *The Queen* (Ont. Gen. Div., Court File No. 79885/94) (sworn June 2, 1994), Exhibit B, Table 2.

children, and 2 per cent had custody.[87] Carolyn Smith surveyed 294 lesbians, gays, and bisexuals in Nova Scotia in 1993, and found that 18 per cent of lesbian women, 13 per cent of bisexual women, 7.6 per cent of gay men, and 21.4 per cent of bisexual men were parents. Of those parents, 77.8 per cent of the lesbian women had custody of their children, and 8.8 per cent of the lesbians identified themselves as co-parents. None of the bisexual women, gay men, or bisexual men had custody of their children, but 6.7 per cent of gay men and 7.1 per cent of bisexual men identified themselves as co-parents.[88] Neither of these studies counted the actual number of children being raised by same-sex parents, but these figures suggest that significant numbers of children are being raised both by single queer parents and by same-sex couples.

The Wakkary affidavit in *Rosenberg* provided data that purported to relate to same-sex couples with and without children in various income classes (see table 6.1), although the data are not broken down by sex of the parents or total numbers of children in these modelled queer households. If each of these couples had an average of two children, then the number of children with same-sex parents in Canada in 1994 would have been 9,600, which seems very low.

At the other extreme, Rachel Epstein has estimated that there are approximately 250,000 lesbian parents in Canada, on the basis that 10 per cent of women in Canada are lesbian, and 15 to 20 per cent of all lesbian women are mothers.[89] Using the Blumstein and Schwartz figures to project the number of children per parent, these projected 250,000 mothers might have as many as 345,000 to 447,500 children.

Conclusions

In the end, the real point of this review of the data is that official census policies treat lesbian, gay, bisexual, transgendered, and transsexual people exactly the same way the law treats them – as if they did not exist. The invisibility concretized in the social science research literature is merely the statistical version of the denial of legal personality. Thus the most important and pressing policy objective to take from this review of the literature is that it is urgent for Canada to include detailed and valid questions on sexuality, on sex identity, on relationships, and on parenting in all its general demographic instruments. Especially now that the Department of Justice and the Department of Finance are working in tandem, as in the *Rosenberg* case, to generate litigation data from information not available to others, it has become urgent to develop effective research instruments. Certainly the literature does at least shed a great deal of light on what effective research instruments would look like.

From the perspective of legal and economic policy, however, two other conclusions can be drawn from the research literature, even in its current state. The first conclusion is that legal and economic policy has a huge impact on the extent to which people move from desire to behaviour, and from behaviour to self-identification as lesbian, gay, bisexual, transsexual, or transgender. There may be methodological barriers to counting each and every 'actual' queer in Canada, but the simple step of including sexuality in census forms would, over time, encourage sexual minorities to reveal themselves in their responses. The second conclusion is that it may well be impossible to get an exact and accurate count of all queers in Canada, so long as significant numbers of people do not wish to disclose their sexualities. But that should not matter. Those who are not willing to disclose their identity are less likely to live so openly that they would seek or even wish to have same-sex or family responsibilities or rights of any kind. Openness tends to correlate with a demand for recognition of relationships, whether they be relationships with partners or with children.[90]

People who are so far from acting on desire that they refrain from same-sex behaviour, and people who may experience same-sex desire or attraction but who live, relate, or even marry heterosexually will certainly bear heavy psychic costs as the result of the discrimination that keeps them so far from actualizing their desires. But it is not these people who will bear the full social, legal, or economic costs of official and *de facto* discrimination on the basis of sexuality. Indeed, they will be among the recipients of the innumerable benefits that are now restricted only to those who function as heterosexuals.

I am not suggesting that numbers or data matter more than people, that discrimination is worse if it can be quantified, or that numbers are necessarily the best basis for making decisions about social or legal policy. But I do conclude that people who are ignored in basic census and survey data can be ignored elsewhere as well. If lesbian, gay, bisexual, transgendered, and transsexual people are to be recognized as 'persons' in law, then they will also have to count and be counted for purposes of social and economic policy.

Chapter Seven

The High Costs of Being Queer

> For the category of sex is a totalitarian one ... It grips our minds in such a way that we cannot think outside of it.
> Monique Wittig, 'The Category of Sex,' in *The Straight Mind and Other Essays* (London: Harvester Wheatsheaf, 1992), 8

Categories of 'sex' construct the 'hetero-'sex around which the 'heterosexual economy' is organized. Based on the discursive use of 'women' as units of value, and thus of exchange,[1] the 'heterosexual economy' hierarchically commodifies and appropriates the sexual, productive, and reproductive labour of women as a sex class.[2]

One of the most important dimensions of the 'heterosexual economy' is the tendency to restrict the creation and exchange of value to heterosexual relations, and, conversely, the deployment of the category 'sex' to deny the creation and exchange of value in 'homo'-sex relations. Thus the heterosexual economy simultaneously appropriates women's productive capacities and erases/impoverishes the 'homosexual economy.'[3]

On a functional level, the operation of these two economies of sex imposes heavy costs on human beings on the basis of sex. For people legally described as 'women,'[4] the first and heaviest cost is the appropriation of women's productive capacities, resulting most notoriously in the dual labour economy in which women's incomes are but a small fraction of men's.[5] The second cost is the 'heterosexuals only' social and legal structures that restrict the circulation of value created through heterosexual relations to heterosexuals, and, effectively, to the men who hold and control that value. By denying sex/ual minorities access to the heterosexual economy, value is denied to sexual minorities on every level of existence, impoverishing the 'homosexual economy' to the benefit of the heterosexual economy in much the same way that value is shifted from women to men in the heterosexual economy.

The result of this dynamic – the appropriation of value both from women and from sexual minorities in hierarchies of sex and sexuality – imposes large costs on queers at the same time that it confers vast benefits on 'straights.' The legal category that makes these economies of sexuality possible is 'legal personality,' for that is the conceptual foundation on which queers are systematically excluded from structures of heterosexual hierarchy and appropriation. First-order denial of legal personality translates throughout legal and social structures into the everyday 'discrimination,' 'bias,' 'erasure,' and 'disadvantage' that form the mechanism by which those costs are imposed on queers.

The 'heterosexual economy' is huge and encompasses literally every social and legal structure that touches on relationships. In this chapter and in chapter 8, I have collected qualitative and quantitative measures of the costs of being queer in the heterosexual economy of Canada. I have roughly divided the discussion into the role of the state benefit system (chapter 8) and the role of the state as an organizer/regulator of so-called private relations (this chapter). In chapter 9, I discuss a particular set of state-benefit provisions that are said to 'beneficially' exclude queers, that are said to make it worthwhile for same-sex couples to remain invisible.

My argument here is not simply that lesbian, gay, bisexual, transgendered, or transsexual people should necessarily seek, accept, or even tolerate full admission to the heterosexual economy. For one thing, the impossibility in the dominant order of thinking outside the category 'sex' would presuppose hierarchical appropriative relations where there are none, or make incomprehensible to 'the straight mind' relationships that are not hierarchical or appropriative. For another, dismantling the sexual divisions between the two economies would not necessarily dismantle the underpinnings of the heterosexual economy – hierarchical appropriations of women's capacities – although it would certainly subvert it through mimesis.[6]

My goal here is more modest. I seek merely to give voice to the ways that being forced to think outside the category 'sex' and outside the 'heterosexual economy' burdens queer existence. While I do at some points touch on why queer existence is nonetheless still so empowering, so life-giving, so worth it, that is not my primary purpose here. Instead, my intent is to identify the material implications of denying full legal personality to adults purely on the basis of their sexuality, thereby enriching the 'heterosexual economy' and impoverishing the 'queer economy.'

Unquantifiable Costs of Discrimination

Pervasive denial of the legal personality of queers not only imposes tangible material burdens on queers, but shapes the sense of self, shapes visions of the future, and builds invisible psychic boundaries that sometimes are not even tested by some people. Looking back at my first lesbian relationship, I can now see how it bore the weight of our coming to consciousness of the social and legal consequences of living outside hetero society. We both tried to laugh off the pain of that realization. But in the end, despite trying out several different strategies to get where we felt we wanted to go, what was left was the pain of knowing that our relationship could exist only in the shadows of society. As I became a lawyer, began teaching law, and carried on with my life, I thought that I had forgotten that pain, had put that part of my life behind me. It was not until I saw the headline in the *Globe and Mail* announcing that 'a lesbian mother' had won her child-custody appeal that I realized that I had not gotten past the pain of living with the knowledge that, as a lesbian woman, I was not expected to be able to have a family – I had really only buried it. Even before I read the reasons in *Bezaire* v *Bezaire*,[7] the simple fact that a newspaper had published a headline that read 'Lesbian Mother Is Awarded Custody of Her Two Children'[8] changed how I felt about myself and my life options. It changed the quality of my life. It changed who I could be as a person. It changed the entire rest of my life.[9] It changed what my life could become, merely by articulating that, in Ontario, being lesbian did not *per se* disqualify me from having custody of my children, should I ever become part of a family.[10]

Recognition of how discrimination erases whole paths into the future pervasively affects one's sense of who one is, of what life can be. I have found it painfully ironic that North American culture has recently come to see how deeply the non-recognition of relationships as depicted in, for example, *The Scarlet Letter*, violates human dignity, human integrity. In theatres across the continent, on home televisions, even in the Supreme Court of Canada, the image of hidden, forbidden relationships has evoked widespread sympathy at the same time that it has fuelled dramatic changes in constitutional and family law.[11] *The Well of Loneliness*[12] has never received this kind of attention, nor has a majority of the Supreme Court of Canada ever exhibited this degree of deeply felt sympathy for non-recognition of same-sex relationships. Thus I felt hurt and angry at the inconsistent decisions in *Miron* v *Trudel* and *Egan and Nesbit* v *The Queen*.[13] But it was not until the Hawaii trial court released its decision in *Baehr* v *Miike*[14] on 3 December 1996 that another door in my heart opened. (The court ruled that the State of Hawaii had given no justifiable reason for denying marriage licences to lesbian and gay couples.) Having concluded that, for lesbian and gay couples, attaining legal recognition as non-married cohabitants would be 'good enough,' I thought I had ruled out the serious possibility of plain, old-fashioned marriage for same-sex couples. Thus I was caught by surprise when I reacted to the news of this decision much as I had responded to news of the decision in *Bezaire* v *Bezaire* – I suddenly realized that I could, for the first time in my life, begin to think about someday having the choice of whether to marry my life partner. Quite apart from whether I might ever be legally permitted to marry in Ontario, completely aside from whether I would ever want to marry, simply being able to think about even the possibility of marriage somewhere in the world has again profoundly changed how I think about my life.

Because I have now gone through the emotional process of realizing how much of myself I have had to shut down in order to function as a lesbian woman in Canadian society, I know that other doors must still lock important parts of my heart. And now that I am a member of a family, I know that important parts of my children's hearts are under lock and key as well. They know, as do I, that many areas of concrete discrimination and social disapproval still affect all of us. They know, as do I, that our entire family is still legally incapacitated in many ways that would never even occur to other people.

It is impossible to quantify these effects of discrimination. Indeed, it is only now becoming possible to say that they exist, to describe them qualitatively. But the language of law is still inadequate to describe this effect fully. Some justices of the Supreme Court of Canada have made a genuine effort to construct an equality jurisprudence that can adequately apprehend 'fundamental attributes ... essential to our popular conception of "personhood" or "humanness".' Justice L'Heureux-Dubé has warned that non-recognition of same-sex relationships gives the 'meta-message' that such relationships are 'less worthy of respect, concern and consideration,'[15] Justice Cory has spoken of how forcing 'homosexual common-law couples' to function as individuals 'imprisons them in their choices,'[16] while Justice McLachlin has concluded that 'discrimination on the basis of marital status touches the essential dignity and worth of the individual.'[17] These expressions of understanding give me hope that someday the gap between the outcomes in the *Miron* v *Trudel* and *Egan and Nesbit* cases can be bridged. But even these expressions of understanding do not begin to apprehend all the costs that are imposed on sexual minorities in the heterosexual economy.

I discuss some of these unquantifiable costs of being queer under three general headings: effects on health and security; burdens on family functioning; and constraints in living with crisis situations, old age, and death.

Health and Security

Economic, emotional, social, legal, and spiritual factors all affect the health of human beings. In day-to-day functioning, people who have open and unrestricted access to health care, hospitalization benefits, drug plans, dental plans, and so on, will generally enjoy better health than those who do not. When one or more members of a family are denied health services because of their or their parents' sex or sexual orientation, discrimination on the basis of sexuality will certainly have a negative effect on their health. Same-sex partners and children who do not have relationship status are not assured of hospital visitation rights,[18] nor do they automatically qualify for damages or benefits under criminal injury-compensation schemes or worker-compensation legislation.[19]

The exclusion of same-sex relationships from the 'heterosexual economy' undermines the stability of queer couples and families in many ways. Everything from denial of full parental status in relation to children born or adopted within same-sex relationships[20] to the rights of family members to change their names or sponsor members for immigration purposes affects family stability.[21] Children who have access to all the resources of all their parents experience more stability and security, and tend to do better when both adults are able to share in the responsibilities of child-rearing.[22] Recognition of family structure gives the family an in-built stability during tough times,[23] while the right to petition family courts for dissolution of relationships, spousal support, child custody, child support, and support enforcement sets up 'rules' that give even the post-breakdown family unit greater stability and helps insulate it from protracted litigation.[24] Although British Columbia has now enacted same-sex support and child-support rules, and the decisions in *M.* v *H.* have created the possibility of same-sex support for former partners in Ontario, those are just two of the myriad provisions that help create family security.

Lesbian, gay, bisexual, transgendered, and transsexual people are almost by definition socially insecure. Living with open hatred and intolerance promotes insecurity.[25] When open and widespread hatred gives way to hate-motivated violence,[26] the refusal of some families to tolerate or even support their queer members, and fear on the part of openly queer people to involve themselves with adolescents and young adults as role models, social insecurity gives way to constant danger. The lack of social security is especially acute for younger people. Youths who are ostracized from their families receive inadequate emotional and social support, and completely lose their families as 'social safety nets.'[27] This leaves them to the streets, vulnerable to involvement in the sex trades, use of drugs, and unhealthy relationship patterns.[28] Thus it is no surprise that the suicide rates among lesbian and gay teenagers and young adults is the highest in Canada, a vivid demonstration that they have no sense of social security at all.[29]

Even when loss of family support, physical safety, or continued ability to survive is not the issue, queer lives are fraught with further insecurities. Sexual minorities live with constant awareness of disclosure issues that affect not only themselves, but their relationships and children. Many situations in which 'outing' is an issue have important legal consequences, such as the relatively simple act of naming a witness to an automobile accident or an assault, if the witness happens to be a someone who has not disclosed his or her sexuality.[30] There is the further insecurity of knowing that there literally are no words in the English language to describe a life partner with the same seriousness as one would describe a spouse or cohabitant: 'For gays, there is no counterpart to words like "boyfriend," "husband," or "fiance" that heterosexuals use to describe their partners. The connotations are different. Vague terms only momentarily delay identification of the friend's gender and understate the depth of the relationship.' Instead, sexual minorities are locked into the same social space approximately labelled as 'going steady,'[31] and attempts to formulate terms that do realistically describe intimate relationships like 'lover' seem to be extremely irritating to some heterosexuals.[32]

Relationship Functioning

The combined effects of discrimination on family stability and social security can be, to a certain extent, moderated by careful planning and documentation. Cohabitation agreements, parenting contracts, wills, trusts, powers of attorney, and various consent forms can be drafted to protect relationships, children, and interests in property. But the fact that sexual minorities cannot simply marry when they choose to, or at least obtain limited legal recognition for long-term cohabitation, means that these expensive legal documents are not just an option – they are a necessity for those who take their relationship and family responsibilities seriously. Thus the costs of these solutions to everyday problems become part of the costs of living outside the 'heterosexual economy.'[33] La Croix and Badgett have estimated that the one-time costs of the entire documentation package are, in the United States, $6,800 per couple.[34]

These solutions are, of course, class-sensitive. Lower-income queers have less access to the kinds of legal services needed to formulate these types of documents. They also have less access to the best legal representation in other contexts as well.[35] The cumulative effects of lack of information or knowledge on how to safeguard or pursue rights are, in turn, even higher costs.[36] Thus it is not surprising that even though the numbers of human rights complaints relating to sexuality have increased in the last ten years, those numbers remain quite low. This reflects the hopelessness that many lesbians, gays, bisexuals, and trans people feel when told that they should seek legal recognition of their rights.[37]

Crisis, Age, and Death

The effects of discrimination become acute in crisis situations and as life ends. Although some provincial legislation will at least get same-sex partners in the door of the hospital, if there is a conflict between a partner and another member of the family of the ill person, substitute-decision-maker legislation no longer gives clear-cut primacy to powers of attorney or consent-to-treatment certificates executed in favour of a life partner. Hostile families of origin can disrupt treatment plans, emergency measures, and countless other contexts in a crisis merely by asserting their primary right to make decisions for someone who is ill or injured.[38] Nor do life partners or children have obvious rights in relation to a wide range of compensation or survivor schemes.

Whether the context is a crisis, illness, old age, or death, same-sex couples can be separated at the very times when they need each other the most. Numerous provincial statutes guarantee elderly residents of nursing homes, charitable institutions, and retirement homes full rights to privacy with their spouses or former cohabitants, and even the right to share a room if they are in the same facility. But same-sex couples are carefully excluded from all these provisions, leaving same-sex couples with the knowledge that, at the end of their lives, they have no guarantee of intimate privacy.[39] Upon the death of a life partner, same-sex partners do not have clear-cut rights to claim their partner's body; to make decisions about donor tissue;[40] to demand an inquest into cause of death or obtain access to information on post-mortem findings if there is no inquest;[41] to make funeral arrangements or arrangements for interment or cremation; to obtain their partner's vital statistics, service record, or death certificate; or to receive notice of proceedings in probate.[42]

Same-sex partners can protect their partner's and children's interests with trusts or wills, but they cannot extend any of the more ordinary statutory projections to them. Surviving partners have no rights under intestacy legislation,[43] nor under family law legislation, nor rights to assume the office of personal administrator. Even if a surviving partner were to be named personal administrator on intestacy, he or she could be removed by a court in favour of a relative of the deceased; the surviving partner would not qualify for exemption from the requirement to post a bond, an exemption which is automatically extended to all spouses or surviving cohabitants,[44] nor would he or she, nor all of the children, necessarily qualify as deemed beneficiaries under insurance policies[45] or as family members who are entitled to select and retain chattels exempt from seizure on execution by judgment creditors of the deceased partner.[46]

To be fair, courts are aware of some of these unquantifiable effects of discrimination. For example, Justice Cory in *Egan and Nesbit* drew attention to the cumulative effects of public harassment, verbal abuse, crimes of violence, employment discrimination, denial of access to services, exclusion from some aspects of public life, closetry forced by stigmatization, criminalization of sexuality, psychiatrization of sexuality, and non-recognition of relationships, and connected them with the high rates of youth suicide in queer communities.[47] However, Justice Cory himself remains in the minority when it comes to judicial understanding of how devastating these forms of discrimination can be.

Employment Discrimination

One of the key ways in which the heterosexual economy maintains the dual appropriation of wealth through sex hierarchies and 'heterosexuals only' social/legal/economic structures is through employment discrimination. A critical element of legal personality, the right to work is played out in attitudes towards employment discrimination, in the ways in which sexual minorities attempt to cope with employment discrimination, and in the effects of employment discrimination on queer incomes.

Attitudes and Discrimination

Surveys of public opinion generally, and of lesbian and gay communities in particular, demonstrate that discrimination in employment takes many forms. On the general social level, queers have to live with the knowledge that there is by no means widespread support for their right to work. Between 20 and 25 per cent of the U.S. population appears to believe that employment discrimination against lesbians and gays should be legal,[48] and 59 per cent believe that they should not be permitted to teach school.[49] Social prejudice obviously has to affect the employment climate. Extending Becker's theory of discrimination to sexual orientation, Klawitter and Flatt have hypothesized that lesbians and gays 'might be denied jobs, fired, or segregated into lower-paying positions because employers dislike homosexuals, or because employers want to avoid dissatisfaction among workers or customers.'[50] Indeed, several studies have found that the levels of employment discrimination reported by lesbians and gays – between 16 and 46 per cent – are consistent with the levels of discrimination reflected in attitudinal studies.[51] In other words, people in the United States who believe that lesbians and gays should not have the right to work appear to be putting their beliefs into action.

These results are also consistent with direct studies of employer attitudes. Badgett reports that a survey of 191 employers revealed a high level of intent to discriminate: 27 per cent of employers said that they would not hire homosexuals, 18 per cent said that they would fire them, and 26 per cent said they would not promote them.[52] While Canadian attitudinal studies have not focused so specifically on employer attitudes, they have documented the existence of significant levels of prejudice in Canada.[53]

Coping with Discrimination

Not surprisingly, many sexual minorities choose to stay as far in the closet as necessary (or, in some cases, as possible) in order to minimize or avoid employment discrimination. Between 10 and 20 per cent of the lesbians and gays who were open enough about their sexuality to respond to a survey on the subject reported that they remain completely in the closet in their work lives. Only 20 to 30 per cent were out to everyone in the workplace.[54] Another survey found that 11 per cent of respondents were completely closeted in all aspects of their lives, and that some 26 per cent of respondents had not disclosed their sexuality to their physicians even when they were open with other people.[55] Pressure to remain in the closet thus has to be counted as one of the most damaging effects of widespread employment discrimination.

It is not easy to remain invisible in the workplace. Homophobic attitudes not only force people to remain silent about their sexuality, but also put them under pressure to adhere as fully as possible to traditional sexual stereotypes. For women, this means trying to avoid or counter suspicions of lesbianism by adopting the standards of female appearance that correlate with success in the workplace.[56] Men experience similar pressures. These pressures have to be seen as differentially affecting lesbian women, who also experience greater barriers to workforce participation simply on the basis of their sex in the first place, and, as demonstrated below, earn far less than men across all age and employment categories because of their sex.

Some studies have found that, perhaps to compensate for anticipated discrimination, lesbians and gays have higher levels of education than others holding similar positions.[57] Lesbians and gays are also less likely to be employed in a family business or to own their own business, which suggests that family attitudes and customer attitudes also play an important role in shaping the way in which lesbians and gays plan their work lives. Schneider has found a correlation between degree of outness and income levels: lesbians with higher incomes were less likely than those with lower incomes to disclose their sexuality.[58] This suggests that there is a clear trade-off between income and openness. Higher incomes can be earned at the price of remaining invisible as a lesbian, while the price of openness in the workplace is choosing or staying in lower-paying jobs.

Discrimination and Income

Social prejudice has created barriers to the measurement of lesbian and gay earnings and incomes. As discussed in chapter 6, statistical analysis of any aspect of lesbian or gay life must begin with the collection of representative and reliable data. But until Census Canada and the Survey of Consumer Finances begin to include questions on sexuality in their statistical instruments, it will be impossible to carry out the kinds of research that are needed in this area. Once reliable data exist, and researchers can develop representative samples randomly chosen from the population of the country as a whole, it will be possible to overcome the limitations of univariate studies and conduct multivariate analysis of incomes that control for sexuality, education, age, and other important determinants of earning capacity.

Thus the literature on incomes and sexuality can be divided into two categories: Studies that are based on data collected only from queer respondents (univariate studies), and studies that collect data on a wide-enough range of independent variables such as education, occupation, race, location, marital status, and experience to make it possible to control for sexuality and sex in the analysis (multivariate studies). There are quite a few univariate studies, and only a few multivariate studies. Understanding the differences between these types of studies makes it possible to use them critically.

Univariate Surveys

Selective univariate surveys of exclusively lesbian or gay respondents can provide data that are very useful, for example, to advertisers who wish to gauge the income levels of those who read specific magazines or newspapers. However, univariate surveys of lesbians or gays do not form a valid basis for comparing lesbian or gay incomes with heterosexual incomes, for example, if heterosexual people with similar levels of education and so on are not included in the sample too.

Uncritical use of univariate surveys can lead to inaccurate conclusions about sexual minorities. For example, on the basis of univariate income surveys, Justice Scalia concluded in a United States Supreme Court case that gay men have higher average incomes, and thus higher 'disposable' incomes, than the average male.[59] Lee Badgett has demonstrated how uncontrolled sampling can seriously distort findings on national incomes by sexuality. Table 7.1 compares univariate survey data on incomes reported by lesbian, gay, and bisexual people with data on all national incomes. The results of the univariate surveys have deviated by as much as 34 percentage points in some studies.

As Badgett has explained, even the least biased of these surveys, the *Examiner* survey, which used random dialling to obtain interviews with self-identified lesbians, gays, and bisexuals, did not collect any data on comparable heterosexual men or women. Data like these may help businesses that might want to cultivate lesbian or gay clientele assess the income levels of queers who live in a particular geographic area and have telephones, but it does not shed any light on how lesbian or gay incomes

Table 7.1. Survey Data on Lesbian, Gay, and Bisexual Incomes and National Incomes

Survey	Year	Gender	LGB income	National income	LGB/NI
OUT/LOOK	1988	Men	$25,000–$29,000	$27,343	99%
		Women	$20,000–$24,000	$18,823	117%
Simmons	1988	Both	$36,900		N/A
San Fran. Examiner	1989	Men	$29,129	$28,605	102%
		Women	$26,331	$19,643	134%

SOURCE: M.V. Lee Badgett, 'The Wage Effects of Sexual Orientation Discrimination' (1995), 48 *Industrial and Labor Relations Review* 4: 726, 729.

compare with incomes of non-queer people. The other two studies were even more biased because they used newspaper inserts and magazine surveys to collect their data, thereby excluding from the potential sample anyone who did not read that newspaper or magazine.[60]

Multivariate Analysis of Random Samples

Several recent studies have attempted to generate more valid profiles of queer earnings and incomes by using multivariate analysis of random samples. Because the 'spiral of fear' affects self-disclosure of sexuality in any survey, the numbers of queer people in these samples are not necessarily representative of the population as a whole. However, these studies do have the great advantage of making it possible for researchers to control for sexuality, sex, education levels, experience, and other factors that have been shown to affect earnings.

These multivariate studies reach conclusions that completely contradict the results of the univariate studies: Lesbians and gays are overrepresented in low-income classes, and, when compared with heterosexual people with similar levels of education and experience, lesbians, gays, and bisexuals have significantly lower incomes. (None of these studies touched on transgendered or transsexual people's incomes.) Even within the category of multivariate studies, however, methodology can affect findings.

Philip Blumstein and Pepper Schwartz conducted an early couples survey that found correlations between low incomes and sexuality. Surveying some 6,000 married, cohabiting, and lesbian/gay couples, they found that married men were overrepresented in the high-income brack-

Table 7.2. Annual Incomes by Sexuality, Marital Status

Incomes	Husbands	Wives	Cohab. men	Cohab. women	Gay	Lesbian
Under $5,000	4%	47%	13%	22%	10%	17%
$5,000–$9,999	6	17	15	26	18	25
$10,000–$14,999	15	18	21	26	27	27
$15,000–$24,999	35	13	28	21	28	23
$25,000–$49,999	31	4	18	4	14	7
$50,000 and up	9	1	5	1	3	1
Number of people	3,608	3,577	644	651	1,909	1,550
Percentage	30.2	30	5.4	5.5	16	13

SOURCE: Philip Blumstein and Pepper Schwartz, *American Couples: Money, Work, Sex* (New York: William Morrow 1983), Table 9, 598.

ets, while gay men and lesbian women were overrepresented in low-income brackets and underrepresented in high-income brackets (see table 7.2).[61]

These figures reveal that income is allocated hierarchically by sex, marital status, and sexuality. More men in the sample have high incomes than any women in the sample, and more women have low incomes than any men in the sample. They also contradict the popular perception that, because gay couples have access to two 'male' wages, they will have the highest incomes of all couples. Blumstein and Schwartz found that all the heterosexual men – whether married or cohabiting – had fewer low incomes and more high incomes than did gay men. With the exception of the lowest income bracket, gay men had more of the lowest incomes, and fewer of the middle and highest incomes. The same percentage of cohabiting and gay men fall into the middle bracket (incomes of $15,000 to $24,999), but the pattern immediately above and immediately below this turning point strongly reveals the sexuality hierarchy. Married men definitely received significantly higher incomes than cohabiting men, and cohabiting heterosexual men in turn had much higher incomes than gay men.

Although table 7.2 reveals an income hierarchy among women as well, there are some significant differences. Dependency on a male income appeared to play an important role in the allocation of low and high incomes among women. Equally small percentages of women in each category had the highest incomes, but more lesbian women fell into the highest income brackets, while more heterosexual women fell into the

Table 7.3. Incomes by Sexual Behaviour, 1989–1991

	Lesbian/ Bisexual	Hetero. Women	Gay/ Bisexual	Hetero. men
Annual earnings	$15,056	$18,341	$26,321	$28,312
0–$9,999	29.4%	21.2%	10.6%	8.8%
$10,000–$19,999	35.3	36.2	29.8	22.5
$20,000–$29,999	29.4	25.8	21.3	26.2
$30,000–$39,999	5.9	12.0	17.0	19.4
$40,000–$49,999	0.0	4.7	21.3	23.1

SOURCE: M.V. Lee Badgett, 'The Wage Effects of Sexual Orientation Discrimination' (1995), 48 *Industrial and Labor Relations Review* 4: 726, 734.

lowest income brackets. At the lowest income levels, married and cohabiting women vied for overrepresentation, although the state-supported dependency of married women would appear to account for the very large percentage of married women who reported incomes of less than $5,000. Some 47 per cent of married women fell into this income category.

Blumstein and Schwartz recorded raw data in this table, and did not weight the sample for relative education levels or other factors that have been demonstrated to affect income levels. Since lesbian women clearly had higher average levels of income than any other category in this study, such a weighting could be expected to affect the allocation of income levels.[62] When Lee Badgett used a multivariate regression analysis of the effect of sexual activity on incomes, she weighted factors other than sexuality in order to more accurately measure the impact sexuality might have on income levels as measured by the General Social Survey.[63] Although the survey collected information on sexual activity rather than sexual identity and used income brackets instead of specific income figures, Badgett was able to get a more precise picture of how sexuality affects income hierarchies. She found that heterosexual men had the highest incomes, followed by gay/bisexual men, heterosexual women, and lesbian/bisexual women, in that order. As table 7.3 indicates, this hierarchy is reflected across the four income classes Badgett used: No lesbian/bisexual women and only 4.7 per cent of the heterosexual women in the sample earned $40,000 or more, while only 8.8 per cent of the heterosexual men earned incomes of $9,999 or less as compared with 29.4 per cent of lesbian/bisexual women.

When Badgett included controls for other factors influencing income, she found that being behaviourally lesbian, gay, or bisexual reduced income, but that the difference was statistically significant only for men. She concluded that the income penalty for gay or bisexual men could be as much as 24.4 per cent, and increased to as much as 26.7 per cent when occupation variables were included.[64]

It is in Badgett's findings relating to lesbian/bisexual women that the intersection of the heterosexual and homosexual economies becomes most visible. Badgett found that lesbian/bisexual women earned only 57.2 per cent of the average gay/bisexual man's income, compared with a ratio of 64.8 per cent for heterosexual women and men. This means that lesbian/bisexual women appear to be even more disadvantaged by their sexuality relative to men of the same sexuality than are heterosexual women. But, when Badgett included occupation and other variables, she found that they were not statistically significant for lesbians and bisexual women. This meant that it was not sexuality *per se* that predicted lesbian women's low incomes, but some other factor. Badgett speculated that this might be due to several factors – sexual behaviour might not be as good a proxy for sexual identity for lesbians as for gay men; gender might be more important in determining income for lesbian and bisexual women than is sexual identity; gay/bisexual men might face greater discrimination than lesbian/bisexual women; lesbian/bisexual women may not fear sexual-orientation discrimination as much as gay men do because women already face sex discrimination in the workplace; double jeopardy might encourage lesbian women to work harder to offset the effects of discrimination; the lesbian/bisexual women sample might be too small; or, the model did not adequately control for unobservable differences between lesbian and heterosexual women in regard to experience or workforce attachment.[65]

Although the data that Badgett used do leave some questions unanswered, and although some of the results cannot be fully explained without further research, Badgett's multivariate analysis has demonstrated that behaviourally gay/bisexual men earn from 11 to 27 per cent less than behaviourally heterosexual men, and that behaviourally lesbian/bisexual women earn between 12 and 30 per cent less than behaviourally heterosexual women. However, as predicted by the theory that women are disadvantaged first and most dramatically by institutions of heterosexuality and then, secondarily, by the devalued status of the 'homosexual economy,' these data demonstrate that, if lesbian women became 'straight' and gay men became 'straight,' now-straight lesbian women would still have the lowest incomes of any group, while now-straight gay men would have the same high incomes as heterosexual men.

Table 7.4. Individual and Household Incomes by Sexuality, 1990

	Lesbian couples	Gay couples	Cohabit. hetero.	Married hetero.
Household income	$45,166	$58,366	$37,505	$47,193
Individual men	–	$23,037	$18,445	$24,949
Individual women	$17,497	–	$11,857	$9,308

SOURCE: Marieka M. Klawitter and Victor Flatt, *Antidiscrimination Policies and Earnings for Same-Sex Couples* (Working Papers in Public Policy Analysis and Management) Seattle: University of Washington Graduate School of Public Affairs, 1995), Table 2.

Beginning in 1990, the U.S. Census added 'unmarried partner' to the list of categories under 'householder relationships.' This enabled the householder (the owner or lessee of the residence polled) to identify an unmarried partner. Because the sex of the unmarried partner could also be recorded, researchers have been able to construct samples of same-sex couples out of this data.[66] When Marieka M. Klawitter and Victor Flatt used the 1990 census data to analyse the income levels and race/gender composition of same-sex couples, they confirmed Badgett's findings (see table 7.4).[67]

Although Klawitter and Flatt were primarily concerned with the effects of anti-discrimination laws on the wage gap associated with sexuality, these data also offer further information on how sexuality, relationship status, and sex affect income levels, because Klawitter and Flatt were able to develop data on cohabiting heterosexual couples, a group that was omitted from Badgett's study.[68] They concluded that, after controlling for other regression factors, household incomes were highest for married couples and male same-sex couples, followed by unmarried different-sex couples, and lowest for female same-sex couples.[69] I have calculated the predicted earnings for each type of couple at the household and individual levels in my table 7.5, using the regression results obtained by Klawitter and Flatt.[70] These results reveal that, in contrast with the raw data summarized in table 7.4, cohabiting heterosexual earnings at the household level were higher than those of both lesbian and gay couples at the household level.

When the results of the Blumstein and Schwartz, Badgett, and Klawitter–Flatt studies are read together, not only do the data confirm the existence of measurable income hierarchies among lesbian, cohabiting heterosexual, and married heterosexual women, but it also becomes clear that the

Table 7.5. Predicted Earnings Differences for Couple Type, 1990

	Lesbian same-sex	Gay same-sex	Cohabit. hetero.	Married hetero.
Household income	$37,754	$45,777	$41,530	$46,721
Individual men	–	$18,462	$18,213	$24,450
Individual women	$15,823	–	$10,611	$9,866

SOURCE: Calculated from data Klawitter and Flatt, *Antidiscrimination Policies and Earnings for Same-Sex Couples*, Tables 2 and 4, using 'private employment' lines.

further women are removed from formal marital relations, the higher their incomes. There are many possible explanations for this result, but the hypothesis that rings truest is that the more certain women are that they will never have access to any of the myriad benefits allocated to heterosexuals by the heterosexual economy, the more they tend to optimize earnings however they can.[71] Even at their most optimal, the highest women's incomes (lesbian women's) are but 86.9 per cent of the lowest men's incomes (those of cohabiting men). Comparing women and men in the same types of relationships, the ratios are all lower: Lesbian women's earnings are only 85.7 per cent of gay men's; cohabiting women's earnings are but 58.3 per cent of cohabiting men's; married women's earnings are only 40.4 per cent of married men's. The strong effects of sex on earnings levels confirms that, for lesbian women, the heterosexual economy is still probably a stronger determinant of women's low earnings than is sexuality.

These income hierarchies persist even when income data are adjusted for education. Using data collected by Voter Research and Surveys in 1992, Kenneth Sherril found that, in the unweighted sample, lesbians, gays, and bisexuals together were overrepresented in low income categories when compared with heterosexual men and women. Only 14.2 per cent of heterosexual respondents had incomes below $15,000, while 20.8 per cent of lesbian, gay, and bisexual respondents had incomes below $15,000. However, queers were underrepresented in the high income categories, with only 7.5 per cent of lesbian, gay, and bisexual respondents reporting incomes over $75,000, while 12.5 per cent of heterosexual respondents had incomes over $75,000. The same imbalances were apparent in other income categories, with the most evident equality in the $30,000–$49,999 income range (28.6 per cent queer versus 29.9 per cent heterosexual). These unweighted data did not adjust for any labour-market factors such as education, experience, and sex.

Table 7.6. Family Income by Sexual Orientation and Education, 1991

Family income	Lesbian/ gay/bi	Hetero- sexual	Ratio
0–$15,000	9.9%	6.1%	63%
$15,000–$29,999	27.0	16.4	65
$30,000–$49,999	27.9	29.2	(4)
$50,000–$74,999	21.6	26.1	(17)
$75,000 and up	13.5	22.3	(39)

SOURCE: Derived from data generated by Voter Research and Surveys exit poll, Election Day, 1992, and analysed in Sherrill, 'Testimony,' para. 67, 68.
Note: '()' indicates that the percentage of lesbian/gay/bisexual respondents in income class is less than the percentage of heterosexual respondents by the figure in the parentheses.

When Sherrill noted that the lesbian, gay, and bisexual respondents had higher levels of education than the heterosexual respondents (43.4 per cent of the lesbians, gays, and bisexuals had college degrees of some sort, compared with 38.4 per cent of the heterosexual respondents), he weighted the sample for education to control for equivalent levels of education. The results of this weighting, in table 7.6, reveal that, even when the data are controlled for education, sexuality will affect income changes for people with the same levels of education.

Sherrill concluded that lesbian, gay, and bisexual people are nearly two-thirds more likely to have family income of less than $15,000 than are heterosexual college graduates, and two-thirds more likely to fall into the next-lowest income category as well. At the higher income levels, they are 17 per cent less likely to earn between $50,000 and $74,999, and over one-third less likely to have incomes of more than $75,000. Sheer will and energy (here, as reflected in higher education) are evidently not enough to close the wage gaps between the two sexual economies.

Methodologically, the best studies would collect data in a way that would overcome the 'spiral of silence'; would embrace a large-enough sample to test all the salient labour-market determinants; would include identifiable lesbian, gay, bisexual, transgendered, and transsexual people both as individuals and in their family configurations; and would collect comparable data on heterosexuals. No such studies have been carried out yet, because, in the absence of census or government survey data, the costs of such private research are prohibitive.

One strategy for cutting these costs would be to use the same survey instruments as are used in census or consumer surveys, but such a strategy overcomes only some of the methodological problems in this area. For example, the Gay and Lesbian Equality Network and Nexus Research in Ireland used the Economic and Social Research Institute's 1987 household survey instrument to compare queer poverty with heterosexual data collected earlier. While this did create a basis for comparisons, the two surveys were carried out in different years, which certainly resulted in changes in the value of money, the employment context, and so on, and the two surveys selected respondents differently. Thus results obtained in such studies would also have to be used with some caution.[72]

Canadian Data

There are as yet no valid Canadian studies of the earnings or incomes of lesbian, gay, bisexual, transgendered, or transsexual persons. Although it might be possible to abstract some potential queers from some of the government-collected data in the census or the Survey of Consumer Finances, no one who is in a position to see the raw data has done so yet. Alan Cornwall's small 1986 survey of fifty-one lesbians and gays in the Windsor and Detroit area did collect some income data. The distributions of incomes in this univariate study are roughly consistent with the U.S. findings, with lesbian incomes clustered at the very lowest levels and gay incomes falling rather more heavily into the lower- and middle-income ranges than average male incomes for that year (see table 7.7).[73]

Albert Wakkary did present some purported earnings data to the court in *Rosenberg* v *The Queen*. But these data are highly suspect. First, they are strictly univariate data – as is obvious from table 7.8, there is nothing against which to compare the supposed same-sex earnings. Although Wakkary testified that these data were abstracted by adjusting the 1991 Survey of Consumer Finances for 1994 levels, the same operations were not performed on comparable heterosexual-couple earnings. So these data remain purely univariate. Second, the couples described as 'same-sex couples' in this table may be queer, or they may be friends, roommates, distant relatives, or other groupings. There is nothing in the SCF upon which the Department of Finance economist who prepared this table could have relied to divine either the sexuality or the relationship of the two people described as being in a couple.

Third, all the studies reviewed above make it very clear that the incomes of lesbian women are markedly lower than the incomes of gay men, whether measured as incomes of individuals or of same-sex couples. Even if there are two gay men for every lesbian in Canada, the

Table 7.7. Lesbian and Gay Incomes, 1986

Income	Lesbians	(%)	Gays	(%)
Under $10,000	4	(45.5)	1	(2.9)
$10,000–$20,000	3	(27.3)	4	(11.4)
$20,000–$30,000	1	(0.9)	8	(22.3)
$30,000–$40,000	–		8	(22.3)
$40,000–$50,000	2	(18.2)	6	(17.1)
$50,000–$75,000	–		4	(11.4)
Over $75,000	–		4	(11.4)
Total respondents	11*		35	

SOURCE: Alan Cornwall, 'Personal and Estate Taxation for Gay and Lesbian Individuals and Couples: Survey and Selected Topics' (Windsor, Ont.: Faculty of Law, University of Windsor, 1986), 6–10. (Manuscript on file with author.)
* Five responses by lesbians were missing.

Table 7.8: Same-Sex Couples by Number of Earners, Household Income, 1994

Total household income	One earner	Two earners	Total
Under $10,000	1,100	–	1,100
$10,000–$20,000	2,800	2,400	5,200
$20,000–$30,000	1,700	11,500	13,200
$30,000–$40,000	1,700	15,100	16,800
$40,000–$50,000	700	18,500	19,200
$50,000–$75,000	1,200	43,000	44,100
Over $75,000	–	35,000	34,900
Total households	9,200	125,500	134,700
Average household income	$27,850	$63,070	$60,670
Percentage of all couples	6.8%	93.2%	100%

SOURCE: Affidavit of Albert Wakkary, filed in *Rosenberg* v *The Queen* (Ont. Gen. Div., Court File No. 79885/94) (sworn 2 June 1994), Exhibit B, Table 2.

incomes in table 7.8 would not be so skewed towards the higher brackets if lesbian and gay couples were both represented in this sample. Not only do these data not disaggregate female same-sex couples from male same-sex couples, but they are not at all consistent with the findings above as to the distribution of incomes by sex among sexual minorities. Fourth, these data are markedly inconsistent with the data in any of the U.S. studies. Without sources and without comparators, they should not be treated as reliable or valid.

Net Worth and 'Disposable' Incomes

Logic suggests that disadvantaged people – people who have lower overall earnings and incomes; people who have to struggle every day with widespread levels of hatred, lack of social, economic, family support, and discrimination; and people who have to incur greater transaction costs in order to safeguard themselves, their children, and their property against as many of the effects of discrimination as possible – will have less wealth than those who do not have to struggle with those disadvantages.

Because of the almost complete invisibility of the queer population in governmental research studies, and because researchers are still trying to solve the problem of accurately measuring the effects of discrimination, concepts of net worth or disposable incomes have not been the focus of research as yet.

Two factors do suggest, however, that when valid data do become available, sexual minorities will not be found to have significantly more 'disposable' income than their heterosexual counterparts, and will also have lower overall net worth. The first factor is the effect of decades of government and private-sector subsidies directed at heterosexual couples, discussed in the next chapter. The second factor is simply that queer people do have children too – almost as many children as heterosexuals.[74] To the extent that beliefs about 'procreative potential' lie behind assumptions about 'disposable' income, the reality is that sexual minorities procreate in all the ways that heterosexuals do.

Conclusions

Life options affect the dreams, goals, and choices people create for themselves. The combined effects of widespread social opprobrium in relation to lesbian, gay, bisexual, transgendered, and transsexual people, and the very real costs of discrimination mean that sexual minorities have to fashion their dreams, goals, and choices around the limited spaces that are permitted to them. All sexual minorities know that they have to shape their lives around the innumerable unquantifiable and quantifiable effects of discrimination. Health care, family stability, social security – defined as everything from simple physical safety to knowing what to call ourselves and the people dearest to us – documenting relationships, and day-to-day living are more complex, more laden with risk, for those who are characterized primarily by their sexuality. These unquantifiable effects are again compounded when sexual minorities have to deal with crisis, advancing age, or death.

Although the popular myth seems to be that gays – and, increasingly, lesbians – are 'rich' and lead unbounded child-free lives, this is simply not true. Research has demonstrated that fewer lesbian and gay people are self-employed, which means that they are thus more dependant upon employment earnings for support. Yet employment discrimination is widespread, resulting both in pressure to stay in the closet and in lower incomes for both men and women. There are no research data yet on employment patterns of bisexual, transgendered, or transsexual people in Canada. Despite the shortcomings of the social science research data, several careful studies have revealed that, when compared with heterosexual women and men of similar age, experience, and education, lesbian women and gay men earn significantly less than their heterosexual counterparts – as much as 27 per cent less for gay men, and at least 12 per cent less for lesbian women.

Since all the studies that have led to these results are U.S., it is still uncertain whether these findings will be replicated in Canada. But one thing is clear: By leaving sexual minorities out of the Canada Census and the Survey of Consumer Finances, the government has put itself in the position of being able to take advantage as a litigant of its control over non-published data it has collected at the taxpayers' expense in its role as census taker. The result of the abuse of control over the data-collection process has been the production of data that are dramatically inconsistent with the findings of non-governmental researchers, that deliberately obscure the issues, and that appear to be designed purely for the purpose of defending the government against charges of discrimination in Charter challenges brought by queer folk.

Until non-governmental researchers step in to fill in the data gap between the Department of Finance figures and the U.S. research data, there is the risk that the courts and legislatures in Canada will treat these highly unreliable figures as uncontroverted and, given the chance, will continue to leave queers impoverished in the 'homosexual economy' while heterosexual males continue to reap the massive benefits of the 'heterosexual economy.'

Chapter Eight

The High Costs of Heterosexuality and the 'Queer Penalty'

neutrality n. the quality or state of being neutral; *adj.* assisting or siding with neither of two opposing sides in a war, dispute, controversy etc.
New Lexicon Webster's Encyclopedic Dictionary (Canadian Edition)

Alterity A form of otherness irreducible to and unable to be modelled on any form of projection of or identification with the subject ... outside of, unpredictable by and ontologically prior to the subject.
Elizabeth Grosz, *Sexual Subversions: Three French Feminists* (Sydney: Allen & Unwin, 1989), xiv

The 'costs of being queer' outlined in chapter seven are generated by a mix of 'private' and 'public' factors that mirror the dominant image of sexuality as binary and 'hetero.' Some of those 'public' forces are, of course, state/social actions expressed in laws. So-called private forces seemingly emerge prior to laws and thus are thought to (legitimately) form the ground on which laws are constructed.

But the role of the state goes beyond merely mirroring the ground upon which 'private' actors stand. As the state has become increasingly involved in material economies of allocation, production, and consumption, and in symbolic economies of creating and circulating value, something like 40 to 43 per cent of the national domestic product flows into the hands of Canadian governments each year, and government expenditures are 46 to 48 per cent the size of the gross national product.[1] This means that 'the state' has come to be just as much 'the ground' as civil society and its private arrangements.[2] From the perspective of sexual minorities in Canada, that ground is far from neutral in relation to either sex or sexuality.

It is difficult to uncover the non-neutrality of the state so long as it is impossible to find other 'ground' exterior to the state from which it can be viewed. Without 'alterity,' without the self-consciousness of some irreducible 'other,' there is nothing to see, because there is no one to see it and nowhere to see it from. Queer struggles in Canada for 'personhood' as conceived in legal discourse began with the search for that alterity that makes personality credible, for the status of other outside the binary oppositions of hetero society from which that society can be seen. That struggle has been made arduous not only because of the deployment of legal invisibility, non-personhood, and discrimination, but because in its day-to-day operations the state itself has blocked the formation of those knowledges out of which alterity can emerge.

Simply put, the invisibility of queers in statistical data and the complete refusal to recognize sexual minorities as categories of existence in legal, political, or economic discourse has meant that there has been literally no information on which to base a study of how massive government expenditure patterns, for example, disadvantage sexual minorities compared with heterosexuals. On the 'private' employment side, it is possible to see that discrimination on the basis of sexuality imposes costs on lesbians and gays in a heterosexual economy. But on the 'public' expenditure or revenue-raising side, it is virtually impossible to measure the effects of discrimination without knowing how many queers there are, how much money they earn, what their demographic locations look like, and so on, relative to the rest of the population.

Seeking a standpoint from which to view the effect of state operations on sexual minorities, I have traced state/social policy through the revenue/expenditure process as it turns, like a Möbius band, from being about the recognition of or subsidy of heterosexual relationships into being about excluding, penalizing, and depowering those whose relationships are not heterosexual. As the recognition and subsidy of heterosexual relationships create disincentives to the formation of other, non-'hetero'sexual relationships, it becomes apparent that the two policies are the same.[3] Like the Möbius band, this policy effect is neither an inversion nor an 'inside-out' move. As with the Möbius band, both edges are one edge, both sides are one side, and edges and sides seamlessly flow in a continuous, unbroken twist unmarred by internal divisions, demarcations, or gaps. If one were to try to colour one 'side' of a Möbius band orange to mark the 'heterosexual' side, the whole band would end up being orange. If one were to try to start on the other 'side' to mark the 'queer' side green, the whole band would end up being green. So I envision the relationship between policies about sex/ualities, which construct that which they appear to ignore while constructing that which they expressly address.

In this chapter I have thus treated the presence of heterosexual policies as marking the absence of queers in those policies. By treating this absence, this negation, as an autonomous standpoint from which to observe the effect of state policies on civil society, I have been able to interrogate the difference in the two sets of policies and thereby measure the value assigned to queer existences by the state.[4]

In order to gain this view, I have looked at social/economic legal policies specific to 'spouse' or 'opposite-sex' cohabitants in order to see where the privileging or recognition of hetero-partnering must, through the absence of opposing terms, operate to hierarchically dichotomize hetero- and homo-partnering at the same time that it excludes homo-. Instead of looking merely at the positive reasons for sexuality-specific legislation, I have deconstructively read back into these texts those who are only there by implication – queers.

Expanding the question to ask 'What is the state/society doing when it recognizes hetero-identities?' has helped reveal the policy objectives promoted by the various types of sexuality-specific provisions used in law. And where this question can be answered quantitatively, this strategy makes explicit what must remain unsaid in order for heterosexual domination of the economy to continue: that the entire state/society pays a high price to maintain hetero-privilege, a price that simultaneously imposes quantifiable penalties on queer existences.

I began this deconstruction by collecting all the provisions in Canadian law that depended upon boundary terms like 'spouse,' 'husband' or 'wife,' 'opposite-sex' or 'marriage/ed' for application,[5] and then used an iterative process to identify the main functions they appeared to fulfil. I was left with four main categories:

1 Provisions that recognize family sharing, or that are designed to promote redistribution of incomes or wealth within the family unit;
2 Provisions that subsidize or promote economic dependency of some heterosexual adults through the provision of state-funded benefits;
3 Provisions that function as a contemporary version of the older 'family wage' system to selectively enhance the economic power of families through both 'private' and 'public' benefit systems;
4 Provisions that prevent members of couples from collaborating together to obtain unintended advantages from any of the above.

Although each of the many statutory provisions that turn on relationship status for application serves its own distinct policy objectives, they are all linked by one of these four fundamental objectives. On a functional level, there are no others that make sexual/ity divisions coherent.

The provisions that fall into the first three categories benefit hetero-sex couples, and correspondingly disadvantage queers who are coupled in all the relevant ways except the legal sex of their partner. I focus on these three types of provisions in this chapter. Taking up the types of provisions that fall into each of the first three categories in turn, I attempt to quantify in as much detail as possible the costs of these 'for heterosexuals only' benefits to the Canadian state. By using some of the projective data explored in chapter 6, I also attempt to quantify the size of the 'queer penalty' that is thereby imposed on same-sex couples by these provisions. Although the lack of reliable data on the size of the queer population, the number of same-sex couples in Canada, their incomes and family configurations, and the responsibilities they assume in relation to each other make accurate calibration of the 'queer penalty' manifestly speculative, even the claim that there is a 'queer penalty' helps create the alterity from which difference and perhaps change can proceed.

The 'anti-avoidance' or 'unintended advantages' provisions in the fourth category obviously do not 'benefit' heterosexuals in the same way as do the provisions in the first three categories. Their beneficial impact is expressed through safeguarding the integrity of the entire regulatory/incentive system and discursively reiterating the primacy of the 'hetero-' ground, even though some of them are embedded in larger legal structures that do confer some benefits on some subclasses of couples. Some commentators have described the (implied) exemption of queers from these provisions as one of the 'benefits of exclusion.' I would disagree. Queers are not 'exempted' from these types of provisions by design, decision, or expression; they are not addressed in this type of legislation because they are absent, not present, denied, and non-existent in most legal policy. This absence is merely the ([un]intended) consequence of directing massive levels of state support and regulation at favoured groupings. Thus this absence is really symptomatic of the social undesirability and political non-existence of same-sex couples – it is not a positive benefit that the body politic, after deliberation, has decided to confer on queers. Because these types of provisions raise unique and complex policy issues of their own, and have become woven into queer discourse in surprising ways, I discuss them separately in chapter 9.

Recognizing Family Sharing

Many legal provisions have come to be contingent on sexuality because all levels of government have become increasingly involved in regulating the distribution of economic power among family members. Most government policies and schemes that fall into this category were enacted in order to redress the worst effects of the almost complete concentration on economic power in male hands, and reflect the specificities of male-dominant heterosexual relationships. Other provisions that fall into this category are intended to render neutral some areas of law – such as taxation law – with regard to prior redistributional provisions. As they stand now, these private redistributional provisions touch the full range of family property issues:

a. ownership of the family home;
b. ownership of other family property;
c. rights to income support and a share of family assets on relationship breakdown;
d. forced shares of decedents' estates;
e. taxation provisions that ensure that transfers consistent with the above principles are exempt from tax liability.

By themselves, provisions that are intended to regulate how incomes and assets are shared during the relationship, with children, at the end of relationships, or at death, do not change the net wealth of the couple – they merely affect who controls or is considered to 'own' that wealth. They have a purely redistributional function, with the desired redistribution being within 'family' units as defined in the relevant legislation and the penalized redistribution being outside such units. Thus some members of couples – those who receive increased shares of family income or assets – will feel that these provisions 'benefit' them, while those whose shares are reduced will feel burdened.

Not so the last category of provisions. Taxation provisions that appear to relate to redistribution of wealth among family members generally permit that redistribution to take place on a tax-deferred basis. This ensures that such 'sharing' transfers are not treated like market-value dispositions that give rise to taxable income, but are treated, from the government's perspective, as if they had never taken place. This reduces the government's 'share' otherwise claimable in the transaction, and ensures that even partial redistribution to those outside the unit will not occur through the medium of the taxation system. Now it is true that some taxation provisions that were originally enacted merely to insulate intra-family transfers from ordinary taxation operate so predictably across differing income levels that they actually confer a financial benefit on the family unit as a whole.[6] However, this effect is generally not the most significant consequence of relationship-contingent taxation provisions, so I have discussed all of them together here.

Redistributional Provisions

Generally, redistributional provisions reconcile the claims between three distinct factions within the 'family': families of origin (the lineage represented by each of the two adult partners); the adult partners (as against each other); and their children (as against older generations). The point of balance among these three groups that is reflected in law is in an almost constant state of flux. However, it is fair to say that, over the last twenty-five years in Canada, the main direction of policy change has been to equalize the shares of property and income that can be claimed as between adult partners, which has brought Canadian family property law closer to the 50 per cent–50 per cent husband–wife model associated with European community-property regimes.[7] Thus Ontario family property law, for example, provides for equal ownership of the matrimonial home no matter how title to that home is held,[8] and presumptively splits other family assets between the two partners on relationship breakdown or death.[9]

Even though Ontario property law creates a global presumption of equality of ownership between spouses, the interests of each spouse's family of origin are nonetheless represented to a considerable extent. The Family Law Act excludes assets and incomes that can be traced to a spouse's family of origin from the net family property that is presumptively divided between spouses.[10] This ensures that property which comes to a spouse from their family of origin will at least stay with that spouse, go to their children, or be available to be redirected in testamentary dispositions to some other branch of the family of origin, if the recipient so desires. Even though all interests in the matrimonial home are reserved for spouses, courts can exercise discretion to take contributions from families of origin into account in dividing up the spouses' interests in the home.

The interests of children are represented in Ontario family property law by provisions that require parents to assume equal responsibility for the support of their children, whether during cohabitation, marriage, or separation.[11] Children's interests are also represented in the forced share of decedents' estates to which children are entitled,[12] and in the right to contest testamentary dispositions that unfairly prejudice them.[13] Although these examples are drawn from Ontario statutes, other Canadian jurisdictions have adopted similar regimes.[14]

These redistributional types of provisions are not restricted to family incomes or assets. For example, spouses and other relatives can bring actions in tort when another family member is injured or killed, the measure of their damages being lost support, services, or companionship,[15] and spouses can assume a lease signed by a spouse.[16]

Taxation Provisions

While family law makes it look like individual members of families are given legal rights as against each other, taxation provisions make it look like the family unit as a whole is exempt from tax liability for transactions in which income or assets are being 'kept in the family.' Both types of provisions are designed to promote the equitable distribution of wealth within the family; property law provisions do so by giving all family members a legal basis to claim interests in each other's property, while tax provisions protect incomes or assets that are being 'kept in the family' from erosion by taxation. So long as income/assets are not transferred outside the family unit, no tax liability will be imposed. Thus, for example, if a vehicle is transferred to a spouse or another member of the family, no one has to pay a vehicle transfer tax or obtain new safety certification.[17] This will be true even if the transfer is pursuant to separation or divorce, at which time the partners theoretically become 'individuals' again as the 'couple' is terminated. There are similar exemptions in other taxation statutes. Transfer of real estate will be exempt from land transfer taxes if the transferee is a spouse or other family member.[18] Transfers of income- or gain-producing property will not trigger liability under the Income Tax Act if the transfer is to a spouse or child.[19]

The Income Tax Act is riddled with these types of exemptions. Not only are *inter vivos* transfers of property exempt, but incomes flowing from property – such as interest income or dividends – are treated as if no transfer had taken place.[20] The types of property that can be transferred on an exempt basis is quite long, and includes deferred compensation, tax-assisted savings,[21] and even tax exemptions or tax benefits.[22]

Same-Sex Couples

Although these property and taxation provisions may appear, at first glance, to be irrelevant to same-sex couples, they actually create a system of disincentives to forming or maintaining same-sex relationships. These types of statutory provisions not only signify the non-existence of queer families, but they actually impose higher costs on property/income arrangements for queers. Heterosexual spouses and cohabitants can count on being able to resort to legislative frameworks to resolve conflicts over ownership of property, and do not have to worry about sharing family wealth with the state every time income or assets are transferred between them. In contrast, same-sex partners are subject to each other's personal power and personal sense of sharing in the allocation of rights as between them, and, no matter how fair-minded a partner might be either in life or in death, wills can be challenged, trusts can be disrupted, and taxes will have to be paid as the consequence of any transfers, *inter vivos* or testamentary.

It is difficult to quantify these costs in the aggregate. Not only does the persistent direction of assets towards families or origin under Canadian property law tend to diminish the wealth of same-sex partners, but the costs of private litigation are very high on the individual level. Unlike the reaction of the provinces after the Supreme Court of Canada decision in *Murdoch* v *Murdoch*,[23] which led to speedy enactment of family property laws codifying many of the equitable principles applied in these cases,[24] it has been twelve years since the decision in *Anderson* v *Luoma*, recommendations such as those made in the Ontario Law Reform Commission's 1993 report relating to same-sex couples have not led to any discernible legislative action,[25] and even when same-sex partners are able to share property during life or at death, they are taxed on those transfers as if they were ordinary market transactions. Even the principal-residence exemption, which is one place where same-sex couples can at least achieve tax-exempt or low-tax savings as a couple (because they each get one full exemption), will not be available to former or surviving partners to the same extent as for heterosexual couples.[26]

These are not incidental or unintended effects. Some of the first tax policies designed to promote heterosexuality and to discourage sharing economic power with same-sex partners were enacted by Augustus in Rome from 30 B.C. to A.D. 14. Augustus devised a number of taxation measures to buttress the Julian Laws, which promoted heterosexual marriage and reproduction, and created disincentives for men to live unattached to women. Preferred beneficiaries (family members) paid no taxes on bequests, whereas unrelated beneficiaries were taxed heavily.[27] The contemporary disparities in the tax treatment of sharing transactions between heterosexual and same-sex partners are not trivial. Table 8.1 outlines the 'rollovers' that are available to heterosexual partners under federal and provincial income tax legislation who make *inter vivos* or testamentary arrangements to share their property with their families.

As table 8.1 illustrates, every form of property that is recognized in income tax law can be transferred from one spouse to another on a completely tax-deferred basis during life, on relationship breakdown, or upon death. This means that tax liability deferred on the spousal transfer will not crystallize until the spouse who receives the property disposes of it or dies. For tax purposes, such transfers between spouses are treated as if the items remained within the same legal entity continuously. The assets that can be transferred on such a tax-deferred basis include not only all forms of capital property (the home, farming property, and eligible capital property), but also assets held in registered plans, by partnerships, and as life insurance policies. Even tax benefits can be transferred between spouses without any loss of the value of the benefit, turning the many tax benefits 'owned' by one spouse into forms of property that can be shared with the other spouse as well.

It is important to stress that these provisions do not bring new wealth into the family unit. They are not 'tax benefit' items in the sense that taxpayers who do certain things will receive some sort of tax subsidy. On the contrary, these rollover provisions treat family sharing as normative, and thus are designed to make sure that technical transfers are not treated like non-family market-based transactions. These rollovers suspend the rules that would ordinarily apply to transactions between strangers. Some of these rollovers are doubly advantageous because, in the long run, they take potential income out of the hands of the taxpayer and place it in the hands of the taxpayer's spouse. This establishes an income split down the road, which is a second tax benefit flowing from the original tax-deferred rollover of property from one spouse to another.

Same-sex partners cannot take advantage of any of these family-sharing tax rules. Thus same-sex partners who may actually share incomes and assets in exactly the same ways as heterosexual couples bear heavy tax penalties for that sharing. Because the federal government has not included any estimates on the magnitude of the tax forgone because of these family rollovers, it is difficult to speculate on just how much

The High Costs of Heterosexuality and the 'Queer Penalty' 223

Table 8.1. Income Tax Benefits for Sharing Income or Wealth with Heterosexual Partner, 1997

Provision	Description
\multicolumn{2}{l}{Provisions that make it possible to transfer assets between spouses without tax liability:}
24	Tax-deferred rollover for transfer of eligible capital property to spouse
40	Tax-deferred rollover for transfer of farming property to spouse
40	Capital gain on home held in trust for spouse can be tax exempt under principal-residence exemption
54	Capital gain on home owned by one spouse for use and occupation by other spouseexempt from taxation as principal residence
60(j.2)	Tax-deferred rollover for transfer of funds from registered pension plan or deferred-profit-sharing (DPSP) plan to spousal RRSP
70	Tax-deferred rollover for transfer of property to surviving spouse or spousal trust
70, 73	Tax-deferred rollover for transfer of farming property used by spouse
73	Tax-deferred rollover for transfer of capital assets to spouse or spousal trust during life
74.5	Tax-deferred rollover for transfer of capital assets to spouse living apart
96	Non-recognition of partnership income and gains when spouse takes over other spouse's partnership interest
118.2	Credits for payment of medical expenses of spouse
118.2(2)(q)	Credits for payment of premiums for medical insurance covering spouse
146	Tax-deferred transfer of RRSP assets to surviving spouse's RRSP
147	Tax-deferred rollover of spouse's DPSP to other spouse's own registered plans
47.3	Tax-deferred rollovers from deceasedor separated spouse's registered pension plan (RPP) to other spouse's own RRSP, or DPSP
148	Tax-exempt transfer of life insurance policies between spouses
\multicolumn{2}{l}{Provisions that make it possible to transfer tax benefits from one spouse to another:}
104	Flow-through of tax benefit items where property is held in spousal trust, but income is paid to spouse personally
110.6	Flow-through of enhanced capital gainexemption where property is rolled over to spouse

SOURCE: Income Tax Act, R.S.C.1985, c. 1 (5th Supp.), as amended.

exclusion from these provisions costs same-sex taxpayers.[28] But they form one of the material costs to same-sex couples flowing from denial of queer existences.

Subsidizing Adult Dependency

While family-sharing provisions do not create any new wealth as such, but instead preserve family wealth from taxation when it is shared, some statutory provisions are designed to deliver positive government subsidies to heterosexual couples. Conceptually, these 'heterosexuals only' provisions are of two types: Some of them can be claimed only if one of the partners is economically dependent on the other; some can be claimed by couples no matter what their income levels. I discuss the first category in this section; the second type of subsidy, which I think of as a contemporary version of the 'family wage,' is discussed in 'The New "Family Wage" System' below.

Costs of Dependency Benefits

The federal and provincial governments provide a large number of subsidies for single-income heterosexual couples. The most important ones are outlined in table 8.2, and include three major income tax credits (the married tax credit, the transferable income tax credits, and the alimony deduction) and two direct transfers (the federal spousal pension allowance [SPA] and the CPP survivor pensions and death benefits). All these benefits are available to formally married spouses and to opposite-sex cohabitants who meet the relevant statutory definition of 'spouse.'[29]

None of these provisions is actually labelled 'for dependent partners only.' But they achieve that effect by setting up eligibility criteria that in fact exclude partners who could be considered to be economically self-sufficient. Each statute contains its own mechanism for restricting these benefits to dependent adult partners, or, in the case of alimony, courts must find that the recipient requires some financial assistance in order to maintain an adequate standard of living.

The full married tax credit, worth approximately $1,372.50 to a supporting spouse in 1993, could be claimed only if the dependent spouse's income for the year was less than $538.[30] The transferable tax credits are not all contingent on the incomes of the dependent spouse, but no spouse who has enough income to take full advantage of these credits will transfer them to the other spouse. Thus the actual transfer of credits from

Table 8.2. Cost to Government of Subsidies for Dependants of Heterosexual Adults, 1993

Provision	Federal (mill.)	Provincial	Total
Married credit	$1,680.2	840.1	2,520.3
Transferable credits	243.0	121.5	364.5
Net alimony deductions[a]	61.9	30.9	92.8
Spousal pension allowance	684.9	–	684.9
CPP survivor pension[b]	1,474.9	–	1,474.9
All	4,144.9	992.5	5,137.4

SOURCE: SPSD/M version 5.2, adjusted to 1993; the figures for the CPP survivor pension were derived from Human Resources Development Canada, *Social Security Statistics, Canada and Provinces: 1968–69 to 1992–93* (Ottawa: Queen's Printer, 1994), Table 214, at 60, because the SPSD/M did not have a variable for survivor pensions or death benefits under the CPP.
a Reconciled with figures reported in Revenue Canada, *Taxation Statistics, 1993* (Ottawa: Minister of Supply and Services Canada, 1995), Table 10, at 142, 144.
b Payments to surviving spouses and children are not broken down in the statistical reports; I have arbitrarily assumed that half went to each.

one spouse to another has to be seen as a symptom of low income.[31] Alimony is paid only when there is a sufficient income disparity between the payer and recipient, and reflects the pre-existence of economic dependency before the relationship came to an end. The tax benefit flows to the payer,[32] the theory being that this benefit will be shared with the former partner, but the amount of the payment will be cut down in the recipient's hands by their own income tax liability.[33] The federal spousal pension allowance is paid to a very particular segment of the low-income population: To qualify, an opposite-sex spouse or cohabitant must be between the ages of sixty and sixty-five, and must either be married to the recipient of Old Age Security (OAS) benefits with an income of less than $21,360 if the spouse receives the Guaranteed Income Supplement (GIS), or be widowed and have income less than $15,672. It is worth $710.89 per month (if spouse is alive) or $784.71 (if widowed).[34] The maximum CPP survivor pension is $436.25 per month.[35]

On the fiscal level, these subsidies for dependent partners are very expensive. In 1993, the total cost of these five programs came to $5.1 billion. They accounted for 3.6 per cent of total government spending on social security and 1.5 per cent of overall government spending in that year.[36] I find this latter figure especially interesting: It suggests that subsidizing dependent heterosexual relationships is one of the sixty-seven most important functions of the Canadian state.

Distributional Data

Proponents of these dependency subsidies sometimes claim that they are intended to ensure that women's non-waged work in the home does not go entirely unrewarded. That claim does not have a lot of credibility: most of these subsidies pre-dated by decades the emergence of political consciousness around 'women's unpaid work.' In fact, the functional effects of these subsidies – especially the married tax credit – actually undercut the economic autonomy of women, because they encourage women to substitute non-waged domestic work for waged work.[37] This 'substitution effect' contributes to the impoverishment of women as a class. As dependency benefits create an incentive for low-income workers (who tend overwhelmingly to be female workers) to leave waged work and work in the non-waged domestic economy, they help support higher wages for the remaining workers. At the same time, they provide cheap domestic labour to their supporting partners, which in turn increases their ability to earn money incomes. At the end of this process, the 'substitution effect' leaves more money and wealth in the hands of supporting partners (mostly males) and less in the hands of dependent partners. Because the government benefits that help promote this process are paid to and 'owned' by supporting partners, these government benefits intensify that impoverishment.

Other arguments are sometimes brought out to explain the 'rationality' of maintaining the 'heterosexuals only' limits on these dependency benefits. It has been argued that women who do have children should remain in the home to care for them while they are young; that women whose spouses can afford to support them should work in the home even if they have no children; and that women who probably did withdraw from waged labour deserve some support later in life, even after the children are gone, in order to help maintain the dependent lifestyle as an option literally until death. None of these justifications squares with the distributional data on the relationship between being married, having children, and qualifying for these benefits. Not all married couples have children. Not all children are raised by married couples. Not all children raised by married couples are young enough to need someone home with them. Many married couples are too old to be likely to have children. And there is nothing about being in same-sex relationships that suggests that same-sex couples do not have children, that children with same-sex parents do not benefit from having an adult home with them, or that same-sex parents would not in any event qualify as economically dependent.

Table 8.3. Distribution of Married/Equivalent Tax Credit, by Census Family, 1993

Census family category ($ million)	Married credit amt.	%	Marr/Equiv amt.	%
Married couple, no children	407.4	24.2	407.4	18.5
Married couple, young children	900.3	53.6	900.3	40.9
Married couple, old children	208.8	12.4	208.8	9.5
Married couple, one elderly	163.8	9.8	163.8	7.5
Single parent family, young chld.	0.0	0.0	506.7	23.0
Single parent family, old children	0.0	0.0	12.0	0.6
Unattached individual, not elderly	0.0	0.0	0.0	0.0
Unattached individual, elderly	0.0	0.0	0.0	0.0
Total	$1,680.2	100.0	$2,198.9	100.0

SOURCE: SPSD/M version 5.2, adjusted to 1993.

Table 8.3 demonstrates how badly targeted the married tax credit actually is, whether it is considered on its own merits or whether it is considered in conjunction with the equivalent-to-married credit. Looking at the two credits together, only 40.9 per cent of the total benefit goes to married couples with young children. Although 23.0 per cent goes to single-parent families with young children, that means that only some 64 per cent of the benefit goes to families with young children.

Married couples with no children account for the bulk of this target inefficiency. Looking just at the allocation of the married credit, some 24.2 per cent of the credit went to married couples with no children in 1993. Another 12.4 per cent went to couples whose children were grown, and 9.8 per cent went to couples that could not be expected to have more children because of their age. If the real justification for the married credit is to promote heterosexual biological reproduction, then it has missed the mark rather wildly. Not all dependent adults are women. As family forms have changed, 'dependency' is no longer allocated almost exclusively on the basis of sex, age, and ability. The spousal pension allowance is also overinclusive if the real objective is to compensate women who have substituted non-waged domestic work for waged work. Not all recipients of this allowance will necessarily have raised children earlier in life. It would not be at all difficult to amend section 118(1)B(a) to limit this credit to taxpayers whose dependent spouses or partners had forgone waged work in order to care for children, nor would it be difficult to remove the opposite-sex limitations from it.

The dependency benefits delivered through the income tax system are

Table 8.4. Distribution of Married/Equivalent Tax Credit, by Income Class, 1993

Base consumable income class	Number in class (%)	Equivalent credit (%)	Married credit (%)
Up to $10,000	23.8	44.0	15.8
$10,001–$30,000	36.8	35.8	30.7
Over $30,000	39.4	20.2	53.5
Total	100.0	100.0	100.0

SOURCE: SPSD/M version 5.2, adjusted to 1993.

also very poorly designed in terms of the class distribution of claims. Unlike the SPA, which is means-tested on the basis of both partners' incomes on a continuing basis, the only relevant test for eligibility under the Income Tax Act is the income of the dependent partner. Thus a couple with one middle or high income can still take full advantage of the tax dependency benefits, no matter how high that one income might be. Not surprisingly, low- and middle-income individuals cannot afford to support their partners as easily as can high-income individuals. As table 8.4 demonstrates, the equivalent-to-married credit claimable by single parents is distributed on a bottom-up basis, with the largest percentage of credits going to taxpayers with the lowest incomes, but, in contrast, the distribution of the married credit is 'upside down'– supporting spouses with the lowest incomes receive the smallest benefits under the credit and spouses with the highest incomes receive the largest benefits.

Irrationally, income class correlates more strongly with receipt of the married credit than does marital status or presence of young children in the home. In addition, the large numbers of claims for the equivalent-to-married credit in the lower income brackets suggest that there are significant numbers of single-parent families in Canada.[38] Thus it is clear that denying the married tax credit to same-sex couples on the basis of sexuality or on the basis of the biological sex of their partner is both overinclusive of couples who are thought to need it because one of them has withdrawn from waged work to work in the home, and is also underinclusive of those who do satisfy the most fundamental reason for economic dependency – working in the home.[39]

Whether the 'real' purpose of dependency benefits is to promote substitution of non-waged domestic work for waged work, or to create a class of women who are more likely to have children if they withdraw from waged work, or to encourage partners whose spouses can afford to

Table 8.5. Tax Subsidies for Supporting Partners, 1993

Item	Wife (Divorced)	Husband (Married)	Husband (Divorced)	Husband (Remarr'd)
Salary	$3,620	$30,820	$30,820	$30,820
Alimony	1,262	–	(1,262)	(1,262)
Child support	5,135	–	(5,135)	(5,135)
Taxable income	10,017	30,820	24,423	24,423
Federal tax liability	(1,703)	(5,350)	(4,152)	(4,152)
Personal tax credits	1,830	1,830	915	1,830
Child tax benefit[a]	2,040	775	–	–
GST credit[a]	608	363	304	398
Net federal tax	–	(2,382)	(2,933)	(1,924)
Combined federal and Ont. taxes	–	(3,764)	(4,634)	(3,040)
After-tax income	12,665	27,057	19,789	21,138
Standard of living[b]	0.6	1.1	1.6	1.2

SOURCE: Income Tax Act Annotated, R.S.C. 1985, c. 1 (5th Supp.), as amended.

a Because these tax credits are fully refundable, they form part of the after-tax cash flow the wife in this example has available to her. Because the husband's income is high enough to attract positive tax liability in each variation illustrated in this table, it will merely be used to offset his excess tax liability, instead of being refunded to him in cash.

b These ratios were calculated with the low-income measures attached to the Working Draft of Bill C-41, the federal child-support guidelines, at 56. The measures were based on household configuration, and were to be applied to post-support incomes. One person: $12,299; two persons: $17,219; one adult and two children: $20,908; two adults and two children: $24,598. (The final legislation used lower cut-offs because the formula was modified to apply to post-tax income. These are relevant to pre-tax incomes.)

support them to withdraw from waged work, either to provide in-home services to the wage-earning partner or to care for their children and home, then the class bias built into these benefits still makes them difficult to justify. In a country where child poverty is recognized as a widespread problem, and where poverty overall is a major justification for the government's increasing intervention into the social security area, providing subsidies for general domestic services to middle- and high-income couples does not seem like a rational solution to any problem.[40]

Looking at the distributional implications of support deductions and the tax credit system, an alternative hypothesis appears plausible: both the dependency credits and the support deductions help maintain the supply of non-waged domestic labour. Table 8.5 demonstrates that the married tax credit interacts with the alimony/child deduction to cushion the effects of divorce on men's after-tax incomes, to make it economically more attractive for men to remarry after divorce than to remain single, and to encourage women to focus their work efforts on the domestic non-waged sector whether divorced or married.

Table 8.5 reflects three assumptions: that the husband in this example earns a constant salary of $30,820 in each scenario; that, before divorce, the wife worked exclusively in the home; and that, after divorce, the wife received occasional earnings of $3,620, child support of $5,135, alimony of $1,262, and refundable tax credits of $2,648 for a total income of $12,665.[41]

On these assumptions, it can be seen that, during his first marriage, the husband received the benefit of the married tax credit and of his wife's non-waged work, which enhanced his income-earning capacity and made it unnecessary to spend money on child care. The husband lost both those tax benefits and the economic benefits of his wife's non-waged work when the couple divorced. The husband's net standard of living nonetheless increased dramatically after divorce – despite paying alimony and child support – because he was no longer providing his family's entire support. This increase in his standard of living was enhanced by the fact that, in this type of situation, it can be expected that the wife would continue to devote most of her energies to caring for their children, because her income would be completely inadequate to cover such expenses, and because the deductions for the support payments will almost always provide a net subsidy to the husband for making those payments.

When the divorced husband remarried, his standard of living fell again because two people had to live on the same income he had as a single divorced person. But it did not fall to its previous level, because the continued deductions for alimony and child support provided an element of subsidy of his lifestyle that persisted despite his remarriage. Indeed, with the subsidies for dependency available in relation to the second wife, combined with other subsidies available to the various elements of the family as reconstituted, the husband was literally supporting two separate families by the time he remarried. Yet his standard of living at the end of the process actually increased, and, he then had two women focusing most of their productive labours on non-waged work that benefited him and the children.

Separating the various subsidy elements in situations like these can be complicated, but it helps reveal the very real effects of the various dependency- and family-focused government benefits. Overall, these benefits make it easier for dependent adults to choose to work in the non-waged sector, and the adults who move into or stay in those relations of economic dependency overwhelmingly tend to be women. This means that relations of economic dependency are not merely motivated by altruism, or even by social tradition, but actually make the gendered appropriation of labour routine in Canada.

The New 'Family Wage' System

The 'family wage' movement arose earlier in this century in reaction to the demand by women workers for equal pay and as one of the ways governments perpetuated the economic disadvantage of racially identified groups. The 'family wage' was conceived as a way to meet women's demands for apparent wage equality while continuing to pay men more, not on the basis of their sex, but on the basis that they had a social obligation to support themselves as well as their wives and children on their earnings.[42] The family wage system was gradually abolished, beginning in the middle of this century, although the considerable differentials in the rates of pay that women and men continue to receive is evidence that the belief that men are entitled to higher rates of pay – even when they do not support anyone else – continues to be widespread.

Despite the apparent abandonment of the 'family wage' system, employment contracts and statutory provisions continue to confer significant benefits on heterosexual couples, whether married or merely cohabiting, specifically to increase the economic power of workers who have families. Functionally, these benefits are gender-neutral variants of the older 'family wage.' These benefits are structured differently than was the 'family wage.' Instead of taking the form of flat wage increments, they are usually contingent on family composition, activities, or needs. In the so-called private employment sector, these 'family wage'–type benefits include employment benefits for members of the employee's family, such as extended hospitalization benefits, dental benefits, counselling benefits, tuition waivers, retirement health insurance benefits, insurance pricing, employee discounts, survivor's benefits, and death benefits. These types of benefits are also found in the public employment sector, because the labour market has tended to produce competitive levels of compensation and packages of fringe benefits in both areas.

'Family wage'–type benefits are not conditioned on proof that a partner or child is in fact economically dependent on the recipient.[43] Regardless of dependency, regardless of income levels, and regardless of need, 'family wage' benefits are paid to the qualifying partner purely because of the existence of the spousal or parent–child relationship. Family wage benefits generally come into existence as incidents of private contracts. However, as both provincial and federal fiscal policy has become increasingly enmeshed with the private sector, both for regulatory purposes and in order to fine-tune the interface between the allocation of the tax burden and the distribution of all forms of economic power, more and more statutory provisions have come to reflect the values that underlie the creation of family benefits. In particular, the income tax treatment of employment-based family benefits has come to play a crucial role both in allocating these benefits and in enhancing their financial value to recipients. In essence, the income tax system 'magnifies' the financial value of these new family wages whenever it grants them any special tax treatment.[44]

As an aside, I find it interesting that, although the older family wage system that emerged in the 1920s was at least in part a reaction against the increased visibility of gay men and lesbian women in Canada, same-sex couples appear to have had more success in gaining access to these types of 'heterosexuals only' benefits than they have in relation to other types of relationship benefits. Family wage types of benefits are delivered in three distinct ways: through pension plans, in the form of employment benefits, and through the income tax system.

Pension-based family wages arise in quite diverse circumstances. At one extreme, the federal government extends a family wage type of payment to survivors of CPP/QPP contributors. This benefit takes the form of a death benefit plus survivor pensions when the contributor leaves a spouse or dependent children who qualify to receive the benefit. In the aggregate, these survivor pensions and death benefits cost a total of $2,949.9 million to fund in 1992–3.[45] The CPP/QPP plans are not the only public pension plans in Canada. Each province and the federal government have their own public-sector retirement plans, and all of these plans extend survivor benefits like those found in the CPP/QPP legislation.[46]

The CPP/QPP survivor/death benefits of the public social security system have their private analogues. Every private pension plan in Canada – including RRSPs and RPPs – contains similar provisions. These pension survivor options are also examples of the new family wage system, because they actually allocate pension or revenue funds out of the general fund to surviving spouses and children. Contributors who

The High Costs of Heterosexuality and the 'Queer Penalty' 233

have spouses or children make the very same contributions to these plans as other contributors. The difference arises at the other end, when pay-outs commence. Contributors whose spouse or children qualify for survivor pensions or death benefits have notionally received larger returns on their contributions than those whose families do not qualify for any benefits.

Employee benefits also enhance the family wage. Services or payments to spouses or children received under dental, health, hospitalization, or drug plans are examples of these forms of the new family wage system, as are employee discounts, low-interest loans, and education benefits. Most of these employment benefits are subsidized to some extent by the income tax system, which treats many of them as tax exempt. This increases the after-tax value of these forms of compensation to the employee, and the income tax system adds an increment of value to the new family wage system.

In addition to the preferential tax treatment of employment benefits, the income tax system also extends various forms of preferential tax treatment to taxpayers on the basis of their marital status. These types of provisions, outlined in table 8.6, have nothing to do with employment benefits, with the economic status of the spouse or cohabitant, or with any children the taxpayer might have – they are available merely on the basis of 'spouseness' without regard to the economic dependency or capacity of that spouse.

Very few of the tax benefits listed in table 8.6 are contingent on the dependency of the spouse, family income levels, or having had children. The provisions that facilitate income-splitting between partners deserve special comment. Sharing income during marriage or cohabitation is considered to be a 'non-event' for most tax purposes, because support of another member of the family is considered to be a consumption choice that has been equated with keeping a pet elephant.[47] That is, in terms of tax policy, income is actually shared, or is presumed to be shared, but the spouse with the higher income does not get to remove the amount shared from his or her income – sharing is treated as being no different from other personal consumption transactions. Nor does the partner who is being supported have to pay any tax on that support. Because the Canadian income tax system uses the individual as the tax unit, income-splitting between spouses is deliberately countered by numerous provisions of the Income Tax Act,[48] and can even be considered to constitute tax avoidance or tax evasion, depending on the circumstances.[49]

However, some provisions in the Income Tax Act nonetheless permit

234 Are We 'Persons' Yet?

Table 8.6. Tax Provisions that Deliver or Magnify Family Wages for Opposite-Sex Couples, 1997

Provisions that make it possible to split incomes between spouses:

8	Deduction for cost of maintaining home for spouse (railway workers)
62, 64	Costs of moving spouse's personal property can be deducted as part of 'household' moving expenses
104, 108	Income splitting by way of use of trust
146	Taxpayer can receive tax deductions for contributions to spouse's RRSP
146	Joint and survivor benefits can be paid out of RRSP assets
Reg. 8501	Permits redirection of RPP benefitsto separated or divorced spouse

Provisions that differentially benefit opposite-sex partners:

15	Tax exemption for employee shareholder loan taken out to provide housing for spouse
248(1)	Tax-exempt payment of up to $10,000 death benefit to spouse

Provisions that organize and/or subsidize survivor pensions:

60(j.2)	Surviving spouse can roll deceased spouse's RPP or DPSP into own RRSP
146.3	Surviving spouse benefits can be paid out of retirement income funds (RIFs)
Reg. 8503, 8506	Surviving spouse benefits can be paid out of RPPs

SOURCE: Income Tax Act, R.S.C. 1985, c. 1 (5th Supp.), as amended.

income-splitting between opposite-sex partners in some specific circumstances. The alimony payments which function as dependency benefits also give rise to legitimate forms of income splitting.[50] Because husbands usually receive tax benefits for alimony deductions that are larger than the tax liability incurred by wives in relation to those payments, not only does the payer enjoy the tax benefits of income-splitting, but part of that tax benefit actually comes out of the public fisc.[51] This type of income-splitting is not limited to separation or divorce. A taxpayer can obtain the tax benefits of income-splitting without resulting tax liability in the other spouse's hands by making deductible contributions to the other spouse' RRSP.[52] Some taxpayers can even deduct the costs of maintaining the family home.[53]

To the extent that family wage types of increments are available to heterosexuals only, and to the extent that the value of these increments may be magnified by tax-exemption or tax-deferral, these benefits subsidize heterosexual existence. The 'wage' portions of these types of benefits are paid by both the private employment sector and each level of government that extends them to workers. The costs of tax benefits for these types of benefits are borne directly by the public sector, and thus by the taxpayers who fund it.

The 'Queer Penalty'

Viewed from the alterity of queer existences, the purposes of the many 'heterosexuals only' provisions are not actually relevant. Whether they are designed to recognize sharing of economic power within the family, to subsidize economic dependency, or to construct a new 'family wage' system, each of these provisions works a penalty on same-sex couples who would otherwise – but for the biological sex of one of them – be qualified to receive them. Thus every one of these provisions, programs, or benefits forms part of what I think of as 'the queer penalty'– the actual economic penalty that sexual minorities pay for living outside the 'heterosexual economy.'

The queer penalty has two important dimensions. One dimension is grounded in the present: What programs, what benefits, what legal norms exclude same-sex couples this year, and at what costs to them? The other dimension is longitudinal, and relates to the fact that, as people live year after year with the queer penalty, their own economic resources remain unsubsidized in the myriad ways that heterosexual resources are subsidized. This not only affects well-being in the most fundamental sense of the terms, but it also affects, over time, the capacity of all sexual minorities in Canada to care for themselves, to care for their families, and to contribute to their communities.

When what I have called the measurable costs of heterosexuality and the queer penalty are placed next to each other, it becomes possible to bring into focus the huge benefit–penalty system that addresses at the micro-economic level of each person in Canada their sexual choices, their sexuality, their relationship options, the value of their feelings. I know it is crass and not very sensitive of me to put all this in monetary terms, but it awes me to see how much time, effort, and money go into maintaining this critically important yet largely invisible hierarchy of privilege. Unlike 'the wage gap,' 'sex discrimination,' 'pay equity,' or even the race-linked poverty of many groups in Canada that has begun to come into view in national statistics, there is no public awareness of how much of the economic activity in this country is directed at who we love, who we sleep with, who we make our lives with. Call me naïve, but I think that if people were aware of these dynamics, they might not agree that these are appropriate priorities.

The figures in table 8.7 estimate the costs of the aggregate subsidy to the 'heterosexual economy' and the consequent 'queer penalty' in 1993. Yes, these figures are speculative: No one really knows how many queers there are in Canada, nor does anyone really know how many queers are coupled, would couple, or would like to couple. Nor does anyone know anything about the demographics of queer communities. No one is permitted to know, at a very fundamental level. But even without the knowledges that are crucial to true alterity, these figures cannot be criticized as being too generous. They are projected on a very conservative basis. I have assumed that for every thousand heterosexual couples in Canada, there is at least one queer couple. That estimate is conservative. In the alternative, I have assumed, still conservatively, that if only 9 per cent of the population is queer and only one-third of all queers are coupled, then there is one same-sex couple for every 33.3 heterosexual couples.[54]

Even these very conservative figures reveal the vastness of the sexual privilege that has been constructed in Canada in just two short decades. These provisions are not so old or so steeped in tradition that their true origins or purposes lie shrouded in the mists of time. On the contrary, all the pieces of legislation that have constructed this sexual hierarchy have been amended – often quite recently – to ensure that, although they may now extend to cohabitants who have not married, they still apply only to cohabitants of the opposite sex. The first such definition of 'spouse' was not enacted until 1974,[55] and the wave of amendments extending this principal to most federal legislation, for example, were not enacted until 1975.[56] Even modest attempts to challenge the universality of this hierarchy in 1993 failed utterly.[57]

It is important to stress that this preliminary tabulation of the costs of heterosexuality and the 'queer penalty' actually leaves out much more than it includes. I have made no attempt to quantify any of the effects of discrimination discussed in chapter 7, even though many of them do have monetary as well as emotional, physical, or spiritual impact. I have no way to even think about how much tax-deferred rollovers of family

The High Costs of Heterosexuality and the 'Queer Penalty' 237

Table 8.7. The Costs of Subsidizing the 'Heterosexual Economy' and the 'Queer Penalty,' 1993

Item ($ million)	Heterosexual benefits	Queer penalty if .1%	if 3%
Married tax credit	$2,520.3	2.5	75.6
Transferable credits	364.5	.4	10.9
Spousal RRSP contribs.	small	small	small
Survivor pensions/RRSP rollovers	n.a.	3.0	3.0
Employment health benefits	n.a.	8.0	8.0
Net alimony deductions	92.8	0.1	2.8
SPA	684.9	0.7	20.6
CPP survivor pensions/death benefits	1,474.9	1.5	44.2
Total	5,137.4	16.2	165.1

SOURCES: Tables 8.2, 8.4, and 8.5, derived from SPSD/M version 5.2, adjusted to 1993 (projecting same-sex couple take-up rates of 0.5 per cent and 3 per cent of reported heterosexual claims); Affidavit of Albert Wakkary, filed in *Rosenberg* v *The Queen* (Ont. Gen. Div., Court File No. 79885/94) (sworn 2 June 1994), Exhibit C (Department of Finance column, adjusted to 1994).

property are worth to heterosexual couples. These items are not tabulated in any of the published statistics, nor can they be modelled convincingly. Similarly, land-transfer-tax exemptions for transfers to family members, insurance discounts, exemptions from vehicle transfer fees, and so on, cannot be quantified easily.

But perhaps they do not need to be quantified. Surely it is difficult to ignore the fact that all these provisions – the ones that can be quantified and those that cannot, beyond the individual level – all run in the same policy direction: exclusion, invisibility, debasement, denial, erasure, trivialization. In the aggregate, all the provisions that exclude same-sex couples consistently ensure that those who are denied the monetary relief distributed by the heterosexual benefit system receive no other forms of succour either, but are burdened consistently by this culture, not only psychically, but materially as well.

Conclusions

In this chapter, I have concluded that legislation makes reference to spousal status or other relationship status in order to achieve one of four fundamental policy objectives:

1 Recognize or promote the redistribution of incomes or wealth within the family unit;
2 Provide subsidies for couples in which one partner is economically dependent on the other;
3 Give expression to the 'new family wage system' that selectively enhances the economic power of families;
4 Support the boundaries of the above categories with appropriate 'anti-avoidance' provisions.

All of these types of provisions are restricted to opposite-sex couples only, and, by excluding same-sex couples, all of them burden queer existences.

In addition, by excluding same-sex couples from the first three categories of legislation, the state imposes, in effect, a quantifiable 'queer penalty' on lesbian, gay, bisexual, transgendered, and transsexual people to the extent that they form relationships with people who are of the same legal sex. At the very least, and using the most conservative assumptions possible (that there are between 0.1 per cent and 3 per cent as many same-sex couples as there are heterosexual couples in Canada), I have concluded that just in relation to those heterosexual benefits that can be quantified in some way, the 'queer penalty' for 1993 was no less than $16.2 million, and probably more on the order of $165.1 million. In the same year, I have estimated that the various subsidies routinely given to opposite-sex couples in the 'heterosexual economy' in that same year came to at least $5.1 billion – and that is just in relation to eight of the most important of the heterosexual benefit programs.[58]

Not to state the obvious, but if heterosexuality were so 'natural' and normative, the state surely would not be called upon to subsidize it so heavily. And these items have nothing to do with supporting families with children; not one single item in this calculation relates to expenditures for the benefit of children. They relate only to the support of heterosexual relations as between adults. This $5.1 billion of federal and provincial money represents 1.5 per cent of overall government expenditures for the 1993 year, and suggests that supporting and promoting heterosexuality without regard to whether heterosexuals so subsidized are having or raising children is one of the sixty-seven most important things the Canadian state considers that it should be doing at this juncture in history.

The alterity of queer existences has made the dichotomous hierarchy of sexualities in Canada visible, has constituted it as 'difference.' In an ethical social/political system, making visible the previously invisible effects of the 'heterosexual economy' on sexual minorities should lead to negotiation between the heterosexual state/society and those 'others' over the terms of recognition.[59] The discourse to date, of course, has had the state/society resisting this negotiation by continuing to deny the alterity of queer existences wherever possible. Ironically, the call to negotiation has been answered by sexual minorities themselves, who have taken responsibility for looking closely at the costs attached to the apparent gains and losses flowing from the recognition some of them seek. It is to this calculus of recognition that I turn in chapter 9.

Chapter Nine

The 'Benefit' Conundrum and the Politics of Exclusion

> If we don't invent a language, if we don't find our body's language, it will have too few gestures to accompany our story. We shall tire of the same ones, and leave our desires unexpressed, unrealized. Asleep again, unsatisfied, we shall fall back upon the words of men – who, for their part, have 'known' for a long time. But not our body. Seduced, attracted, fascinated, ecstatic with our becoming, we shall remain paralyzed. Deprived of our movements. Rigid, whereas we are made for endless change. Without leaps or falls, and without repetition.
> Luce Irigaray, *This Sex Which Is Not One*, trans. Catherine Porter and Carolyn Burke (Ithaca, NY: Cornell University Press, 1985), 214

Not all legal provisions that apply to 'spouses' or cohabitants confer benefits on them. Many such provisions actually burden in one way or another people who are in opposite-sex relationships. When these 'burdening' provisions are pulled out and isolated from the vast array of provisions that give shape to and subsidize the 'heterosexual economy,' the fact that they do not apply to same-sex couples can easily be made to look like legal policy already 'benefits' queers in some ways that are not available to 'straights.' For example, when Elaine Schachtschneider, a married woman, tried to claim the equivalent-to-married credit in relation to one of her children when she filed her income tax return, she argued that restricting this credit to non-married taxpayers violated her Charter rights.[1] In trying to explain why limiting this tax benefit to single parents did not violate Schachtschneider's Charter rights, the court agreed that both unmarried heterosexuals and lesbian/gay parents could claim this credit when married partners could not, because married couples did not constitute an historically disadvantaged group.

'Straight' objections to the spectre of lesbian couples 'getting away with' benefits denied to heterosexual couples intersect with recent queer commentaries on the 'benefits' of being excluded from the heterosexual economy. For example, Patricia LeFebour has called attention to how recognition of same-sex relationships would interact with hierarchies of race, class, and health, to disadvantage people living with AIDS.[2] Nitya Duclos has demonstrated how recognizing same-sex relationships would intersect hierarchically with sex and family composition.[3] In these tellings, the stories of queer status in law become not about the costs of being excluded, but about the advantages of exclusion, the substance of absence, the negativity of presence. I differentiate these two turns of queer analysis because they signal a critical juncture in the queer deconstruction of the 'heterosexual economy.' I consider this juncture to be 'critical' because it exposes the limits of the 'either–or' paradigm that drives dualist legal thought, and, at the same time, it necessitates further deconstruction of these dichotomies if the analysis is not to end in stasis or mere reversal.

The new dichotomy of which I speak is the divergence between 'heterosexual provisions' that currently 'benefit' queers versus those that currently burden queers – the 'queer penalty' discussed in chapter 8. At the level of legal theory, exposing how hierarchized dualisms might result from granting new rights to members of disadvantaged groups tends all too easily to become a reason to continue to deny those claims. For example, the Supreme Court of Canada eagerly embraced Audrey Macklin's critical feminist analysis of Beth Symes's Charter challenge to the classification of child-care expense deductions. Macklin had demonstrated how granting Symes's claim would privilege Symes relative to some other classes of women, because gaining the right to deduct the cost of child care as business expenses would do nothing to improve the position of women who were treated as employees for tax purposes.[4] The Macklin–Supreme Court interchange did not inspire the Department of Finance to revise section 63 of the Income Tax Act in order to address the issues raised by *Symes* and simultaneously to ameliorate their impact on low-income employed taxpayers. Nor have women's groups taken the initiative of following up with Charter challenges involving low-income women. That is the stasis or paralysis to which Irigaray refers.

By analogy to what happened in *Symes*, attempts to describe the specificities of lesbian, lesbian mother, HIV-positive, living with AIDS, or raced existences can become the next justification for continuing to deny the existence of all queers for all purposes, instead of opening up negotiations over the terms on which queers are to be treated as autonomous members of society.

Still at the level of theory, an alternative, deconstructionist, route around stasis would be strategic reversal of the binary term ('repetition') to displace the negativity associated with it, and to express the claim in terms that encompass and exceed the original binary terms. When applied to the current legal status of sexual minorities, that would involve moving out of the 'victim' position, in which queers who need particular benefits try to remain hidden in the gaps of the law, and moving into a position that 'inhabits' the dichotomy from both the 'inside' and the 'outside.'[5]

The strategy of inhabiting a dichotomy will not work if it collapses into mere reversal of power relations. For example, if the strategy sought to privilege queers at the expense of 'straights,' it would continue the paralysis. (When power is hierarchically allocated, that is not likely to happen anyway, except, perennially, in the minds of those who hold power.) The trick is to find discursive elements that encompass both binary/dichotomized categories ('benefits of recognition' versus 'benefits of exclusion'; 'heterosexual burdens' versus 'queer benefit') at the same time that they move beyond them.[6] This movement can occur only when the 'others' who have joined the discourse – queers – are able to speak out of self-affirmation.

In this chapter, I plumb the contradictory dimensions of the benefit/burden dichotomy for ways in which queers can 'inhabit' it instead of being ruled by it. Part of 'inhabiting' has already happened, of course. By being named, by entering the discourse as different but autonomous, by declaring queer existences to be not negative but positive, lesbian and gay existences (and, one hopes, soon trans/bi existences as well) provide perspectives from which to pull the dichotomy of 'benefit' and 'burden' apart to reveal their architecture.

As I demonstrate in this chapter, the 'heterosexual burdens' that are the 'benefits' of (queer) exclusion simply re-enact heterosexual privilege by 'paying' queers to hide, to remain invisible, absent, negated. On a distributional level, the more disadvantaged some sectors of queer communities are, the more 'beneficial' invisibility becomes to them. On a structural level, there is great concern that once queers can gain access to the massive heterosexual benefit system, the unequal and appropriative nature of marital relations, race-based hierarchies, sexuality, and class will then place irresistible pressures on queers to assimilate to dominant relationship models instead of creating more egalitarian or non-monogamous forms of relationship. Taking this second concern to its extreme, the fear is that if same-sex relationship benefits are available only to those whose relationships fit dominant legal models of heterosexual relations, then the current system of 'heterosexual benefits' and the 'queer penalty' will be transformed into, for example, 'monogamy benefits' or the 'egalitarian penalty.' Paralysis – not 'movement.'

I also explore how the complexities of existing hierarchies of wealth, sex, and race intertwine with the continuing denial of full legal personality to women as a class to construct the 'benefits of exclusion' to which critical feminists and queers have drawn attention, whether those benefits have been defined in monetary terms or in terms of exclusion from the hierarchical, appropriative pairing of recognized heterosexual unions.

After exploring these complexities, I look at how power-holders in both the heterosexual economy and the queer economy have attempted to deploy critical readings of the 'benefits of exclusion' not in order to deconstruct the hierarchies which make them possible, but in an attempt to reinforce and defend those hierarchies against queer incursions. The deployment of exclusion in these diverse situations makes 'repetition' and 'encompassing' all the more elusive, yet necessary.

'Benefits' of Being Excluded

Along with the vast array of government benefits that are designed to support, regulate, and subsidize heterosexual relations, many legal provisions have been designed to make sure that members of couples cannot simply step out of the 'couple unit' and present themselves as individuals in order to escape some of the larger responsibilities associated with relationship recognition, or to escape some of the mechanisms designed to deliver hetero benefits to those who are thought to need them most. These provisions function more or less as 'anti-avoidance' provisions, and take one of three general shapes:

1 Provisions that are designed to prevent spouses from collaborating to optimize benefits of various kinds;
2 Provisions that reflect the economies of consumption
thought to arise from cohabitation –'the tax on marriage'; and
3 Provisions that are designed to induce family members
to turn first to each other for economic support, and then to the state only if that level of support falls below some official cut-off point.

The third category has received the most attention in litigation, but the other two categories are also important in getting a clear picture of how being excluded from the definition of 'spouse' or 'cohabitants' can be considered to 'benefit' same-sex couples.

Although issues of privilege and hierarchy are discussed in detail later in this chapter, it is important to stress before outlining the 'beneficial exclusion' provisions that, if they were extended to apply to same-sex couples, many of them would differentially burden low-income couples when compared with middle- and high-income couples. This differential burden would itself be sexed, raced, classed, and based on ability, because members of queer communities bring their full selves to their economic lives. Queers who experience the greatest disadvantages would be burdened most heavily by these forms of inclusion.

Conflict-of-Interest Provisions

Some spouse-based legislative provisions are designed to prevent spouses from collaborating to optimize benefits of various kinds. This includes conflict-of-interest provisions, disclosure-of-family-interest legislation, and numerous taxation provisions that are intended to force family members to deal at arm's length with each other or to block tax-planning schemes in which family members can be presumed to have collaborated to reduce their overall tax liability. Some of the most obvious of these types of provisions are the Ontario Municipal Conflict of Interest Act[7] and the Loan and Trust Corporations Act,[8] which either place an absolute prohibition on some kinds of dealings with spouses by those in positions of power and responsibility, or require that spouses declare conflicts of interest and remove themselves from decision making in relation to the conflict.[9]

Conflict-of-interest provisions do not all work in the same way. For example, the principal-residence provisions in the Income Tax Act flatly prohibit spouses (including, since 1993, opposite-sex cohabitants) from designating more than one building per year as a principal residence of any of them. There is no room for negotiation there, no room for proof that the two spouses did not live together, and so on. Heterosexual couples can exercise some control over whether they will be affected by this rule, simply because couples who do not marry and who do not actually live together conjugally will not be deemed to be spouses. Although it is difficult to imagine anyone getting a divorce in order to enjoy the benefit of an extra principal-residence exemption, this is one of the myriad heterosexual benefits – and one of the limits on those benefits – that some people scrutinize before deciding whether to marry, cohabit, or live separately.

Other conflict-of-interest or anti-avoidance rules not only look to the legal relationship between members of couples, but also are buttressed by factual tests of 'relatedness' or 'connection.' To use another example drawn from the Income Tax Act, even if same-sex couples are not permitted to marry and cannot be deemed to be spouses by virtue of cohabitation,[10] they may still be considered to be 'related persons' who are deemed not to deal at arm's length for purposes of some 500 anti-avoidance provisions in the Income Tax Act. Because married and cohabiting couples are considered to be 'related persons,' they are irrebutably deemed not to deal at arm's length.[11] But the statute further stipulates that 'it is a question of fact whether persons not related to each other were at a particular time dealing with each other at arm's length.'[12]

Thus it is fair to say that, although same-sex couples would be burdened by some of these kinds of provisions by being deemed to be married, some of those 'burden' provisions can already be applied to same-sex couples when the facts warrant – despite the fact that same-sex couples are currently denied the benefits of ascribed marital status.

The 'Tax on Marriage'

Some 'benefit' programs confer greater benefits on single individuals than on married/cohabiting couples, while other programs use benefit 'grind-down' formulas or low-income cutoffs (LICOs) to balance benefits against the couple's income. Most social-assistance eligibility formulas operate in this way, as does the refundable GST tax credit. The GST credit is a good example of both the 'tax on marriage' and LICO formulas (LICOs are discussed in detail later in this chapter). The GST tax credit in section 122.5 of the Income Tax Act was devised to ameliorate the admittedly regressive incidence of flat-rated consumption taxes like the sales tax or the GST, which bear most heavily on low-income taxpayers. Because the GST tax credit reflects the assumption that economies of consumption enable couples to live more cheaply than individuals, this credit actually confers larger benefits on individuals than on spouses and cohabitants.[13]

Table 9.1 illustrates how this 'tax on marriage' operates for people whose incomes are low enough to qualify for the full credit. For 1993, the full adult GST credit was $199. Single adults also received a single-adult

Table 9.1. Effect of Family Configuration on GST Credit, 1993

	Individuals	Couple
One adult	$304	–
Two adults	608	398
One adult, one child	503	–
Two adults, one child	807	503
Two adults, two children	1,006	609

SOURCE: Income Tax Act, section 122.5, adjusted for 1993 taxation year.

supplement of $105, and single parents could claim, in addition to their own $199 adult credit and $105 single-adult supplement, a second adult credit of $199 for one dependent child plus a supplement of $105 for each additional child. In contrast, couples could claim $199 per adult, for $398 per couple, but did not receive the $105 single-adult supplement for either of them, nor the $199 adult credit for any dependent child.

Table 9.1 illustrates how family configuration affects the distribution of this credit. The amount of the 'tax on marriage' depends on the specific configuration of the family. When two adults are deemed to be 'spouses' for purposes of the GST credit, they lose $210 each year between them. When they have one child, the reduction is $304 per year; if they have two children, the reduction is $397 in credit per year. In the aggregate, this 'tax on marriage' feature of the GST credit system offsets the dependency-transferable credit system outlined in chapter 8. Although it has never been described in the policy literature as such, it represents a sort of 'side door' reduction in the tax benefits of marriage. Interestingly, it is not a very visible reduction in the dependency credits, because it arises from a completely different set of provisions in the Income Tax Act, and it is administered separately as a refundable tax.

The implications of this 'tax on marriage' for queers in Canada are very interesting. It is safe to say that most queers in Canada whose incomes fall below $30,000 per year are receiving at least part of the GST credit. The differential between the size of the couple credits and the individual credits assumes that the economies of consumption are approximately 40 per cent. This means that, depending on family configuration, if same-sex couples and their children come to be recognized as 'family' for purposes of the GST credit, they would lose something on the order of 35 to 40 per cent of the GST credits they could receive if they could continue to be treated as 'individuals' for purposes of the GST credit.

Because of the probable demographics of same-sex couples, it may well be that this 'tax on marriage' would burden same-sex couples more than it does opposite-sex couples. Because of the differences between lesbian incomes and gay incomes, this burden would be greater for lesbian couples than for gay couples. Further, to the extent that either lesbian or gay couples may not practise the same appropriations of non-waged work associated with heterosexual couples, any 'economies of consumption' or 'economies of scale' queer couples do enjoy are unlikely to be so large that they would offset the monetary loss of the full individual-level GST credits. Nor are queer couples as likely to qualify for dependency credits that would at least partially ameliorate the loss of GST credits. From a policy perspective, it is highly likely that this system would be extended to same-sex couples. This 'tax on marriage' came into effect during the same time that federal and provincial income tax legislation was being amended to expand the definition of 'marriage' to include opposite-sex cohabitants. What better time to introduce a 'tax on marriage' than when more 'married' people have suddenly been added to this tax base. The Tax Policy branch of the Department of Finance has already realized that, if the Income Tax Act were amended to treat same-sex couples as spouses, many of them will then have to pay this 'tax on marriage.'[14]

'Family Income' Means Testing

Many of the 'heterosexual benefit' provisions discussed in chapter 8 also contain low-income cut-off clauses (LICOs). These LICOs are designed to restrict eligibility for some spousal benefits to those people who need them the most. The theory behind these LICOs is that these benefits are, in effect, forms of social assistance that thus should be made available only to low-income people. LICOs are found not only in direct government expenditure schemes, but also in indirect-expenditure programs delivered through income tax legislation. Examples include the LICOs in direct social-assistance legislation, old-age spousal pension allowances, child benefits, the equivalent-to-married tax credit, some of the transferable tax credits, child-care expense deductions, unemployment insurance, worker compensation, and medicaid provisions.

LICOs for individual recipients of government benefits are not particularly controversial. When LICOs are not only calculated and administered by reference to the income of the individual applicant, but are further contingent on the incomes of other family members, via 'family income' concepts, however, many people who would qualify for benefits as individuals are denied benefits because their spouse's or cohabitant's income is large enough to take the couple or the family over the group-based LICO. From a policy perspective, the use of 'family income' concepts to control eligibility for government benefits is really just the flip side of the effect of dependency benefits: An income-earning adult who supports an economically dependent spouse can receive dependency benefits to help carry that burden. But if that economically dependent spouse wants to escape his or her dependency by taking advantage of some of these means-tested benefits, 'family income' limits will prevent him or her from qualifying for those benefits as an 'individual' unless the supporting spouse's income is low enough that together they still fall under the family LICO for that type of program.

The actual mechanics of LICOs can take various forms. Some LICO formulas merely look to the couple's aggregated incomes, so that an individual will receive social assistance if his or her own income falls below the relevant level, but will be denied assistance if his or her spouse's or cohabitant's income can be presumed to offset that low personal income. Tax-based LICOs can work the same way: an individual who had income of $25,921 or less in 1993 would have received the full federal child tax credit of $601, but if his or her spouse/cohabitant's income took the couple over that threshold, then they would not have qualified for the credit at all. Other LICO formulas work in more subtle ways. For example, the LICO in the child-care expense deduction provisions can shift between spouses, depending on their relative income levels. A single individual can deduct the full amount of child-care expenses, but a married/cohabiting taxpayer can deduct the full amount only if two conditions are met: their combined income is large enough to take advantage of the full deduction, and the taxpayer's individual income is lower than his or her spouse's income. If the partner's income is the lower of the two, then section 63 of the Income Tax Act requires that partner to claim the deduction. This type of LICO is designed to measure benefits by reference to the 'need' of a coupled taxpayer. The formula appears to allocate the deduction to an 'individual' member of a couple, but by forcing the spouse with the lower income to be that individual, it ceases to be a 'real' individual benefit.[15]

The policy objective behind the use of family- or couple-based LICOs is simple: Family-income concepts force family members to turn first to each other for economic support, and then to the state only if the level of support they can receive from their family does not meet some minimum. The expectation that family members will support each other is backed up not only by family law, but by the Criminal Code.[16]

Like all the spousal benefit provisions themselves, family/couple LICO clauses are expressed in relentlessly heterosexual terms. None of them applies to same-sex couples, because all the relevant definitions of 'spouse' in these statutes are expressly limited to 'opposite-sex' couples. No matter how long same-sex couples have been together, and no matter how many children they may have, they will never be affected by couple-based LICOs. The same opposite-sex definitions of 'spouse' in dependency provisions that deny same-sex couples access to couple-based benefits also ensure that couple-based LICO clauses will not apply to same-sex couples either. Nor does factually dealing 'not at arm's length' with a same-sex cohabitant bring queers within the application of these rules.

Thus denial of dependency benefits to same-sex couples imposes a penalty on same-sex couples, but family-income concepts actually appear to benefit same-sex couples. Where cohabiting heterosexuals might lose unemployment insurance benefits, social assistance, medicaid, child benefits, child tax benefits, the equivalent-to-married tax credit, or the maximum value of the child-care expense deduction under the Income Tax Act simply because of the presence of an income-earning partner in the household, same-sex couples can as much as double their benefits while living together, because their partners' incomes do not have to be taken into account in calculating their eligibility.

It is quite difficult to speculate on how much these 'beneficial exclusions' are worth to same-sex couples. For example, in the case of the GST credit, deemed marriage will reduce the net benefit that can be claimed by each partner, and the LICO applied to this benefit will further constrain it as household income rises. The GST credit is reduced by 5 per cent of the extent to which family income exceeds the relevant LICO. Thus aggregation of family incomes can reduce the already-reduced GST credit faster for couples than would occur on the individual level. This of course depends on the specific make-up of family incomes.[17]

Distributional Concerns

As the legal status of sexual minorities in Canada has begun to change, views on the appropriateness of relationship recognition have begun to polarize at the community level as well as in the formal political process. The two levels of the debate reveal quite different dynamics, but they do have one thing in common: Hierarchies of class, race, gender, and sexuality tend to take over at every level, whether the focus is on individual cases, on the way communities have organized, or on the formal political level.

Queer communities in Canada have been particularly concerned with the distributional and hierarchical effects of recognition of same-sex relationships. These concerns arise directly out of queer experience with the effects of class, sex, race, and sexual hierarchies throughout life, and they have become intense as people have realized that, intended or not, there are some important advantages to being denied relationship recognition. Same-sex couples have been concerned that these 'beneficial exclusions' are not income-neutral, but differentially burden low-income couples whose incomes are at or near the various LICOs. They have also been concerned that the combination of the gender-specificity and the income-specificity of most 'beneficial exclusions' would differentially impact on those who are already the most vulnerable members of vulnerable communities. People living with HIV/AIDS, people disadvantaged by race or ability, women in lesbian relationships, and couples raising children would be most adversely affected by these types of provisions. Thus it is fair to say that queer communities are concerned – and advisedly so – that inclusion of same-sex couples in couple-based benefit programs would benefit some couples at the expense of others. In this section, I expand on these concerns to demonstrate that no one demographic characteristic can completely predict how relationship recognition will affect sexual minorities. Even from the relatively narrow perspective of distributional concerns, relationship recognition has complex implications for all sexual minorities.

Low-Income Queers

Many of the legal incidents of relationship recognition transcend class, race, gender, and sexual divisions. The sense of security that comes with knowing that, whether in little or big events of day-to-day life, one cannot be excluded merely on the basis of sexuality is important at any income level. Having a legal framework within which to identify and define relationship responsibilities and rights; being able to receive employment benefits; enjoying the security of knowing that, at the very least, CPP survivor benefits may be available to one's partner in old age; being able to put one's partner on title to the family car without paying vehicle transfer taxes, or on the family automobile insurance policy – all these legal rights are of more or less equal value regardless of economic power. Indeed, they grow more valuable as money incomes drop, and conflict or crisis of any kind makes proportionately bigger demands on scarce energy and resources. Thus CPP survivor benefits, for example, would be more valuable to low-income partners than to partners who have substantial income and assets of their own.

Class differences exacerbated by race, gender, and sexual differences mean that, even among themselves, lesbians, gays, bisexuals, and transgendered/sexual persons have quite mixed feelings about the general issue of inclusion versus exclusion. In this regard, lesbian, gay, bisexual, transgendered, and transsexual persons, whether in relationships or not, are not very different from heterosexuals. That is so because the rights and responsibilities that go along with legal recognition of relationships are a mixed blessing: heterosexual couples value being treated as each other's next of kin, but they do not necessarily value the legal obligation to support each other, or being required to share support of children after their own adult relationship ends.

Low-income individuals who expect to form stable relationships may welcome the opportunity to seek support if the relationship were to terminate, to receive the proceeds of life insurance policies, to be treated as 'spouse' for purposes of intestate succession, guardianship of children, or medical care. They may also find some of the employment benefits that extend to families quite valuable precisely because of income constraints. However, low-income individuals or couples will not be particularly interested in being able to make deductible contributions to each other's RRSPs or in the tax advantages of legalized income-splitting. Nor would those who do not earn large enough incomes to take full advantage of the married tax credit or transferable credits benefit from ascribed spousal status to the same extent as those with higher incomes. And in some situations, the benefits of inclusion could well outweigh the burdens of inclusion, at least at some points in life, such as when low-income lesbians would otherwise be entitled to the child tax benefit.

The overall calculus of relationship recognition is most pressing for the poorest sectors of queer communities, which includes women, raced people, and people with impaired health. As discussed in chapter 7, lesbian women earn the lowest incomes, married men earn the highest incomes, and gay/bisexual men earn significantly more than heterosexual women but measurably less than heterosexual men. Because of these income disparities at the individual level, lesbian couples have less combined income than any other type of couple, and heterosexual married couples have the most, despite women's quite low earnings relative to men. Cohabiting heterosexual couples and gay couples rank quite close to each other, with gay couples receiving somewhat higher incomes than cohabiting opposite-sex couples.[18]

The fact that the lowest-income people in queer communities are lesbian women is particularly significant, for, more than many other social benefits, income supports for women with children tend to be subject to low-income cut-offs. The child tax benefit, social assistance, the equivalent-to-married credit, health care benefits delivered through social assistance programs, and child-care expense deductions are all subject to LICOs that would differentially disadvantage lesbian women if they were to be deemed to be cohabitants or spouses.

When race is taken into consideration, it can skew income disparities, often pushing incomes downward. Data on average employment income by place of birth and sex demonstrate the magnitude of the effect of ethnic origin/place of birth on incomes, with both women and men from Southeast Asia, South America, Central America, East Asia, the Caribbean, and Western Asia receiving the lowest incomes on raw data and when the data are adjusted for age and education.[19] When the effect of gender is considered along with area of origin, however, the disparities are pronounced, even within the groups with the lowest incomes. For example, in a 1988 study, average employment incomes adjusted for age and education for South and Central American women were $11,411, compared with men's average incomes of $17,362. And even though men from Southeast Asia were ranked lowest in incomes (fifteenth) and women from Southeast Asia were ranked only fourteenth, the adjusted average income for men was significantly higher than the women's – $16,429, compared with $11,419. When it becomes possible to factor sexuality into this kind of detailed data, it may well be that the combined effects of gender, race, and sexuality will result in even lower incomes for racially identified lesbian couples than for non–racially identified lesbian couples, for example.[20]

Health issues intensify income hierarchies as well. People living with HIV or AIDS who depend on social assistance may find that they would not be able to afford adequate medication or treatment if they were to lose the medical coverage extended to those on social assistance. When the 'couple' is used as the benefit unit, such couples go over the low-income cut-offs more rapidly than if they were assessed as individuals. This concern was originally raised by Patricia LeFebour, who explored, from a class perspective, how the extension of provincial family health coverage to same-sex couples would differentially disadvantage people with AIDS.[21]

Middle- and High-Income Queers

Lesbians and gays with higher incomes also have mixed feelings about legal recognition of relationships. Some people feel that their property or income might be at risk, while some welcome the opportunity to obtain increased tax benefits as well as to secure their partner's and children's financial interests. Those who expect to form successful long-term relationships tend to be interested in obtaining the economic and tax benefits that flow from relationship recognition. These benefits include employment-related benefits, the dependent-spouse credit in the Income Tax Act, the availability of rollovers for inter-partner transfers of property, the opportunity to effectively double their pension benefits, and various exemptions from liability that would otherwise be triggered under tax legislation, as well as benefits flowing from pension plans, RRSPs, and public retirement schemes. In contrast, higher-income lesbians and gays who may not be in relationships or who anticipate relationship breakdown are concerned that legal recognition of their relationships might fetter their financial autonomy, force them to share property, their homes, or their incomes. Or, if they have arranged their investments so that both partners can take advantage of couple-based benefits such as the principal-residence exemption,[22] they may feel that the disadvantages of ascribed status outweigh the advantages.

To a certain extent, these concerns are not entirely unlike the concerns that heterosexuals have in relation to ascribed status. While heterosexuals could once exercise some choice over the legal incidents of their relationships by choosing between marriage or cohabitation, the inclusion of 'opposite-sex' cohabitants in a growing number of statutory definitions of 'spouse' has deprived both married couples and cohabitants of the chance to make that choice. Ascribed status is always imposed involuntarily, and the only way to avoid it is to live separately.

Hierarchical Concerns

The other set of concerns voiced by members of queer communities arises not out of mere distributional issues, but out of critical understanding of the deep historical connections between the institution of marriage, gender privilege, the formation of private property, and the role of the state in maintaining all hierarchies of privilege, be they hierarchies that turn on race, gender, sex, sexuality, relationship status, reproductive status, ability, economic class, or other such characteristics.

It is absolutely true that marriage and heterosexual cohabitation are very often unequal and even appropriative relations. Biological sex remains the single most important predictor of low incomes throughout life, low or negative net worths, disproportionate responsibility for the care of children, low access to middle- and high-paying jobs, disproportionately heavy levels of taxation, and low incomes even after division of assets and incomes upon separation or divorce.[23] Thus marriage is almost always an unequal relationship to the extent that the partners do not make choices at the micro level to ensure that all disparities of incomes, opportunities, or wealth are evened out over the years. And it is appropriative to the extent that many husbands continue to take advantage of the ceaseless unpaid labour of their wives to advance in their careers; make educational, career, recreational, and health choices that optimize their long-term earning capacities; yet resist the equalization of assets or incomes even upon divorce. Despite advances in family property law, the continued discretion given to courts in allocating assets, incomes, and child custody on relationship breakdown continues to leave women with well less than half of the family estate, and well over half the work of raising children.[24] And even if, despite all this, two partners sought to construct for themselves a perfectly 'equal' relationship, the massive array of benefits offered by the heterosexual economy would make it difficult to achieve in practice.

Queer communities across North America are thus engaged in the so-called marriage debate. But instead of lumping all strands of this debate together and treating them as if they were all discussing the same issue, I find it useful to begin by separating the U.S. version of the debate from the Canadian version. Generally (to the extent that any generalization is accurate), the debate in the United States is over 'marriage' versus 'not marriage.' This definition of the issue is due to the legal specificities of U.S. relationship laws, which really do not recognize alternative legal categories like 'cohabitation' in any systematic way. Interestingly, even those activists in the United States who characterize themselves as being 'anti-marriage' often point to extension of employment spousal benefits, for example, as a better political goal than obtaining formal marriage rights, because that would give same-sex couples the advantages of marriage without the disadvantages. In Canada, however, the success of the 'opposite-sex' movement has given *de facto* relationships such high visibility that the legally recognized category of 'opposite-sex' cohabitation has come to be seen as a viable middle ground between formal marriage and complete lack of legal recognition. Combined with a less ideological and more materialist approach to policy formation on this issue, the Canadian debate has centred on asking 'What form of recognition?' rather than on debating 'marriage' versus 'not marriage.' The deconstructivist atmosphere in which cohabitation has emerged as a marriage alternative has perhaps created a more open context within which the 'marriage debate' has been enacted in Canada.

I am not suggesting that queer critics on the two sides of the border do not have anything to offer each other. However, given the nature of cultural hegemony, it should not be surprising that there is a tendency in Canada to hear U.S. voices quite clearly, and sometimes without awareness of the differences in cultural contexts.

U.S. 'Marriage Debate'

As relationship-recognition issues began to work their way through legal structures in the United States, the language of 'marriage' was quickly inserted into that area of rights discourse. Passage of registered partnership legislation in Denmark in mid-1989 and the decision in *Braschi* v *Stahl Associates*,[25] in which the court ruled that a gay male couple was a 'family' for purposes of survivor rights under rent control legislation, focused mainstream media attention on the legal status of same-sex relationships. The issue was quickly framed as being about 'marriage' instead of about 'relationship recognition,' and as a confrontational 'debate' rather than as a discussion both within queer communities and in the larger community. Anti-queer/anti-marriage proponents approached the issue as related primarily to 'morality,' 'family values,' and the 'sanctity of marriage.' Queer debate appeared to polarize around two seemingly irreconcilable positions, with Tom Stoddard, executive director of Lambda, for example, arguing that the lesbian/gay community should give top priority to marriage rights for a number of practical and ethical reasons, and Paula Ettelbrick, a radical feminist lesbian who was at the time legal director of Lambda, arguing that marriage not only was not a 'path to liberation,' but would constrain, assimilate, undermine, homogenize, and silence lesbians and gays.[26]

One reading of the resulting developments is that critical queers tried to open up more nuanced discursive space within which to plumb these contradictory views, but that the press of political and legal events crowded nuance out of the picture and silenced those voices. For example, Nan Hunter, a libertarian feminist lesbian who participated in numerous symposia on the issue of queer marriage, attempted to open up a deconstructive materialist analysis of those elements of marriage that might be beneficial to queers, those that might be problematic, and the transformative potential of queer marriage. Nitya Duclos, a Canadian critical feminist who was invited to respond to Hunter's paper, began to particularize that materialist analysis.[27] Neither of these disruptions had much impact on the polarized characterization of the 'debate.'

Another less flattering view is that critical interventions were simply not tolerated in the charged atmosphere surrounding the U.S. 'marriage debate.' When Hunter was legal director of the queer caucus of the national American Civil Liberties Union (ACLU), she heard that the local Hawaii ACLU office had been asked to support *Baehr* v *Lewin*[28] in the early stages, and allegedly used her position to convince the local state office to canvass local queer opinions on marriage before committing itself. This move was seen by some pro-marriage advocates as an attempt to block ACLU support of the case and to stall the decision long enough to mobilize opposition to marriage litigation.[29] Critical assessment of the issue was further squeezed out in other areas of the country, where local 'debates' were staged by 'touring companies' made up of pro-marriage gay men and anti-marriage lesbian women, and the legal literature quickly began to reflect this polarized dynamic.[30]

Whether critical materialist nuance was drowned out because it was a minority view all along, because it was a largely lesbian feminist view,[31] because it got in the way of dominant queer agendas, or because anti-queer/anti-marriage pressure was really more urgent, the result of this three-way dynamic was the emergence of a massive constitutional confrontation that will take years to sort out. The celebration of *Baehr I* was short-lived[32] as the federal government formulated the Defense of Marriage Act (DOMA)[33] even before *Baehr* v *Miike* was decided. Designed to deprive same-sex marriages of portability in the United States and to insulate federal legislation against similar lawsuits, a wave of DOMA-like statutes began to wash across the United States. The result of this escalation has muffled the 'marriage debate' in queer communities as activists across the United States have begun to focus on opposing these state DOMAs – whether they would have priorized marriage rights in the absence of DOMA or not. A similar effect can be seen in the legal literature, which has all but completely dropped its critical consideration of the merits of marriage and has now become preoccupied with the constitutional and legal status of DOMA legislation.[34] Proponents of same-sex marriage now seem to be searching for ways to justify having taken control of the national political agenda,[35] and the appeals in

Baehr II appear to be taking up much of the discursive space that might have been devoted to the materialist deconstruction that Hunter and Duclos began back when this debate first surfaced.

Canadian Debate

It is of course an oversimplification to claim that the discussion of relationship recognition in Canada is completely different and separate from the 'marriage debate' in the United States. For one thing, Canadians who have engaged this issue have routinely referred to points made by U.S. commentators, usually without elaborating on the cultural or legal specificities within which the 'marriage debate' or other critical issues have unfolded and developed there.[36] For another, Nitya Duclos certainly attempted to inject Canadian experience (although it was not contextualized as such) into the U.S. 'marriage debate.'[37] However, the realities of cultural hegemony have meant that, while the voices of U.S. commentators have been heard fairly clearly in Canada, the opposite has not been true. This has resulted in a rather markedly one-way integration of both sets of concerns on the Canadian side.

Having said that, the Canadian context is still structurally different in many important regards. First, the Charter of Rights now entrenches equality on the basis of sex and sexual orientation. In the United States, sex equality is entrenched in some state constitutions, but not in the federal constitution, and sexual orientation has no constitutional protection (except in Hawaii) under the heading 'sex.' Second, a much larger sector of the queer population is protected by human rights non-discrimination clauses in Canada than in the United States. Third, Canadian queers began to make some inroads into categories like 'family' as early as 1989,[38] holding out the hope that queers could gain equality with opposite-sex cohabitants, a strategy that has involved lower levels of confrontation with conservatives and less risk than all-or-nothing marriage litigation. Fourth, the cohabitants with whom some queer litigants would be equal have already received vastly more legal recognition in Canada than they have in the United States, so that this strategy has offered a concrete alternative to formal marriage for some same-sex couples. And finally, although Canada enacted its own variant of DOMA back in the mid-1970s, the 'opposite-sex' definitions of 'spouse' are more cryptic and muted, and have now already begun to be attacked successfully in Charter litigation.[39]

Because of these differences, and also because litigation over formal marriage rights did not ripen quite as quickly in Canada as in the United States, Canadian activists have, for the time being, backed off on the formal marriage issue. After the trial court turned down a Charter challenge to the Ontario Marriage Act[40] on the basis that, at common law, people of the same sex did not have the legal capacity to marry each other, and after the Supreme Court of Canada ruled in *Egan and Nesbit* v *Canada*[41] that exclusion of same-sex couples from the definition of 'opposite-sex' cohabitants was constitutionally valid, an appeal in that Charter challenge was withdrawn for fear that it would push the courts into negative rulings before cases involving cohabitant rights (such as *M.* v *H.* and *Rosenberg*) could be pursued.[42] Unlike the U.S. debate over the formal marriage issue, this decision was not made because of community opposition to marriage for queers (although some people involved in that discussion may have been motivated by anti-marriage sentiments), but because of timing and strategic considerations.

Because the legal and strategic context in Canada has been different, the framing of relationship recognition issues at the community level in Canada has also been different. The concerns about 'assimilation' into the unequal and appropriative relations of marriage are certainly still significant in Canada, but Canadians have raised the more subtle and, I think, important question of how legal recognition of same-sex relationships inevitably reinforces the many hierarchies of privilege that are already apparent in queer communities.[43] These critiques do not fall into the trap of the 'either–or' dynamic dictated by the current legal context in the United States, but explore in realistic fashion how power differences in lesbian and gay couples and in the larger lesbian and gay community are constructed, and how those power differences will be affected by changes in the legal context.[44]

One hierarchy of privilege that has particularly concerned the Women's Legal Education and Advocacy Fund (LEAF) is the hierarchy between monogamous and non-monogamous relationships that is reinforced every time two-person relationships are given legal recognition. This has remained the strongest argument in Canada for avoiding any legal recognition of same-sex relationships whatsoever, even when concerns over hierarchies of wealth, privilege, and dependency might be addressed. The organizers of the national LEAF consultation with lesbian communities across Canada wrote papers and briefs, presented panels, and proposed policy positions that pointed out the inherent limitations of including same-sex couples in policies now limited to opposite-sex couples.[45] Although the organizers reported that the consultation process helped raise awareness of how the myriad relationship benefits offered by the state would privilege one type of relationship over another if extended to same-sex couples, they recognized that they were to some extent attempting to move against the larger tide of political events, which included the extension of surviving spouse benefits to same-sex couples in *Leshner* by the time their report was published. Thus they did not make any final recommendations on this or other issues, and instead emphasized the importance of continual consultation with all communities affected by proposed litigation or legislation.[46]

The LEAF lesbian consultations have been misused by litigants,[47] and did not develop some of the most challenging issues such as the role of non-monogamous relationships in queer communities very fully,[48] with the result that some of the most creative ideas that emerged in the consultations have been largely ignored. However, they have helped expose the main point of the lesbian critique of relationship recognition: Both marriage and opposite-sex cohabitation are inherently unequal and appropriative legal institutions, and unless all the rights and responsibilities that will flow from recognition of same-sex relationships are examined carefully, the assimilation of lesbian or gay existence to either the marriage model or the common-law model would make it more difficult for lesbians and gays to develop more egalitarianism relationships. This structural concern merges with the concern about privileging some forms of relationships at the expense of others, and with concerns over the distributional impact of inclusion.

Consider this concrete example of how distributional and hierarchical, structural issues merge. If same-sex couples were given the ascribed status of 'spouse' for purposes of the Income Tax Act, then lesbian women could find themselves in the same position as the taxpayer in *Poulter* v *M.N.R.*: Lesbian women who receive the child tax benefit by virtue of their low incomes could lose those benefits if they and their cohabitant were deemed to be spouses. It would be completely irrelevant that such partner might not actually contribute to the support of the child, or that they lived together but were not in monogamous relationships, or that they might not think of themselves as a 'family.' Obviously, denial of the child tax benefit in such circumstances would place considerable pressure on lesbian women to couple, to couple monogamously, to seek or accept support from their cohabitant, to raise children with a partner even if they would rather remain single parents, or to continue, even though living outside the heteropatriarchal economy, to seek support as a means of economic survival.

To take this example further, the survival strategy promoted by the family-income testing in the child tax benefit would never work as well for lesbian women as it does for heterosexual women, because lesbian women are economically situated both as lesbians and as women. The 'pay-off' for being induced to seek support would be less for lesbian women than it is for heterosexual women, and would become just one more factor that would add up to the greater costliness of life as lesbian. Nor is this factor insignificant. The loss of the child tax benefit litigated in *Poulter* came to some $1,600 in tax credits per child in 1993. The loss of this tax benefit would be financially significant for a person whose income was less than $25,921 (the family income threshold for 1993) – but it would have been largely offset by the value of the dependent-spouse credit that the other partner could have claimed if the taxpayer were a dependent spouse.[49] Deemed marriage provisions and the differential allocation of poverty to women would certainly contribute to the relentless pressure on all women in Canada to seek out and remain in economically dependent relationships.

Nor is this example particularly fanciful. Although the LEAF lesbian consultations revealed that lesbians engage in and value a wide diversity of relationship forms, and although social science research has demonstrated that same-sex couples often express the strong belief that both partners should work outside the home,[50] many lesbian couples do in fact divide labour along lines very much like those characteristic of heterosexual couples. The evidence led by the parties in *Anderson* v *Luoma*[51] illustrate these similarities. Penny Anderson and Arlene Luoma had two children conceived by alternative insemination. Luoma, the older and more established partner, supported the entire family during Anderson's child-bearing years and managed their real estate investments. Luoma gave Anderson a gold wedding band with a solitaire diamond, and they took what was described by the court as a 'honeymoon' for a month in Central America shortly after they began living together. When Anderson returned to waged work after their children were a few years old, it was as a secretary in Luoma's notary business. Anderson's salary payments may have been structured to generate the tax benefits of income-splitting, and Luoma appeared to be in charge of what was done with the after-tax proceeds of that income. Anderson also spent considerable time supervising renovations of their home, keeping house, and caring for Luoma and the children. When the relationship broke down, Luoma held title to most of their property, and talked Anderson into signing over her interest in the family home to help them get off to a 'fresh start' by moving to a farm. As soon as Anderson signed the deed, Luoma convinced Anderson to move out of the house with the children, moved her new partner into the house and into her business, and refused to share her assets or income with Anderson on the basis that she was under no legal obligation to do so.

Nor are the relationship dynamics revealed in *Anderson* v *Luoma* merely artefacts of lesbian practice in the long-ago 1980s. Although the partners in *M.* v *H.* never had any children, there were many similar power imbalances. The economically dominant partner (H.) was again older, appeared to have more business experience, and relied on her relationship with M. to induce her to form a business together. When their business began to fail, H. continued to work for wages, while M., having less experience and fewer prospects, found that she could best contribute to their undertakings by taking on more responsibility for the care of their home and the care of H. Then, when the relationship broke down – apparently partly because H. did not want to see herself as supporting M., did not want to memorialize their relationship in a cohabitation agreement – H. locked M. out of their properties, took all their business records, and refused to share either assets or income with her.

On the basis of the record in these two cases, I think it fair to say that at least some lesbian women model unequal and appropriative behaviour in their relationships. Thus the extension of dependency benefits or 'family wage' types of benefits to lesbian couples would undoubtedly set some lesbian women up to respond to inducements to dependency at the same time that they would deprive them of some of the benefits they may receive now. Women who are lesbian are not insulated from these types of pressures: The partners in *Anderson* v *Luoma* may well have tried to act in concert to take advantage of opportunities to split business income that were at the time denied to married couples, and that are now denied to opposite-sex cohabitants.[52]

Deploying Exclusion

If queer communities had the political power or freedom to shape relationship regimes to meet the particular needs of each sector of these communities, they might be able to solve the hierarchical and distributional problems that divide people on the basis of class, race, sex, ability, family composition, as well as on the basis of sexuality.

But perhaps not. What is startling is that there is a decided gap between what queer people say in political contexts and what they seem to be doing to each other in individualized conflicts. It is almost as if the alienation that springs from the 'inside/outside' figuration of enclosed cultural boundaries – heterosexism – has taught some sexual minorities how to deploy exclusion against others to their own advantage. In fact, at the same time that some members of specific communities are decrying relationship recognition as assimilationist, other members of the same communities are deploying the empty space of non-assimilated 'outsider' locations against their former partners.

The deployment of exclusion for the personal advantage of some queers is consistent with the deployment of exclusion at the level of formal politics as well. In at least one case – *Egan and Nesbit* v *The Queen* – the litigants essentially told the government that they did not care whether the price of relationship recognition was (possibly) the loss of some increment of provincial social welfare support. And on the larger political level, some sectors of the queer community have actually tried to show how it would be financially in the interests of the state to recognize same-sex relationships, if only to bring same-sex couples within the rubric of 'couples' for purposes of applying LICOs. Instead of engaging with the deeper structural issues that these offers have opened up, however, some governments appear to have taken the position that they do not want 'queer' money, and, in the recent appeal in *Rosenberg v. M.N.R.*,[53] seem to be going so far as to say in legal argument that lesbians and gays are really much better off in the unboundaried unregulated space of 'outsider.'

'You Were Never a "Real" ____'

Much of the relationship litigation in both Canada and the United States reveals that less-powerful members of same-sex couples are often forced to pay the price of exclusion at a very personal level. Going back to the examples in *Anderson* v *Luoma,* Luoma successfully defended the claim for child support by basically arguing that she was not a 'real' parent. Although she won on issues of parentage and implied agreement to support, with the court ruling that she was not a 'parent' within the meaning of various provincial statutes and had never undertaken to provide support on a continuing basis, she also argued that factually she had never functioned as a 'parent' either. Thus, Luoma took the position that, far from having agreed with or supported Anderson in her decision to conceive through alternative insemination, she testified that 'the plaintiff was on a frolic of her own' and that she was not present at the births of the children – one of whom bore her given name – as parent, but merely as '"coach" in the delivery room' (135).[54] She further tried to distance herself from the decision to form a family with Anderson by saying 'if a woman wanted a child, she should be allowed to have a child'– a statement that was quite inconsistent with evidence that she herself had explored single parent adoption as part of the family-formation process (130–2).

Some of the terror that goes along with living as an 'outlaw' comes through the text of the reported decision, which makes Luoma's denial of her parental role even sadder. Luoma appeared to fear having full continuing responsibility for supporting the entire family, and seems to have tried, from time to time, to interest or support Anderson in starting a business, getting a job, or doing something to increase family income. This is quite credible in light of the fact that lesbian women certainly are doubly disadvantaged in terms of earning capacity, and are disadvantaged further by lack of access to state-funded benefit programs. Yet the 'outlaw' status of their relationship not only made it possible for Luoma to deny all responsibility for Anderson and their two children, but also supported her in taking the position that she never intended to 'live together ... in economic partnership,'[55] and thus thought that she should keep all the couple's considerable property – which was largely in her sole name at the time of trial – as her own. (In addition to the family home, they had two investment properties and recreational property.)

This aspect of the case helps illustrate how power imbalances in unregulated 'outlaw' relationships affect life choices and litigation strategies. While Luoma clearly did not want, after the fact, to 'live together ... in economic partnership,' she apparently did not mind having had a partner who had lived with her in economic partnership. Anderson withdrew from waged work shortly after she commenced her relationship with Luoma; she did all the housework; she renovated Luoma's house, even borrowing money from her own family to finance the renovations; she contributed all her income to their joint enterprises; she traded her car in for their newer one; and, at the end of their relationship, while she was struggling to overcome Luoma's sudden involvement with a new secretary in her office, she agreed to sign off her interest in the family home in order to help Luoma carry out her sudden plan to move the family to a farm to make a 'fresh start.'[56]

Nor was Arlene Luoma unique in having deployed exclusion in an attempt to gain litigation advantage from 'outlaw' status. Numerous lesbian women in the United States who have conceived through alternative insemination in exactly the way Anderson did have successfully contended that the heterosexual language of parentage law has excluded their former partners from the category 'parent.' In case after case, courts have accepted this position, ruling that lesbian co-mothers are not entitled to seek joint custody or access because they are literally strangers to their own children.[57] In some cases, birth mothers have actually obtained restraining orders preventing their former partners from ever contacting their children again.[58] While there is certainly a contrary line of authority on this point in the United States,[59] and while the courts in Canada have declined to follow suit on the basis of sexual-orientation clauses in provincial human rights legislation and the sexuality-neutral language of children's law, being able to deny the parental status of the other parent is a powerful negotiation and litigation strategy that has effectively driven many women right out of their children's lives. 'You are not a "real" parent' is just one way members of queer communities have deployed exclusion against each other.

More recently in Canada, the defendant in *M.* v *H.* attempted to justify this deployment of exclusion by invoking the 'anti-assimilation' arguments expressed in numerous passages in the LEAF lesbian consultations. As recounted by the trial court in this support action,[60] the plaintiff and defendant had lived together for ten years, formed two businesses together, purchased two properties together, and, when the economic climate impaired their businesses, divided income-earning and household work between them as best they could: M. took over household responsibilities when H. was able to find paid work, but M. could not. When the relationship broke down, H. began signing M.'s signature on business documents without her knowledge, refused to let M. see their business records, locked her out of all their properties, shut down the incorporated business, took possession of all records and assets, and began operating the remaining business as a sole proprietorship.

In submissions on behalf of H., her lawyer quoted extensively from the LEAF consultations. Statements that had been made in the consultations to illustrate the diversity of lesbian opinion were used by the lawyer to make it appear that the entire lesbian community in Canada monolithically opposed relationship recognition. Thus she argued that Canadian lesbians have serious reservations about 'marriage,' and that H. should not be subject to family law remedies because '[a]t a [LEAF] panel in Vancouver on the family, concern was expressed about the traditional definition that [sic] structure of the family, which was identified as "heterosexist, patriarchal and deeply oppressive".' This statement was taken completely out of the context in which it was used in the report; it had actually related to concerns that recognizing lesbian relationships might privilege lesbians in monogamous or cohabiting or economically mutual relationships 'at the expense of others.'[61]

H.'s apprehension over being responsible for the support of another adult comes through very clearly in other submissions made on behalf of H. In examination for discovery, H. had apparently testified that, '[i]f she had known that letting the plaintiff live in her home would mean that she could be characterized as a "spouse", she either would not have let her move in, or she would have entered a written agreement.'[62] But instead of arguing that H. was already disadvantaged as a woman and as a lesbian, or that there had never been a clear expectation that she would support M., H.'s lawyer went on to contend that forcing her to *ex post facto* 'assimilate' her relationship to 'heterosexual norms' would 'deprive her of choice' and 'run counter to the choices which she and the plaintiff made during their association,'[63] that their relationship was more like that of 'best friends' who lived together,[64] and that she has never looked 'for a "heterosexual" characterization with respect to past or future relationships.'[65] To this end, H. initiated an extremely costly Charter challenge to defend her refusal to pay support or divide any assets under the Family Law Act[66] which has now gone before the Supreme Court of Canada.[67]

The deployment of exclusion against other members of queer communities is deeply damaging not only on the doctrinal level, but also on the economic level. M.'s legal bills must be over $100,000 by now, and she has been extremely fortunate to find a lawyer who would be able to carry an account of that size for several years. It is entirely likely that the net assets held by H. will be entirely exhausted by the legal fees H. has incurred in trying to avoid an order to pay support to M. for some period of years. Both women started out economically disadvantaged as women and as lesbians. They are now additionally disadvantaged by having become caught in protracted, painful, and costly litigation over their net relationship estate. In the end, no matter how the case ends up, they will both have lost probably all they ever had as the result of this litigation.

Can we assume that women who have lower net worths necessarily behave more ethically towards each other? I know on the basis of my own experience and those of friends that biological lesbian mothers frequently threaten their lesbian co-mothers that 'you will never see the children again' because 'no court would award you access, you are not a "real" parent.' Other partners have helped themselves to furniture, credit cards, houses, clothing, pets, knowing that between the invisibility of lesbian women and gay men in family law and the costs of invoking the legal system, their former partners had no effective power to oppose them. Extended families reinforce the power dynamics thus set up, often supporting a birth mother or a partner in claiming that there never was any 'real' relationship.

I am not suggesting that the 'rule of law' will magically stop queers from deploying their own exclusion against each other, no more than it has solved all the problems in heterosexual relationships. But I am suggesting that the overall costs of forcing same-sex couples to remain 'outlaws' must be treated as one of the many complex factors that enter into the assessment of the best overall direction for strategy. The distribution of the benefits of inclusion along class, race, sexual, ability, and gender lines would certainly reinforce the appropriation and dependency paradigms associated with heterosexual relationships. But the allocation of the costs of exclusion also disproportionately burden those who are already disadvantaged by class, race, sexuality, gender, and ability as well. Nor is alternative dispute resolution the solution. Lesbian communities tend to polarize around former partners, which would certainly make it difficult to find disinterested mediators.[68]

'We Will Pay for Our Rights'

I do not believe that it will be possible to extend full legal personhood to lesbian, gay, bisexual, transgendered, and transsexual people without re-enacting at least some hierarchies of privilege. So long as Canadian society depends on unequal and appropriative relations, privilege will not have to be challenged in any meaningful way. The best progressives can hope for, in my opinion, is that once queer communities are fully empowered to participate in every political debate on equal terms, more of the implications of hierarchy will become visible and less tolerable to the body politic.

Having said that, I find it disheartening that, even if queer communities could agree on the appropriate moral stance to take in relation to the inclusion/exclusion debate, and even if all queers could pay for and wanted to pay higher costs for their rights, the state does not seem to want their money. This aspect of the debate over inclusion has not yet come sharply into focus. But it is there, a loose subtext that surfaces from time to time as expedience dictates. In the United States, it has emerged most clearly in the work of the economist Lee Badgett. In 1995 testimony before the Hawaii Commission on Sexual Orientation and the Law, Badgett and La Croix made submissions on the economic consequences of non-recognition of same-sex relationships. In addition to spelling out how non-recognition burdens same-sex partners, they demonstrated how giving same-sex partners the right to marry would actually increase tax revenues because same-sex partners with two incomes would pay higher taxes if their relationship were recognized. The more 'couples,' the higher the revenues from the 'tax on marriage.'[69] Elsewhere Badgett and Goldfoot have speculated that, so long as same-sex couples continue to prefer to form two-earner households, they will be more likely to pay the 'marriage tax' if they were legally permitted to marry.[70] Projecting that as many as 85 to 90 per cent of same-sex couples might marry if they could, and that each couple that did marry would pay $1,244 more in federal and state income taxes, they conclude that, if 10,000 two-earner same-sex couples married, the federal government would collect $12 million in additional revenues in California alone.[71] Badgett and Goldfoot have also argued that because 'marriage is the most common route off welfare,' the State of California could have saved as much as $3.3 million in 1994 if only some 750 families went off welfare due to marriage. As they stated, 'if a marriage is not legally recognized, no spousal support can be expected, increasing the state's financial burden for that family.'[72] This is, of course, the familiar 'spouse in the house' rule turned upside down: By arguing that the state would profit from the recognition of *de facto* relationships, Badgett and Goldfoot are actually arguing in favour of the 'spouse in the house' rule, and support the fact that relationship recognition would differentially burden low-income same-sex couples – here, by depriving one or both partners of social assistance. This strategy becomes somewhat less startling when it is remembered that, in the context of the U.S. 'marriage debate,' the status of marriage would be assumed voluntarily, unlike the status automatically ascribed on the basis of cohabitation in Canada.

This type of argument has also been made in the Canadian context, although in much more nuanced form. In *Egan and Nesbit*, it appeared that Egan and Nesbit might lose larger provincial social assistance benefits than they might receive under the old age security system if they were to qualify for the spousal allowance. In ruling that denying them the spousal allowance under such circumstances nonetheless violated section 15(1) of the Charter, the Court implicitly rejected the government's position that they had not been 'burdened' by exclusion from the federal program. However, when another majority of the Court went on to rule that excluding same-sex couples from this program was justifiable, the option of choosing 'to pay for their rights' was taken away.

'We Don't Want Your Money'

In the Charter challenges that have been brought against some elements of the heterosexual benefit system, the government (so far, the federal government) has attempted to establish that exclusion is actually better for queers, and that inclusion would actually burden same-sex relationships. So, in addition to the genuine uncertainty among lesbians versus gays, for example, or among HIV- positive versus HIV-negative people, government lawyers are basically telling queer communities that they should be glad that they are excluded from benefit programs, because the demographics of queer communities suggest that inclusion would actually result in higher tax bills and reduced government benefits for most same-sex couples. Government control over demographic data used to formulate these arguments unfortunately means that no one else can access this information in order to scrutinize it or challenge these propositions.

Thus the politics of inclusion and exclusion are being played out at several different levels. While hierarchies of class, race, and gender play a big role in identifying who will gain and who will lose as the result of policies of either inclusion or exclusion, more powerful members of same-sex relationships are deploying exclusion against their partners, relatively advantaged members of communities are offering to 'pay for their rights,' and the government is simply shrugging the problem off, contending that same-sex couples will not benefit from recognition, and that the government does not want the extra revenue in any event.

In defence of the state, it would be extremely unfair to queer people to impose increased costs on same-sex couples before redressing the widespread homophobia that has resulted in centuries-long exclusion, violence, and economic discrimination. But that is not the type of 'incrementalism' that the Supreme Court seemed to endorse in *Egan and Nesbit*. Rather, the Court appeared to support the foot-dragging variety of 'incrementalism' without regard to the sequence in which various rights and responsibilities should be extended to same-sex couples. It was for this reason that many lesbian couples in Canada sighed in relief when the federal government declined to include same-sex cohabitants in the definition of deemed spouses that was adopted in the wake of *Schachtschneider* v *The Queen*.[73] Although the court in that case ruled against the taxpayer, it explicitly referred to the fact that unmarried heterosexuals and lesbian/gay partners could claim the equivalent-to-married credit in relation to dependent children when married partners could not. Parliament responded with alacrity to the perception that unmarried couples were receiving tax benefits that were denied to married couples. Effective in 1993, the definition of 'spouse' was expanded to include non-married opposite-sex cohabitants for purposes of the entire Income Tax Act.[74] But the government drew the line at deeming same-sex couples to be 'spouses' too. There is a strong sense that the government did not mind collecting increased revenues from heterosexual cohabitants, but that it was not interested in receiving increased revenues from the queer population if the price of that revenue was having to recognize same-sex relationships.[75]

The Canadian state again told lesbians and gays that 'we don't want your money' in *Rosenberg* v *A.-G. Canada*. One of the reasons the Department of Justice gave in defence of Revenue Canada's refusal to extend survivor benefits to same-sex partners under employment pension plans was that, far from 'discriminating' against same-sex couples, the 'opposite-sex' definition of 'spouse' actually benefited same-sex couples because it exempted them from the GST credit 'tax on marriage' and other tax burdens. Using non-published statistical data (described in chapter 6), the government contended that more same-sex couples would pay higher taxes than would benefit from relationship recognition, to the tune of some $10 million to $36 million per year in the aggregate, and, at the individual level, some $290 per year.[76] The effect is almost entirely due to the GST 'tax on marriage.'

The data produced by the government strongly suggest that it is eager to make it look like it is magnanimously telling queer couples to keep their money. As table 9.2 indicates, however, those projections are extremely vulnerable to attack. Using government data on the tax expenditures associated with many of the same items, and using the very conservative take-up rates I employed in table 8.7, I have come to quite different conclusions: Only if the take-up rate were an absurdly low 0.1 per cent of the heterosexual population, and only if most same-sex couples had such low incomes that they would pay the GST 'tax on marriage' would same-sex couples pay more in taxes if recognized than if not recognized. My 3 per cent take-up rate is more realistic, and, on that basis, same-sex couples might experience as much as $108.3 million in tax benefits. Unlike the Department of Justice projections, my projections take into account some of the other major 'heterosexual benefits'– chief of

Table 9.2. Competing Projections on Net Federal Costs of Recognition to Same-Sex Couples, 1993/1994

Provision	Department of Finance	($ million)	This study
Married credit			($1.7) to (50.4)
Equivalent credit Net credits	(5.0)		
Transferable credits	(2.0)		(0.2) to (7.3)
GST credit	28.0		27.0
Child benefits (CTB, CCED)	small		small
Spousal RRSP contribs.	small		small
Survivor pensions/RRSP rollovers	(3.0)		(3.0)
Employment health benefits	(8.0)		(8.0)
Net alimony deductions	not calc.		(0.1) to (1.9)
SPA	not calc.		(0.7) to (20.5)
CPP survivor pensions/death benefits	not calc.		(1.5) to (44.2)
Net costs to same-sex couples	10.0		11.8 to (108.3)

SOURCES: Affidavit of Albert Wakkary, filed in *Rosenberg* v *The Queen* (Ont. Gen. Div., Court File No. 79885/94) (sworn 2 June 1994), Exhibit C (Department of Finance column, adjusted to 1994); Table 8.7 derived from SPSD/M version 5.2, adjusted to 1993 (projecting same-sex couple take-up rates of 0.5 and 3 per cent of reported heterosexual claims).
( ) indicates net benefits to same-sex couples.

which are the net alimony deduction delivered through the Income Tax Act, the SPA delivered through the Old Age Security Act, and the CPP survivor pensions and death benefits delivered through the Canada Pension Plan Act.

Quite apart from the many criticisms that can be made of the Department of Finance's analysis, treating all the spouse-related provisions of the Income Tax Act themselves as if they were an undifferentiated unit ignores the very different policy objectives that they serve. The income tax rollovers for transfers of property among members of families, for example, reflect the assumption that both members of a couple have an ownership interest in property owned by either of them, and ensure that transfers in compliance with provincial family property law do not attract income tax liability. In contrast, the dependency credits reflect the belief that those who support dependent adults are entitled to extra public assistance without regard to their actual wealth. The Department of Finance blurred the policy differences among these types of spouse-based provisions in the Income Tax Act by repealing the definition of 'spouse' in section 146.1 and moving it to the global definition in the new section 252(4). However, the fact that there is one definitional section for the entire statute does not mean that the government or the courts have to rule on all the policy issues affected by that definition in one fell swoop. By refusing to disaggregate the policy objectives of various spouse-related provisions in the Income Tax Act, and by drawing attention instead to the alleged global costs to queers of relationship recognition, the federal government appears to be saying not that it is concerned with the possibly regressive distributive impact of relationship recognition, but that it simply does not want queer money on any terms.

Rethinking the Benefit Unit

'Inhabiting' the dichotomies of 'benefit' and 'burden' helps reveal that, like the various 'benefit' provisions discussed in chapter 8, many different types of 'burdens' flow from relationship recognition. Because of the complexities of relationship forms and legal policies, no easy generalizations can resolve any of these complexities. Having said that, however, it is clear that gendered and sexualized economic hierarchies lie at the heart of most of the 'burdens' I have discussed. So long as legal policy is shaped around the heterosexual presumption, and so long as social assistance–type benefits are shaped around the appropriative nature of male–female pairing, the non-recognition of queer relationships will continue to represent an 'escape hatch' from that whole system. Factors of race, ability, economic class, age, and education intensify this effect whenever they are present.

To state this conclusion in another way, one of the main causes of the 'benefits' of exclusion analysed in this chapter is the continuing denial of women's full legal personality by the structure of the 'benefit unit.' Whenever state policies can 'see' women only as part of a household unit or married couple instead of as autonomous individuals, and whenever notions like 'two can live cheaper than one' or 'spouses have an obligation to support each other' are used to fine-tune benefit levels, many same-sex couples will find that it is actually to their advantage to stay outside the heterosexual 'benefit' system. Thus whenever conflict of interest–type provisions use the 'spouse' as a proxy for people who can be presumed to deal out of self-interest, to cheat, or to collaborate, lesbian or gay couples who want to give the appearance of dealing at arm's length are permitted to hide behind their lack of 'couple' status. Similarly, when benefit provisions like the principal-residence exemption restrict families to one benefit per couple, lesbian or gay couples find that they can still get double benefits because they are considered to be strangers in law, not spouses. And whenever sliding scales or benefit clawbacks are used to adjust social assistance, tax credits, or other benefits to family composition in order to reflect 'economies of scale,' same-sex couples can apply for benefits as separate individuals even if they in fact live together, consume together, enjoy economies of scale, and still live more cheaply together than they could singly. LICOs and 'family income' cut-offs similarly treat queer couples as if they were single.

Although the legal issue in *Thibaudeau v The Queen* was not framed in terms of women's 'legal personality,' the effect was the same: Even divorced women were not permitted to escape the category 'spouse' and to be taxed as economically autonomous 'individuals' in law. Before the Income Tax Act was amended to repeal the income-shifting mechanism Suzanne Thibaudeau had challenged, the only couples who were not caught in this involuntary post-divorce 'couple' were same-sex couples. Whether the feature of heterosexual coupling that has attracted this treatment is described as 'appropriation of women's non-waged labour,' 'recognition of economies of scale,' or 'dependency,' the fact is that a century of shaping 'benefit' programs around the expectation that husbands (dominant wage-earners) will support wives (secondary wage-earners) and that spouses should turn first to each other for support instead of to the state has resulted in the construction of systematic barriers to opportunism that also act as inducements to queer couples to avoid recognition.

There are two problems with this status quo. First, it actually promotes the continued denial of queer legal personality, holding out the powerful inducement of money as the pay-off for this denial. The second is that it leaves intact the social, economic, and sexual hierarchies that initially justified these structures and created this seemingly safe space for queers within larger structures of appropriation and oppression. To go back to the image of the Möbius band, the heterosexual benefit/queer penalty system is a unitary, unifying, one-sided whole that either burdens queer existences by exclusion or simply denies queer existences absolutely. But within the twisting encircling boundaries of the band itself, tucked away in the shadows of the curves, hidden in the folds and loops of this system, are little enclosed spaces within which queer existences are denied, it is true, but benefited by that denial.

These encircling boundaries can be turned inside out, yet the shadowed little spaces in the 'middle' continue to be re-created no matter which way the boundaries are moved. Sexuality and burden cannot be separated from each other in this image; slicing the band lengthwise would merely increase the complexity of the twisting boundaries and place more of the social universe in these new shadows.[77] Partially severing the boundary itself would relieve some of the pressure making up the twists, and would help reduce the size of the unburdened 'middle.' But only when the band or strip is totally severed would this 'safe space' disappear completely.

Severing the boundaries to eliminate these 'safe shadows' can be done only by abolishing the allocation of benefits and burdens around the categories of 'sex' and their organizers, 'sexuality.' Because hierarchies of sex and sexuality themselves turn on the 'individual–household' dichotomy, it is within those two models that strategies for addressing the problem of the 'unburdened shadows' exposed here can be found.

The Individual Principle

Monique Wittig has described the path towards the full legal personality of queers with brilliant clarity: To become a 'person' in law is to become an 'individual subject,' she has argued, and 'the advent of individual subjects demands first destroying the categories of sex, ending the use of them, and rejecting all sciences that still use those categories as their fundamentals.'[78]

It is the massive heterosexual benefit/queer penalty system that creates the shadows in which some 'individual' queer subjects who are in relationships are forced to hide. No egalitarian modification of that system will eliminate the shadows. At best, the topography of the shadowed middle can be altered, the space enclosed can hold more people or fewer, but so long as the benefit system hinges on heterosexuality, the structural problem remains unsolved.

Unhinging this system then depends on replacing the relationship or household base with the individual base. It involves the destruction of 'sex' as the organizing principle of social and legal policy. The destruction of the category 'sex' in policy would in turn abolish social/legal categories of sexuality and relationship, leaving in its place subjects who are defined not by reference to men, or by reference to relationships, assumed dependency, presumed support, or economic functioning, but by virtue of existing as adult human beings. Such a policy move would complete the process begun centuries ago with the struggle against the legal erasure of women's legal personality and the transfer of all their civil capacities to husbands who exercised complete domain over them and their needs. Such a move would also eliminate the hierarchy of privilege that heterosexuality has become.

In concrete and practical terms, adoption of the 'individual' as the 'benefit unit' of social, economic, and legal policy would return attention to the urgency of completing each human being's path to full 'personhood.' Eliminating state benefits to those who support the dependent, the non-waged, and the appropriated would shift government resources away from funding the massive system of 'heterosexual benefits' and direct them to the people who need them the most. Where the subject matter of state regulation continues to be of concern to the body politic, new rules could be fashioned to address such issues directly, instead of mediating them through the categories of 'sex,' 'sexuality,' and 'legal status.' For example, conflict-of-interest rules would no longer have to contain presumptions of conflict where certain relationships or status existed, but could set out substantive descriptions of ethical conduct to be applied responsively to the context: 'Whenever a person is in fact not dealing with another person at arm's length, such person must disclose that conflict in writing and remove him/herself from the relevant decision-making process.' Or, in income tax legislation: 'Whenever a transaction is not factually at arm's length, all valuations must be supported by independent certification.' Presumptions of economic unity would also be eliminated, resulting, for example, in the restoration of the right of each individual to his or her own principal-residence exemption, so long as he or she factually did reside principally in that property when residing as an individual.

The individual principle is most urgently needed in relation to social assistance–type benefits, whether delivered through direct social legislation or indirectly through tax expenditures like the GST credit. Arguments that 'economies of scale' or 'two can live more cheaply than one' are not convincing when some cohabitants – room-mates, friends, siblings, other housemates – are legally permitted to share space without triggering reduction in their individual benefit levels. There would appear to be no reason to tailor benefit levels to types of relationships. This would also involve abolition of legal obligations to support other adults. Thus application of the individual principle would mean, on a practical level, that sliding-scale benefits, family-income means testing, and 'tax on marriage' types of provisions would have to be dropped from benefit-eligibility formulas.

Adoption of the individual as the benefit unit would offer an escape from the economic dependency and appropriation that is built into the present revenue-expenditure system. It would ensure that the state has no place in the 'bedrooms' of people in Canada, and would presumptively establish each adult as economically autonomous, as the 'subject' of social, economic, and legal policy, no matter who was in his or her bedroom. It would break male monopoly over 'individualism' and ensure that, when people live in community, everyone bears equal obligations towards everyone else, instead of allocating obligations just to those whose productive capacities are appropriated for the benefit of the 'community.'

This proposal is neither new nor particularly radical. When the first income tax act was being debated in Parliament in 1917, the government had decided against offering dependency exemptions of any kind, whether for a spouse or for children. The government had decided to offer generous individual exemptions rather than detailed dependency exemptions because of the diversity of households already evident in Canadian society: 'It would be unfair to base the distinction solely on the number of the members of a family, because there are many citizens who have not only children to take care of, but other dependents as well. [T]here are many citizens who have not only their own family to take care of, but also the family of a brother or a sister, or perhaps they have to look after an aged father or mother.'[79]

This proposal was met with howls of outrage from the 'family' lobby. Incredulous at the suggestion that single men and 'spinsters with taxable income' with no dependants might receive the same personal exemptions as married men, many members insisted vehemently that heterosexual, dependency, and reproductivist 'hinges' all be inserted into the system to make it 'fair': 'I think it is absolutely unfair to put the man with no children on the same footing as the father of a big family, with the children to feed and clothe and send to school, and so forth.'[80] The touchstones for these arguments were 'single men,' 'spinsters with taxable incomes,' and married women with no children. Single men were described as being 'lax,'[81] as 'escaping too lightly';[82] spinsters were assumed to have no dependants; and married women with no children were accused of being 'free,' of being able to 'go out whenever [they want] ... to,' work for wages, or 'save a lot of disbursements' by working in the home.[83] As the arguments piled up, the members became more and more incensed at the image of married men, with all their dependants, being treated the same as all these other groups. In the end, the government agreed to reduce the $3,000 individual exemption to $1,500 for unmarried men and women, and some consideration was given to raising the exemption to $4,000 for men with six or more children.[84]

That this 'hinge' is sexist/heterosexual is undeniable. Social commentators have recorded the prevalence of 'homosexuality' in the first part of the century, and some of the very pointed comments made in the 1917 debate described above had to be heterosexist in intent: 'We have some striking examples of unmarried men in this House. I am not in favour of encouraging a man to laxity in that regard, because I believe a man should get married, if possible, when he reaches a certain age. Of course, with some of them, it is not their fault.'[85] A short time later, one commentator wrote of the 'modern' era, 'homosexuality ... has become a recognized part of modern urban life. Homosexual practices are lampooned on the state and in the "smart" magazines, and the large homosexual dances or "drags" have become the equivalent of the circus for the "ultra-sophisticated".'[86]

The rampant sexism, racism, heterosexism, and reproductivism of the intervening decades submerged the 'individual principle' so deeply that it has all but disappeared from sight in Canadian legal policy. Even statutes that still pay lip service to the 'individual principle' are so riddled with special provisions relating to sexuality and relationship status that income tax liability is functionally imposed more on the basis of relationships than on the basis of individual autonomy.

But the individual principle emerges when the social benefit system is 'unhinged' from sexuality, as illustrated by Danish law. At the same time that Denmark enacted registered-partnership legislation in 1989, it took the less-well-known step of adopting the individual as the basic unit of legal policy. The reasons given for taking that step were essentially the exact opposite of those given in Canada seventy years earlier when inserting the 'heterosexual hinge'– they included recognition of women's greater involvement in waged work, the desire to remove disincentives to marriage, the goal of treating all relationships equally, and concern that any form of household-based benefit unit would involve too much administrative complexity.[87] Although implementation of this policy has been gradual and the areas of continuing compromise are still significant, cost was thought to be less important than making sure that social policy was consistent with the economic realities of women's lives and the diversity of relationship forms.

Relationship-Based Alternatives

As demographers keep demonstrating, households in Canada are becoming increasingly diverse. If nothing else, to continue to legislate as if every adult lives either as a single individual or as a member of a monogamous heterosexual couple is highly unrealistic, and offers incentives to others besides queers to seek escape from heterosexual burdens in the seductively shadowed spaces bounded by heterosexual privilege/queer burden.

Where it is thought important to retain some relationship-based eligibility criteria, then a completely different strategy for removing the sexual/heterosexual 'hinge' from Canadian legal policy would involve removing either criteria relating to sexuality or criteria relating to conjugality from legislation. That is, strategies for blunting the hierarchical and appropriative impact of the present system have focused either on bringing more types of conjugal relationships into the benefit calculus, or on shifting away from sexual or familial connection as the test and adopting non-conjugal criteria. Bringing more types of conjugal relationships into benefit criteria really boils down to including same-sex partners and perhaps multiple partners of all sexualities. Lesbian and gay activists have not surprisingly tended to prefer this strategy because of the frequent similarities between same-sex couples and opposite-sex couples. The argument is simply that, due to these similarities, the most logical place to begin extending benefit criteria is with couples similarly located. While cost factors remain elusive and speculative, there is some perception that this would be the most cost-effective approach to revising benefit criteria along relationship lines. This approach would imply the continued use of formulas that take into account economies of consumption arising from shared space, equipment, incomes, and responsibilities when economies of scale are thought to justify reduced benefits. At the margins, of course, this is where proposals for sexuality-neutral versions of the benefit unit cross feminist and race-based critiques of benefit legislation, for the non-waged work factored into 'economies of scale' tables is not distributed equally.

As the heterosexual benefit unit has come under increasing attack, it has been interesting to see that there is actually considerable support for removing conjugality criteria and moving in the direction of letting recipients of benefits choose their own co-beneficiaries. The best Canadian example of this approach is seen in the new 'designated traveller' benefits given to federal politicians. Instead of limiting benefits for travel companions to spouses or opposite-sex cohabitants, parliamentarians can take anyone they chose with them.[88] In the United States, a variant of this model has been adopted in Hawaii, which permits literally any type of couple – even two acquaintances – to receive benefit certificates that entitle them to receive benefits ordinarily reserved to married couples, such as medical insurance coverage, joint property ownership, inheritances, and employment spousal benefits.[89]

Both the Canadian 'designated traveller' and the Hawaii 'reciprocal beneficiary' examples have received considerable criticism from queer activists who feel that this model is really designed to accommodate homophobic attitudes. It is no secret that although some members of Parliament would have had no hesitation in declaring a gay lover or partner to be a 'spouse' or 'partner' for purposes of parliamentarian travel benefits, other members were concerned that, if they did extend those benefits to another person of their same sex, they would be perceived as being lesbian or gay. Similarly, it has been suggested that the 'same-sex' hinge in the Hawaii reciprocal benefits bill was removed at the last minute because of religious objections to extending benefits expressly to same-sex couples in state legislation.[90]

Thus it does seem fair to say that at least some of the popularity of 'designated beneficiary' types of models may reflect continuing prejudice against queers. I find it interesting that, although the additional costs of extending benefits to same-sex couples appears to trouble many people, the even greater costs of extending benefits to other non-conjugal partners or individuals does not seem to bother critics at all.

Some commentators have proposed non-conjugal benefit units not in order to avoid affirming same-sex couples, but in order to shift the focus of benefit entitlement away from relationships and onto the social 'good' that is thought to entitle people to benefits. For example, Nancy Polikoff has suggested that if what the state/society finds so valuable about married couples is their stability, then any unit that exhibits the desirable degree of stability ought to receive tax credits or benefits. Similarly, if raising children is the social 'good' that justifies benefits, then that should be the 'hinge' that attracts legal consequences, benefits, or burdens, rather than the 'hinges' of sex, sexuality, or legal status.[91] Other feminist commentators have suggested other ways of expanding the benefit unit, although there is general agreement that the individual principle should play a greater role in allocating benefits.[92]

While I certainly agree that greater consistency between policy objectives and the contours of the benefit unit is important, I have noticed that these discussions of the benefit unit tend to focus on the distribution of positive benefits in the sense of, for example, dental coverage or family housing perquisites of employment. But the problem at the core of the benefit-unit conundrum is the fact that when couples, families, or other groupings are used as the qualifying unit for income-tested benefits such as social assistance, what is being allocated through the definition of the 'benefit unit' is not more money, but disentitlement and cut-offs. Thus suggestions that benefits should be extended to 'nurturers' or 'affectional units' have not included as much sustained attention to the 'down' side of benefit allocation, which is that two non-conjugal friends sharing space, for example, could cut off each other's eligibility for social assistance in some circumstances at the same time that one of them may be permitted under an expanded benefit menu plan to extend his or her 'family' benefits of some sort to the other. This problem could be minimized by ensuring that all individuals who form stable households, nurture, and so on, were to be subject to the same LICOs, 'economies of scale,' and anti-avoidance rules, and if those LICOs, and so on, were to look to economic realities rather than to assumptions about how some kinds of relationships work, then the shadowed safe centre of the boundary would shrink considerably. For example, going back to the *Poulter* case, the child tax credit for non-married parents would be available regardless of relationship form, so long as the other adult did not factually contribute to the support of the child. If the other adult(s) did contribute, then the fact that they might be heterosexual lovers, queer partners, friends, room-mates, relatives, or boarders would be completely irrelevant.[93]

Bringing the tyranny of 'sex' to an end does not necessarily imply the rejection of all relationship criteria in allocating benefits and burdens. However, untangling critical feminist and critical race reasons for expanding benefit units from homophobic reasons for going in the same direction will not be easy. The individual model is most consistent with the recognition of the full personhood of each adult human being, but one of the most exciting things about the prospect of the fuller political enfranchisement of sexual minorities is that, perhaps in the future, everyone will be able to join this complex debate, instead of leaving it to be decided by those who are privileged by sex, sexuality, ability, race, and/or class.

Conclusions

The 'heterosexual economy' confers scores of benefits, privileges, rights, and subsidies on its subjects every year. Looking just at the few benefits that can be quantified with any reliability, the costs ran to some $5.1 billion in 1993 alone. These benefits were paid just to support adult heterosexual relationships – none of these benefits had anything to do with the support of children. In contrast, the 'queer economy' is an economy of penalties, burdens, extra costs, lower incomes, and greater challenges. In the aggregate, same-sex couples in the 'queer economy' bore a 'queer penalty' of between $16 million and $165 million in 1993.

In the face of this material oppression, it is no wonder that lurking in the 'shadows' of the official economy to escape some of the burdens of coupledness looks good to some couples at least some of the time. Indeed, the lower the couple's income, the more alluring these shadows can look. These shadows serve the interests of the state/society well too. The state merely has to point to the shadows, and assert their value to an otherwise invisible group of people, and evidence of concrete discrimination is transformed into evidence that the government cares so much about the welfare of same-sex couples that it would never – no, not ever – want to recognize their relationships for policy purposes.

Queer communities have reacted rationally and logically to the choices being given to them by this structure. Those who would pay higher taxes, lose social assistance, or otherwise be disadvantaged if they were deemed to be spouses, and those who would run the risk of being forced out of the closet by ascribed status, have quite sensibly pointed out that they have nothing to gain from relationship recognition. Therefore they oppose it. Those who recognize that relationship benefits are premised on the appropriative, hierarchical, or monogamous features of heterosexual relationships have also opposed relationship recognition, and are sometimes joined by those who find that making those arguments helps mask their own self-interest with the guise of anti-establishment values. And splitting queer communities very neatly down a deep fault line, those who have something to gain from relationship recognition endorse it, seek legislation, bring test litigation, seek funding, and try to organize around that goal.

By continuing to attach a mix of benefits and burdens to recognized relationships, the state/society has virtually ensured that queer communities themselves will deadlock along lines of gender, race, sexuality, relationship form, and family structure. It is only by thinking simultaneously inside and outside the categories of (hetero/same-)sex that queer communities can challenge these structures.

The 'relationship-recognition debate,' as it has become in this telling, can be subverted and encompassed in two dramatically different ways. The first subversion would be to abandon the sex, sexist, sexual, and reproductivist 'hinges' that construct these hierarchies in the first place.

Systematic implementation of the 'individual principle' would both complete the project of abolishing ancient legal incapacities that are the expression in law of hierarchies, and promote the autonomy of all adults in this society, making relationship, reproduction, and other forms of affiliation a matter of personal choice rather than a strategy for survival. In this way, the destruction of categories of 'sex' would not destroy queer existence, but would expand the escape now available to queers to all others who are oppressed by the massive heterosexual benefit/queer penalty system. As Monique Wittig has urged, 'our survival demands that we contribute all our strength to the destruction of ... heterosexuality as a social system.'[94] This would be a good way to do it.

For a culture so focused on dependency relations, whether they be the dependency of adult on adult, child on adult, households on the state, however, replacement of the heterosexual benefit/queer penalty system//queer-friendly shadows with the 'individual principle' might be too much too fast. The Canadian state is structured around focusing resources on relational units, and those who have constructed queer variants of those units are understandably invested in gaining access to the benefits even as they lament the loss of the shadows. Restructuring benefits around more encompassing 'hinges' like raising children, providing care for incapacitated adults, or factual dependency might represent a humane and politically feasible way to begin the process of recognizing the full legal personality of all adults in Canada.

Although the debate over the 'benefits of exclusion' has been critical to seeing the full dimensions of how the sex/uality system affects sexual minorities, now that the system of heterosexual privilege has become more visible, the two choices of 'existing' or 'not existing' have become 'not exist' versus 'not exi(s)t.' 'You see they only give us two choices. Assimilate or get lost ... We need to make a third choice.'[95] That 'third choice' might end up looking like assimilation of heterosexual existence to queer existence, or vice versa. But whatever it becomes, it will dialectically result in rethinking how the state subsidizes and thereby regulates human connections.

Chapter Ten

The Costs of 'Incrementalism'

[W]e still have a class of children that are being treated like that ugly old-fashioned word 'bastard.' They are bastardized. And that is stupid ... public policy.
> Lee McKay, Lesbian and Feminist Mothers Political Action Group, in testimony before Parliamentary Committee on Equality (27 June 1985), 9: 26

The Attorney General of Canada has taken the position ... that 'the means chosen does not have to be necessarily the solution for all time. Rather there may always be a possibility that more acceptable arrangements can be worked out over time'. Viewed in this light, the impugned legislation can be regarded as a substantial step in an incremental approach to include all those who are in serious need ...
> Justice Sopinka, in *Egan and Nesbit*, [1995] 2 S.C.R. at 575

Significant changes in the social, legal, and economic status of lesbians and gays are beginning to take place, and the need for changes in the status of bisexual, transgendered, and transsexual people is coming to be recognized. The Ontario government added the category 'partner' to the Substitute Decision Act and related statutes in the early 1990s, which gives same-sex partners the status of kin in medical emergencies. The Ontario Court of Appeal has now ruled that same-sex partners can apply for support under the provisions of the Family Law Act,[1] and that federal legislation denying survivor options to lesbian or gay employees under employee pension plans is constitutionally invalid.[2] A federal Human Rights Board of Inquiry has ruled that all provisions of federal law that deny same-sex couples any of the spousal benefits given to federal employees have to be extended to include them, including provisions of the

Income Tax Act.[3] And British Columbia has become the first jurisdiction in Canada to amend a large number of its family-related statutes to give same-sex partners the same legal status as opposite-sex cohabitants.[4]

Although these developments are all extremely exciting, they extend only to selected legal issues that touch the lives of sexual minorities. On the whole, sexual minorities currently live in a situation of legal chaos. Not only are two of the key rulings affecting relationship status still under final appeal – *M. v H.* and *Dwyer*[5] – but the extent to which the policy of 'incrementalism' adopted by the Supreme Court of Canada in *Egan and Nesbit v The Queen*[6] will be applied to other specific legal contexts is far from clear. Legislative changes continue to occur sporadically, inconsistently, and in isolated areas of law, leaving other areas of change to be accomplished through the customary practices of sexual minorities; selected, risky, and expensive litigation; and the exercise of government discretion. Caught between the heightened expectation of 'equality,' on the one hand, and continuing denial of legal status in a wide array of specific situations, on the other, surrounded by conflicting opinions on the implications of cases like *Egan and Nesbit*, and confronted with reluctance by most governments to clarify the law, even sexual minorities who celebrate these isolated victories still have to construct their lives and hopes for the future around the status quo.

In this chapter, I discuss how the checkerboard of legal rights produced by *ad hoc* incremental change sets up second-order problems, 'Catch 22s', inconsistencies, and uncertainties that continue to make it very difficult for lesbian, gay, bisexual, transgendered, and transsexual people to get on with their lives. The first general situation relates to income tax law, where the federal government first used its administrative discretion to delay extension of employment benefits to same-sex couples, and now has withdrawn its appeal in *Rosenberg* without giving any indication of how far it intends to apply the ruling in *Rosenberg* to other areas of income tax law. The resulting uncertainty leaves same-sex couples in a vulnerable position in relation to income tax reassessments and objections. The other general area relates to the second-class status ascribed to children with same-sex parents, a status that is a direct reflection of the lack of legal recognition given to their families in many areas of law. Both of these examples demonstrate that leaving sexual minorities to flounder in legal chaos reinforces the message that they and their responsibilities are of so little political significance that they do not deserve government consideration. I conclude that the continuing refusal to examine any of these issues in a systematic fashion has given rise to 'incremental dis-

284 Are We 'Persons' Yet?

crimination' – tolerance of inconsistent and generally burdensome legal provisions that seriously misrepresent the realities of queer existences in Canada today.

Same-Sex Benefits

Because income tax law reduces to dollars and cents the values that implicitly shape a great deal of legal policy, it is not surprisingly on the cutting edge of Charter challenges and legal scrutiny relating to sexuality. Two major trends in the taxation of same-sex couples emerging from Charter challenges to various Revenue Canada positions are quickly coming to a collision point as Revenue Canada's discriminatory exercise of administrative discretion has been exposed and as the federal government has quietly dropped its appeal in *Rosenberg*. The convergence of these two processes has now left open to speculation just how far the inclusion of same-sex couples in the definition of 'spouse' in the Income Tax Act can go or should go at the present time. Given Revenue Canada's history of using its administrative discretion in relation to same-sex benefits as aggressively as possible, lesbians and gays are understandably apprehensive of how Revenue Canada is going to proceed either in rejecting claims to spousal status in areas other than employment pensions or in reassessing those lesbians and gays who have decided to continue filing as individuals. Unless clarifying policy is formulated in the very near future, a great deal more litigation may be needed to settle this difficult area of law.

Employees can bargain for a growing range of contractual benefits, many of which can become quite valuable in their own right. Some 26 per cent of Canadian corporations now offer same-sex benefits,[7] a significant breakthrough in an area that was once but a pipe dream to most same-sex couples. However, the income tax system plays an important role in structuring and conferring value on the whole system of employment benefits, and because the income tax treatment of benefits has not changed to reflect changes in employment practices or the legal status of same-sex couples, the tax treatment of same-sex benefits actually sets up a 'Catch 22' that is not obvious at first glance.

That 'Catch 22' is this: Employment benefits are forms of employment compensation that are bargained for by employers and employees. Income tax law has grown up around these contractual arrangements, and, for a combination of more-or-less 'legal' and policy reasons, does not recognize some employment benefits as 'income,' defers recognition of others, and contains numerous elaborate codes by which to avert tax avoidance in this area. The resulting complex legal structure has left Revenue Canada with enormous administrative power that can be challenged only at great cost and great risk.

So murky has the law of employment benefits become that employers who have wanted to offer same-sex employment benefits, whether out of a genuine sense of fairness or because required to do so by human rights legislation or the terms of collective agreements, have actually been blocked by Revenue Canada from doing so. Employers thus have been faced with three unattractive choices: violate human rights law and/or collective agreements by refusing to extend spousal benefits to same-sex employees; incur the increased costs of offering 'alternative' plans; or undergo expensive and high-profile litigation opposed by the federal government. The more conservative practice of seeking to resolve contentious issues by way of advance rulings has not been useful in clarifying these issues, because requests for advance rulings have merely provided Revenue Canada an opportunity to give unfavourable rulings on a formal level, and have forced the employer to give full notice of issues of which Revenue Canada might otherwise remain unaware.[8] This three-way bind among Revenue Canada, employers, and employees has thus re-created the very forms of discrimination against sexual minorities that the legal system is supposedly trying to eradicate, with Revenue Canada powerfully backing up the anti-queer lobby.

At the heart of this set of 'Catch 22s' has been uncertainty over how far Revenue Canada would be willing to go in relation to some of the positions it has taken over the years. Revenue Canada took the wholly unsupportable position that extension of health coverage to same-sex partners resulted in taxable benefits for queer employees, but suddenly withdrew that position when it was challenged in litigation. Until challenged in court, Revenue Canada persistently took the position that it would not accept amendments to registered pension plans that extended survivor benefits to same-sex partners, and appears to have threatened to use its administrative discretion to 'deregister' plans so amended.

Moore and Akerstrom, Rosenberg, Dwyer v *Toronto (Metropolitan)*,[9] and the recent amendments to the Canadian Human Rights Act[10] have all contributed to the clarification of the tax treatment of same-sex benefits. However, what needs to be emphasized about the status quo is that, with the exception of the registered pension plan provisions, there is actually nothing in the Income Tax Act, in the reported cases, or even in Revenue Canada's own publications that have ever formed a 'legal' basis for treating employment benefits received by same-sex employees differently from those of opposite-sex employees. Until recently, Revenue Canada has simply given expression to the presumed non-personhood of queer employees on the basis of general political expectations, and has used its administrative power to do so.

In order to disclose the extent to which presumed lack of status can produce quite concrete practices of inequality, I outline how this power has been used in relation to tax-exempt benefits and deferred forms of compensation. I also explore the implications of the federal government's abandonment of its appeal in *Rosenberg* for both same-sex survivor options and for future exercises of administrative discretion on income tax issues relating to sexuality.

Tax-Exempt Benefits

Many 'fringe benefits' are fully taxable. Revenue Canada has taken the position that the following types of employment benefits will be taxable: board and lodging; rent-free or low-rent housing; travel benefits; personal use of employer's motor vehicle; holiday trips; prizes; incentive awards; frequent-flyer benefits; travelling expenses for the employee's spouse; wage-loss replacement plans; interest-free and low-interest loans.[11] To this list could be added cash allowances for meals or travel, additional compensation designed to equalize costs of living in new locations, and other cash payments that are made in special circumstances.[12] Whether taxable benefits are paid in cash or in kind, they can be considered to be 'free' in the sense that employees do not pay for them. But because they are taxable benefits, they have hidden costs attached. On the employee's side, the cost of taxable benefits is equal to the amount of tax the employee has to pay on the benefit. On the employer's side, the cost is equal to the after-tax expense of providing the benefit, so long as the cost can be considered to have been incurred as a form of compensation to the employee.

In contrast, tax-exempt benefits bring no hidden tax liabilities with them. Revenue Canada has taken the position that the following items can all be considered to be tax-exempt: uniforms or special clothing; subsidized school services; transportation to the job site; recreational facilities; moving expenses; payment of premiums for private health services plans; employer contributions under provincial hospitalization and medical care insurance plans; transportation passes (except for airline passes, which can give rise to small taxable benefits); subsidized meals (if the employee pays 'reasonable cost' for the meals); reimbursement for setting up trusts to avoid conflicts of interest; and employee counselling services.[13] When employment benefits are non-taxable, the financial value of the benefit is considered to be equal to the amount of revenue the government could have collected in respect of that item had it been taxable.

Despite the fact that none of the provisions of the Income Tax Act concerning private health services plans, one of the most important employment benefits, has ever contained any language that relates to marital status, relationship status, marriage, cohabitation, spouses, or words denoting 'husband' or 'wife,' Revenue Canada took the position until late in 1996 that extension of these non-taxable benefits to same-sex partners of employees would give rise to taxable income to the employee, and could even threaten the tax-exempt status of all other employees' benefits as well. Although that was an unsupportable position, at least one case – the human rights complaint brought by Mary-Woo Sims against Metropolitan Toronto – actually went through a protracted hearing on that understanding. Revenue Canada changed its reading of those provisions just two weeks before that decision was released,[14] although the board, which did not appear to be aware of that development, ruled against Revenue Canada anyway.

Section 6(1)(a)(I) of the Income Tax Act governs the taxation of employer-financed benefit plans. Its basic function is to exempt most such benefits from income taxation: registered pension plans, group sickness or accident insurance plans, private health services plans, supplementary unemployment benefit plans, deferred profit-sharing plans, group term-life insurance policies, and counselling services are thus all tax-exempt. With the obvious exception of the rules relating to registered pension plans discussed below, nothing in the Income Tax Act limits or conditions any of these exemptions by reference to sexuality, marital status, or family relationship. Out of the entire list of exempt benefits, the only type of benefit that involves any 'relationship' criteria is the counselling services described in section 6(1)(a)(iv), which extends benefits to the employee or any individual 'related to' the employee.[15]

In particular, the reference to the exemption for premiums paid by employers in relation to 'private health services plans' makes absolutely no mention of family connection or relationship status. This is one of the most important categories, because it affects private health insurance plans that underwrite medical, hospitalization, drug, chiropractic, massage, vision, dental, and physiotherapy benefits. Nor do the regulations under the Income Tax Act, Revenue Canada interpretation bulletins, or Department of Finance publications elaborate on this definition.[16] Nonetheless, despite this complete silence on the crucial point of sexuality, family connection, or relationship status, Revenue Canada took the position in private rulings that benefits received by same-sex partners were taxable income to lesbian and employees. As employers and employees began to challenge this position, Revenue Canada apparently put requests for reconsideration or for new rulings on hold while *Egan and Nesbit* was being appealed. The same day the Supreme Court of Canada issued its ruling in that case, Revenue Canada began to take those requests off the back burner and reaffirmed its position: Same-sex health coverage can 'taint' an entire plan, must be 'tracked' separately in order to segregate same-sex coverage from the rest of the coverage in order to minimize the tax benefits flowing from such coverage, and must not be 'cross-subsidized' by the main plan in any way, even if the segregated plan were managed separately.[17]

Revenue Canada devised complex and confusing rules for setting up segregated plans, how to tell whether plans were 'tainted,' how to avoid 'cross-subsidization,' guidelines on when it would be acceptable to keep queer employees in the same plan but account for their benefits separately, and suggestions that even basic coverage for queer employees could itself become a taxable benefit. By mid-1996, some 20 to 30 per cent of all employers were jumping through these administrative hoops in order to offer same-sex benefits, or were quietly forgoing tax deductions they were legitimately entitled to claim in calculating their own tax liability in order to avoid confrontation with Revenue Canada. Many queer employees continued to go without same-sex benefits, however. Some personnel administrators turned down requests for same-sex coverage because of the extra administrative hassles involved, and human rights commissions began to worry about seeking remedies that might 'trigger' 'deregistration' of employee benefit plans, leaving many queer employees to solve the problem of family health coverage on their own.

Fortunately, this problem was eventually addressed in litigation. But even in litigation, the mystique of legitimacy surrounding Revenue Canada's position was never really challenged. Instead, the proceedings were brought on the assumption that Revenue Canada's reading of the statute was legally correct, and that this 'law' violated the Charter. Even the expert witnesses for the complainants in these cases did not question the legality of Revenue Canada's position. Thus in *Moore and Akerstrom* v

Canada,[18] two gay couples, supported by the Canadian Human Rights Commission, had brought a complaint against the Treasury Board, the Department of Foreign Affairs, Canada Immigration, and the unions to which the employee complainants belonged, for refusal to extend the full range of employment benefits to them and their partners. In the hearing, the government presented evidence that including same-sex partners in the definition of 'spouse' would mean 'deregistration' of the plan, or that off-side plans such as was devised in *Leshner* could be set up (para. 33). Although the tribunal did not make any findings on this point, it ordered the government to prepare an inventory of all provisions of the Income Tax Act that would treat any employment-related benefits given to same-sex common-law couples as taxable (para. 109). After failing to convince the tribunal that such same-sex benefits should be 'tracked' separately for tax purposes,[19] Revenue Canada apparently realized how it would look if it tried to explain its position on health benefits in legal terms. In a private ruling dated 14 September 1996, Revenue Canada thus advised that 'a plan which provides coverage for same sex couples can meet the definition of a "private health services plan".'

Nothing had changed. The statute had not been amended in any way. Although the letter outlining this new position cited *Moore and Akerstrom*, that decision did not make any comments about the constitutionality of this definition, nor did the tribunal make any remarks on what aspect of the definition offended the Charter. According to the ruling, the only thing that had changed was that Revenue Canada had asked its legal counsel for 'an analysis' of the definition.

Unfortunately for Mary-Woo Sims, this process did not unfold in time to save her, her counsel, or her adjudicator the trouble of challenging the tax treatment of same-sex health benefits under the Ontario Human Rights Code.[20] As in *Moore and Akerstrom*, the complainant did not challenge the government's evidence that Revenue Canada would force same-sex employees to report taxable benefits in relation to partner coverage if they were ordered by the tribunal, and the entire hearing then proceeded on the basis that this legal state of affairs discriminated against queer employees. In the end, the adjudicator apparently realized that extension of health benefits to same-sex partners could not in fact result in the 'deregistration' of those plans, for she simply ordered the province and municipality to provide insured benefits – including health plans – for same-sex partners and children. Ironically, Revenue Canada had already 'changed its position' by then.

Many other non-taxable benefits are available to the partners and children of lesbians, gays, bisexuals with same-sex partners, and transgender or transsexual people whose partners are of the same legal sex as they. The use by family members of employer-provided recreational facilities and transportation passes provided by an employer is tax exempt.[21] The new tax exemption for employer-funded counselling services provided by employers does not make any reference to sexuality.[22] Nor is there any legal basis for reading the moving-expense deduction, which extends to expenses relating to 'members of the taxpayer's household,' as somehow excluding same-sex households.[23] It is unlikely that Revenue Canada will attempt at this late date to deny exemption of these benefits on the basis of sexuality, but knowing the history of Revenue Canada's behaviour in relation to other exempt benefits, taxpayers and their advisers should be prepared to defend themselves against such an exercise of administrative power.

Deferred Compensation

The tax treatment of deferred compensation plans is handled quite differently from other employment benefits. All these income tax provisions contain sexuality-specific language that has prevented employees with same-sex partners from taking advantage of the survivor options available to heterosexual employees when planning for their retirement and death. The denial of survivor benefits to queer employees has been very troubling, because deferred-compensation plans have become increasingly important components of the employment compensation package, and in many families accumulated pension rights are now one of the biggest assets the family has, second only to the family home.

In present-day income tax law, deferred compensation is generally thought to fall into three basic categories. Either employees will bargain for 'registered' plans such as pension plans, retirement savings plans, employee profit-sharing plans, deferred-profit-sharing plans, supplementary unemployment-benefit plans, education savings plans, and retirement income funds, or they will agree on stock-option plans or other salary-deferral arrangements. Of the 'registered' plans, pension plans involve the most employees and have attracted the most legal attention. The 'registered' feature of deferred-compensation plans has given rise to fundamental confusion over the tax status of these forms of compensation. Two opposing views of the tax character of deferred compensation have emerged in the technical literature, which, when combined with Revenue Canada's insistence that same-sex couples are not recognized for purposes of income tax legislation, has resulted in complete administrative refusal to give queer employees the benefits received by heterosexual employees under registered plans.

The 'legal' view is that deferred compensation paid into trusteed plans and held legally outside the reach of employees is not 'income' to employees until disbursements are actually made to them from the fund. Investment income accumulating in the fund is also considered to be not 'income' to employees for the same reason, although it could be taxable to the fund itself unless explicit tax exemption were given to the fund. This older view can be traced back to the very first British income tax statute enacted in 1799,[24] it was the rule in Britain during all but thirteen years between 1799 and 1917, and it has formed the basis for the tax treatment of employee pension plans in Canada since 1917.[25] The legal view of the tax status of employee pension contributions is based squarely on the legal definition of income for tax purposes. In income tax jurisprudence, income does not exist until it 'comes in' to the hands of the taxpayer. Monies paid into the hands of a third party who is under a legal duty to keep it until stipulated conditions are met is not 'received' by employees until those conditions are met. These are the 'realization' and 'receipt' principles that are central to the judicial definition of income, and that have been consistently and universally applied in British, Canadian, and other Anglo-based income tax systems.[26] The Canadian tax treatment of contributions to employee pension plans has never deviated from the legal model.[27] What has changed, however, has been the elaboration of this basic model to clarify its application to related situations. Thus employers were permitted to deduct lump-sum contributions to pension plans as well as ongoing annual contributions; anti-avoidance rules were enacted to counter use of pension structures to minimize tax liability in non-pension commercial transactions; and the principles of 'realization' and 'receipt' have been extended to apply to non-employment plans such as private RRSPs.[28]

The government's view of income tax rules relating to registered employee pension plans is that these provisions exist as a mechanism for delivering 'tax benefits' or 'state subsidies' to selected classes of taxpayers. This view is often attributed to the Carter Commission on Taxation, which adopted Stanley Surrey's post–Second World War notion that some special tax rules should be thought of as generating 'tax benefits' or 'incentives' for desirable forms of behaviour.[29] According to this view, employees receive a 'tax benefit' when their tax liability on pension contributions and accumulations is deferred until retirement, and the government considers this 'tax benefit' to be functionally identical to direct social assistance payments. Thus the federal government began in the 1970s and 1980s to refer to registered pension plans as the 'tax-assisted' part of the overall retirement income system,[30] and even began treating the 'tax forgone' as the result of the deferred nature of pension plan contributions and accumulations as 'tax benefits' and 'tax expenditures.'[31]

This assertion of 'side door' federal jurisdiction via the income tax structure over 'registered' pension plans is inaccurate. As early as the 1960s, it had become evident that the federal government lacked constitutional jurisdiction to regulate pensions, being provincial matters of property rights.[32] Even the Carter Commission concurred in this view, and thus found that the only objectives the federal government could legitimately pursue in relation to employee pension plans were to help foster pension 'consciousness' via the Income Tax Act and to ensure as a matter of revenue production that each registered plan is 'a bona fide arrangement to provide retirement income for employees, not a disguised form of temporary savings plan.'[33] This is in fact what happened, and this is the basis on which the courts have subsequently interpreted the employee pension plan rules.[34] Because of these jurisdictional issues, the substantive rules governing security of funds, portability, and terms are located in provincial pension regulatory legislation and are incorporated in the Income Tax Act. That substantive regulation is not located in the Income Tax Act itself because the federal government lacks jurisdiction to regulate those aspects of pension plans.[35]

The conflict between the 'legal' and 'subsidy' views of deferred employment compensation is important, because one of the many features of 'registered' employee pension plans are survivor pension options, which Revenue Canada asserted had to be restricted to heterosexual employees. Until it lost its appeal in *Rosenberg*, Revenue Canada took the position that governmental 'tax assistance' delivered through RPPs has turned registered plans into government benefits like the spousal allowance litigated in *Egan and Nesbit*, and thus that employers were not permitted to extend survivor benefits to same-sex partners of employees. Revenue Canada thus refused to accept such amendments to existing plans for registration, and threatened to 'deregister' entire plans if they did extend survivor options to lesbian or gay employees.

Unfortunately, the plaintiff's success in *Rosenberg* has not settled this contentious issue completely. Although the board in *Dwyer* did constitutionally correct all the provisions that supported the denial of same-sex survivor benefits for municipal employees in Ontario, it was afraid to trigger 'deregistration' of the entire RPP by ordering such benefits in that case. Thus it only contingently ordered that such benefits be extended if and when the Income Tax Act were amended. Now that the government has abandoned its appeal in *Rosenberg*, of course, that contingent remedy can come into effect if Ontario's appeal in *Dwyer* is resolved in favour of the complainant. The parties in *Moore and Akerstrom* had all agreed on consent that the RPP issue would be omitted from that case, so it is not yet clear how *Rosenberg* will affect those types of human rights complaints. Uncertainly over this issue has in the meantime been compounded by *Laessoe* v *Air Canada*,[36] a human rights complaint in which the complainant sought an order for survivor options in the Air Canada employee pension plan trust agreement. That complaint was resolved in favour of the employer not because of Revenue Canada's threat of 'deregistration,' but on the basis that it was financially and legally impossible to structure 'alternative' survivor benefits that would achieve even rough equality with ordinary RPP survivor benefits without creating imponderable administrative conflicts, inequality with other members of plans, and uncontrollable costs. As a private-sector ruling, *Laessoe* suggests that employers who are unwilling to extend same-sex survivor benefits do not yet have to.

Quite apart from the confusion and inconsistencies reflected in these cases, what is striking about the way they have been handled is the deep fear of Revenue Canada that appears to have shaped the issues, the arguments, and the remedies even in the successful cases. The spectre of 'deregistration' of RPPs appears to have struck terror in the hearts of all these complainants, their lawyers, and even the courts and boards that have dealt with them. The 'fear' factor shaped the way the complaint was framed from the very beginning in *Leshner*. The board in *Leshner* recognized that the exclusion of same-sex survivors from the RPP rules violated section 15 of the Charter.[37] In both sets of reasons released by the board,[38] however, it pointed out that the Ontario Human Rights Commission had recommended that the federal government be left out of any order, and uncritically agreed that the commission's fear of 'deregistration' was reasonable and urgent.[39] So great has this fear been that no one, so far as I can tell, ever filed a conditional amendment that would protect the plan from retroactive 'deregistration,' even though that is one of the options available when the administration of a plan does not conform to the regulations.[40]

This 'fear factor' is evident in the other cases as well. When the federal government refused to accept the Canadian Union of Public Employees (CUPE)'s amendment to its RPP trust agreement, it threatened to 'deregister' the CUPE plan if the union went ahead and extended those benefits under the main plan anyway. After a special appeal to the Federal Court of Appeal under the Income Tax Act failed to override the minister's position, CUPE was forced to embark on protracted and very expensive litigation (*Rosenberg*) to challenge the RPP survivor rules directly under the Charter. When the Ontario Human Rights Commission struck a board of inquiry to deal with the complaints in *Dwyer*, *Dwyer* had been told that he should not even pursue the pension plan issue in the face of *Leshner* and threatened deregistration, and counsel for the parties had accepted unquestioningly that extension of even health-related employment benefits could trigger 'deregistration' of those plans. Dwyer found this construction of the issues intolerable, and, to his credit, he engaged separate counsel to pursue an order for alternative survivor benefits. However, by this time, all parties had convinced themselves that a board order to extend survivor benefits to same-sex partners would somehow trigger immediate 'deregistration' of the entire plan, and thus Dwyer was persuaded to ask only for an order contingent upon eventual change of the Income Tax Act; he did not even ask for an 'offside' plan like the one ordered in *Leshner*.[41]

The RPP survivor rules are not the only income tax provisions that discriminate incrementally against same-sex couples. As discussed in chapter 8, wherever division of assets, rollovers of other deferred plans, or support provisions are permitted to opposite-sex cohabitants on a tax-favoured basis, same-sex partners experience further discrimination. Taking the impact of those provisions to their logical conclusion, same-sex partners who are ordered to share family assets with former partners are forced to treat those divisions as if the assets were sold to strangers, because they cannot be transferred on a tax-deferred basis. In these situations, 'incremental change' leads to intensified disadvantage in contexts where Parliament rushed to ease the situation of opposite-sex cohabitants.[42]

Lesbian and gay struggles to obtain same-sex employment benefits of all kinds have been significantly impeded by Revenue Canada's use of its administrative discretion to interpret and apply the Income Tax Act. To date, these struggles have been most successful where there were in fact no legal barriers to equal treatment, and have been only partially successful in relation to RPPs, where the legislative context did actually support Revenue Canada's position. Now that the federal government has abandoned its appeal in *Rosenberg*, the conflict between *Laessoe* and *Rosenberg* means that the scope of the *Rosenberg* decision in relation to RPPs remains unclear. Does *Rosenberg* apply only when the employer is willing to extend same-sex survivor benefits to employees? Or does it mean that it is now clearly a violation of the federal human rights code to deny such benefits? On the more general level, however, *Rosenberg* radically casts the meaning of 'spouse' in the rest of the Income Tax Act into question. But will Revenue Canada acquiesce in the extension of the rest of the benefit provisions to same-sex couples? Or will it reassess couples who claim such benefits on the basis that they are deemed to be spouses only for purposes of the RPP rules? And, if Revenue Canada decides to read *Rosenberg* narrowly in that regard, does that mean that it will not be reassessing same-sex couples who report as individuals for purposes of the child-benefit or other means-tested provisions? Or does it mean that Revenue Canada will now be ascribing spousal status to all same-sex couples in order to extend the reach of the GST tax credit 'tax on marriage' and other penalty provisions?

Status of Children

It is not only sexual minorities who are subject to 'incremental' discrimination – children with same-sex parents are also burdened by inconsistent and chaotic laws surrounding their status, rights, and relationships. This is not a trivial problem. Growing numbers of queers in Canada have children, yet, at this time, only British Columbia has made an effort to clarify legal policy relating to children with same-sex parents.[43] The sheer numbers of statutes relating to children in Canada means that legal issues abound.[44] Legal issues relating to children are potentially more serious as well. While adults can usually act in their own interests when they face discrimination, children have to depend on the larger culture – usually as represented by schools, hospitals, government agencies, and courts – and on the adults in their lives to safeguard their interests.

I describe the types of discrimination experienced by children with same-sex parents as 'incremental' because there are some places where Canadian law has admitted the possibility that 'same-sex parents' could exist, and thus that 'children with two parents of the same sex' can also exist. The moment Canadian courts began to award custody to lesbian or gay parents, that eventuality became possible. And then, when the B.C. tribunal declared it discriminatory to deny access to artificial insemination on the basis of sexuality,[45] legal culture accepted the possibility that lesbian couples might become parents of children conceived through artificial insemination. But this type of 'incremental' change – 'yes, you can exist, but we will define your rights and responsibilities "incrementally"' – means that as children with same-sex parents have come into life, they have faced a world governed by legal rules that sometimes treat them as if they have two parents, sometimes as if they have only one parent, and sometimes as if they have three or four. The process of living under conditions of incremental change means, for children with same-sex parents, living under conditions of frequent discrimination and legal chaos.

This incremental discrimination unfolds in the many small events of daily life. When schools do not recognize both same-sex parents, when camp counsellors demand that only a birth parent sign consent forms, when hospitals attempt to restrict visits to biological or adoptive relatives, or when government agencies deny benefits on the basis of biological connection, this is discrimination against children with same-sex parents. The homophobic values that underlie this 'everyday' discrimination can undermine family security, as, for example, same-sex parents who have separated try to appeal to 'biology,' 'law,' or 'normal practices' to convince children themselves that they have but one parent. This sort of 'everyday' discrimination gives way to life-altering catastrophe when children of same-sex parents are denied continuing contact with a non-biological parent, when they are denied inheritance rights, or when they are denied immigration status.[46]

Definitions of 'Parent'

All these legal problems stem from the same source: the law of parentage. At the present time in Canada, there is a huge gap between narrow traditional definitions of 'child' and 'parent' and wider contemporary definitions. Narrow traditional definitions tend to construct the parent–child relationship around presumptive biological connection or formal legal adoption, while wider contemporary definitions tend to look to the existence of a factual, 'in fact,' or *de facto* parent–child relationship. To complicate matters, there are many variants of both basic models. Wider definitions have come to be used in a growing number of statutes over the last few decades, and there are many places in legal policy where wider factual definitions essentially override older definitions. Nonetheless, the resulting differences between definitions means that children with same-sex parents move into and out of this life-defining relationship many times during their lives – sometimes even in the course of just one day. And each child with same-sex parents faces the inevitable realization, which will dawn at some point in their lives, that one of their parents may well be, for some legal purposes, a 'stranger' to them in law.[47]

What must be emphasized in analysing the narrow and wider approaches to defining 'child' is that no approach used in Canada is based purely on the existence of biological connection. Like every other culture, Canadian culture has left a great deal of room for people to decide for themselves how they will live and how they will create their families. However, even the narrow traditional approach to defining parentage incorporates millennia of cultural practices that augment bare legal doctrine. Upon close examination, it becomes obvious that there is a great deal of room even under the narrow traditional approach for people to make their own decisions – independent of biological fact – as to who will be legally recognized as 'parent' and who will not.

Presumptive Parentage: Taking Ontario law as an example, the starting point for defining the parent–child relationship is section 1 of the Children's Law Reform Act,[48] which provides that 'a person is the child of his or her natural parents' (section 1[1]) or 'a person is the child of the adopting parents as if they were the natural parents'(section 1[2]). All other 'kindred relationships' are considered to flow from the parent–child relationship with either the 'natural parents' or 'adopting parents' (section 1[3]). These provisions make it look as if parentage is simply and exclusively a function of either biological connection or formal legal adoption. This impression is reinforced by section 2 of the act, which stipulates that references in Ontario law to 'relationship by blood or marriage' are to be construed as including the relationship between a child and 'natural parents' (section 2[1]). In fact, parentage can be established not only by biology or by legal act, but also by the nature of the relationship between the adults in the household and the way they decide to relate to the child. Even more interesting, presumptions of parentage operate to create the legal status of parent both within formal marriage and within non-married cohabitation.

Within marriage, the Children's Law Reform Act contains a number of presumptions that operate to impose a parent–child relationship in many situations in which there is neither formal legal adoption nor actual biological connection. These presumptions essentially codify common-law doctrine. The central presumption in Ontario law is that a male person will be recognized in law to be the father of a child – and therefore the 'natural' father of the child – merely by virtue of being married to the mother at the time the child is born. It will not make any difference in the law of parentage that he might not be the actual biological father of the child (section 8[1][1]). This codifies long-standing common-law doctrine: *Pater is est quem nuptiæ demonstrant* (The father is he whom the marriage points out).[49] This presumption is given wide application. It extends to children born during a marriage that was in some way terminated as much as ten months before the child was born, and to children born before a male who acknowledges the child as his actually marries the mother (section 8[1][2], [3]). Thus a child born to a married woman as the result of an extramarital affair, or as the result of alternative insemination, or as the result of other reproductive technologies, whatever they might be, will be considered to be the 'natural child' of and related 'by blood or marriage' to her husband – regardless of the lack of biological connection between the husband and the child. This legal fiction is so powerful that, even when mothers subsequently try to negative the parental relationship on the basis of artificial insemination, for example, the courts have rejected such moves.[50] And before non-married cohabitants began to acquire some of the legal status of married couples in Ontario law, a male who wished to achieve the status of 'father' over the objections of the mother had to bring an application in court for a finding and declaration of paternity (section 5[1]).

During cohabitation, much the same presumptions operate. As non-married cohabitants began to be equated with married couples, the presumption of parentage flowing from the fact of marriage has been extended to men who merely cohabit with a woman who has a child. Section 8(1)(4) of the act sets out this presumption of parentage in these terms: 'The person was cohabiting with the mother of the child in a relationship of some permanence at the time of the birth of the child or the child is born within 300 days after they ceased to cohabit.' Legally, this presumption is just as durable as the presumption of parentage flowing from the fact of formal marriage: A male person presumed to be the father of a child must take the same steps as a married person to disavow parentage. If he does nothing to rebut the presumption, then he becomes, by operation of law and without any reference to biology, a 'natural parent' of the child.

Looking at the rules governing parentage from the perspective of how legal fictions create legal 'facts,' it is obvious that even the narrow traditional definition of 'parent' and 'child' in Ontario law does not turn strictly on biological connection or formal legal adoption. Even the definition of 'natural parents' leaves a great deal of room for a man and a woman to permit these presumptions to operate, and for the man to assume the social, economic, and legal role of father merely by virtue of this presumption. Thus Ontario law permits consensual *de facto* parent–child relationships to be classified as legal parent–child relationships.

Once these legal presumptions of parentage come into effect, they define the parent–child relationship for all purposes and in all contexts relevant to Ontario law. The Children's Law Reform Act (CLRA) stipulates that all other family relationships flow from the 'fact' that a person is a child of a natural parent (section 1[3]). This means that the presumptive father's family of origin will become the child's family, giving the child grandparents, aunts, uncles, cousins, and so on, who are conclusively presumed without any legal proceedings whatever to constitute the child's 'kin.'

There are no exceptions to these rules. All these relationships are declared by the act to apply 'for all purposes of the law of Ontario' (section 1[1]).[51] The CLRA further provides that any reference to a relationship by blood or marriage includes the 'natural' parent–child relationship defined in section 1 of the act, and extends this rule of construction to every act of the legislature, any regulation, any order, any by-law made under an act, and any instrument made in Ontario (section 2[1], [2][a], [b]).

It is true that there is one loophole in this presumed universality: If legislation, regulations, and so on, indicate a contrary intention, this statutory definition of 'parent' will be suspended and the contrary intention will govern the determination of parentage in that context (section 1[1]). However, no contrary intention does appear anywhere in Ontario law. Thus the fact that parents are married or cohabit will conclusively establish that both of them are the 'natural' parents and the 'legal' parents of any child born to the woman.

The definitions of 'parent' and 'child' in the CLRA are thus the cornerstone on which other narrow definitions are built. For example, the Succession Law Reform Act merely states that '"child" includes a child conceived before and born alive after the parent's death' and '"parent" means the father or mother of a child.'[52] The finer details of parentage addressed by the CLRA are simply incorporated into the Succession Law Reform Act by virtue of the statutory direction set out in section 2 of the CLRA.[53] Anyone who is a 'child' within the meaning of section 1 of the CLRA will fall within the definitions of 'relative' ('related by blood, marriage or adoption') in the Substitute Decision Act, 1992,[54] and 'child ... of the incapacitated person' and 'relative' under the Health Care Consent Act, 1996.[55]

One of the noteworthy features of the CLRA definition of the parent–

child relationship is the firmness with which the common-law category of 'illegitimacy' has been abolished. The title of the first part of the act is 'Equal Status of Children,' and sections 1 and 4 ensure that the legal status of the relationship between the parents will not affect the child's legal relationship with either of them. Section 1(1) stipulates that 'his or her status as their child is independent of whether the child is born within or outside marriage,' and section 1(4) provides that the common-law distinction between 'children born in wedlock' and 'born out of wedlock' is abolished.

The abolition of the common-law status of 'illegitimate child' ensures that even federal statutes that might not have addressed that issue yet will not override provincial legislation. For example, the Citizenship Act defines 'child' as including 'a child adopted or legitimized in accordance with the laws of the place where the adoption or legitimation took place.'[56] The CLRA can be read as having irrebuttably 'legitimized' all children born outside of formal legal marriage. That 'legitimation' is then read into the federal application of the Citizenship Act.[57]

Common-Law Parentage: Narrow definitions of parentage have been augmented by wider *de facto* concepts of parentage for various policy reasons. Even the Ontario Children's Law Reform Act contains some examples of these expanded *de facto* or common-law concepts of parentage: Any person who is entitled to custody of a child in Ontario is declared to have 'the rights and responsibilities of a parent in respect of the person of the child' (section 20[2]).[58] A same-sex parent can become entitled to custody in one of two ways: through *de facto* custody, or through court order. *De facto* custody, or physical custody, can be established merely by living with the child apart from the other parent, so long as it is with the consent, implied consent, or acquiescence of that other parent (section 20[4]). Such *de facto* custody will trigger the recognition of parental rights and responsibilities. In the alternative, a parent or 'any other person' may apply for an order of custody.[59] If a same-sex parent were not considered to be 'a parent' for purposes of this provision, then he or she would certainly be 'any other person.' Once an application for custody is filed with a court, the court is required to make the custody determination 'in the best interests of the child.' Although 'relationship by blood or through an adoption order' is relevant to a determination of the best interests of the child, it is but the seventh of eight major factors enumerated in the 'best interests' test (section 24[2][a]–[g], [3]). And in any event, the entire purpose of the 'best interests' analysis is to assist the court in reaching a custody determination that best suits 'all the needs and circumstances of the child' (section 21[2]).

A same-sex parent who has acceded to 'all the rights and responsibilities of a parent' by virtue of the Children's Law Reform Act will be considered to be a 'parent' for purposes of most if not all of the narrow definitions of the parent–child relationship in Ontario law. The fact of being a custodial parent would overcome any problems arising from the limited language of the Health Care Consent Act; consent to health care treatment would certainly be considered to be 'in the best interests of the child.'[60] Other statutory provisions resolve these types of uncertainties in favour of those who have either physical custody or legal custody of children. For example, the Family Law Act contains an expanded definition of 'child' and 'parent':

> 'child' includes a person whom a parent has demonstrated a settled intention to treat as a child of his or her family, except under an arrangement where the child is placed for valuable consideration in a foster home by a person having lawful custody;
> 'parent' includes a person who has demonstrated a settled intention to treat a child as a child of his or her family, except under an arrangement where the child is placed for valuable consideration in a foster home by a person having lawful custody.[61]

These definitions, which apply only to the Family Law Act, are designed to ensure that responsibility for child support is a not a function of provable biological connection, formal legal adoption, or presumptions arising from marriage or cohabitation, but instead is a function of the social and psychological reality created by the adults in the household.[62] In assessing whether that reality supports a finding of 'settled intention,' courts have looked to factors such as the depth of love and affection between the person to be charged with support and the child, forms of address ('mom' or 'dad'), degree of ongoing financial support, involvement in the education and guidance of the child, and the duration of the relationship.[63] The same expansive definition is found in other Ontario statutes. For example, the Succession Law Reform Act reiterates the above definitions for purposes of Part V of the act, which charges decedents' estates with support for dependants for whom the decedent has not made adequate provision (sections 57–73).

Other statutes use different formulations to include social parentage. The Canada Pension Plan Act, which confers important benefits on surviving children, uses an extremely wide definition of 'child':

> 'child' of a contributor means a child of the contributor whether born before or after the contributor's death, and includes an individual adopted legally or in fact by the contributor while the individual was under twenty-one years of age, and an individual of whom, either legally or in fact, the contributor had, or immediately before the individual reached twenty-one years of age did have, the custody and control, but does not include a child of the contributor who is adopted legally or in fact by someone other than the contributor or his spouse prior to the death or disability of the contributor unless the contributor was maintaining the child, as defined by regulation.[64]

This definition treats parentage as arising from *de facto* adoption ('adopted ... in fact'), physical custody, or court-ordered custody. Other federal statutes take similar approaches, although not necessarily in the same words. The Canadian Forces Superannuation Act includes step-children, 'illegitimate' children being supported by the contributor, and children 'adopted ... in fact' in the definition of 'child' for purposes of survivor benefits under the RCMP pension.[65] The Income Tax Act achieves the same effect, including a 'natural' child (section 252[1][a]), a wholly dependent child of whom the taxpayer had the custody and control 'in law or in fact' (section 252[1][b]), a child of the taxpayer's spouse (section 252[1][c]), and an adopted child (section 252[1][d]). Reciprocal definitions of 'parent' and other relationships complement this definition of 'child' for purposes of the entire Act (section 252[2][a],[g]).

At the federal level, the trend is very markedly in the direction of expanded social or 'common-law' concepts of 'child.' Some federal statutes may use rather outmoded language to achieve that effect (such as references to 'illegitimate children'), but the effects are substantially similar.[66] The British Columbia amendments to the Family Relations Act via Bill 31, of course, markedly depart from all the existing models by creating the new category of 'step-parent' and stipulating that a 'same gender' partner can become a step-parent by virtue of cohabitation with the other parent for at least two years (section 1), frankly placing same-sex parents on the same footing as opposite-sex cohabitants who have assumed the parental role in that way.

The Gap between Definitions

There is a huge gap between these two types of definitions of 'child' in Canadian law. The narrow definition encompasses biological children (including formerly 'illegitimate' children), formally adopted children, and non-biological children born to a cohabiting or formally married couple. Wider social definitions encompass children adopted 'in fact' as well as legally, children of whom the adult has physical or legal custody, step-children, and children in relation to whom the adult 'stands in the place of parent.'[67]

There are obvious areas of overlap between these two definitional approaches. For example, the extension of the presumptions of male parentage to cohabiting partners overlaps with the wider notions of *de facto* adoption, physical custody, and *in locis parentis*. However, the wider notions do not just bring males who cohabited with a birth mother at the time of birth into the category of 'parent'– parentage can now be established not only at the birth of a child, but at almost any time during minority; same-sex partners can become parents either at birth or during minority of the child; people who are not conjugally involved with 'natural' parents can become a 'parent' under these definitions.

Despite the increasing reliance on the wider expansive definition of parentage, however, the narrow definition still operates in several key areas of provincial law. A child who does not fit within the definition in the Ontario Succession Law Reform Act will not be entitled to receive a child's share of an intestate estate, nor share in the estate of a relative who dies without a surviving spouse or children. In such a situation, such a child will be entitled, at best, to apply for dependent's relief under Part V of that act. Not only is this 'share' qualitatively different from a share of the net assets of the estate, in that it is really just a charge against the income of the estate, but receipt of relief is entirely conditional upon the child's financial situation and prospects in life (sections 57–73). It may be that the parent can safeguard the child against some of these effects by making provision for the child in his or her will, but that is only a partial solution. If the testator has other children who do fall into the narrow definition of child, they can take the entire estate in priority to the dependant, who may only apply for relief, causing serious problems between siblings. Wills have been challenged on numerous grounds, have been lost, misconstrued, and even deliberately destroyed by adverse parties. And in any event, no testamentary disposition can control the devolution of the estates of other relatives.

A child who is not 'related by blood, marriage or adoption' within the narrow terms of the Ontario Children's Law Reform Act will not be considered to be a 'relative' for purposes of legislation like the Substitute Decision Act, 1992,[68] will not be permitted to participate in making decisions about the care of a parent or other family member, and will not even be entitled to notice of guardianship proceedings (section 69[5][2]). The reverse propositions also flow from this restrictive definition: A same-sex parent would not be a 'relative' and thus could not make decisions about the care of a child who became incapacitated. The same types of problems are also posed by the narrow definitions of 'child' and 'relative' in the Health Care Consent Act, 1996.[69]

The execution of general or limited powers of attorney would overcome many of limitations posed by the Substitute Decision Act and the Health Care Consent Act. But they do not necessarily solve every problem. There are many situations in which parents will not want to hand over powers unless absolutely necessary, which could well be too late if the reason for handing power over is incipient incompetency. And not everyone in the health care professions is as impressed with powers of attorney in relation to children as lawyers might like to think. Even the recognition of same-sex parentage in some contexts – such as for purposes of awarding child custody or access[70] – will not necessarily extend to all of Ontario law. For example, the court in *Re K.*[71] speculated that children born into same-sex relationships would not be able to share in the estate of the non-biological parent on intestacy unless that parent had formally adopted the child. Federally, a child cannot gain citizenship with a parent unless he or she meets the restrictive definition in that statute,[72] and the benefits flowing from jurisdiction under the Divorce Act may be beyond the reach of a child who does not fall within the only somewhat expansive definition in that statute.

The abolition of 'illegitimacy,' especially when combined with the extension of presumptions of parentage to cohabiting males, was designed to ensure that all children have equal status, and that no children are burdened by the lack of legal recognition of their relationships with their parents. However, the sex-specific reference to presumptive fathers in the current law of parentage continues to leave children with same-sex parents without legal status in relation to their non-biological parent, a form of 'illegitimacy' that has not yet been abolished in Canadian law. To date, this gap between the narrow and wider definitions of 'parent' can be bridged in three ways: by seeking the extension of 'step-parent' adoption to same-sex parents; by challenging the sex-specific definition of 'natural parent'; and by relying on the effects of legal custody.

Some same-sex parents have attempted to deal with the lack of status accorded same-sex parents by formal 'step-parent' adoption, adopting their own children jointly with their partner. As the result of Charter challenges to the Ontario adoption rules[73] and legislative amendments to British Columbia adoption legislation,[74] same-sex 'step-parent' adoptions are now available in at least two jurisdictions, and a 'same gender' partner can become a step-parent by virtue of two years cohabitation in British Columbia as well.[75] In such jurisdictions, 'step-parent' adoption orders give same-sex parents the status of deemed 'natural parent' by way of section 1 of the Children's Law Reform Act. It is not clear at this time whether *de facto* step-parentage will have such an effect.

While this strategy does clarify and confirm parent–child relationships in same-sex families, it does not solve all the problems for all families. First, 'step-parent' adoption will not be a realistic option for every same-sex couple. Economic, class, race, health, and other factors can serve as deterrents or barriers to successful adoption. 'Step-parent' adoption may be viable when a child was conceived in a relationship by alternative insemination, but numerous factors can impede such a plan in other cases. Children born as the result of heterosexual relationships or conceived by other means as yet to be explored may not be adopted easily. It is not necessarily an option for the thousands of children born before 1995, the year in which *Re K.* was first decided, especially if the relationship between the parents broke down before that year. Nor is it an option when the birth parent is incapacitated or deceased. It will not be an option when the birth or adopting parent is ambivalent about sharing parenting, being queer, being out as queer (being a same-sex parent is a very 'out' thing to do), or uncertain about the relationship, even though parentage in fact is established. In short, it is an option that is available only to some same-sex parents.

Second, 'step-parent' adoption is not necessarily the best way to confirm parentage after a child has reached the age of social awareness. Children who have been raised since birth by same-sex parents have expressed the belief that being adopted later in life somehow says that their parents were not always their parents, and that adoption somehow detracts from that relationship, making it seem as if they were not 'really' their parents before the adoption took place. These views suggest that same-sex parents should look at *Re K.* with a more critical eye. Was the court correct in saying that children of same-sex parents could not inherit from their non-biological/non-adopting parent outside a will? Is it correct that this is the only way for non-biological lesbian mothers to 'become' a parent of their child? Questioning those aspects of *Re K.* will not be easy. The legal imagination thrives on solid legal fictions like those created by legal adoption. For example, the authors of an article on the tax treatment of support payments between same-sex spouses became quite excited at the implications of step-parent adoption for the deductibility of child-support payments should the couple ever split up.[76] More recently, a Vermont state court denied an application for visitation rights to a lesbian mother who it said could have gone through a step-parent adoption when she and her former partner were still together. Because they had not, the court concluded that the applicant had at least acquiesced in the position her former partner was taking in the access hearing, which was that the applicant was not in fact a parent.[77]

Challenging the heterosexual presumption embedded in the current understanding of 'natural parents' may offer a better way to bridge the 'sexuality' gap in legal definitions of parent–child relationships. Section 1(1) of the Children's Law Reform Act declares that 'for all purposes' a person 'is the child of his or her natural parents,' and that status as a child 'is independent of whether the child is born within or outside marriage.' The phrase 'natural parents' is itself gender-neutral. Thus it cannot be taken as disqualifying two women or two men from being the 'natural parents' of a child. 'Natural parents' must include the couple that creates and nurtures a child's very life and existence. Such a direct definition is reinforced by the presumptions of parentage found in section 8 of the Children's Law Reform Act, the Ontario Human Rights Code, and the Charter of Rights. Constitutionally corrected, section 8(4) of the Children's Law Reform Act would presume a same-sex cohabitant to be a parent of a child born during (or within 300 days after) cohabitation. This constitutional correction should flow from the reasoning of the Supreme Court in *Egan and Nesbit* and *Miron v Trudel*, and from the reasoning of the Ontario Court of Appeal in *M. v H.*

This reading of Charter equality jurisprudence is backed up by the provisions of the Ontario Human Rights Code and the legislative objectives of the Children's Law Reform Act. The code prohibits discrimination on the basis of 'family status,' on the basis of sex, and on the basis of sexual orientation.[78] The code defines 'family status' as 'the status of being in a parent and child relationship.' 'Family status' must encompass situations in which some types of parent–child relationships are not given legal recognition; the abolition of 'illegitimacy' in sections 1(1) and (4) of the Children's Law Reform Act admits of no other construction of 'family status' in the code. Indeed, no other interpretation of 'family status' would be consistent with the recognition of the 'equal status of children' in Part I of that act. Whichever way a court might want to turn in finding new types of 'family status' that are not covered by the code, the prohibitions on discrimination on the basis of sex and sexual orientation would preclude carving out new categories of legally recognized 'illegitimacy.' Once parentage were established on this basis, both same-sex parents would be 'parents' for all other purposes under Ontario law, and all other kindred relationships would flow from both parents equally (section 1[2][3]).

The language of lesbian parentage is slowly developing in some judicial decisions. In *J.A.L.* v *E.P.H.*,[79] the court ruled that the non-biological lesbian mother could seek joint custody or access of her child. The court wrote that '[t]he inescapable conclusion to be drawn ... is that ... the child was to be a member of their nontraditional family, the child of both of them, and not merely the offspring of EPH as a single parent.' The court emphasized that they were both involved in planning and obtaining alternative insemination, and that they had lived together as a close family unit. And during the trial in *Baehr* v *Miike*,[80] an expert witness for the state admitted in cross-examination that, in some situations, stepparent adoption would not be appropriate when 'a same-sex couple that sought and received reproductive assistance and in which the non-biological parent was fully involved from the beginning of the planning process, was present throughout the nine month period and at birth, and thereafter, raised the child as though they were the biological parents of the child.'[81] The court noted as well that this witness agreed that all the basic civil rights flowing from the parent–child relationship – including inheritance rights and rights to every form of support – were crucial to the well-being of children with same-sex parents.

Lastly, the 'sexuality' gap in definitions of the parent–child relationship can be bridged by reading the legal effects of custody as extending to all legal contexts affecting the status of children. Same-sex parents who have physical or legal custody under the Children's Law Reform Act are declared to have 'the rights and responsibilities of a parent in respect of the person of the child' (section 20[2]). Same-sex parents can establish physical custody through section 20(4) of the act, which provides that, when parents have separated and the child lives with one of the parents 'with the consent, implied consent or acquiescence of the other,' the non-custodial parent's right to exercise custody is suspended until an agreement or order provides otherwise. While this provision primarily functions to clarify the rights and responsibilities of the custodial parent after separation, and to insulate the child from the effects of private processing of custody issues, it also confirms the parental status of the acquiescing non-custodial parent. Legal custody can be established through court order. Same-sex parents clearly have standing to apply for such an order;

section 21 of the act gives the right to apply for custody to parents or to 'any other person.' In such a situation, a court would be obligated to make a custody determination that considers all the needs and circumstances of the child, the 'best interests of the child,' but relationship by blood or marriage to the other parent would be but one of eight major factors the court would be required to consider (section 24[1], [2]). Certainly courts have previously given access as well as joint custody to same-sex parents in Ontario.[82] After establishing physical or legal custody, a parent would still have to persuade a court that section 20(2), which provides that a person entitled to custody has the rights and responsibilities of a parent, actually establishes parentage for purposes of section 1 of the act and thereby for all other purposes of Ontario law. This would be a matter of statutory construction, having reference to both the legislative objective of the custody provisions and the human rights/Charter rights context.

Reading the law of parentage through the prism of the Charter, the gap between the narrow and wide definitions of parentage can be bridged by a declaration that children born during same-sex cohabitation are the children of both parents and that both parents are 'natural parents' for purposes of the general law.[83] This route is preferable to same-sex stepparent adoption, because it is most consistent with the lived reality of the family and with the Charter guarantee of equal protection of the law, and it would affect all children with same-sex parents, not just those whose parents have separated. Same-sex couples are still a long way from convincing legislatures to give their unique customary arrangements statutory status. But that is what is happening: It has been customary now for almost two decades for same-sex couples to have children together through alternative insemination.[84]

The legal status of parents is but one of the many challenging legal issues surrounding children in alternative families. How to characterize the legal relationship between sperm donors and children in lesbian families, the partners of sperm donors and children, siblings who have different biological origins, and new partners of the original same-sex parents are also pressing concerns to same-sex families. It is obvious that jurisdictions that have already set up more fluid and fact-based categories, such as Ontario and British Columbia, will be able to serve the interests of children in those jurisdictions more effectively than jurisdictions that still limit the inquiry to biological connection and formal marriage. Negotiating these issues will not be simple. Conflicts between lesbian mothers and gay sperm donors, between old partners and new partners of both, and between children in the same families of origin are inevitable. Reality has a way of outstripping legal norms, but the danger right now is that, in the absence of clarifying legislation, those who can point to legally recognized connections such as the biological connections of sperm donors will predictably attempt to deploy narrow common-law precepts in order to gain legal advantage, while those whose claims are based in actual relationships rather than on law or biology will remain more vulnerable to disruption of their connections. Thus, for example, the case of *Thomas S. v Robin Y.*[85] pitted a sperm donor against two lesbian co-mothers when the donor decided to pursue judicial recognition of his paternity and independent custody or access to the one child in the family who had been conceived as the result of his donation. Although the two mothers were fully involved in all aspects of their children's lives from conception, the reasoning of the court repeatedly verged on weighing the rights of the donor against the rights of the birth mother, and very little emphasis was put on the role or status of the non-biological co-mother. As the justice who dissented from the order recognizing the donor's paternity pointed out, the daughter who was the focus of this litigation was forced to become 'aware that her family is vulnerable to attack on a number of fronts,' became aware that her non-biological mother's status was 'ambiguous,' and had her sense of security in the composition of her family fundamentally shaken when she learned, at age nine, that the court had declared that she – and only she – had a legal 'father.'[86]

Incremental Discrimination

To give courts and legislators the benefit of the doubt, perhaps they are just not aware of how completely the realities of queer existences have moved beyond current legal doctrine. But until law catches up with reality, forcing lesbians, gays, bisexuals, transgendered people, transsexual people, their partners, and their children to all wait for 'incremental change' to reach them is just another way of enforcing 'incremental' discrimination. Although there is legitimate concern among queer communities over how partners and parents should relate to each other, and although there is quite understandable distrust on all sides of many legal issues, it is becoming clear that growing numbers of couples of all kinds are trying to make sensible arrangements for their lives together. Part of making those arrangements is being able to make adequate provision for retirement, old age, death, care and education of children, devolution of property, and all the events that naturally occur in life.

All levels of government are remiss in not moving more quickly to examine and rationalize the complex areas of law that are triggered whenever life unfolds. The Income Tax Act is long overdue for reform in this regard. Revenue Canada has gotten away with positions affecting same-sex couples that would not have lasted a minute with heterosexual couples. Of even greater seriousness is the fact that the ever-increasing numbers of children with same-sex parents are growing up aware that they are vulnerable to becoming a new generation of dispossessed, 'illegitimate,' second-class citizens, denied legal connection to some of the people in their families. Children grow up very fast. In the decade it took the federal government to actually take the step of including 'sexual orientation' in the human rights code, children who were in grade school at the beginning of that period of time have grown up and become voters by now. Children who were raised on books like *Heather Has Two Mommies* are now studying law in high school, and are beginning to realize that, depending on where they are and what they are doing at any one time, they are not even sure who their 'legal' parents are. What might seem like isolated and strange issues to heterosexuals are in fact life-defining for many young people and their families in Canada.

Chapter Eleven

The Future of Queer Personhood

person n. a man, woman or child, regarded as having a distinct individuality or personality, or as distinguished from an animal or thing | | (law) a human being or a collection of human beings considered as having rights and duties.
New Lexicon Webster's Encyclopedic Dictionary , Can. ed.
(New York: Lexicon Publishers, 1988), 749

As this typical dictionary definition makes clear, the word 'person' is usually used to distinguish human beings from non-humans. In law, however, 'person' is used to classify human beings and other entities by rights and duties. Thus 'person' can include a long list of non-human entities, including business corporations, territorial corporations, foreign corporations, partnerships, a county, or the estate of a decedent, at the same time that it can be used to exclude some human beings: 'Not every human being is necessarily a person, for a person is capable of rights and duties, and there may well be human beings having no legal rights.' And '[a] person is such, not because he [*sic*] is human, but because rights and duties are ascribed to him.'[1]

What is interesting about the way the concept of 'personhood' operates in law is that, once courts have established through common-law doctrine that some classes of human beings are excluded from terms like 'person' or 'citizen,' there are only two ways to retrieve the rights and duties thereby lost. One way is through the piecemeal restoration of rights and duties by way of statutory enactments and judicial interpretations of selected provisions. Married women's property legislation is an example of this form of restoration, as are interpretation statutes that give courts direction on how to read some undefined terms in statutes. (The term 'person' can be statutorily defined as including both men and women, for example, reversing judicial presumptions that 'person' refers only to men.)

The other way is through the doctrine of 'constitutional personhood,' in which constitutional pronouncements are interpreted inclusively instead of narrowly. Depending on the scope of application of such pronouncements, they can go a long way towards reversing presumptions of non-personhood. This is what happened with the Privy Council ruling in *Edwards* v *A.G. Canada*[2] when it reversed the Supreme Court of Canada decision in *Reference as to the meaning of the word 'persons' in section 24 of the British North America Act, 1867.*[3] Common-law expectations that women would be excluded from terms such as 'person' were reversed by the higher authority of the Privy Council decision, and, until statutory processes of clarification took over, the new principle of constitutional personhood reached as far as analogy and context could bear.[4]

While the doctrine of constitutional personhood does rely to a certain extent on domestic legislation and policies for material expression of general principles, constitutional recognition of personhood can reverse not only existing common-law declarations of non-personhood, but earlier constitutional declarations as well. And in a political climate in which domestic legislation is used not to recognize legal rights and duties, but to constrain or nullify them, the doctrine of constitutional personhood can be invoked to invalidate such incapacitating classifications.

To a great extent, the doctrine of constitutional personhood emerged in response to the inadequacies of legislation that purported to restore some legal capacities to 'civilly dead' groups. Although it took well over a century to work out the relationship between legislative powers to impair or shape legal capacities on the basis of race, and constitutional guarantees of legal capacity in the United States, through the repetitive interplay of legislation and constitutional challenges, the result has been the emergence of a body of jurisprudence that now offers a principled basis from which to seek the restoration of civil capacities of other groups – including people characterized by their sexuality.

In this chapter, I outline how the use of legislative powers to stave off the restoration of the full legal personality of African Americans in the United States actually incited the emergence of a constitutional doctrine of personhood powerful enough to invalidate such legislation. I then explore how this doctrine of constitutional personhood has recently come to be applied to lesbian, gay, and bisexual people in the United States in the face of similar legislative, and even constitutional, attempts to nullify their legal personality. I contrast the resulting U.S. constitutional model of queer personhood with the purely legislative models of queer rights/duties that have been developed in some European countries, and point out the differences in legal capacities that can be expected to flow from both models.

Within this framework, I then examine current legislative models and constitutional decisions in Canada. I conclude that legislatures in Canada appear to prefer legislative models that simultaneously extend and constrain fundamental legal capacities to models that would restore full civil capacities across the board. Courts, however, appear to be reaching consensus that the equal protection clause in section 15(1) of the Charter requires them to invalidate such constraints as come before them, and to formulate orders that restore full legal personality.

What hangs in the balance in these two processes – legislative 'reform' that both grants and constrains rights versus judicial application of the constitutional doctrine of personhood – is which presumption is to govern: the presumption that sexual minorities continue to occupy the essentially rightless/dutiless jurisprudential space labelled 'sexual orientation,' which can be furnished with some narrowly selected rights/duties only as dictated by political will, or the presumption that sexual minorities are constitutionally guaranteed the full legal capacities associated with legal 'personhood,' a presumption that can be overcome only in the most compelling and least burdening of circumstances.

If the presumption of heterosexual privilege and queer non-existence continues to operate, then the process set in motion when the first Canadian court ruled that gay men lack some legal capacities[5] will permit legislatures and courts to continue to reinscribe the rightless/dutiless existence of sexual minorities even as they appear to extend them selected rights. But if the doctrine of constitutional personhood is seen as now having primacy, then sexual minorities are constitutionally no longer 'other,' resigned to *locus nullius juris* – the place of no laws even beyond outlawry – but are presumed to have all the ordinary legal rights of adult humans.

Constitutional Personhood

The history of the civil rights of African Americans in the United States makes it perfectly clear that 'civil rights' provisions do not necessarily have to protect or extend the civil capacities of disadvantaged groups. Indeed, many of the earliest civil rights statutes enacted on this continent had the opposite purpose – to limit, or even nullify, important civil capacities. In this section, I outline how this dynamic affected the civil capacities of African Americans in the United States between the mid-1800s – the era in which the Emancipation Proclamation abolished slavery – and 1967 – the year in which the last legal disability imposed on African Americans was invalidated on the basis that it violated constitutional guarantees of full legal personality. I then explore how the same dynamic has affected the recognition of the legal capacities of sexual minorities in the United States, beginning with tentative legislative extensions of legal capacities to lesbians and gays, and ending, as of this writing, with the emergence of constitutional protection for the legal personality of people characterized by sexuality.

Race and Civil Status

Before the end of the Civil War in the United States, the status of involuntary servitude was legally constructed by 'slave codes' that systematically nullified all the legal capacities ordinarily accorded to adult human beings. By using statutory provisions to erase all these elements of legal personality, human beings were turned into property or 'things' because they had been denied all those capacities that in legal discourse were considered to be the hallmarks of human existence.

The Code of Alabama, 1852, provides a clear example of how this was done. The laws of Alabama contained provisions that denied slaves the right of employment, the right to own property, the right of movement, the right to assemble, the right to bear arms, the right to hunt, all backed up with elaborate provisions for the maintenance of 'slave patrols' charged with enforcing these prohibitions at the community level. Slaves were expressly declared to be the 'property' of their masters, and other provisions gave the master the express legal right to enforce obedience. These same codes set out the legal incidents of 'freedmen,' a category that applied only to African Americans. Contrary to what the term 'freedmen' might seem to suggest, people who fell into that category were not permitted to stay in Alabama for more than thirty days at a time, on pain of imprisonment, and were also subject to severe limitations on their rights of speech, association, movement, trade, and religion. In addition, contact between freedmen and slaves was severely prohibited.[6]

If U.S. constitutional law had ever contained any presumption that slaves or freedmen were included in the concept of 'people of the United States' or 'citizens,' that presumption was decisively rebutted in the 1857 decision in *Dred Scott* v *Sandford*,[7] which arose out of constitutional challenges to federal legislation purporting to exclude slavery from new territories. In the course of ruling that African Americans had 'no rights which the white man [sic] was bound to respect,' Chief Justice Taney treated this as a constitutional condition:

> The words 'people of the United States' and 'citizens' are synonymous terms, and mean the same thing. They both describe the political body who form the sovereignty, and who ... hold the power ... The question before us is, whether the class of persons described in [this] plea compose a portion of this people, and are constituent members of this sovereignty? We think they are not, and that they are not included, and were not intended to be included, under the word 'citizens' in the Constitution, and can therefore claim none of the rights and privileges which that instrument provides for and secures to citizens of the United States. On the contrary, they were at that time considered as a subordinate and inferior class of beings, who ... had no rights or privileges but such as those who held the power and the government might choose to grant them ...
> [N]either the class of persons who had been imported as slaves, nor their descendants, whether they had become free or not, were ... acknowledged as a part of the people, nor intended to be included in the general words used in that memorable instrument [the Declaration of Independence].

The purpose of the Emancipation Proclamation, which became the Thirteenth Amendment to the U.S. Constitution in 1865, was to abolish the legal status of involuntary servitude by overcoming this negative presumption. The assumption behind the language of the Thirteenth Amendment ('Neither slavery nor involuntary servitude ... shall exist ...') seemed to be that, if the status of involuntary servitude were abolished constitutionally, then the state slave codes would be invalidated automatically. This in turn would restore the full civil capacities of former slaves.

Far from acquiescing in this new constitutional stance, the U.S. southern states attempted to circumvent the effect of the Thirteenth Amendment by replacing their old slave codes with new statutes labelled 'civil rights' codes that reinstated, as much as possible, the material and legal conditions of slavery. These statutes did in fact give declaratory effect to some elements of legal personality for former slaves. The preambles to these new codes thus declared that they were intended to recognize and secure the new 'civil capacities' of former slaves. However, even a cursory examination of these texts – known as the 'Black codes' – reveals that they were clearly designed to re-establish the legal incidents of slavery and to limit the effect of the Thirteenth Amendment as much as possible. Thus the Laws of Mississippi, 1865, for example, opened with the following declaration:

> AN ACT to confer Civil Rights on Freedmen, and for other purposes.
>
> Section 1
>
> *Be it enacted by the Legislature of the State of Mississippi,* That all freedmen, free negroes and mulattoes may sue and be sued,... in all the courts of law and equity of this State, and may acquire personal property ... by descent or purchase, and may dispose of the same, in the same manner ... that white persons may.[8]

This legislation then went on to secure a few other fundamental civil capacities: It deemed former cohabitants to be legally married, it permitted freedmen to testify as competent witnesses in civil and criminal proceedings involving white persons as parties or accused, and it recognized contracts of employment. However, these few civil capacities were extended at the same time that numerous other provisions reconstructed the material conditions of slavery. The act went on to prohibit 'freedmen' from renting or leasing real property except in designated areas, intermarrying with any 'white person,' living or working in any area without police or municipal permits, working without contracts approved by local authorities, quitting a contract of employment without good cause, unlawful assembly, holding weapons, or preaching. The new legislation also deemed any unemployed freedmen, any freedman with no licensed home, and any child of a freedman not being cared for 'adequately' to be a 'vagrant,' provided for the arrest of such 'vagrants,' and authorized local sheriffs to sell their labour to the highest bidder. Preference in such a sale of 'labour' was to be given to the 'worker's' former owners. Numerous other provisions imposed heavy penalties on anyone who interfered with any such 'employment contracts' or helped a 'freedman' who was in breach of a contract escape the jurisdiction.[9]

It is not difficult to see how such new legal disabilities re-created the material and legal conditions of involuntary servitude. The extension of some previously denied elements of legal capacity to African Americans was not sufficient to offset the effects of these many continuing disabilities. When coupled with deeply seated social prejudice and intolerance, it is no wonder that the Emancipation Proclamation by itself and even in conjunction with the Thirteenth Amendment did not dramatically improve the social and economic conditions of former slaves.

The continued imposition of civil incapacities in legislation like this led eventually to the enactment of the Civil Rights Act of 1866, which made concrete provision for social assistance and land rights for former slaves. Because there were already suggestions that even mere relief legislation might be found to be unconstitutional despite the language of the Thirteenth Amendment, the federal government initiated the adoption of the Fourteenth and Fifteenth amendments to the U.S. Constitution. These constitutional amendments – especially the due-process and equal-protection clauses of the Fourteenth Amendment – were designed to invalidate specially disabling provisions in the laws themselves in order to restore the full elements of legal personality to former slaves, and to ensure that the federal government would have the constitutional authority to enact ameliorative civil rights legislation.

The adoption of the Fourteenth and Fifteenth amendments certainly did not immediately have this effect. So deeply entrenched were the values reflected in the 'Black codes' of the southern states that it took more than a century to eradicate the last of these legal disabilities. Courts persisted in interpreting these restoration provisions narrowly; legislatures kept devising new and different ways to incapacitate people by race; and social/economic discrimination of all kinds depowered racially identified people, which made it more difficult for them to derive the maximum benefit from the legal rights they did have.

During the rest of the nineteenth century, the courts participated in the deep struggle to continue denying all but the most formal elements of civil capacity to African Americans. In case after case, the U.S. Supreme Court found ways to read the Thirteenth, Fourteenth, and Fifteenth amendments to the federal constitution in ways that continued to erase the very rights and duties those amendments had been designed to restore,[10] but as time passed, the Court abandoned its assertion that African Americans were not 'people' or 'citizens' and instead followed the example of the 'Black codes'– paying lip service to the civil and political equality of racialized groups, but refusing to apply that equality to discriminatory legislation or practices.

Thus in the key Civil Rights Cases of 1883,[11] the majority of the Court declared federal civil rights anti-discrimination legislation to be unconstitutional at the same time that it purported to recognize the legal personality of African Americans: 'When a man has emerged from slavery, and by the aid of beneficent legislation has shaken off the inseparable concomitants of that state, there must be some stage in the progress of his elevation when he takes the rank of a mere citizen, and ceases to be the special favourite of the laws, and when his rights as a citizen, or a man, are to be protected in the ordinary modes by which other men's rights are protected ...' With the decisions in *Hall* v *De Cuir*[12] and *Plessy* v *Ferguson*,[13] shortly thereafter, the Court continued to affirm the 'absolute equality of the two races before the law,' but concluded that manifestly inferior segregated facilities satisfied the requirement of 'absolute equality,' and continued to declare even state anti-segregation laws to be unconstitutional. As the result of this line of decisions, the plethora of segregationist and discriminatory state and federal laws that came to be known as 'Jim Crow' laws were immunized from constitutional review, and all forms of social, political, economic, and legal discrimination against racialized groups continued without any effective challenge up until the mid-1900s in the United States.

It is interesting to note that, during this period, one of the last of the civil disabilities to be abolished was the prohibition on marriage between African Americans and 'whites.' Prohibitions on interracial marriage or cohabitation were found in statutes and state constitutions, civil laws, and criminal laws.[14] The number of such provisions grew steadily after the Civil War. By 1910, some thirty-five states had enacted these 'racial purity' laws. The 'anti-miscegenation' movement was not just a southern political reaction; many northern and western states readily adopted this type of legislation as well.[15] The fact that these anti-'miscegenation' laws predated the first full-blown 'Jim Crow' laws by several decades suggests that integration on the intimate level was perhaps even more threatening to the dominant classes than integration in 'public' institutions. However, once the racial line had been drawn in the 'private' sphere, legislators then moved on to draw similar lines in 'public' spheres of social existence.

From our vantage point, the virulence of the criminal penalties imposed on those who married or cohabited across racial lines is shocking. State statutes uniformly declared such marriages to be void, and imposed criminal penalties not only on the parties to the marriage, but on anyone who performed them as well.[16] The language with which courts rejected challenges to those penalties is also stunning, difficult to take literally. Some of the most profound appeals to a sense of the 'natural order of the races' are found in these cases. One of the earliest cases upholding 'miscegenation' laws appealed both to the importance of the racially homogeneous home to the nurture of future ('white') generations and to 'the Creator' to justify this form of racial segregation:

> It is through the marriage relation that the homes of a people are created – those homes in which, ordinarily, all the members of all the families of the land are, during a part of every day, assembled together;... where ... the young become imbued with the principles, and animated by the spirit and ideas, which in a great degree give shape to their characters and determine the manner of their future lives ... Who can estimate the evil of introducing into their most intimate relations, elements so heterogeneous that they must naturally cause discord, shame, disruption of family circles and estrangement of kindred?...
>
>> 'Why the Creator made one white and the other black, we do not know; but the fact is apparent, and the races are distinct, each producing its own kind, and following the peculiar law of its constitution.... The natural law...is as clearly divine as that which imparted to them different natures"...
>
> And surely there can not be any tyranny or injustice in requiring both alike, to form this union with those of their own race only, whom God hath joined together by indelible peculiarities, which declare that He has made the two races distinct ...
>
> [Marriage] is a public institution established by God himself, is recognized in all Christian and civilized nations, and is essential to the peace, happiness, and well-being of society ... The right ... to regulate and control, to guard, protect, and preserve this God-given, civilizing, and Christianizing institution is of inestimable importance ...[17]

Over the following decades, courts devised other justifications to buttress this appeal to Christian values and 'natural order.' Racial amalgamation, it was claimed, would produce a 'mongrel population and a degraded civilization.'[18] Academics developed arguments based on fear of transmission of disease, 'imperious sexual impulse,' and 'retardation' in support of strict segregation on every level of society.[19] The principle of 'purity of blood' was even extended to the management of the blood supply: Blood banks were required to identify blood by the race of donors, and were prohibited from using 'blood from a person of a different racial classification' except in 'certified' emergencies.[20]

That anti-miscegenation laws denied important elements of legal personhood is clear. Nonetheless, anti-miscegenation laws were not finally declared unconstitutional even in lower courts until 1948, in *Perez* v *Lippold*.[21] In *Perez*, a California court declared that miscegenation laws were not valid unless they employed a 'reasonable means' to prevent a social evil, but that if they arose merely 'out of earnest belief, or out of irrational fears,' they 'reason in a circle' which lacked 'compelling justification.' The court also concluded that the 'right to marry is as fundamental as ... the right to have offspring' and thus cannot be infringed on the basis of mere prejudice. Despite the clarity of this reasoning, the U.S. Supreme Court did not follow suit until 1967, in the same year that the poll tax was finally abolished.[22] In *Loving* v *Virginia*,[23] the court concluded that the 'freedom to marry has long been recognized as one of the vital personal rights essential to the orderly pursuit of happiness by free men,' and ruled that 'the freedom to marry, or not to marry, a person of another race resides with the individual and cannot be infringed by the State.'

Although racial discrimination in the United States continues to affect the social, economic, and political rights of African Americans and other racially identified people, what is striking about the legal context now is that the restoration of legal personality has been accomplished not by legal provisions that have given people characterized by 'race' specified rights (and obligations), but by the use of the Fourteenth Amendment to invalidate and remove many specially disabling provisions from laws that have been expressed in terms of race. While special structures such as federal civil rights legislation still offer remedies for some forms of discrimination such as in employment or education, the restoration of legal personhood has not proceeded by way of, for example, special 'interracial partner' provisions, but by applying the general constitutional principle of equal protection of the laws to invalidate provisions that purport to place legal limits on people who are characterized by their race.

Romer v *Evans*

The constitutional status of people characterized by their sexuality has gone through a similar history in the United States, although this history has unfolded over a relatively short period of time. With the first assertions of ordinary legal rights – notably, the right to marry again – the common-law presumption that sexual minorities did not have full legal capacities was relied upon, as in Canada, to assign them to the right-less space labelled 'sexual orientation.' In the first case under the Fourteenth

Amendment to raise issues of sexuality before the U.S. Supreme Court, *Bowers* v *Hardwick*,[24] a gay man claimed that a state sodomy statute violated his constitutional rights to privacy and due process of law. The Court flatly refused to rule on those issues, and instead reframed the issue as the existence of a 'homosexual right to sodomy.' Not surprisingly, the Court found that the constitution contained no such right.

Efforts to obtain the enactment of federal or state constitutional measures to combat discrimination on the basis of sexuality have consistently failed. So have efforts, beginning in 1975, to pass federal civil rights legislation to protect employment and housing rights on the basis of sexual orientation. As a result, activists have concentrated on lobbying for state and municipal anti-discrimination or human rights provisions.[25] Only a dozen or so jurisdictions have enacted some form of statutory human rights provisions to prohibit discrimination on the basis of sexual orientation,[26] and activists found that their best hopes were often to seek the adoption of municipal anti-discrimination ordinances. Thus, by the early 1990s, some sixty cities had enacted municipal ordinances that prohibited discrimination on the basis of sexual orientation.[27] Unusual instruments for the protection of human rights, these ordinances were designed to safeguard the classical elements of legal personality. The best ordinances have usually prohibited discrimination in a wide range of situations, including housing, education, credit, union practices, private employment, and public employment. Most of them do prohibit discrimination in public employment, but only half offer coverage in private employment, bank credit, or public accommodation.[28]

When compared with statutory human rights provisions and constitutional provisions, municipal ordinances offer relatively limited protection. Municipal councils have limited jurisdiction in terms of both territorial reach and subject matter. Courts do not give municipal ordinances as much deference as to statutory or constitutional provisions, which has resulted in decisions 'reading down' remedies won in municipal litigation.[29] Municipalities do not have the power to change marriage laws, and thus the most they have been able to in relation to same-sex marriage has been to extend same-sex employment benefits to their own employees and to place pressure on local employers to follow suit.[30]

Despite the limited nature of protection extended by municipal ordinances, they have sparked widespread political backlash in the United States. This backlash has taken several different forms. Lobbyists in many communities pursued the local repeal of such human rights ordinances,[31] either by proposing referendum measures to repeal municipal ordinances or state-wide measures to nullify ordinances, educational initiatives, and negotiated agreements. Some of these referenda have merely generated discriminatory municipal ordinances or state statutes.

By far the most devastating attacks have been by way of state constitutional referendum measures. In Oregon, for example, the adoption of an anti-discrimination ordinance in Portland led quickly to Measure 13, a referendum ballot item that was designed to result in immediate amendment to the Oregon state constitution. This referendum proposal would have prohibited the state from protecting civil rights on the basis of sexuality, prohibited extension of marital status or spousal benefits to same-sex couples, prohibited schools from addressing homosexuality, prevented governments from making personnel decisions on the basis of sexuality, restricted access to library materials relating to homosexuality, and insulated private industry from liability for discriminatory conduct.[32] In short, Measure 13 would have resulted in the immediate nullification of a wide range of legal capacities previously enjoyed by sexual minorities, and would have limited the power of governments and courts alike to restore other capacities such as marriage in the future. In effect, Measure 13 would have achieved by way of constitutional amendment what the 'Black codes' of the southern states sought to achieve after the Emancipation Proclamation came into effect – express nullification of legal capacities that were extended by other legal or constitutional provisions.

Amendment 2 to the Colorado state constitution, similar to Measure 13 but drafted in more general terms, was proposed in reaction to the adoption of civil rights ordinances in the municipalities of Aspen, Boulder, and Denver. These ordinances prohibited discrimination in housing, employment, education, public accommodations, health, and welfare on the basis of sexual orientation. 'Sexual orientation' was defined as including heterosexuality, homosexuality, and bisexuality.[33] Amendment 2 was adopted in a state-wide referendum in 1992. Entitled 'No Protected Status Based on Homosexual, Lesbian, or Bisexual Orientation,' it provided that no level of government nor any arm of government could adopt or enforce any provisions or policy 'whereby homosexual, lesbian or bisexual orientation' could receive any legal protection. The amendment automatically came into effect as soon as it received sufficient votes, thus bypassing the state legislature completely.

It was the passage of Amendment 2 that finally resulted in the application of the Fourteenth Amendment to sexual minorities. Challenging Amendment 2 on the basis that it denied lesbian, gay, and bisexual people the 'equal protection of the law,' the plaintiffs argued that despite the fact that Amendment 2 had created a new state constitutional provision, it imposed legal incapacities on people characterized by their sexuality. The U.S. Supreme Court agreed with the plaintiffs.

The Court based its ruling squarely on the constitutional protection of personhood expressed in the Fourteenth Amendment. Quoting directly from Justice Harlan's dissent a century earlier in *Plessy* v *Ferguson*, Justice Kennedy admonished that 'the Constitution "neither knows nor tolerates classes among citizens",'[34] and concluded that the amendment unconstitutionally violated the guarantee of equal protection of the law because it 'imposes a special disability upon [lesbians, gays, and bisexuals] alone' (1627), and 'make[s] them unequal to everyone else.' The Court concluded that such 'class legislation ... [is] obnoxious to the prohibitions of the Fourteenth Amendment' and that the state 'cannot so deem a class of persons a stranger to its laws' (1629). The Court found that there was no explanation for Amendment 2 other than the expression of animus against lesbian, gay, and bisexual people, and therefore could find no rational basis to sustain it. In the face of the decision in *Romer* v *Evans*, Measure 13 in Oregon and other referendum measures were withdrawn shortly after the decision was published.[35]

Baehr v *Miike, Defense of Marriage Act, and 'Reciprocal Benefits'*

Constitutional protection of legal capacity has been extended not only to personal rights in *Romer* v *Evans*, but also to relational rights in *Baehr* v *Miike*,[36] in which a Hawaii court ruled that denial of marriage licences on the basis of the sex of the partners violated the state constitution. The Hawaii state constitutional provision was worded somewhat differently from the federal Fourteenth Amendment. Like the Fourteenth Amendment, the Hawaii constitution prohibits denial of the equal protection of the laws, but, unlike the Fourteenth Amendment, it goes on to provide that no person shall 'be denied the enjoyment of the person's civil rights or be discriminated against in the exercise thereof because of race, religion, sex, or ancestry.'[37]

Baehr v *Miike* arose when local officials refused to give lesbian and gay couples marriage licences because of the sex/uality-specific language in the marriage statute, which stipulated that a valid marriage contract 'shall be only between a man and a woman.'[38] Treating the limitation of marriage to 'a man and a woman' as a sex-based classification, the state court concluded that there was no rational connection between the purpose of the legislation and this classification, and that the state did not have a compelling interest in denying marriage licences to same-sex couples. The court concluded that this classification violated the equal protection clause in the Hawaii constitution and thus ordered that marriage licences be issued. This order has now been stayed pending appeals.

Separated by more than a century from the earliest cases involving state anti-intermarriage laws, the state's purported justifications for opposing same-sex marriage nonetheless sounded very similar to the justifications for the older race-based laws. The state argued that limiting the right to marry served five 'substantial and compelling' state interests: It protected the health and welfare of children; it fostered procreation within a marital setting; it ensured that Hawaii marriages would be recognized in other jurisdictions; it protected the public fisc; and it protected civil liberties, which included the 'reasonably foreseeable effects of State approval of same-sex marriages, on its citizens.'[39]

After hearing extensive testimony from experts on each of these points, the court found that the state had not presented sufficient evidence to support any of these contentions. The court's central finding was that family structures were quite diverse, with children being raised by 'natural parents, single parents, step-parents, grandparents, adopted parents, hanai parents, foster parents, gay and lesbian parents, and same-sex couples.'[40] Having also found that children were better off in families that received full recognition under all laws, including laws that conferred benefits or subsidies on families, and that marriage between adults made many forms of social and economic support available to both parents and children that would not otherwise be available, the court concluded that the exclusion of same-sex couples was neither justifiable nor 'narrowly tailored to avoid unnecessary abridgments of constitutional rights.'[41]

Even before the hearing of this matter was concluded, opponents of same-sex marriage began to deploy political power at both the federal and state levels to try to block it. On 21 September 1996, the federal congress approved the Defense of Marriage Act (DOMA).[42] The DOMA purports to give states and other levels of government the right to refuse to give effect to same-sex marriage,[43] and, for federal purposes, has defined 'marriage' and 'spouse' in the following terms: '[T]he word "marriage" means only a legal union between one man and one woman as husband and wife, and the word "spouse" refers only to a person of the opposite sex who is a husband or a wife.'[44] According to one commentator, the non-recognition clause of DOMA gives states the power to conduct themselves in a fashion far more discriminatory than they ever had in relation to intermarriage.[45]

Shortly after the decision in *Baehr v Miike* was released, the Hawaii state legislature considered a proposal for a constitutional amendment relating to marriage framed in similar language.[46] However, the proposed state constitutional amendment went even further than DOMA; it defined 'marriage' as being limited 'to the union of only one man and one woman,'[47] and proposed an exception to the Hawaii equal protection clause itself. Thus the Hawaii equal rights amendment would contain the following exception: 'Regulations, laws, rules, orders, decrees and legal doctrines that define or regulate marriage, the parties to marriage, or the benefits of marriage shall not be deemed in violation of this section or any other section of this constitution by virtue of a limitation of the marriage relationship to the union of only one man and one woman.'[48] The legislative version of this proposal contained its justification right in its text: '[T]he unique social institution of marriage involving the legal relationship of matrimony between a man and a woman is a protected relationship of fundamental and unequaled importance to the State, the nation, and society.'[49]

In the meantime, pending the appeal in *Baehr v Miike*, while waiting for constitutional challenges to the DOMA to be decided by the courts, and while the Hawaii proposals that would limit marriage to men and women remained pending,[50] the Hawaii legislature ended up enacting the first U.S. 'reciprocal benefits' legislation. This new statutory provision permits any type of couple (same sex, opposite sex, non-conjugal, etc.) to receive benefit certificates that entitle them to receive benefits ordinarily reserved to married couples, such as medical insurance coverage, joint property ownership, inheritances, and employment spousal benefits. Originally designed to give same-sex couples some of the benefits associated with marriage while continuing to prevent them from marrying, the same-sex limitations in the bill were removed at the last minute in deference to religious objections to any formal recognition of same-sex relationships.[51]

At the other end of the debate, strategists who have noticed how effective the 'sex' clause in the Hawaii state constitution has been in attacking the validity of provisions that discriminate on the basis of sexuality have begun to rethink the federal Equal Rights Amendment (ERA) movement. Recasting the proposed ERA as the inclusive Constitutional Equality Amendment (CEA) with clauses relating to sexual orientation, marital status, 'ethnicity,' national origin, colour, indigence, and pregnancy, organizers have begun to attract coalition support for this new congressional lobbying effort.[52]

The two cases discussed here – *Romer* v *Evans* and *Baehr* v *Miike* – both illustrate how the constitutional doctrine of personhood has been applied to protect sexual minorities from the impairment of their civil capacities by statutory enactments as well as by state constitutional provisions. While the existence of the 'sex' clause in the Hawaii state constitution was probably critical to the ruling in *Baehr* v *Miike*,[53] the unmodified language of the federal Fourteenth Amendment equal protection clause easily invalidated the state constitutional provision challenged in *Romer* v *Evans*.

Perhaps even more important, these two cases demonstrate that the fundamental strategy pursued in the racial civil liberties movement – the restoration of full constitutional personhood – can work in relation to sexuality as well. Thus both decisions stand for the proposition that it is not necessary for queers to settle for limited sexuality-specific rights in the search for full legal personality. It is possible, where the incidents of 'personhood' are constitutionally protected, to invalidate the incapacitating provisions themselves, instead of having to settle for the incorporation of selected and constrained rights into that jurisprudential space known as 'sexual orientation.'[54]

European Models

Several European countries have adopted a very different approach to queer existences than that found in the United States. There is generally less drama over the 'sanctity' or 'unique' nature of heterosexual marriage. Nor are there movements to deprive sexual minorities of the basic civil rights that have been safeguarded in legislation or multilateral treaties.[55] Indeed, Denmark enacted legislation that assimilated same-sex couples to marriage at the end of the 1980s, and Sweden has since extended the legal status of recognized cohabitation to same-sex couples. While not all countries in Europe have completely decriminalized queer sexual expression, some countries have begun, through anti-discrimination legislation and judicial decisions, to fill in the gaps between decriminalization and the recognition of civil capacities.[56]

Although some European legislation relating to sexuality – especially the relationship-recognition provisions – has been ground-breaking, it does still fall short of securing to sexual minorities the same legal capacities accorded heterosexual couples. In an admittedly muted way, European statutes relating to the civil capacities of sexual minorities have done somewhat the same thing that the old 'Black codes' of the post–Civil War southern states did in the mid-1800s – they have extended some civil capacities to lesbians and gays in the legislation, but they have also taken the opportunity to statutorily nullify or limit the exercise of other elements of legal personhood at the same time. Primarily these incapacities relate to parentage, assisted conception, and formal legal marriage.

The 'Marriage' Model

In 1989, Denmark enacted 'registered partnership' legislation that was intended to give same-sex partners status similar to that of marriage.[57] Registration of partnerships is performed civilly after the issuance of a 'partnership certificate,' and, as with marriage, the partners do not have to prove that they will live together or that they have a sexual relationship. The consequences of the relationship flow not from the substantive nature of the relationship, but from the fact of partnership. Once the partnership registration is completed, many of the incidents of marriage are automatically extended to the couple. This includes mutual obligations of support; community-property rules; insurance rules; separation, divorce, maintenance, and inheritance regimes; death duties; the right to the home; social security benefits; and pensions.[58] Literally all provisions of Danish law that refer to 'marriage' or 'spouse' are now interpreted to include registered partnerships and registered partners.[59]

Registered partnerships are not completely assimilated to the marriage model; they still lack many of the legal incidents of heterosexual marriage. First and foremost, same-sex partners are not permitted to marry formally; registered partnerships have been devised in order to offer some legal basis for the recognition of same-sex relationships, but that relationship is not considered to be 'marriage.' It is a form equivalent to marriage in legal effect only. Thus the formation of a registered partnership cannot be carried out religiously, because registration can only be performed by public authorities. Similarly, because registered partnerships are purely civil relationships, registered couples have no claim to mediation performed by the clergy. Unlike heterosexual marriage, which can be entered into in Danish law by two people who are merely visiting the country, at least one of the parties to registration of a partnership must be a Danish citizen. Along the same lines, parties to a registered partnership between a Danish citizen and a person from a treaty country will not be considered to be 'spouses' for the purpose of such treaties until agreement on that variation is received from the contracting country.

Perhaps most important of the differences between registered partnerships and the heterosexual marriage model to which the legislation purports to assimilate same-sex couples, however, is the prohibition on joint adoption of children during the relationship and joint custody of children after relationship breakdown. Apparently the legislature 'assumed' that registered partners could have children 'separately' but not 'together.' Nor can registered partners seek parentage in relation to children born during the relationship, adopted by one of them during the relationship, or raised together by the couple, for the rules relating to parentage are biologically based and expressed in sex-specific terms, which thus precludes the extension of registered-partnership status to issues of parentage.[60] Registered partners are not permitted access to assisted conception for similar reasons.[61] Because legal recognition of the parent–child relationship is thus withheld, there is no legal basis, on relationship breakdown, for an application for joint custody, access, or child support.[62]

From the perspective of the legal capacities conferred on same-sex couples by legislation and those that are withheld, registered partnerships are second-class forms of relationships. But the particular legislative context in Denmark appears to have made it impossible to extend the legal recognition of non-married cohabitation to same-sex couples, because cohabitation does not at present have any status. Interestingly, the government appears to be considering extending the principle of individual liability and benefits to married couples in order to equalize the status of married couples and cohabitants if cohabitation were to be legally recognized. This would be done in order to ensure that the use of the couple as the benefit unit in allocating tax liabilities and distributing social benefits would not burden married couples in comparison with nonmarried cohabitants. It also explains why relationship recognition in Denmark has been conferred by extending the marriage model – until the tension around the use of the couple as the benefit unit is resolved, deeming same-sex couples to be married was the only way to legitimize the extension of the heavier burden of income taxation borne by married couples to same-sex couples.[63] Although not all Danish couples would appear to agree, the government is still of the opinion that marriage is the best legal framework for relationship recognition.[64]

The 'Cohabitation' Model

In 1987, Sweden extended some of the heterosexual cohabitation provisions to same-sex couples, preferring this route to the politically more controversial route of granting same-sex couples marriage rights. The resulting legal framework is primarily focused on property rights rather than on the incidents of the relationship itself, and was not, at the time the legislation was enacted, accompanied by any civil rights or human rights guarantees.[65]

The legal framework governing heterosexual cohabitants was extended to same-sex couples in two steps, both of which were taken at the same time: Legislation was enacted to place 'joint homes' of cohabitants on much the same basis as the matrimonial home of Canadian matrimonial property law,[66] and a separate act extended the provisions of this legislation to same-sex cohabitants.[67] This legislative regime ensures that a home acquired for the joint use of a same-sex couple can be alienated or encumbered only with the written consent of both partners, or on court order. Even if a predeceasing partner disposes of his or her interest in the joint home by will, the surviving partner is entitled to a statutory forced share in both the home and the household goods. Partners can opt out of the joint home provisions by written contract, which is consistent with the community-property regime that applies to married couples in Sweden.[68]

As in Denmark, one of the biggest legal disabilities still imposed on same-sex partners is the denial of adoption rights. Unlike Denmark, however, Sweden achieved that result by limiting adoption to married couples and single persons.[69] Since same-sex couples fall into neither category, they, like cohabiting heterosexuals, are not permitted to adopt children. This, then, has obviated the need to address parentage, child-custody, access, or child- support issues, since apparently the legislation has not contemplated that same-sex couples might have children together through assisted conception.

Although same-sex couples in Sweden appear to have most of the same legal rights to property as heterosexual cohabitants, they, along with heterosexual cohabitants, are still expressly denied other incidents flowing from marriage. Thus they are also second-class citizens in relation to this cluster of fundamental civil capacities. Like Danish activists,

Swedish strategists have been lobbying for changes in the laws relating to assisted conception, adoption, and parentage.[70] And if the Finnish 'recognized companionship' legislation is enacted, activists are demanding that those rights will be extended to same-sex couples.[71]

Judicial Remedies

The creation of second-class legal status for same-sex relationships in Europe does not appear to be the work of legislatures alone. The Hungarian Constitutional Court ruled in 1995 that a new law on common-law marriages[72] unconstitutionally excluded same-sex cohabitants. The law was sent back to the legislature with instructions to extend it to same-sex couples. However, the court also ruled that same-sex couples did not have the right to formal civil marriage, and a constitutional lawyer who was interviewed by the media after the decision was released speculated that the court might accept legislation that prohibited same-sex couples from adopting children together.[73]

It has been suggested that the European reluctance to extend adoption rights to same-sex couples whose relationships otherwise have some legal status can be traced to the provisions of the 1967 Council of Europe Convention on Adoption.[74] This convention stipulates: 'The law shall not permit a child to be adopted except by either two persons married to each other, whether they adopt simultaneously or successively, or by one person.'[75] My own sense is that this adoption provision is symptomatic of the deep reluctance to accord sexual minorities the full incidents of legal personality. Segregating same-sex couples in special domestic regimes, whether they be called 'registered partners' or '"homosexual" cohabitees,' produces a legal framework within which the state can continue to deny selected incidents of legal personality in response to popular opinion.

Canadian Models

Legislative models in both the United States and some European countries suggest that, when politicians have addressed the legal status of sexual minorities, they have tended to focus their attention not on general concepts of legal personhood, but on the most pressing of specific current issues. Not surprisingly, legislative models in Canada bear a strong resemblance to those in the United States and Europe, sharing with them the use of separate statutory markers such as 'partner,' 'same-sex couples,' 'stepparent,' or 'same gender' couples to create a separate system of rights for queers, and the use of piecemeal statutes to extend only selected rights to people who fall into these categories.

Against this trend, however, is the growing trend in Canada for courts to use their powers under the Charter of Rights to invalidate and remove statutory markers that violate the equal protection clause in section 15(1) of the Charter. In this section, I conclude that these courts are giving expression to the doctrine of constitutional personhood that is embedded in the Charter, and are forming a principled basis upon which the presumption that sexual minorities are not 'persons' in law is being reversed.

Legislative Models

In Canada, legislation relating to sexuality has taken three identifiable forms. The first form, and still the most prevalent, has been the inclusion of 'sexual orientation' clauses in human rights legislation. The second form has been the inclusion of terms such as 'partner' in selected statutes to solve specific legal problems. The third form has consisted of omnibus legislation designed to inject lesbians and gays into a large number of statutes all at once.

Not all jurisdictions in Canada have as yet added 'sexual orientation' clauses to their human rights statutes. In those jurisdictions that have taken this step, the effect of this legislative extension has been to give people covered by these clauses recourse to human rights commissions when they experience discrimination in employment, housing, accommodation, or services. Although some human rights commissions and tribunals have treated the exclusion of lesbians or gays from other statutes in that jurisdiction as constituting discrimination based on 'services' or 'employment,'[76] it is unlikely that the jurisdiction of commissions will be seen as extending to every statutory exclusion in concurrent legislation in the near future. In any event, human rights legislation itself can contain definitions that exclude sexual minorities from some provisions. For example, the Ontario human rights statute still contains 'opposite-sex' definitions of 'marital status' and 'spouse'[77] despite the ruling in *Dwyer* v *Toronto (Metropolitan)*.[78] While section 15(1) of the Charter can be invoked to overcome that definition in specific complaints, it is yet another obstacle to overcome in litigation.

The second form of legislative reform, the amendment of selected statutes to extend their application to sexual minorities, is still rare in

Canada. Only two statutes in Ontario have been amended in this way, using the term 'partner' to give same-sex couples the kind of decision-making and management authority associated with spouses in the event of the illness or incapacity of one of them.[79] (I take perverse pleasure in the other 162 statutory provisions in Ontario that use the term 'partner' in a wide range of other contexts. Some of those usages appear to have been drafted with a view to making sure that they are not confused with the queer usage of 'partner,' using adjectives like 'business' or 'limited,' but most do not. I look forward to litigation over the extent to which the queer meaning of 'partner' is to be read into those other usages.)

The third form of legislation is also rare, no doubt because there is still so much social and political controversy surrounding queer existences. Both times omnibus legislation has been drafted, it has resulted in bills that only selectively include sexual minorities. The first time omnibus legislation was proposed in Canada, by the NDP government in Ontario, it was defeated. Although Bill 167 did give expression to many of the recommendations of the Ontario Law Reform Commission in a 1993 report that had considered the situation of both same-sex cohabitants and opposite-sex cohabitants, chief of which was adoption of the limited provisions of the European registered-partnership model,[80] the government began to whittle the scope of Bill 167 down even more as it moved through the legislative process. When Bill 167 was proposed in 1994, the original draft would have deemed same-sex cohabitants to be 'spouses' in the same way that 'opposite-sex' cohabitants are and would have included same-sex couples in statutory definitions of 'marital status,' making them members of the same family and giving them the status of next of kin.[81] Bill 167 would also have amended over fifty other statutes to place same-sex cohabitants and opposite-sex cohabitants on an equal footing, and sometimes to place both types of cohabitants on the same footing as formally married couples.

Despite the wide reach of Bill 167 as originally drafted, amending nearly sixty statutes over all, it would have left unamended some twenty other statutes that use the word 'spouse' or that govern the rights and responsibilities of married couples. Some of these twenty-odd statutes would have consequentially applied to both same-sex and opposite-sex cohabitants upon the enactment of Bill 167, because some of those statutes depended for their operation on definitions that would have been changed by the bill.[82] Other provisions were excluded from Bill 167 because it was obvious that changes to the definitions of 'spouse' and 'marriage' in the Human Rights Code and the Interpretation Act made in Bill 167 would have applied inferentially to them.[83]

However, Bill 167 would still have stopped short of giving either opposite-sex or same-sex cohabitants the same rights and responsibilities as formally married couples. Several important statutes were left out of Bill 167 in order to ensure that, for various policy reasons, they could not be considered to apply to same-sex couples. In taking this step, the government made it perfectly clear that it did not think same-sex couples should have the right to chose between marriage and cohabitation.[84] One of the most important of these exclusions was the parentage provisions of the Children's Law Reform Act. The presumptions of parentage flowing from the fact of formal legal marriage or from opposite-sex cohabitation would have remained completely unaffected by Bill 167, and would have left the status of children with same-sex parents unclarified. Although the government made much of its proposal to permit same-sex couples to adopt children jointly, it did not even broach the question of how parentage should be defined in relation to children born to same-sex parents.[85]

Another important area of provincial law that was excluded from Bill 167 was the matrimonial property provisions located in Part II of the Family Law Act.[86] Part II contains the special rules relating to the interests of married persons in the 'matrimonial home,' and also provides for a presumptive sharing of the net matrimonial estate on death or relationship breakdown. Although Part III of the act would have been amended by Bill 167 to apply to same-sex cohabitants, the only property right it creates as between non-married cohabitants is a right to support after relationship breakdown; remedies in relation to property interests can be obtained only in court proceedings.[87] Lastly, it was clear that the province did not feel that it should risk contradiction between provincial and federal definitions of 'spouse' in income tax legislation. Thus provincial income tax statutes that make any reference to definitions of 'spouse' in the federal Income Tax Act were also excluded from the schedule of amendments to other acts.[88]

In short, Bill 167 would have given all couples in Ontario – whether married or unmarried, same-sex or opposite-sex – many of the same rights and responsibilities. However, the special status of formal marriage would have remained unaffected in several key regards: Same-sex couples would not have gained the right to formally marry under Bill 167; neither same-sex nor opposite-sex cohabitants would have acquired any greater rights in relation to each other's property than they already had under equitable doctrine; the parentage of children would not have been clarified in any way; and the income tax treatment of couples – which federally had treated non-married cohabitants as if they were married since 1993 – would not have been extended to same-sex cohabitants in provincial income tax law.

The differences in treatment between same-sex cohabitants, opposite-sex cohabitants, and married couples would have been even more pronounced had Bill 167 been enacted, because as the legislative process unfolded, the government proposed last-minute amendments designed to placate right-wing opponents of the entire package. (The government had already agreed to permit a free vote on this legislation, which meant that it was certain to fail in any event.) These changes would have ensured that same-sex couples would not be able to adopt children jointly, and would have dropped the provision that would have deemed same-sex couples to be married, leaving them to be included in the more limited 'cohabitation' provision.[89] In one version of this announcement, it appears that the government considered itself to be offering the Swedish 'domestic partner' model instead of its original proposal.[90]

Many lesbian and gay activists – some of whom were already dissatisfied with the narrow terms of the legislation in the first place – were greatly relieved when Bill 167 was defeated on 9 June 1994. The feeling was that Bill 167 was beginning to look entirely too much like the European models by restricting the concept of 'the family' to 'the couple.'

When Bill 31[91] was enacted early in 1998 in British Columbia, it also borrowed a number of features from European models. Bill 31 extended legal recognition to same-sex partners by adding the categories 'stepparent' and 'persons of the same gender' to family law legislation. The effect of this change has meant that same-sex partners who are deemed to be 'step-parents' have standing in custody, access, and support proceedings, and that same-sex partners who meet the cohabitation requirements can be considered to be spouses for purposes of cohabitation agreements and support provisions. (Same-sex couples had already obtained adoption rights in British Columbia by legislation in 1996.) However, this statute did not go even as far as Bill 167 would have gone in terms of amending the rest of the B.C. statutes that employ terms like 'spouse' or 'husband and wife,' although the government has confirmed that it is studying remaining statutes to prepare further legislation.

Standing back from the legislative models that have been developed in Canada, it is clear that, if the legal rights and duties of sexual minorities were left up to politicians, these rights and duties would remain quite constrained and partial. The legislative models that have been developed have not moved in the direction of eliminating opposite-sex markers like the words 'opposite-sex' or 'husband and wife' from statutes so much as they have added new categories such as 'same sex' or 'same gender' to existing legislation.

The least offensive example of this approach is found in Bill 31 in British Columbia, which has replaced the old definition of 'spouse'[92] with completely gender- and sexuality-neutral language that includes living with 'another person in a marriage-like relationship for a period of at least 2 years' and 'persons of the same gender.' By including 'persons of the same gender' in the basic definition of 'spouse,' it could be said that the definition does not really create new categories so much as it removes old barriers to existing categories. However, two things detract from this view. First, nothing in this definition or the amended act as a whole enables same-sex partners to marry, so that persons of the same gender are still denied full legal capacity in that regard. Second, while persons of the same gender are now placed on an equal footing with others who become considered to be spouses by living in a marriage-like relationship for two years, both sets of cohabitants continue to be denied access to the family property and division of pension provisions in the statute.

While it is true that this legislation has not gone so far as to set up a third-class category of relationships such as 'registered domestic partnerships,' it has created, for example, a third-class form of parentage with the category 'stepparent.' The first class of parents are those considered by marriage to be the parents of a child, even if the husband of the birth mother has had nothing to do with the conception or actual parenting of the child. The second class of parents are those who are deemed by virtue of cohabitation to be parents, as when the male person cohabiting with a birth mother is deemed to be a parent.[93] The third class of parents are those partners of the 'same gender' who cannot be classified as 'males' or as 'fathers' under the parentage and paternity provisions of the legislation even if they were in a permanent conjugal relationship with the birth mother at the time of conception and birth, and even if they played the role of committed parent from the beginning. These same-sex partners can be considered to be a 'parent' only by meeting the new definition of 'step-parent' in Bill 31: 'a person is the stepparent of a child if the person and a parent of the child ... lived together in a marriage-like relationship for a period of at least 2 years and [includes] persons of the same gender.'[94] When a same-sex partner has become a parent some time after the child is born, this definition of parentage treats that partner the same as it does a heterosexual partner who establishes a relationship with a parent who has already had children. But when the parent has been involved with the conception, birth, and parenting of the child from the very beginning, as is the custom in growing numbers of lesbian and some gay as well as bisexual couples, it is third-class parental status.

It is certainly not a bad idea in legislative amendments to vacate the common-law presumption that same-sex relationships cannot be recognized in law, lest future courts say again when reading gender-neutral and sexuality-neutral language that the legislature could have expressly included same-sex couples if that is what they had intended, this can be done without setting up new second-class and third-class categories. For example, Australian amendments to inheritance and intestacy provisions have set up the categories 'domestic partner' and 'eligible partner' to deal with the rights of non-married cohabitants. But instead of limiting 'domestic partner' to same-sex couples, that category has been defined as including 'a person other than the person's legal spouse who – whether or not of the same gender as the deceased – lived with the deceased at any time as a member of a couple on a genuine domestic basis ...'[95] Although the Australian model does continue to separate married couples from non-married couples, it defines the second category in terms that are clearly intended only to erase common-law exclusions and not to establish an entirely separate third class of relationships. In fact, in some circumstances, a same-sex partner is actually given preference over a formally married spouse of the same person in matters of intestacy.[96] Legislation proposed in Québec takes a similar approach, sometimes replacing phrases like 'the man or the woman' in definitions of 'spouse' with 'the person' and sometimes inserting phrases like 'or the same sex' to expand 'opposite-sex' definitions.[97]

Judicial Charter Remedies

The equal protection clause in section 15(1) of the Charter is, like the U.S. Fourteenth Amendment upon which it was patterned, a constitutional guarantee of 'personhood' that prohibits the use of legislative classifications to impair or constrain legal personality. As Justice L'Heureux-Dubé has recently stated in *Vriend* v *Alberta*, the central function of section 15 is to protect human beings from denial of their fundamental legal personality: 'Integral to the inquiry into whether a legislative distinction is in fact discriminatory within the meaning of s. 15(1) is an appreciation of both the social vulnerability of the affected individual or group, and the nature of the interest which is affected in terms of its importance to human dignity and personhood.' Justice L'Heureux-Dubé went on to connect this general concern with the problems of legislative classification of human beings: '[E]very legislative distinction (including, as in this case, a legislative omission) which negatively impacts on an individual or group ... the impact of which deprives the individual or group of the law's protection or benefit in a way which negatively affects their human dignity and personhood, does not treat these persons or groups with "equal concern, respect and consideration".'[98]

Ironically, while it was the Supreme Court of Canada that finally confirmed, in *Egan and Nesbit*, that people characterized by their 'sexual orientation' are among those whose legal capacities are protected in section 15(1) of the Charter, it was that same Court that had agreed, in *Mossop*, that sexual minorities were properly assigned to that jurisprudential space labelled 'sexual orientation,' a space that would be presumed to be *nullius juris* unless specifically stated to the contrary. Against the backdrop of *Mossop* and in light of the fact that the Court agreed in *Egan and Nesbit* that violations of section 15 protections could be 'justified' under section 1 of the Charter, the scope of the constitutional personhood of sexual minorities thus remains in question.

While the majority decision in *Vriend* has demonstrated that queer personhood is fully protected in the human rights context, this ruling still stops short of full restoration of queer legal capacity if only because the scope of human rights legislation itself still remains quite limited. Touching on 'private' relations that have a 'public' dimension in employment, accommodation, or services, and touching also on the 'private' role of 'public' entities as in employment or accommodation, the full scope of human rights codes in relation to redressing the legal status of sexual minorities has yet to be determined.

However, the Charter decisions that have invalidated classifications based on sexuality suggest that courts are prepared to apply the equal protection clause in section 15(1) to remove discriminatory language entirely when it cannot be justified under section 1 of the Charter. In those situations, provisions become neutral as to sexuality, and the obvious presumption is that this sexuality-neutral language will apply both to heterosexual and non-heterosexual people. In this way, lower courts appear to be giving effect to the doctrine of constitutional personhood in relation to issues of sexuality. Not all successful lower-court Charter challenges have resulted in these kinds of orders. Looking just at those direct Charter challenges that have resulted in judicial orders amending statutory provisions, remedies appear to have taken two distinct forms – reading in words like 'same sex' or 'sexual orientation,' or reading statutes down to eliminate discriminatory terms like 'opposite sex.'

The cases in which courts have read 'sexual orientation' into human rights statutes have reinforced the boundaries of the jurisprudential space labelled 'sexual orientation' despite the fact that they have done so in order to alleviate exclusion.[99] However, since the Supreme Court of Canada refused in *Mossop* to read existing classifications such as 'sex' in human rights legislation as extending to issues of sexuality,[100] courts that have wanted to remedy this problem have really had no choice but to continue this process of exclusion and segregated rights in the curative mode.

In Charter challenges to general non-human rights legislation, courts that have found language excluding sexual minorities to be invalid have tended to remove all sexuality-specific classifications from discriminatory legislation instead of adding special 'sexual orientation' clauses to the statutes. These orders have been fashioned either by by reading sexuality-specific language that excluded sexual minorities down or out of the statute ('reading down'), or by reading the provision as if it applied to the excluded group, but without ordering judicial amendment of the provision itself ('reading "as if"').[101]

Reading statutes, regulations, policies, or practices 'as if' they did not exclude people based on their sexuality or the nature of their relationships, or reading them 'as if' they included sexual minorities, is consistent with the view that the only way the full legal capacities of sexual minorities will ever be restored is by removing of all sexuality-based boundaries from law, policy, and practice. Quite literally, this is the remedy that was provided by the Privy Council in the 'Persons' Case, and it can be used to create authoritative interpretations of words that appear everywhere in life, with or without Charter challenges to bring them into issue. When used consistently, this approach can reverse the presumption that words silent as to sexuality exclude sexual minorities and establish the opposite presumption that silence as to sexuality is to be read inclusively.

The remedy of reading statutes 'as if' they applied to lesbians and gays has been ordered in at least three Charter challenges to classifications based on sexuality. Leaving aside the special problem created by the Supreme Court of Canada ruling in *Mossop*, the B.C. Supreme Court granted this remedy in *Knodel* v *B.C. Medical Services Commission*,[102] the Federal Court of Appeal used it in *Veysey* v *Correctional Service of Canada*,[103] and the tribunal in *Dwyer* v *Toronto (Metropolitan)* relied on it in making a complex order encompassing several statutes and regulations that were not sexuality-specific.

In *Veysey*, the court concluded that the literature setting out the details of a Corrections Canada 'family visiting program' involving 'relatives' or 'connections' 'opens the door to applications by common law partners of the same sex.' The court expressly disavowed any reliance on the Charter to reach this conclusion, although it did read the program description in light of what it described as 'the reintegrative purpose' of the program. The court was careful to explained how the uniqueness of the program and circumstances had led it to this conclusion: 'We are here dealing with very special and unusual expressions found in a unique document obviously not drafted by legal experts and directed at a specific program of integration of inmates in society.'[104] Nonetheless, this decision does stand for the proposition that courts do not have to read policies, documents, or statutes restrictively in relation to sexuality. In *Knodel*, which also dates from the early 1990s, the B.C. Supreme Court ruled that the government had violated section 15(1) of the Charter when it denied coverage to a gay man's partner the provincial medical services program. At that time, the Medical Service Act[105] provided that the term 'spouse' 'includes a man or woman who, not being married to each other, live together as husband and wife.' Relying on the Charter, the court ordered the government to interpret the definition of 'spouse' to include the applicant and his partner, reasoning that the claimant had lived with his partner 'as husband and wife' in terms of commitment and continuity, and that excluding the partners purely on the basis of their sexuality violated their equality rights.[106] The board of inquiry in *Dwyer* was faced with a large number of discriminatory statutes that all stood in the way of extending survivor options to lesbian and gay employees. In dealing with those statutory provisions and regulations that did not actually limit their definitions of 'spouse' to persons of the opposite sex, the board ordered the relevant arm of government to read them 'as if' they included same-sex partners. The board considered that it had the authority to make this order by virtue of the Charter, since this complaint contained Charter challenges to these various statutes.

The other remedy that achieves essentially the same effect – reversing the heterosexual presumption – is the Charter remedy of 'reading down.' This appears to be the main trend in those decisions that have invalidated provisions that discriminate on the basis of sexuality. The first case in which this remedy was used was *Leshner* v *The Queen*,[107] in which the majority of the board concluded that the 'opposite-sex' definition of 'marital status' in the Ontario Human Rights Code, which permitted pension plans to discriminate on the basis of sexuality, unjustifiably violated section 15 of the Charter.[108] The board ordered the offending words in that definition to be read down, removing the words 'of the opposite sex' from the definition. Thus the definition became sexuality-neutral: '"marital status" means the status of being married, single, widowed, divorced or separated and includes the status of living with a person in a conjugal relationship outside marriage.'[109] The board in *Dwyer* followed *Leshner* when it was confronted with an almost identical complaint several years later. That board also granted the remedy of 'reading down' the offending portions of the definitions, this time reading the definition of 'spouse' in the Human Rights Code in the way the board in *Leshner* recommended it be amended: '"spouse" means the person to whom a person is married or with whom the person is living in a conjugal relationship outside marriage.'

These board decisions have now been backed up by the authority of two court decisions that have also removed sexuality-specific classifications from the impugned provision. In *M. v H.*,[110] Charron J., writing for the majority, ordered that the words 'a man and a woman' be severed from the definition of 'spouse' in the cohabitant support provisions of family legislation, and that the words 'two persons' be read in instead. This produced the following definition of 'spouse' for that purpose:

'spouse'... includes either of two persons who are not married to each other and have cohabited,
  (a) continuously for a period of not less than three years, or
  (b) in a relationship of some permanence, if they are the natural or adoptive parents of a child.

In *Kane v Ontario (A.-G.)*,[111] the court also used the remedy of reading down to produce exactly the same constitutionally corrected definition of 'spouse' for purposes of insurance legislation.

Not all courts have been able to eliminate discriminatory classifications by removing sexuality-specific language. Not only have courts literally been forced to read 'sexual orientation' into human rights codes that have continued to exclude sexual minorities, but the courts in three direct Charter challenges have had to inject new sexuality-specific language into ordinary statutes in order to correct their discriminatory impact. This third form of remedy('reading in') has been used only when necessitated by the statute being challenged. For example, in *Re K.*[112] and *Re C.E.G.*,[113] the particular way in which 'spouse' was defined in the offending legislation made it impossible to read the sexuality-specific language down: '"spouse" means the person to whom a person of the opposite sex is married or with whom the person is living in a conjugal relationship outside marriage.'[114] The definition of 'spouse' as it related to married couples was not in issue in that case, and if the court had simply removed the words 'of the opposite sex,' the resulting definition would have lifted the heterosexual requirement from the marriage branch of the definition as well as from the cohabitation branch. While that might be considered by some to be a desirable result in a case like this, only the 'cohabitant' limb of this definition of 'spouse' had been in issue in this case. In order to retain grammatical consistency and to avoid letting down the 'marriage bar,' the court injected the words 'or the same' into the second branch of the definition instead of removing the 'opposite-sex' language. Thus the definition of 'spouse' as constitutionally corrected in *Re K.* and followed in the two *Re C.E.G.* rulings is as follows: '"spouse" means the person to whom a person of the opposite sex is married or with whom a person of the same or opposite sex is living in a conjugal relationship outside marriage.'

In *Rosenberg v Canada*,[115] the same kind of drafting problem made it difficult for the court to employ the remedy of reading down. The definition of 'spouse' in the Income Tax Act that was challenged in *Rosenberg* stated, in pertinent part, that 'words referring to a spouse at any time of a taxpayer include the person of the opposite sex who cohabits at that time with the taxpayer in a conjugal relationship ...'[116] Because this type of definition of 'spouse' did not neatly separate formally married couples from cohabitants, merely removing the words 'of the opposite sex' would have achieved more than had been requested in this case, and certainly more than the court would have wanted to have achieved with its order. Nor could the court have turned the challenged definition into a provision aimed only at cohabitants, because the Income Tax Act consistently employs this 'includes' style of expression even when identifying formally married couples: The 'extended' meaning of 'spouse' simply says that '"spouse" and "former spouse" of a particular individual include another individual of the opposite sex who is a party to a voidable or void marriage with the particular individual.'[117]

Because of the particular terms on which the statutes on *Rosenberg*, *Re K.*, and *Re C.E.G.* were drafted, these courts found it grammatically inappropriate to sever and remove the offending words, and really had little choice but to inject new 'same-sex' clauses into these statutory provisions in order to constitutionally correct them. Thus these decisions are not inconsistent with the judicial recognition of the constitutional personhood of lesbians and gays, but illustrate how deeply divisions on sexuality affect legal concepts.

While the Supreme Court of Canada appears to be reluctant to give the doctrine of constitutional personhood full application to sexual minorities, at least to the extent of denying financial benefits funded out of 'public' revenues to same-sex couples on an equal basis, lower courts appear to have been giving this doctrine literal application in provisions that still employ sexuality-specific language to exclude sexual minorities. Given a choice between injecting new 'same-sex' clauses into statutes versus invalidating language that creates classifications based on sexuality, Canadian courts have demonstrated a pronounced preference for eliminating classifications based on sexuality as completely as possible.

Conclusions

In this study, I have found that sexual minorities in Canada have, in the last decade, made great strides in bringing and winning human rights and Charter challenges to discriminatory legislation. However, when these gains are interrogated to identify the extent to which lesbian, gay, bisexual, transgendered, and transsexual people have gained the full incidents of 'legal personality,' I have concluded that the presumption of heterosexual privilege continues to operate unless challenged directly, and continues to support provisions and practices that impair their legal 'personhood' in myriad ways.

Because being queer is very much (although certainly not exclusively) a 'relational' condition, it is not surprising that the incidents of legal personality that touch most directly on relationship recognition have been most systematically denied in this way. Looking particularly at the costs of discrimination to sexual minorities and at the critical role the state has come to play in Canada in supporting the 'heterosexual economy,' I have found that sexual minorities in Canada start out with greater obstacles in life, are disproportionately burdened by discriminatory norms throughout their lives, have lower incomes, thereby accumulating fewer assets, and receive less legal, social, and economic support for their relationships or for their children. Despite the extension of the Charter to sexuality in growing numbers of cases, sexual minorities are now being overwhelmed by the continuing uncertainties of 'incremental discrimination' as the result of the Supreme Court of Canada decision in *Egan and Nesbit* and the responses of lower courts to the ambivalence enacted in that decision.

As the twentieth century C.E. ends, it seems unlikely to me that lesbian, gay, bisexual, transgendered, and transsexual people will enter the next millennium as full 'persons' in law. Anti-queer opponents have learned the lessons of history far too well, and will undoubtedly attempt to continue to limit the remedies available under human rights codes and the claims that queers can make against the state as severely as possible. At best, sexual minorities may only be able to hope for clarification of their rights and responsibilities against each other, if not against the state.

As the difficulties of attaining full 'personhood' become ever more apparent, it may be that measures like those developed in Europe or reflected in Bill 167 – which extend partial recognition to same-sex relationships – will come to look more attractive, at least in contrast to the very heated political atmosphere that has built up in the United States around the Hawaii decision in *Baehr and Miike*, the Defense of Marriage Act, and the emerging movement in the United States to constitutionally limit 'marriage' to people of the opposite sex.[118]

With this less than optimistic view of the future, however, it seems clear to me that despite the fact that Canada did not develop a tradition of protecting 'constitutional personhood' until very recently, the detailed provisions of section 15(1) of the Charter, the careful analysis that has grown up around its application even to issues of sexuality, and the development of Charter remedies designed to invalidate classifications by sexuality all make it possible that the Charter guarantee of 'equal protection' will eventually reverse the heterosexual presumption, replacing it instead with the presumption that sexual minorities are fully persons in law.

The barriers to such a goal are significant. Charter discourse has as yet to begin breaking down the artificial contours of legally defined 'sex' in a way that opens issues of sex or sexual identity up to more than bipolar or dichotomous 'either–or' analysis. Issues of bisexual, transgender, or transsexual existence remain invisible in Charter discourse, not aided either by the growing deployment of 'sexual orientation' as a category of protection any more than they are aided by the inclusion of terms such as 'same-sex' or 'same-gender' relationships in legislation. Legislatures appear to be most comfortable when creating second- and third-class status for lesbians and gays, and to date have shied away from legislative structures that abolish categories of sex or sexuality instead of multiplying them.

Courts bear a great deal of responsibility for having created this overly regulated status quo, and for having constructed the heterosexual presumption that has so powerfully eaten away at any ordinary legal rights that could be claimed by sexual minorities. But ultimately I do think it will be the courts that can dismantle that jurisprudential space labelled 'sexual orientation,' a space that continues to be but furnished barely with a hodge-podge of special rights and limited duties, and enable sexual minorities to exercise the full legal capacities presumptively flowing from the fact of being human. With the constitutional power to invalidate all classifications by sexuality in legal policy, in the end, it really is the courts that hold the power to restore all sexual minorities to full legal personhood.

Notes

Preface

1 Stephanie Coontz and Peta Henderson, 'Property Forms, Political Power, and Female Labour in the Origins of Class and State Societies,' in *Women's Work, Men's Property: The Origins of Gender and Class*, ed. Stephanie Coontz and Peta Henderson, 108–55 (London: Verso, 1986).
2 At various times in China, including in the seventeenth, nineteenth, and twentieth centuries, accounts of same-sex cohabitation contracts involving both women and men have been published: See James McGough, 'Deviant Marriage Patterns in Chinese Society,' in *Normal and Abnormal Behavior in Chinese Culture*, ed. Arthur Kleinman and Tsung-Yi Lin, 171–201 (Dordrecht, Netherlands: Kluwer Academic, 1981). The essayist Michel de Montaigne recorded an account of the nuptial mass of two Portuguese men celebrated in Rome in the sixteenth century: Michel de Montaigne, 'A Strange Brotherhood' (Travel Journal, entry of 18 March 1581), in *The Complete Works of Montaigne: Essays, Travel, Journals, Letters*, trans. Donald M. Frame (Stanford, CA: Stanford University Press, 1958). Aboriginal peoples in North America have traditionally recognized some same-sex relationship rituals, described in Will Roscoe, *The Zuni Man–Woman* (Albuquerque: University of New Mexico Press, 1991), and African cultures have recognized same-sex marriages in customary law, as documented by Edward Evans-Pritchard in *The Azande: History and Political Institutions* (Oxford: Oxford University Press, 1971), 199–200. For data on the status of same-sex relations in Greece and Rome, see Michel Foucault, *The History of Sexuality*, trans. Robert Hurley (New York: Pantheon, 1978), vols. 2 and 3. Further references to such practices are collected in Andrew Sullivan, ed., *Same-Sex Marriage: Pro and Con* (New York: Vintage, 1997), 3–42, and John Boswell, *Same-Sex Unions in*

Premodern Europe (New York: Vintage, 1994), xxvi, notes 17–25. Anthropological references to same-sex relations or to marriage do not easily correlate with contemporary practices in Euro-American culture. Often, they were motivated by kin structures rather than by notions of romantic 'love' or 'sexuality': See Claude Lévi-Strauss, 'The Family,' in *Man, Culture and Society*, ed. Harry Shapiro, 261–85 (New York: Oxford University Press, 1956).

3 For example, the Ibo and Nuer in Africa still celebrate woman–woman marriage in exactly the same way as they do man–woman marriage, and Ngozi Oti has reported that no opprobrium attaches to either the partners or their children, who are conceived by relations with a man selected by the couple but not parented by him: Ngozi Oti, 'Same-Sex Marriage' (Kingston, ON: Queen's University, Faculty of Law, Law and Sexuality Seminar, 13 November 1996; paper on file with author). And see Ifi Amadiume, *Male Daughters, Female Husbands: Gender and Sex in an African Society* (London: Zed, 1987), and Barry Adam, 'Age, Structure, and Sexuality,' (1985), 11 *Journal of Homosexuality* 19–33. The Hawaiian trial court in the *Baehr* case received evidence on the importance of common law in the Aboriginal state that continued into the nineteenth century there, under which same-sex unions between men were recognized: See *Baehr* v *Miike*, [1996] Westlaw 694235, 1996 Haw App LEXIS 138 (Haw Cir Ct, 1st Cir, 3 Dec. 1996), per Chang J., aff'g *Baehr* v *Lewin*, 74 Haw 530, 852 P 2d 44 (1993), clarified on grant of reconsideration in part, 74 Haw 645, 852 P 2d 74 (1993).

4 John Boswell, *Christianity, Social Tolerance and Homosexuality: Gay People in Western Europe from the Beginning of the Christian Era to the Fourteenth Century* (Chicago: University of Chicago Press, 1980), 70–1, 127–8, has documented how Christianity became the conduit through which the 'narrower morality' of the later Roman Empire was deployed throughout Europe in the fourth and fifth centuries.

5 See Barry D. Adam, *The Survival of Domination: Inferiorization and Everyday Life* (New York: Elsevier, 1978), 18–20, 24–5.

6 See Hannah Arendt, *Rahel Varnhagen: The Life of a Jewish Woman* (New York: Harcourt Brace Jovanovich, 1974), for a detailed fictional evocation of this dynamic.

7 See generally Adam, *Survival of Domination*, 18–26, and Barry D. Adam, *The Rise of a Gay and Lesbian Movement* (New York: Twayne, 1995), ch. 1.

8 Josiah Strong, *Our Country* (New York, 1885), 208–27, quoted in Richard Bardolph, ed., *The Civil Rights Record: Black Americans and the Law, 1849–1970* (New York: Thomas Y. Crowell, 1970), 27.

9 Claudia Koonz, *Mothers in the Fatherland: Women, the Family and Nazi Politics* (New York: St Martin's, 1987), chs. 1 and 2.

10 SO 1944, c 51; *Re Drummond Wren* (1945), 4 DLR 674 (Ont H Ct), per Mackay J.
11 Not that 'entrenchment' is necessarily any guarantee of progressive application. See generally the cycles of judicial disregard documented in the pages of Bardolph's *The Civil Rights Record*.
12 *Egan and Nesbit v The Queen*, [1995] 2 SCR 513.
13 (1998), 156 DLR (4th) 385, [1998] SCJ No. 29 (QL) (SCC), rev'g (1996), 132 DLR (4th) 595 (Alta CA), per McClung, O'Leary, JJ A, Hunt JJ A dissenting, rev'g [1994] 6 WWR 414 (Alta. QB), per Russell J.
14 See the facta filed with the Supreme Court in the *Vriend* appeal by the Evangelical Fellowship of Canada, the Christian Legal Fellowship, Focus on the Family (Canada) Association, and the Province of Alberta: Didi Herman, *Rights of Passage: Struggles for Lesbian and Gay Legal Equality* (Toronto: University of Toronto Press, 1994), chs. 5 and 6.
15 John D. Whyte, 'Rights without Remedies' (Toronto: Canadian Bar Association (Ontario) Lesbian and Gay Legal Issues Committee, 1997).
16 *Reference as to the meaning of the word 'persons' in section 24 of the British North America Act, 1867*, [1928] SCR 276, rev'd by *Edwards v A.G. Canada*, [1930] AC 124 (PC).
17 See Respondent's Factum in *Rosenberg v A.G. Canada* (Ont CA File No. C22807), paragraphs 47–9.
18 See Statistics Canada, *1996 Census Consultation Report number 2* (Ottawa: StatsCan, 1997), 18–19.
19 See for example Carl Stychin, *Law's Desire: Sexuality and the Limits of Justice* (New York: Routledge, 1995), 48–53. Stychin has emphasized that this result is usually inadvertent, and that it is not sufficient to prevent queers from finding creative ways to fill in 'gaps' in the law that do burden them or constrain expressions of self.
20 My inspiration for this type of analysis continues to be the work of Christine Delphy, whose critical reconstruction of marxian methodology remains, in my opinion, some of the best materialist feminist work of this era. Her critique of heterosexual and racist structures opens up connections between materialist feminism and materialist analysis of sexuality: See Christine Delphy, *Close to Home: A Materialist Analysis of Women's Oppression*, trans. and ed. by Diana Leonard (Amherst: University of Massachusetts Press, 1984).
21 Two critical lesbians who have contributed to this project are Monique Wittig and Luce Irigaray. Both employ radical deconstructive strategies to contest the necessity of sexual categories in law at all, although Wittig appears to be more receptive to using law to achieve change under some circumstances than Irigaray: See Luce Irigaray, *This Sex Which Is Not One*,

trans. Catherine Porter and Carolyn Burke (Ithaca, NY: Cornell University Press, 1985); Monique Wittig, 'One Is Not Born a Woman,' in *The Straight Mind and Other Essays*, trans. Marlene Wildeman (Boston: Beacon, 1992), 9–20, at 20. Critical queers (many of whom are critical lesbian feminists who have become disenchanted with essentialist lesbian theory and with non-lesbian feminist theory) tend to focus their deconstructive energies on naturalist connotations of terms like 'lesbian,' 'gay,' 'bisexual,' 'transgender,' and 'heterosexual' and on the political/legal strategies that containment within that vocabulary tends to generate. Critical lesbians tend to focus on how hierarchies of gender, class, and race privilege some queers at the expense of others. For a general discussion of queer theory and its diverse and fluid relationships to lesbian theory, see Annamarie Jagose, *Queer Theory: An Introduction* (New York: New York University Press, 1996), especially 116–19, 126. One of the most important works in this area continues, in my opinion, to be Adam, *Survival of Domination*, who has traced these themes through their parallel expression in relation to race, religion, and sexuality in historical context and from a sociological/legal perspective.

22 Judith Butler has played a major role in developing this area of queer theory: See Judith Butler, *Gender Trouble: Feminism and the Subversion of Identity* (New York: Routledge, 1990); *Bodies That Matter: On the Discursive Limits of 'Sex'* (New York: Routledge, 1993); 'Critically Queer' (1993), 1 *GLQ: A Journal of Lesbian and Gay Studies* 17–32.

23 Nancy D. Polikoff, 'The Child Does Have Two Mothers: Redefining Parenthood to Meet the Needs of Children in Lesbian-Mother and Other Nontraditional Families' (1990), 78 *Georgetown Law Review* 459.

24 Brad Sears, 'Winning Arguments/Losing Themselves: The (Dys)Functional Approach in *Thomas S. v. Robin Y.*' (1993), 29 *Harvard Civil Rights–Civil Liberties Law Review* 559, 572–3; Fred A. Bernstein, 'The Child Does Have Two Mothers ... And a Sperm Donor with Visitation' (1996), 22 *Review of Law and Social Change* 1, 38–45.

25 Sears, 'Losing Themselves,' 573; Berstein, 'Donor Visitation,' 43.

26 The phrase coined by Jagose, *Queer Theory*, 126.

27 Toni A. H. McNaron, Gloria Anzaldúa, Lourdes Arguëlles, and Elizabeth Lapovsky Kennedy, eds., 'Theorizing Lesbian Experience' (1993), 18 *Signs* have collected a large number of articles that reflect the diversity of lesbian existence. One of my favourites is Lisa M. Walker, 'How to Recognize a Lesbian: The Cultural Politics of Looking Like What You Are' (866–90), discussing how reliance on visible signifiers of difference in lesbian communities to express identities and preferences renders invisible 'femme' lesbians.

28 For a wonderful study of transgender identities, see Leslie Feinberg, *Transgender Warriors: Making History from Joan of Arc to RuPaul* (Boston: Beacon, 1996).
29 I tend to use both 'queer' and another inclusive phrase –'sexual minorities'– out of concern that too frequent use of 'queer' may alienate readers who have issues with that term. For an analysis of the coalescence of 'sexual minorities' over the past twenty-five years and the relationships among queer legal theory, feminist critical theory, and critical race theory, see Francisco Valdes, 'Coming Out and Stepping Up: Queer Legal Theory and Connectivity' (1995), 1 *National Journal of Sexual Orientation* 1–34.
30 See Ronald Dworkin, *Taking Rights Seriously* (London: Duckworth, 1977).
31 See for example Nicholas Bamforth, *Sexuality, Morals and Justice: A Theory of Lesbian and Gay Rights Law* (London: Cassell, 1997).
32 Patricia Williams, *The Alchemy of Race and Rights* (Cambridge, MA: Harvard University Press, 1991).
33 Shane Phelan, *Getting Specific: Postmodern Lesbian Politics* (Minneapolis: University of Minnesota Press, 1994), 129–30, arguing that 'full citizenship' is a precondition to lesbian participation in democratic processes.
34 John Casey, *Pagan Virtue: An Essay in Ethics* (Oxford: Clarendon Press, 1990), ch. 1, arguing that an ethic founded on virtues that constitute 'personhood' points to the continued vitality of a 'pagan' ethical tradition.
35 Luce Irigaray, 'How Do We Become Civil Women,' in *Thinking the Difference: For a Peaceful Revolution*, trans. Karin Montin (New York: Routledge, 1994), 39–64.
36 Roberta Kevelson, 'Problems of Civil Membership: Pragmatism, Semiotics, and the Jural State,' in *States, Citizens, and Questions of Significance*, ed. John Brigham (New York: Peter Lang, 1997), 82–99, at 94. For a demonstration of how the 'zero significance' given to non-citizens ('aliens') and racially identified people generates hierarchies of citizenship, consider the federal government's response to the decision in *Francis v Canada (Minister of Citizenship and Immigration)*, [1998] OJ No. 1791 (Ont Ct Gen Div) (QL), per McNeely J., in which the court quashed a deportation order against a woman of colour from Grenada on the basis that it would infringe the rights of her young children, citizens by birth in Canada, as citizens of Canada to remain in Canada: '[The ruling] raises a more fundamental issue here and it is the question to give citizenship to children who are born in Canada when their parents are not Canadians': Bruce Cheadle, 'Robillard wants to revisit automatic citizenship for newborns' CP Ottawa (8 May 1998). For an analysis of 'the citizenship debate' and Canadian immigration policy, see Abigail B. Bakan and Daiva Stasiulis, 'Foreign Domestic Worker Policy in

Canada and the Social Boundaries of Modern Citizenship,' in *Not One of the Family: Foreign Domestic Workers in Canada*, ed. Abigail B. Bakan and Daiva Stasiulis (Toronto: University of Toronto Press, 1997), 29–52, esp. 44–7.

Chapter One: 'Full Life,' Human Rights, and Sexuality

1 Muriel Rukeyser, from 'Letter to the Front VII,' in *The Norton Anthology of Literature by Women: The Tradition in English*, ed. Sandra M. Gilbert and Susan Gubar (New York: W.W. Norton, 1985), 1781.
2 If it were not for Elly Bulkin, '"Kissing/Against the Light": A Look at Lesbian Poetry,' in *Lesbian Studies, Present and Future*, ed. Margaret Cruikshank (Old Westbury, NY: The Feminist Press, 1982), 32, 35, I would not have known what to listen for in Rukeyser's poems.
3 Muriel Rukeyser, 'The Poem as Mask,' in *The Speed of Darkness* (New York: Random House, 1968), 3.
4 See *Re Drummond Wren*, [1945] 4 DLR 674 (Ont H Ct), per Mackay J. The court quoted extensively from the political speeches of the day made by the heads of all the Allied states to establish the links between human rights legislation and the Jewish genocide in Nazi Europe; after making this link, the court then declared restrictive covenants prohibiting the transfer of real property to Jewish persons to be invalid. For information on Muriel Rukeyser's life and career, see Louise Kertesz, *The Poetic Vision of Muriel Rukeyser* (Baton Rouge: Louisiana State University Press, 1980).
5 See, for example, the work of Harold Lasswell, who has defined 'human dignity' as being shaped by eight 'value' categories – power, respect, affection, rectitude, well-being, wealth, skill, enlightenment – which themselves give rise to the fundamental values of 'deference' and 'welfare.' This elaborate scheme of values has had considerable influence in both political theory and legal theory during this century. See Harold D. Lasswell, 'Politics: Who Gets What, When, How,' in *The Political Writings of Harold D. Lasswell* (Glencoe, IL: The Free Press, 1951), 276–480. Also see generally Harold D. Lasswell and Abraham Kaplan, *Power and Society: A Framework for Political Inquiry* (New Haven, CT: Yale University Press, 1950); Harold Lasswell and Myres McDougal, *The Jurisprudence of a Free Society: Studies in Law, Science and Policy* (New Haven, CT: Yale Law School, 1968); Myres S. McDougal and H.D. Lasswell, 'Legal Education and Public Policy,' in *The Analysis of Political Behaviour: An Empirical Approach* (New York: Oxford University Press, 1947).
6 [1995] 2 SCR 513. *Egan and Nesbit* is discussed in detail in chapter 3.
7 This was not always or consistently the case. The Napoleonic Code had

emancipated gay people in Europe, and homosexuality had been decriminalized after the French Revolution: Barry D. Adam, *The Survival of Domination: Inferiorization and Everyday Life* (New York: Elsevier, 1978), 24–5.

8 See ibid., 24–7, and Lillian Faderman, *Surpassing the Love of Men: Romantic Friendship and Love between Women from the Renaissance to the Present* (New York: Morrow, 1981). In *Odd Girls and Twilight Lovers: A History of Lesbian Life in Twentieth-Century America* (New York: Penguin, 1991), 39–51, Lillian Faderman details the medical-scientific construction of the category 'lesbian' in North American. Myriam Everard, 'Lesbian History: A History of Change and Disparity,' in *Historical, Literary, and Erotic Aspects of Lesbianism*, ed. Monika Kehoe, 123–37 (New York: Harrington Park, 1986), has demonstrated that many of Faderman's findings applied to lesbian relationships and the medical-legal regulation of women's sexuality in the Netherlands in the nineteenth century, and Louis Crompton, 'The Myth of Lesbian Impunity: Capital Laws from 1270 to 1791' (1981), 6 *Journal of Homosexuality* 11, has documented the use of criminal laws to regulate lesbian existence, contrary to the more popular belief that lesbian existence had never been subject to criminal regulation.

9 In 1935, German criminal law had been revised to extend the concept of 'criminally indecent activities between men,' and the courts had published a landmark ruling to the effect that any act was punishable as a crime 'if the inborn healthy instincts of the German people demand it.' Nearly 50,000 homosexuals had been interned in concentration camps between 1931 and 1944. Reported in Richard Plant, *The Pink Triangle: The Nazi War against Homosexuals* (New York: Henry Holt, 1986), 110, 231–2.

10 Randy Shilts, *Conduct Unbecoming: Gays and Lesbians in the U.S. Military* (New York: St Martin's, 1993), 381.

11 Plant, *Pink Triangle*, ch. 5. For further information on the queer Holocaust, see generally G. Grau, *Hidden Holocaust? Gay and Lesbian Persecution in Germany 1933–45* (London: Cassell, 1995).

12 Alfred C. Kinsey, Wardell B. Pomeroy, and Clyde E. Martin, *Sexual Behavior in the Human Male* (Philadelphia: Saunders, 1948).

13 Alfred C. Kinsey, Wardell B. Pomeroy, Clyde E. Martin, and P.H. Gebhard, *Sexual Behavior in the Human Female* (Philadelphia: Saunders, 1953).

14 See H.L.A. Hart, *Law, Liberty and Morality* (London: Oxford University Press, 1968), text accompanying notes 16–18.

15 *Report of the Committee on Homosexual Offences and Prostitution*, Cmd no. 247, 1957 [Wolfenden Report], paragraphs 14, 24.

16 Patrick Devlin, *The Enforcement of Morals* (Oxford: Oxford University Press, 1965; originally presented as the Maccabean Lecture to the British Academy,

1959), attacked the notion that law could adequately maintain order without reference to 'Christian morals.' This elicited the vigourous critique of Devlin by H.L.A. Hart in *Law, Liberty and Morality* (Oxford: Oxford University Press, 1963; originally published in 1959, and developed over the next several years). Ronald Dworkin later joined the 'Hart–Devlin' debate in 'Liberty and Moralism,' in *Taking Rights Seriously* (London: Duckworth, 1977). This debate continues to rage on in contemporary constitutional litigation over the legal status of sexual minorities: See Daniel Mendelsohn, 'The Stand' (1996), *Lingua Franca* (October), 34–46, which summarizes the debate between classicists John Finnis and Martha Nussbaum, who gave expert testimony on the relationship between religion and morality in *Romer v Evans*, 116 S Ct 1620 (U.S.SC, 1996), per Kennedy J. Nicholas Bamforth provides an excellent summary and analysis of these debates in *Sexuality, Morals and Justice: A Theory of Lesbian and Gay Rights Law* (London: Cassell, 1997), chs. 4 and 5.

17 See Leslie J. Moran, *The Homosexual(ity) of Law* (New York: Routledge, 1996), who sets out the history leading up to and flowing from the Wolfenden Report in the United Kingdom.

18 Section 157 of the Criminal Code had previously made the commission of 'an act of gross indecency with another person' an indictable offence. The Trudeau amendment created an exception to that offence for acts engaged in privately, between two persons, both over the age of twenty-one, with consent: Gary Kinsman, *The Regulation of Desire: Sexuality in Canada* (Montreal: Black Rose, 1987), 139–77, esp. 161–4, discusses this important change in the legal status of gay sex. In 1987, the age of consent was lowered to age eighteen in section 159(2), but, at the same time, section 157 was repealed and section 159(1) made 'anal intercourse' an indictable offence. What has been perceived as the wholesale 'decriminalization' of gay sex was actually quite selective, and the federal government has resiled from that 'decriminalization' in important regards since then. See chapter 5 for further discussion of criminal provisions affecting sexual minorities.

19 See *University of Saskatchewan v Saskatchewan Human Rights Commission*, [1976] 3 WWR 385 (Sask. QB).

20 See Andrea Weiss and Greta Schiller, *Before Stonewall: The Making of a Gay and Lesbian Community* (Tallahassee, FL: Naiad, 1988) and John D'Emilio, *Sexual Politics, Sexual Communities: The Making of a Homosexual Minority in the United States, 1940–1970* (Chicago: University of Chicago Press, 1983), 231–3, for detailed accounts of the Stonewall uprising. The precipitating event was a police raid on the Stonewall Inn, a popular bar in the New York East Village. When the police arrested the bouncer, three drag queens, and a

lesbian, the large crowd that gathered attacked the police, torched the bar, and began a series of riots out of which emerged the assertion of 'Gay Power.' Although it is often described as a lesbian and gay uprising, transvestite Puerto Rican men, young street people, drag queens, and other queers actually led the action. For the impact of the riots on lesbian communities, see Faderman, *Odd Girls*, 191–6, for the impact of the riots on lesbian communities. Annual Pride celebrations in countries around the world now mark the anniversary of the Stonewall uprising.

21 Del Martin and Phyllis Lyon, *Lesbian/Woman* (New York: Bantam, 1972).
22 See Steven Maynard, 'In Search of "Sodom North": The Writing of Lesbian and Gay History in English Canada, 1970–1990' (1994), 21 *Canadian Review of Comparative Literature* 117–32, 118–19, for a short history of the beginnings of the Canadian movement and collected research references.
23 Barry D. Adam, 'Structural Foundations of the Gay World,' in *Queer Theory/Sociology*, ed. Steven Seidman, 111–26 (Cambridge, MA: Blackwell, 1996). See also D'Emilio, *Making Homosexual Minority*, 23–39, discussing the Second World War and afterward in the United States; Faderman, *Odd Girls*, 159–87, discussing lesbian cultures in the 1950s and 1960s in the United States; and Becki L. Ross, *The House That Jill Built: A Lesbian Nation in Formation* (Toronto: University of Toronto Press, 1995), documenting the emergence of self-affirming lesbian communities in Toronto in the 1970s.
24 (Garden City, N.Y.: Blue Ribbon, 1928). According to Lillian Faderman, Radclyffe Hall compiled a set of notes based on the works of the sexual 'inversion' theorists around which she fashioned the psychological profile of Stephen Gordon, and the introduction to the book was written by Havelock Ellis: See Lillian Faderman, 'Love between Women in 1928: Why Progressivism Is Not Always Progress,' in *Historical, Literary, and Erotic Aspects of Lesbianism*, ed. Monika Kehoe (New York: Harrington Park, 1986), 23–42, 40, note 4.
25 Hall, *Well of Loneliness*, 506.
26 Family Law Act, RSO 1990, c F3, section 1(2).
27 A.C. Sullivan, 'Same-Sex Marriages 1975 (Colorado)' <104607.2767@compuserve.com> (25 June 1996).
28 See *Adams v Howerton*, 486 F Supp 119, 673 F 2d 1036 (CCA 9, 1983), cert den 458 U.S. 1111, 102 S Ct 3494 (U.S. SC, 1985).
29 *Re North and Matheson* (1974), 52 DLR (3d) 280 (Man. Co Ct), per Philp Co Ct J.
30 *Corbett v Corbett*, (1970), 2 All ER 33. The applicant, a cross-dressing male, sought annulment on the basis that his marriage to a male-to-female transsexual was invalid. Contesting the application, the respondent pleaded

that she was legally female. The court found that the wife remained male despite her surgery, and granted the annulment. See the discussion at the end of this chapter of Ontario cases involving legal reassignment of sex.
31 See V. Muller, '"Trapped in the Body"– Transsexualism, the Law and Sexual Identity' (1994), 3 *Australian Feminist Law Journal* 103–17, for a collection of references to the literature.
32 Kirsten Thompson has developed a detailed table showing how, despite the dozens of combinations of pre-operative and post-operative chromosomal and anatomical characteristics, all transsexual persons are forced into the categories 'male' or 'female' and, based on the sex of their partner, into the categories 'heterosexual' and 'homosexual': See Kirsten Thompson, 'Bodies of Law: The Discursive Creation of Sexed Bodies in the Legal Context' (unpublished, 1996), 25.
33 See Z. Nataf, *Lesbians Talk Transgender* (London: Scarlet, 1996), for discussion of the fluidity of sex, sexuality, and identity. There is a real shortage of good terminology for these kinds of discussions. I have settled for 'queer' as a universal referent, even though I recognize that this term itself needs to be and is being deconstructed along numerous lines: See David Halperin, *Saint Foucault – Towards a Gay Hagiography* (New York: Oxford University Press, 1995), 62, who defines 'queer' as 'whatever is at odds with the normal, the dominant.'
34 *Damien* v *Ontario Human Rights Commission* (1976), 12 OR (2d) 262 (HCJ), per Osler, Callon, and Holland, JJ.
35 Donald Casswell, *Lesbians, Gay Men, and Canadian Law* (Toronto: Emond Montgomery, 1996), 194–5 and note 75, reporting on information received from Harry Kopyto, Damien's lawyer, in November 1995.
36 *Damien* v *Ontario Racing Commission* (1975), 11 OR (2d) 489 (HCJ).
37 Ontario Human Rights Commission, *Life Together: A Report on Human Rights in Ontario* (Toronto: Queen's Printer, 1977), 81. The commission recommended in this report that 'sexual orientation' be added to the code, at least in relation to services, employment, and housing.
38 [1976] 3 WWR 385 (Sask. QB).
39 Doug Wilson, a gay lecturer in the Education department at the University of Saskatchewan, had been prohibited from supervising practice teaching in public schools because of his sexuality. He filed a complaint with the provincial human rights commission for discrimination on the basis of 'sex.'
40 (1978), 87 DLR (3d) 609 (Sask. CA), per Culliton, CJS, Woods and Hall, JJ.
41 *Re North and Matheson*, discussed above.
42 *Vogel* v *Government of Manitoba* (1983), 4 CHRR D/1654 (Bd of Adj) [*Vogel I*].
43 Human Rights Code of British Columbia, section 3.

44 *Gay Alliance Toward Equality* v *Vancouver Sun*, [1979] 2 SCR 435, (1979), 97 DLR (3d) 577 (SCC), aff'g (1977), 77 DLR (3d) 487, [1975] 5 WWR 198 (B.C. CA), rev'g Board of Inquiry (unreported). For criticisms of the GATE decision, see Richard Goreham, 'Comment' (1981), 59 *Canadian Bar Review* 165; Jeff Richstone and J. Stuart Russell, 'Shutting the Gate: Gay Civil Rights in the Supreme Court of Canada' (1981), 22 *McGill Law Journal* 92.
45 (1989), 10 CHRR D/6064 (Can. HR Trib).
46 *A.-G. Canada* v *Mossop*, [1993] 1 SCR 554, L'Heureux-Dubé, Cory and McLachlin JJ. dissenting, aff'g [1991] 1 FC 18, (1990), 71 DLR (4th) 661 (FCA), rev'g (1989), 10 CHRR D/6064 (Can. HR Trib).
47 See, for example, Jody Freeman, 'Defining Family in *Mossop* v. *DSS*: The Challenge of Anti-Essentialism and Interactive Discrimination for Human Rights Litigation' (1994), 44 *University of Toronto Law Journal* 42–96; Mary Eaton, 'Patently Confused: Complex Inequality and *Canada* v. *Mossop*' (1994), 1 *Review of Constitutional Studies* 203–45; Blain Donais, 'Three Strikes and Human Rights Is Out [*Mossop*]' (1993), 57 *Saskatchewan Law Review* 363–79.
48 *Haig and Birch* v *The Queen* (1991), 5 OR (3d) 245 (Ont. Gen Div), per McDonald J., aff'd (1992), 9 OR (3d) 495 (Ont. CA), per Lacourcière, Krever, and McKinley JJ A. This decision is discussed in detail in chapter 2.
49 For accounts of the effect the John Damien Defence Committee had on the growing consciousness of lesbians and gays of their legal vulnerability, see Didi Herman, *Rights of Passage: Struggles for Lesbian and Gay Legal Equality* (Toronto: University of Toronto Press, 1994), 21, and Ross, *Lesbian Nation*, 32. Contradictorily, the commission continued until at least 1977 to act informally on complaints brought by lesbians and gays.
50 Québec Charter of Human Rights and Freedoms, RSQ 1977, c C-12, section 10.
51 *L'Association A.D.G.Q.* v *Catholic School Commission of Montreal* (1979), 112 DLR (3d) 230 (Que. SC). This victory was seen as particularly significant because traditional religious organizations were emerging as formidable opponents of gay liberation. In this case, the school had argued strenuously that forcing it to accommodate the gay group forced it to violate its religious values, and the court had rejected this contention on the basis that the school had not applied any of its 'religious' values when it had rented the premises to other organizations.
52 Activists tend to forget how difficult it is for some people to say 'the "L" word' or 'the "G" word.' After presenting a paper on lesbians and gays in law to a law faculty a few years ago, I was shocked when a senior colleague well respected for his progressive views and his personal risk-taking on

political issues came up to me and asked very seriously: 'How can you say those words so easily?' At first I had no idea what he was talking about, but finally realized that he was asking how he might get over his long-standing inability to say the words 'lesbian,' 'gay,' or 'queer.'

53 For example, Minneapolis passed an ordinance in 1975 that prohibited discrimination on the basis of 'affectional preference.' St Paul passed an almost identical ordinance relating to 'sexual or affectional orientation.' The Minneapolis ordinance gave the following definition: '"Affectional preference" means having or manifesting an emotional or physical attachment to another consenting person or persons, or having or manifesting a preference for such attachment, or having or projecting a self-image not associated with one's biological maleness or one's biological femaleness.'

54 The scope of what lesbians and gays could hope to achieve with human rights legislation had been progressively narrowed over the years. Compare the protection eventually gained under Canadian human rights statutes (contracts, services, housing, and employment) with the comprehensive list of demands that the queer movement had started out with, reported in Adam, *Rise of Movement*, 123. Also see Becki Ross, 'Sexual Dis-Orientation or Playing House: To Be or Not to Be Coded Human,' in *Lesbians in Canada*, ed. Sharon Dale Stone, 133–45 (Toronto: Between the Lines, 1990), for a critique of the shortcomings of human rights legislation.

55 For accounts of these conflicts, see Herman, *Rights*, 49, and Ross, *Lesbian Nation*, 33–7, 169.

56 See Mary Eaton, 'Theorizing Sexual Orientation,'LL.M. thesis, Queen's University Faculty of Law, Kingston, ON, 1991. Eaton and other lesbian women later raised this issue for discussion at the community level in the consultation process funded by LEAF National: See LEAF, *Litigating for Lesbians: LEAF Report on Consultations with the Lesbian Community* (Toronto: LEAF, 1993). This was by no means the dominant view of the community. Some lesbian women continued to favour more relationally focused terms such as 'affectional preference,' while other groups took the position that a strong lobby around 'sexual orientation' was necessary. The Lesbian Organization of Toronto (LOOT) supported the inclusion of 'sexual orientation' in the code: Ross, *Lesbian Nation*, 164 and 286, note 21. More recently, Eaton has argued that Charter equality jurisprudence might offer another opportunity to seek a wider construction of 'sexual orientation': Mary Eaton, 'Lesbians, Gays and the Struggle for Equality Rights: Reversing the Progressive Hypothesis' (1994), 17 *Dalhousie Law Journal* 130–86.

57 Royal Commission on the Status of Women, *Report* (Ottawa: Information Canada, 1970).

58 The first such definition of 'spouse' was enacted in 1974: Bill C-4, 1st Sess, 30th Parl, 23 Eliz II, 1974, amending the War Veterans Allowance Act, RS, c W-5, c 34 (2d Supp) (Royal Assent given November 1974). This was followed by an omnibus federal statute that made the same changes to programs such as the Canada Pension Plan, the Old Age Security Act: Bill C-16, Statute Law (Status of Women) Amendment Act, 1974, 1st Sess, 30th Parl, 23–24 Eliz II, 1974–5 (Royal Assent given 30 July 1975).

59 Previously, common-law spouses were treated as single people unless they met fairly onerous criteria – seven years of cohabitation, public representations by a man that a woman was his wife, and so on. Under the new criteria, they were deemed to be spouses after cohabiting for three years when there was a bar to marriage and after only one year when there was not.

60 For example, in the debate over the amendment to the War Veterans Allowance Act, Mr Jones stated in expressing his concern with the new formula: 'Once you open the door on a thing like this, then you open the door on common law marriages and the recognition of them and a lot of other things': House of Commons Standing Committee on Veterans Affairs, First Sess, 30th Parl, 1974, 31-10-1974, 3: 35. In ridiculing the effect of the same change in the Old Age Security Act, Mr Fortin obliquely supported the heterosexual values reflected in the formula when he stated: 'A man and a woman, of course it is important that they be of different sex, and this bill says it also, put forms in the same envelope, and send it to the Minister ...': House of Commons Debates, First Sess, 30th Parl., 24 Eliz II, vol. VII, 1975, 18 June 1975, 6901.

61 David Rayside, 'Gay Rights and Family Values: The Passage of Bill 7 in Ontario' (1988), 26 *Studies in Political Economy* 109, 112. Federal recommendations were made in Parliamentary Committee on Equality Rights, Equality for All (Ottawa: Queen's Printer, 1985).

62 Equality Rights Statute Law Amendment Act, 1986, SO 1986, c 64.

63 Now found in Human Rights Code, RSO 1990, c H.19, section 10.

64 Legislative Assembly of Ontario, 2d Sess, 33rd Parl (2 Dec. 1986), at 3839, Hon Mr Wrye, Minister Responsible for the Human Rights Code. The government was challenged quite strongly on the 'sexual orientation' amendment on the basis that '[h]omosexual "marriages" with the corresponding right to adopt children would run contrary to the father/mother/child relationship that most psychologists (indeed, most people) recognize as being vital to a child's well-being': Hudson T. Hilsden, Chairman, Coalition for Family Values, letter dated 4 October 1986, 2 (copy on file with author).

65 This is of course the 'belief-practice' distinction of constitutional religious freedom doctrine or the 'orientation-conduct' distinction of lesbian/gay cases in United States jurisprudence. See Affidavit of Meredith Cartwright, in *M. v H.* (1996), 27 OR (3d) 593, 132 DLR (4th) 538 (Ont. Gen Div), Epstein J; Eaton, *Theorizing*, 149, for a fuller discussion of these distinctions and their implications in the Canadian context.

66 Legislative Assembly of Ontario, 19 January 1987, 4665–6; 25 November 1986, 3622.

67 *Bailey v The Queen* (1980), 1 CHRR D/193, at D/199, D/221, D/222 (Hum Rts Trib), per Cumming P.

68 It is worth noting that one of the first human rights decisions to establish this point was later written by Peter Cumming. See the discussion of Michael Leshner's human rights complaint and Charter challenge in chapter 2.

69 See Québec Charter of Human Rights and Freedoms, RSQ 1977, c C-12, section 10; Human Rights Code, SM 1987–8, c H175, section 9; Human Rights Act, SYT, c 3, section 6(g); Human Rights Code, 1981, SO 1981, c 53, as am SO 1986, section 4(1). Some commissions, such as the federal commission, had recommended addition of 'sexual orientation' clauses to their statutes for years. See for example *Sexual Orientation: A Policy Planning Report Prepared for the Canadian Human Rights Commission* (August 1979), upon which the commission relied in making policy recommendations. Canadian Human Rights Commission, *Annual Report, 1982* (Ottawa: Queen's Printer, 1983), 9.

70 *Haig and Birch v The Queen* (1991), 5 OR (3d) 245 (Ont. Gen Div), per McDonald J., aff'd (1992), 9 OR (3d) 495 (Ont. CA), per Lacourcière, Krever, and McKinley JJ.A. This decision is discussed in chapter 2.

71 See Saskatchewan Human Rights Code, SS 1979, c S.24.1, as amended by Bill 38, SS 1993, c 61, sections 4–15, 18 (passed 22 June 1993); Human Rights Act, SBC 1992, c 42; Human Rights Act, RSNS 1989, c 213, as amended by SNS 1991, c 12; Human Rights Act, RSNB 1973, c H-11, as amended by SNB 1992, c 30, sections 1–8.

72 *Newfoundland (Human Rights Commission) v Newfoundland* (1995), 127 DLR (4th) 694 (Nfld. TD), per Barry J. The Newfoundland House of Assembly voted to add 'sexual orientation' to its Human Rights Code on 2 December 1997.

73 Canadian Human Rights Act, RSC 1985, c H-6, section 3(1), as amended by SC 1996, c 14, sections 1 and 2.

74 *Vriend v Alberta* (1998), 156 DLR (4th) 385 (SCC), per Cory and Iacobucci JJ, rev'g (1996), 132 DLR (4th) 595 (Alta. CA), per McClung, O'Leary, JJ A, Hunt J A dissenting, rev'g [1994] 6 WWR 414 (Alta. QB); Human Rights Act,

SPEI, c 92, amended by Bill 121 to add 'sexual orientation' (Royal Assent 11 June 1998).
75 It is unlikely that these amendments and rulings would all have come into existence if it were not for section 15(1) of the Charter of Rights. With the exception of the Québec clause, every one of these rulings and amendments can be traced back to the influence of the Charter, by way of policy recommendations, application of the Charter to human rights legislation in Charter challenges, or political desire to act before litigation might be launched. For example, the inclusion of sexual orientation in Bill 7 was somewhat easier to promote once the federal Equality Rights Committee recommended that human rights legislation should be so amended in order to be consistent with the Charter. See Parliamentary Committee on Equality Rights, *Equality for All* (Ottawa: Queen's Printer, 1985), recommendation 10.
76 *L'Association A.D.G.Q.* v *Catholic School Commission of Montreal* (1979), 112 DLR (3d) 230 (Que. SC); *Waterman* v *National Life Assurance Co. of Canada* (1992), 18 CHRR D/173 (preliminary hearing); (1993), 18 CHRR D/176 (Ont. Bd of Inquiry), per Plaut, Bd; *Mercedes Homes Inc.* v *Grace*, [1993] OJ No. 2610 (Action Nos. 92-L-42090, 92-L-43302) (Ont. Ct of J–Gen Div), per Sutherland J.
77 *Re Carleton University and C.U.P.E., Local 2424* (1988), 35 LAC (3d) 96, aff'd on judicial review, unreported (Div Ct) (4 June 1990); *Re Treasury Board (Indian and Northern Affairs) and Watson* (1990), 11 LAC (4th) 129, 17 CLAS 98 (PSSR Bd); *Vogel* v *Manitoba* (1992), 90 DLR (4th) 84, 16 CHRR D/242, [1992] 3 WWR 131, 79 Man. R (2d) 208, 32 ACWS (3d) 114 (Man. QB), per Hirschfield J, dismissing an application for judicial review of the dismissal of the applicants' complaints under the Human Rights Code (Man.), rev'd [1995] MJ No. 235 (Man. CA), per Scott, CJM, Philp and Helper JJ A [*Vogel II*]; *Re Treasury Board (Public Works) and Hewens* (1992), 28 CLAS 627 (Pub Serv Staff Rels Bd); *Roberts* v *Club Exposé* (1993), 21 CHRR D/60 (Ont. Bd Inq), per Hartman, Bd of Inq; *Clinton* v *Ontario Blue Cross* (1993), 93 CLLC par 17,026 (Ont. Bd of Inq); rev'd [1994] OJ No. 903 (Action No. 543/93); *Re Cami Automotive Inc. and C.A.W., Local 88* (1994), 45 LAC (4th) 71.
78 *Carleton, Watson, Vogel II, Hewens,* and *Clinton.*
79 See Lynne Pearlman, 'Theorizing Lesbian Oppression [*Waterman* v *National Life Assurance*]' (1994), 7 *Canadian Journal of Women and Law/Revue juridique 'La femme et le droit'* 454–508 for a detailed analysis of the deficiencies in this decision.
80 In this case, the gay men had filed a complaint with the Ontario Human Rights Commission, and the court did stay the termination of their tenancy pending the outcome of that complaint. The abatement was set off against rent they had withheld. This is a very troubling decision, filled with

preoccupation with their HIV status and the supposed effects of AIDS on their conduct. See chapter 5 for further discussion of this case.
81 See the discussion of *Roberts* in Andrea Timoll, 'The Erasure of Women of Colour from Canadian Jurisprudence,' LL.M. thesis, Queen's University, Faculty of Law, Kingston, ON, 1996, 196–8.
82 *Vogel v Manitoba* (1992), 90 DLR (4th) 84, 16 CHRR D/242, [1992] 3 WWR 131, 79 Man. R (2d) 208, 32 ACWS (3d) 114 (Man. QB), per Hirschfield J, dismissing an application for judicial review of the dismissal of the applicants' complaints under the Human Rights Code (Man.), rev'd [1995] MJ No. 235 (Man. CA), per Scott, CJM, Philp and Helper JJ A (14 June 1995). North and Vogel had litigated the right to marry in *Re North and Matheson* (1974), 52 DLR (3d) 280 (Man. Co Ct), and had lost their claim for same-sex employment benefits in *Vogel v Government of Manitoba* (1983), 4 CHRR D/1654 (Bd of Adj), per Rothstein, Marshall [*Vogel I*]. The Manitoba Court of Appeal decision did reverse the Queen's Bench after the Supreme Court of Canada in *Egan and Nesbit* was released in 1995; see chapter 3.
83 SM 1987–8, c 45 (CCSM, c H175), section 9.
84 The same reading of the 'sexual orientation' and 'marital status' clauses of the Ontario Human Rights Code had been reached in *Leshner v The Queen* (1992), 92 CLLC para 16,329 (Ont. Bd of Inq), in which the board ordered the Province of Ontario to create an off-side pension arrangement for a gay employee who had pleaded the Charter in his human rights complaint, and in *Dwyer v Toronto (Metropolitan)*, File No. BI-0056-93 (27 September 1996) (Ont. Bd of Inq).
85 See William Flanaghan, 'People with HIV/AIDS, Gay Men, and Lesbians,' in *Legal Inversions: Lesbians, Gay Men, and the Politics of Law*, ed. Didi Herman and Carl Stychin (Philadelphia, PA: Temple University Press, 1995), 195. If this hypothesis is correct, then it would explain the favourable decision in *Pacific Western Airlines Ltd. and Canadian Air Line Flight Attendants Association*, unreported arbitration (16 April 1987), per Hope, Page, and Cameron (dissenting), Arbitrators. The grievor had been suspended with pay from his position as flight attendant when it was suspected that he had contracted AIDS. Even though the grievor had died by the time the grievance came on for hearing, the panel found in favour of the union simply on the basis of the collective agreement, without relying on human rights provisions or the Charter equality provisions.
86 [1989] CHRD No. 14 (Action No. TD 14/89) (Can. Hum Rts Trib).
87 For discussion of this ruling, see Sherry S. Liang, '*Centre d'Accueil Sainte-Domitile v. Union des Employes de Service, Local 298* (FTQ): A Case Comment' (1990), 2 *Education and Law Journal* 3: 342.
88 [1994] FCJ No. 364 (FCTD).

89 See Casswell, *Canadian Law*, 192–4, for an excellent discussion of the *Thwaites* case in the larger context of the military's harassment and expulsion of lesbians and gays. When viewed in this context, and remembering that the government did settle all the military discrimination cases, the fact that Simon Thwaites had to live through a board hearing and an appeal in order to get redress appears much less comforting. As Casswell recounts, Thwaites spent long years unemployed, bankrupt, and waiting.
90 [1994] BCJ No. 2104 (B.C. SC), per Meiklem J.
91 On appeal, the court concluded that this finding had not been supported by direct evidence, and that the complainant had had the opportunity to lead evidence on this issue during the hearing. Thus it vacated the award. However, this did not detract from the board's ruling on constructive refusal to treat.
92 See Vicky D'Aoust, 'Competency, Autonomy, and Choice: On Being a Lesbian and Having Disabilities' (1994), 7 *Canadian Journal of Women and Law/Revue juridique 'La femme et le droit'* 564–78.
93 See Paula Gunn Allen, 'Beloved Women: Lesbians in American Indian Cultures' (1981), *Conditions* 70; Judy Grahn, 'Strange Country This: Lesbianism and North American Indian Tribes,' in *Historical, Literary, and Erotic Aspects of Lesbianism*, ed. Monika Kehoe, 43–58 (New York: Harrington Park, 1986).
94 See the many essays collected in Joan Nestle, ed., *The Persistent Desire: A Femme–Butch Reader* (Boston: Alyson, 1992), and Gayle Rubin, 'The Leather Menace: Comments on Politics and S/M,' in Samois, *Coming to Power*, 2d ed., 194–229.
95 See for example Cherie Moraga, 'Preface,' in *This Bridge Called My Back: Writings by Radical Women of Color*, ed. Cherie Moraga, xiv–xix (New York: Kitchen Table: Women of Color Press, 1983); Steven Seidman, 'Identity and Politics in a "Postmodern" Gay Culture: Some Historical and Conceptual Notes,' in *Fear of a Queer Planet: Queer Politics and Social Theory*, ed. Michael Warner, 105–42 (Minneapolis, MN: University of Minneapolis Press, 1993).
96 Consider Monika Kehoe, 'Lesbians Over 65: A Triply Invisible Minority,' in *Aspects of Lesbianism, Historical, Literary, and Erotic*, ed. Monika Kehoe, 139–52 (New York: Harrington Park, 1986).
97 Minnesota Statutes 1992, subdiv 45, section 363.01. The first part of the definition is also more expansive than that found in Canadian jurisprudence: 'Sexual orientation means having or being perceived as having an emotional, physical or sexual attachment to another person without regard to the sex of that person or having or being perceived as having an orientation for such attachment ...' This definition is unique among the state statutes that currently provide legal protection for the civil rights of sexual minorities.

98 See *Brown* v *Minister of Health* (1990), 66 DLR (4th) 444 (B.C. SC); *Canadian AIDS Society* v *Ontario*, [1995] OJ No. 2361 (Ont. Ct of J–Gen Div), per Wilson J (4 August 1995); *Piche* v *Canada*, [1994] FCJ No. 1008 (FCTD), Nitikman D J (2 November 1984). These cases, all involving the Charter of Rights, are discussed in the next chapter. See also *D.* v *D.* (1978), 88 DLR (3d) 578, 20 OR (2d) 722 (Co Ct), per Smith J, a custody case in which a father was described interchangeably as 'bisexual' and 'homosexual.'

99 See for example *Guppy* v *Guppy*, [1992] NJ No. 133 (Nfld. SC, Unified Fam Ct), per Barry J (15 May 1992), in which a father contested custody of a three-year-old daughter on the basis of the mother's bisexualism.

100 Vital Statistics Act, RSO 1990, c V-4, section 36, sets out the conditions under which a transsexual person may legally change his or her sex as reported on his or her birth certificate and other documentation.

101 (1990), 1 OR (3d) 569 (Ont. Ct. (Master)), per Cork, Master.

102 (1992), 10 OR (3d) 254 (Ont. Gen Div), per Jenkins J.

103 Jenkins J concluded that the marriage licence was obtained under 'false pretences' using a driver's licence that used a male name. However, L.C.'s change of name and her driver's licence were completely legal: See *Re Reid* (1986), 56 OR (2d) 61 (Ont. Dist Ct), per Vannini DCJ, in which a pre-surgical male who planned to have transsexual surgery was permitted to legally adopt female names to permit him to begin living as a woman.

104 (1996), 27 OR (3d) 593, 132 DLR (4th) 538 (Ont. Gen Div), Epstein J, aff'd (1996), 31 OR (3d) 417, 142 DLR (4th) 1 (Ont. CA), per Doherty and Charron J, Finlayson J dissenting, leave to appeal granted 24 April 1997, per L'Heureux-Dubé, Sopinka, and Iacobucci JJ, on condition that government pay all costs in any event of the cause (argued 18 March 1998).

105 [1993] FCJ No. 1263 (FCTD), per Rouleau J.

106 RSO 1990, c V-4, section 36.

107 Section 36(1). Such a change is to be documented by the production of two medical certificates, one from the practitioner who 'performed transsexual surgery' and one from a practitioner who has concluded, on the basis of examination, that transsexual surgery was performed. See section 36(2)(a), (b).

108 Given the language of the Vital Statistics Act and the ruling in *Re Reid* (1986), 56 OR 2d 61, I do not see how counsel could have made this concession. In *Re Reid*, the court permitted a pre-surgical male who planned to have transsexual surgery to legally adopt female names. Part of the process of beginning to live as a woman would then be to obtain documentation such as a driver's licence in that new name. Once a transsexual person moves so far through the process that 'the anatomical

Notes to pages 26–32   363

sex structure ... is changed [through] transsexual surgery,' as required by the act, legal sex reassignment carries with it the legal prerogatives of that new sex. All that seems to have really happened in this case is that Mrs Owen had lived for two decades under the mistaken belief that she had met the statutory requirements for legal sex reassignment.

109 There are numerous other cases like these. In *L.A.C.* v *C.C.C.*, [1986] BCJ No. 2817 (B.C. SC), per Gow LJSC, the court concluded, in granting a divorce to a woman whose husband had begun the transsexual process, that 'intercourse by means of an artificial cavity constructed by surgical intervention did not amount to consummation of the marriage.' In *M.* v *M.(A.)* (1984), 42 RFL (2d) 55 (P.E.I. SC), the court awarded a divorce to a husband whose wife had begun the transgender process on the grounds that because of 'a latent physical incapacity,' the wife lacked 'capacity for natural sexual intercourse [which] was an essential element of a marriage.' Neither of these cases was framed as a human rights case or Charter challenge. In the case of the Charter, the events giving rise to the litigation presumably pre-dated 1985, which is when section 15 of the Charter of Rights came into effect, and in the early 1980s it may well have seemed futile to look to human rights legislation for any type of relief in what were essentially divorce proceedings.

110 *P.* v *S.*, Case C-13/94 (Ct of J of the EC, Luxembourg, 30 April 1996), The Times Law Report (7 May 1996).

111 'Women make legal history as same-sex spouses' (Nanaimo, BC) (3 November 1997). The marriage was performed before George Scott completed transsexual surgery. But see *Sheridan* v *Sanctuary Investments Ltd.* (B.C. Hum Rts Trib, unreported, 11 Jan. 1999), in which a complaint brought by a preoperative transsexual woman was resolved under the headings 'sex' and 'disability.'

Chapter Two: Chart(er)ed Rights

1 For a cogent overview of the origins of liberatory bills of rights in constitutional democracies versus parliamentary democracies, see Francesca Klug, *A People's Charter: Liberty's Bill of Rights* (London: National Council for Civil Liberties, 1991), 3–13.

2 Anne Bayefsky, 'Defining Equality Rights,' in *Equality Rights and The Canadian Charter of Rights and Freedoms*, ed. Anne F. Bayefsky and Mary Eberts (Toronto: Carswell, 1985), 1–80, at 49 and references in note 228.

3 There has as yet been no indication as to whether transgendered or transsexual persons might be able to bring Charter challenges under the heading

of discrimination on the basis of 'sex.' But see *P. v S.*, European Communities, Court of Justice (7 May 1996), in which the court treated discrimination against a transsexual person as discrimination on the basis of 'sex.'
4 [1991] BCJ No. 2588 (B.C. SC), per Rowles J.
5 (1992), 9 OR (3d) 495 (Ont. CA), per Lacourcière, Krever, and McKinley JJ A.
6 (1991), 87 DLR (4th) 320, 30 ACWS (3d) 979 (FCTD), per Martin J, aff'd (1993), 103 DLR (4th) 336 (FCA), per Mahoney and Robertson JJ A, Linden J A dissenting, aff'd [1995] 2 SCR 513 (SCC).
7 SC 1960, c 44.
8 Section 1.
9 For the texts of each of these drafts, see Bayefsky, 'Equality Rights,' 5–11.
10 SC 1977–8.
11 For example, Kenneth Smith and other members of the Vancouver Gay and Lesbian Community Centre made submissions to the Special Joint Committee on the Constitution of Canada in 1980 that explained why the Charter should expressly prohibit discrimination on the basis of sexual orientation. The committee received similar submissions from Gordon Fairweather, Chair of the Canadian Human Rights Commission, and from other lesbian and gay organizations: See James E. Jefferson, 'Gay Rights and the Charter' (1985), 43 *University of Toronto Faculty of Law Review* 70–89, at 75.
12 Barry D. Adam, *The Rise of a Gay and Lesbian Movement* (New York: Twayne, 1995), 128.
13 Recounted by Svend Robinson in House of Commons Sub-Committee on Equality Rights of the Standing Committee on Justice and Legal Affairs, First Sess, 33rd Parl, 1984–5, 27-5-1985, 9: 75.
14 Emphasis added.
15 Anne Bayefsky, in 'Defining Equality Rights,' 48, notes 226 and 227, has collected references to committee proceedings and policy submissions that document these two points. See also Peter Hogg, *Canada Act 1982 Annotated* (Toronto: Carswell, 1982), 51. The strongest argument given for reading the open-ended language as including 'sexual orientation' is set out in Jefferson, 'Gay Rights,' 74–6: Because the other additional heads of discrimination that had been lobbied to the committee along with 'sexual orientation' were added to section 15(1) during the drafting process, there was nothing to which the open-ended language could refer if it were not taken to refer to 'sexual orientation.'
16 RSQ 1977, c C-12, section 10.
17 Human Rights Act, SO 1987, section 18 [Bill 7], adding 'sexual orientation' to sections 1, 2(1), 3, 5(1), and 6 of the Ontario human rights code.
18 Arnold Bruner, 'Sexual Orientation and Equality Rights,' in *Equality Rights*, 457–92, 464, note 32, quoting private correspondence dated 11 February 1983.

Notes to pages 35–40 365

19 See Penny Kome, *The Taking of Twenty-Eight: Women Challenge the Constitution* (Toronto: Women's Press, 1983), for an account of women's lobbying efforts around the sex equality provisions of the Charter.
20 Charter of Rights, section 32(2).
21 This bias is consistent with some of the dynamics reported in Becki L. Ross, *The House That Jill Built: A Lesbian Nation in Formation* (Toronto: University of Toronto Press, 1995), 8.
22 For a detailed history of Gigantes's role, see David Rayside, 'Gay Rights and Family Values: The Passage of Bill 7 in Ontario' (1988), 26 *Studies in Political Economy* 109, 112. The 'opposite-sex' movement and its relationship to Bill 7 is discussed in chapter 1.
23 Saskatchewan, Department of Justice, *Compliance of Saskatchewan Laws with the Canadian Charter of Rights and Freedoms* (Regina: Department of Justice, 1984), 11.
24 Ministry of the Attorney General, *Sources for the Interpretation of Equality Rights Under the Charter: A Background Paper* (Toronto: Ministry of the Attorney General, 1985), 300, 301 (emphasis in original).
25 Department of Justice, *Equality Issues in Federal Law: A Discussion Paper* (Ottawa: Department of Justice, 1985), 10 (Sessional Paper No. 331-4/6, tabled in the House of Commons on 31 January 1985).
26 Ibid., 63.
27 Ibid.
28 House of Commons Sub-Committee on Equality Rights of the Standing Committee on Justice and Legal Affairs, First Sess, 33rd Parl, 1984–5, 27-3-1985, 1: 3. This non-partisan committee consisted of Patrick Boyer (Chair), Pauline Browes, Maurice Tremblay (Vice-Chairs), Roger Clinch, Mary Collins, Sheila Finestone, and Svend Robinson (Members).
29 'Race, national or ethnic origin, colour, religion, sex, age or mental or physical disability.'
30 House of Commons, Minutes of Proceedings and Evidence of the Sub-Committee on Equality Rights of the Standing Committee on Justice and Legal Affairs, First Sess, 33rd Parl, 1984–5, Issue No. 6, 1-5-1985, 6: 8 (Mr Robinson, quoting Commr Simmonds).
31 Ibid., 6: 10.
32 Ibid., 6: 11.
33 'I do not talk about my husband as my lover; I talk about him as my partner. How I manifest my relationship with him is my personal, in-my-bedroom business. I may suggest to you that the use of the term "lover" at all times in your presentation, is counter productive in society, and may I recommend to you some consideration of using the term "my partner", "my friend", or other terminology ... I can tell you that it has created for me some difficulty

in being supportive of the cause I believe you have every right to promote': No. 10, 29-5-1985, 10: 30–1. Svend Robinson defended the witness, at 10: 32. Robinson's presence clearly made a difference. When Ms Finestone gave the same admonition to another witness later on in the hearings, Robinson was not in attendance. Perhaps emboldened by his absence, she actually accused the witness of creating 'backlash' by using the term 'lover': Ibid., No. 21, 26-8-1985, 21: 15.
34 See No. 9, 27-5-1985. 9: 19.
35 See for example Vancouver Gay and Lesbian Community Centre, Brief to Committee on Equality Rights (n.d.) (available through Box 2259, Main Post Office, Vancouver, BC V6B 3W2) (copy on file with author).
36 Doug Wilson, Chris Vogel, Rick North, and Penny Anderson all testified in these hearings about their own cases.
37 See Parliamentary Committee on Equality Rights, *Equality for All* (Ottawa: Queen's Printer, 1985).
38 Recommendations 12 and 13.
39 Recommendations 10 and 11.
40 Recommendation 17.
41 Department of Justice, Canada, *Toward Equality: The Response to the Report of the Parliamentary Committee on Equality Rights* (Ottawa: Mimistry of Supply and Sewrvices Canada, 1986). While the title of the committee report – *Equality for All* – overstated the real content of its recommendations, I think it is very telling that the federal government was not willing to commit to equality, but merely to moving (at some unspecified pace) towards equality.
42 Response to Committee, at 13.
43 Ibid., at 14.
44 Ibid.
45 See Charter of Rights Amendment Act, 1985 (B.C., Bill 33); Charter Omnibus Act, (Alta., 1984, Bill 95, and 1985, Bill 42); Canadian Charter of Rights and Freedoms Consequential Amendment Act (Sask., 1984–5, Bill 41); Statute Law Amendment Act (N.S., 1985); An Act to Amend certain Ontario Statutes to conform to section 15 of the Canadian Charter of Rights and Freedoms (Ont., 1985, Bill 7); An Act Respecting Compliance of Acts of the Legislature with the Canadian Charter of Rights and Freedoms, S.N.B. 1984, c 4; federal Bill C-27 (1985).
46 Thus scholarly efforts at that time were devoted to attempting to construct arguments that would convince courts to apply section 15 to discrimination on the basis of sexuality: See Jefferson, 'Gay Rights,' and Leopold and King, 'Compulsory Heterosexuality.'
47 [1994] 6 WWR 414 (Alta. QB), per Russell J, rev'd (1996), 132 DLR (4th) 595

(Alta. CA), per McClung, O'Leary, JJ A, Hunt JJ A dissenting, reinstated (1998), 156 DLR (4th) 385 (SCC), per Cory and Iacobucci JJ.
48 *Stiles* v *Canada* (1986), 3 FTR 234 (FCTD), per Dubé J, (1986), 2 FTR 173 (FCTD), per Martin J; *Sylvestre* v *Canada* (1986), 30 DLR (4th) 639 (FCA), per Pratte, Marceau, and Lacombe JJ, rev'g [1984] 2 FC 516 (FCTD); *Bordeleau* v *Canada*, [1989] FCJ No. 553 (FCTD) (QL), per Dubé J.; *Veysey* v *Correctional Service of Canada* (1990), 109 NR 300 (FCA), per Iacobucci CJ, Urie and Decary JJ, aff'g on different grounds (1989), 29 FTR 74; *Glad Day Bookshop Inc.* v *M.N.R.* (1992), 90 DLR (4th) 527 (Ont. Ct J–Gen Div), per Hayes J; *Haig and Birch* v *Canada* (1992), 9 OR (3d) 495 (Ont. CA), per Lacourcière, Krever and McKinley JJ A, aff'g (1991), 5 OR (3d) 245 (Ont. Gen Div), per McDonald J; *Egan and Nesbit* v *The Queen* (1991), 87 DLR (4th) 320, 30 ACWS (3d) 979 (FCTD), per Martin J, aff'd (1993), 103 DLR (4th) 336 (FCA), per Mahoney and Robertson JJ A, Linden J A dissenting, aff'd [1995] 2 SCR 513 (SCC); *Douglas* v *Canada* (1992), 12 CRR (2d) 284, 98 DLR (4th) 129, [1993] 1 FC 264, 93 CLLC 17,004 (FCTD), per MacKay J; *R.* v *Lalo*, [1993] NSJ No. 369 (N.S. CA), per Clarke CJNS, Hart and Freeman JJ A, aff'g [1993] NSJ No. 26 (N.S. Co Ct), per Bateman Co Ct J; *Halm* v *Minister of Employment and Immigration*, [1995] 2 FC 331 (FCTD), per Reed J. The case involving the bisexual plaintiff was *Piche* v *Canada (Sol. Gen.)*, [1984] FCJ No. 1008 (FCTD), per Nitikman D J.
49 In *Stiles* v *Canada*, the Federal Court – Trial Division granted a stay of one of two actions brought by a gay RCMP officer who had been advised by the Canadian Security Intelligence Service that he would not be considered for employment by CSIS because of his admitted homosexual experience. In *Bordeleau* v *Canada*, the court rejected the government's motion to dismiss a claim of discrimination on the basis of sexual orientation, which the government had argued was obviously bound to fail. The complainant had been dismissed from the armed forces because of sexual orientation.
50 In *R.* v *Lalo*, the court rejected a Charter challenge to section 156 of the Criminal Code brought by a man who had been charged with the offence of indecent sexual assault. The court concluded that the conduct leading to the charge had been completed before section 15 came into effect in 1985.
51 After Michelle Douglas's lesbian identity came to be known, she was informed that Canadian Armed Forces policies provided that she was no longer eligible for promotion, conversion of her existing years of service, posting outside the geographic area, transfer to the reserve force, or other training or qualification courses. She was then denied security clearance on the basis of her presumed loyalties to the homosexual community, and, after she lost her security clearance, her release was recommended on the basis

that she could not obtain the requisite security clearance. After she brought a section 15(1) challenge to the validity of these policies and administrative decisions, the government offered to settle her suit for $100,000, on the condition that it not be considered to be binding precedent in relation to other parties. The court accepted the settlement, but declared that the terms of the settlement were supportable on the basis of its own reading of the jurisprudence, even if the terms of the settlement agreement extended only to the immediate parties. Thus, *Douglas* does have some precedential value in future litigation.

52 *Glad Day Bookshop Inc.* v *M.N.R.* and *Piche* v *Canada (Sol. Gen.).*
53 *Veysey* v *Correctional Service of Canada* (1990), 109 NR 300 (FCA), aff'g on different grounds (1989), 29 FTR 74.
54 *Halm* v *Minister of Employment and Immigration*, [1995] 2 FC 331 (FCTD), per Reed J.
55 (1989), 29 FTR 74 (FCTD), per Dubé J.
56 (1990), 109 NR 300 (FCA), per Iacobucci C J, Urie, and Decary JJ, aff'g on different ground.
57 *Egan and Nesbit* v *The Queen* (1991), 87 DLR (4th) 320, 30 ACWS (3d) 979 (FCTD), per Martin J.
58 *Egan and Nesbit* v *The Queen* (1993), 103 DLR (4th) 336 (FCA), per Mahoney and Robertson JJ A, Linden J A dissenting.
59 Human Rights Act, RSC 1985, c H-6, section 3.
60 *Halm* v *Canada (Minister of Employment and Immigration)*, [1995] FCJ No. 1565 (Action No. IMM-1901-95) (FCTD), per Rothstein J (23 November 1995).
61 *Anderson* v *Luoma* (1986), 50 RFL (2d) 126 (B.C. SC), per Dohm J.; *Andrews* v *Minister of Health* (1988), 64 OR (2d) 258 (HCJ), per McRae J; *Brown* v *Minister of Health* (1990), 66 DLR (4th) 444 (B.C. SC), per Coultas J; *Knodel* v *B.C. Medical Services Commission*, [1991] BCJ No. 2588 (B.C. SC), per Rowles J; *Leshner* v *The Queen* (1992), 92 CLLC 16,329 (Ont. Bd of Inq), per Cumming and Plaut, Bd, Dawson, Bd dissenting in part; *Layland* v *Ontario (Minister of Consumer & Commercial Relations)* (1993), 14 OR (3d) 658, [1993] OJ No. 575 (Ont. Div Ct), per Southey, Sirois, and Greer JJ; *Vriend* v *Alberta*, [1994] 6 WWR 414 (Alta. QB), per Russell J; *Re K.* (1995), 23 OR (3d) 679, per Nevins Prov Div J. In 1996, the Alberta Court of Appeal reversed the trial court in *Vriend* v *Alberta* (1996), 132 DLR (4th) 595 (Alta. CA), per McClung, O'Leary, JJ A, Hunt JJ A dissenting, but it was reinstated by the Supreme Court of Canada; see (1998), 156 DLR (4th) 385 (SCC), per Cory and Iaco-bucci JJ. The two *Vriend* appeals are discussed in chapter 3, since they both involved close readings of the Supreme Court decision in *Egan and Nesbit*.

62 *Knodel* v *B.C. Medical Services Commission, Leshner* v *The Queen, Vriend* v *Alberta* (this decision was held in abeyance during appeals), and *Re K*.
63 Anderson had already been told by the court that, under provincial family law, there was no legal basis for her support claims because of her sexuality, and she was denied exclusive possession of the family home pending other action. The court suggested that her only remedy lay in an action for breach of contract: See *Anderson* v *Luoma* (1984), 42 RFL (2d) 444 (B.C. SC), per Wallace J. Of course, this application pre-dated the effective date of section 15(1) of the Charter.
64 This case is one of the 'denial of relationship' cases that has tended to crop up in the absence of legal rights. The defendant took the position that the plaintiff had basically had the two children 'on a frolic of her own,' and denied her own parental status as a strategy for avoiding liability for support payments. However, the evidence at trial included artifacts of lesbian co-parenting such as birth announcements naming 'Penny and Arlene' as the proud parents.
65 Luoma's subsequent applications for leave to appeal and stay of proceedings pending appeal were dismissed in *Anderson* v *Luoma*, [1987] BCJ No. 600 (B.C. CA), per Carrothers J A.
66 Health Insurance Act, RSO 1980, c 197.
67 Ont. Regs 452, section 1(c)(i).
68 (1974), 52 DLR (3d) 280 (Man. Co Ct), per Philp Co Ct J.
69 *Andrews*, (1988), 64 OR (2d) at 263.
70 This case began as an effort to solve an immigration problem, because Todd Layland could not gain landed immigration status to live with his partner through any other avenue. See Christine Donald, *Immigration and Refugee-Status Issues for Lesbians, Gay Men, and Bisexuals* (Toronto: Coalition for Lesbian and Gay Rights in Ontario, 1995), 3. For a discussion of this case, see Robert Wintemute, 'Sexual Orientation Discrimination as Sex Discrimination: Same-Sex Couples and the Charter in *Mossop, Egan* and *Layland*' (1994), 39 *McGill Law Journal* 429–78.
71 Medical Service Act, RSBC 1979, c 255, section 2.01, provided that '"spouse" includes a man or woman who, not being married to each other, live together as husband and wife.'
72 The court also awarded increased costs to Knodel because it agreed that limiting costs to the usual scale would have been unjust, given the complexity and difficulty of the legal issues involved in the case. See *Knodel* v *B. C. (Medical Services Commission)*, 6 CPC (3d) 340 (B.C. SC), per Rowles J.
73 Income Tax Act, RSC 1985, c 1, sections 147.1(1), 146(1.1).
74 (1992), 92 CLLC, at 16,346-7.

75 Employment Standards Act, SO 1989, c 73, section 3(1)(b), 9(c); Public Service Superannuation Act, RSO 1980, c 419, as amended; Public Service Pension Act, SO 1989, c 73; Pension Benefits Act, SO 1987, c 35.
76 For Leshner's account of this case, see Michael Leshner, 'Achieving Equality and the Leshner Case: Is Anyone Listening?' (1992), 12 *Windsor YearBook of Access to Justice* 398–401. *Leshner* should be treated with some caution when it is read as a Charter challenge. Because the order in that case was so contingent and so personalized to the complainant, it should not be taken as having invalidated all the legislative provisions in issue in that case. It does not appear to have established, either, that the definitions of 'marital status' or 'spouse' in the Ontario human rights code have been read down for all time by the reasons in *Leshner*. Thus formal notice of constitutional question should always be given when attempting to take advantage of the reasoning in *Leshner*. See for example *Clinton* v *Ontario Blue Cross*, (1993), 93 CLLC par 17,026 (Ont. Bd of Inq), rev'd [1994] OJ No. 903 (Action No. 543/93) (QL), per Carruthers, Dunnet, and Adams JJ, in which an Ontario court ruled that a board of inquiry could not order Blue Cross of Ontario to extend health insurance benefits to the lesbian partner of an employee on the basis of the code alone. And because the complainant had not given notice of constitutional question, it could not apply section 15 of the Charter to reach the result it had ordered.
77 *Vriend* v *Alberta* (1996), 132 DLR (4th) 595 (Alta. CA), per McClung, O'Leary, JJ A, Hunt JJ A dissenting, rev'g [1994] 6 WWR 414 (Alta. QB), per Russell J. For a detailed discussion of the trial-court decision in *Vriend*, see Shirish Chotalia, 'The *Vriend* Decision: A Case Study in Constitutional Remedies in the Human Rights Context' (1994), 32 *Alberta Law Review* 825–34.
78 *Vriend* v *Alberta* (1998), 156 DLR (4th) 385 (SCC), per Cory and Iacobucci JJ, rev'g (1996), 132 DLR (4th) 595, per McClung, O'Leary, JJ A, Hunt JJ A dissenting, and reinstating [1994] 6 WWR 414 (Alta. QB), per Russell J.
79 RSO 1990, c C.11, section 136(1).
80 See Human Rights Code, RSO 1990, c H.19, Parts I and II.
81 This ruling has been followed in *Re C.E.G. (No. 1)*, [1995] OJ No. 4072 (Ont. Gen Div) (QL), per Aston J (17 August 1995).
82 For example, when the issue was harassment on the basis of sexuality. See *Re Cami Automotive Inc. and C.A.W., Local 88* (1994), 45 LAC (4th) 71, discussed in chapter 1.
83 *Laessoe* v *Air Canada*, [1996] CHRD No. 10 (Can. Hum Rts Trib, 13 September 1996), per Armstrong, Kaluzny, and Pitzel, Members.
84 *A.-G. Canada* v *Mossop*, [1993] 1 SCR 554, L'Heureux-Dubé, Cory and McLachlin JJ dissenting (1990), 71 DLR (4th) 661 (FCA), aff'g [1991] 1 FC 18,

71 DLR (4th) 661 (FCA), rev'g (1989), 10 CHRR D/6064 (Can. Hum Rts Trib), discussed in chapter 1.
85 *Re Parkwood Hospital and McCormick Home and London and District Service Workers' Union* (1992), 24 LAC (4th) 149, 25 CLAS 472 (Ont.) (17 January 1992); *Re Treasury Board (Transport Canada) and Smith* (1993), 29 CLAS 620 (Can.) (9 February 1993); *Re Canada Post Corp. and P.S.A.C.* (1993), 34 LAC (4th) 104, 30 CLAS 477 (Can.) (16 April 1993) [*Canada Post I*]; *Re Canada (Treasury Board–Environment Canada) and Lorenzen* (1993), 38 LAC (4th) 29, 32 CLAS 396 (Pub Serv Staff Rel Bd) (24 September 1993); *Re Canada Post Corp. and P.S.A.C.* (1993), 38 LAC (4th) 333, 33 CLAS 4 (Can.) (5 October 1993) [*Canada Post II*]; *Re Canada Post Corp. and P.S.A.C.* (1994), 35 CLAS 469, 35 CLAS 469 (Can.) (8 March 1994) [*Canada Post III*]; *Re University of Lethbridge and University of Lethbridge Faculty Assn.* (1994), 48 LAC (4th) 242, 39 CLAS 398 (Alta.) (31 October 1994); *Re Bell Canada and C.T.E.A.* (1994), 43 LAC (4th) 172, 37 CLAS 20 (Can.) (23 November 1994); *Re Canadian Broadcasting Corp. and Canadian Media Guild* (1995), 45 LAC (4th) 353, 37 CLAS 449 (Can.) (1 February 1995), suppl. award (1995), 52 LAC (4th) 350, 42 CLAS 98 (6 December 1995); *McAleer* v *Canada (H.R.C.)*, [1996] 2 FC 345, 132 DLR (4th) 672 (FCTD), per Joyal J, aff'd [1996] 1 FC 804 (FCA), per Pratte, Strayer, and Linden JJ A, aff'd [1998] SCJ No. 31 (SCC), per L'Heureux-Dubé, Gonthier, McLachlin, Major, and Bastarache JJ. (9 April 1998), sub nom *Canada (Canadian Human Rights Commission)* v *Canadian Liberty Net*; *O'Neill and Coles* v *The Queen*, Unreported (Bd of Inq, 13 October 1994), per Hovius, Bd.
86 *Parkwood*, *Smith*, *Canada Post I*, and *Canada Post II*.
87 *Egan* v *Canada* (1991), 87 DLR (4th) 320, [1992] 1 FC 687, 47 FTR 305 (FCTD), aff'd 103 DLR (4th) 336, [1993] 3 FC 401, 153 NR 161, 124 DLR (4th) 609, 95 CLLC 210-025, 29 CRR (2d) 79 (FCA), per Robertson J. The federal court had concluded that Egan and Nesbit belonged to the category of 'non-spouses' even though they lived together conjugally.
88 [1996] 2 FC 345, 132 DLR (4th) 672 (FCTD), per Joyal J, aff'd [1996] 1 FC 804 (FCA), per Pratte, Strayer, and Linden JJ A, aff'd [1998] SCJ No. 31 (SCC), per L'Heureux-Dubé, Gonthier, McLachlin, Major, and Bastarache JJ (9 April 1998), sub nom *Canada (Canadian Human Rights Commission)* v *Canadian Liberty Net*.
89 Unreported (Bd of Inq, 13 October 1994), per Hovius, Bd.
90 [1997] 3 FC 920 (FCA), per Marceau, Linden, and Robertson JJ A, rev'g (1995), 97 FTR 282 (FCTD), per Joyal J (20 June 1995), aff'g the federal commission's refusal to process Nielsen's complaint after *Haig and Birch* had been released.

91 In *Nielsen* v *Canada* (1992), 5 Admin LR (2d) 278 (FCTD), per Muldoon J, the court refused to read sexual orientation into the federal human rights code, and instead endorsed the commission's decision to hold Nielsen's complaint in abeyance while awaiting the result of the appeal to the Supreme Court of Canada in *Mossop*. Nielsen's complaint arose out of the denial of same-sex employment benefits, and she had brought it under the headings 'sex' and 'marital status' because at that time 'sexual orientation' was not included in the code. *Haig and Birch* had been released by the time the appeal in *Mossop* had been decided, so despite the negative ruling in *Nielsen*, the commission had become empowered to process her complaint under the heading 'sexual orientation.' In the 1995 decision, the Federal Court Trial Division had concluded that it could not apply the new law arising from *Haig and Birch* to a complaint that had been filed before that decision was released, treating the date of decision in *Haig and Birch* as being equivalent to the date of enactment of a legislative amendment.

Chaptre Three: 'Demonstrably Justifing' Discrimination

1 [1995] 2 SCR 513 (SCC), aff'g (1993), 103 DLR (4th) 336 (FCA), per Mahoney and Robertson JJ A, Linden J A dissenting, (1991), 87 DLR (4th) 320, 30 ACWS (3d) 979 (FCTD), per Martin J.
2 *Douglas* v *Canada* (1992), 12 CRR (2d) 284, 98 DLR (4th) 129, [1993] 1 FC 264, 93 CLLC 17,004 (FCTD), per MacKay J; *Bordeleau* v *Canada*, [1989] FCJ No. 553 (FCTD) (QL), per Dubé J.; *Stiles* v *Canada* (1986), 3 FTR 234 (FCTD), per Dubé J., (1986), 2 FTR 173 (FCTD), per Martin J; cf. *Sylvestre* v *Canada* (1986), 30 DLR (4th) 639 (FCA), per Pratte, Marceau, and Lacombe JJ, rev'g [1984] 2 FC 516 (FCTD). These cases are all discussed in chapter 2.
3 [1994] 6 WWR 414 (Alta. QB), per Russell J, rev'd (1996), 132 DLR (4th) 595 (Alta. CA), per McClung, O'Leary, JJ A, Hunt JJ A dissenting, reinstated (1998), 156 DLR (4th) 385 (SCC), per Cory and Iacobucci JJ.
4 (1992), 9 OR (3d) 495 (Ont. CA), per Lacourcière, Krever, and McKinley JJ A, aff'g (1991), 5 OR (3d) 245 (Ont. Gen Div), per McDonald J.
5 See Kristin Bumiller, 'Victims in the Shadow of the Law: A Critique of the Model of Legal Protection' (1987), 12 *Signs* 3, who has demonstrated why potential claimants avoid using civil rights protections in the United States; Marguerite Russell, 'Human Rights: Contradictions and Realities,' LL.M. thesis, Queen's University Faculty of Law, Kingston, ON, 1993, who demonstrates how the reluctant recognition of civil and human rights in Canada has resulted in segregation in administrative law and limited remedies for proven discrimination.

6 [1991] BCJ No. 2588 (B.C. SC), per Rowles J.
7 (1988), 64 OR (2d) 258 (HCJ), per McRae J.
8 (1990), 66 DLR (4th) 444 (B.C. SC), per Coultas J.
9 (1990), 109 NR 300 (FCA), per Iacobucci, C J, Urie and Decary JJ, aff'g on different grounds (1989), 29 FTR 74.
10 (1992), 92 CLLC 16,329 (Ont. Bd of Inq), per Cumming and Plaut, Bd, Dawson, Bd dissenting in part.
11 (1995), 23 OR (3d) 679, per Nevins Prov Div J.
12 [1995] 2 FC 331 (FCTD), per Reed J.
13 (1986), 50 RFL (2d) 126 (B.C. SC), per Dohm J.
14 In fact, the federal government conceded that sexual orientation was a 'non-enumerated' ground of protection in section 15(1) of the Charter. [1995] 2 SCR 513, at 528, per La Forest J.
15 [1995] 2 SCR 418 (SCC), per McLachlin J.
16 *The Queen* v *Thibaudeau*, [1995] 2 SCR 627 per Gonthier J.
17 *M.* v *H.* (1996), 27 OR (3d) 593, 132 DLR (4th) 538 (Ont. Gen Div), Epstein J, aff'd (1996), 31 OR (3d) 417, 142 DLR (4th) 1 (Ont. CA), per Doherty and Charron J, Finlayson J. dissenting, leave to appeal granted 24 April 1997, per L'Heureux-Dubé, Sopinka, and Iacobucci JJ, on condition that government pay all costs in any event of the cause; argued 18 March 1998.
18 *Rosenberg* v *A.-G. Canada* (1995), 127 DLR (4th) 738, 25 OR (3d) 612 (Ont. Gen Div), per Charron J, rev'd [1998] OJ No. 1627 (OCA) (QL), per McKinley, Abella, and Goudge JJ A.
19 As soon as the older of two spouses or heterosexual cohabitants reaches age sixty-five, a younger spouse between the ages of sixty and sixty-four can receive the spousal allowance, so long as the aggregate income of the two spouses is below the statutory cut-off. This spousal allowance is available to all married heterosexuals and to non-married heterosexuals who have cohabited for one year and a day. It does not matter which spouse is the primary income earner or what the relative contribution of each is to their aggregate income, so long as the total income falls below the cutoff.
20 *Miron* v *Trudel*, [1995] 2 SCR 418, and *The Queen* v *Thibaudeau*, [1995] 2 SCR 627.
21 For a detailed discussion on how to find the majority decision in plurality opinions, see Ken Kimura, 'A Legitimacy Model for the Interpretation of Plurality Decisions' (1992), 77 *Cornell Law Review* 1593. For criticism of the confusion created by these plurality decisions, see Dianne Pothier, 'M'Aider, Mayday: Section 15 of the Charter in Distress' (1996), 6 *National Journal of Constitutional Law* 295.
22 *Andrews* v *Law Society of British Columbia*, [1989] 1 SCR 143.

23 *R.* v *Turpin*, [1989] 1 SCR 1296.
24 *Symes* v *Canada*, [1993] 4 SCR 695.
25 *R.* v *Oakes*, [1986] 1 SCR 103, at 139, per Dickson C J.
26 [1990] 2 SCR 229, at 317–18, per La Forest J.
27 [1986] 2 SCR 713, at 772, per Dickson C J.
28 348 U.S. 483 (U.S. SC 1955).
29 *McKinney* involved exceptions to age-discrimination provisions in human rights legislation that permitted universities to force professors to retire at age sixty-five. The universities had persuaded the Court that younger professors could be hired only when older professors retired, and that the overall mission of university education depended upon this type of compulsory faculty renewal. That case thus involved balancing private-sector management-type interests against the human rights of some workers. *Edwards Books* involved balancing employer's rights to religious observance versus the rights of workers to a common pause day. In *Lee Optical*, 'balancing' pitted commercial opticians who were barred from adjusting eyeglass frames against licensed ophthalmologists and optometrists, and arose under the due-process clause of the Fourteenth Amendment to the U.S. Constitution. Most of the compelling quotes Justice Sopinka used in his section 1 analysis were drawn from the persuasive language with which Justice Douglas explained why the legislature could regulate eye care 'one step at a time.'
30 Justice Sopinka, remarks from the bench, *Wilson Moot*, Final Round (24 February 1996).
31 Justice Sopinka had made a similar 'flexibility' argument the year before, reasoning that the government was entitled to move at its own pace in responding to changing social conditions: See *Native Women's Association of Canada* v *The Queen*, [1994] 3 SCR 627, at 655–6.
32 'It may be suggested that the time has expired for the government to proceed to extend the benefits to same-sex couples and that it cannot justify a delay since 1975 to include same-sex couples. [T]here is some force to this suggestion ...': [1995] 2 SCR, at 576.
33 [1995] 2 SCR at 569, citing *Bliss* v *A.-G. Canada*, [1979] 1 SCR 183, 190, and *Brooks* v *Canada Safeway Ltd.*, [1989] 1 SCR 1219, at 1243–4.
34 For other critiques of *Egan and Nesbit*, see Paul B. Schabas, 'Sexual Orientation Protected by the Charter' (1995), 7 *Immigration and Citizenship* 5: 52–3; Carl F. Stychin, 'Essential Rights and Contested Identities: Sexual Orientation and Equality Rights Jurisprudence in Canada' (1995), 8 *Canadian Journal of Law and Jurisprudence* 49–66.
35 [1995] 2 SCR 627.

36 This was not a contentious point because the legislature had already amended the legislation in question in precisely that way before the date of this decision.
37 See generally [1995] 2 SCR at 590–1.
38 See Kathleen A. Lahey, 'Developments in Tax Law: The 1994-95 Term' (1996), 7 *Supreme Court Law Review* (2d) 381, for a detailed analysis of the dissenting opinions written by Justices McLachlin and L'Heureux-Dubé. Also see their discussion of how the submersion of divorced women in the 'fractured family' continues to deny the 'personhood' of women in the Charter.
39 It is interesting that none of these cases involved people who had formed family groupings on the basis of other cultural norms. Thus we do not have any indication of how the Supreme Court would have evaluated evidence relating to other family forms, such those which have their origins in other cultures or have been severely affected by long-standing conditions of poverty and powerlessness: See for example Nancy Tanner, 'Matrifocality in Indonesia and Africa and among Black Americans'; Carol B. Stack, 'Sex Roles and Survival Strategies in an Urban Black Community,' in *Woman, Culture and Society*, ed. Michelle Zimbalist Rosaldo and Louise Lamphere (Stanford, CA: Stanford University Press, 1974), 129, 113.
40 [1993] FCJ No. 1263 (FCTD), per Rouleau J.
41 During argument, Lillian Owen had conceded that she had not had the legal capacity to marry her husband, and that her marriage was a nullity. Neither of these concessions appeared to be inevitable, but the court then built on them in its reasoning.
42 As of 1 April 1996, 88 of these provisions were contained in the Income Tax Act, many of which themselves confer a wide range of different benefits; the other 274 provisions were contained in other federal statutes.
43 See *Moge* v *Moge* (1992), 43 RFL (3d) 345 (SCC), referring to the 'unmitigated parsimony' of courts when setting levels of self-sufficiency for divorced or separated women, the continuing disparities in levels of incomes and assets between women and men, wives and husbands, the differential responsibilities of wives and husbands in relation to the care of minor children. This decision collects most of the statistical and academic sources that document these findings in Canada and similar countries.
44 *Rosenberg* v *A.-G. Canada* (1995), 25 OR (3d) 612 (Ont. Gen Div), per Charron J, rev'd [1998] OJ No. 1627 (OCA) (QL), per McKinley, Abella, and Goudge JJ A; *R.* v *Silva* (1995), 26 OR (3d) 554 (Ont. Gen Div), per Zelinski J; *Little Sisters Book and Art Emporium* v *Canada (Minister of Justice)*, [1996] BCJ No. 71 (B.C. SC), per Smith J, inj. granted [1996] BCJ No. 670 (B.C. SC) (QL), per

Smith J; *Minister of Employment and Immigration* v *Hodder*, No. 104-241-492 (8 January 1997) (Canada Pension Plan Rev Trib), per Dempsey, Chair, Siscoe and Richard, Members; *Boulais* v *Minister of Employment and Immigration*, No. 105-655-781 (3 March 1997) (Canada Pension Plan Rev Trib), per Dempsey, Chair, Marks and Johnson, Members; *Minister of Human Resources and Development* v *Fisk*, Appeal CP 04471 (25 September 1997) (Canada Pension Plan App Bd), per Foisy J A, Dureault J, and McMahon, Member.

45 (1996), 25 OR (3d) 612 (Ont. Gen Div), per Charron J.

46 *Leshner* v *The Queen*, 92 CLLC 16,329 (31 August 1992) (Bd of Inq).

47 The *Leshner* board had rejected stronger options, at least in part because it felt that ordering the province to litigate with the federal government was really a political decision, and because it felt that the provincial government could be counted on to come up with funding on a current-income basis to provide equal benefits as surviving spouse claims actually arose. At that time, the *Leshner* board felt that it might be enough to 'ask' the province 'to put the province's case strongly and continually to the federal government for the necessary amendments to the Income Tax Act,' and to 'ask' the Ontario Human Rights Commission 'to monitor the progress of these efforts.' The board thus gave the province permission to provide the ordered surviving spouse benefits on an unfunded basis for three years, but to implement a funded arrangement after three years and to keep it in place until the necessary amendments could be made to the Income Tax Act: 92 CLLC, at 16,356-7.

48 This definition is located in section 252(4) of the Income Tax Act, and applies to the pension provisions as the result of section 146(1)(1.1).

49 This decision is reported as *Canadian Union of Public Employees (CUPE)* v *M.N.R.* (1993), 93 DTC 5099 (FCA), per Pratte J. In this appeal, the court took the position that while the minister did have the power to refuse to apply a provision of the ITA he or she considered to be unconstitutional, once the minister had decided that the opposite-sex definition of spouse did not violate the Charter, the Federal Court could not go outside that view. This decision was not appealed; instead, CUPE challenged the ITA provision directly under the Charter.

50 If CUPE had amended its plan to include same-sex surviving spouse benefits in order to comply with its collective agreement, human rights law, and the Charter of Rights, the Minister of National Revenue could have served CUPE with notice of intent to revoke the registration of the plan as soon as such change became effective (ITA section 147.1[12]). The revocation of registration provisions do provide that notice of actual revocation cannot be served until thirty days after mailing the notice of intent to revoke (ITA

section 147.1[12][b]), that the administrator of the plan has the right to appeal to the Federal Court of Appeal or to any judge thereof for an order suspending the revocation (ITA sections 147.1[13], 172[3]), and the right to set up a new plan for non-offending contributions, but the administrative costs of taking any of those routes would have been considerable. Nothing in the Income Tax Act nor human rights law gives plan administrators any grace period within which to test out changes to plans designed to implement Charter guarantees. Thus the Minister of National Revenue had CUPE in a serious bind. See also ITA section 147.1(11), ITR section 8501. These provisions and dynamics – including alternative provisions that could have been made in the face of threatened 'deregistration'– are discussed in chapter 10.

51 (1995), 25 OR (3d) at 622. This analysis is quite limited. Compared with direct assistance programs like the old age security system, the only cost to the government of private pension plans is the cost of deferred taxation on contributions and accumulations in the plan. These deferred taxes account for but a tiny portion of the eventual pay-out received by beneficiaries. By treating the deferral of current tax liability as absolute and permanent, the government had presented a highly distorted picture of how registered plans actually work from the financial perspective. In addition, increasing the number of qualified beneficiaries actually increases the rate at which funds in registered plans enter the tax base, reducing the government's tiny 'costs' even further.

52 *Rosenberg* v *A.-G. Canada*, [1998] OJ No. 1627 (OCA) (QL), per McKinley, Abella, and Goudge JJ A, rev'g (1995), 25 OR (3d) 612 (Ont. Gen Div), per Charron J.

53 For a detailed analysis of the policy issues surrounding the income tax RPP rules, see chapter 10.

54 *Egan and Nesbit*, [1995] 2 SCR 513, at 530–1, 532–3, per La Forest J; *Miron* v *Trudel*, [1995] 2 SCR 418, at 435, 453–4, per Gonthier J.

55 *Little Sisters*, [1996] BCJ No. 71, at para 136.

56 In *Little Sisters Book and Art Emporium* v *Canada (Minister of Justice)*, [1996] BCJ No. 670 (B.C. SC) (QL), per Smith J, the court granted an immediate injunction on Canada Customs's method of surveilling shipments to the plaintiff, concluding that continued intrusion threatened immediate harm.

57 *Canadian AIDS Society* v *Ontario*, [1995] OJ No. 2361 (Ont. Ct of J–Gen Div) (QL), per Wilson J, aff'd [1996] OJ No. 4184 (OCA) (QL), per Morden ACJO, Catzman and Carthy JJ A; *Re C.E.G. (No. 1)*, [1995] OJ No. 4072 (Ont. Ct of J– Gen Div) (QL), per Aston J; *Newfoundland and Labrador Human Rights Commission* v *Nolan and Barry*, [1995] NJ No. 283 (Nfld. SC) (QL), per Barry J;

M. v H. (1996), 27 OR (3d) 593, 132 DLR (4th) 538 (Ont. Gen Div), per Epstein J, aff'd (1996), 31 OR (3d) 417 (Ont. CA), per Doherty and Charron JJ A, Finlayson J dissenting; *Obringer v Kennedy Estate*, [1996] OJ No. 3181 (Ont. Gen Div) (QL), per Sheard J; *Dwyer v Toronto (Metropolitan)*, File No. BI-0056-93 (27 September 1996) (Ont. Bd of Inq); *Kane v Ontario (A.-G.)*, [1997] OJ No. 3979 (Ont. Gen Div) (QL), per Coo J; *Vriend v Alberta*, [1994] 6 WWR 414 (Alta. QB), per Russell J, rev'd (1996), 132 DLR (4th) 595 (Alta. CA), per McClung, O'Leary, JJ A, Hunt JJ A dissenting, reinstated (1998), 156 DLR (4th) 385 (SCC), per Cory and Iacobucci JJ.

58 Para 53.

59 (1996), 132 DLR (4th) at para 37–8. Justice McClung, the grandson of Nellie McClung of the 'Persons' Case, wrote an even more extreme opinion in which he concluded that the silence on sexual orientation in the legislation was not even reviewable by the courts under the principle of judicial deference.

60 The Court was also influenced by the U.S. Supreme Court decision in *Romer v Evans*, 116 S Ct 1620 (U.S. SC, 1996), in which Kennedy J ruled that state constitutional provisions invalidating all state or municipal actions designed to protect people from discrimination on the basis of sexuality violated the equal-protection clause of the Fourteenth Amendment. That court concluded that such provisions had the unconstitutional effect of depriving one class of persons of ordinary legal protections that most people have come to take for granted. The provincial appellate decision in *Vriend* attracted widespread criticism in the legal literature. See for example Ritu Khullar, '*Vriend*: Remedial Issues for Unremedied Discrimination' (1997), 7 *National Journal of Constitutional Law* 232; Shannon K. O'Byrne and James F. McGinnis, 'Case Comment: *Vriend v. Alberta*; Plessy Revisited: Lesbian and Gay Rights in the Province of Alberta' (1996), 34 *Alberta Law Review* 892; Dianne Pothier, 'The Sounds of Silence: Charter Application When the Legislature Declines to Speak' (1996), 7 *Constitutional Forum* 113; Wayne N. Renke, 'Case Comment: *Vriend v. Alberta*: Discrimination, Burdens of Proof, and Judicial Notice' (1996), 34 *Alberta Law Review* 925.

61 Albertans appear to be sensitive to the risk that they will be seen as turning anti-Charter sentiment into justification for targeting lesbian women and gay men, for there is now discussion of putting the issue of legislative overrides to section 15 of the Charter to a provincial referendum: 'It would look as though the province is targeting a particular group for discrimination. [A referendum] would ... lend legitimacy to the process': 'Power to the people, not the judges,' *Alberta Report* (11 March 1996), 20–6, at 26, quoting Christopher Manfredi. Drawing on the analogy to *Romer v Evans*, if a

Notes to pages 84–90   379

referendum were used to justify or even trigger an override, it might open the door to a Charter challenge to such a use of section 33.
62 (1996), 27 OR (3d) 593, 132 DLR (4th) 538 (Ont. Gen Div), per Epstein J.
63 Family Law Act, RSO 1990, c F.3, Part III, section 29.
64 (1996), 31 OR (3d) 417 (Ont. CA), per Doherty and Charron JJ A, Finlayson J dissenting.
65 RSO 1990, c S.26.
66 RSO 1990, c F.3.
67 He also sought to be appointed trustee of the estate under section 29 of the Estates Act, RSO 1990, c E.21.
68 (1993), 14 OR (3d) 658 (Ont. Div Ct), per Southey and Sirois, J, Greer J. dissenting.
69 For a more detailed discussion of these policies, see chapter 5.
70 In roughly chronological order, the successful cases were *Re Memorial University of Newfoundland and N.A.P.E.* (1995), 39 CLAS 13 (Nfld.); *Vogel v Manitoba* (1995), 126 DLR (4th) 72 (Man. CA), per Scott CJM, Philp and Helper JJ A, rev'g (1992), 90 DLR (4th) 84, 79 Man. R (2d) 208, per Hirschfield J [*Vogel II*]; *Re Metro Toronto Reference Library and Canadian Union of Public Employers, Local 1582* (1995), 51 L.A.C. (4th) 69 (Ont.); *Re Treasury Board (Agriculture and Agri-Food Canada) and Yarrow* (1996), 43 CLAS 309 (Can.); *Re Treasury Board (Canadian Grain Commission) and Sarson* (1996), 42 CLAS 337 (Can.); *Moore and Akerstrom v The Queen*, [1996] CHRD No. 8 (Can. Hum Rts Trib), per Norton, Chair, Ellis, and Sinclair, Members; *Korn v Potter and Benson* (1996), 134 DLR (4th) 437 (B.C. SC), aff'g (1995), 23 CHRR D/319 (Bd of Inq); *Re Canadian Pacific Ltd. and Brotherhood of Maintenance of Way Employees* (1996), 57 LAC (4th) 89, 44 CLAS 410 (Can.); *Re Chrysler Canada Ltd. and Canadian Auto Workers* (1996), 57 LAC (4th) 81, 44 CLAS 351 (Ont.); *Re Boutilier and Treasury Board (Natural Resources)* (1997), 31 PSSRB Decisions 15, [1997] CPSSRB No. 54 (Can. Pub Serv Staff Rels Bd), per Tarte, Chair; *McCallum v Toronto Transit Commission*, [1997] OHRBID No. 19 (Ont. Bd of Inq) (QL), per McNeilly, Bd; *Hudler v London (City)*, [1997] OHRBID No. 23 (Ont. Bd of Inq) (QL), per McKeller, Bd; *Bewley v Ontario*, [1997] OHRBID No. 24 (Ont. Bd of Inq) (QL), per McNeilly, Bd; *Nova Scotia (Minister of Finance) v Hodder*, [1998] NSJ No. 125 (N.S. CA) (QL), per Chipman, Freeman, and Flinn JJ A; *Nova Scotia (Minister of Finance) v MacNeil Estate*, [1998] NSJ No. 124 (N.S. CA) (QL), per Chipman, Freeman, and Flinn JJ A. The federal tribunal ruled against the gay complainant in *Laessoe v Air Canada* [1996] CHRD No. 10 (Can Hum Rts Trib), per Armstrong, Kaluzny, and Pitzel, Members.
71 RSC c 377.

72 The medical practitioner had refused the complainant AI because he claimed that he did not want to run the risk of being called into legal proceedings by the women; he had been subpoenaed in the proceedings in *Anderson* v *Luoma* (1986), 50 RFL (2d) 127 (B.C. SC), because he had given the plaintiff in that case artificial insemination.
73 Para. 36. The other decision of significance in this group is *Re Chrysler Canada Ltd. and Canadian Auto Workers*, in which the adjudicator ruled that denial of same-sex survivor options under the employee pension plan, a registered pension plan, was grievable.
74 Nitya Iyer, 'Categorical Denials: Equality Rights and the Shaping of Social Identity' (1994), 19 *Queen's Law Journal* 179–207, at 204.
75 Audre Lorde, *Zami: A New Spelling of My Name* (Trumansburg, NY: The Crossing Press, 1982), 182.
76 Anne Bayefsky, 'Defining Equality Rights,' in *Equality Rights and The Canadian Charter of Rights and Freedoms*, ed. Anne F. Bayefsky and Mary Eberts (Toronto: Carswell, 1985), 1–80, at 48 and references in notes 226 and 227.
77 See *P.* v *S.*, Case C-13/94 (Ct of J of the EC, Luxembourg, 30 April 1996) The Times Law Report (7 May 1996), in which the court treated discrimination against a transsexual person as discrimination on the basis of 'sex.' And see Robert Wintemute, *Sexual Orientation and Human Rights: The United States Constitution, the European Convention, and the Canadian Charter* (Oxford: Clarendon Press, 1997), 12 note 31, who provides a detailed legal basis for that position.
78 Stonewall Think Tank (12 June 1997).
79 See, for example, references collected in Cynthia Petersen, 'Envisioning a Lesbian Equality Jurisprudence,' in *Legal Inversions: Lesbians, Gay Men, and the Politics of Law*, ed. Didi Herman and Carl Stychin, 118–37 (Philadelphia, PA: Temple University Press, 1995), notes 1 and 2.
80 This approach was successful in *Sheridan* v *Sanctuary Investments Ltd.* (B.C. Hum Rts Trib, unreported, 11 Jan. 1999).
81 *Baehr* v *Miike*, [1996] Westlaw 694235, 1996 Haw App LEXIS 138 (Haw Cir Ct, 1st Cir, 3 Dec. 1996), per Chang J, aff'g *Baehr* v *Lewin*, 74 Haw 530, 852 P 2d 44 (1993), clarified on grant of reconsideration in part, 74 Haw 645, 852 P 2d 74 (1993).
82 Legal change and Charter challenges may well be sparked by barbara findlay, Sandra Laframboise, Deborah Brady, Christine Burnham, and Septima (Ron) Skolney-Elverson, *Finding Our Place: Transgendered Law Reform Project* (Vancouver, B.C.: High Risk Project Society, 1998),

Notes to pages 96–101   381

a comprehensive review of legal issues faced by transgendered persons.

83 See Didi Herman, 'The Good, the Bad, and the Smugly: Sexual Orientation and Perspectives on the Charter,' in *Charting the Consequences: The Impact of Charter Rights on Canadian Law and Politics*, ed. David Schneiderman and Kate Sutherland (Toronto: University of Toronto Press, 1997), 201–17, at 213; Mary Eaton, 'Lesbians, Gays and the Struggle for Equality Rights: Reversing the Progressive Hypothesis' (1994), 17 *Dalhousie Law Journal* 130–86, at 185–6.

84 The numbers of human rights complaints are growing quickly. The federal Human Rights Commission reported that as of 5 December 1996, it had pending ninety-six complaints relating to same-sex employment benefits, most of which related to pension benefits, and had already stood down seventeen of these complaints pending the resolution of the *Rosenberg* appeals: Affidavit of John Hucker, Secretary General of the Canadian Human Rights Commission, filed with Ontario Court of Appeal in *Rosenberg* appeal (5 December 1996).

85 Ellen Degeneres, 'Ellen' (30 April 1997) skilfully conveyed this 'lesbian coffee house' view of queer existence in a scene involving her recently homophobic boss and his wife. She was sitting in a lesbian coffee house with her friends after a tense coming-out scene with the boss. Suddenly the boss came into the coffee house with his wife and sat down. After they looked around expectantly for what seemed like an uncomfortably long time, Ellen finally broke the tension by asking: 'Okay, what are you doing here?' Her boss replied: 'You've seen our lives, now we would like to see yours.' Ellen's rejoinder: 'My life is a lesbian coffee house?'

Chapter Four: Human Rights, Charter Rights, and 'Legal Personality'

1 (1996), 132 DLR (4th) 595 (Alta. CA), per McClung, O'Leary, JJ A, Hunt JJ A dissenting, rev'g [1994] 6 WWR 414 (Alta. QB), per Russell J, rev'd (1998), 156 DLR (4th) 385 (SCC), per Cory and Iacobucci JJ.

2 Richard Bardolph, *The Civil Rights Record: Black Americans and the Law, 1819–1970* (New York: Thomas Y. Crowell, 1970).

3 Kristin Bumiller, 'Victims in the Shadow of the Law: A Critique of the Model of Legal Protection' (1987), 12 *Signs* 3, has demonstrated why potential complainants avoid using civil rights protections in the United States. The essays collected in David Kairys, ed., *The Politics of Law: A Progressive Critique* (New York: Pantheon, 1982), put those who place complete faith in 'rights' on notice of the futility of doing so.

4 Patricia Williams, *The Alchemy of Race and Rights* (Cambridge, MA: Harvard University Press, 1991).
5 Compare Justice Scalia's dissent in *Romer* v *Evans*, 116 S Ct 1620, at 1630, in which he claimed that the anti–anti-discrimination provisions in Amendment 2 merely prevented the enshrinement of 'special rights' for queers, with this passage from the 1883 Civil Rights Cases, 106 U.S. 3 (1883), per Bradley J. Justice Bradley was explaining why the Thirteenth and Fourteenth amendments to the U.S. Constitution could not be applied to invalidate state statutes excluding African Americans from theatres and other public places:

> When a man has emerged from slavery, and by the aid of beneficent legislation has shaken off the inseparable concomitants of that state, there must be some stage in the progress of his elevation when he takes the rank of a mere citizen, and ceases to be the special favourite of the laws, and when his rights as a citizen, or a man, are to be protected in the ordinary modes by which other men's rights are protected.

6 The 'civil death' resulting from marriage meant that women could not own property, make contracts, sue or be sued, alienate or administer her own property, divorce her husband, or even inherit her own dowry. See J. H. Baker, 'Baron et Feme: Unity of Person,' in *An Introduction to English Legal History* (London: Butterworths, 1971), 258–66.
7 For example, Justice L'Heureux-Dubé in her dissenting opinion in *The Queen* v *Thibaudeau*, [1995] 2 SCR 627, at 543.
8 This view is not entirely unique. J.D.C. Galloway, 'Three Models of (In)Equality' (1993), 38 *McGill Law Journal* 64, at 83–4, seemed to see 'human dignity' as premised upon 'self-respect' or 'personhood,' and 'The Constitutional Status of Sexual Orientation: Homosexuality as a Suspect Classification' [Note] (1985), 98 *Harvard Law Review* 1285, 1300, proposed that the application of the equal-protection clause of the Fourteenth Amendment to issues of sexuality be framed not in terms of 'irrelevant characteristics,' but around the denial of full 'personhood.'
9 It has also lurked under the surface of feminist criticism, moral philosophy, and equality theory. See, for example, Luce Irigaray, 'How Do We Become Civil Women,' in *Thinking the Difference: For a Peaceful Revolution*, trans. Karin Montin (New York: Routledge, 1994), 39–64; John Casey, *Pagan Virtue: An Essay in Ethics* (Oxford: Clarendon Press, 1990), especially 1–50; Galloway, 'Three Models of (In)Equality,' 83–4.
10 See Bardolph, *Civil Rights Record*; and 'Declaration of Sentiments,' in *The Feminist Papers*, ed. Alice Rossi, 415–19 (New York: Bantam, 1972).

11 *The Queen* v *Thibaudeau*, [1995] 2 SCR 627; *Egan and Nesbit* v *The Queen*, [1995] 2 SCR 513; *Miron* v *Trudel*, [1995] 2 SCR 627.
12 For example, minors are still considered to be 'legally incapacitated,' as are those declared mentally 'incompetent.' And corporate legislation constitutes corporations as entities that can act in law by deeming them to be 'natural persons.' See Derek Mendes da Costa, Richard J. Balfour, and Eileen E. Gillese, 'The Anglo-Canadian System of Landholding: A Historical Introduction,' in *Property Law: Cases, Text and Materials*, 2d ed. (Toronto: Emond Montgomery, 1990), 7: 33, 8: 9–13.
13 *Reference as to the meaning of the word 'persons' in section 24 of the British North America Act, 1867*, [1928] SCR 276, rev'd by *Edwards* v *A.G. Canada*, [1930] AC 124 (PC) (hereinafter referred to as the 'Persons' Case).
14 In *Loving* v *Virginia*, 388 U.S. 1, 18 L Ed 2d 1010 (1967), per Warren CJ, the Court ruled that race-based 'miscegenation' statutes violated the equal-protection and due-process clauses of the Fourteenth Amendment to the U.S. Constitution.
15 See, for example, Urukagina's Code (Sumer, *c.* 2350 B.C.E) and Ur-Nammu Lawcode (Ur, *c.* 2050 B.C.E.), both of which are described in Samuel Noah Kramer, *The Sumerians: Their History, Culture, and Character* (Chicago: University of Chicago Press, 1963); Lipit-Ishtar Code (Sumer, *c.* 2000 B.C.E.), discussed in Samuel Noah Kramer, trans., 'The Lipit-Ishtar Lawcode,' in *Ancient Near Eastern Texts Relating to the Old Testament*, 2d ed., ed. James B. Pritchard, 159–61 (Princeton, NJ: Princeton University Press, 1955); Laws of Eshnunna (Ammurrite state, *c.* 1760 B.C.E.), found in Albrecht Goetze, trans., 'The Laws of Eshnunna,' in *Ancient Near Eastern Texts Relating to the Old Testament*, ed. Pritchard, 161–3; Hammurabi Code (Babylon, *c.* 1750 B.C.E.) and Assyrian Code (Assyria, *c.* 1300 B.C.E.), in Elizabeth M. MacDonald, *The Position of Women as Reflected in the Semitic Codes of Law* (Toronto: University of Toronto Press, 1931).
16 See generally Stephanie Coontz and Peta Henderson, 'Property Forms, Political Power, and Female Labour in the Origins of Class and State Societies,' in *Women's Work, Men's Property: The Origins of Gender and Class*, ed. Stephanie Coontz and Peta Henderson, 108–55 (London: Verso, 1986).
17 'Laws of Hammu-Rabi,' in *The Babylonian Laws*, trans. J.C. Miles and G.R. Driver (Oxford: Clarendon Press, 1960), 2: 15, 19, 51, 57 (sections 6, 15–20, 129, 143). Two of these provisions refer to binding and casting into the water, or casting into the water, which may not necessarily be a death penalty so much as a method of determining whether the transgressor was live or die. The effect was very likely death, especially when the accused was bound.
18 Hammu-Rabi Code, sections 138–40.

19 During the *unitas personae*, the son was, in legal terms, a chattel, and his father's legal rights in relation to him were found in the law of possessions. See Samuel Parsons Scott, *Corpvs Jvris Civilis: The Civil Law* (Cincinnati: Central Trust Co., 1973, orig. publ. 1932), vol. I, at 64, note 2. Women and slaves were similarly chattels. It is interesting that the fiction of the *unitas personae* itself was a transformation of the earlier legal fiction of the joint undivided family, which gave expression to the communal nature of family ownership of property, but which allocated authority on the basis of biological descent and sex – the oldest living son in any generation was the title holder of the communally owned family property, and no one else in the family, including his mother, had any authority. See C.W. Westrup, 'The Joint Undivided Family,' in *Introduction to Early Roman Law* (London: Oxford University Press, 1934), 5–6, 67–8.

20 Alan Watson, 'Family Law,' in *The Law of the Ancient Romans* (Dallas: Southern Methodist University Press, 1970), 32–9.

21 See Ch. Letourneau, 'Slavery in Rome,' in *Property: Its Origin and Development* (London: Walter Scott, 1892), 272–5. The domestic nature of early owner–slave relations in early Rome undoubtedly made it easy to apply this principle to slaves as well as to children and women. See Max Kaser, 'The Legal Position of Slave,' in *Roman Private Law*, trans. Rolf Dannenbring (Durban: Butterworths, 1965), 69.

22 For example, under Justinian, relationships between slaves (*contubernium, de facto* marriage) came to be recognized: Ibid., 69–71. The contemporary law of master–servant or principal–agent grew out of these attributes of the *unitas personae*.

23 Thus the legal fiction of marital unity between husband and wife, which was just another application of the doctrine of *unitas personae*.

24 See Watson, *Ancient Romans*, 32–6. Like slaves and sons, women did have some *de facto* capacities, the most predominant of which was the right to administer some property as if it were their own. This property, known as the *peculium*, whether administered by women, slaves, or children, however, was legally considered to be owned by the father/husband/owner – whoever held *potestas* over that person. And, like slaves, women did not own the fruits of their own labour; for example, if a woman made goods with wool provided by her husband, he continued to own those goods, even if they were the clothes on the wife's back.

25 See generally Watson, *Ancient Romans*, 32–9.

26 Hopkins, 'Brother–Sister Marriage in Roman Egypt' (1980), 22 *Comparative Studies in Society and History* 2: 303–54, at 312, noted that. in Roman Egypt, there is evidence 'of husbands calling wives "sister" and of wives calling

husbands "brother".' See also Susan Treggiari, 'Consent to Roman Marriage: Some Aspects of Law and Reality' (1982), 26 *Classical Views* 34–44, at 34–5.
27 See Watson, *Ancient Romans*, 32.
28 Only marriages between Roman citizens were legally recognized: See Treggiari, 'Roman Marriage,' 43.
29 John Boswell, *Same-Sex Unions in Premodern Europe* (New York: Vintage, 1995), 97–106. See also Eva Cantarella, *Bisexuality in the Ancient World*, trans. Cormac O'Cuilleanain (New Haven, CT: Yale University Press, 1992), 78–93.
30 Boswell, *Same-Sex Unions*, 99.
31 Ibid., 98.
32 As early as 195 B.C.E., Roman women had won the right to administer their own dowries and to divorce their husbands: Durant, *Caesar*, 89, 135.
33 A woman found guilty of adultery could be exiled, she could lose as much of half her dowry, and up to one-third of any property she had acquired through gifts or family inheritance could be confiscated: Durant, *Caesar*, 223–4. Augustus was forced to begin loosening these controls within a few years of introducing them.
34 Boswell suggests that the only same-sex weddings so banned were 'those involving traditional gender roles,' because the law applied only '[w]hen a man marries [a man] as if he were a woman': See Boswell, *Same-Sex Unions*, 85–6, and note 163, citing the Theodosian Code, 9.7.3, which Boswell has dated at 342 C.E. (Theodosius was the same emperor who ended the Olympic games: Durant, *Caesar*, 486.)
35 See Durant, *Caesar*, 598, for Tertullian's account of the rise of Christian sexual morality and the condemnation of homosexual practices, and 625–7, for a description of Alexander's 'deportation of homosexuals' as part of his censorship of public morals in the 220s; John Boswell, *Christianity, Social Tolerance and Homosexuality: Gay People in Western Europe from the Beginning of the Christian Era to the Fourteenth Century* (Chicago: University of Chicago Press, 1980), 70–1, 127–8. The relationship between the role of Christian doctrine in law and legal policy is also highly controversial. Right-wing scholars have attempted to establish that Western civilizations disapproved of same-sex relations long before Christianity emerged as a significant movement: See Daniel Mendelsohn, 'The Stand' (1996), *Lingua Franca: The Review of Academic Life* (September/October): 34–46, which recounts how John Finnis, an Oxford University moral philosopher, and Robert George, a politics professor at Princeton University, testified in *Romer* v *Evans* that moral disapproval of homosexuality existed prior to the Christian era, while Martha Nussbaum, a classicist at the University of Chicago, demonstrated how the translations upon which Finnis relied were themselves distorted by

homophobic values. See also Mark Jordan, *The Invention of Sodomy in Christian Theology* (Chicago: University of Chicago Press, 1997).

36 This tabulation is my own, based on my reading of Roman civil law at successive stages of development. Not all citizens enjoyed all of these rights at all times; 'public morality,' for example, was under the control of the censors at key points in Roman history. But see generally Ch. Letourneau, 'Slavery in Rome,' in *Property: Its Origin and Development* (London: Walter Scott, 1892), 272–5; Max Kaser, 'The Legal Position of Slaves,' in *Roman Private Law*, trans. Rolf Dannenbring (Durban: Butterworths, 1965), 69–71; Alan Watson, 'Family Law,' in *The Law of the Ancient Romans* (Dallas: Southern Methodist University Press, 1970), 32–9, for discussions of these elements in relation to the categories of 'slaves' and women.

37 Boswell, *Same-Sex Unions*, 100, who recounts the case in which the non-citizen status of an adopted brother appears to have formed the basis for invalidating the inheritance and freeing the estate to pass to the son of the deceased. A great deal of controversy has surrounded the reading of this situation, but the point here is that civil status of the surviving partner seems to have offered an early and convenient basis for curtailing the inheritance rights of some male partners. Boswell frankly admitted that he did not have any particular insight into the nature of the relationship between the two men involved.

38 This period lasted roughly from 400 C.E. until the Arabic invasion of 711 C.E.

39 Durant, *Caesar*, 479.

40 See John Boswell, *Christianity, Social Tolerance, and Homosexuality: Gay People in Western Europe from the Beginning of the Christian Era to the Fourteenth Century* (Chicago: University of Chicago Press, 1980), 61–90, 171–4.

41 Samuel Parsons Scott, trans., *The Visigothic Code* (Boston: Boston Book Co., 1910), Titles II and III. Jewish persons were forced to stone other Jewish persons and required to take their property after they died: ibid., xii–xv. Exorbitant special taxes imposed on Jews were remitted only upon 'true conversion': P.D. King, *Law and Society in the Visigothic Kingdom* (Cambridge: Cambridge University Press, 1972), 131, 143. Jewish persons were forced to give enormous amounts of money and property to Arian Christians, and to pay their taxes: Scott, *Visigothic Code*, xiii.

42 Scott, *Visigothic Code*, xv.

43 Thus married women could not sue or be sued, testify in court, sit on juries, hold public office, own property, enter into contracts, establish a legal domicile separate from their husbands, or have custody of their children: See J.H. Baker, 'Baron et Feme: Unity of Person' and 'Succession,' in *An*

Introduction to English Legal History (London: Butterworths, 1971), 144–9, 258–66. Of course, these general statements were subject to geographic, temporal, and class variations. Some customary capacities enjoyed by women were never completely expunged by English common law, and some exceptions were found in various areas of law: See generally G.D.G. Hall, trans., *Tractatus de Legibus: The Treatise on the Laws and Customs of the Realm of England Commonly Called Glanvill* (London: Thomas Nelson and Sons, 1965, orig. written *c.* 1187–9).

44 See Baker, 'Baron et Femme: Unity of Person,' and 'Succession,' 258–66, 144–9.

45 Married women's property legislation was enacted as early as 1790, but it was of such limited form that it made little difference to the overall status of women as a class.

46 French law, which traced its origins more directly from customary law and then from the Roman civil code after the Revolution, only slowly acquired the notion that married women were under any disabilities, and the doctrine of coverture never gained the hold on legal doctrine in France that it did in England. The best compilation of laws relating to the status of women in Canada remains Susan Altschul and Christine Carron, 'Chronology of Some Legal Landmarks in the History of Canadian Women' (1975), 21 *McGill Law Journal* 476. Common-law presumptions about the civil capacities of women were given statutory expression as early as 1831 and 1849 in Canada.

47 See Bardolph, *Civil Rights Record*.

48 See An Act to prevent the future introduction of Slaves and to limit the Term of Enforced Servitude within the Province, SUC 1793 (2d sess.), c 7.

49 Legislation enacted in 1850 put Aboriginal peoples in the legal position of minors by defining membership in the category 'Indian,' controlling allocation and use of property by 'Indians,' setting up rules on marriage to non-'Indians,' and establishing a framework of social and economic control that eventually deprived Aboriginal peoples of all effective civil rights. See An Act for the protection of the Indians in Upper Canada from imposition and the property occupied or enjoyed by them from trespass and injury, SC 1850, 13 & 14 Vic, C 74; An Act for the better protection of Lands and Property of the Indians in Lower Canada, SC 1850, 13 & 14 Vic, C 42; cf. Indian Act, RSC 1985, c 149, as it stood until recently. In addition to the blanket incapacities imposed on Aboriginal persons under the Indian Act, and despite the partial nullification of the status rules of old section 12(1)(b) by Bill C-31, the Indian Act continues to deprive Aboriginal women who are status Indians from dealing equally with men in relation to property. See

Derrickson v *Derrickson*, [1984] 2 WWR 754 (B.C. CA), [1986] 1 SCR 285; *Paul* v *Paul*, [1986] 1 SCR 306; *Sampson* v *Gosnell Estate*, [1989] BCJ No. 426 (B.C. CA), which ruled that Aboriginal women who were denied claims to property located on reserves (property which was their before marriage, in some cases) and which was thus under the jurisdiction of the Indian Act, had no remedies under provincial property law – and thus no remedies at all.

50 An Act to prevent Chinese from acquiring Crown lands, BCS 1884, c 2; An Act to prevent the immigration of Chinese, BCS 1884, c 3; An Act to regulate the Chinese population, BCS 1884, c 4.

51 See the various statutory amendments and Orders in Council collected in Appendices III through XI of Ken Adachi, *The Enemy That Never Was* (Toronto: McClelland and Stewart, 1979), which ordered everything from the internment of Japanese-Canadian persons during the Second World War to appropriation of real and personal property and deportation of Japanese nationals who 'manifested their sympathy with or support of Japan' 'by making requests for repatriation to Japan and otherwise.'

52 See Richard H. Bartlett, 'Parallels in Aboriginal Land Policy in Canada and South Africa' (1988), 4 *Canadian Native Law Reporter* 1–35, for a detailed comparison of these two sets of apartheid laws; see also the various legal provisions of the Third Reich in Germany in the 1930s and 1940s, such as Reich Citizenship Law (15 September 1935) and other documentation in J. Noakes and G. Pridham, eds., *Nazism: A History in Documents and Eyewitness Accounts, 1919–1945* (New York: Stocken, 1983).

53 The Declaration referred directly to the following elements of legal personhood: voting, public office, ownership of property, ownership of wages, the doctrine of marital unity, prohibitions on divorce, child custody, and access to education. See 'Declaration of Sentiments,' in *Feminist Papers*, 415–19.

54 Ibid.,' 418.

55 Article XIV, U.S. Constitution, Bill of Rights.

56 Mabel Raef Putnam, *The Winning of the First Bill of Rights for American Women* (Milwaukee, WI: Frank Putnam, 1924), 65–6.

57 For the laws of the Third Reich that imposed civil disabilities on Jewish persons, see the documents collected in Noakes and Pridham, eds., *Nazism*. This legal history is discussed in some detail in chapter 5.

58 See Kathleen A. Lahey, 'Feminist Theories of (In)Equality,' in *Equality and Judicial Neutrality*, eds. Sheilah L. Martin and Kathleen E. Mahoney, 71–86 (Toronto: Carswell, 1987), for some of this legal history.

59 SA, c I-2.

60 For a detailed history of the legal protection of human rights in Canada, see

Walter S. Tarnopolsky and William F. Pentney, *Discrimination and the Law* (Don Mills, ON: De Boo, 1985).
61 Section 1.
62 *Edwards* v *A.-G. Canada*, [1930] AC 124, 136 (PC).
63 As Andrea Timoll has demonstrated, the 'Persons' Case has never been applied substantively in a case involving civil disabilities: See Andrea Timoll, 'The Erasure of Women of Colour in Canadian Jurisprudence,' LL.M. thesis, Queen's University, Kingston, ON, 1996. For discussions of the racism, classism, and heterosexism of Emily Murphy, one of the women who brought the 'Persons' Case, see Christine Mander, *Emily Murphy: Rebel* (Toronto: Simon and Pierre, 1985); Annalise Acorn, 'Snapshots Then and Now: Feminism and the Law in Alberta' (1996), 35 *Alberta Law Review* 140.
64 This should not be particularly surprising. Hon. John Crosbie appealed to the 'Persons' Case in urging that governments and people base their actions and policies not on section 15 of the Charter as a 'legal minimum,' but as needed to offer 'new protection where necessary': Hon. John Crosbie, *Toward Equality* (Ottawa: Minister of Supply and Services Canada, 1986), 3.
65 41 OR (2d) 113 (OCA), per MacKinnon ACJO, Jessup and Martin JJ A. This language was subsequently adopted in the later appeal from the Ontario Court of Appeal. See *Southam Inc.* v *The Queen*, [1984] 2 SCR 145 (SCC), per Dickson J.
66 (1983), 41 OR (2d) at 123.
67 See, for example, *Reference re Section 94(2) of the Motor Vehicle Act*, RSBC. 1979, c 288, [1985] 2 SCR 486, per Lamer J, in which the Court invoked the image of the 'living tree' but gave no indication that the image had arisen in any earlier judicial decision. The closest citation that appears in the opinion is to *Law Society of Upper Canada* v *Skapinker*, [1984] 1 SCR 357, but the Court simply drew from that case the proposition that narrow interpretations of the Charter, 'if not modulated by a sense of the unknowns of the future, can stunt the growth of the law.' The Court gave no source for that concept either, but may have been alluding to the 'growth' aspect of the 'tree' image.
68 [1991] 2 SCR 158 (SCC).
69 [1992] 3 SCR 813, at 848 (SCC), per L'Heureux-Dubé J.
70 [1993] 1 SCR 554 (SCC).
71 See, for example, *Duval* v *Sequin*, [1972] 2 OR 686 (Ont. HCJ), per Fraser J, following *Montreal Tramways Co.* v *Leveille*, [1933] SCR 456 (SCC) (tort liability for injury to unborn foetus); *Morgentaler* v *The Queen*, [1976] 1 SCR 616 (SCC) (unborn foetus not person for purposes of criminal provisions regulating abortion).

390 Notes to pages 118–23

72 *Borowski* v *A.-G. Canada (Sask.)*, [1984] 1 WWR 15, per Matheson J, aff'd [1989] 1 SCR 343 (foetus not included in 'everyone' in section 7 of the Charter); *R.* v *Morgentaler* (1985), 52 OR (2d) 353 (Ont. CA), [1988] 1 SCR 30 (SCC) (foetus given no legal personality by Charter, but rights of pregnant women included in 'security of the person'); *R.* v *Sullivan*, [1988] BCJ No. 1494 (B.C. CA) (QL), per Nemetz CJBC, Hinkson and Macdonal JJ A (stillborn child not person for purposes of charging midwife); *Tremblay* v *Daigle*, [1989] 2 SCR 530 (SCC) (unborn foetus not 'human being' within the meaning of Charter of Human Rights and Freedoms, RSQ, c C12, preamble, ss. 1, 2, or 'juridical person' within meaning of Civil Code of Lower Canada so as to give father standing to seek injunction on mother's abortion.
73 See *R.* v *Moyer*, [1994] 2 SCR 899 (SCC), per Lamer CJ (no 'notion of personhood' in Criminal Code reference to 'offering indignities to human remains'); *R.* v *Bernardo*, [1995] OJ No. 1472 (Ont. Ct J–Gen Div) (QL), per LeSage ACJOC (family could not assert privacy or security interests re videotape evidence on behalf of deceased victims even if surviving victim did have privacy interests therein).
74 [1989] 1 SCR 143 (SCC).
75 [1989] 1 SCR at 195.
76 [1993] 2 SCR 689 (SCC).
77 [1992] 2 SCR 731 (SCC).
78 [1992] 2 SCR 731, 808 (SCC), citing Mari Matsuda, 'Public Response to Racist Speech: Considering the Victim's Story' (1989), 87 *Michigan Law Review* 2320, at 2338, 2379.
79 [1988] OJ No. 51 (Ont. CA)(QL), per Brooke, Blair and Morden JJ A.
80 [1993] 3 SCR 519 (SCC).
81 116 S Ct 1620 (U.S. SC, 1996), per Kennedy J.
82 [1993] 3 FC 401, 103 DLR (4th), aff'g [1992] 1 FC 687, 87 DLR (4th) 320 (FCTD).
83 (1856), 19 How 393, at 404, per Tanney CJ.
84 *Egan* v *The Queen*, [1993] 3 FC 401, at 428–9, per Linden J, dissenting, citing *Reference as to the meaning of the word 'persons' in section 24 of the British North America Act, 1867*, [1928] SCR 276, rev'd by *Edwards* v *A.-G. Canada*, [1930] AC 124 (PC).
85 See *Hunter* v *Southam Inc.*, [1984] 2 SCR 145, at 155.
86 [1993] FCJ No. 1263 (FCTD)(QL), per Rouleau J.
87 Social benefit legislation running the gamut from the Old Age Security spousal allowance to indirect benefits to married couples under the Income Tax Act uses the married couple as the benefit unit, and that unit has now been expanded to include cohabiting couples as well as married couples.

The problem with this method of allocating and measuring social benefits is that it proceeds on the assumption that women have equal control and enjoyment of such benefits, which is patently not the case. For an example of how this assumption affects women on a practical, individual level, see *Collins* v *M.N.R.*, [1994] TCJ No. 929 (TCC)(QL), in which family allowance payments were deemed to be the wife's income and taxed at her 26 per cent marginal rate, while the wife's child-care expenses were deemed to be incurred by her husband and generated benefits at his marginal rate, which was only 17 per cent. Appeals from both aspects of this assessment failed, the court reasoning that neither provision discriminated against the taxpayers because any disparate impact generated by either provision related merely to 'family status.' See also the discussion of *Poulter* v *M.N.R.*, [1995] TCJ No. 228 (TCC)(QL) in chapter 9.
88 116 S Ct 1620 (U.S. SC, 1996), per Kennedy J, with Stevens, O'Connor, Souter, Ginsburg, and Breyer JJ, Scalia J dissenting with Rehnquist CJ and Thomas J.
89 163 U.S. 537, 16 S Ct 1138, 41 L Ed 256 (1896), Harlan J dissenting.
90 Technically, the principle of separate-but-equal accommodation began to crumble in 1938, when the U.S. Supreme Court ruled that paying the tuition for African Americans to attend universities out of state was not 'equal' accommodation. See *Missouri ex rel. Gaines* v *Canada*, 305 U.S. 337 (1938). *Brown* v *Board of Education of Topeka*, 347 U.S. 483 (1954), is considered to have deprived *Plessy* of any further authority.
91 The United States subsequently denied *certiorari* in relation to the *Cincinnati Issue 3* case, which involved an amendment to the municipal charter similar in intent to Amendment 2. The Court commented that denial of *cert*. did not reflect on the merits, but was due to the fact that the Court 'does not normally make an independent examination of state law questions that have been resolved by a court of appeals': see *Equality Foundation of Greater Cincinnati, Inc.* v *City of Cincinnati*, File No. 97-1795 (U.S. Supreme Court, 13 October 1998), per Stevens J, denying cert. from 128 F. 3d 289 (CA6 1997).
92 File No. BI-0056-93 (27 September 1996) (Ont. Bd of Inq) (municipal employers ordered to extend employee benefits to same-sex partners, including pension benefits when Income Tax Act amended).
93 (1996), 27 OR (3d) 593, 132 DLR (4th) 538 (Ont. Ct Gen Div), Epstein J, aff'd (1996), 31 OR (3d) 417, 142 DLR (4th) 1 (Ont. CA), per Doherty and Charron J, Finlayson J dissenting, leave to appeal granted 24 April 1997, per L'Heureux-Dubé, Sopinka, and Iacobucci JJ, on condition that government pay all costs in any event of the cause.
94 See *Handyside* v *United Kingdom (European court)*, at 754, concluding that

freedom of expression was an 'essential foundation' of democratic society and human development.
95 See for example H.L.A. Hart, *The Concept of the Law* (Oxford: Oxford University Press, 1961); Donna Greschner, '(comment) Quebec Association of Protestant School Boards' (1984–5), 49 *Saskatchewan Law Review* 336.
96 (1986), 44 Alta. LR (2d) 1 (Alta. CA), per Lieberman, Kerans, and Stevenson JJ A (denying partners of Ontario law firm right to become non-resident members of Alberta bar).
97 [1985] 1 SCR 295.

Chapter Five: Are We 'Persons' Yet?

1 [1995] 2 SCR 513 (SCC).
2 [1995] 2 SCR 627 (SCC).
3 From the perspective of the citizenship question, the tendency in contemporary legal culture to grant those sexual minorities who remain most fully 'in the closet' the fullest access to the social goods conferred by Canadian society is not dissimilar to the fact that immigrant women who come to Canada as 'foreign domestic workers' have to leave much of themselves 'at home' in order to gain access through immigration to some of these social goods: Abigail B. Bakan and Daiva Stasiulis, 'Foreign Domestic Worker Policy in Canada and the Social Boundaries of Modern Citizenship,' in *Not One of the Family: Foreign Domestic Workers in Canada*, ed. Abigail B. Bakan and Daiva Stasiulis (Toronto: University of Toronto Press, 1997), 29–52, esp. 44–7. The comparison must admit of differences as well, however, because the poverty faced by foreign domestic workers in both countries far exceeds the poverty faced just because of sexuality, and accounts for the perception that, when compared with other groups, sexual minorities are relatively privileged.
4 For example Katherine O'Donovan, *Sexual Divisions in Law* (London: Weidenfeld and Nicolson, 1985), 2, has distinguished between 'private' civil society unregulated by law within the family, home, and women's domain, and the rest of civil society. This of course completely ignores the extensive intrusion by law of the state into that sphere, turning it into an extension of the 'public' at the same time that the 'public' realm has become increasingly ordered through 'private' processes. See also Susan Moller Okin, 'Gender, the Public and the Private,' in *Political Theory Today*, ed. David Held (Cambridge: Polity Press, 1991), 67–90, at 83; Jürgen Habermas, *The Structural Transformation of the Public Sphere* (Cambridge, MA: MIT Press, 1994), 6.
5 Stephanie Coontz and Peta Henderson, 'Property Forms, Political Power,

and Female Labour in the Origins of Class and State Societies,' in *Women's Work, Men's Property: The Origins of Gender and Class*, ed. Stephanie Coontz and Peta Henderson (London: Verso, 1986), 108–55, at 148–51, detail the replacement of kinship groups with citizenship in territorially defined states as the organizing principle of civil society in early Mesopotamian and Greek states.

6 *Andrews* v *Law Society of British Columbia*, [1989] 1 SCR 143, the first Charter equality case to reach the Supreme Court of Canada, established landed immigrants as a 'non-enumerated' group for purposes of the right to practise law.

7 See for example Canada Elections Act, RSC 1985, c E-2, section 50(1)(b).

8 It is worth noting that the Federal Court has recently confirmed that federal prisoners cannot be denied the right to vote in federal elections: See *Sauvé* v *Canada*, [1997] FCJ No. 594 (FCTD, 16 May 1997) (File No. T-2257-93, T-1084-94), per Wetson J (stay of order permitting voting denied while further appeal pending; section 51(d) of the Canada Elections Act had purported to deny federal voting rights to inmates serving sentences of more than two years).

9 Reich Citizenship Law, German, 15 September 1935, section II.3, reprinted in J. Noakes and G. Pridham, eds., *Nazism: A History in Documents and Eyewitness Accounts, 1919–1945* (New York: Stocken, 1983). Within a few months of Adolf Hitler's election in 1933, special legislation on a huge range of subjects began to withdraw other legal capacities from Jewish persons. The 'Decree on the Practice of Dentists and Dental Technicians under the Health Insurance Plan' (2 June 1933) removed Jewish persons and Communists from the national health insurance plan. This was followed in 1934 by the 'Aryanization of Private Insurance,' which was designed to prevent Jewish medical practitioners from receiving payment under private health insurance plans. The April 1933 'Law against the Overcrowding of German Schools and Universities' placed limits on the numbers of 'non-Aryan' students who could attend any one school. The Citizenship Law of 1935 was the culmination of a long process of withdrawing civil capacities. Jewish persons were not the only targets of Nazi oppression. The Third Reich used the power of the state to 'wipe away' Slavs, Gypsies, disabled people, Jehovah's Witnesses, and criminals as well: See Barry Adam, *The Rise of a Gay and Lesbian Movement* (Boston: Twayne, 1987), 49.

10 First Supplementary Decree of Reich Citizenship Law, Germany, 14 November 1935, sections I.1, III, IV.1, 2, reprinted in Noakes and Pridham, eds., *Nazism*.

11 Law for the Protection of German Blood and German Honour, German, 16 September 1938, reprinted in ibid.

12 Richard Plant, *The Pink Triangle: The Nazi War Against Homosexuals* (New York: Henry Holt, 1986), 133; see also 110–13 generally. Others have described Paragraph 175 as criminalizing 'a kiss, an embrace, even homosexual fantasies.' See references collected in Adam, *Rise of Movement*, at 168, note 4, and text at 52.
13 Samuel Parsons Scott, trans., *The Visigothic Code* (Boston: Boston Book Co., 1910), Titles II, III.
14 First Supplementary Decree, section V.2. Some Jewish persons did of course 'pass' for at least some time.
15 See Erica Fischer, *Aimée and Jaguar: A Love Story, Berlin 1943*, trans. Edna McCown (New York: HarperCollins, 1994), for a account of the investigation of a German lesbian that was triggered by her attempts to see her lover after she had been sent to a concentration camp.
16 See Criminal Code, RSC 1985, c C-46, section 159(2)(a)(b), (3)(a).
17 During the McCarthy era in the United States and in parallel developments in Canada during the same period of time, targeting of 'homosexuals' in public service and other public spheres was justified in part on the basis that homosexuality was considered to be criminal, and many police forces routinely kept lists of suspected or identified 'homosexuals': See Adam, *Rise of Movement*, 53, 56–60, 133; Lillian Faderman, *Odd Girls and Twilight Lovers: A History of Lesbian Life in Twentieth-Century America* (New York: Penguin, 1991), 140–50; Becki L. Ross, *The House That Jill Built: A Lesbian Nation in Formation* (Toronto: University of Toronto Press, 1995), 13.
18 The American Law Institute, an organization devoted to studying legal policy and recommending model legislation, had recommended in the mid-1950s that all consensual relations between adults in 'private' should be excluded from the scope of the criminal law. A few years later, the U.K. Report of the Committee on Homosexual Offenses and Prostitution, Cmd no. 247, 1957 (Wolfenden Report), made a similar recommendation: See H.L.A. Hart, *Law, Liberty and Morality* (London: Oxford University Press, 1968), text accompanying notes 16–18.
19 Leslie J. Moran, 'The Homosexualization of English Law,' in *Legal Inversions: Lesbians, Gay Men, and the Politics of Law*, ed. Didi Herman and Carl Stychin (Philadelphia, PA: Temple University Press, 1995), 3–28, at 8. Submissions to the committee suggested that someone could be considered to be 'homosexual' if he or she engaged in 'homosexually motivated masturbation,' or had poor relations with his wife, had unsuccessful heterosexual love affairs, exhibited various neuroses or psychopathologies, or had 'latent' homosexual tendencies. But same-sex sexual activity was in some circumstances considered to be 'false' homosexuality, as in incarcerated populations, adolescence, prostitution, or hypersexuality. These references are collected in ibid., 6–9.

20 Adam, *Rise of Movement*, 67. By this time, policing of 'cross-dressing' appears to have fallen off. For accounts of older police practices, see Gary Kinsman, *The Regulation of Desire: Sexuality in Canada* (Montreal: Black Rose, 1987), 122–3.
21 This list is taken from Moran, 'Homosexualization,' 10.
22 Criminal Code, RSC 1985, c C-46, sections 159(1), (2).
23 Section 160.
24 Sections 271–3, replacing the gender-specific charges of attempted indecent assault (section 156), indecent assault on a male (section 156), and gross indecency (section 157).
25 Section 210.
26 Part XXIV, section 753 *et seq.*
27 See section 150.1. For detailed discussions of the criminalization of queer sexual expression in Canada, see A.K. Gigeroff, 'The Evolution of Canadian Legislation with Respect to Homosexuality, Pedophilia and Exhibitionism' (1965–6), 8 *Criminal Law Quarterly* 445; Donald Casswell, *Lesbians, Gay Men, and Canadian Law* (Toronto: Emond Montgomery, 1996), ch. 5; Mary Eaton, 'Lesbians and the Law,' in *Lesbians in Canada*, ed. Sharon Dale Stone, 109–32 (Toronto: Between the Lines, 1990).
28 See Subcommittee on Equality Rights, Equality for All (Ottawa: Ministry of Supply and Services Canada, 1986), Recommendation 13.
29 Canada, Department of Justice, *Toward Equality: The Response to the Report of the Parliamentary Committee on Equality Rights* (Ottawa: Ministry of Supply and Services Canada, 1986), 14.
30 For information on the continued use of police powers under various provisions of the Criminal Code against queer communities, particularly gay men, see Adam, *Rise of Movement*, 132–3; Kinsman, *Regulation of Desire*.
31 (1995), 23 OR (3d) 629, 98 CCC (3d) 481 (Ont. CA), per Goodman, Catzman, and Abella JJ A, aff'g (1992), 75 CCC (3d) 556 (Ont. Gen Div). The charges arose out of the appellant's three-year relationship with the teenaged niece of his fiancée. See also the earlier decision in *R. v L.A.* (1986), 24 CRR 158 (Ont. Prov Ct–Fam Div), in which the court ruled that denying the defence of consent to charge of anal intercourse on basis of age violated section 15 of the Charter.
32 *R. v Jewell and Gramlick* (Ont. CA, 21 July 1995) (Doc. CAC18639, C18641); *R. v McGowan* (1995), 102 CCC (3d) 461 (Ont. Ct–Prov Div); cf. the pre–*Carmen M.* decision in *R. v Keen* (Ont. CA, 13 May 1996) (Doc. CAM18146).
33 [1995] 2 FC 331 (FCTD), per Reed J.
34 [1998] AQ. no 935 (Que. CA) (QL), per LeBel, Proulx, and Chamberland JJ.
35 Before the offence of indecent assault upon a male was abolished with the repeal of section 156, a B.C. court ruled that the offence did not violate

section 15(1) of the Charter because it did not discriminate against men or on the basis of sexual orientation: *R. v Stymiest (No. 2)* (1993), 81 CCC (3d) 141 (B.C. CA), per Legg, Wood, and Goldie JJ A. When buggery was still included in section 155 of the Criminal Code, an Ontario court ruled that the differential ages of consent applicable to that charge did not violate section 15 of the Charter. This decision pre-dated the application of section 15(1) to discrimination on the basis of sexual orientation: See *R. v Robinson*, [1988] OJ No. 2592 (Ont. Dist Ct, 19 February 1988), per Carnwath DCJ.
36 For example, the court in *R. v McLaren* (1982), 1 CCC (3d) 573 (Ont. Co Ct), allowed a new trial of charges laid under section 193(2)(b) of the Criminal Code (being found in a common bawdy-house) after police raided a gay bath; the appellate court concluded that the trial judge had failed to apply community standards of public decency or tolerance and had erred in failing to consider whether purely social reasons for attending the premises satisfied the element of *mens rea*.
37 (1988), 41 CCC (3d) 163, 25 OAC 1 (Ont. CA), per Brooke, Blair, and Morden JJ A.
38 Section 157 was repealed by RSC 1985, c 19 (3d Supp.), section 2.
39 (1995), 26 OR (3d) 554 (Ont. Gen Div), per Zelinski J.
40 In *Silva*, a gay man who had been charged with public indecency challenged the use of videotapes obtained in non-consensual police surveillance of public washrooms as evidence in his trial under sections 7 and 8 of the Charter. The court allowed the appeal, concluding that he had had a 'reasonable expectation of privacy' in the public washroom, and that even intermittent videotape surveillance directed only at gay men suspected of using the cubicles for sexual purposes brought the administration of justice into disrepute and thus constituted an unreasonable search and seizure. The court was influenced by *R. v Wong*, [1990] 3 SCR 36 (SCC), in which the court was critical of surreptitious videotape surveillance of washrooms because of the 'reasonable expectation of privacy' there, but section 487.01, added to the Criminal Code by SC 1993, c 40, section 15, may provide police with a way to get around the ruling in *Silva* where they can obtain a warrant containing terms that a judge considers will be adequate to ensure that privacy is respected as much as possible under the circumstances. This provision obviously gives courts and police a great deal of latitude.
41 [1967] SCR 822.
42 Complete analysis of the criminal status of queer sexual expression would include discussions of cross-dressing, criminal obscenity provisions, prostitution, the bawdy-house laws in section 179 of the Criminal Code, and

sentencing practices. For further references to some of these areas, see Casswell, *Lesbians and Gay Men*, ch. 5; Kinsman, *Regulation of Desire*; Douglas Saunders, 'Note: Sentencing of Homosexual Offenders' (1967), 10 *Criminal Law Quarterly* 25; Eaton, 'Lesbians and Law'; B.C. Civil Liberties Association, Position Paper: Private Offenses (Prostitution, Solicitation, Bawdy Houses and Related Matters<http://www.bccla.org/positions/privoff/prostitution.html> (1982, 1996); Jeff Lindstrom, <au834@freenet.carleton.ca> has compiled an incredible collection of histories, newspapers articles, and other information on the bathhouse raids before, during, and after 1981 (current to 1996), which can be accessed through his web page at <http://www.ncf.carleton.ca/~au834/*.html>. For the historical account of John White, a Tory member of Canadian Parliament from 1871 to 1887 who was the cross-dressing Eliza McCormack, see Donald H. Akenson, *At Face Value: The Life and Times of Eliza McCormack/John White* (Montreal: McGill-Queen's University Press, 1990).

43 Even something as seemingly innocuous as use of public parks becomes a high-risk activity for gay men. Barry Adam has recounted the differential enforcement of park curfew laws, with twenty-four men being ticketed in 1997 for being in gay cruising areas, while heterosexuals found in those same areas received none (Personal communication, on file with author).

44 Immigration Act, 1952, sections 5, 19(1)(e). Other groups so excluded included prostitutes, pimps, vagrants, and beggars. Philip Girard has concluded that these provisions were enacted in solidarity with the rise of anti-lesbian and gay sentiment during the U.S. 'cold war' and the McCarthy era in the early 1950s: See Philip Girard, 'From Subversion to Liberation: Homosexuals and the Immigration Act 1952–1977' (1987), *Canadian Journal of Law and Society* 3.

45 (1972), 5 Imm App Cases 185 (Imm App Bd).

46 See generally Rob Tielman and Hans Hammelburg, *The Third Pink Book: World Survey on the Social and Legal Position of Gays and Lesbians*, ed. Aart Hendriks et al. (New York: Prometheus, 1993).

47 This case is noted in Christine Donald, *Immigration and Refugee-Status Issues for Lesbians, Gay Men, and Bisexuals* (Toronto: Coalition for Lesbian and Gay Rights in Ontario, 1995), 2, 3.

48 [1995] 2 FC 331 (FCTD), per Reed J.

49 *Halm v Canada (M.E.I.)*, [1996] 1 FC 547 (FCTD), per Rothstein J.

50 Immigration Act, RSC 1985, c I-2, section 2(1), giving effect to Canada's obligations under the U.N. Convention Relating to the Status of Refugees (1951), 189 U.N. TS 2545 (in force in Canada 2 September 1969).

51 *A.-G. Canada v Ward*, [1993] 2 SCR 689. The Federal Court Trial Division

subsequently confirmed that refugee claims could be brought on the basis of sexual orientation: See *Pizarro* v *M.E.I.* (1994), 75 FTR 120 (FCTD).
52 EGALE, Sexual Orientation Cases (1997) (this document was compiled by the Parliamentary Library Staff at the request of Svend Robinson, and is available on <http://www.egale.ca/~egale/legal/cases.htm>.
53 See generally *Jorge Inaudi*, No. T9104459 (9 April 1992, Imm Ref Bd, Conv Refugee Det Div) (refugee status granted); *Pizarro* v *M.E.I.* (1994), 75 FTR 120 (FCTD) (Convention refugee claimant from Argentina; application successful); *Artur Lasha* (May 1994, Imm Ref Bd, Conv Refugee Det Div) (refugee status granted); *Jose Luis Ortigoza* (January 1995, Imm Ref Bd, Conv Refugee Det Div) (refugee status granted).
54 [1995] FCJ No. 894 (FCTD), per Noël J (No. IMM-5088-94, 9 June 1995).
55 Cf. *Dykon* v *The Queen* (1994), 25 Imm L R (2d) 193 (FCTD), per McKeown J, which reversed the board's denial of refugee status to a man from Ukraine; the court concluded that the board was in error when it speculated on the effect of the dissolution of the Soviet Union on laws prohibiting homosexuality in Ukraine, and because the applicant was perceived to be gay.
56 *Polyakov* v *M.C.I.*, [1996] FCJ No. 300 (FCTD) (No. IMM-1140-95, 9 February 1996) (refugee status denied to Russian claimant alleging fear of persecution in Moldova on basis of sexuality because claim lacked credibility).
57 See Donald, *Immigration and Refugee-Status Issues*, 1–7, for short reports of other refugee cases which are at various stages in the immigration or appeal process; see also *Zhu* v *M.C.I.*, [1995] FCJ No. 1396 (FCTD) (No. IMM-3395, 20 October 1995) (claimant from People's Republic of China denied humanitarian and compassionate decision because government appeared to have taken sufficient account of his sexual orientation).
58 [1996] FCJ No. 1042 (FCTD) (QL), per Simpson J (No. IMM-2833-95, 29 July 1996).
59 Casswell, *Lesbians and Gay Men*, ch. 13, at 575–602, has an excellent and detailed discussion of most of the queer refugee cases, including details of redeterminations, and so on, which should be consulted for information up to 1997. However, he does not appear to have collected all the cases involving lesbian women, or to have seen the situation of lesbian women as significantly different from that of gay men.
60 *Van Vulpen* v *M.E.I.*, File No. V-79-6100 (Imm App Bd, 29 August 1980), rev'd No. A-179-81 (FCA, 1982), per Thurlow, Heald, and Primrose JJ A.
61 See for example Joe Serge, 'Lesbian's family unit can't be sponsored,' *Toronto Star*, 12 January 1991, J4, part of a regular advice column on immigration matters. Serge advised a Canadian lesbian applicant, whose relationship with her British partner and three children had been recognized by the

family division of the Royal Courts of Justice in London, that she could not sponsor her family but should suggest that her 'mate' explore the entrepreneur program.
62 *Morrissey and Coll* v *Canada*, filed January 1992, Federal Court Trial Division; *Carrott and Underwood* v *Canada*, filed February 1992, Federal Court Trial Division. These applications are discussed in EGALE, Sexual Orientation Cases.
63 M. Davidson, *Processing of Same Sex and Common Law Cases*, ORD0150 (Hull, PQ: Department of Immigration, 3 June 1994).
64 EGALE, Sexual Orientation Cases.
65 See Donald, *Immigration and Refugee-Status Issues*, 1–7, for details of cases reported in the media. *Re Layland and Beaulne* (1993), 14 OR (3d) 658 (Ont. Ct [Gen Div] Div Ct), per Southey, Sirois, and Greer JJ, leave to appeal granted by the Ontario Court of Appeal (7 June 1993); appeal withdrawn (1995).
66 OUT/LAW has set up an Internet database containing official information on same-sex sponsorship: <http://www.smith-hughes.com/olim.html>. However, users of this information are advised to consult with experienced queer or queer-friendly lawyers before approaching Immigration Canada under this program. The way an initial application is framed and the office to which it is submitted will have a tremendous impact on the outcome. This review has been published as: Robert Trempe, Susan Davis, and Roslyn Kunin, *Immigration Legislative Review: Not Just Numbers: A Canadian Framework for Immigration* (Ottawa: Minister of Public Works and Government Services, 1997). Chapter 5, Recommendation 32, proposes that 'spouse' be defined as including 'a partner in an intimate relationship, including cohabitation of at least one year in duration, with the burden of proof resting on the applicant,' and Recommendation 40 proposes the creation of a new class of close personal acquaintances of the sponsor's choice, excluding a spouse, which would encompass closeted same-sex partners, *de facto* children, and others. The government has indicated that it will not be pursuing this report for other reasons. The report can be found on the Internet at http://cicnet.ci.gc.ca/english/about/policy/lrag/erecomm.html.
67 *Edwards* v. *A.-G. Canada*, [1930] AC 124 (PC), rev'g *Reference as to the meaning of the word 'persons' in section 24 of the British North America Act, 1867*, [1928] SCR 276, discussed in chapter 4.
68 'Mayor Klein and the gays,' *Alberta Report*, 23 January 1981, 7.
69 As Adam, *Rise of Movement*, 130–1, points out, in some parts of the United States unprecedented numbers of gays and some lesbians have been elected or appointed to high public office. But the same thing has not happened anywhere in Canada.

70 Elizabeth Aird, 'Transsexual stands out in municipal race,' *Vancouver Sun*, 7 October 1996.
71 *Re Damien and Ontario Human Rights Commission* (1976), 12 OR (2d) 262 (Ont. Div Ct).
72 EGALE, Sexual Orientation Cases, reported that a Santa Claus association was required to modify its ad when it stipulated that recruits should not have homosexual tendencies. Commission des droits de la personne du Québec, *Bulletin*, File No. M-M 00, 040-257. But perhaps playing Santa Claus is not a public office?
73 In the federal Charter discussion paper, the Attorney General of Canada (by then, Hon. John Crosbie) gave these reasons for excluding queers from the military and intelligence forces: fear of offending the laws of other countries to which personnel might be posted; security risks; and the disruption to the institution that flows from violent attacks on gay personnel that their presence invites: Department of Justice, *Equality Issues in Federal Law: A Discussion Paper* (Ottawa: Department of Justice, 1985), 63 (Sessional Paper No. 331-4/6, tabled in the House of Commons on 31 January 1985). In the hearings before the Parliamentary Committee on Equality, the Chief Commissioner of the RCMP, R.H. Simmonds, stressed that in addition to all the other reasons for excluding queers from the RCMP, there was the very real concern that it would not be possible to 'manage' the RCMP if queers were hired: House of Commons, Minutes of Proceedings and Evidence of the Sub-Committee on Equality Rights of the Standing Committee on Justice and Legal Affairs, First Sess, 33rd Parl, 1984–5, Issue No. 6, 1-5-1985 6: 9 (Commr Simmonds).
74 See *R. v Sylvestre* (1986), 30 DLR (4th) 639 (FCA) (dismissal of lesbian from armed forces did not deprive her of 'liberty to be a homosexual' but merely of right to be in armed forces); *Stiles v Canada* (1986), 2 FTR 173 (FCTD), per Martin J (File No. T-2284-85, 20 March 1986) (denial of motion to stay action pending the outcome of a similar proceeding in Ontario); *Stiles v A.-G. Canada* (1986), 3 FTR 234 (FCTD), per Dubé J (File No. T-2284-85, 2 May 1986) (denial of transfer to CSIS on basis of sexuality settled); *Bordeleau v Canada* (1989), 32 FTR 21 (FCTD), Dubé J (settled); *Douglas v The Queen*, [1992] FCJ No. 1100 (FCTD) (QL), per MacKay J (action by lesbian settled); *Minister of National Defence v Security Intelligence Review Committee* (1990), 34 FTR 161 (FCTD), per Cullen J (earlier unsuccessful appeal in *Douglas*).
75 *Haig and Birch v The Queen* (1992), 9 OR (3d) 495 (Ont. CA), per Lacourcièr, Krever, and McKinlay JJ A; Canadian Human Rights Act, RSC 1985, c H-6.
76 File No. T-2396 (FCTD, 17 December 1991), aff'd File No. A-19-92 (FCA, 7 March 1994).

77 [1994] FCJ No. 364 (FCTD).
78 *Vriend* v *Alberta* (1998), 156 DLR (4th) 385 (SCC), per Cory and Iacobucci JJ, rev'g (1996), 132 DLR (4th) 595 (Alta. CA), per McClung, O'Leary, JJ A., Hunt JJ A. dissenting, rev'g [1994] 6 WWR 414 (Alta. QB).
79 See also *Fontaine* v *Canadian Pacific Ltd.*, [1989] CHRD No. 14 (Action No. T.D. 14/89) (Can Hum Rts Trib), in which a tribunal awarded damages to a Canadian Pacific cook who had been dismissed because of his HIV status. For a case comment on this ruling, see Sherry S. Liang, *'Centre d'Accueil Sainte-Domitile* v. *Union des Employes de Service, Local 298 (FTQ)*: A Case Comment' (1990), 2 *Education and Law Journal* 3: 342.
80 An Act to confer Civil Rights on Freedmen, Laws of Mississippi, 1865, c. IV, sections 1, 4:
81 *Seneca College of Applied Arts and Technology* v *Bhadauria*, [1981] 2 SCR 181; see also *Alpaerts* v *Obront* (1993), 45 CCEL 218 (Ont. Gen Div).
82 See Kerry Lobel, ed., *Naming the Violence: Speaking Out about Lesbian Battering* (Seattle: Seal Press, 1986).
83 See Eric Heinze, 'Gay and Poor,' (1995) *Howard Law Journal* 38: 433–48.
84 (1990), 59 CCC (3d) 432 (B.C. CA).
85 See also *R.* v *Taylor* (1982), 135 DLR (3d) 291 (Ont. CA), in which the court allowed a new trial because the trial court erred in treating the accused's admission that he was gay as having probative value in relation to guilt.
86 [1995] BCJ No. 1032 (B.C. SC) (QL), per Low J, aff'd [1998] BCJ No. 126 (B.C. CA) (QL), per McEachern CJBC, Cumming and Hollinrake JJ A.
87 *R.* c *P.(D.)*, File No. CA Québec 200-10-000105-937 (CAQ).
88 Section 626(2).
89 (1993), 84 CCC (3d) 353 (Ont. CA), per Krever, Doherty, and Abella, JJ A., leave to appeal denied, [1994] 1 SCR x.
90 The trial court judge had refused to allow such questions because potential jurors could be 'presumed' to do their duty and decide the facts without personal bias or prejudice once they had been duly chosen and sworn. *Parks* questions have become routine in cases involving raced defendants.
91 *R.* v *Alli*, [1996] OJ No. 3032 (Case No. C18720, 10 September 1996) (Ont. CA), per Doherty, Charron, and Moldaver JJ A.
92 *Alli* is summarized in Craig Harper, '*Parks* Challenge Not Extended to Other Minorities, Gays: Ont. C.A.,' *Lawyer's Weekly*, 11 October 1996, 13.
93 I am not to be taken as subscribing to the 'public–private' dichotomy, because 'public' laws are fully constitutive of so-called private rights, but I am using this terminology here out of expediency.
94 See for example Code of Alabama, 1852, Title 13, chs. 3 and 4, section 983-998 ('Patrols').

95 See for example Ellen Faulkner, *Anti-Gay/Lesbian Violence in Toronto: The Impact on Individuals and Communities* (Ottawa: Department of Justice Canada, 1997) (Technical Report TR1997-5e), unique in that it collected data from bisexual and transgendered persons as well as from lesbians and gays, found high lifetime rates of violence, ranging from 78 per cent experiencing verbal assaults to 21 per cent being battered, 21 per cent experiencing harassment by police, and 7 per cent being assaulted with a weapon. The reported cases demonstrate that anti–gay/lesbian violence is often extremely vicious and even fatal: See Canadian Bar Association (Ontario), *Submission on Bill C-41* (Ottawa: CBA, 1995). Gary D. Comstock, *Violence against Lesbians and Gay Men* (New York: Columbia University Press, 1991), has collected data on perpetrators as well as on victims in this U.S. study.

96 Bill C-41, adding section 718.2 to the Criminal Code. This was thought to be necessary because very few courts ever directly addressed the 'hate crime' nature of attacks on queers. One of the few cases to have done so is *R. v Atkinson, Ing and Roberts* (1979), 43 CCC (2d) 342 (Ont. CA), in which the court increased the sentence because of the 'gay bashing' nature of the assaults.

97 See for example 'Two men arrested in St. Catharines gay-bashing,' *Québec–Ontario Regional General News*, 20 June 1995 (two accuseds allegedly went out for the purpose of 'fag' bashing); 'Gay-bashing psycho,' *Western Regional General News*, 3 June 1995 (Vancouver gay community concerned over police failure to locate murder suspect).

98 A recent human rights case has taken hate propaganda against sexual minorities very seriously: See *McAleer v Canada (H.R.C.)*, [1996] 2 FC 345, 132 DLR (4th) 672 (FCTD), per Joyal J, aff'd [1996] 1 FC 804 (FCA), per Pratte, Strayer, and Linden JJ A, aff'd [1998] SCJ No. 31 (SCC), per L'Heureux-Dubé, Gonthier, McLachlin, Major, and Bastarache JJ (9 April 1998), sub nom *Canada (Canadian Human Rights Commission) v Canadian Liberty Net*.

99 The leading works are Lobel, *Naming the Violence*, and David Island, *Men Who Beat Men Who Love Them* (New York: Harrington Park, 1991). See also RuthAnn Robson, 'The Violence among Us,' in *Lesbian (Out)Law: Survival Under the Rule of Law* (New York: Firebrand, 1992), ch. 12, documenting historical and contemporary disregard, distortion, or minimization of violence between lesbian women. Claire M. Renzetti, 'Building a Second Closet: Third party Responses to Victims of Lesbian Partner Abuse' (1988), 38 *Family Relations* 157–63, has documented how the tendency of lesbian communities to disbelieve victims of lesbian battering and to support batterers compounds such abuse.

100 Vital Statistics Act, RSO 1990, c V-4, section 36; Vital Statistics Act, RSBC 1974, c 66, section 21; Vital Statistics Act, RSA 1980, c 384, section 21.1. Under Vital Statistics Act, RSQ 1979, c 10, sections 16–22, the change of legal sex applies only from the date of the court order.
101 Vital Statistics Act (Ont.), section 36.
102 See *Re Reid* (1986), 56 OR (2d) 61 (Ont. Dist Ct), per Vannini DCJ, in which a pre-surgical male who planned to have transsexual surgery was permitted to legally adopt female names to permit him to begin living as a woman.
103 *B. v A.* (1990), 1 OR (3d) 569 (Ont.), per Cork, Master (bilateral mastectomy, pan-hysterectomy, and full hormonal treatment did not entitle woman to change legal sex to male); *Canada v Owen*, [1993] FCJ No. 1263 (FCTD), per Rouleau J, rev'g Old Age Security Review Board (unreported) (woman denied Old Age Security surviving spouse allowance when disclosed that she had not had final transsexual surgery; *L.C. v C.C.* (1992), 10 OR (3d) 254 (Ont. Gen Div), per Jenkins J (marriage declared void *ab initio* when woman decided not to have final transsexual surgery).
104 In *Sherwood Atkinson (Sheri de Cartier)*, (1972), 5 Imm App Cases 185 (Imm App Bd), a male-to-female transsexual person who related to men was considered to be 'homosexual.'
105 *Gay Alliance Toward Equality* v *Vancouver Sun* (1979), 27 NR 117 (SCC), aff'g [1977] 5 WWR 198 (B.C. CA). A board of inquiry had initially found in favour of the complainants under human rights legislation, but the Court of Appeal had reversed the board.
106 See for example *Commission des droits de la personne du Québec c Le Progrès du Saguenay Ltée et Paul Bergeron*, File No. 150-02-000354-79 (CPQ, 24 April 1979) (complaint arising out of newspaper refusal to public advertisement for gay conference settled out of court); *Commission des droits de la personne du Québec*, File M-M-02, 325-1 was also settled (7 September 1980) (newspaper refused to publish advertisement for gay club).
107 *C.D.P.Q.* v *Anglsberger* (1982), 3 CHRR D/892 (CPQ) (transsexual man received damages for refusal of service in restaurant; decision based on 'civil status').
108 *Commission des droits de la personne du Québec*, File No. Q-Q -1, 018-1, 019-1 (no date).
109 Christopher Lefler Complaint, Saskatchewan Human Rights Commission, filed in October 1996 (discussed in EGALE, Sexual Orientation Cases), arose when the University of Saskatchewan removed a gay man's art from a student exhibition.
110 See *Haig v Durrell*, [1990] OJ No. 1350 (Ont. H Ct J) (QL), per Austin J;

Oliver v *Hamilton (City) (No. 2)* (1995), 24 CHRR D/298 (Ont. Bd of Inq) (mayor's refusal to proclaim Gay Pride Week discriminated on the basis of sexual orientation).

111 In *Reimer* v *Saskatchewan Human Rights Commission*, [1991] SJ No. 360 (QBM No. 425 of AD 1991 JCR) (QB), per Wimmer J, the court granted a writ of prohibition against the commission, barring its inquiry, because the applicant had produced some evidence suggesting pro-gay bias on the part of one commission staff and because of the publicity surrounding the issue, which the applicant claimed had been generated improperly by the complainants. In *Reimer* v *Saskatchewan Human Rights Commission*, [1992] SJ No. 547 (Appeal No. 954) (CA), per Bayda, Vancise, and Jackson JJ A, the Court of Appeal lifted the order of prohibition and awarded costs to the appellant. Thus it was not until the board of inquiry could rule on the complaint that the issue was resolved. See *Geller* v *Reimer* (1994), 21 CHRR D/156 (Sask. Bd of Inq), which ruled that denial of a parade permit violated freedom of expression and right to peaceful assembly on the basis of sexual orientation.

112 *Hudler* v *London (City)*, [1997] OHRBID No. 23 (Ont. Bd of Inq) (QL), per McKeller, Bd.

113 Ken Watson, 'City Council Refuses Pride Day,' *PIC Press Kingston*, July 1991, 1.

114 *Re Priape Enrg. and M.N.R.* (1979), 52 CCC (2d) 44 (Que. SC).

115 [1992] 1 SCR 452 (SCC).

116 See *Little Sisters Book and Art Emporium* v *The Queen*, [1992] BCJ No. 2351 (B.C. SC), per Collver J (application to strike out statement of claim on basis of Charter sections 15 and 2(b) dismissed; (1996), 131 DLR (4th) (B.C. SC), appeal pending (Customs Act did not violate Charter, but Customs application of the legislation did); (1996), 134 DLR (4th) 293 (B.C. SC) (court subsequently enjoined Customs Canada from continuing to systematically inspect plaintiff's deliveries); *Glad Day Bookshop Inc.* v *M.N.R.* (1992), 90 DLR (4th) 527 (Ont. Ct J–Gen Div), per Hayes J (Charter section 2 not violated because 'some' of the material was 'degrading' and the dominant characteristics in 'some of them' was 'undue exploitation of sex). See also *R.* v *Pink Triangle Press Inc.* (1980), 51 CCC (2d) 485 (Ont. Co Ct), vacating acquittal in (1979), 45 CCC (2d) 385 (Ont. Prov Ct) and ordering new trial. Although I find paedophilia unacceptable in both heterosexual and lesbian/gay material, the standard applied by the Crown in this case clearly was stricter than that applied to similar heterosexual material. Even quick perusal of the sexual- fantasy columns and other material in magazines like *Playboy* or *Hustler* makes that obvious.

117 (1996), 131 DLR (4th) (B.C. SC), appeal pending.
118 *Little Sisters Book and Art Emporium* v *The Queen*, (1996), 134 DLR (4th) 293 (B.C. SC).
119 (1990), 66 DLR (4th) 444 (B.C. SC), per Coultas J. *Brown* is one of the few cases that refer to bisexuals, although the term seems to have been used as a synonym for 'homosexual.'
120 See also *Wood* v *Hinkel*, [1994] BCJ No. 2104 (B.C. SC), dismissing an appeal from a board award of damages to a complainant with AIDS whose dentist had refused to treat him.
121 [1995] OJ No. 2361 (Ont. Gen Div) (QL), per Wilson J, aff'd [1996] OJ No. 4184 (OCA) (QL), per Morden ACJO, Catzman, and Carthy JJ A.
122 The fact that blood donors had not given express or implied consent to HIV testing years after making their donations was held not to bar testing or distribution of results. Charter guarantees were considered to have been 'justifiably' violated in this situation.
123 (1996), 134 DLR (4th) 437 (B.C. SC), aff'g (1995), 23 CHRR D/319 (Bd of Inq).
124 (1995), 127 DLR (4th) 738, 25 OR (3d) 612 (Ont. Gen Div), per Charron J, rev'd [1998] OJ No. 1627 (OCA) (QL), per McKinley, Abella, and Goudge JJ A.
125 *Commission des droits de la personne du Québec* c *Camping & plage Gilles Fortie Inc.*, File No. 95-287 (P.Q. TD) (campground denying accommodation to two *or* more adults of same sex unless part of family group violated Québec Charter); *L'Association A.D.G.Q.* c *La Commission des écoles catholiques de Montréal* (1979), 112 DLR (3d) 230, [1980] CS 93 (CSQ) (Catholic school's refusal to rent school facilities to gay group when other community groups had rented it violated Québec Charter).
126 With notable exceptions, of course. The Indian Act still deprives Aboriginal persons of most of the legal capacities of persons, to give just one example.
127 *525044 Alberta Ltd. (c.o.b. Tony C's 21 Club & Restaurant)* v *Triple 5 Corp.*, [1993] AJ No. 728 (Action No. 9303-17350) (Alta. QB), per McDonald J.
128 [1993] OJ No. 2610 (Action Nos. 92-L-42090, 92-L-43302) (Ont. Ct of J–Gen Div), per Sutherland J.
129 After the complainants filed with the Human Rights Commission and refused to pay rent because of the harassment, their landlord made an application to terminate their tenancy. The court refused to stay the landlord's action until the human rights complaint could be resolved on the basis of the tenants' health status, but ordered them to pay only half the amount of rent they had withheld. The court did order a stay of judgment pending the outcome of the human rights complaint. For a thorough review of the issues and legal literature relating to sexual minorities and

HIV/AIDS, see Ralf Jürgens, *Legal and Ethical Issues Raised by HIV/AIDS; Literature Review and Annotated Bibliography* (Montreal: Canadian AIDS Society, 1995), especially 21–6, 88–92, and cases collected therein.
130 *Janz v Harris*, [1993] MJ No. 262 (Action No. FD 90-01-24244) (Man. QB Fam Div), per Goodman J. However, the court did award lump-sum support out of the proceeds of the sale of the matrimonial home, which it described as a 'reasonable alternative.' See also *Gillis v Gillis* (1980), 14 RFL (2d) 147 (P.E.I. SC), in which the lesbianism of the former wife did not affect her right to receive an equal share of the family assets in question.
131 (1986), 50 RFL (2d) 127 (B.C. CA).
132 The children had been conceived through artificial insemination while the couple were together.
133 The court described the defendant as being merely a 'third party to the children and their mother.' Cf. *W. v G.* (N.S.W. S Ct, 1996), ordering a former lesbian partner to pay $150,000 in a lump sum to the biological mother of their two children. The award was calculated to cover expenses relating to the two children until they reached adulthood. The award was based not on statute, but on promissory estoppel, after the court accepted evidence that the defendant had implicitly promised to support the children while the two women were together.
134 See also *Forrest v Price* (1992), 48 ETR 72 (B.C. SC), per Boyd J (similar facts re gay couple). In *Brunet v Davis*, [1992] OJ 1586 (Ont. Gen Div) (Action No. 4633/89, 16 April 1992), the court awarded one gay partner a 25 per cent interest in the profit on a building the two of them had renovated together, based on their relative contributions to labour and materials.
135 (1996), 27 OR (3d) 593, 132 DLR (4th) 538 (Ont. Gen Div), Epstein J, aff'd (1996), 31 OR (3d) 417, 142 DLR (4th) 1 (Ont. CA), per Doherty and Charron J, Finlayson J dissenting, leave to appeal granted 24 April 1997, per L'Heureux-Dubé, Sopinka, and Iacobucci JJ, on condition that government pay all costs in any event of the cause. See also *M. v H.* (1994), 17 OR (3d) 118 (Ont. Gen Div), per Epstein J (dismissing motion by defendant for summary judgment); (1994), 20 OR (3d) 70 (other couples with similar claims denied intervenor status).
136 *M. v H.* (1993), 15 OR (3d) 721 (Ont. Gen Div), per Epstein J.
137 RSO 1990, c F.3.
138 This was accomplished by cases like *Rathwell v Rathwell*, [1978] 2 SCR 436, and, in Ontario, the matrimonial home provisions of statutes like the Family Law Reform Act, 1978, SO 1978, c 2.
139 See *Pettkus v Becker*, [1980] 2 SCR 834 (SCC).
140 (1990), 1 OR (3d) 569 (Ont.), per Cork, Master.

141 *Sleeth* v *Wasserlein* (1991), 36 RFL (3d) 278 (B.C. SC).
142 [1996] OJ No. 3181 (Ont. Gen Div) (File No. 01-1716/95, 15 August 1996), per Sheard J.
143 Estates Act, RSO 1990, c E.21, section 29.
144 Succession Law Reform Act, RSO 1990, c S.26, section 44.
145 Family Law Act, RSO 1990, c F.3, section 5.
146 Succession Law Reform Act, Part V.
147 *Re Layland and Beaulne* (1993), 14 OR (3d) 658 (Ont. Ct [Gen Div] Div Ct), per Southey, Sirois, and Greer JJ, leave to appeal granted Ontario Court of Appeal (7 June 1993); appeal withdrawn (1995) (this case is discussed in detail below).
148 (1980), 17 RFL (2d) 376, Kurisko DCJ. The formula looks to some twenty-two factual points relating to these seven relationship features: shelter; sexual and personal behaviour; services; social activities; societal presentation; economic support; and children.
149 Unless, perhaps, one residence were maintained strictly in order to facilitate child access: See *Thauvette* v *Malyon*, unreported (Ont. Gen Div, 4 April 1996), per Roy J, which the court in *Obringer* distinguished from being separated by employment and nationality without legal possibility of sponsored immigration.
150 20 App Div 2d 464, 247 NYS 2d 664 (1964), aff'd 15 N.Y. 2d 825, 205 NE 2d 874 (N.Y. SC, 1965).
151 In *In re Kaufman's Will*, a New York court held that the will of a wealthy gay man which left the bulk of his estate to his partner of ten years was invalid because of undue influence. This decision is widely regarded by commentators in the United States as reflecting homophobia at the level of applying the doctrine of undue influence. See, for example, Jeffrey G. Sherman, 'Undue Influence and the Homosexual Testator' (1981), 42 *Pittsburgh Law Review* 2250; Roberta Achtenberg, *Sexual Orientation and the Law* (New York: Clark Boardman, 1989), 405; 'Existence of Illicit or Unlawful Relation Between Testator and Beneficiary as Evidence of Undue Influence' (1977), 76 *American Law Reports* 3d; *Estate of Spaulding*, 83 Cal. App 2d 15, 187 P 2d 889 (194); *In re Anonymous*, 75 Misc 2d 133, 347 NYS 2d 263 (1973).
152 (1993), 80 BCLR 2d 393 (B.C. SC).
153 See *Patterson* v *Lauritsen*, [1984] 6 WWR 329 (B.C. SC), which documents the existence of this prejudice in relation to testamentary dispositions generally. In that case, a deceased mother had excluded her son from her will because of homosexuality and drug addiction; however, the court ruled that disinheritance on the basis of sexual orientation was unjustified,

and that there was no evidence that the son was in fact addicted to drugs; thus he received an equal share of the estate along with his siblings.
154 *Vriend v Alberta*, [1994] 6 WWR 414 (Alta. QB), per Russell J, rev'd (1996), 132 DLR (4th) 595, 18 CCEL. (2d) 1 (Alta. CA), per McClung, O'Leary, JJ A, reinstated (1998), 156 DLR (4th) 385 (SCC).
155 RSA 1980, c I-2.
156 (1992), 18 CHRR D/176 (Ont. Bd of Inq).
157 [1995] BCJ No. 1203 (Action No. C906406) (B.C. SC), per Hood J.
158 (1994), 45 LAC (4th) 71.
159 (1994), 22 CHRR D/244 (Ont. Bd of Inq).
160 But cf. *A. v Colloredo-Mansfeld (No. 3)* (1994), 23 CHRR D/328 (Ont. Bd of Inq), in which a board concluded that it did not have jurisdiction over sexual-orientation harassment of employees because sexual orientation was omitted from the protected grounds in the harassment clause of the Ontario Human Rights Act.
161 *Case C-13/94* (Ct of J of the EC, Luxembourg, 30 April 1996) The Times Law Report (7 May 1996).
162 *Case v Case* (1974), 18 RFL 132 (Sask. QB); *Bezaire v Bezaire* (1981), 20 RFL (2d) 358 (Ont. CA); *Monette c Sylvestre*, [1981] CS 731.
163 *Droit de la famille-31* (1983), 34 RFL (2d) 127 (CSQ).
164 *Bezaire v Bezaire* (1981), 20 RFL (2d) 358 (Ont. CA).
165 *Monk v Doan* (1990), 94 Sask. Rev 316 (Sask. QB) (custody given to lesbian aunt who was in a 'discreet' and 'dignified' long-term relationship).
166 *Elliott v Elliott* (1984), 25 ACWS (2d) 304 (B.C. SC) (father who was engaged received custody even though lesbian mother was already living in a 'discreet' relationship); *Elliott v Elliott*, [1987] BCJ No. 43 (Richmond No. 57-83) (B.C. SC) (seventeen-year-old son helped convince court to make mother's custody of younger sister contingent upon living alone).
167 *S. v S.*, [1992] BCJ No. 1579 (Action No. 02278 (Cranbrook)) (B.C. SC) (lesbian mother who wanted to relocate denied custody because court concerned how relationships she might form in future would affect children); *Boucher v Boucher* (1986), 72 NBR (2d) 100 (N.B. QB) (husband denied custody because other 'homosexual acts' had resulted in criminal record and loss of employment; court concerned with effect of potential unemployment on children).
168 *Bernhardt v Bernhardt* (1979), 10 RFL (2d) 32 (Man. QB).
169 *K. v K.* (1976), 23 RFL 58 (Alta. Prov Ct); *B. v B.* (1980), 16 RFL (2d) 7 (Ont. Prov Ct); *Droit de la famille-14*, File No. 750-12-002454-82 (CSQ, 22 December 1982); *Daller v Daller* (1988), 18 RFL (3d) 53, 22 RFL (3d) 96 (Ont. CA); *N. v N.* [1992] BCJ No. 1507 (Vancouver No. D076135) (B.C. SC).

170 *Palmer* v *Palmer* (1981), 15 Sask. R 20 (Sask. QB) (former alcoholic mother in heterosexual relationship given custody in preference to unemployed father with 'homosexual tendencies').
171 *Robertson* v *Geisinger* (1991), 36 RFL (3d) 261 (Sask. QB) (court based decision on best interests of child).
172 *Worby* v *Worby* (1985), 48 RFL (2d) 369 (Sask. QB); *Saunders* v *Saunders* (1989), 20 RFL (3d) 368 (B.C. Co Ct), per Wetmore, Co Ct J; *E.(A.)* v *E.(G.)* (1989), 77 Nfld. & P.E.I. R; 240 APR 142 (Nfld. UFC). In *Worby*, the court also required the father to see his children either at the mother's home or in public places, because the court agreed with the mother that the father's 'lifestyle' could be 'harmful,' 'highly confusing, disruptive, and contrary to their moral upbringing.'
173 *P.B.* v *P.B.* (Ont. Prov Ct Fam Div, 6 April 1988).
174 *Johnston* v *Rochette* (1982), 27 RFL (2d) 380 (Que. SC).
175 [1992] NJ No. 133 (Action No. 1002/1991, F/91/0278) (Nfld. SC Unif Fam Ct, 15 May 1992).
176 *D.* v *D.* (1978), 3 RFL (2d) 327 (Ont. Co Ct).
177 Doc. A5602/94 (Ont. Gen Div, 9 May 1996).
178 [1995] BCJ No. 2136 (Nanaimo No. 5920/009596 (B.C. SC, 11 October 1995).
179 [1990] BCJ No 1487 (B.C. SC, 27 June 1990).
180 [1994] BCJ No. 2824 (Quesnel No. 5869) (B.C. SC, 6 December 1994), per de Villiers Prov Ct J.
181 (Unreported) File No. 195/89 (Ont. Prov Ct Prov Div), per Pedlar J.
182 See also *Holtzman* v *Knott*, 520 NW 2d 91 (Wis. SC, 1994), per Abrahamson, J, cert den. 116 S Ct 475 (U.S. SC, 1995), in which the Supreme Court ruled that a non-biological co-mother of an AI child was permitted to seek visitation of her son. The Court based its ruling on its equitable power to protect the best interest of a child by ordering visitation under circumstances not included in the statute. The Court ruled that a 'parent-like relationship' would be recognized when four elements were factually established: (1) that the biological or adoptive parent consented to and fostered the formation of a parent-like relationship with the child, (2) that the petitioner and child lived together in the same household, (3) that the petitioner assumed significant obligations of parenthood without expectation of financial compensation, and (4) and that the relationship was of sufficient time to become a 'bonded, dependent relationship parental in nature.'
183 [1997] OJ No. 2646 (Ont. Gen Div) (QL), per Benotto J.
184 *Re K.* (1995), 23 OR (3d) 679 (Ont. Prov Div), per Nevins Prov Div J.
185 This ruling has been followed in *Re C.E.G. (No. 1)*, [1995] OJ No. 4072 (Ont. Ct of J–Gen Div), per Aston J (17 August 1995).

186 See *W. v G.* (New South Wales, unreported, 1996), in which a trial court ordered lump-sum child support of $150,000 for two children on the basis of an implied promise to support.

187 [1994] BCJ No. 485 (Vancouver Action No. F03410) (B.C.Prov Ct), per Collings Prov Ct J.

188 Cf. *Benson v Korn*, [1995] CHRR D/319 (4 August 1995) (B.C. Council of Human Rights), per Patch, Council Member, which held that a doctor's refusal to provide artificial insemination to a lesbian couple constituted discrimination on the basis of sexual orientation under British Columbia human rights legislation.

189 No. 21380/93 (Eur Comm Hum Rts, 27 June 1995).

190 For further discussion of this issue, see chapter ten.

191 *North v Matheson* (1974), 20 RFL 112, 53 DLR (3d) 280 (Man. Co Ct) (denial of capacity to marry did not violate Manitoba Human Rights Act); *Re Layland and Beaulne* (1993), 14 OR (3d) 658 (Ont. Ct [Gen Div] Div Ct), per Southey, Sirois, and Greer JJ, leave to appeal granted by the Ontario Court of Appeal (7 June 1993); appeal withdrawn (1995) (denial of marriage certificate to two gay men did not violate section 15[1] of the Charter because homosexuals can marry persons of the opposite sex, and because lack of legal capacity is simply natural consequence of lack of procreative capacity).

192 *Re Treasury Board (Public Works) and Hewens* (1992), 28 CLAS 627 (Pub Serv Staff Rels Bd).

193 See *Canada v Owen*, [1993] FCJ No. 1263 (FCTD), per Rouleau J; *C.L. v C.C.* (1992), 10 OR (3d) 254 (Ont. Gen Div), per Jenkins J; *B. v A.* (1990), 1 OR (3d) 569, per Cork, Master; *M. v M.* (1984), 42 RFL (2d) 55 (P.E.I. SC).

194 *Corbett v Corbett*, [1970] 2 All ER 33, per Ormond J, which was followed in the first marriage case in Canada, *North and Matheson* (1974), 20 RFL 112, 53 DLR (3d) 280 (Man. Co Ct).

195 [1993] FCJ No. 1263 (FCTD), per Rouleau J, rev'g Old Age Sec Rev Bd (unreported).

196 *Van Vulpen v M.E.I.*, File No. V-79-6100 (Imm App Bd, 29 August 1980), rev'd No. A-179-81 (FCA, 1982), per Thurlow, Heald, and Primrose JJ A; *Sherwood Atkinson (Sheri de Cartier)* (1972), 5 Imm App Cases 185 (Imm App Bd).

197 The court in *Re Layland and Beaulne* (1993), 14 OR (3d) 658 (Ont. Ct [Gen Div] Div Ct), per Southey, Sirois, and Greer JJ, leave to appeal granted by the Ontario Court of Appeal (7 June 1993); appeal withdrawn (1995), has held that lesbians and gays do have the legal capacity to formally marry people of the opposite sex, so this would presumably cover the recognition as an opposite-sex cohabitant as well.

198 The earlier decision in *Mossop* v *Canada (Sec'y State)*, [1993] 1 SCR 554 (SCC), also established that same-sex relationships do not fall within the meaning of 'family status' in federal human rights legislation. This was a pre-Charter case.
199 [1995] 2 SCR 418 (SCC), per McLachlin J.
200 (1995), 126 DLR (4th) 72 (Man. CA), per Scott CJM, Philp, and Helper JJ A, rev'g (1992), 90 DLR (4th) 84, 79 Man. R (2d) 208, per Hirschfield J [*Vogel II*].
201 [1994] BCJ No. 2588 (Action No. A893414) (B.C. SC), per Rowles J.
202 The Federal Court of Appeal ruled in *Veysey* v *Correctional Service of Canada*, (1990), 109 NR 300 (FCA), per Iacobucci CJ, Urie, and Decary JJ, aff'g on different ground (1989), 29 FTR 74 (FCTD), per Dubé J, that a gay male penitentiary inmate's partner was improperly excluded from the 'private family visiting program' established by Corrections Canada. This decision was based on section 15(1) of the Charter at the trial court level, but the appellate court affirmed on the basis that the program guidelines were drafted so loosely that they could include 'relatives' that went beyond 'the traditional family circle' to include even 'uncles and godfathers.' Thus this case is of limited value as a precedent on the recognition of same-sex relationships.
203 See Family Relations Amendment Act, 1997, SBC 1997, 2d sess, 36th Parl, 46 Eliz. II, 1997 [Bill 31], passed third reading 23 July 1997, which includes same-sex partners in the definition of 'spouse' for purposes of most family-related legislation in British Columbia. Also consider the inclusion of the term 'partner' in Substitute Decisions Act, 1992, SO 1992, sections 1(2), 10(2), which is defined as follows: 'Two persons are partners for the purpose of this Act if they have lived together for at least one year and have a close personal relationship that is of primary importance in both persons' lives.' And see the new policy for free airline travel for members of Parliament, which replaced the term 'spouse' with the term 'designated traveller': Tim Naumetz, 'Free travel for MPs' spouses now includes gay partners,' *Ottawa Citizen*, 6 December 1997, A5.
204 See Ontario Law Reform Commission, *Report on the Rights and Responsibilities of Cohabitants Under the Family Law Act* (Toronto: LRCO, 1993), 43–5.
205 See *Connolly* v *Woolrich* (1867), 11 LC Jur 197; *Johnstone* v *Connolly* (1869), 17 RJRQ 266; cf. *Jones* v *Fraser* (1886), 12 QLR 327 (Que. QB), aff'd in passing (1886), 13 SCR 342, in which one member of the court insisted that the Christian ideal of marriage should be applied to the exclusion of customary marriage: 'In Christian countries ... marriage ... is the union for life of one man with one woman, to the exclusion of all others; any intercourse without these distinctive qualities cannot amount to a Christian marriage.'

206 See Walter Williams, *The Spirit and the Flesh: Sexual Diversity in American Indian Culture* (Boston: Beacon, 1986), 94–5; Will Roscoe, *The Zuni Man–Woman* (Albuquerque: University of New Mexico Press, 1991) (describing the Zuni berdache).
207 E.E. Evans-Pritchard, 'Sexual Inversion among the Azande' (1970), 72 *American Anthropologist* 1428–34.
208 E.E. Evans-Pritchard, *Kinship and Marriage among the Nuer* (Oxford: Clarendon Press, 1951), at 108–9. According to Ngozi Oti, 'The History of Gay and Lesbian Marriages' (paper prepared for 1995 Law and Sexuality seminar), 12, the validity of customary Ibo 'woman marriages' has been upheld in 1978 and 1981 Edicts of the Customary Courts in Anambra State and Imo State, Nigeria.
209 Robert J. Morris, 'Configuring the Bo(u)nds of Marriage: The Implications of Hawaiian Culture and Values for the Debate about Homogamy' (1996), 8 *Yale Journal of Law and the Humanities* 105, at 118, 127, 133–6, 143. Morris documents the long-standing recognition of aikāne relationships (aikāne are the partners in a same-sex relationship) in Hawai'ian premodern customary law. As Morris recounts, aikāne can achieve marriage by adoption or cohabitation plus intent, and acceded to all the incidents of marriage, including inheritance rights, agency, inclusion in the partner's family of origin, raising children, and being considered to be a relative.
210 See generally Boswell, *Same-Sex Unions*, xxvi, especially references collected in notes 17–25.

Chapter Six: Counting Queers

1 As John Maynard Keynes observed, people who are still trying to get enough to eat and stay warm are not really concerned with much else: See J.M. Keynes, 'Economic Possibilities for Our Grandchildren,' in *Essays in Persuasion* (London: Macmillan, 1931), 358–73.
2 *Egan and Nesbit v The Queen*, [1995] 2 SCR 513.
3 For an excellent version of these arguments, see Herek, 'The Tyranny of the 10%: Does it Really Matter How Many Americans are Gay?' *The Advocate*, 1 August 1989, 46, 48. See also Arnold Bruner, 'Sexual Orientation and Equality Rights,' in *Equality Rights and the Canadian Charter of Rights and Freedoms*, ed. Anne Bayefsky and Mary Eberts (Toronto: Carswell, 1985), 457–92, at 458 note 4, who suggests that it is really not worthwhile to try to go beyond the general 10 per cent figure ordinarily used.
4 Personal communication; I have not received permission to name the source.

Notes to pages 175–8   413

5 See Statistics Canada, *1996 Census Consultation Report number 2* (Ottawa: Statistics Canada, 1997), 18–19.
6 Maureen Baker, *Canadian Family Policies: Cross-National Comparisons* (Toronto: University of Toronto Press, 1995).
7 Ibid., 9–10.
8 Justice Sopinka's 'novelty' contention is a variant of the 'too few to matter' view: [1995] 2 SCR, at 576.
9 Justice Scalia made a variation on this argument in his dissenting opinion in *Romer v Evans*, 116 S Ct 1620, at 1630.
10 *Andrews v Minister of Health* (1988), 64 OR (2d) 258 (HCJ).
11 *Layland v Ontario (Minister of Consumer & Commercial Relations)* (1993), 14 OR (3d) 658, [1993] OJ No. 575 (Ont. Div Ct), per Southey, Sirois (concurring), and Greer JJ (dissenting).
12 [1996] Westlaw 694235, 1996 Haw App LEXIS 138 (Haw Cir Ct, 1st Cir, 3 Dec. 1996), per Chang J, aff'g *Baehr v Lewin*, 74 Haw 530, 852 P 2d 44 (1993), clarified on grant of reconsideration in part, 74 Haw 645, 852 P 2d 74 (1993).
13 For a current example, see Respondent's Factum in *Rosenberg v A.-G. Canada* (Ont. CA File No. C22807), paragraphs 47–9, which laid the basis for assertions about numbers that eventually resulted in unquestioned judicial assertions. See statements by the courts in *Rosenberg v Canada* (1995), 127 DLR (4th) 738, 25 OR (3d) 612 (Ont. Gen Div), per Charron J, rev'd [1998] OJ No. 1627 (OCA) (QL), per McKinley, Abella, and Goudge JJ A.
14 Alfred C. Kinsey, Wardell B. Pomeroy, and Clyde E. Martin, *Sexual Behavior in the Human Male* (Philadelphia: W.B. Saunders, 1948); Alfred C. Kinsey, Wardell B. Pomeroy, Clyde E. Martin, and P.H. Gebhard, *Sexual Behavior in the Human Female* (Philadelphia: W.B. Saunders, 1953).
15 Kinsey et al., *Sexual Behavior in the Human Male*, 651.
16 Ibid., 650.
17 Defined as two to six homosexual experiences during a three-year period between ages sixteen and fifty-five: ibid.
18 Ibid., 651.
19 Ibid., 357–61, 610–66.
20 Kinsey et al., *Sexual Behavior in the Human Female*, 474–5.
21 Drawn from table in John C. Gonsiorek and James D. Weinrich, 'The Definition and Scope of Sexual Orientation,' in *Homosexuality: Research Implications for Public Policy*, ed. John C. Gonsiorek and James D. Weinrich (Newbury Park, CA: Sage, 1991), 1–12, at 3. The table itself was taken from another source that summarized the Kinsey results.
22 For discussions of methodological issues raised by the Kinsey studies, see

William G. Cochran, *Statistical Problems of the Kinsey Report on Sexual Behaviour in the Homosexual Male: A Report of the American Statistical Association Committee to Advise the National Research Council Committee for Research in Problems of Sex* (New York: Greenwood Press, n.d.); John Bancroft, ed., *Researching Sexual Behaviour: Methodological Issues* (Bloomington: Indiana University Press, 1997); Liz Stanley, *Sex Surveyed, 1949–1994: From Mass-Observation's 'Little Kinsey' to the National Survey and the Hite Reports* (London: Taylor & Francis, 1995) (feminist perspectives on sex surveys). For an engaging biography of Kinsey's life and critique of his work, see James H. Jones, *Alfred C. Kinsey: A Public/Private Life* (New York: W.W. Norton, 1997).

23 P.H. Gebhard, 'Incidence of Overt Homosexuality in the United States and Western Europe,' in *NIMH Task Force on Homosexuality: Final Report and Background Papers* (Rockville, MD: National Institute of Mental Health, 1972). Gebhard was one of the Kinsey collaborators in the 1950s.

24 J.K. Meyer, 'Ego-dystonic Homosexuality,' in *Comprehensive Textbook of Psychiatry*, ed. H. Kaplan and B. Sadock, 1056–65 (Baltimore, MD: Williams and Wilkins, 1985).

25 Cited in M.V. Lee Badgett, 'The Wage Effects of Sexual Orientation Discrimination' (1995), *Industrial and Labor Relations Review* 48(4): 726–39, at 728.

26 R.L. Sell, J.A. Wells, A.-J. Valleron, A. Will, M. Cohan, and K. Umbel, 'Homosexual and Bisexual Behaviour in the United States, the United Kingdom and France' San Francisco, Sixth International AIDS Conference, 1990.

27 'Percentage of gay men difficult to assess,' *National General News*, 21 April 1993.

28 Edward O. Laumann, John H. Gagnon, Robert T. Michael, and Stuart Michaels, *The Social Organization of Sexuality: Sexual Practices in the United States* (Chicago: University of Chicago Press, 1994), 293.

29 Carol Ness, '3.2% of U.S. Voters are Gay, Survey Reports,' *San Francisco Examiner*, 25 April 1996, 1.

30 'Homosexual Attraction Is Found in 1 of 5,' *New York Times*, 6 September 1994, A12.

31 Gonsiorek and Weinrich, 'Definition,' 4–5.

32 Laumann et al., *Social Organization*, 292–301.

33 Ibid.

34 Ibid., 295.

35 Sell et al. 'Homosexual Behaviour.' See also Laumann et al., *Social Organization*, 295, who reported that 4 per cent of the women in their sample had indicated that they had had sex with another woman sometime since

turning eighteen, but that the response level fell to a little over 2 per cent when asked about the last five years, and to approximately 1.3 per cent in relation to the year immediately before being interviewed.
36 Kenneth S. Sherrill, Testimony in *Equality Foundation of Greater Cincinnati, Inc.* v *City of Cincinnati*, No. C-1-93-0773, 16 June 1994 (U.S. DC, Ohio So Dist, West Div).
37 Sherrill, Testimony, para. 29, citing Kinsey et al., *Sexual Behavior in the Human Male*, 53.
38 After Elisabeth Noelle-Neumann, *The Spiral of Silence* (Chicago: University of Chicago Press, 1984), 6–7. Noelle-Neumann concluded that research subjects who feel that their opinions are unpopular are afraid to reveal them even in a research context, for fear of isolation or retaliation.
39 Voter Research and Services, 6 November 1990, conducting research for ABC, CBS, CNN, and NBC television networks.
40 Cf. Philip Blumstein and Pepper Schwartz, *American Couples* (New York: Pocket Books, 1983), Table 17, 602, in which the authors report that 36 per cent of gay men and 23 per cent of lesbian women indicated on their questionnaire that they 'do not care who knows I am gay.' The relative openness of these respondents may have to do with the fact that these couples were sufficiently open to have formed a long-term intimate relationship, and were so open that they voluntarily participated in the Blumstein–Schwartz study.
41 Sherrill, Testimony, para. 34.
42 The practice of keeping lists of queers appears to have originated with the Third Reich in Germany: Barry Adam, *The Rise of a Gay and Lesbian Movement* (Boston: Twayne, 1987), 53, 56–60, 85, 133; Lillian Faderman, *Odd Girls and Twilight Lovers: A History of Lesbian Life in Twentieth-Century America* (New York: Penguin, 1991), 140–50; Becki L. Ross, *The House That Jill Built: A Lesbian Nation in Formation* (Toronto: University of Toronto Press, 1995), 13. The effect of age on the composition of the 'out' queer population is also seen the Blumstein and Schwartz study. The bulk of the 6,000 respondents in that study were well under age 45, with an average age for gay men and lesbian women of 33.3 and 30.6 years, respectively: See Blumstein and Schwartz, *American Couples*, Table 4, 595. This would be a factor in the relative openness reported in Table 17 of that study.
43 *Report on the Rights and Responsibilities of Cohabitants under the Family Law Act* (Toronto: Ontario Law Reform Commission, 1993), 7.
44 *Homosexuality: Research Implications.*
45 See OLRC, *Report*, 7, note 14.
46 See for example Affidavit of Mariana Valverde, filed in *Rosenberg* v *The*

Queen (Ont. Gen Div, Court File No. 79885/94) (sworn 15 December 1993), para. 11, pp. 7–8.
47 Dr Valverde was asked to comment on media coverage on the figures published by the Battelle Research Centre, which were very much lower than the global Kinsey figures; 1.5 per cent men identified as 'exclusively homosexual,' and only 2.3 per cent disclosed sex with a man in the last ten years.
48 Laumann et al. left the question about sexuality until the rest of the interview was over, and permitted respondents to write their answers down and seal them in an anonymous envelope. Laumann et al. used a probability study involving a representative sample of 3,500 women and men.
49 These figures were derived by using 7 per cent of males over the age of eighteen (of which there were 10,991,110 in 1995) and 4.4 per cent of females (11,440,206): See Statistics Canada, *Annual Demographic Statistics, 1995* (Ottawa: Minister for Statistics Canada, 1996), Table 1.4, 'Special Age Groups,' 67.
50 *Globe and Mail*, 30 June 1997, at A1.
51 Kathy Roberson, 'Domestic Partnerships Raise New Questions About Benefit Equity' (1993), 20 *Pension & Benefits Reports (BNA)*, 2478, 2478 (22 November).
52 See Marieka M. Klawitter and Victor Flatt, *Antidiscrimination Policies and Earnings for Same-Sex Couples* (Seattle: University of Washington Graduate School of Public Affairs, 1995) (Working Papers in Public Policy Analysis and Management), using 1990 U.S. census data.
53 See M.V. Lee Badgett and Josh A. Goldfoot, 'For Richer, For Poorer: The Freedom to Marry Debate – The Cost of Nonrecognition of Same Gender Marriages' (1996), *Angles, The Policy Journal of the Institute for Gay and Lesbian Strategic Studies* 1(2): 1, 3.
54 Australian Bureau of Statistics, 1996 Census of Population and Housing (Canberra), Table 1, p. 18 (Australia, 1996 Census). The question that led to the collection of this data stated: 'what is your relationship to householder #1?– the same formulation that is being sought for the Canadian census. The total population over the age of fifteen in that census was found to be 13,914,897.
55 Klawitter and Flatt, *Earnings for Same-Sex Couples*, 11–12.
56 Philip Blumstein and Pepper Schwartz, *American Couples*, especially Table 3, 594.
57 See for example Letitia Anne Peplau and Susan D. Cochran, 'A Relational Perspective on Homosexuality,' in *Homosexuality/Heterosexuality: Concepts of Sexual Orientation*, ed. David P. McWhirter, Stephanie A. Sanders, and June

Machover Reinisch (New York: Oxford University Press, 1990), 321–49, at 332, who report that an estimated 60 per cent of lesbian women are coupled, compared with 40 per cent of gay men.
58 Australia, 1996 Census, Table 1, p. 18.
59 Ted Myers, G. Godin, L. Calzavara, J. Lambert, and D. Locker, *The Canadian Survey of Gay and Bisexual Men and HIV Infection: Men's Survey* (Ottawa: Canadian AIDS Society, 1993), 28–30.
60 Stephen Michael Samis, '"An Injury to One is an Injury to All": Heterosexism, Homophobia, and Anti-Gay/Lesbian Violence in Greater Vancouver' M.A. thesis, Sociology and Anthropology, Simon Fraser University, 1995, 69–70. Samis reported that 25.3 per cent of relationships were five years in duration or longer; 39.6 per cent were one to four years; 21.8 per cent were less than one year old.
61 Coalition for Lesbian and Gay Rights in Ontario, *Systems Failure: A Report on the Experiences of Sexual Minorities in Ontario's Health-Care and Social-Services System* (Toronto: CLGRO, 1997) (Project Affirmation).
62 Numbers of adults were drawn from Statistics Canada, 1995 Statistics, Table 1.4, 'Special Age Groups,' 67.
63 Statistics Canada, *Age, Sex and Marital Status: The Nation* (Ottawa: Minister for Statistics Canada, 1992), Table 10, p. 140.
64 Statistics Canada, *1996 Census Consultation Guide* (Ottawa: Statistics Canada, 1992), 36.
65 The report went on to conclude that comments from all sectors, from within lesbian and gay communities and elsewhere, 'recognized that inclusion of a question on same-sex relationships would generate a negative reaction from the public,' and merely recommended focus-group and questionnaire testing in which lesbian and gay respondents could make use of the write-in space provided: Statistics Canada, *1996 Census Consultation Report number 2* (Ottawa: Statistics Canada, 1997), 18–19.
66 Ibid.
67 People who wanted to know how to get their relationships to 'count' in the 1996 census were told to write in 'same-sex partner of Person 1' or 'same-sex partner of Person ' with choices for up to six persons per household if they wished to select 'Other–Specify' in answering Question 2 (relationships of members of the household): Statistics Canada Memorandum, received by EGALE in 1996.
68 Statistics Canada Memorandum, received by EGALE in 1996.
69 See Statistics Canada, 'List of files on the FTP site' <http://100.2.22.222/english/Dii/ftp.html>, relating to the Data Liberation Initiative (also described on the website).

418 Notes to pages 185–7

70 Statistics Canada, *2001 Census Consultation Guide* (Ottawa: Statistics Canada, 1997), 38, 39, 26.
71 See EGALE, [Press release] 'Nation-wide survey of lesbians, gays and bisexuals launched today,' 7 May 1998.
72 See CLGRO, *Systems Failure*, surveying 1,233 respondents.
73 Statistics Act, RSC 1985, c S-19, section 19(1).
74 Ibid., sections 7, 17–18.
75 See Affidavit of Albert Wakkary, filed in *Rosenberg* v *The Queen* (Ont. Gen Di., Court File No. 79885/94) (sworn 2 June 1994), para. 8-9, at 7–8, and Exhibit B.
76 CLGRO, *Systems Failure*, summary at 9, demonstrates how powerfully the 'spiral of silence' operates even in urban-based queer communities: 11 per cent of the 1,233 respondents reported that they were not out as lesbian, gay, or bisexual; 35 per cent of the men/42 per cent of the women reported that they did not feel safe being out in their communities; 26 per cent have not disclosed their sexuality to their physicians.
77 'The Gap between Psychosocial Assumptions and Empirical Research in Lesbian-Mother Child Custody Cases,' in *Redefining Families: Implications for Children's Development*, ed. Adele Eskeles Gottfried and Allen W. Gottfried, 131–56 (New York: Plenum, 1994).
78 Ibid., 132; M. Kirkpatrick, 'Clinical Implications of Lesbian Mother Studies' (1987), 14 *Journal of Homosexuality* 1–2: 201–11, and C. Pies, 'Lesbians Choosing Children: The Use of Social Group Work in Maintaining and Strengthening the Primary Relationship' (1987), 5 *Journal of Social Work and Human Sexuality* 2: 79–88; Rhonda R. Rivera, 'Our Straight-Laced Judges: The Legal Position of Homosexual Persons in the United States' (1979), 30 *Hastings Law Journal* 799–955.
79 Citing J.S. Gottman, 'Children of Gay and Lesbian Parents' (1989), 14 *Marriage and Family Review* 3–4: 177–96; P.H. Turner, L. Scadden, and M.B. Harris, 'Parenting in Gay and Lesbian Families' (1990), 1 *Journal of Gay and Lesbian Psychotherapy* 3: 55–66.
80 Robert L. Barret and Bryan E. Robinson, 'Gay Dads,' in *Redefining Families: Implications for Children's Development*, ed. Adele Eskeles Gottfried and Allen W. Gottfried (New York: Plenum, 1994), 156–70, at 159, citing F. Bozett, 'Parenting Concerns of Gay Fathers' (1984), 6 *Topics in Clinical Nursing* 60–71.
81 J. Harry, 'Gay Male and Lesbian Relationships,' in *Contemporary Families and Alternative Lifestyles*, ed. E. Macklin and R. Rubin (Beverly Hills, CA: Sage, 1983), 216–34; A. Bell and M. Weinberg, *Homosexualities: A Study of Diversity Among Men and Women* (New York: Simon and Schuster, 1978).

82 Bell and Weinberg, *Homosexualities*.
83 Blumstein and Schwartz, *American Couples*, Table 12, 600.
84 With 1,568 lesbian women in the sample, 220 had a total of 392 children, and 125 lived with 173 children at least six months of the year: Ibid.
85 Australia, 1996 Census, Table 1, 18.
86 Alan Cornwall, 'Personal and Estate Taxation for Gay and Lesbian Individuals and Couples: Survey and Selected Topics,' Faculty of Law, University of Windsor, 1986 (manuscript on file with author).
87 Samis, 'Injury to One,' 69–70.
88 Carolyn Gibson Smith, *'Proud but Cautious': Homophobic Abuse and Discrimination in Nova Scotia* (Halifax: Nova Scotia Public Interest Research Group, Dalhousie University, 1993), 11–13.
89 Rachel Epstein, 'Lesbian Families,' in *Voices: Essays on Canadian Families*, ed. Marion Lynn (Scarborough, ON: Nelson Canada, 1996), 107–30, at 108, 127, note 1.
90 See for example the data on registered partners in Denmark, 1989 to 1996: Only 0.2 per cent as many men register as partners as marry; only 0.19 per cent as many women register as partners as marry: '"I do"' in Denmark,' *Honolulu Star-Bulletin*, 22 January 1997, B1, B4. And consider the data from the Office of Labor Relations, New York City, which in 1995 found that fewer than 1 per cent of all employees enrolled a domestic partner of either the same or the opposite sex after adoption of such programs.

Chapter Seven: The High Costs of Being Queer

1 See Margaret Benson, 'The Political Economy of Women's Liberation' (1969), 21 *Monthly Review* 13–27; Gayle Rubin, 'The Traffic in Women: Notes on the "Political Economy" of Sex,' in *Toward an Anthropology of Women*, ed. Rayna Reiter, 157–210 (New York: Monthly Review Press, 1975), who extended to lesbians Lévi-Strauss's analysis of the exchange of women in his *The Elementary Structures of Kinship* (London: Eyre and Spottiswoode, 1969). See also Janet Rifkin, 'Toward a Theory of Law and Patriarchy' (1980), 3 *Harvard Women's Law Journal* 83–95, who built upon Lévi-Strauss's and Rubin's work to illustrate the role of law in maintaining these relations.
2 For a one of the earliest accounts of the multifaceted ways in which heterosexual relations create the 'heterosexual economy,' see Christine Delphy, 'Our Friends and Ourselves: The Hidden Foundations of Various Pseudo-Feminist Accounts,' in *Close to Home: A Materialist Analysis of Women's Oppression*, trans. Diana Leonard (Amherst: University of Massachusetts Press, 1984), 106–37, at 113–16. For a discussion of how the tax-expenditure

system in Canada replicates and reinforces this process, see Kathleen A. Lahey, *The Taxation of Women in Canada* (Kingston, ON: Queen's University Faculty of Law, 1988).

3 Luce Irigaray has played on the double meaning of 'homo' ('homme') in using 'homosexual economy' to refer to the relations between the men in the 'heterosexual economy' who appropriate the property into which women's production has been collapsed. That is not the meaning I give the term here. I use 'homosexual economy' or 'queer economy' to refer very literally to the economic relations surrounding people who are characterized by their sex/ualities: See Luce Irigaray, 'Commodities among Themselves,' in *This Sex Which Is Not One*, trans. Catherine Porter and Carolyne Burke (Ithaca, NY: Cornell University Press, 1985), 192.

4 For an engaging analysis of the biological and social indeterminacy of 'sex,' see Leslie Feinberg, *TransGender Warriors: Making History from Joan of Arc to RuPaul* (Boston: Beacon Press, 1996).

5 In any one year in Canada, women as a sex class receive approximately 25 per cent of all post-tax incomes; men receive the other 75 per cent: See Lahey, *Taxation of Women* generally. Other structures of privilege such as race, ability, culture, education, and class function in similar ways.

6 See Irigaray, *Sex Not One*, at 161, discussing change through transformed 'mimesis' or 'historical reversal' of relations of domination.

7 Some of the various proceedings in this custody case are reported in *Bezaire v Bezaire* (1980), 20 Fam L Rev 50 (Ont. Co Ct), (1980), 20 RFL (2d) 358 (Ont. CA).

8 *Globe and Mail*, 18 January 1979, 12.

9 I have tried to describe some of these changes in Kathleen A. Lahey, 'Reasonable Women and the Law,' in *At the Boundaries of Law: Feminism and Legal Theory*, ed. Martha Fineman and Nancy Sweet Thomadsen (New York: Routledge, 1991), 10.

10 Nor did the court's revocation of custody several months later undo any of this. Seeing the headline 'Lesbian mother loses custody of two children' in *The Globe and Mail* (25 April 1979, 11) merely reinforced the fact that Gail Bezaire had had legal custody to begin with.

11 In *Miron v Trudel*, [1995] 2 SCR 418, at 498 (SCC), per Justice McLachlin, writing for the majority: 'Those living together out of wedlock no longer are made to carry the scarlet letter. Nevertheless, the historical disadvantage associated with this group cannot be denied.'

12 By Radclyffe Hall (New York: Blue Ribbon Books, 1928).

13 [1995] 2 SCR 513.

14 [1996] Westlaw 694235, 1996 Haw App LEXIS 138 (Haw Cir Ct, 1st Cir, 3

Dec. 1996), per Chang J, aff'g *Baehr* v *Lewin*, 74 Haw 530, 852 P 2d 44 (1993), clarified on grant of reconsideration in part, 74 Haw 645, 852 P 2d 74 (1993).
15 [1995] 2 SCR at 567.
16 *Egan and Nesbit*, [1995] 2 SCR at 594, per Cory J (dissenting).
17 *Miron* v *Trudel*, [1995] 2 SCR 418, at 497, per McLachlin, J (writing for the majority).
18 M.V. Lee Badgett and Josh A. Goldfoot, 'For Richer, For Poorer: The Freedom to Marry Debate' (1996), 1 *Angles: Policy Journal for Gay and Lesbian Strategic Studies* 2: 1–4, at 2. But see Substitute Decisions Act, 1992, SO 1992, c 30, sections 1(2), 17(1). References to U.S. authorities are used only when the law is the same in both the United States and Canada and I have not been able to document the precise legal point in the Canadian legal context.
19 See for example Victims' Bill of Rights, 1995, SO 1995, c 6, which permits spouses of victims to sue for damages. The definition of 'spouse' in this legislation includes opposite-sex cohabitants, but it does not include same-sex cohabitants who would otherwise meet all the elements of the statutory definition of 'spouse.'
20 For a fuller discussion of this issue, see chapter 10.
21 Sumner J. La Croix and Lee Badgett, *A Brief Analysis of Important Economic Benefits Accruing from Same-Sex Marriage* (Hawaii: Commission on Sexual Orientation and the Law, 1995), 1, 2.
22 Badgett and Goldfoot, 'For Richer,' 1.
23 Ibid.
24 La Croix and Badgett, *Economic Benefits*, 1, 2.
25 Kenneth S. Sherrill, Testimony, *Equality Foundation of Greater Cincinnati, Inc.* v *City of Cincinnati*, No. C-1-93-0773, 16 June 1994 (U.S. DC, Ohio So Dist, West Div), para. 14.
26 See generally the data on hate crimes against lesbians and gays in Committee on Lesbian and Gay Legal Issues and Rights, *Submissions on Bill C-41* (Ottawa: Canadian Bar Association, 1995).
27 Eric Heinze, 'Gay and Poor' (1995), *Howard Law Journal* 38: 433–48, at 443.
28 Eli Coleman, 'The Development of Male Prostitution Activity among Gay and Bisexual Adolescents,' in *Gay and Lesbian Youth*, ed. Gilbert Herdt (New York: Columbia University Press, 1989), 131.
29 See *De l'illégalité à l'égalité: Rapport de la consultation publique sur la violence et la discrimination envers les gais et lesbiennes* (Commission des droits de la personne du Québec, May 1994), at 125, quoted in *Egan and Nesbit*, [1995] 2 SCR at 601, per Cory J.
30 See generally Heinze, 'Gay and Poor.'
31 Ibid., 437.

32 See the discussion of Sheila Finestone's reaction to that term during the hearings of the Parliamentary Committee on Equality in chapter 2.
33 Badgett and Goldfoot, 'For Richer,' 2.
34 La Croix and Badgett, *Economic Benefits*, 2.
35 Heinze, 'Gay and Poor,' at 446–7.
36 See generally Heinze, 'Gay and Poor.'
37 Marieka M. Klawitter and Victor Flatt, *Antidiscrimination Policies and Earnings for Same-Sex Couples* (Seattle: University of Washington Graduate School of Public Affairs, 1995) (Working Papers in Public Policy Analysis and Management), 10.
38 In Ontario, same-sex partners do have the capacity to make decisions for each other in such cases. A partner is defined in this way: 'Two persons are partners for the purpose of the Act if they have lived together for at least one year and have a close personal relationship that is of primary importance in both persons' lives.' A partner has all the rights of a spouse under this legislation, including the right to notice in various proceedings relating to the other partner's capacity and care, and the right to give consent when the other is unable. Substitute Decisions Act, 1992, SO 1992, c 30, sections 1(2), 17(1). In the absence of such legislation, family members as identified by the traditional markers of blood, marriage, or adoption hold those capacities.
39 See Nursing Homes Act, RSO 1990, c N.7, section 2(2)(14); Homes for the Aged and Rest Homes Act, RSO 1990, c H.13, section 1.1(2(14); Charitable Institutions Act, RSO 1990, c C.0, section 3.1(2)(14).
40 Human Tissue Gift Act, RSO 1990, c H.20, sections 5(1), (2); Coroners Act, RSO 1990, c C.37, section 29(2).
41 Coroners Act, sections 18(2), 26(1).
42 La Croix and Badgett, *Economic Benefits*, 1.
43 *Obringer v Kennedy Estate*, [1996] OJ No. 3181 (Ont. Gen Div) (File No. 01-1716/95, 15 August 1996), per Sheard J.
44 Estates Act, RSO 1990, c E.21, section 36(2).
45 Insurance Act, RSO 1990, c I.8, sections 179(a), (b), 305.
46 Execution Act, RSO, 1990, c E.24, sections 5(2), (3), (6).
47 [1995] 2 SCR at 600–2.
48 David W. Moore, 'Public Polarized on Gay Issue,' *Gallup Poll Monthly* (April 1993), 34; Larry Hugick, 'Public Opinion Divided on Gay Rights,' Gallup Poll Monthly (June 1992), 2–6.
49 Hugick, 'Opinion Divided.'
50 Klawitter and Flatt, *Earnings*, 4, discussing Gary S. Becker, *The Economics of Discrimination* (Chicago: University of Chicago Press, 1971).

51 M.V. Lee Badgett, 'The Wage Effects of Sexual Orientation Discrimination' (1995), 48 *Industrial and Labor Relations Review* 4: 726, at 728, reporting on twenty-one studies reviewed in Lee Badgett, Colleen Donnelly, and Jennifer Kibbe, *Pervasive Patterns of Discrimination against Lesbians and Gay Men: Evidence from Surveys Across the United States* (Washington, DC: National Gay and Lesbian Task Force Policy Institute, 1992). See also Klawitter and Flatt, *Earnings*, 4, discussing studies by the Seattle Commission for Gays and Lesbians, OUT/LOOK, and the National Gay and Lesbian Task Force.

52 Badgett, 'Wage Effects,' 728, summarizing Jay Brause, 'Closed Doors: Sexual Orientation Bias in the Anchorage Housing and Employment Markets,' in *Identity Reports: Sexual Orientation Bias in Alaska* (Anchorage, AK: Identity Inc., 1989).

53 See David Rayside and Scott Bowler, 'Public Opinion and Gay Rights' (1988), 25 *Canadian Review of Sociology and Anthropology* 4: 649–60.

54 Klawitter and Flatt, *Earnings*, 5.

55 Coalition for Lesbian and Gay Rights in Ontario, *Systems Failure: A Report on the Experiences of Sexual Minorities in Ontario's Health-Care and Social-Services System* (Toronto: CLGRO, 1997) (Project Affirmation), summary at 9.

56 See Heinze, 'Gay and Poor,' 443–4; *Waterman v National Life Assurance Co. of Canada*, (1992), 18 CHRR D/173 (preliminary hearing); (1993), 18 CHRR D/176 (Ont. Bd of Inq), per Plaut, Bd.

57 Klawitter and Flatt, *Earnings*, 6, reporting on the sample of same-sex couples drawn from the 1990 U.S. census data. However, they report that other studies do not consistently reflect this finding, leading to the possibility that selecting for 'coupleness' may produce different results than selecting for 'lesbian or gay.' But see also Philip Blumstein and Pepper Schwartz, *American Couples: Money, Work, Sex* (New York: William Morrow, 1983), Table 6, 598, reporting that lesbian women had more average years of education than any other group in the study; gay men had slightly less average years of education than husbands, but more than cohabiting men.

58 Beth E. Schneider, 'Coming Out at Work: Bridging the Private/Public Gap' (1986), *Work and Occupation* 13(4): 463–87, at 479.

59 *Romer v Evans*, 116 S Ct 1620 (U.S. SC, 1996), at 1634.

60 See Badgett, 'Wage Effects,' 729. The results of the OUT/LOOK survey are reprinted in William B. Rubenstein, ed., *Lesbians, Gay Men, and the Law* (New York: New Press, 1993), 257. Even a cursory examination of this report will reveal the analytic limitations of such studies for other than pure marketing purposes. A more recent study conducted by Simmons Market Research Bureau reported that 21 per cent of all gay men and lesbians have household incomes of more than $100,000, 22 per cent have graduate degrees, and

58 per cent hold management positions. See David Armstrong, 'Study finds affluent, educated gay market,' *San Francisco Examiner*, 4 February 1997, D1. As Kenneth Sherrill pointed out, however, this study was for pure marketing purposes, and was heavily biased by the fact that all respondents were magazine readers – a very affluent sector of the population: Kenneth Sherrill, 'More misleading data from Simmons Research [Letter to editor]', *San Francisco Examiner*, 5 February 1997.
61 Blumstein and Schwartz, *American Couples*.
62 Ibid., Table 6, 598.
63 Badgett, 'Wage Effects,' analysing data from James Allan Davis and Tom W. Smith, *General Social Surveys 1972–1991* (Chicago: National Opinion Research Center, 1991).
64 Badgett, 'Wage Effects,' 736.
65 Ibid., 737.
66 The way in which the questions are framed has made the resulting census data more or less useless for studying lesbians, gays, or bisexuals who are not in couples. Non-coupled respondents, whether 'householders' or otherwise, had no way to record their sexuality.
67 Using the United States Census 5% Public Use Microdata Sample (PUMS) to carry out their analysis, they found 6,800 same-sex couples in the 5 per cent sample. This figure suggests that, in the entire country, there are only 136,000 'out' couples, one member of which is classified as a 'householder.' This figure seems far too low to be realistic.
68 Recently released 1996 Australian census data on self-identifying same-sex couples may produce some of the same results. On a preliminary analysis of the data, it is clear that the household incomes of lesbian couples are markedly lower than those of gay couples, both in terms of the pattern of distribution along the income range for both lesbians and gay, and in terms of the size of median incomes. The largest percentage of gay household incomes fall into the highest income bracket, while the largest percentage of lesbian household incomes fall into the next bracket down. However, a full analysis of the data would be required in order to be able to compare the results with those generated with U.S. data: See Australian Bureau of Statistics, *1996 Census of Population and Housing* (Canberra), Table 1, 18.
69 Klawitter and Flatt, *Earnings*, 20, discussing data in their tables 3 and 4.
70 These regression results are expressed relative to the base case and is calculated as exp(coeff.)-1.
71 Badgett, 'Wage Effects,' 733, has developed a much richer set of hypotheses

in trying to explain why lesbian women have the highest female earnings, but the factors she posits come down to much the same thing.
72 Reported in Eoin Collins, 'Lifting the Lid on Discrimination and Poverty' (1996), *Poverty Today* (December/January) 7.
73 Cf. Lahey, *Taxation of Women*, Table 4-1, 159, reporting that average male incomes for 1981 were $18,122 and average female's were $9,768.
74 Sherrill, 'Testimony,' para. 66, summarizing findings of a recent Yankelovich study: While 66 per cent of heterosexuals in that study were found to be parents, 50 per cent of the gay and lesbian respondents were also found to be parents. About a third of heterosexuals had children under eighteen living with them, and about a quarter of the lesbian and gay people had children under eighteen living with them.

Chapter Eight: The High Costs of Heterosexuality and the 'Queer Penalty'

1 *The National Finances 1992* (Toronto: Canadian Tax Foundation, 1992), 3: 13, 3: 15.
2 For a recent deconstruction of the 'public'–'private' divide that takes account of the nature of the contemporary 'state,' see Jürgen Habermas, *The Structural Transformation of the Public Sphere* (Cambridge, MA: MIT Press, 1994), 6. He analyses the 'societization' of the state and the 'statization' of civil society in concluding that the 'public/private' divide has come to be more or less useless as a critical concept.
3 Eric Heinze has described this process from the political perspective: '[C]ontemporary statist societies have largely converged on the exclusive, biological mother–father–children paradigm, a normative-heterosexual paradigm of social organization': Eric Heinze, *Sexual Orientation: A Human Right* (Dordrecht, Neth.: Martinus Nijhoff, 1995), 33.
4 In critical deconstruction, 'difference' drags the denied, the erased, the repressed up into the light of day by treating it as if it exists 'in its own right' and not merely as absence. 'Difference' in this sense treats 'lesbian,' for example, as existing not as pure gap or negativity, but as an autonomous identity: See Grosz, *Subversions*, xvii.
5 As of 17 June 1998, a QuickLaw search produced the following numbers of sections that referred to 'spouse': Federal legislation: 283 provisions (up from 276 in 1997); Ontario: 248; British Columbia: 258; Alberta: 242; Saskatchewan: 314; Manitoba: 126; New Brunswick: 116; Yukon Territory: 93. This is just the tip of the iceberg; in Manitoba, for example, another 102 provisions refer to 'husband' or 'wife,' and 230 refer to 'marry/iage/ed,'

and about half the jurisdictions also use 'opposite sex' in 2 to 28 provisions. There is a great deal of overlap among these provisions, of course. Federal legislation contained a total of 343 heterosexual-specific provisions; Ontario legislation, 343.

6 The most notorious example of this effect is found in *The Queen* v *Thibaudeau*, [1995] 2 SCR 627, in which a majority of the Supreme Court ruled that the appellant was not disadvantaged by the inclusion of child-support income in her taxable income because her husband received not only a deduction for the payment, but a tax benefit that exceeded her tax burden. Thus the 'former family' received a net tax benefit as the result of the overall effect of these tax rules.
7 W. Friedmann, 'A Comparative Analysis,' in *Matrimonial Property Law*, ed. W. Friedmann (Toronto: Carswell, 1955), 433–53, at 451–3.
8 Family Law Act, RSO 1990, c F.3, Part II.
9 Ibid., Part I, section 5(1), (2); section 6(1)–(13); Succession Law Reform Act, RSO 1990, c S.26, Part I, sections 44–6.
10 Family Law Act, RSO 1990, c F.3, Part I, section 4(2)(1), (2), (5); section 5(2).
11 Ibid., Part III, sections 31, 33, 34 .
12 Succession Law Reform Act, RSO 1990, c S.26, Part I, sections 45, 46.
13 Ibid., c S.26.
14 See generally Family Relations Act, RSBC, c 121; Domestic Relations Act, SA, c O-37; Maintenance Orders Act, SA, c M-1; Family Maintenance Act, SM, c F-6.1; Family Maintenance Act, SM, c F.20; Code civil du Québec, LQ 1991, c 64; Family Services Act, SNB, c F-2.2; Family Maintenance Act, RSNS, c 160; Family Law Act, SPEI 1995, c 12; Family Law Act, RS Nfld., c F-2; Divorce Act, RSC 1985, (2d Supp.), c 3.
15 Family Law Act, RSO 1990, c F.3, section 61(2)(e).
16 Landlord and Tenant Act, RSO 1980, c 237, section 7.
17 Highway Traffic Act, Regulations 744/82, section 2. But see *O'Neill and Coles* v *The Queen*, (unreported Bd of Inq, 13 October 1994), per Hovius, Bd of Inq, an Ontario board of inquiry ruled that same-sex partners were entitled to transfer ownership of vehicles between themselves without obtaining new safety certification, just like opposite-sex cohabitants and married couples.
18 Land Transfer Tax Act, RSO 1990, c L.6, section 1(1).
19 Income Tax Act, sections 73 (transfers of property between spouses), 70 (transfers to surviving spouse), 70 and 73 (transfers to child).
20 See, for example, ITA section 82 (dividend income from shares transferred to spouse treated as income of transferor).
21 See ITA sections 60 and 146 (RRSPs), 146.3-147 (other pension-type benefits), 96 (partnership interest), 148 (life insurance policies), 248 (death benefits).

22 See ITA sections 110.6 (permitting interspousal transfers of the capital gains exemption), 118 (transfer of pension tax credit), 118.2 (transfer of medical expense tax credits), 118.8 (transfer of other tax credits).
23 (1973), 41 DLR (3d) 367 (SCC); see also *Murdoch v Murdoch* (1976), 26 RFL 2 (Alta. SC), per Bowen J.
24 See Family Law Reform Act, SO 1978, c 2, enacted on the recommendations made by Ontario Law Reform Commission, *Report on Family Law: Family Property Law* (Toronto: Ministry of the Attorney General, 1975), vol. IV.
25 Brenda Cossman and Bruce Ryder, *Gay, Lesbian and Unmarried Heterosexual Couples and the Family Law Act* (Toronto: Ontario Law Reform Commission, 1993).
26 See Income Tax Act, section 40(4), relating the surviving spouse's period of ownership of the family home back to include the period of ownership by the other spouse.
27 The Julian Laws required men under the age of sixty and women under the age of fifty to be married, and voided bequests to many who were not actively participating in heterosexual relations: See Mary R. Lefkowitz and Maureen B. Fant, *Women's Life in Greece and Rome* (Baltimore: Johns Hopkins University Press, 1982), 182. See also James Coffield, *A Popular History of Taxation: From Ancient to Modern Times* (London: Longman Group, 1970), 25–6. Special inheritance taxes were imposed on bequests to unmarried men, childless married men, and unmarried women with fewer than three children: Will Durant, *Caesar and Christ* (New York: Simon and Schuster, 1944), 224.
28 See Canada, Department of Finance, *Government of Canada Tax Expenditure 1995* (Ottawa: Department of Finance, 1995), Table 1, reporting on tax expenditures for the taxation years 1993 and 1995. The amounts listed for all these items are 'n.a.' (not available).
29 In the Income Tax Act, this definition is found in section 252(4). In the Old Age Security Act, this definition is located in RSC 1985, c O-9, section 2, and in the Canada Pension Plan Act, it is found in RSC 1985, c C-8, section 2.
30 ITA, section 118(1)B(a). For 1993, the federal component of this credit was $915. When the provincial income tax rate is 50 per cent of the federal tax payable, the value of the married tax credit at the provincial level is $457.50. The higher the provincial tax rate, the higher the provincial layer of this credit will be.
31 See ITA section 118.8, transferring unused credits for age ($592, subject to low income cut-offs section 118[2]), mental/physical impairment ($720; section 118.3[1]), education expenses (section 118.6), tuition (section 118.5), and pension income ($170; section 118[3]).

32 Sections 60, 60.1.
33 Amendments to the Income Tax Act made in 1997 exempt future child-support payments from the tax base, but these amendments have no effect on alimony payments unless taxpayers attempt to rename child support as 'alimony' in order to gain access to this tax treatment.
34 These are the benefit levels as at January 1997.
35 As of 1996. The precise level of benefit payable depends on the age of the survivor and the number of dependent children. A death benefit may also be payable: Department of Finance, *The Canada Pension Plan: Basic Facts* (Internet: CPP Publications, February 1996).
36 Human Resources Development Canada, *Social Security Statistics: Canada and the Provinces, 1968–69 to 1992–93* (Ottawa: Queen's Printer, 1994), Table 2, 18.
37 See generally Patricia Apps, *A Theory of Inequality and Taxation* (Cambridge: Cambridge University Press, 1981); Norma Briggs, 'Individual Income Taxation and Social Benefits in Sweden, the United Kingdom, and the U.S.A. – A Study of Their Inter-Relationships and Their Effects on Lower-Income couples and Single Heads of Household' (1985), *International Bureau of Fiscal Documentation* 243; Eden Cloutier, *Taxes and the Labour Supply of Married Women in Canada* (Ottawa: Economic Council of Canada, 1986).
38 This is true even when the cohabiting opposite-sex couples are taken out of the data, which they were effective in 1993.
39 The federal government appears to be afraid to address the irrationality of dependency benefits directly. Note, however, that the GST tax credit, delivered through the income tax system, is structured in a way that offsets some of the excesses of the dependency benefits. The GST credit for couples is actually less than for two individual adults, plus it is scaled out as incomes rise. The sheer size of the GST credit goes some distance to offsetting the effects of the dependency credits.
40 Human Resources Development Canada, *Social Security Statistics, Canada and Provinces: 1968–69 to 1992–93*, Table 1, 13: total social security expenditures accounted for 42.3 per cent of overall government expenditures in 1992–3.
41 These figures are demographically representative. See *Taxation Statistics 1993*, Table 10, for levels of alimony and child support; see Louise Dulude, *Love, Marriage and Money* (Ottawa: Canadian Advisory Council on the Status of Women, 1984), 40–2, for levels of occasional earnings associated with this scenario, adjusted to 1993 levels.
42 See Julie A. Matthaei, *An Economic History of Women in America: Women's Work, the Sexual Division of Labor, and the Development of Capitalism* (New

York: Schocken Books, 1982), 121, 134–5, 195. Black males, for example, never gained enough political power to obtain the same differential. And as the distribution of incomes by gender and ethnic origin demonstrates all too clearly, the presumption that families could be supported on one male income alone is deeply biased against racially identified groups: See Statistics Canada, Cat. no. 93-154, 93–155, tabulating incomes by ethnic origin and gender for 1986.

43 However, over age eighteen, children can still be included in many benefit plans if they are actually economically dependent on the relevant parent, either by virtue of disability or by virtue of enrolment in post-secondary educational programs.

44 I am not including things like the child tax benefit, child-focused subsidy programs, or child-related deductions, in this category, since those programs are contingent not so much on sexuality or even marital status, but on the parent–child relationship. For discussion of related issues, see chapter 9.

45 Human Resources Development Canada, *Social Security Statistics, Canada and Provinces: 1968–69 to 1992–93*, Table 214, 60, reporting for 1992–3.

46 See, for example, Members of Parliament Retiring Allowances Act, RSC 1985, c M-5; Public Sector Pension Reform Act, SC 1992, c 46 [unofficial c P-31.8]; Public Service Superannuation Act, RSC 1985, c P-36; Pension Act, RSC 1985, c P-6; Royal Canadian Mounted Police Superannuation Act, RSC 1985, c R-11; War Veterans Allowance Act, RSC 1985, c W-3; and so on. Provinces all have similar arrays of statutes.

47 'No one would suggest that the costs of caring for a pet elephant are deductible, simply because it is impossible to go to work and leave the elephant alone': *Symes* v. *The Queen*, [1993] 4 SCR at 741, per Iacobucci J, quoting Michael J. McIntyre, 'Evaluating the New Tax Credit for Child Care and Maid Service' (1977), 5 *Tax Notes* 7, at 8.

48 Thus see ITA section 39 (capital gains on shares transferred to spouse included in income of transferor when realized); section 74.1 (income on assets transferred to spouse included in income of transferor); section 74.2 (gains or losses on assets transferred to spouse treated as gains or losses of transferor); sections 84.1, 85 (shares owned by spouse included in determination of control of corporation by other spouse); section 97 (includes partnership interest of spouse in determination of whether other spouse is majority partner); section 108 (contributions to trust by spouse of settlor treated as contributions by settlor); section 146 (contributions to spousal RRSP withdrawn within three years treated as income of contributor).

49 See generally sections 245, 246, and section 251, which deem spouses to be

'related' for purposes of a huge number of specific anti-avoidance provisions.
50 See sections 60, 60.1, 56, and 56.1 of the ITA.
51 See also the provisions relating to the division of pension assets with separated or divorced spouses in Regulations 8501.
52 Section 146. See the discussion of RRSPs later in this section.
53 Section 8 (railway workers are entitled to deduction for cost of maintaining home occupied by spouse).
54 See chapter 6 for a detailed discussion of the barriers to obtaining reliable data on the queer community.
55 Bill C-4, 1st Sess, 30th Parl, 23 Eliz II, 1974, amending the Veterans and Civilian War Allowances Act, RS, c W-5, c 34 (2d Supp) (Royal Assent given November 1974).
56 Bill C-16, Statute Law (Status of Women) Amendment Act, 1974, 1st Sess, 30th Parl, 23–4 Eliz II, 1974–5 (Royal Assent given 30 July 1975).
57 Ontario Bill 167, discussed in chapter 11.
58 There are literally hundreds more at the present time.
59 Elizabeth Grosz again: 'Ethics means being called by and responding to the other's otherness ... Only when each ... is recognized as an independent otherness by the other is an ethical relation between them possible': Ibid., xvii–xviii.

Chapter Nine: The 'Benefit' Conundrum and the Politics of Exclusion

1 *Schachtschneider* v *The Queen* [1991] TCJ No. 1023 (TCC), aff'd 93 DTC 5298 (FCA), leave to appeal den. [1995] SCCA No. 335 (1 June 1995). Schachtschneider wanted to be able to claim this roughly $1,400 tax credit in relation to one of her children, just as lesbian women with children can each claim this credit because they are not 'married' or (since 1993) 'opposite-sex' cohabitants.
2 Patricia LeFebour, 'Same-Sex Spousal Recognition in Ontario: Declarations and Denials: A Class Perspective' (1993), 9 *Journal of Law and Social Policy* 272–89; Patricia LeFebour and Michael Rodrigues, *Estate Planning for Same-Sex Couples* (Toronto: Canadian Bar Association [Ontario], 1995) (Eleventh Semi-Annual Estate Planning Institute).
3 Nitya Duclos, 'Some Complicating Thoughts on Same-Sex Marriage' (1991), 1 *Law and Sexuality: A Review of Lesbian and Gay Legal Issues* 31.
4 See Audrey Macklin, 'Where Sex Meets Class' (1992), 5 *Canadian Journal of Women and Law* 498–517, relied upon in *Symes* v *The Queen*, [1993] 4 SCR

695, at 743, 744, 766, per Iacobucci J; cf. L'Heureux-Dubé J, at 803, 827. Symes tried to treat the full amount of her child-care expenses as ordinary business expenses. Women who are not carrying on a business are limited to the much smaller deductions under section 63 of the Income Tax Act. What the Court missed was that the policy objective behind imposing those low-income cut-offs was itself class-specific, designed to keep middle- and high-income women like Symes in the home while encouraging low-income women to work outside the home.
5 Jacques Derrida, *Of Grammatology*, trans. Gayatri Chakrovorty Spivak (Baltimore: Johns Hopkins University Press, 1976), 24.
6 Jacques Derrida, *Speech and Phenomena and Other Essays on Husserl's Theory of Signs*, trans. Alan Bass (Evanston: Northwestern University Press, 1973), 129.
7 RSO 1990, c M.50, sections 1 'spouse,' 3.
8 RSO 1990, c L.25, sections 141(2), 142(1), (2).
9 See also for example Business Development Bank of Canada Act, SC 1995, c 28, sections 31, 33.
10 Section 252(4), effective after 1992.
11 Section 251(1)(a), incorporating definition of 'related persons' in section 251(2)(a).
12 Section 251(1)(b).
13 The low-income measures used in the draft federal child-support guidelines under the Divorce Act indicated that in 1997 it took $12,299 per year to support a single individual, but only $17,219 to support two persons, regardless of whether the second person is an adult or a child. Thus, for two individuals living in separate households to achieve the same standard of living of a couple living on $17,219, the two individuals would need $12,299 times two ($24,598). 'The couple' is presumed to be able to live together on 70 per cent of what the two separate individuals would need. These 'economies of consumption' reflect unstated assumptions that do not necessarily apply to all couples.
14 See the data collected and analysed in Affidavit of Albert Wakkary, filed in *Rosenberg* v *The Queen* (Ont. Gen Div, Court File No. 79885/94) (sworn 2 June 1994), especially paras. 11–14, at 8–9.
15 This subtler form of LICO is a hangover from the days when women were expected to stay home to care for children instead of engaging in waged work. Forcing the spouse with the lower income to claim the deduction increases the overall tax benefits of substituting non-waged domestic work for waged work, at the margin, but minimizes the benefits given to women who really 'need' to work because their husbands cannot adequately

support them, and so on. For an extended discussion of the history and policies reflected in such child-care deduction rules, see Kathleen A. Lahey, '1995 Term – Taxation Developments' (1996), 7 *Supreme Court Law Review* (2d) 381, at 415–16.

16 RSC 1985, c C-46, section 215(1)–(4).
17 For an example of how rigidly this 'deemed' spouse system operates, see *Poulter* v *M.N.R.*, [1995] TCJ No. 228 (TCC) (Action No. 94-2119(IT)I, 16 March 1995), per Christie TCJ. Also, this case is noteworthy because of the arguments concerning sexuality that were made in it. The taxpayer had attempted to argue in that case that she was being penalized for being heterosexual, because two lesbian women would not have been deemed to have been spouses in the same circumstances. The court rejected that argument.
18 See chapter 7, tables 7.4 and 7.5.
19 R. Beaujot, K.G. Basavarajappa, and R.B.P. Verma, *Current Demographic Analysis: Income of Immigrants in Canada* (Ottawa: Statistics Canada, 1988), 66–7, Tables 23, 24, analysing census data.
20 Beaujot et al., *Income of Immigrants*, 67, Table 24.
21 LeFebour, 'Same-Sex Spousal Recognition in Ontario'; see also LeFebour and Rodrigues, *Estate Planning for Same-Sex Couples*.
22 Section 54 stipulates that married couples may designate only one principal residence per family per year. This provision also applies to opposite-sex cohabitants by virtue of section 252(4) of the act.
23 See generally Kathleen A. Lahey, *The Taxation of Women in Canada* (Kingston, ON: Queen's University Faculty of Law, 1988).
24 See for example Jean Keet, 'The Law Reform Process, Matrimonial Property, and Farm Women: A Case Study of Saskatchewan, 1980–1986' (1990), 4 *Canadian Journal of Women and the Law* 2: 166–89.
25 74 NY 2d 201, 543 NE 2d 49 (1989).
26 See for example Walter Isaacson, 'Should Gays Have Marriage Rights? On Two Coasts, the Growing Debate Produces Two Different Answers,' *Time*, 20 November 1989, 101; *OUT/LOOK: National Lesbian and Gay Quarterly*, presented their views in polarized form under the heading 'Gay Marriage: A Must or A Bust?': Thomas B. Stoddard, 'Why Gay People Should Seek the Right to Marry' (1989), 6 *OUT/LOOK* 8; Paula L. Ettelbrick, 'Since When Was Marriage a Path to Liberation? (1989), 6 *OUT/LOOK* 8.
27 See Nan D. Hunter, 'Marriage, Law, and Gender: A Feminist Inquiry' (1991), 1 *Law and Sexuality* 1: 9–30; Duclos, 'Complicating Thoughts.'
28 852 P 2d 44 (Haw. 1993), motion for reconsid. granted in part 852 P 2d 74 (Haw 1993) [*Baehr I*].

29 See William B. Rubenstein, 'Divided We Litigate: Addressing Disputes Among Group Members and Lawyers in Civil Rights Campaigns' (1997), 106 *Yale Law Journal* 6:1623–81, at 1637, and notes 68–70.

30 Ibid., 1637, and note 67. The American Bar Association published a symposium on the issue in (1990), 76 *American Bar Association Journal* 42. Nancy D. Polikoff, 'We Will Get What We Ask For: Why Legalizing Gay and Lesbian Marriage Will Not "Dismantle the Legal Structure of Gender in Every Marriage"' (1993), 79 *Virginia Law Review* 1535, was a radical lesbian feminist response to Nan Hunter's paper, and in turn evoked Evan Wolfson, 'Crossing the Threshold: Equal Marriage Rights for Lesbians and Gay Men and the Intra-Community Critique' (1994), 21 *Review of Law and Social Change* 567–615, who powerfully attacked the 'anti' position. (Wolfson represented Lambda in the Hawaii marriage case.) For larger examinations of the issue, see Andrew Sullivan, ed., *Same-Sex Marriage: Pro and Con* (New York: Vintage, 1997) and Suzanne Sherman, ed., *Lesbian and Gay Marriage: Private Commitments, Public Ceremonies* (Philadelphia, PA: Temple University Press, 1992). Sherman is fairly uncritical of her subject, and focuses in great detail on how and why couples she interviewed arrived at the positions they did. Sullivan is an articulate advocate for recognition of same-sex marriage, and the 'con' material collected in his book does not really stand up well to the 'pro' material.

31 I do not mean to suggest that the lines followed strict political, gender, or sexual divisions. For example, Patricia A. Cain, a lesbian feminist tax lawyer, moved directly into a demonstration of how non-recognition of lesbian and gay couples in income tax law disadvantages them in 'Same-Sex Couples and the Federal Tax Laws' (1991), *Law and Sexuality* 1: 97–131, while Steven K. Homer argued in 'Against Marriage' (1994), 29 *Harvard Civil Rights–Civil Liberties Law Review* 2: 505–30, at 530, that by pursuing the right to marry 'we valorize the mechanism of our oppression.'

32 For celebratory case comments, see Marty K. Courson, '*Baehr* v. *Lewin*: Hawaii Takes a Tentative Step to Legalize Same-Sex Marriage' (1994), 24 *Golden Gate University Law Review* 1: 41–66, and Scott K. Kozuma, '*Baehr* v. *Lewin* and Same-Sex Marriage: The Continued Struggle for Social, Political and Human Legitimacy' (1994), 30 *Willamette Law Review* 891–916.

33 Pub L No. 104-199, section 2(a), 1996 USCCAN (110 Stat) 2419 [1 USC section 7] (DOMA).

34 See for example Larry Kramer, 'Same-Sex Marriage, Conflict of Laws, and the Unconstitutional Public Policy Exception' (1997), 106 *Yale Law Journal* 7: 1965–2008; Thomas M. Keane, 'Aloha, Marriage? Constitutional and Choice

of Law Arguments for Recognition of Same-Sex Marriages' (1995), 47 *Stanford Law Review* 499–532.
35 Rubenstein, 'Divided/Litigate.'
36 See for example Brenda Cossman, 'Family Inside/OUT' (1994), 44 *University of Toronto Law Journal* 1–39; Mary Eaton, 'Lesbians and the Law,' in *Lesbians in Canada*, ed. Sharon Dale Stone, 109–32 (Toronto: Between the Lines, 1990).
37 Duclos, 'Complicating Thoughts.'
38 *Veysey* v *Canada*, [1990] 1 FC 321 (FCTD), aff'd on other grounds (1990) 109 NR 300 (FCA).
39 Bill C-16, Statute Law (Status of Women) Amendment Act, 1974, 1st Sess, 30th Parl, 23–4 Eliz II, 1974–5 (Royal Assent given 30 July 1975), extending the definition of 'spouse' to include 'opposite-sex cohabitants' in most federal statutes.
40 RSO 1990, c M.3, section 8(4). The Charter challenge was rejected in *Layland and Beaulne* v *Ontario (M.C.C.R.)*, (1993), 14 OR (3d) 658 (Ont. Ct Gen Div), per Southey and Sirois JJ, Greer J (dissenting).
41 [1995] 2 SCR 513 (SCC).
42 Karen Patrick, 'Going to the chapel? Activists warn timing is wrong for same-sex marriage case' (1995) *Capital XTRA!* 26: 10.
43 For example, Nitya Duclos argued that the mixed benefits and burdens of marriage may reinforce differences in power, status, and wealth among an already hierarchized lesbian and gay community: Duclos, 'Complicating Thoughts.'
44 See also Didi Herman, 'Are We Family?: Lesbian Rights and Women's Liberation' (1991), 28 *Osgoode Hall Law Journal* 4: 789–815; Ontario Law Reform Commission, *Report on the Rights and Responsibilities of Cohabitants under the Family Law Act* (Toronto: OLRC, 1993), especially 46–7 and references in notes 70, 71.
45 LEAF, *Litigating for Lesbians: LEAF Report on Consultations with the Lesbian Community* (Toronto: LEAF, 1993), 11.
46 Ibid., 22. The organizers also reported that there were mixed feelings by the end of the consultations on pursuing 'sexual orientation' language in human rights codes. Ironically, within a few years of these consultations, lesbian litigants began achieving really significant victories under the rubric of 'sexual orientation' in Charter cases. These cases include *Re K.* (1995), 23 OR (3d) 679 (Ont. Prov Div), per Nevins Prov Div J; *M.* v *H.* (1996), 27 OR (3d) 593, 132 DLR (4th) 538 (Ont. Ct Gen Div), Epstein J aff'd (1996), 31 OR (3d) 417, 142 DLR (4th) 1 (Ont. CA), per Doherty and Charron J, Finlayson J dissenting, leave to appeal granted 24 April 1997, per L'Heureux-Dubé, Sopinka, and Iacobucci JJ, on condition that government pay all costs in any event of the cause.

47 See the discussion of *M. v H.* in the next section.
48 For an excellent overview of this issue, see Elizabeth Kassoff, 'Nonmonogamy in the Lesbian Community,' in *Loving Boldly: Issues Facing Lesbians*, ed. Esther D. Rothblum and Ellen Cole, 167–82 (New York: Harrington Park, 1989), and references collected therein.
49 The combined federal and provincial value of the child credit in 1993 was as much as $1,612; the value of the combined federal and provincial married tax credit was roughly $1446 for 1993. Note, however, that low-income couples can rarely afford for one partner to withdraw completely from waged work. In order for the supporting spouse to have qualified for the full married tax credit in 1993, the taxpayer would have to have had income of less than $538 for that year.
50 See Philip Blumstein and Pepper Schwartz, *American Couples* (New York: Wm. Morrow, 1983); L. Kurdek, 'Lesbian and Gay Couples,' in *Lesbian , Gay, and Bisexual Identities Over the Lifespan*, ed. Anthony R. D'Augelli and Charlotte J. Patterson, 243–61 (New York: Oxford University Press, 1995).
51 (1986), 50 RFL (2d) 127 (B.C. SC), per Dohn J.
52 Note, however, that such action is susceptible to Revenue Canada review on the basis that they did not in fact deal at arm's length: See section 251(1)(b) of the Income Tax Act. And note that not all same-sex couples are necessarily motivated by such power imbalances, or act with such calculation to take advantage of them in the current legal context; See generally Nicole Tellier, 'Support and Property Issues for Same Sex Couples: Domestic Contract, Court Challenges and Remedies,' Toronto, Special Lecture, 1995.
53 (1995), 127 DLR (4th) 738, 25 OR (3d) 612 Ont. Ct Gen Div), per Charron J (opposite-sex definition of common-law spouse in Income Tax Act pension provisions violates section 15(1) of the Charter, but is justified under section 1).
54 *Anderson* v *Luoma* (1986), 50 RFL (2d) 127 (B.C. SC), at 135.
55 This is the language used in LEAF, *Consultations*, at 10, setting out one of the reasons that some lesbian women in Canada do not seek relationship recognition.
56 Also see *Forrest* v *Price*, (1992), 48 ETR 72 (B.C. SC), per Boyd J, in which the defendant also appeared to be taking the position that all the property belonged to him.
57 See for example *Curiale* v *Reagan*, 222 Cal App 3d 1597, 272 Cal Rptr 520 (1990); *Nancy S.* v *Michele G.*, 228 Cal App 3d 831, 279 Cal Rptr 212 (1991).
58 See Elizabeth A. Delaney, 'Statutory Protection of the Other Mother: Legally Recognizing the Relationship Between the Nonbiological Lesbian Parent and her Child' (1991), 43 *Hastings Law Journal* 177–216, for a review of the leading cases in the United States.

59 See *Holtzman* v *Knott*, 193 Wis 2d 649, 533 NW 2d (Wisc. SC 1995), cert denied 133 L Ed 2d 404, 116 S Ct 475 (U.S. SC 1995), in which the Court relied on equitable powers to protect the best interests of a child in ordering visitation by a non-biological lesbian co-mother.
60 *M.* v *H.* (1993), 15 OR (3d) 721 (Ont. Ct Gen Div), per Epstein J.
61 Factum of the Defendants, Court File No. FC-804/93, para. 95, at 34, quoting LEAF, *Consultations*, 10–11.
62 Ibid., para. 52, at 19.
63 Ibid., paras. 53–4, at 19–20.
64 Ibid., para. 50, at 18–19.
65 Ibid., para. 53, at 19.
66 See Family Law Act, RSO 1990, c F.3, Parts I, III.
67 This Charter challenge was not initiated by the plaintiff. H.'s lawyer filed a motion to strike the application for interim support on the basis that section 29 of the Family Law Act does not apply to same-sex cohabitants, that section 15(1) of the Charter would not support such a reading of section 29, or, in the alternative, that continued exclusion of same-sex cohabitants from the definition of 'spouse' in section 29 would be found to be demonstrably justified in a free and democratic society. This motion has carved a new path into Charter litigation, because now presumably any court that is being asked to extend legislative provisions to same-sex couples can be forced by the defendant to rule on the probable outcome of a Charter challenge before dealing with the merits. That is, it is no longer only the victims of discrimination who can bring Charter challenges, but those who deny that discrimination has occurred can precipitate them as well. Ontario has carried the appeal to the Supreme Court of Canada, because H. has dropped out of the action.
68 Nor is mediation. See Claire M. Renzetti, 'Building a Second Closet: Third Party Responses to Victims of Lesbian Partner Abuse' (1988), 38 *Family Relations* 157–63, who has documented how lesbian communities tend to withhold support for victims of lesbian-relationship abuse, and sometimes actually support the abusers.
69 Badgett and La Croix concluded, on the basis of current federal and state income tax tables, that two-earner couples with children would pay approximately $2,213 more in combined taxes if married than if unmarried, and that two-earner couples without children would pay $806 more. In contrast, they found that the combined tax burden for single earners with children would actually fall by $1,226 if married, and for single-earner couples without children, would fall by $2,879: See Sumner J. La Croix and Lee Badgett, *A Brief Analysis of Important Economic Benefits Accruing from*

Same-Sex Marriage (Hawaii: Commission on Sexual Orientation and the Law, 1995), Table, at 6.
70 M.V. Lee Badgett and Josh A. Goldfoot, 'For Richer, For Poorer: The Freedom to Marry Debate' (1996), 1 A*ngles: Policy Journal for Gay and Lesbian Strategic Studies* 2: 1–4, at 3.
71 They did not run any projections for the entire country.
72 Badgett and Goldfoot, 'For Richer,' at 2–3.
73 [1991] TCJ No. 1023 (TCC), aff'd 93 DTC 5298 (FCA), leave to appeal den. [1995] SCCA No. 335 (1 June 1995), discussed in the introduction to this chapter.
74 SC 1993, c 24, section 140(3), adding section 252(4) effective after the 1992 taxation year. Section 252(4) now deems unmarried couples to be 'spouses' if they are of the opposite sex and have cohabited in a conjugal relationship for twelve months or are parents of a child. See also *Landon* v *M.N.R.*, [1991] TCJ No. 1037 (TCC).
75 It is ironic that non-married cohabitants had challenged the injustice of excluding them from spousal benefit provisions under the Income Tax Act for years, without any success whatsoever. Yet the first time a taxpayer claimed that a measure designed to assist single parents disadvantaged a married couple, the legislation was changed immediately. See for example *Christoffersen* v *M.N.R.*, [1993] TCJ No. 164 (TCC), in which the minister had denied a common-law wife's claim for the disability credit in relation to her partner; her Charter challenge failed. See also *The Queen* v *Scheller*, 75 DTC 5406 (FCTD); *McPhee* v *M.N.R.*, 80 DTC 1034 (TRB); *Toutant* v *M.N.R.*, 78 DTC 1499 (TRB).
76 Affidavit of Albert Wakkary, filed in *Rosenberg* v *The Queen* (Ont. Gen Div, Court File No. 79885/94) (sworn 2 June 1994), paras. 11–14, at 8–9.
77 If a Möbius strip is sliced from what used to be one end to the other former end, the strip itself remains intact and is still one-sided – but it has twice as many twists and is twice as long.
78 Monique Wittig, 'One Is not Born a Woman,' in *The Straight Mind and Other Essays*, trans. Marlene Wildeman (Boston: Beacon Press, 1992), 9–20, at 20.
79 Canada, House of Commons, Debates and Proceedings, 7th Sess, 12th Parl, IV: 4102, 4103 (3 August 1917), Thomas White.
80 Ibid., IV: 4103, Mr Verville.
81 Ibid., IV: 4104, Mr Graham.
82 Ibid., IV: 4106, Mr Middlebro.
83 Ibid., IV: 4105, Mr Knowles.
84 Ibid., IV: 4109, Thomas White.
85 Ibid., IV: 4104, Mr Graham.

86 Erwin Wexberg, *The Psychology of Sex: An Introduction*, trans. W. Béran Wolfe (New York: Blue Ribbon Books, 1931), vi. I am grateful to Kate Lahey Salter for drawing this text to my attention.
87 Ingrid Lund-Andersen, 'Moving Towards an Individual Principle in Danish Law' (1990), 4 *International Journal of Law and the Family* 328–42, at 329.
88 The new policy for free airline travel for members of Parliament replaced the term 'spouse' with the term 'designated traveller.' Initially opened up to extend this benefit to same-sex partners, the benefit was extended even further so that a travelling companion of the same sex would not necessarily be assumed to be gay, but the new framing of the benefit enables other non-intimate companions to receive the benefit too: Tim Naumetz, 'Free travel for MPs' spouses now includes gay partners,' *Ottawa Citizen*, 6 December 1997, A5.
89 Meki Cox, 'Law Providing Reciprocal Benefits for Unmarried Couples goes into Effect,' Associated Press, 9 July 1997.
90 Ibid.
91 Interview with Polikoff reported in Fenton Johnson, 'Wedded to an Illusion: Do gays and lesbians really want the right to marry?', *Harper's Magazine*, November 1996, 43–50, at 48–9. Didi Herman, *Rights of Passage: Struggles for Lesbian and Gay Legal Equality* (Toronto: University of Toronto Press, 1994), 147–8, also finds this approach appealing, although she considers all of these types of policy structures to be not alternative strategies in themselves, but the inevitable 'next stage' in the process of 'troubling' heterosexual family norms.
92 Julie A. Nelson, 'Tax Reform and Feminist Theory in the United States: Incorporating Human Connection' (1991), 18 *Journal of Economic Studies* 11–29, an economist, has argued against either the 'pure' individual or relational approach to the benefit unit. However, she has concluded that, to the extent that the individual model is to be given fuller expression, household composition should be treated as a private consumption decision and not as a basis for calculating benefits. On balance, she urges moving closer to the individual model at the same time that relationship-based provisions are modified to recognize a wider range of qualifying relationships. The Women and Taxation Working Group of the Ontario Fair Tax Commission came to a similar conclusion, primarily because some members of the Working Group saw existing dependency benefits as offering an opportunity to put some government benefits directly in the hands of dependent adults: See Fair Tax Commission, *Discussion Paper Searching for Fairness* (Toronto: Fair Tax Commission, 1993), 60–2. Cossman, 'Inside/Out,' has concluded that when sufficient attention is paid to context, discussion of both individual and

relationship-based models can lead to the creation of new 'deconstructive' legislative structures that offend neither the 'we are family' nor the 'we are not family' queer lobbies, and that diverse strategies – including modified forms of benefit units – can be pursued across the range of policy issues. Gwen Brodsky, 'Out of the Closet and Into a Wedding Dress? Struggles for Lesbian and Gay Legal Equality' (1994), 7 *Canadian Journal of Women and the Law* 523–35, has concluded that activists can develop purposive and progressive approaches to the benefit unit by beginning with the context and by refusing to adopt or fit into existing models of 'family.' Claire Young, 'Taxing Times for Lesbians and Gay Men: Equality at What Cost?' (1994), *Dalhousie Law Journal* 534–59, has similarly urged that by beginning with the larger context and then addressing issues from the specificities of lesbian and gay existence, law-reform approaches can be worked out carefully.

93 However, see Shelley A. M. Gavigan, 'Paradise Lost, Paradox Revisited: The Implications of Familial Ideology for Feminist, Lesbian, and Gay Engagement to Law' (1994), 31 *Osgoode Hall Law Journal* 3: 589–624. Gavigan not only traces both sides of the 'paradox' of the benefit unit, but also looks critically at proposals for expanded benefit units in the context of a race-, sex-, class-, and sexuality-sensitive analysis. Gavigan's purpose here would be to eliminate 'family' as a site of legal contest, and to eliminate judicial control over relationship recognition.

94 Wittig, *Not Born Woman*, 20.

95 Jeannette Armstrong, *Slash* (Penticton, BC: Theytus, 1985), 70.

Chapter Ten: The Cost of 'Incrementalism'

1 *M. v H.* (1996), 27 OR (3d) 593, 132 DLR (4th) 538 (Ont. Ct Gen Div), Epstein J, aff'd (1996), 31 OR (3d) 417, 142 DLR (4th) 1 (Ont. CA), per Doherty and Charron J, Finlayson J dissenting, leave to appeal granted 24 April 1997, per L'Heureux-Dubé, Sopinka, and Iacobucci JJ, on condition that government pay all costs in any event of the cause. This decision means that in addition to being able to claim a share of accumulated relationship property via equitable remedies, same-sex cohabitants can also claim a share of their former partners' income for a period after relationship breakdown.

2 *Rosenberg v A.-G. Canada* (1995), 127 DLR (4th) 738, 25 OR (3d) 612 (Ont. Gen Div), per Charron J, rev'd [1998] OJ No. 1627 (OCA) (QL), per McKinley, Abella, and Goudge JJ A.

3 *Moore and Akerstrom v The Queen*, [1996] CHRD No. 8 (Can Hum Rts Trib, 13 June 1996), per Norton, Chair, Ellis, and Sinclair, Members. This order did exclude the employee pension plan survivor provisions, on consent of the

parties, but one hopes that the Supreme Court of Canada ruling in *Rosenberg* will fill in that gap.
4 Family Relations Amendment Act, 1997, SBC 1997, 2d Sess., 36th Parl, 46 Eliz II, 1997 [Bill 31], passed third reading 23 July 1997, includes same-sex partners in the definition of 'spouse' for purposes of most family-related legislation in British Columbia.
5 See *Dwyer* v *Toronto (Metropolitan)*, Ontario Board of Inquiry (Human Rights Code), Decision No. 96-0033 (27 September 1996), per Tacon, Adj (unreported).
6 [1995] 2 SCR 513.
7 Randy Bauslaugh, 'Sex, Money and Family Values' (1994), 4: 1 *Employment and Labour Law Reporter* 2.
8 See generally Bauslaugh, 'Sex, Money.'
9 File No. BI-0056-93 (27 September 1996) (Ont. Bd of Inq).
10 RSC 1985, c H-6, as amended by SC 1996, c 14, section 1, adding 'sexual orientation' to the prohibited grounds of discrimination.
11 Revenue Canada, Interpretation Bulletin IT-470R, 'Income Tax Act Employees' Fringe Benefits' (8 April 1988), amended by Special Release, 'Employee Fringe Benefits' (11 December 1989).
12 See generally Income Tax Act, sections 5, 6(1).
13 Interpretation Bulletin IT-470R.
14 Reported as *Dwyer* v *Toronto (Metropolitan)*.
15 See SC 1990, c 39, section 1(1), applicable to 1988 et seq.
16 See ITA section 6(1)(a)(I); section 248(1) 'private health services plans'; Interpretation Bulletin IT-339R2, 'Income Tax Act Meaning of 'Private Health Services Plan' (8 August 1989); Interpretation Bulletin IT-470R (8 April 1988), 'Employee's Fringe Benefits,' paras. 39, 40, 41; Special Release, 'Employee Fringe Benefits' (11 December 1989); ATR-23, 'Private Health Services Plan' (14 July 1987).
17 Revenue Canada, 'Same Sex Benefits' (Private ruling 9502935) (25 May 1995); Revenue Canada, 'PHSP within a Flex Plan for Same Sex Benefits' (Private ruling 9505605) (30 June 1995); Revenue Canada, 'Effect of the Egan (S.C.C.) decision on Same Sex Partners Health Plan' (Private ruling 9518245) (22 November 1995); Revenue Canada, 'Private health services plans' (Private ruling 9532815) (6 February 1996).
18 [1996] CHRD No. 8 (Can Hum Rts Trib, 13 June 1996), per Norton, Chair, Ellis and Sinclair, Members.
19 *Moore and Akerstrom* v *Canada (Treasury Board)*, supplementary order (10 April 1997).
20 See *Dwyer* v *Toronto (Metropolitan)*.

21 Interpretation Bulletin IT-470R, paras. 33-8, 42.
22 Section 6(1)(a)(iv) stipulates that they are tax exempt if they are provided to 'an individual related to the taxpayer.' There is plenty of interpretive room to read that language as including same-sex partners. There is no definition of 'individual related to the taxpayer' anywhere in the Income Tax Act. Section 251(2)(a) defines 'related persons' or 'persons related to each other' as 'individuals connected by blood relationship, marriage or adoption,' but this definition was enacted for purposes of giving effect to section 251(1), an anti-avoidance provision. (Section 251[1] provides that 'related persons' are deemed to not deal at arm's length with each other, but that it will be a question of fact whether 'persons not related to each other' deal at arm's length with each other.)
23 Section 62(3)(a)–(e) defines 'moving expenses' as including those relating to 'members of the taxpayer's household.' 'Household' is not a defined term.
24 *Halsbury's Statutes of England* (1949, 2d ed.), vol. 12, at 231, General Note.
25 Laurence E. Coward, 'Some History on Pensions in Canada,' in *Pensions in Canada*, ed. Laurence E. Coward (Don Mills, ON: CCH Canadian, 1964), 199-212, at 199; A. R. Ilersic, 'Pension Plans for All' (1954), 2 *Canadian Tax Journal* 75–82, at 75, note 2.
26 F.E. LaBrie, *The Principles of Canadian Income Taxation* (Don Mills, ON.: CCH Canadian, 1965), 25; Seligman, 'Income Tax,' 7 *Encyclopedia of the Social Sciences* at 629 (1932); *Eisner v Macomber*, 252 U.S. 189 (U.S. SC, 1919), at 207, per Pitney J.
27 See Income War Tax Act, 1917, SC 1917, c 28, section 3(7), added by 9–10 Geo V, c 55, section 2(7); Income War Tax Act, RS 1927, c 97, section 5(g).
28 See *British Insulated and Helsby Cables, Ltd.* v *I.R.C.*, [1926] AC 205 (HL); *C.I.R.* v *The Duke of Westminster*, [1936] AC 1 (HL); Income War Tax Act, as amended by 1 Ed VIII 1936, c 38, section 5; Income War Tax Act, as amended by 6 Geo VI 1942, c 28, sections 3(1)(c), 5(5); Coward, 'History on Pensions,' 203.
29 *Report of the Royal Commission on Taxation* (Ottawa: Queen's Printer, 1966), vol. 2: 7–19.
30 Task Force on Retirement Income Policy, *The Retirement Income System in Canada: Problems and Alternative Policies for Reform* (Ottawa: Minister of Supply and Services Canada, 1979), 309.
31 Department of Finance, *Pension Reform: Improvements in Tax Assistance for Retirement Saving* (Ottawa: Minister of Supply and Services Canada, 1989), especially Chart 1, at 4; Canada, Department of Finance, *Government of Canada Tax Expenditure 1995* (Ottawa: Queen's Printer, 1996), 'Defining tax expenditures.'

32 Robert M. Clark, 'The Pension Benefits Act of Ontario and Its Relation to Federal Pension Proposals,' in *Pensions in Canada*, ed. Coward, 27–44, at 31; W.R. Latimer, 'Pension Plan – *Filius Nullius*?' (1962), 10 *Canadian Tax Journal* 190–5, 193.
33 Carter Commission Report, vol. 3, at 428–9, paragraph 11.
34 See Income Tax Act, SC 1970–71–72, c 63, sections 6(1)(a)(i), 56(1)(a)(i); *West Hill Redevelopment Co. Ltd.* v *M.N.R.* (1969), 69 DTC 5358 (Exch Ct, per Kerr J; *Susan Hosiery Ltd. [No. 2]* v *M.N.R.* (1969), 69 DTC 5346 (Exch Ct), per Gibson J; *MacIntyre* v *M.N.R.* (1972), 72 DTC 1134 (TRB), per Boisvert QC.
35 ITA section 147.1(15).
36 [1996] CHRD No. 10 (Can Hum Rts Trib, 13 September 1996), per Armstrong, Kaluzny, and Pitzel, Members.
37 *Leshner*, at 16,357.
38 *Leshner* v *Ontario*, 92 CLLC 16,129 (7 April 1992) (granting intervenor status to provincial insurer (*Leshner I*); *Leshner* v *Ontario*, 92 CLLC 16,329 (decision on the merits of the complaint) (*Leshner II*).
39 *Leshner I*, at 16,129–30; *Leshner II*, at 16,332.
40 In addition, the Income Tax Regulations provide for return of contributions in order to avoid revocation of plan (Regulations para. 8502[d][iii]) and reduction of benefits in order to avoid revocation of a plan (Regulation para. 8502[f][ii]). Thus if the tribunal had ordered a course of action that was eventually reversed by a court, and if the minister did seek retroactive revocation of registration under such circumstances, and if the court would permit the revocation to go ahead in such circumstances, then, even after receiving notice of intent to revoke registration, the plan administrator could salvage the registration in order to avoid revocation.
41 In *OPSEU Pension Plan Trust Fund* v *Ontario*, [1998] OJ No. 5075 (Ont. Gen Div) (File No. 98-cv-157212), per Rivard J., the court confirmed that separate plans for lesbian and gay employees violate the Charter.
42 See, for example, the 1979 amendments to the Income Tax Act to sections 56, 60, and 73(1)(d), which were enacted to ensure that provincial recognition of equitable claims brought by non-married cohabitants would not lead to onerous income tax consequences. The policy objectives of these amendments are discussed in David M. Sherman, ed., *Department of Finance Income Tax Act Technical Notes* (Scarborough, ON: Carswell, 1992), 244–5, 267–8, 377–8.
43 See Family Relations Amendment Act, 1997, SBC 1997, 2d Sess, 36th Parl, 46 Eliz II, 1997 (passed 3rd reading 23 July 1997) [Bill 31].
44 As of 10 February 1997, 68 federal statutes contained 339 provisions relating

Notes to pages 295–9 443

to children. Of the 68 federal statutes, no fewer than 16 related in some way to the pension or support rights of surviving children. Provincial law contains even more provisions: Ontario: 636; Manitoba: 360; Alberta: 339; British Columbia: 487.

45 *Korn* v *Potter* (1996), 134 DLR (4th) 437 (B.C. SC), per Holmes J.
46 For a good overview of how legal status has affected many children with same-sex parents in the United States, see Joseph P. Shapiro, 'Kids with gay parents' (1996), 121 *U.S. News and World Report* 11: 75–9.
47 See *Re Ramer*, [1971] OR 350–3 (Ont. H Ct J), per Houlden J, in which the daughter of a man who remarried after the daughter became an adult was not a preferred beneficiary for purposes of succession duty, but was a 'stranger' in law to her despite the closeness of their relationship.
48 RSO 1990, c C.12.
49 1 *Blackstone's Commentaries* 446.
50 See section 4(2). Thus in *Low* v *Low* (1994), 114 DLR (4th) 709, 4 RFL (4th) 103 (Ont. Gen Div), per Ferrier J, and *Zegota* v *Zegota-Rzegocinski* (1995), 53 ACWS (3d) 95, [1995] WDFL 683, [1995] OJ No. 204 (Ont. Gen Div), per Yates J, husbands whose wives conceived by artificial insemination were declared to be parents under these filiation provisions, and were awarded access; in *Keeping* v *Pacey*, [1995] OJ No. 1982 (Ont. Ct of J) (Cobourg Registry No. 13/95, 1 June 1995), per Ingram Prov J, parentage was not in issue, and access was denied on the basis that the husband had made no effort to establish or maintain a relationship with the child for three years before bringing the application; the court referred to the husband as 'a stranger to this child,' and did not appear to be aware how the parentage presumptions related to the 'best interests' test in section 24(2). See also *Levin* v *Levin*, 645 NE 2d 601 (Ind. 1994) (husband could not avoid paying child support on basis child conceived by artificial insemination); *Sleeper* v *Sleeper*, 145 Ore. App 165, 929 P 2d 1028 (Ore. CA 1996) (husband retained custody of two children biologically conceived with other men during marriage; wife estopped from denying parentage).
51 Section 1(1).
52 RSO 1990, c S.26, section 1(1).
53 See also the definition of 'issue' in section 1(1) of the Succession Act: '"issue" includes a descendant conceived before and born alive after the person's death.'
54 SO 1992, c 30, section 1(2).
55 SO 1996, c 2, Schedule A, sections 20(1)(5), 20(10). Each jurisdiction handles the issues relating to parentage slightly differently. For example, Family Relations Act, RSBC 1996, c 128, sections 94 and 95, discuss presumptions of

paternity in terms of 'the male person' who is 'the father' by virtue of either marriage or cohabitation. The inclusion of partners of the 'same gender' in the definition of 'stepparent' by virtue of Bill 31 would appear to not affect the definition of 'parent' in a way that would change the exclusion of women from the application of these presumptions.
56 RSC 1985, c C-29, section 2(1).
57 The prohibition on discrimination on the basis of 'family status' in human rights legislation reinforces this policy. See for example Human Rights Code, RSO 1990, c H.19, sections 1, 2, 3, 5, 6.
58 Children's Law Reform Act, section 20(2).
59 Section 21. Note that this is not necessarily the case in every jurisdiction. For example, in Newfoundland, a person does not have standing to apply for custody unless they have 'demonstrated a settled intention to treat the child as a child of his or her family.' See Children's Law Act, RSN 1990, c C.-13, sections 31(1), 69(4).
50 CLRA, section 20(2).
61 RSO 1990, c F.3, section 1(1).
62 See for example *R.R.C. v A.E.F.*, [1996] OJ No. 675 (Ont. Ct Gen Div, 21 February 1996) (London Registry No. D0712/94), per Campbell J; *Laro v Laro*, [1995] OJ No. 2738 (Ont. Ct Prov Div, 11 September 1995) (Sudbury Registry No. D331/94), per Guay Prov J.
63 See *Barclay v Santucci*, [1994] OJ No. 2803 (Ont. Un Fam Ct, 24 November 1994) (File No. V-1014/93), Vanduzer UFCJ.
64 RSC 1985, c C-8, section 42(1), defining 'child' for purposes of Part II, pertaining to pensions and supplementary benefits.
65 RSC 1985, c C-17, section 2(2). The definition also includes children who were formally adopted during minority, but that clause is found in all the traditional definitions of 'child' as well. If a person falls into this definition of 'child,' they must meet a further age and dependency test to qualify for survivor allowances: See section 25(1)(b), (4)(a), (b).
66 Cf. the Divorce Act, RS, 1985, c 3 (2d Supp), section 2(1), (2), which defines 'child of the marriage' as 'a child of two spouses or former spouses,' and does not include children of cohabitants. This definition is consistent with the wider social concept of parentage, for it includes any child in relation to whom a couple stands 'in the place of parents' or the stepchild of one of them. However, it is narrower than other definitions in that it does not include children of non-married cohabitants. This unique narrowness is, of course, due simply to the fact that the Divorce Act by its very terms of reference applies only to formally married couples. Cohabitants do not need to seek divorce, but can simply cease cohabiting.

67 There is also a huge gap between Canadian law relating to parentage and U.S. law. Thus it would be important to carefully distinguish legislative regimes in Canadian litigation, should any of the parties seek to introduce U.S. authorities. See for example Elizabeth A. Delaney, 'Statutory Protection of the Other Mother: Legally Recognizing the Relationship between the Nonbiological Lesbian Parent and Her Child' (1991), 43 *Hastings Law Journal* November: 177–216; cf. *Holtzman v Knott*, 193 Wis. 2d 649, 533 NW 2d (Wisc. SC 1995), cert denied 133 L Ed 2d 404, 116 S Ct 475 (U.S. SC 1995), in which the Court relied on equitable powers to protect the best interests of a child in ordering visitation for a non-biological lesbian co-mother; the Court found that the co-mother had established a 'parent-like' relationship.
68 SO 1992, c 30, section 1(2).
69 SO 1996, c 2, Schedule A, section 20(1)(5).
70 CLRA, section 20.
71 (1995), 23 OR (3d) 679, per Nevins Prov Div J.
72 Citizenship Act, section 5(2)(a).
73 *Re K.* (1995), 23 OR (3d) 679, per Nevins Prov Div J; followed in *Re C.E.G. (No. 1)*, [1995] OJ No. 4072 (Ont. Ct of J–Gen Div), per Aston J (17 August 1995).
74 Adoption Act, SBC 1995, c 48, sections 1, 29(1), effective November 1996 in relation to same-sex adoptions.
75 Bill 31, section 1.
76 See 'More on Taxation and Same-Sex Couples' (June 1995), *Money and Family Law* 46–8.
77 *Titchenal v Dexter*, 693 A 2d 682 (Vt. SC 1997), per Allen CJ. The dissenting member of the court pointed out, to no avail, that 'step-parent' adoption by lesbian mothers had not been available while the couple was still together.
78 Human Rights Act, RSO 1990, c H.19, sections 1, 2, 3, 5, 6, 10(1).
79 (1996), 13 *Lambda Update* 3: 6 (Penn. Super Ct).
80 [1996] Westlaw 694235, 1996 Haw App LEXIS 138 (Haw Cir Ct, 1st Cir, 3 Dec. 1996), per Chang J, aff'g *Baehr v Lewin*, 74 Haw 530, 852 P 2d 44 (1993), clarified on grant of reconsideration in part, 74 Haw 645, 852 P 2d 74 (1993).
81 At para. 50, quoting transcript (11 September 1996), 114–15.
82 *Re L. and S.* (Unreported) File No. 195/89 (Ont. Prov Ct Prov Div), per Pedlar J.
83 But see *Buist v Greaves*, [1997] OJ No. 2646 (Ont. Gen Div), per Benotto J, in which the court refused a declaration that a non-biological co-mother was 'also Simon's mother.' The court concluded that it did not have jurisdiction to declare that Simon had more than one mother, and that she had failed to establish a mother–child relationship. The problem in this case may have

revolved around the request for a finding that Simon had two 'mothers' instead of asking that the non-biological co-mother be declared to be a 'parent.' While a 'father' is pointed out by the marriage or cohabitation, the mother is pointed out by the birth, and as early marriage litigation demonstrated, common-law doctrine is more resistant to Charter challenge than statutory categories.

84 Cf. Cree-Naskapi (of Québec) Act, SC 1984, c 18, section 174, which defines 'child' for purposes of succession of property as including a child adopted 'in accordance with Cree or Naskapi custom.'
85 618 NYS 2d 356 (App Div, 1994), rev'g 599 NYS 2d 377 (Fam Ct, 1994).
86 For an outline of the case and of the arguments made by Nancy Polikoff in her *amicus curiae* brief to the court in this case, see Nancy D. Polikoff, 'The Social Construction of Parenthood in One Planned Lesbian Family'(1996), *Review of Law and Social Change* 203–11.

Chapter Eleven: The Future of Queer 'Personhood'

1 'Person,' *Black's Law Dictionary* (St Paul, MN: West Publishing, 1968), 1299–1300.
2 [1930] AC 124 (PC).
3 [1928] SCR 276.
4 The constraints that were still placed on the civil capacities of women despite the 'Persons' Case were an important factor in the eventual formulation of the terms of section 15(1) of the Charter. The way in which this movement affected women of colour, Aboriginal women, and other hierarchically disadvantaged women is another story that remains to be fully told.
5 *University of Saskatchewan* v *Saskatchewan Human Rights Commission*, [1976] 3 WWR 385 (Sask. QB).
6 The Code of Alabama, 1852, Title 13, chapters 3 and 4; Part II, Title 5, chapters 3 and 4.
7 19 How 393 (U.S. SC, 1857).
8 Laws of Mississippi, 1865, chapter IV, section 1.
9 Ibid., sections 1, 3–9; chapter VI, section 2; chapter XXIII, sections 1, 2.
10 These cases and the reasoning used by the courts are reproduced in pertinent part in Richard Bardolph, *The Civil Rights Record: Black Americans and the Law, 1819–1970* (New York: Thomas Y. Crowell, 1970), 58–72, 144–53.
11 109 U.S. 3 (U.S. SC, 1883).
12 95 U.S. 485 (U.S. SC, 1878).
13 163 U.S. 537 (U.S. SC, 1896).

14 See for example Constitution of Alabama, 1865, in Alabama Revised Code, 1867, article IV, section 31.
15 Bardolph, *The Civil Rights Record*, 130–1.
16 See for example *North Carolina Public Laws, 1865–1866*, c 40, section 8. Elsewhere this legislation also made it a criminal offence for cohabiting former slaves who became deemed to be married to fail to register that relationship. See sections 5, 6.
17 *Green v State*, 58 Ala. 190 (Ala. SC, 1871), quoting an earlier case.
18 *Pace and Cox v Alabama*, 69 Ala. 231 (Ala. SC, 1881) aff'd 106 U.S. 585 (U.S. SC, 1882).
19 Frederick L. Hoffman, 'Race Traits and Tendencies of the American Negro' (1896), 11 *Publications of the American Economic Association* 95, 327, 329.
20 See Acts of Louisiana, Reg Sess, 1958 (No. 519), sections 1, 2, 3.
21 32 Cal. 2d 711, 198 P. 2d 17 (Calif. SC, 1948).
22 The poll tax was abolished when the Twenty-fourth Amendment was finally ratified. The poll tax was routinely used to prevent African Americans from exercising their right to vote in Southern states. See Constitution of the United States, Article XXIV, sections 1, 2.
23 388 U.S. 1 (1967).
24 478 U.S. 186 (U.S. SC, 1986).
25 See Barbara Case, 'Repealable Rights: Municipal Civil Rights Protection for Lesbians and Gays' (1989), 7 *Law and Inequality* 441, 444, and note 18.
26 See for example Wisc. Stat Ann, sections 111.22, 111.31–6 (West Publishing, 1988) (added in 1982), which contains some of the most complete protection. The other jurisdictions are California, Connecticut, District of Columbia, Hawaii, Maine, Massachusetts, Minnesota, New Hampshire, New Jersey, Rhode Island, and Vermont. The Maine and New Hampshire statutes were passed in 1997.
27 See Note, 'Domestic Partnership Recognition in the Workplace: Equitable Employee Benefits for Gay Couples (and Others)' (1990), 51 *Ohio State Law Journal* 1067; Case, 'Repealable Rights,' at 445, note 25.
28 Case, 'Repealable Rights,' at 453.
29 See for example *Big Brothers, Inc. v Minneapolis Commission on Civil Rights*, 284 NW 2d 823 (Minn. SC, 1979), in which the court ruled that red-flagging gay volunteers was not discriminatory, because mothers of boys in the program had a legitimate need for information on their sexuality.
30 Note, 'Workplace Recognition,' at 1070, points out that some local organizations have also extended insurance benefits to same-sex partners.
31 Case, 'Repealable Rights,' 452–3.

32 See *Mabon* v *Keisling*, 317 Or. 406, 856 P 2d 1023 (1993); *Lewis* v *Keisling*, 320 Or. 13, 879 P 2d 857 (Or. 1994).
33 See Aspen Municipal Code (1977), section 13-98; Boulder Rev. Code (1987), sections 12-1-1 to 12-1-11; Denver Rev. Municipal Code (1991), art. IV, sections 28-91 to 28-116.
34 *Romer* v *Evans*, 116 S Ct 1620 (U.S. SC, 1996), per Kennedy J, quoting *Plessy* v *Ferguson*, 163 U.S. 537, 559, 16 S Ct 1138, 41 L Ed 256 (U.S. SC, 1896), per Harlan J (dissenting from approval of 'separate but equal' doctrine).
35 See Suzanne B. Goldberg, '*Romer* v. *Evans* Update' (1996), 13 *Lambda Update* 3: 12. See, however, *Equality Foundation of Greater Cincinnati* v *City of Cincinnati*, File No. 97-1795 (U.S. Supreme Court, 13 October 1998), per Stevens J, denying cert. from 128 F 3d 289 (CA6 1997), the effect of which was to leave a similar amendment to a municipal charter untouched.
36 1996 Westlaw 694235, 1996 Haw App LEXIS 138 (Haw Cir Ct, 1st Cir, 3 Dec. 1996), per Chang J, aff'g *Baehr* v *Lewin*, 74 Haw 530, 852 P 2d 44 (1993), clarified on grant of reconsideration in part, 74 Haw 645, 852 P 2d 74 (1993).
37 Hawaii Constitution, Article I, section 5.
38 HRS Ann, Div 3, Tit 31, c 572, section 572-1.
39 *Baehr* v *Miike*, [1996] Westlaw 694235, 1996 Haw App LEXIS 138, Findings of Fact and Conclusions of Law, para. 18.
40 Ibid., para. 123.
41 Ibid., para. 19.
42 United States Public Laws, 110 Stat 2419 (104th Congr, 2d Sess), adding to U.S. CA title 28, c 115, a new section 1738C, and adding to U.S. CA title 1, c 1, new section 7.
43 U.S. CA title 28, c 115, new section 1738C.
44 U.S. CA title 1, c 1, new section 7.
45 Andrew Koppelman, 'Why Discrimination against Lesbians and Gays Is Sex Discrimination' (1994), 69 *New York University Law Review* 197. Lawyers have already begun to search for ways to minimize the impact of DOMA. See for example Cynthia M. Reed, 'When Love, Comity, and Justice Conquer Borders: INS Recognition of Same-Sex Marriage' (1996), 28 *Columbia Human Rights Law Review* 97–134, at 102–10.
46 House Bill 117, House of Representatives, 19th Legisl, 1997, State of Hawaii (15 January 1997).
47 Hawaii House Bill 117, section 1.
48 Hawaii House Bill 117, section 2, to be added to Constitution of the State of Hawaii, article I, section 5.
49 Hawaii House Bill 117, section 1.
50 As of 26 March 1996, three states had enacted anti-marriage bills (Indiana,

South Dakota, and Utah), sixteen other states were still considering anti-marriage bills, and eleven such bills had been defeated, withdrawn, or killed: Evan Wolfson, 'Economic Arguments for the Freedom to Marry' <EWLLDEF@aol.com> (26 March 1996).

51 Meki Cox, 'Law Providing Reciprocal Benefits for Unmarried Couples goes into Effect,' Associated Press, 9 July 1997.
52 Constitutional Equality Amendment (CEA), adopted in July 1995 by the National Organization for Women (NOW) at its annual conference. The text of the CEA and CEA Frequently Asked Questions (FAQs) are available from NOW at http://www.now.org.
53 Ideologies of difference are deeply seated. In ruling on a constitutional challenge to opposite-sex marriage laws in the 1970s, and without the benefit of a 'sex' clause, the Minnesota Supreme Court rejected the analogy between same-sex marriages and interracial marriages litigated in *Loving* v *Virginia*: 'There is a clear distinction between a marital restriction based merely upon race and one based upon the fundamental difference in sex': *Baker* v *Nelson*, 191 NW 2d 185, at 187 (Minn. SC, 1971).
54 The recent decision in *Brause and Dugan* v *Alaska*, Case No. 3AN-95-6562 CI (Alaska Sup Ct, 3d Dist, 1998), per Michalski J (27 February 1998), has followed *Baehr* v *Miike* in finding that marriage being a fundamental right, sex-based classifications restricting the right to marriage violate the equal protection clause of the Alaska constitution.
55 See Douglas Sanders, 'Getting Lesbian and Gay Issues on the International Human Rights Agenda' (1996), 18 *Human Rights Quarterly* 67–106, 78–87, surveying legal developments at the European regional level.
56 See Kees Waaldijk, 'Standard Sequences in the Legal Recognition of Homosexuality – Europe's Past, Present and Future' (1994), 4 *Australasian Gay and Lesbian Law Review* 50–72.
57 Act No. 372 of 7 June 1989, effective 1 October 1989, cited in Marianne Hojgaard Pedersen, 'Denmark: Homosexual Marriages and New Rules Regarding Separation and Divorce' (1991–2), 30 *Journal of Family Law* 289, note 2.
58 Pedersen, 'Homosexual Marriages,' 290–1. See also Deborah M. Henson, 'A Comparative Analysis of Same-Sex Partnership Protections: Recommendations for American Reform' (1993), 7 *International Journal of Law and the Family* 282–313, at 286–7, for some of the details of community property, inheritance, and intestacy provisions.
59 See Linda Nielsen, 'Family Rights and the 'Registered Partnership' in Denmark' (1990), 4 *International Journal of Law and the Family* 29–307.
60 Pedersen, 'Homosexual Marriages,' 290. According to Pederson, the reason

for the citizenship requirement is that registered partnerships will probably not be recognized elsewhere. That does not make any sense to me; it seems more likely that the government was reluctant to become a 'marriage haven' internationally.

61 Linda Nielsen, 'Denmark: New Rules Regarding Marriage Contracts and Reform Considerations Concerning Children' (1992–93), 31 *Journal of Family Law* 309, 314. According to Nielsen, activism around these exclusions has not yet produced any changes in the legislation.
62 Pedersen, 'Homosexual Marriages,' 290–1.
63 See Ingrid Lund-Andersen, 'Moving Towards an Individual Principle in Danish Law' (1990), 4 *International Journal of Law and the Family* 328.
64 Nielsen, 'Family Rights,' 300.
65 This is also the model being considered in Finland. The organization promoting the bill has rejected the phrase 'registered partnership' in favour of 'recognized companionship' or 'legalized spouses' in order to make sure that people do not think that couples are listed in a public register somewhere: Paula Kuosmanen and Kati Mustola, 'Lesbian Motherhood in Finland' <Kati.Mustola@Helsinki.FI> (20 February 1997).
66 Cohabitees (Joint Homes) Act, SFS 1987: 237, amended by SFS 1987: 815, cited in Henson, 'Comparative Analysis,' 287, 307, note 26.
67 SFS 1987: 813, cited in Henson, 'Comparative Analysis,' 287, 309, note 28.
68 Henson, 'Comparative Analysis,' 287.
69 Ibid., 288.
70 Bjoern Skolander, 'RFSL Presents Report on Gays and Children' <skolander@bahnhof.se> (18 February 1997).
71 Kuosmanen and Mustola, 'Finland Motherhood.' See also Kate Griffin and Lisa Mullholland, eds., *Lesbian Motherhood in Europe* (London: Cassels, 1997). Kees Waaldijk and Andrew Clapham, eds., *Homosexuality: A European Community Issue – Essays on Lesbian and Gay Rights in European Law and Policy* (Dordrecht: Martinus Nijhoff, 1993), report that, although Norway and Iceland already recognize registered partnerships, and the Netherlands and Spain are in the process of adopting such legislation, only Iceland currently has provisions that deal with parentage of same-sex couples. The Netherlands legislation is expected to follow suit, but in a separate bill.
72 Ptk. 578/G.
73 Blaise Szolgyemy, 'Hungary high court gives blessing to gay couples' (Budapest, Hungary: Reuters, 8 March 1995), obtained from <mszymczy@urm.gov.pl> (9 March 1995).
74 Henson, 'Partnership Protections,' 288.

75 European Convention on the Adoption of Children, Europ TS No. 58 (24 April 1967), article 6(1).
76 For example, in *Bewley* v *Ontario*, [1997] OHRBID No. 24 (Ont. Bd of In.) (QL), per McNeilly, Bd, a lesbian woman filed a complaint with the Ontario Human Rights Commission when she and her partner were not permitted to register their new hyphenated last names after going through a commitment ceremony. The commission and board treated the complaint as arising out of the 'denial of the right to equal treatment with respect to services because of sexual orientation,' and the board ruled in favour of the complainant.
77 Human Rights Code, RSO 1990, c H.19, section 10(1).
78 File No. BI-0056-93 (27 September 1996) (Ont. Bd of Inq), per Tacon Bd.
79 See Health Care Consent Act, 1996, SO 1996, c 2, Sched A, section 20(1), (9), which permits partners to make health care decisions for each other on the same footing as spouses, and Substitute Decisions Act, 1992, SO 1992, sections 1(2), 10(2). In both these statutes, 'partner' is defined as follows: 'Two persons are partners for the purpose of this Act if they have lived together for at least one year and have a close personal relationship that is of primary importance in both persons' lives.'
80 Ontario Law Reform Commission, *Report on the Rights and Responsibilities of Cohabitants Under the Family Law Act* (Toronto: OLRC, 1993), 53–6.
81 Bill 167, An Act to amend Ontario Statutes to provide for the equal treatment of persons in spousal relationships, 3rd Sess, 35th Legisl (Ontario), 43 Eliz II, 1994, sections 1(1)–(3), 2 (lost on division following debate on second reading, 9 June 1994).
82 See for example Child and Family Services Act, RSO 1990, c C.11, section 136(1), which incorporates the definition of 'spouse' in the Human Rights Code, the definition of which would have been changed by Bill 167 to include same-sex and opposite-sex cohabitants; Land Transfer Tax Act, RSO 1990, c L.6, section 1(1), which incorporates the expanded definition of 'spouse' in Part III of the Family Law Act for purposes of exempting transfers of real estate between cohabitants from land transfer taxes; Toronto Islands Residential Community Stewardship Act, 1993, SO 1993, c 15, section 1, which incorporates the expanded definition of 'spouse' in Part III of the Family Law Act; Rental Housing Protection Act, RSO 1990, c R.24, section 1(1), the definition of 'spouse' in which depends on the definition in the Landlord and Tenant Act, which in turn was to have been expanded by Bill 167; Mortgages Act, RSO 1990, c M.40, section 53, depending on changes made in Landlord and Tenant Act.

83 See for example Assessment Act, RSO 1990, c A.31, section 19, exempting property held by a surviving spouse from reassessment; Consumer Reporting Act, RSO 1990, c C.33, section 1(1), which merely refers to 'spouse's name and age' for identifying purposes; Conveyancing and Law of Property Act, RSO 1990, c C.34, section 13(1), which merely refers to 'spouse' in clarifying how grants to concurrent owners are to be construed; Independent Health Facilities Act, RSO 1990, c I.3, section 1(1), which refers to spousal relationships in setting out conflicts of voting interests; Marriage Act, RSO 1990, c M.3, section 9(1), relating to presumptions of death when spouse is missing; Municipal Health Services Act, RSO 1990, c M.57, section 6(1), which relates to liability for personal taxes levied by municipality; Municipal Tax Sales Act, RSO 1990, c M.60, section 4(2), which relates to the interface between notice of arrears in payment of property taxes and family property law; Ontario Guaranteed Annual Income Act, RSO 1990, c O.17, section 1, which already included opposite-sex cohabitants in the definition of 'spouse' for purposes of eligibility for benefits; Ontario Pensioners Property Tax Assistance, RSO 1990, c O.33, section 1, which already defined 'family unit' as including not only spouses, but any other individuals occupying the same principal residence, whether related or not. But see Retail Sales Tax Act, RSO 1990, c R.31, section 4.2, which provides an exemption from liability for retail sales tax in relation to transfers of used vehicles to another member of the family or received from a spouse in satisfaction of claims under the Family Law Act; although the intention here might have been to limit this exemption to formally married couples, the fact that this provision makes no reference to Part II of the Family Law Act makes it highly unlikely that this provision would have continued to be applied only to married couples after Bill 167 had become effective.
84 Legislative Assembly of Ontario, 3rd Sess, 35th Parl (27 April–8 June 1993), 6572, 6573 (Hon. Marion Boyd, Attorney General and Minister Responsible for Women's Issues).
85 Debates, Boyd, 6574–7. For a detailed discussion of these issues, see chapter 10.
86 RSO 1990, c F.3.
87 Other provisions which back up Part II of the Family Law Act would also have remained unaffected by Bill 167. See, for example, Land Titles Act, RSO 1990, c L.5, section 44(1), which stipulates that a spouse's interest in real estate is not considered to be an 'encumbrance'; 'spouse' in this provision is defined by reference to Part II of the Family Law Act. See also Registry Act, RSO 1990, c R.20, section 47(5), (6), which requires an affidavit of marital status for purposes of Part II of the Family Law Act to be filed whenever registering real property.

88 These statutes are Income Tax Act, RSO 1990, c I.2, section 7(3), which incorporates the definitions of 'cohabiting spouse' and 'qualified dependant' in section 122.6 of the federal act by reference for purposes of calculating provincial income tax liability; Ontario Home Ownership Savings Plan, RSO 1990, c O.20, section 1(1), which limits tax credits for OHOSPs to spouses as defined in federal income tax legislation, even though the federal government no longer extends tax credits in relation to home ownership savings plans; Corporations Tax Act, RSO 1990, c C.40, section 1(1), which incorporates many of the definitions in the federal statute by reference.
89 James Rusk and Martin Mittelstaedt, 'Boyd buys one day of time to win votes for same-sex bill,' *Globe and Mail*, 8 June 1994, A6; William Walker and Leslie Papp, 'NDP alters same-sex bill,' *Toronto Star*, 9 June 1994, A1; Craig McInnes, 'Boyd backs off on gay spouses,' *Globe and Mail*, 9 June 1994), A1.
90 Walker and Papp, 'NDP alters,' A1.
91 Family Relations Amendment Act, 1997, SBC 1997, 2d Sess, 36th Parl, 46 Eliz II, 1997 [Bill 31], passed third reading 23 July 1997.
92 In Family Relations Act, RSBC 1996, c 128, section 1(c), as amended by Bill 31, section 1(c).
93 Family Relations Act, RSBC 1996, c 128, sections 94 and 95, set out rules of parentage and presumptions of paternity in terms of 'the male person' who is 'the father' by virtue of either marriage or cohabitation.
94 Family Relations Act, RSBC 1996, c 128, section 1(c), as amended by Bill 31, section 1(d).
95 Family Provision (Amendment) Bill 1996, An Act to amend the Family Provision Act 1969, 1996, Legislative Assemb Australian Cap Terr, section 5, 'domestic partner,' 'domestic relationship,' 'eligible partner,' 'legal spouse,' and 'spouse.' See also the same definitions in Administration and Probate (Amendment) Bill 1996, An Act to amend the Administration and Probate Act 1929, 1996, Legislative Assemb Australian Cap Terr, section 8.
96 Administration and Probate (Amendment) Bill 1996, section 10, amending section 45A in the legislation to provide that an eligible partner who lived with an intestate for more than the five years immediately preceding death would take the whole of the spousal share, even to the exclusion of a surviving formally married spouse.
97 An Act to amend various legislative provisions concerning de facto spouses, Draft Bill, 1998, sections 1, 2.
98 *Vriend v Alberta* (1998), 156 DLR (4th) 385 (SCC), per L'Heureux-Dubé J, at paras. 183, 184.

454   Notes to pages 338–40

99 See *Haig and Birch* v *Canada (A.-G.)* (1992), 9 OR (3d) 495 (Ont. CA), per Lacourcière, Krever, and McKinley JJ A, aff'g (1991), 5 OR (3d) 245 (Ont. Gen Div), per McDonald J; *Vriend* v *Alberta*, [1994] 6 WWR 414 (Alta. QB), per Russell J, rev'd (1996), 132 DLR (4th) 595 (Alta. CA), per McClung, O'Leary, JJ A, Hunt JJ A dissenting, reinstated (1998), 156 DLR (4th) 385 (SCC), per Cory and Iacobucci JJ; *Nfld. and Labrador Human Rights Commission* v *Nolan and Barry*, [1995] NJ No. 283 (Nfld. SC) (QL), per Barry J.
100 *A.-G. Canada* v *Mossop*, [1993] 1 SCR 554, L'Heureux-Dubé, Cory, and McLachlin JJ dissenting (1990), 71 DLR (4th) 661 (FCA), aff'g [1991] 1 FC 18, 71 DLR (4th) 661 (FCA), rev'g (1989), 10 CHRR D/6064 (Can Hum Rts Trib). This decision is discussed in detail in chapter 1.
101 Two of these are among the five remedies Lamer CJ outlined in *Schachter* v *Canada*, [1992] 2 SCR 679, 93 DLR (4th) 1, 1 NR 1 (SCC). The other three he listed are striking down the entire provision, severance, and either striking down or severance coupled with temporary suspension of the declaration of invalidity. The declaration reading a provision 'as if' it included an excluded group is more of an interpretive process than a Charter remedy as such, and has been used by courts granting Charter remedies as well as by those that have declared that they are not basing their decision on the Charter. An example of the latter type of order is the Federal Court of Appeal order in *Veysey*, discussed below.
102 [1991] BCJ No. 2588 (B.C. SC), per Rowles J.
103 (1990), 109 NR 300 (FCA), per Iacobucci CJ, Urie and Decary J., aff'g on different grounds (1989), 29 FTR 74.
104 (1990), 109 NR 300 (FCA), per Iacobucci CJ, Urie and Decary JJ, aff'g on different ground.
105 RSBC 1979, c 255, section 2.01.
106 This decision was based in part on the lower-court ruling in *Veysey*, which had relied on the Charter to extend the family visiting program to the claimant, and of course the Federal Court of Appeal did not affirm the lower court in *Veysey* on that ground. But that does not detract from the use of *Knodel* as an example of the 'reading as if' remedy, which is as much a creature of ordinary principles of statutory interpretation as it is of the Charter equality provisions.
107 (1992), 92 CLLC 16,329 (Ont. Bd of Inq), per Cumming and Plaut, Bd, Dawson, Bd, dissenting in part.
108 (1992), 92 CLLC, at 16,346-16,347.
109 (1992), 92 CLLC, at 16,355.
110 (1996), 27 OR (3d) 593, 132 DLR (4th) 538 (Ont. Gen Div), per Epstein J,

aff'd (1996), 31 OR (3d) 417 (Ont. CA), per Doherty and Charron JJ A, Finlayson J dissenting.
111 [1997] OJ No. 3979 (Ont. Gen Div) (QL), per Coo J.
112 (1995), 23 O.R. (3d) 679, per Nevins Prov. Div. J.
113 *Re C.E.G. (No. 1)*, [1995] OJ No. 4072 (Ont. Gen Div) (QL), per Aston J.
114 Human Rights Code, RSO 1990, c H.19, section 10(1) 'spouse,' incorporated by reference into section 136(1) of the Child and Family Services Act, RSO 1990, c C.11.
115 (1995), 25 OR (3d) 612 (Ont. Gen Div), per Charron J, rev'd [1998] OJ No. 1627 (OCA) (QL), per McKinley, Abella, and Goudge JJ A.
116 RSC 1985, c 1 (5th Supp), section 252(4), added effective for the 1993 taxation year.
117 Section 252(3).
118 As this debate intensifies, some same-sex couples have begun to look to corporate law instead of family law as a way to protect mutual interests. See GeoCities, 'Better Than Marriages, Gay or Straight,' <rllc@geocities.com>. Corporate remedies are available: see *M. v H.* (1993), 15 OR (3d) 721 (Ont. Gen Div), per Epstein J, in which the court used the corporate oppression remedy to extend an interest-free loan to the plaintiff because family law did not provide for interim support for same-sex cohabitants.

Index

In this index, cases and statutes are referenced in the following manner: When the name of a case or statute is given in the text, the text page number is cited. When the name of the case or statute is given in a note but not in the text, the note number and the page on which the note appears are cited, followed by the number of the related text page in parentheses. For example, '359n. 77 (19)' refers to note 77 on page 359 and to page 19 of the text. This method of referencing takes the reader to the page on which the case is discussed, with the note number as a guide to the precise location.

Full case and statute citations are provided in the notes, but not in the index.

A. v Colloredo-Mansfeld (No. 3), 408n. 160 (162)
Aboriginal persons, suspension of legal personality, 112
Act for the better protection of Lands and Property of the Indians in Lower Canada, An, 387n. 49 (112)
Act for the Protection of the Indians in Upper Canada from imposition and the property occupied or enjoyed by them from trespass and injury, An, 387n. 49 (112)
Act to Confer Civil Rights on Freedmen, An, Laws of Mississippi, 1865, c. IV, 40n. 80 (146)
Act to prevent Chinese from acquiring Crown lands, An, 388n. 50 (112)

Act to prevent the future introduction of Slaves and to limit the Term of Enforced Servitude within the Province, An, 387n. 48 (112)
Act to prevent the immigration of Chinese, An, 388n. 50 (112)
Act to regulate the Chinese population, An, 388n. 50 (112)
Acts of Louisiana, Reg Sess, 1958, 447n. (319)
Adams, Richard, 8–9
Adams v Howerton, 353n. 28 (9)
Administration and Probate (Amendment) Bill 1996 (Australia), 453nn. 95, 96 (336)
administrative proceeding: distinguished from Charter challenge,

458   Index

89; more successful than court proceedings, 98–9
Adoption Act (British Columbia), 304
African Americans, civil rights of; Black codes, 315–17; Civil Rights Act of 1866, 317; cohabitation, interracial, prohibition of, 318; constitutional restoration, 320; *Dred Scott* decision, 314–15; early statutes, limiting purpose, 313, 315–16 ; erasure of rights by courts, 317–20; and Fourteenth Amendment, 317; marriage, interracial, prohibition of, 318; re-creation of conditions of servitude, 316–17; slave codes, 314; and Thirteenth Amendment, 315
A.-G. Canada v *Mossop*, 355n. 46 (13), 55, 56, 59, 117, 411n. 198 (168), 337–8
A.-G. Canada v *Thwaites*, 22, 145
A.-G. Canada v *Ward*, 119, 397n. 51 (140)
Alpaerts v *Obront*, 401n. 81 (147)
Amendment 2 (Colorado), 322–3
American Civil Liberties Union, 256
American Law Institute, 6
Anderson v *Luoma*, 51–3, 65, 157, 221, 260–3
Andrews v *Law Society of British Columbia*, 45–50, 58, 68, 118
Andrews v *Law Society of Upper Canada*, 393n. 6 (133)
Andrews v *Minister of Health*, 51–3, 58, 61–2, 65, 413n. 10 (176)
Anglo-Norman law, 111
Anonymous, Re, 407n. 151 (160)
anti-miscegenation laws, 318–20
armed forces, exclusion from, 144–5
Artur Lasha, 398n. 53 (140)

Assessment Act (Ontario), 452n. 83 (332)

B. v *A.*, 24, 403n. 103 (152), 410n. 193 (167)
Baehr v *Lewin*, 256
Baehr v *Miike*, 380n. 81 (95), 176, 195, 256, 307, 323–6
Bailey v *The Queen* (1980), 358n. 67 (17)
Baker v *Nelson*, 449n. 53 (326
Barclay v *Santucci*, 444n. 63 (301)
Bardolph, Richard, 100
Beaulne, Pierre, 143
Bell Canada and C.T.E.A. (Re), 371n. 85 (55), 58
benefit system, social-good criteria, 278
benefit units, 271–3, 279
Benson v *Korn* (Board of Inquiry), 410n. 188 (166)
Bernhardt v *Bernhardt*, 408n. 168 (163)
Bewley v *Ontario*, 379n. 70 (87), 89, 451n. 76 (331)
Bezaire v *Bezaire*, 408n. 164 (163), 194, 195
Big Brothers v *Minneapolis Commission on Civil Rights*, 447n. 29 321
Big M Drug Mart v *R.*, 125
Bill C-4 (1974), 430n. 55 (236)
Bill C-4 (sentencing for hate-motivated crimes), 402n. 96 (151)
Bill 31 (Family Relations Amendment Act) (British Columbia): limited scope of, 334; marriage not available in, 335; parentage provisions of, 335; property not shared in, 335; spouse, definition of, 335; and stepparent, 334
Bill 167 (Ontario): amendments to,

334; deemed spouses in, 332; income tax provisions excluded from, 333; formal marriage excluded from, 333; opposite-sex cohabitants, equality with, 332; parentage restrictions in, 333; property restrictions in, 333; spouse, opposite-sex definition of, 430n. 57 (236)
Birch, Joshua, 49
bisexual persons, invisibility of, 92–6
Black v *Law Society of Alberta*, 125
Bliss v *A.-G. Canada*, 374n. 33 (72), 82
Bordeleau v *Canada*, 367n. 48 (46), 372n. 2 (64), 400n. 74 (144)
Borowski v *A.-G. Canada (Sask.)*, 390n. 72 (118)
Boulais v *Minister of Employment and Immigration*, 375n. 44 (78), 80, 90
Boutilier and Treasury Board (Natural Resources) (Re), 379n. 70 (87), 92
Bowers v *Hardwick*, 321
Braschi v *Stahl Associates*, 255
Brause and Dugan v *Alaska*, 449n. 54 (326)
British Insulated and Helsby Cables, Ltd. v *I.R.C.*, 441n. 28 (291)
Brooks v *Canada Safeway*, 374n. 33 (72)
Brown v *B.C. Minister of Health*, 155
Brown v *Board of Education of Topeka*, 391n. 87 (123)
Brown v *Minister of Health*, 65, 368n. 61 (51), 53
Brunet v *Davis*, 406n. 134 (157)
Buist v *Greaves*, 165, 445n. 83 (308)
Business Development Bank of Canada Act, 431n. 9 (244)

Cami Automotive Inc. and C.A.W., Local 88, Re, 18, 359n. 77 (19), 370n. 82 (55), 162

Canada v *Owen*: generally, 25, 403n. 103 (152), 410n. 193 (167), 167; read with 'trilogy' cases, 75–7
Canada (Canadian Human Rights Commission) v *Canadian Liberty Net*, 402n. 98 (151)
Canada Elections Act, RSC 1985, c E-2, 393n. 7 (133)
Canada Pension Plan Act, 301–2, 427n. 29 (224)
Canada Post Corp. and P.S.A.C. [Canada Post I], 371n. 85 (55), 56
Canada Post Corp. and P.S.A.C. [Canada Post II], 371n. 85 (55), 57
Canada Post Corp. and P.S.A.C. [Canada Post III], 371n. 85 (55), 57
Canada (Treasury Board–Environment Canada) and Lorenzen (Re), 371n. 85 (55), 56–7
Canadian AIDS Society v *Ontario*, 155, 377n. 57 (81), 83
Canadian Bill of Rights, 32–3
Canadian Broadcasting Corp. and Canadian Broadcasting Guild (Re), 371n. 85 (55)
Canadian Forces Superannuation Act, 302
Canadian Human Rights Act, 358n. 73 (17), 49; sexual orientation as prohibited ground of discrimination, 285
Canadian Pacific Ltd. and Brotherhood of Maintenance of Way Employees (Re), 379n. 70 (87)
Canadian Union of Public Employees (CUPE) v *M.N.R.*, 376n. 49 (78–9)
capacity to sue: limitations on, 146–7; risk of 'outing,' 147
capacity to testify: social and legal risks of testifying, 148

Carleton University and C.U.P.E., Local 2424, Re (1988), 18, 359n. 77 (20)
Carrott and Underwood v *Canada*, 399n. 62 (142)
Carter Commission on Taxation, 291
Case v *Case*, 408n. 162 (162)
C.D.P.Q. v *Anglsberger*, 403n. 107 (153)
C.E.G. (Re), 340–1, 445n. 73 (304)
C.E.G. (Re) (No. 1), 377n. 57 (81), 83, 409n. 185 (165)
Charitable Institutions Act (Ontario), 422n. 39 (199)
Charter of Human Rights and Freedoms (Québec), 34
Charter remedies: judicial amendment of legislation; reading in, 337–8, 340–1; reading down, 338, 339–40; reading as if, 338–9; scope of protection, 337
Charter of Rights (Canada): drafting process of equality provisions, 32–4; equality provisions applied to sexual orientation, 44; exclusion of sexual minorities in equality provisions, 30–4; generally, 4–5, 17, 359n 75 (27), 65, 121, 136, 257, 293, 306, 331, 336–42; lesbians in compliance process, 36–8; lobbying process, 29–31; open-ended language of equality provisions, 33–4, 38, 43; political tensions in compliance process, 35–8; sexual minorities, marginalization of, in compliance process, 35–9
Chaychuk v *Best CTV*, 161
Chernoff v *Pyne*, 164
child: diversity of definitions of, 296–7; gap between narrow and wide definitions, 302–4; illegitimacy of abolished, 299–300; incremental discrimination against same-sex parents defined, 295–6; lack of legal status of non-biological parent, 304; not purely biological definitions, 297–8; stepparent adoption of, 304–6; *see also* parent
Child and Family Services Act (Ontario), 54–5, 451n. 82 (332)
Children's Law Act (Newfoundland), 444n. 59 (300)
Children's Law Reform Act (Ontario), 165, 297, 299–300, 301, 303, 306, 307, 333
Christoffersen v *M.N.R.*, 437n. 75 (269)
Christopher Lefler Complaint, Saskatchewan Human Rights Commission, 403n. 109 (153)
Chryler Canada Ltd. and Canadian Auto Workers (Re), 379n. 70 (87), 380n. 73 (92)
CIP Paper Products Ltd. and Saskatchewan Human Rights Commission, Re (1978), 12
C.I.R. v *The Duke of Westminster*, 441n. 28 (291)
citizenship, 133–4
Citizenship Act, 300, 304
civil death, forms, 133
Civil Rights Act of 1866 (United States), 317
Civil Rights cases (United States Supreme Court), 317
C.L. v *C.C.*, 410n. 193 (167)
Clinton v *Ontario Blue Cross*, 18, 359n. 77 (21), 370n. 76 (54)
Code of Alabama, 1852, 401n. 94 (150), 314
Code civil du Québec, 426n. 14 (220)
codes of law, early, 103–4
cohabitant, opposite-sex definition

Index 461

of, 15–17; transgendered persons excluded by, 23–6; transsexual persons excluded by, 23–6
cohabitation, opposite-sex, unequal and appropriative, 259
collective agreements: and spousal rights, extension of, 92
Collins v *M.N.R.*, 391n. 87 (123)
Commission des droits de la personne du Québec, File No. Q-Q-1, 018-1, 019-1, 403n. 108 (153)
Commission des droits de la personne du Québec, File M-M-02, 325-1, 403n. 106 (153)
Commission des droits de la personne du Québec v *Camping & plage Gilles Fortie Inc.*, 405n. 125 (155)
Commission des droits de la personne du Québec c *Le Progrès du Saguenay Ltée et Paul Bergeron*, 403n. 106 (153)
common-law spouse: opposite-sex definition of, 15–17; same-sex definition of, 56; transgendered persons excluded by definition of, 23–6; transsexual persons excluded by definition of, 23–6
Connolly v *Woolrich*, 411n. 204 (170)
Constitution of Alabama, 447n. 14 (318)
Constitutional Equality Amendment movement, 325–6
Consumer Reporting Act (Ontario), 451n. 82 (332)
Conveyancing and Law of Property Act (Ontario), 451n. 82 (332)
Corbett v *Corbett*, 353n. 30 (9–10), 410n. 194 (167)
Coroners Act (Ontario), 422nn. 40, 41 (199)

Corporations Tax Act (Ontario), 453n. 88 (333)
Criminal Code, 7, 135–7, 148
criminalization: as means of oppression, 133–42; 'homosexual offences,' 135
criminal law: anti-queer bias, 135–8; 'homosexual offences,' 235–6
Crozier v *Asselstine*, 162
Curiale v *Reagan*, 435n. 57 (264)

D. v *D.*, 409n. 176 (163–4)
Daller v *Daller*, 408n. 169 (163)
Damien v *Ontario Human Rights Commission* (human rights complaint), 11, 400n. 71 (144)
Damien v *Ontario Racing Commission* (civil proceedings), 11
Defense of Marriage Act (United States), 256, 324–5
deferred-compensation registered pension plans: constitutional jurisdiction, 292; effect of cases on, 292–3; income tax benefits of, 291–2; income tax character of, 290–1; sexuality-specific language in, 290
demographic data on queers: Australian, 182–3; Canadian, 175–80, 210–11, 213; United States, 182–3
dependency subsidies: class bias in, 229; cost to governments, 225; described, 224; disincentives to waged work, 225; non-waged domestic labour, 220–1; poor targeting of benefits, 226–8; transfer of wealth to males, 226
Derrickson v *Derrickson*, 387n. 49 (112)
desire, criminalization of, 134–5
discrimination, definition of narrowed, 66

discrimination, quantifiable costs of. *See* employment; income
discrimination, unquantifiable costs of, 196, 197–8, 199
Divorce Act, 426n. 14 (220), 444n. 66 (302), 304
domestic partner (Australia), 336
Domestic Relations Act (Alberta), 426n. 14 (220)
Douglas v *Canada*, 367n. 48 (46), 372n. 2 (64), 400n. 74 (144)
Dred Scott v *Sandford*, 120, 314
Droit de la famille-14, 408n. 169 (163)
Droit de la famille-31, 408n. 163 (163)
Drummond Wren (Re), 350n. 4 (4)
Duval v *Sequin*, 389n. 71 (118)
Dwyer v *Toronto (Metropolitan)*, 377n. 57 (81), 86, 89, 90, 125, 283, 285, 440n. 14 (287), n. 20 (289), 292–3, 294, 331, 338–40
Dykon v *The Queen*, 398n. 55 (140)

E.(A.) v *E.(G.)*, 409n. 172 (163)
Edwards v *A.-G. Canada* ('Persons' Case), 116, 119, 120, 399n. 67 (143)
Egan and Nesbit v *The Queen* (Federal Court of Appeal), 65, 119, 120–1
Egan and Nesbit v *Canada* (Supreme Court of Canada): ambiguity of decision, 67–8; applied in *Little Sisters Book and Art Emporium* v *Canada (Minister of Justice)*, 81; applied in *Rosenberg* v *A.-G. Canada*, 79, 80; compared with *Miron* v *Trudel*, 73–4; distinguished in *Dwyer* v *Toronto (Metropolitan)*, 86; distinguished in *M.* v *H.*, 84; generally, 4, 17, 21, 32, 44, 45, 367n. 48 (46), 48, 50–1, 57–9, 61, 63–5, 125, 130, 155, 174, 176, 195–6, 199, 258, 267, 268, 283, 288, 292, 306, 337, 342; impact, 77–8, 80–1, 87–92; incremental change theory and, 70–1, 88; narrow and generous readings of, 168, 169–70; *Oakes* test, interpretation of, 70, 84; section 1 interpretation in, 69–72; section 15(1) interpretation in, 67–9; sexual-orientation clauses, interpretation in, 91–2
Eisner v *Macomber*, 441n. 26 (291)
eligible partner (Australia), 336
Elliott v *Elliott*, 408n. 166 (163)
employment discrimination: as grounds of complaint, 89–90; levels of, 200; limited protection against, 161–2; sexual harassment as, 162
Employment Standards Act (Ontario), 370n. 75 (54)
equal benefit of the law, expansive interpretation of, 69
Equal Rights Amendment (United States), 113
Equality Foundation of Greater Cincinnati, Inc. v *City of Cincinnati*, 391n. 91 (124)
Estate of Spaulding, 407n. 151 (160)
Estates Act (Ontario), 407n. 143 (159), 422n. 44 (199)
Execution Act (Ontario), 422n. 46 (199)

family employment benefits: employee benefit plans, 233; family wage movement, 231; income splitting, 233–4; income tax treatment, 232; not dependency-contingent, 232, 233; pension

survivor benefits, 232; same-sex couples. *See* queer penalty
family sharing provisions: children's interests, 219–20; costs to same-sex partners, 221–2; family-of-origin interests, 219; interspousal equalization, 219; purpose, 218, 222; Roman law, 221–2; tax-deferred redistributions, 218, 220
Family Law Act (Newfoundland), 426n. 14 (220)
Family Law Act (Ontario), 353n. 26 (8), 25, 84–5, 168, 426nn. 8–11, 15 (219–20), 267, 282, 301, 451n. 82 (332), 452 n. 87 (333)
Family Law Act (Prince Edward Island), 426n. 14 (220)
Family Law Reform Act (Ontario), 427n. 24 (221)
Family Maintenance Act (Manitoba), 426n. 14 (220)
Family Maintenance Act (Nova Scotia), 426n. 14 (220)
Family Provision (Amendment) Bill 1996 (Australia), 453n. 95 (336)
Family Relations Act (British Columbia), 426n. 14 (220), 302, 453nn. 92–4 (335)
Family Relations Amendment Act (B.C.), 411n. 203 (170), 440n. 4 (283), 442n. 43 (295)
Family Services Act (New Brunswick), 426n. 14 (220)
family wage system. *See* family employment benefits
federal inmates: double-bunking, 46; visitation program, 47
Fifteenth Amendment (United States Constitution), 317

Fink (Re), 165
525044 Alberta Ltd. (c.o.b. Tony C's 21 Club & Restaurant) v *Triple 5 Corp.*, 405n. 127 (156)
Fontaine v *Canadian Pacific Ltd*, 22, 401n. 79 (145)
Forrest v *Price*, 406n. 134 (157), 435n. 56 (263)
Fourteenth Amendment (United States Constitution), 113, 123, 317, 320–3, 336

gay men: and AZT costs, 53; Boyer Committee hearings, at, 40–2; as common-law couples, 74; discrimination against in armed forces, 39; and freedom of expression, 47; and marriage licence denial, 53
Gay Alliance Toward Equality v *Vancouver Sun*, 355n. 44 (13), 403n. 105 (153)
Geller v *Reimer*, 404n. 111 (153)
Ghidoni v *Ghidoni*, 164
Gigantes, Evelyn, 38
Gillis v *Gillis*, 406n. 130 (157)
Glad Day Bookshop Inc. v *M.N.R.*, 367n. 48 (46), 154
Green v *State*, 447n. 17 (319)
GST (Goods and Services Tax) credit: differential impact of, 247; larger benefits for individuals, 245; offsets couple benefits, 246; overinclusive/underinclusive, 428n. 39 (228)
Guppy v *Guppy*, 362n. 99 (23), 163

Haig and Birch v *The Queen*, 13, 358n. 70 (17), 19, 32, 45, 367n. 48 (46), 64, 82, 89, 92, 400n. 75 (144), 454n. 99

(338); impact of, 49–51, 53–9, 61–2
Haig v *Durrell*, 403n. 110 (153)
Hall v *DeCuir*, 318
Halm v *Minister of Employment and Immigration*, 367n. 48 (46), 51, 61, 65, 137, 397n. 49 (139)
Hamilton, Jamie Lee, 144
Handyside v *United Kingdom* (European Court), 391n. 94 (125)
Hawaii Constitution, 323
Health Care Consent Act (Ontario), 299, 301, 303, 451n. 79 (332)
heterosexual couples. *See* opposite-sex couples
heterosexual economy: benefits of exclusion from, 241; defined, 192–3
heterosexual relationship benefits, limits on: categories, 243; conflict-of-interest provisions, 244–5; economies of consumption, 245; low-income cutoffs (LICOs), 247–9; tax on marriage, 245–7
heterosexual relationships, recognition of: cost of maintaining, 216–17; exclusion of non-heterosexual relationships, 215–16; privileged, 76–7; women, exploitation of, within, 76
hierarchies of privilege: 92–5; 122, 258
Highway Traffic Act Regulations (Ontario), 426n. 17 (220)
H.I.M. v *W.A.M.*, 164
Hodder and Fisk, 155
Holtzman v *Knott*, 409n. 182 (165), 436n. 59 (264), 445n. 67 (303)
Homes for the Aged and Rest Homes Act (Ontario), 422n. 39 (199)
homosexual economy, defined, 192–3

homosexuals, suppression under Visigoth law, 110
Hudler v *London (City)*, 379n. 70 (87), 90, 404n. 112 (153)
human dignity, language of, 113–15
human rights legislation: inadequacy of, 4–5; scope of protection, 337
human rights movement, dual function, 101
Human Rights Act (British Columbia), 358n. 71 (17)
Human Rights Act (New Brunswick), 358n. 71 (17)
Human Rights Act (Nova Scotia), 358n. 71 (17)
Human Rights Act (Yukon), 358n. 69 (17)
Human Rights Code (Manitoba), 358n. 69 (17), 20, 88
Human Rights Code (Ontario): Bill 167 changes, 332; family status, 444n. 57 (300); opposite-sex definitions, 331, 339; parentage presumptions, 306; sexual orientation clause, 358n. 69 (17); spouse, definition, 370n. 80 (55)
Human Rights Code (Saskatchewan), 358n. 71 (17)
Human Tissue Gift Act (Ontario), 422n. 40 (199)
Hunter v *Southam*, 390n. 85 (121)

immigration: barriers to, 138–9; sponsorship bar, 142
Immigration Act, 397n. 50 (140)
income: advantages of multivariate studies of, 203; education and, 205, 209; government use in of univariate studies in litigation, 210–11; hierarchical allocation of, 203–4,

206, 207–8; lack of data on, 201; lack of univariate studies, 210; lesbians/bisexual women and, 206, 208; limitation of univariate studies of, 202–3; study types defined, 202; suspect character of univariate studies, 210–11

Income Tax Act, 369n. 73 (54), 426nn. 19–22 (220), 427nn. 26 (221), 29, 30 (224), 31 (225), 428n. 32 (225), 429nn. 48, 49 (233), 50 (234), 430nn. 52, 53 (234); child care expense deduction, 241, 248; child tax credit, 248; child, definitions, 302; cohabitants' equitable claims, 294; deemed spouses, 78, 245, 259, 269, 283, 284; employment benefits, taxable, 286; employment benefits, tax-exempt, 286–7, 289–90; GST credit, 245–7; non-arm's-length dealing, 435n. 52 (261); parent, definitions, 302; principal residence exemption, 244; pension plans, 442nn. 34, 35 (292); registered pension plan rules, 90–1; related persons, 245; spouse, 341; spouse-related provisions, 270–1

Income Tax Act (Ontario), 453n. 88 (333)

Income Tax Act Regulation 8501, 430n. 51 (234)

Income War Tax Act, 441nn. 27, 28 (291)

incremental discrimination, defined, 283–4, 295–6

Independent Health Facilities Act (Ontario), 451n. 82 (332)

Indian Act, 387n. 49 (112)

individual as benefit unit: in Danish legal policy, 276; escape from dependency, 274; history of, 275; personhood and, 279; replacing relationship base, 273–4; social assistance benefits for, 274; non-conjugal criteria for, 277–8; non-sexual criteria for, 277

Individual's Rights Protection Act (Alberta), 82, 146, 161

Insurance Act (Ontario), 422n. 45 (199)

Interpretation Act (Ontario), 332

J.A.L. v *E.P.H.*, 307

Janz v *Harris*, 406n. 130 (157)

Jewish persons: civil death, 133–4; under Visigoth law, 110

Johnstone v *Connolly*, 411n. 204 (170)

Johnston v *Rochette*, 409n. 174 (163)

Jones v *Fraser*, 411n. 204 (170)

Jorge Inaudi, 398n. 53 (140)

Jose Luis Ortigoza, 398n. 53 (140)

juridical rights: defined, 108; denied to Jewish persons, 110; denied to sexual minorities, 145–9; denied to women, 111

jury, questioning of for bias, 148–9

K. v *K.*, 408n. 169 (163)

K. (Re), 54–5, 61, 65, 82, 165, 434n. 46 (259), 304, 305, 340–1

Kane v *Ontario (A.-G.)*, 377n. 57 (81), 87, 340

Kaufman's Will (Re), 160

Keeping v *Pacey*, 443n. 50 (297)

Kinsey research: findings, 177–8; interview techniques, 180; methodology 178; response rates, factors affecting, 178–80

Klippert v *The Queen*, 137

Knodel v *B.C. Medical Services Com-*

mission, 32, 48, 368n. 61 (51), 53, 56, 57, 59, 61, 65, 169, 338–9
Korn v *Potter and Benson* (B.C. Supreme Court), 379n. 70 (87), 90, 155, 295

L.A.C. v *C.C.C.*, 363n. 109 (26)
L. and S. (Re), 164–5, 445n. 82 (308)
L'Association A.D.G.Q. v *Catholic School Commission of Montreal*, 355n. 51 (14), 359n. 76 (18), 19
L'Association A.D.G.Q. c *La Commission des écoles catholiques de Montréal*, 405n. 125 (155)
Laessoe v *Air Canada*, 370n. 83 (55), 379n. 70 (87), 91, 293, 295
Landlord and Tenant Act (Ontario), 426n. 16 (220), 451n. 82 (332)
Landon v *M.N.R.*, 437n. 74 (269)
Land Titles Act (Ontario), 452 n. 87 (333)
Land Transfer Tax Act (Ontario), 426n. 18 (220), 451n. 82 (332)
Laro v *Laro*, 444n. 62 (301)
Law Society of Upper Canada v *Skapinker*, 389n. 67 (116)
laws of Mississippi, 1865, 316
Layland, Todd, 143
Layland and Beaulne (Re), 368n. 61 (51), 53, 85, 299n. 65 (143), 159, 410n. 191 (166), n. 197 (167), 413n. 11 (176), 434n. 40 (258)
L.C. v *C.C.*, 24, 403n. 103 (152)
LEAF (Women's Legal Education and Action Fund): lesbian consultations, 258–9; misuse of consultations, 264–5
legal personality, concept explained, xv; *see also* personhood
lesbians: adoption by, 54–5; barriers to immigration, 141; at Boyer Committee hearings, 40–2; as common-law couples, 74; critique of relationship recognition, 259; denial of family law support to, 51–2; discrimination against by armed forces, 39, 46; gay groups and, 36–8; health insurance and, 52–3; income levels of, 206, 208; parentage rights, 164–5; as refugees, 140–2; disadvantages of relationship recognition, 247, 252, 260–1; right to seek custody, 307; (non-lesbian) feminists and, 36–8; recognized as spouses, 54–5; sexual orientation lobby and, 356n. 56 (14)
Leshner v *The Queen*, 368n. 61 (51), 53–5, 59, 61, 65, 78, 289, 293, 294, 339–40
Levin v *Levin*, 443n. 50 (297)
Lewis v *Kiesling*, 448n. 32 (322)
Little Sisters Book and Art Emporium v *Canada (Minister of Justice)*, 375n. 44 (78), 81, 154
L.J. v *L.C.I.*, 140
Loan and Trust Corporations Act (Ontario), 244
Loving v *Virginia*, 383n. 14 (103), 320
Low v *Low*, 443n. 50 (297)
low-income cutoffs (LICOs): benefit to same-sex couples, 249; effect on dependent spouse, 248; family income limits, 247–8; and opposite-sex definitions of spouse, 249; policy objectives, 248–4

M. v *H.*, 358n. 65 (17), 24, 373n. 17 (66), 72, 377n. 57 (81), 84–7, 125, 157–8, 258, 434nn. 46, 47 (259), 261,

Index   467

264–5, 439n. 1 (282), 283, 306, 340; critical importance of, 169–70
M. v M., 410n. 193 (167)
M. v M.(A.), 363n. 109 (26)
Mabon v Kiesling, 448n. 32 (322)
Maintenance Orders Act (Alberta), 426n. 14 (220)
marital status, opposite-sex definition of, 8–10, 15–7, 20–1; transgendered persons excluded by, 23–6; transsexual persons excluded by, 23–6
marriage: opposite-sex definition of, 8–10, 15–7, 20; same-sex, 9–10; trans-gendered persons excluded by opposite-sex definition of, 23–6; transsexual persons excluded by opposite-sex definition of, 23–6; unequal and appropriative, 259
Marriage Act (Ontario), 258, 451n. 82 (332)
'marriage debate': Canadian version, 254–5, 257–61; cohabitation not recognized in U.S. version, 254; constitutional confrontation in U.S. version, 256–7; hierarchical issues in Canada, 258–9; legal and strategic context in Canada, 257–8; polarization in U.S. version, 255; pressure towards dependency relationships in Canada, 260–1
McAleer v Canada (H.R.C.), 371n. 85 (55), 58, 402n. 98 (151)
McCallum v Toronto Transit Commission, 379n. 70 (87), 89
McDonough, Alexa, 143
McKinney v University of Guelph, 70
McPhee v M.N.R., 437n. 75 (269)
Measure 13 (Oregon), 322

Medical Services Act (British Columbia), 369n. 71 (53)
Members of Parliament Retiring Allowances Act, 429n. 46 (232)
Memorial University of Newfoundland and N.A.P.E. (Re), 379n. 70 (87)
Mercedes Homes Inc. v Grace, 359n. 76 (18), 19, 156–7
Metro Toronto Reference Library and Canadian Union of Public Employees, Local 1582 (Re), 379n. 70 (87), 91
Minister of Employment and Immigration v Hodder, 375n. 44 (78), 80, 90
Minister of Human Resources and Development v Fisk, 375n. 44 (78), 80
Minister of National Defence v Security Intelligence Review Committee, 400n. 74 (144)
Minnesota Statutes 1992, subdiv 45, section 363.01, 23
Miron v Trudel 66, 373n. 20 (67), 68, 72, 77, 420n. 11 (194), 195–6, 306; applied in *Little Sisters*, 81; effect of, 168; *Egan and Nesbit* distinguished from, 73–4; *Oakes* test, 72–3
Missouri ex rel. Gaines v Canada, 391n. 90 (124)
Moge v Moge, 375n. 43 (77), 117
Molodowich v Penttinen, 159
Monette v Sylvestre, 408n. 162 (162)
Monk v Doan, 408n. 165 (163)
Montreal Tramways Co. v Leveille, 389n. 71 (118)
Moore and Akerstrom v The Queen, 379n. 70 (87), 89, 90, 439n. 2 (283), 285, 288–9, 293
Morgentaler v The Queen (1975), 389n. 71 (118)
Morrissey and Coll v Canada, 399n. 62 (142)

Mortgages Act (Ontario), 451n. 82 (332)
Mossop, Brian, 13
Mossop v Canada. See A.-G. Canada v Mossop
Municipal Conflict of Interests Act (Ontario), 244
Municipal Health Services Act (Ontario), 451n. 82 (332)
Municipal Sales Tax Act (Ontario), 451n. 82 (332)
Murdoch v Murdoch, 221

N. v N., 408n. 169 (163)
Nancy S. v Michele G., 435n. 57 (264)
Native Women's Association of Canada v The Queen, 71
Nazism. *See* Third Reich
Newfoundland and Labrador Human Rights Commission v Nolan and Barry, 377n. 57 (81), 82, 454n. 99 (338)
Newfoundland (Human Rights Commission) v Newfoundland, 358 n 72 (17)
Nielsen v Canada (Employment and Immigration Commission), 59
non-waged work, unequal distribution of, 277
North and Matheson (Re), 9–10, 12, 52, 410n. 191 (166), 410n. 194 (167)
North Carolina Public Laws, 447n. 16 (318)
Nova Scotia (Minister of Finance) v Hodder, 379n. 70 (87)
Nova Scotia (Minister of Finance) v MacNeil Estate, 379n. 70 (87), 90
Nuosci v Canada, 145
Nursing Homes Act (Ontario), 422n. 39 (199)

Oakes test: analysis of in *M. v H.*, 84; incremental change theory and, 70–1; and 'rational connection' step, 72
Oates v Baker Estate, 160, 161
Obringer v Kennedy Estate, 377n. 57 (81), 85–6, 158, 422n. 43 (199)
Old Age Security Act, 66, 168, 427n. 29 (224)
Oliver v Hamilton (City) (No. 2), 403n. 110 (153)
O'Neill and Coles v The Queen, 371n. 85 (55), 58
Ontario Guaranteed Annual Income Act, 451n. 82 (332)
Ontario Home Ownership Savings Plan, 453n. 88 (333)
Ontario Pensioners Property Tax Assistance Act, 451n. 82 (332)
opposite sex, definitions in terms of, 15–17
opposite-sex couples, burdens on, 240
opposite-sex relationships, creation as category, 9–10
Ouellet v Ouellet, 164
'outing,' risk of, 147, 197

P. v S., 363n. 110 (26), 363n. 3 (32), 380n. 77 (95), 162
P.B. v P.B., 409n. 173 (163)
Pace and Cox v Alabama, 447n. 18 (319)
Palmer v Palmer, 409n. 170 (163)
parent: adoptive, 297, 302; and Children's Law Reform Act, 297; cohabitation and presumptive, 298; custodial, 300–1, 307–8; *de facto*, 300–1; diversity of definitions, 296–7; heterosexual definition of

natural, challenge to, 306; marriage and presumptive, 297–8; not purely biological, 297–8; redefinition of natural, 308; sex-specific definition, 304

parental status: and adoption, 165; and Children's Law Reform Act, 165; and gay men disadvantaged, 164, 165–6; and lesbian mothers, 164–6; and transsexual and transgendered persons, 166

Parkwood Hospital and McCormick Home and London and District Service Workers' Union (Re), 371n. 85 (55), 56

Parliamentary Committee on Equality (Boyer Committee): forms of discrimination identified, 41; government response, 43–4; hearings, 31, 39–43; recommendations, 42–3, 60–1, 136; report, 42–3, 366 n. 37

participation rights: centrality of, 132; defined, 108; denied to Jewish persons, 110; denied to women, 111; regulated by citizenship, 133; regulated by criminal conviction, 133

Patterson v *Lauritsen*, 407n. 153 (161)

Paul v *Paul*, 387n. 49 (112)

Pension Act, 429n. 46 (232)

Pension Benefits Act (Ontario), 370n. 75 (54)

Perez v *Lippold*, 320

'person,' legal meanings of, 311

personhood: in Canadian jurisprudence, 116–17; core incidents, 125–6, 130; differentiated from human dignity, 102; of disadvantaged groups, 130–1; equated with legal capacity, 118–23; of targets of hatred, 131; sense of self and, 117

Piche v *Canada (Solicitor General)*, 367n. 48 (46), 92

Pizarro v *M.E.I.*, 397n. 51, 398n. 53 (140)

Plessy v *Ferguson*, 124, 318, 323

police forces, exclusion of queers from, 144–5

Polyakov v *The Queen*, 398n. 56 (140)

Poulter v *M.N.R.*, 391n. 87 (123), 432n. 17 (249), 259–60, 279

Priape Enrg. and M.N.R. (Re), 404n. 114 (154)

Pride Day, municipal government hostility towards, 153

private rights: and business property, 156–7; and cohabitation, 167–9; and custody and access, 162–4; and customary relationships, 170; defined, 109; denied to Jewish persons, 110; denied to women, 111; and employment, 161–2; and estates, 158–61; and family property, 157–8; and marriage, 166–7; parentage, 164–6; and relationship recognition, 166–70; state ordering of, 132; and support, 157–8, 159

public benefits, denial of to same-sex partners, 78

public office, exclusion through political practice, 143–4

public rights: and constraints on sexual minorities, 150–5; defined, 108; denied to Jewish persons, 110; and freedom from violence, 150–1; and identity, 151–2; and speech, 152–4; and cultural expression, 153; and health care, 154–5

470 Index

Public Service Pension Act (Ontario), 370n. 75 (54)
Public Sector Pension Reform Act, 429n. 46 (232)
Public Service Superannuation Act (Ontario), 370n. 75 (54), 429n. 46 (232)
public–private dichotomy, 5–6, 27
public–private distinction, blurring of, 89–90

Québec Charter of Human Rights and Freedoms, 355n. 50 (14), 358n. 69 (17)
queer, usage of term, xxiii, 10
queer existence, as ground of complaint, 95
queers. *See also* sexual minorities
queers: apparent benefits of exclusion, 240; benefit–burden dichotomy, 241–3; Charter compliance process and, 35–6; invisibility of in statistical data, 215; absence from policies, 216; 'exemption' from anti-avoidance provisions, 217; economic penalty, 216–17; racially identified, 92–6

R. v *Alli*, 149
R. v *Atkinson, Ing and Roberts*, 402n. 96 (151)
R. v *Bernardo*, 390n. 72 (118)
R. v *Butler*, 154
R. v *Carmen M.*, 136
R. v *Edwards Books and Art*, 70
R. v *Jewell and Gramlick*, 395n. 32 (136)
R. v *Keen*, 395n. 32 (136)
R. v *Lalo*, 367n. 48 (46)
R v *LeBeau*; R. v *Lofthouse*; 119, 137
R. v *McGowan*, 395n. 32 (136)
R v *McLaren*, 396n. 36 (137)
R. v *Morgentaler* (1985), 390n. 72 (118)
R. v *Moyer*, 390n. 73 (118)
R. v *Oakes*, 374n. 25 (70)
R. c *P.(D.)*, 401n. 87 (148)
R. v *Parks*, 148
R. v *Paterson*, 148, 149
R. v *Pink Triangle Press*, 404n. 116 (154)
R. v *Robinson*, 395n. 35 (137)
R v *Roy*, 137
R. v *Silva*, 375n. 44 (78), 80, 137
R. v *Stymiest*, 395n. 35 (137)
R. v *Sullivan*, 390n. 72 (118)
R. v *Sylvestre*, 400n. 74 (144)
R. v *Turpin*, 68
R. v *Wilson*, 148
R v *Wong*, 396n. 40 (137)
R. v *Zundel*, 119
Ramer (Re), 443n. 47 (297)
reading in, 49–50; retroactive, 59; same-sex definition of spouse, 55; sexual orientation, 49–50, 54, 57
Reference re Section 94(2) of the Motor Vehicle Act, RSBC 1979, c 288, 389n. 67 (116)
Reference re Provincial Electoral Boundaries (Sask.), 116
refugee claims: by lesbians, 140–2; and persecution test, 140; by queers, 139–41
Registry Act (Ontario), 452 n. 87 (333)
Reid (Re), 362nn. 103, 108, 403n. 102 (151)
Reimer v Saskatchewan Human Rights Commission, 404n. 111 (153)
relationship recognition: distributional concerns, 250, 259; and health issues, 252; hierarchical

issues, 253–4, 258–9; impact of race and ethnic origin, impact, 252; lesbian critique of, 259; and lesbians, 252; and low-income queers, 250–1; and middle/high-income queers, 253; same-sex cohabitation, 168–70; *see also* 'marriage debate'
relationship terminology, 40, 197
relationships: heterosexual, and exploitation of women, 76; hierarchies of, 76; limits of Charter protection for, 75; recognized, benefits of, 76–7
Residential Housing Protection Act (Ontario), 451n. 82 (332)
Revenue Canada: anti–same-sex interpretations, 284–95; fear of, 293–4
Roberts v *Club Exposé*, 359n. 77 (18), 19–20, 92
Robertson v *Geisinger*, 409n. 171 (163)
Rodriguez v *A.-G. British Columbia*, 119
Roman law: children and, 105; civil capacity under, 108–9; marriage and, 105–8; slaves and, 105; taxation measures and, 221–2; *unitas personae* doctrine under, 104–5; Visigoth law, influence on, 110; women and, 105–6
Romer v *Evans*, 352n. 16 (7), 378n. 60 (83), 382n. 5 (101), 119, 123–4, 413n. 9 (176), 448n. 34 (323), 326
Rosenberg v *Canada (Attorney General)*, 373n. 18 (66), 79–80, 84–6, 90, 155, 169–70, 413n. 13 (176), 258, 269, 439n. 2 (282), 283–5, 341; effect unclear, 292–5

Rosenberg v *M.N.R.*. *See Rosenberg* v *Canada (Attorney General)*
Royal Canadian Mounted Police Superannuation Act, 429n. 46 (232)
R.R.C. v *A.E.F.*, 444n. 62 (301)

S. v *S.*, 408n. 167 (163)
same-sex couples: estimate of queer penalty, 236–7; immigration sponsorship bar, 142–3; present and longitudinal dimensions of queer penalty, 235; tax on marriage, 268–9; tax penalties for sharing assets, 221–2; tax treatment issues, 284
same-sex employment benefits: lack of legal basis for different treatment, 285–7; Revenue Canada barriers, 285–95; taxable, 286; tax-exempt, 286–7
same-sex families, legal issues for, 308–9
same-sex parents: stranger in law to child, 297; step-parent adoption, 304–6
same-sex relationships: creation as category, 9–10; differential burden on low-income couples, 250–2, 267; exclusion, 261–6; non-recognition, cost to government, 266–7; power imbalances, 262–3; tax benefits of marriage, 269
Sampson v *Gosnell Estate*, 387n. 49 (112)
Saunders v *Saunders*, 409n. 172 (163)
Sauvé v *Canada*, 393n. 8 (133)
Schachter v *Canada*, 454n. 101 (338)
Schachtschneider v *The Queen*, 240, 268–9
Seneca Falls Declaration of Sentiments, 112

Seneca College of Applied Arts and Technology v *Bhadauria,* 401n. 81 (147)
services discrimination as ground of complaint, 89–90
sex: biological, binary image of, 151; legal change of, 151–2
sex discrimination: excludes sexual orientation, 31–2; as ground of complaint, 95
sex identity, 151–2
sex, decriminalization of, 135–6
sexual expression, queer: as barrier to immigration, 138–9; and age of consent, 136; impairment of personhood by, 137; video surveillance, 137
sexual harassment, 20, 56
sexual orientation: analogous ground in Charter, 49, 50, 59; clause in collective agreement, 57–8; defined in Charter terms, 55, 57–9; excluded from Charter, 30–34; protection for, and relationship issues, 32, 46–9, 53–9; read into collective agreement, 57; read into federal human rights code, 32, 57; sex discrimination and, 31–2; sexual harassment and, 56
sexual minorities: 'passing,' 131; *see also* queers
sexual minorities, civil rights of (Canada): Charter remedies. *See* Charter remedies; omnibus legislation, 332–6. *See also* Bill 167, Bill 31; opposite-sex definitions in, 331; 'partner' terminology, 331–2; sexual orientation clauses in, 331
sexual minorities, civil rights of (Europe): adoption prohibition (Sweden), 329; cohabitation, lack of status (Denmark), 328; cohabitation provisions (Hungary), 330; extension/nullification, 326–7; income tax burden (Denmark), 328; marriage compared (Denmark), 327–8; parentage restrictions (Denmark), 328; property rights focus (Sweden), 329
sexual minorities, civil rights of (United States): constitutional personhood doctrine applied, 326; Fourteenth Amendment applied, 322–3; framing of issues, 321; municipal anti-discrimination ordinances, 321; nullification of legal capacities, 322; prohibitions on same-sex marriage, 323–5; sex-based classification of marriage, 323–4, 325; special systems of rights for, 330–1; state anti-homosexual measures, 322–3
sexual orientation: creation as category, 10, 11; disability and, 22; human rights codes and, 13–17; included in Charter language, 64, 78; lobby, 13–15; narrow interpretations, 17–23, 27; refugee claims, ground for, 140; relationship rights protected, 88–9; sex and, as mutually exclusive concepts, 20, 23; sex discrimination and, 11–15; sexual harassment and, 20; unprotected jurisprudential space, as, 10, 13, 27
sexuality, criminal regulation of, 6
sexuality-specific legal provisions: adult dependency subsidies, 224–31; anti-avoidance provisions, 217; family sharing provisions,

218–20; policy objectives, 216, 218–19, 220, 221, 229–31, 237–8; same-sex couples, burdens on, 221–4
Sherwood Atkinson (Sheri de Cartier), 138, 142, 403n. 104 (152), 410n. 196 (167)
slaves: under Roman law, 105; in North America, 112
Sleeper v *Sleeper*, 443n. 50 (297)
Sleeth v *Wasserlein*, 407n. 141 (158)
Southam Inc. v *The Queen*, 116
speech rights, 152–4
spouse: dependency requirement, 56; married-couples definition, 72–3; opposite-sex definition, 8–10, 15–17, 21; —, applied, 52–3; —, constitutes discrimination, 44, 55, 66–9, 78, 88; —, demonstrably justified, 44, 69–71; —, immigration sponsorship, 142–3; —, legislative objective, 70–2; — transgendered persons excluded by, 23–6; — transsexual persons excluded by, 23–6
state, non-neutrality of, 214–15
Statute Law (Status of Women) Amendment Act, 1974, 430n. 56 (236), 434n. 39 (257)
Stiles v *Canada*, 367n. 48 (46), 372n. 2 (64), 400n. 74 (144)
Stonewall uprising, 7
Substitute Decisions Act (Ontario), 411n. 203 (170), 421n. 18 (196), 422n. 38 (198), 282, 299, 303, 304, 451n. 79 (332)
Succession Law Reform Act (Ontario), 85, 299, 301, 303, 407nn. 144, 146 (159), 426nn. 9, 12, 13 (219–20)
suicide rates, 197
survivor benefits, limits in provincial legislation, 86

Sylvestre v *Canada*, 367n. 48 (46), 372n. 2 (64)
Symes v *Canada*, 68, 429n. 47 (233), 241

tax on marriage, 245–7, 268–9; *see also* GST
Tchernilevski v *M.C.I.*, 140
teaching, exclusion of queers from, 144–5
Thauvette v *Malyon*, 407n. 149 (159)
The Queen v *Scheller*, 437n. 75 (269)
The Queen v *Thibaudeau*, 66, 373n. 20 (67), 72, 74, 77, 130, 382n. 7 (102), 383n. 11 (103), 119, 121–3, 426n. 6 (219)
Thibaudeau v *The Queen*. See *The Queen* v *Thibaudeau*
Third Reich, 133–4
Thirteenth Amendment (United States Constitution), 113, 315, 317
Thomas S. and Robin Y., 309
Titchenal v *Dexter*, 445n. 77 (306)
Toronto Islands Residential Community Stewardship Act (Ontario), 451n. 82 (332)
Toutant v *M.N.R.*, 437n. 75 (269)
transgendered persons: absence of human rights complaints, 23; invisibility, 92–6; right to identity denied, 151–2
transsexual persons: absence of human rights complaints, 23; invisibility, 92–6; right to identity denied, 151–2
'trilogy' cases, contradictions in, 77
Treasury Board (Agriculture and Agri-Food Canada) and Yarrow (Re), 379n. 70 (87), 91
Treasury Board (Canadian Grain Com-

474 Index

mission) and Sarson (Re), 379n. 70 (87), 91
Treasury Board (Indian and Northern Affairs) and Watson (Re), 359n. 77 (18), 20
Treasury Board (Public Works) and Hewens (Re), 359n. 77 (18), 20, 410n. 192 (166–7)
Treasury Board (Transport Canada) and Smith (Re), 371n. 85 (55), 56
Tremblay v Daigle, 390n. 72 (118)
Twenty-fourth Amendment (United States Constitution), 447n. 22 (320)

University of Lethbridge and University of Lethbridge Faculty Association (Re), 371n. 85 (55), 58
University of Saskatchewan v Saskatchewan Human Rights Commission, 12, 446n. 5 (313)

Van Vulpen v M.E.I., 398n. 60 (142), 410n. 196 (167)
Veterans and Civilian War Allowances Act, 430n. 55 (236)
Veysey v Correctional Services of Canada, 367n. 48 (46), 47–8, 56, 57, 59, 61, 65, 411n. 202 (169), 434n. 38 (257), 338–9
violence: in lesbian and gay relationships, 151; means of maintaining non-personhood, 150–1; state reluctance to protect queers, 150–1; sentencing provisions, 151
Visigoth law, 110
Vital Statistics Act (Alberta), 403n. 100 (151)
Vital Statistics Act (British Columbia), 403n. 100 (151)
Vital Statistics Act (Ontario), 362n. 100 (23), 26, 403n. 100 (151)

Vital Statistics Act (Quebec), 403n. 100 (151)
Vogel v Manitoba, 379n. 70 (87), 88, 169
Vogel v Government of Manitoba [Vogel I], 360n. 82 (20)
Vogel v Manitoba [Vogel II], 18, 20–1, 359n. 77 (18), 360n. 82 (20)
voting rights, diminished, 145
Vriend v Alberta, 45 (trial ruling), 368n. 61 (51), 54, 64, 66, 72, 377n. 57 (81), 82, 100, 123–4, 146, 161, 170, 336–7, 358n. 74 (17), 454n. 99 (338)

W. v G., 406n. 133 (157), 410n. 186 (165)
War Veterans Allowance Act, 429n. 46 (232)
Waterman v National Life Assurance Co. of Canada, 359n. 76 (18), 19, 423n. 56 (201)
Waterman v National Life Assurance Co. of Canada (No. 2), 161
Williamson v Lee Optical of Oklahoma, 70
Wittig, Monique, 273
Wolfenden Report, 135
women, legal disabilities of: under Anglo-Norman law, 111; link with other groups, 112, 120–2; under North American law, 112–13; under Roman law, 105–6
Wood v Hinkle, 22, 405n. 120 (155)
Worby v Worby, 409n. 172 (163)

X, Y and Z v U.K., 166

Zegota v Zegota-Rzegocinski, 443n. 50 (297)
Zhu v M.C.I., 398n. 57 (140)